I0759631

# DRAWING ARCHITECTURE

# DRAWING ARCHITECTURE

HELEN THOMAS

Throughout history, right up to the present day, architectural drawings have been the means through which architects initiated and developed their ideas and, in turn, they reveal the design processes whereby architectural projects – both real and imaginary – reach fruition. The diversity of the examples collected in this book shows that the definition of an architectural drawing encompasses many and varied approaches: some that have developed systematically over time, and some that have been invented spontaneously to suit specific purposes – from images conceived in the mind's eye to details worked on collaboratively by different members of a team. Polished presentation drawings made to seduce clients, or for publication, sit alongside instructive diagrams and impromptu sketches communicating intense emotion. The possibilities for categorization are endless, and one of these has been taken up at the end of the book – in the illustrated timeline that shows the drawings in chronological order. However, in ordering the drawings, this process of categorization has been sidestepped in favour of an associational approach. The intention is to provide imaginative space for the reader to make their own connections between the images and their stories as they resonate with personal experience and knowledge. This same intention is echoed here, in this introduction, which makes reference to drawings from the book within a flow of themes.

**Shifting perspectives**

Upon reflection, an architectural drawing can transport you into another world. One of the most successful instances of this is Raphael's sixteenth-century drawing of a segment of the Roman Pantheon rotunda's curved interior elevation (page 74). Raphael invites the viewer to stand, in their imagination, within this ancient circular space and experience the sensation of being simultaneously enclosed by architecture and exposed. In the building itself, it is the unseen oculus at the top of the dome from which this feeling of openness emanates, but in the drawing a realm beyond is implied in shadowy niches and doorways. At the sides, the space spins towards a world outside the rectangular confines of the paper's edges. Raphael did not draw the reality that he saw but made variations – in the placement of the columns, for example – to create an image of how he thought it should be seen. His imaginative recreation of the interior of the Pantheon, the most intact ancient building in Europe and the inspiration for many fantasies of the distant past, broke the rules of representation in several ways. Following no previous graphic or projective system, it mingled qualities of orthography and perspective, making it an object of fascination, and one that was much copied and reinterpreted by later draughtsmen. The same wilful, inventive looseness in the interpretation of the ancient world infuses Andrea Palladio's creative reconstruction of the ruins of the Roman Baths of Agrippa (page 176). This imaginative approach continued in Palladio's built work, which did not reproduce but rather extended and experimented with the formal and spatial potential of his Classical precedents, sometimes creating a reality that was deliberately provocative and transgressed the expectations of his contemporaries.

Based, as he was, in the Republic of Venice, Palladio's stance reflected a relationship with the ancient world that was very different to that of the city's mirror on the other edge of Europe, Constantinople. Orhan Pamuk's 1998 whodunnit novel *My Name is Red*, which follows the lives of four sixteenth-century miniaturists and suspects working within the cultural strictures of the Ottoman Empire, captures an essential difference between the West and the East. Pamuk's protagonists aimed to create a perfect work of art that continued an ancient and immutable tradition of idealized representations of reality. At the same time, they were aware, in their peripheral vision, of the Italian inventions of perspective and naturalistic representation, which allowed the idiosyncratic presence of the individual, unique in time and place, to be expressed. In the image called *Tahmina Comes into Rustam's Chamber* (page 96), which came out of the Timurid court workshops of the fifteenth century, this sense of continuity – which intimates eternity – permeates the composition, with its symbolic density and stylized features. The same separation, or abstraction, from the lived world belongs to the instructive Topkapi Scroll (page 296), made in Persia, whose subject is the production of repetitive and complex geometrical syntheses of structure and ornament.

This fluctuating relationship with reality and time, both the deeply historical and the lived time associated with the making and viewing of a drawing, reveals a consistent characteristic of these artefacts. Each one is an interface between the private, inner world of the imagination and the arena of everyday life, where consensual forms of communication create the shared meaning of things. The imaginative potential of the world that a drawing defines belongs not only to its maker and his or her intention but also to anyone contemplating it. In this way, and at different places along a spectrum between two points, it embodies both the nebulous and unformed possibilities of the mind, and the tangible outcomes of an attempt to articulate and communicate them. The painful sensation that sometimes accompanies this labour is eloquently expressed in Marie-José Van Hee's initial drawing for a house design (page 47). The chaos of her mind spills on to the paper in a multitude of lines; sense – legible meaning – only emerges from a responsive ordering, aided by an eraser and overlaid sheets of paper. In many architectural drawings, a further layer is added to this fragile state, one of shared conventions, accrued over the history of their production. They are fraught with rules and codes, some of which are no longer known. Deducing what they might have been is the driver of much scholarly work, and the inspiration for the myriad theories and interpretations that surround old drawings.

**Interpreting the rules**

*De architectura*, a Latin treatise produced at the end of the first century BC and attributed to Marcus Vitruvius Pollio, combines the knowledge and views of many writers of his time. This manuscript comprises the earliest surviving definition of the rules of Classical architecture. Although none of Vitruvius' original illustrations survive, his descriptions have been interpreted many times over the intervening centuries. Leonardo da Vinci's famous drawing of Vitruvian Man, the tips of his standing and outstretched body touching the edges of an enclosing circle, was one of the earliest visual interpretations of Vitruvius' words. In Berardo Galiani's later illustration (page 87), which appeared in his eighteenth-century edition of *De architectura*, Vitruvian Man's ideal proportions are explored in two separate depictions. The influence of Vitruvius' writings spread across the centuries, inspiring Palladio's own treatise, *I quattro libri dell'architettura*, which he used to disseminate his interpretation of Classical architecture. In turn, this became an intimate companion of architects such as Inigo Jones, whose densely annotated edition accompanied his introduction of Palladio's version of Classicism to the English aristocracy (page 164). Claude Perrault sought the idea of beauty in the authority of Vitruvius, as seen in the design for Sainte-Geneviève (page 230). Translating rules found in the treatise into the foundations of French Neo-Classicism, Perrault used the process to question the construction of taste and its relationship with power. This important connection is picked up and considered in several of the drawings in this book – in Léon Krier's and James Stirling's interior perspective for the Olivetti Headquarters (page 209), for example, which plays with the connoisseurial and historical value of objects within a modern architectural environment. This resonates with Percier and Fontaine's view of a bedroom (page 70), in which the presence and disposition of the objects, combined with the room's decorative schema, communicate very specific messages about taste and social position.

Before the rediscovery of Vitruvius, however, other men in different parts of the world were collecting and collating the secret knowledge of craft guilds into instructive, illustrated manuals in which these early conventions were set down. While universal building codes had existed across China since the third century BC, the precise line drawings of the *Yingzao Fashi* (page 116), which showed how these were to be enacted, were not published until the twelfth century AD. The instructive diagrams of this State Building Standard, the outcome of extensive historical research and interviews designed to extract the inherited methods and unspoken practices of construction, were carried out by the Superintendent for State Buildings, Li Jie.

In Europe, medieval lodge books, such as the one kept by Villard de Honnecourt (page 287), collated the methods and observations of its master craftsmen, but these were still relatively protected. It was not until the fifteenth century that a similar exercise to Li Jie's was undertaken, on a considerably smaller scale, by Mathes Roriczer and Hanns Schmuttermayer (page 38). These two German master craftsmen published their gathered knowledge as design books, intended to be used as instruction manuals for the setting out and carving of pinnacles and gables. As such, these publications bear comparison with the intention of the Topkapi Scroll – to instruct. In the German books, however, geometry was a technique for calculating the disposition of elements, rather than an intrinsic system.

**Colour codes**

Over the centuries, the conventions and codes of architectural drawings have responded to the introduction of new technologies, in terms of the ways in which drawings are produced and disseminated, as well as in response to material and structural developments in building construction itself. Karl Friedrich Schinkel's use of a pale red to highlight the structural metalwork in his section of the Kreuzberg Monument (page 214), with specific elements picked out in black, makes reference to earlier French engineering documents. In his delineations of the structure and reinforcement of the church of Sainte-Geneviève in Paris, Jacques-Germain Soufflot uses pink to define masonry sections, but this distinction was lost in engraved reproductions, such as the detail of the armature in the pediment (page 117). Sébastien Le Prestre de Vauban's military plan of Lille (page 46) was drawn in the early eighteenth century with vivid colours distinguishing its component parts, and this tradition is continued in James Gowan's section through a house with mechanical services from his East Hanningfield project (page 179). In this graphic drawing, each of the prefabricated elements that make up the construction kit-of-parts is given its own bright colour. These are classified according to the building trade associated with a specific material – yellow for carpentry, for example, and red for brick and tile work. Ryue Nishizawa's detail of the Moriyama House (page 126) exaggerates this aspect of architectural drawing to make it into an aesthetic object, and a prosaic description becomes a finely balanced composition of colour fields.

In twentieth-century Europe, colour theory was taught in schools of design such as the Bauhaus through teachers like Paul Klee and Johannes Itten. An interesting aspect of Klee's painting, *Architecture* (page 167), is that his sensitivity to colour was, in this case, inspired by a non-European experience. This appreciation of an exotic phenomenon observed from an outsider's perspective is a counterpoint to the appeal of colour as a means of asserting cultural specificity. The much-admired colours of Luis Barragán, for example, came from his own Mexican cultural milieu, which included painters like Chucho Reyes and Diego Rivera. Barragán's drawing of wealthy horsemen traversing the luxury development of Las Arboledas in Mexico City (page 62) radiates the energy of the sandy orange earth and the foliage, breaker-like in appearance, that fill half of the image. Roberto Burle Marx, although his self-proclaimed palette was the natural flora of Brazil, treated his designs as abstracted fields of colour, codified to represent his planting schemes. While more figural than many of his drawings, the site plan of Ibirapuera Park (page 24) is animated by this technique. This twentieth-century enthusiasm for the exotic had its roots much earlier, in the fantasies of archaeological discovery and the Orientalism of Empire. During the nineteenth century, the attraction of the latter became codified in works such as Owen Jones's analysis of the colour and forms of Egyptian pillars from his book *The Grammar of Ornament* (page 240).

**Shared and private languages**

In technical architectural drawings, a general consensus has grown around what certain colours, shading techniques and line weights mean, but there exists a second layer of language. This emerges in the more intimate communications that take place during the design of a specific building project, or even within an architectural office or between a small team of architects working closely together. In the mid-1980s, when they were working as architects on site at Norman Foster's Hongkong and Shanghai Bank (page 39), the overlapping roles and responsibilities of Ken Shuttleworth and David Nelson created the intense communication shown in their drawing for the services and structural coordination around one of the cores of the building. These subtle dialects highlight the important role that architectural drawings have as documents in which the decisions and ideas made by different contributors to the complex task of understanding, designing and constructing a building or landscape are shared and agreed.

Before the use of computers, modifications and comments were made on the paper surface of the original drawing. Special care had to be taken to preserve the integrity of the fragile medium as erasures and changes were made and overlaid. Sometimes, copies of these originals were used to collect comments from different members of the design team and then the information was transferred to the constantly changing and developing live drawing. The extent of this team has grown over the centuries to include not only structural engineers and quantity surveyors but also a myriad specialists concerned with services, conservation and many other aspects of a building's design, each of whom carries a very specific understanding of the task at hand that somehow needs to be conveyed to the other members of the team. Before the middle of the nineteenth century, when mechanical printing methods were developed, there were two methods of reproducing drawings. The original could be literally copied by hand, carefully scaled off using tools such as dividers, compasses and scale rules. The second technique involved the painstaking task of pricking, whereby the original was placed over a blank sheet and perforated at key points by a special needle. The resulting points on the sheet below would then be joined in order to replicate the original.

Since the development of computer aided design (CAD) programs, the use of the architectural drawing as a site of communication has changed in accordance with the logic of production. In many ways, this has been an improvement. David Chipperfield Architects' drawing mapping out the restoration for the Roman Room ceiling in Berlin's ruined Neues Museum (page 192) embodies a code of colours and hatching patterns accompanied by notes included in the document. On the paper surface of a printout, the conservators have added pencil annotations that use different colours to record successive stages of the work or the condition of the existing fabric of the room. This recording of an ongoing conversation is also evident in the drawing produced by 6a architects, with annotations by Gabriel Orozco (page 297), which was shared as a WhatsApp message. As in the Roman Room ceiling plan, past comments have been incorporated into the layers of the computer drawing, on top of which specific elements and thoughts are painted in or noted down. Currently, the contribution of the virtual environment to enabling smooth and efficient communication between diverse members of the design team is epitomized in Building Information Modelling (BIM), made beautiful in a printout of a three-dimensional Building Information Model produced by Herzog & de Meuron (page 17). This colourful image illustrating the technical building services of the Elbphilharmonie in Hamburg takes the discipline of colour coding to a high level, as each type of duct, cable and service element is defined by a different saturated hue, bold against a black background.

### Location of drawings

Among the drawings collected in this book, the earliest representations of buildings are orthographic architectural drawings, or straight-on views with no perspectival distortion – plans, sections and elevations. Lying on the lap of an ancient diorite statue is the earliest example included here, a plan of a shrine made more than 4,000 years ago (page 163). Found in archaeological sites at the heart of early urban civilization in various regions of Egypt and Mesopotamia, which is now Iraq, such depictions, including the remarkable plan of a palace inscribed on to a clay tablet (page 272) and the sophisticated section and elevation of a portable shrine on sheets of papyrus (page 57), reveal the foundations of Western conventions of architectural representation still followed today. These images were made on portable media: on papyrus or small objects; and later, drawings on parchment, hand scrolls and paper, including hand-drawn and printed books. Due to limitations in the maximum dimension of individual sheets, many designs were spread over numerous pieces joined together. One of the most extravagant of these is Meister Arnold's 4 m-high (13 ft) view of the west facade of Cologne Cathedral (page 262), which covers twenty differently sized sheets of parchment. However, this pales in comparison with Albrecht Dürer's woodcut elevation of the Triumphal Arch of Maximilian I (page 141) which, although smaller in extent, is composed of 195 blocks on 36 conjoined sheets. The majority of the architectural drawings in this book were made on two-dimensional supports, but some of the earlier examples are located on more unusual surfaces, such as the frescos and mosaics covering walls of buildings or even caves. The tenth-century depiction of monastic architecture in the Mogao Caves in China is one example (page 130), situated at a crossroads on the ancient southern Silk Road and portraying a scene over 2,000 km (1242 mi) away.

Another important group of architectural representations was uncovered at the archaeological site of Pompeii. Their discovery not only introduced decorative schema that were copied and adapted from then onwards, as in François-Joseph Bélanger's design for a wall elevation (page 30), but also revealed possibilities for composition and depiction of spatial depth that preceded the rediscovery and development of single-point perspective by Filippo Brunelleschi in the early fifteenth century. The murals of architectural landscapes from around AD 40–45, showing two seaside villas near Pompeii (page 229), illustrate these early experiments.

Some important early orthographic drawings are missing from this volume because they are difficult to represent in two dimensions, having been carved into stone pavements or walls. These on-site directions for construction are called *paradeigma*, and examples include a template for setting out masonry joints for the amphitheatre at Capua, near Naples, from around 1,000 BC, and a mason's template near the entrance to the Mausoleum of Augustus in Rome. Later, more portable templates are represented, however, by Michelangelo's enigmatic *modano* (page 80). Both prosaic in its intent – to provide a mason's guide to the construction of a cornice – and esoteric in its embodied knowledge and creative transformation of precedent, *modani* such as this were closely guarded objects. Less mysterious, Studio Mumbai's tape drawing (page 81) is a contemporary interpretation of this archaic tradition.

St Peter's Basilica in Rome, whose construction began at the start of the sixteenth century and continued for 120 years until its completion, was the symbolic site of transfer of architectural design from the master craftsmen, who were intimately connected with the practical construction of a building, to the more academic figure of the architect. But in the building of the new Basilica of St Peter, drawings, including Donato Bramante's parchment plan (page 212), were made by the architect to communicate to the craftsmen – and a new separation between theoretical design and executive construction was set up. Succeeding Bramante as the basilica's chief architect, Raphael promoted orthogonal drawings as the most suitable means of illustrating the design of a building. In this, he was interpreting Vitruvius' terms for architectural projections – *ichnographia*, or the ground plan, and *orthographia*, or the elevation. Vitruvius' third term, *scaenographia*, was usually interpreted as a perspectival view, but Raphael's preference for completing the spatial description was through the device of the measured and scaled section.

### Depicting space

In this regard, Raphael was asserting his position amid a deep and intense debate about the relation of a spatial realm, in which a number of players were battling for validation and which was being viewed from afar by Pamuk's curious protagonists, described at the beginning of this discussion. Following Brunelleschi's proposal for a system of single-point perspective, the first architect to codify its method was Leon Battista Alberti, in *Della pittura*. In his architectural treatise, *De re aedificatoria*, however, he advocated against its use for architectural representation, proposing the ground plan and the model as the best means of determining and communicating measurements and proportions. Leonardo da Vinci challenged Alberti's system of projecting into a plane framed as if observed through an open window, frustrated by its limitations in engaging with the periphery of a field, which led him to develop the bird's-eye view that could encapsulate a whole scene. This can be seen in a limited way in his sketches of a church in plan and as a perspective seen as a complete object, or body, from afar and from above (page 18).

The debates, and the systems for creating the illusion of three-dimensional space through perspectival projection, continued throughout the sixteenth and seventeenth centuries. An important nexus of its development was in Baroque theatre design, where the desire to set up complex and convincing scenery inspired innovations such as those of Ferdinando Galli da Bibiena (page 279). He transformed the traditional seventeenth-century stage, which was organized around a symmetrical view with a single vanishing point along a central axis, by setting up asymmetrical compositions using a two-point perspective from a plan – thereby opening up the confined picture plane of the proscenium to admit potentially endless space. In a different context, but also intent on creating a fictive architecture beyond the real, Andrea Pozzo invented a system for creating *quadratura* perspective on the surface of a vaulted ceiling, in order to create a magical world beyond the framing device of the architectural enclosure (page 186).

Many other systems of depicting the three-dimensional realm existed alongside the Western perspective tradition. In the 12 m-long (39.4 ft) Qing-dynasty scroll depicting *Burgeoning Life in a Resplendent Age* (page 295), the Western technique is transformed by a form of scattered perspective that allows the scene to unfold in time and across space. This phenomenon plays to the Western idea of depicting reality, blending it with the idealized landscape tradition of conventional Chinese painting.

By the twentieth century, the perspective as the principal means of depicting three dimensions in architectural drawings was being challenged by alternatives that had grown up alongside it – specifically, the isometric in its various manifestations. In terms of perspectival representations of space, the end point of the process of invention is marked by JMW Turner's nineteenth-century diagram showing the principles of rectilinear perspective. As Professor of Perspective at the Royal Academy School in London, Turner gave illustrated lectures on the history of perspective, and his image in this book depicts a system devised by Thomas Malton that, in this lecture diagram, creates a deep sense of spatial ambiguity (page 15). The uneasiness with a confined spatial system that is evident in Turner's image is resolved in Theo van Doesburg's isometrically projected *Counter-Construction* (page 71), which makes a deliberate escape from the boundaries of the picture frame – or, indeed, of any confining device. Its coloured interlocking planes suggest relationships between unspecified overlapping spaces that form a continuum with the surrounding spatial field. Taken to its extreme, and moving well beyond the realm of projecting physical elements as three-dimensional objects, Ivan Leonidov's *Schema of Spatial Culture-Organization* (page 173) proposes an architecture of nodes connected by arcs of electro-magnetic waves, in which absolute ideas about space and distance are replaced by the abstract idea of signal strength.

The origin of isometric or oblique drawing is the subject of much erudite discussion, but one of the earliest examples is Baldassare Peruzzi's sixteenth-century plan, section and interior of St Peter's in Rome (page 149), in which the structural mass is projected up from a plan set at a slight angle to the perpendicular. Auguste Choisy's worm's-eye view – an axonometric projection from below – also exploits the objective quality of isometric projection, in this case allowing the scaling and detailed measurement of the quantities and construction techniques of Roman structures (page 151). Rafael Moneo references drawings such as these in his worm's-eye view of the Museum of Roman Art in Mérida (page 150), in which the structural logic is isolated from the larger reality of the building.

A similar process of abstraction – of one aspect of a building isolated from its entire reality, but also treated as a discrete and site-less object as opposed to the building as an integral part of its context – is used to powerful effect in other isometric drawings. These include Walter Gropius's graphically vivid image of Dessau's Törten housing estate (page 88), and James Stirling's axonometric of the Leicester Engineering Building (page 217). In both of these drawings, the buildings are depicted as autonomous objects with no surroundings.

The possibilities for the isometric as a means of exploring the abstract qualities of architectural form and space were pushed further in a wave of late-twentieth-century theoretical architectural practice that questioned the boundaries of architecture – its cultural but also professional role – which was spurred on by post-war Italian Marxists, who possibly perceived the professional architect to be an instrument of capitalism. Works of great formal and academic complexity emerged, such as Daniel Libeskind's *Time Sections* (page 162), which manoeuvred a series of axonometric projections in order to embody the passage of time, as in a Cubist painting; or John Hejduk's *Diamond House A* (page 105), in which he manipulated the implications of the isometric's rotation in order to raise questions about composition and the meaning of form.

Ultimately, the act of looking at an architectural drawing is affected by the fact that it is a representation of something else – a concept, a design problem, a proposal – which brings its status as an autonomous aesthetic object into question. There is another way of looking at these drawings, however, which is to consider the time that is embodied in them: the interval of looking at or even contemplating them, but also the duration of making them. This time is often understood in commercial terms, especially when the drawing is part of the process of producing a building for which the architect charges a fee. Even if it is instrumental to the development of a purely intellectual approach, its value is tied up with the creation of a potentially lucrative public persona.

Sometimes, perhaps often, however, the act of making the drawing has an additional worth to the person making it. It is said that Steven Holl rises early each morning to take a solitary moment to make a drawing in his sketchbook (page 159), but the master of time borrowed for himself was George Aitchison. His design for a wall elevation of the Arab Hall at Leighton House (page 64) is typical of the intricately detailed watercolour drawings he made for the interiors he designed. Despite his success as a busy public figure, and fees that meant he could afford to cover the labour of draughtsmen, he spent many hours in sometimes repetitive, monotonous work, in order to complete fields of miniature wallpaper, decorative tilework or even representations of friezes by other artists. The deliberate but potentially creative boredom that he reclaimed for himself is often lost from everyday life, but taking the time to contemplate drawings that may be beautiful or intriguing, but not always easy to understand, may be a way of retrieving it.

**MADELON VRIESENDORP (1945–)**

**Flagrant Délit, 1975**

Watercolour and gouache on paper

35.3 × 39.9 cm, 14 × 15¾ in

A fragment of a longer, fantastical narrative, *Flagrant Délit* is one of a series of paintings collectively called *Manhattan* made by artist Madelon Vriesendorp, who was a founding member of the Dutch practice Office for Metropolitan Architecture. This image was used on the cover of Rem Koolhaas' book *Delirious New York: A Retroactive Manifesto for Manhattan* in 1978, and depicts two anthropomorphized skyscrapers, the Empire State and Chrysler buildings, post coitus. Other New York landmarks shown include the Statue of Liberty who, armless and accompanied by a vast crowd of serried onlookers, gazes bereft through the grid of the window, for her torch is the bedside lamp. Below the bed, the Manhattan grid is laid out as a carpet, and a Goodyear Blimp mimics a Salvador Dalí clock in its role as a discarded condom. The Rockefeller Building glares from the door, its searching beam of light panning the bed echoed in the lighthouse and headlights on the shore of the painting behind. The image presents a critique of Manhattan as the epitome of the twentieth-century city, in the form of a surrealist dream. Often attributed as an influence is Dalí's paranoid-critical method. Through the invoking of a paranoid state – in this image, enacted through the mass observation of a private act intensified as a moment of discovery – the intention is to dismantle the seeming reality and identity of the subject – here, the city of Manhattan with its principal characters – so that it can be understood on subjective terms, as an experience. This was in contradiction to the objectivity of modernity as it emerged from the Enlightenment, represented in the searching and obtrusive beams of light in the darkness, and the relentless logic of the grid that comprised the city – here made human.

**GIAN LORENZO BERNINI (1598–1680)**

**Louvre, 1664**

Pen and brown ink with a brown wash

16.3 × 27.8 cm, 6½ × 11 in

Gian Lorenzo Bernini's 1665 visit to Paris was a diplomatic coup for King Louis XIV, who invited him to submit proposals for the east facade of the Louvre, the then-headquarters of the French monarchy. Bernini prepared four designs, and this freehand ink drawing describes a fragment of the first – and most striking – proposal, made before his visit, while his imagination was still in Rome. The building is seen from the east; a central, oval pavilion dominates the left-hand side of the drawing, its northern wing extending from it. Close inspection of this detailed perspective sketch, whose vanishing point disappears into the central arch of the pavilion, rather than the centre of the drawing, reveals the complex layering of the facade. The two-storey elevation sits on a tall, stepped plinth, which accentuates the complex shape of the volumetric composition, its curves and changes of direction in plan, while imparting a fortified character to the whole. Between double-height Corinthian pilasters, balconies curve outwards or inwards, mimicking the flow of the facade, while arches between them frame inner vaults and doorways represented in a forest of inky lines. The whole design was symmetrical, with a second, southern wing replicating the one drawn here, the clerestory above the central space appearing as a crown above the heavy cornice line. However, Bernini's animated, robust and grandiose proposal did not conform to the French Enlightenment architecture that was in vogue at that time. His Baroque challenge to static Classical harmony, which he had been developing in his Roman architectural projects, was rejected in favour of a proposal by a French team led by Claude Perrault. Their sober, symmetrical design with its central portico flanked by flat colonnades over a plain lower storey, which has become the Colonnade de Perrault, was chosen by the king instead.

**GOTTFRIED BÖHM (1920–2021)**

**Pilgrimage Church, 1965**

Pencil on tracing paper

67.2 × 62 cm, 26½ × 24½ in

This drawing encapsulates the extraordinary presence that this pilgrimage church exerts in the central German village of Neviges, where the textures of its bare weathered-concrete surfaces echo, but do not relate to, the rendered walls of nearby buildings. Belonging to a monastery, it is sited in the north of the village, near a wood that surrounds a huge meadow, although none of these natural surroundings, and very few clues as to the character of the settlement, are evident in the drawing. Instead the image, which was made for Böhm's competition-winning entry, focuses on the unadorned concrete surfaces of the building, which are textured with graphite lines. Their rendering explores the abstract, volumetric quality of the church through a study of light falling across its faceted planes. These shades range from a pale grey, resulting from the lightest touch, to the blackness of repeated cross-hatching that can be seen on the right-hand side of the drawing. At the bottom left-hand corner, the entrance to the building appears small in relation to the size of the church's volume. The pitched-roof space of the porch is shown in section, bringing into focus the line cut through the stepped terrain around this side of the compound, which traverses a steep slope. A small tree is shown in silhouette against the wall of the church, and a further human element is revealed in two tiny people outlined against a pale wall on a higher street level. The church's scale is of a different order to these figures and the everyday architecture of the village. Instead, it represents a crystalline mountain from another world, and if it were not for the cross at the peak of the Mariendom it would be difficult to know its purpose.

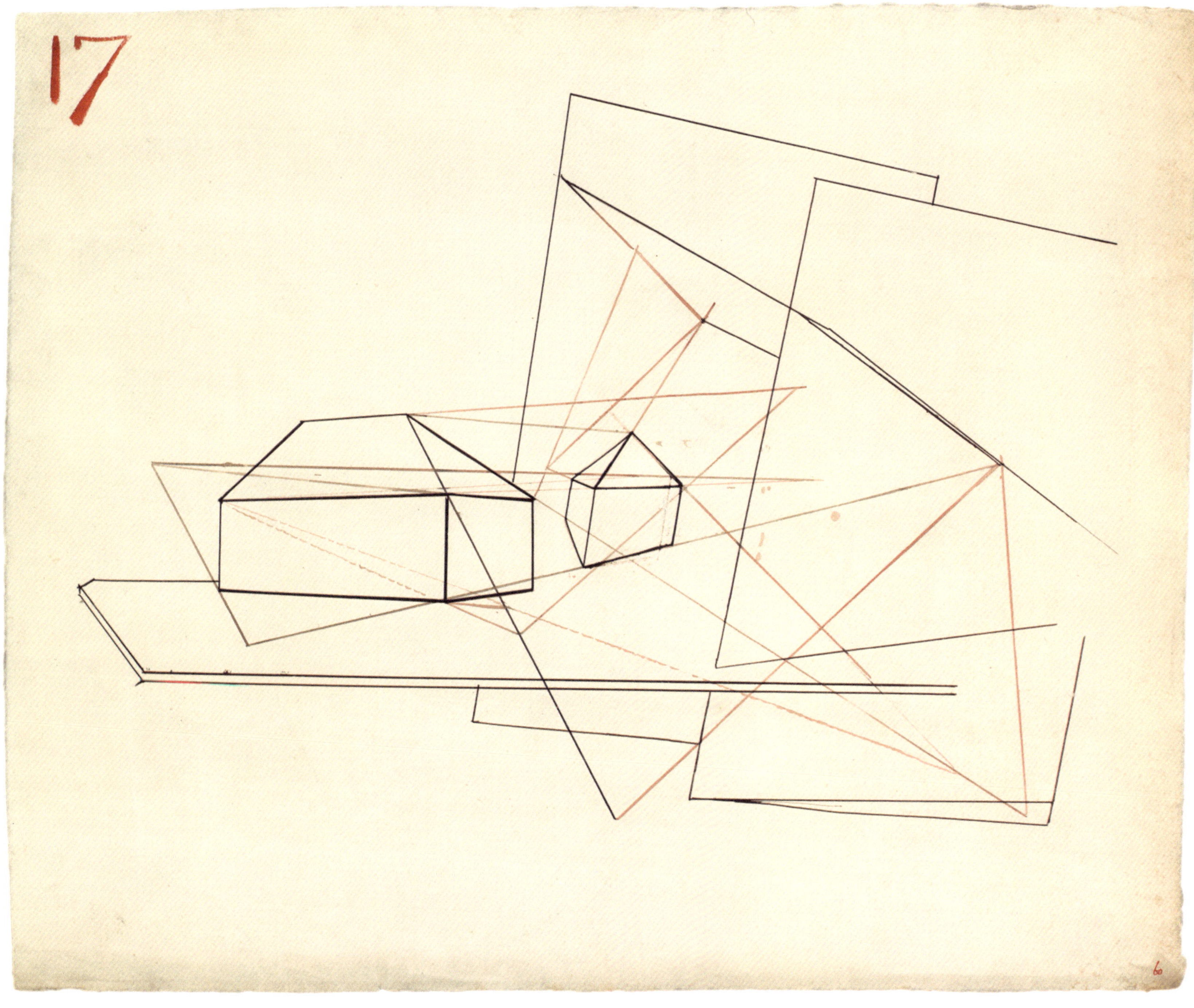


**JMW TURNER (1775–1851)**

**Lecture Diagram 17: Principles of Rectilinear Perspective (after Thomas Malton Senior), 1810**

Pen and ink on paper

48.4 × 60 cm, 19 × 23½ in

Between 1807 and 1837, JMW Turner, famous for sublime landscape paintings whose spaces almost always eschewed traditional perspectival rendering, was Professor of Perspective at the Royal Academy Schools. This image is one of around 170 diagrams that he made to illustrate theories and procedures in his lectures, and is thought to belong to his first series, given in 1811. It shows two simple pitched-roofed volumes, each belonging to its own spatial sphere, despite appearing to share a ground plane. A sense of discomfort is created by the lack of stability in the drawing; there is no vantage point, and the myriad of planes suggested by the triangular shapes and rectangular elements prevents a single, coherent spatial structure from emerging. Without the accompanying notes, it is impossible to understand the diagram within the flow of Turner's argument, but it is interesting for the way it breaks out of the perspective grid's rigid framework while adhering to the principles of one of its interpreters. In demolishing the essential relationship between the two figures, a sense of infinity creeps in that is the essence of Turner's paintings. It is also a precursor to experiments in spatial representation that would emerge at the end of the century, culminating in Cubism and the *Counter-Constructions* of De Stijl polemicist Theo van Doesburg. Many of Turner's diagrams clearly describe practical methods of setting up perspectives. Others reveal a lack of objective consensus through erudite analysis of concepts put forward by others, including British theorists such as seventeenth-century printer and hydrographer Joseph Moxon and eighteenth-century mathematician William Emerson. *Lecture Diagram 17* is an analysis based on the thinking of Thomas Malton Senior, an eighteenth-century draughtsman and writer on geometry who published a treatise on perspective in 1778, and from whose son Turner received early training in architectural drawing.

**JEAN-JACQUES LEQUEU (1757–1826)**

**The Subterranean Labyrinth of the Gothic House, 1800**

Pen, wash and watercolour

51.7 × 36.4 cm, 20¼ × 14¼ in

This fantasy section through an imaginary house described as Gothic, a term more fitting in the literary than architectural sense, shows a strong narrative structure. This is unravelled through the process implied in the other part of its title – the subterranean labyrinth. The section reveals terrible secrets hidden underground, or deep within spaces disguised by the attics and parapets of the surrounding structures. The drawing depicts an architectural promenade that proceeds along undulating tunnels and through enclosed caverns of fire, smoke and shadow – rather like a video game. This quality is enhanced by the glossy character of the finely rendered watercolour, which lusciously evokes the licking flames, pervasive smoke and darkness, and the ritualistic qualities of intricate details, such as the torture-like tools between the chambers of fire, or the cog or wheel beneath the huge seated figure. The architectural style of the rooms is eclectic, and certainly a critique of the rationalist Neo-Classicism of French architecture at that time. The defining narrative concerns the initiation of an Egyptian prince who undergoes trials of fire, water and air, and the corbelled rooms, with their sense of having been excavated rather than constructed, attest to this. Another possible reference are the factories of the Industrial Revolution just coming into being, and the sense of narrative echoes the concept of the linear division of labour, described by Adam Smith in *The Wealth of Nations*, 1776. Lequeu's few biographical details describe an elusive and self-mythologized life, and the date of his death is thought to correspond with the acquisition of his oeuvre by the Bibliotheque Royale in Paris. Recent research suggests that Marcel Duchamp used the name Jean-Jacques Lequeu of Rouen as one of his alter egos, thus adding another layer of mystery to his work and enhancing its surrealist aura.

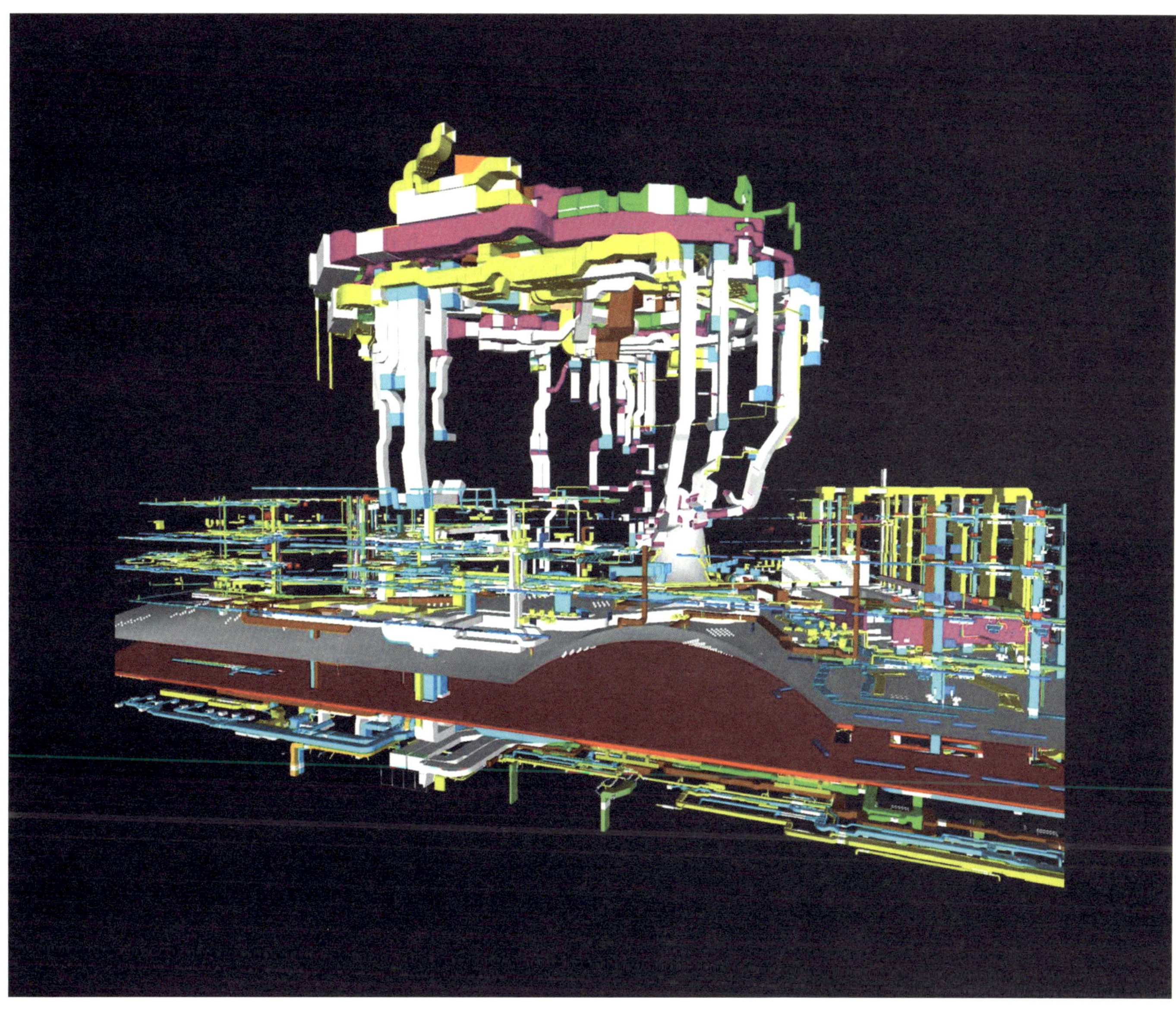

**HERZOG & DE MEURON**

**Elbphilharmonie, 2016**

Computer software

Building Information Modelling (BIM) is a three-dimensional model-based process involving the generation and management of digital representations of the physical and functional characteristics of places and buildings. For an architectural project, everyone on the design and construction team – architect, client, suppliers, engineers, contractors and environmental managers, for example – can work on the model, which becomes a principal design tool. In the office of Herzog & de Meuron, BIM is used during the later stages, when it is essential for different members of a large design team to coordinate. At this juncture, a BIM is made as an assembly of smart objects — predefined architectural elements, already with a value attached and easily quantifiable in the model. Everything is interconnected. Conventional two-dimensional projections (plans, sections, elevations) are extracted as views of the three-dimensional virtual environment. This print is an image taken from a BIM, manipulated to become an aesthetic object, but also communicative of the building that it describes. It shows just one aspect of the complex model made for the Elbphilharmonie, a spectacular extension to an existing warehouse in the Hamburg docks completed in 2016, and was produced in response to an exhibition of architectural drawings that reveal the architect's role as construction coordinator. The layers of the model that relate to the servicing of the project – especially the air supply and extract systems that maintain the fluctuating environments of the large concert hall – have been extracted and coloured to make them legible. The diagram of the building is immediately apparent, where the heavily serviced performance rooms are situated in the new addition on top, and their mop of huge vents and ducts feeds them from the side.

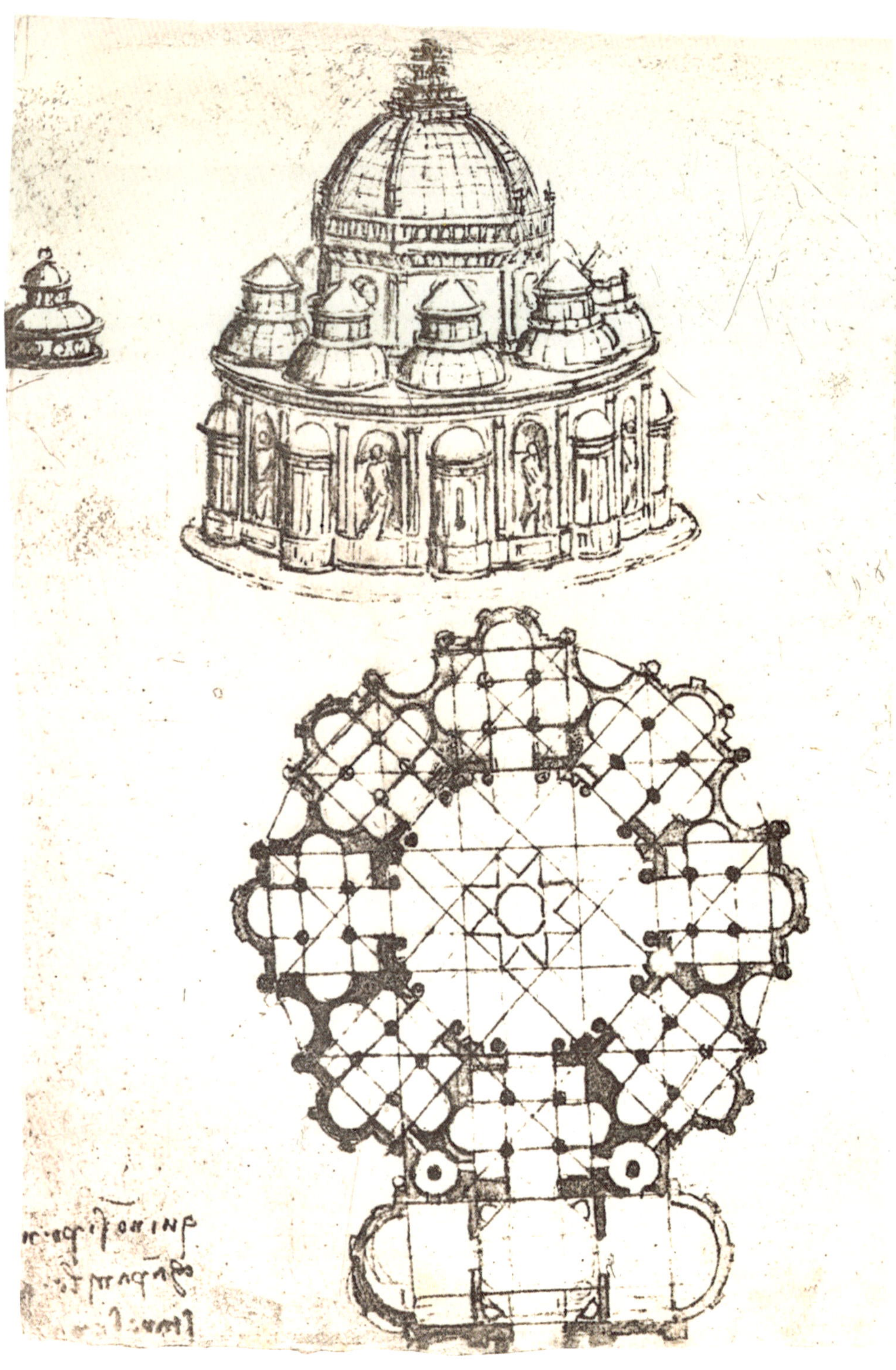

**LEONARDO DA VINCI (1452–1519)**

**Drawing of a church, 1490**

Pen and ink on paper

35 × 26 cm, 13¾ × 10¼ in

This rapid sketch by Leonardo da Vinci, one of a pair and showing the plan and a perspective view of a church, with annotations in mirror script and a tiny sketch of an additional cupola, reveals the Renaissance polymath's analytical skill. Like most of Leonardo's church perspectives, this shows the building viewed from a height, but without the strong modelling of light or shade that he sometimes used to emphasize a sense of three-dimensionality. The complexity of the lines delineating the system of niches and projections of the seven small chapels surrounding the main space, each with their own dome and cupola, could have precluded this. The niches are shaded, but not with the cross-hatching that he often used. This is interesting because it demonstrates a consciousness of space as volumetric, rather than defined by a structural system of columns and walls. The perspective is not formally set up, but made freehand without a vanishing point – like almost all perspectives, or *scaenographia*, in the fifteenth century. Da Vinci made sixty to seventy undated studies for churches – the majority, for centrally planned, domed structures like the one shown here. This preoccupation was consistent with a general movement among artists against the hierarchical, longitudinal naves and aisles of the medieval church with its side chapels, which began with Brunelleschi's Santa Maria degli Angeli in Florence, 1434. For Renaissance and humanist architects, the round or polygonal plan conformed to the perfection of Platonic geometry and represented a microcosm of God's conception of the universe. The clergy's resistance to this innovation, which did not suit the form of the Mass or effect a separation from the congregation, meant that few churches of this type were actually constructed, since they could not respond to ecclesiastical functions. Leonardo's drawings are fantastical explorations of modelling and form, rather than theoretical or design proposals.

**FRANK GEHRY (1929–)**

**Guggenheim Museum, Bilbao, 1992**

Computer software

29 × 10.2 cm, 11½ × 4 in

At the time it was made, this drawing was revolutionary as a design and communication tool for architectural production. In 1989, two years before Frank Gehry made his first visit to the Bilbao site where the new Guggenheim Museum would be situated, his office housed just two computers, used for administration. Resolving and imagining the spatial experiments that Gehry's studio had been working on was confined by the limits of hand drafting, pushing the boundaries of the possible and instigating a search for a way forwards. The solution they found was the CATIA system, computer software developed by the French aerospace industry to make virtual three-dimensional models of complex, multi-axis, curved forms. In the initial analysis and design stages for the Guggenheim, Gehry and his team used conventional means – hand-drawn sketches, plus timber, card and paper models. Once the design began to take on a material form requiring structure and detail, however, CATIA became relevant. This CATIA drawing shows the huge sculptural frames supporting the sheets of titanium cladding that cluster and flow around the museum's solid enclosures – arrived at after a steep learning curve. Initially, the system seemed limited to symmetries and mirror images, but the possibility for visualizing gestural moves soon became evident. With its ability to describe any surface as an equation, and therefore to be able to map and define any part of a complex surface, the software became an invaluable design tool, but more essentially a means of communication, without which the production and coordination of the different elements would have been impossible. CATIA made it possible for the nature of these complex forms to be communicated to subcontractors and manufacturers using the same software, broken down into component parts. This enabled the cutting, moulding and joining of material elements with an unexpected efficiency and accuracy.

**ANGELA DEUBER (1975–)**

**School in Thal, 2013**

Inkjet print on fine art paper

150 × 190 cm, 59 × 74¾ in

This drawing, which architect Angela Deuber calls *Analytique*, is of a school building for the village of Thal. From a distance the surface of the large drawing, which is 1.5 m (4.9 ft) tall and 1.9 m (6.2 ft) long, reads as a composition made of shadows and silhouettes. The darkest zone inhabits the bottom of the sheet. Running diagonally down from a third of the way up the sheet, a dark shape reveals the nature of the ground in a section that cuts through the slope of the site. Just a short way down, it is interrupted by the outline of the building at a large scale that is easy to read from afar. At a much smaller scale, the edge of Lake Constant creates an uneven line behind, rising almost to the upper right-hand corner. A pale circle around a tiny white square indicates that the sheet constitutes a site plan showing the school in relation to its local and regional geographical features, on top of which the other translucent layers have been applied like veils. Behind these shaded zones, the sheet pales into a golden colour, over which a lighter vertical strip and darker-toned rectilinear fields highlight specific elements of the orthogonal drawings that describe the three square floor plans, cross section and four elevations of the building. These are discernible closer up, drawn to the same scale as each other, with a white line running across the top of the dark zone to indicate the surface of the ground. This delicate white line is used to demarcate the plans and the section. The elevations, on the other hand, are drawn in dark shades over the brown background, visible but camouflaged. Floating over the surface of the lake, two different axonometric projections show the organization of the design: the top image dismantles the exterior structure of the facade, while the bottom shows the internal structure and is sited in a garden plot, symbolised by a geometric pattern.

**PIETER SAENREDAM (1597–1665)**

**Nieuwe Kerk in Haarlem, 1653**

Oil on oak

88 × 103 cm, 34½ × 40½ in

Pieter Saenredam's images of seventeenth-century architectural settings resonate today with a minimalist sensibility, selected as favourites by John Pawson and Edmund de Waal. Capturing the essence of plain space by conveying the material, atmosphere and light of large-scale interiors – such as the one in this painting of Haarlem's Nieuwe Kerk, a Protestant Reform church built in the mid-sixteenth century – they depict scenes of everyday life facilitated and protected by a monumental and puritanical architecture. The greater part of Saenredam's oeuvre comprises church interiors that have the open character of public squares rather than the regulated nature of ceremonial buildings. Here, the pavements are inhabited by active figures, and a dog plays near two seated children. The asymmetry of the painting's composition contributes to its informality, and behind the children the enclosure for the pulpit and its canopy sits ship-like on the floor, surrounded by empty space. Nonetheless, the architecture of the church depicted in this image is symmetrical, with a central cross-vault leading into barrel vaults, and a hanging lantern making a vertical line down the centre of the painting. The direction of single-point perspective places the vantage point off-centre, however, and looking towards the corner of the church rather than at the central doorway at the rear. Saenredam was a master of perspective, and his constructions were based on precise measurements. For his interiors, he often made several sketches of overviews, detailed drawings and ground plans, noting the distances between, and the dimensions of, the main architectural elements. This view is unusual in that it includes several elements that existed only in the construction drawings of the church but which, for financial reasons, were not executed in the actual building.

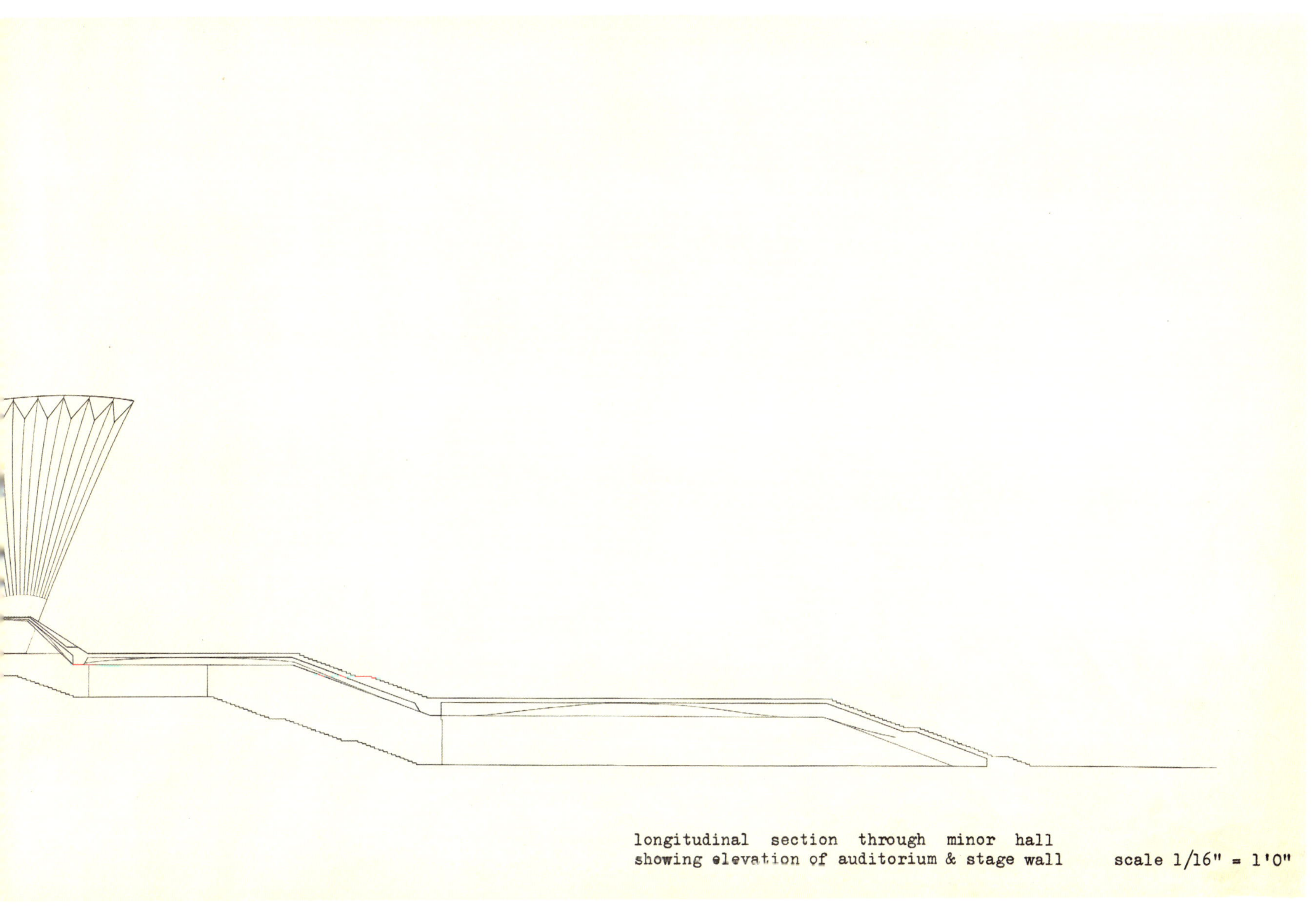


**JØRN UTZON (1918–2008)**

**Minor Hall, Sydney Opera House, 1962**

Ink on paper

26 × 82 cm, 10¼ × 32¼ in

The international competition to design the Sydney Opera House, which accommodates two performance halls, was won by Danish architect Jørn Utzon in 1957. The *Sydney Opera House: Yellow Book* was published in 1962 – three years after construction began, and eleven years before the building opened in 1973. Presented to the Opera House Executive Committee, the drawings shown on its thirty-six pages encapsulated a defining moment in the building's evolution – the resolution of the vaulted shells of the roof, which would be developed over more than a year of design and geometrical study before the construction schedule was prepared. The drawing here features on page 8 of the book, and shows a section through the building looking east and depicting the minor hall. The section line cuts through the floor of the hall, omitting service areas beneath but showing the foyers and staircases to the north of the auditorium facing the sun and the water, with the slope of the seating stepping down gently towards the stage. The dramatic, curved structures that encompass the hall beneath the overarching shells can be seen in elevation, and to the right the performers' entrance descends beneath a large terrace. The point of intersection of the two halls' axes meet on the terrace, and the viewer standing on it can look directly down the centre lines of the halls. It is marked by the Inaugural Plaque, which was laid in 1958 to commemorate the commencement of the podium's construction. Utzon's competition-entry panels had shown schematic designs in which the shell concept was already defined, but its resolution would challenge the building's engineers, led by Ove Arup, for months. Eventually, Utzon himself conceived of the spherical solution, crafting the shells from the surface of an imaginary sphere and imbuing the design with a universal geometry.

**ROBERTO BURLE MARX (1909–94)**

**Ibirapuera Park, 1953**

Gouache and graphite on board

100.3 × 151.1 cm, 39½ × 59½ in

Roberto Burle Marx was the first Brazilian landscape architect to depart from the Classical principles of formal garden design, using the natural world and hybrid culture of his native land to inspire and suffuse his work. In the early 1950s, he was commissioned to design the layout for the first metropolitan park in São Paolo, located on the site of an indigenous village, on a marshy floodplain. Under the direction of Oscar Niemeyer – who designed the park's structures, including an auditorium, gallery and several other pavilions – he developed his plan, and the final scheme was worked on by Otávio Augusto Teixeira Mendes. This drawing reveals Burle Marx's characteristic approach to composition, which he applied to the design of paving, murals, tapestries and reliefs as well as gardens. Trained as a painter, he regarded the creation of landscapes and paintings as intimately connected, and he spoke of his work as a form of painting with vegetation. His colourful, asymmetrical compositions reference paintings by Henri Matisse, Jean Arp and Joan Miró in their free-form lines. In his drawings and painting, these shapes encompass fields of planting and ways through them. The plan of Ibirapuera Park shows these elements overlaid within the larger precinct, which is defined by a flat green. This is outlined by the road system running along the bottom of the plan, its grey colour indicating a paved surface that seeps into the park itself in the form of undulating routes to irregularly shaped plazas. These serve the various buildings designed by Niemeyer, which stand out on the plan with their blank orthogonal shapes that at times break out in strange eruptions. Over the green field, a network of paths is animated by the colour-coded depiction of flowerbeds stuffed with native vegetation, colourful schemes for paved areas and two free-form bodies of water.

**BALKRISHNA V DOSHI (1927–2023)**

**Sangath, 1985**

Coloured pencil on paper

62 × 32 cm, 24½ × 12½ in

The half-buried Sangath complex, in Ahmedabad, is located in a green garden compound, exactly as shown in this colourful, oblique drawing by Balkrishna V Doshi. The composition has been created by projecting the vertical plane upward to scale from a site plan, to show the elevations facing the street to the south. This is a huge, arterial route into the city of Ahmedabad called Drive In Road, whose traffic is represented by the cars at the bottom of the drawing, but also by a striding blue pedestrian and a camel, revealing the more inclusive attitude that the inhabitants of Ahmedabad have to animals compared to those of European and North American cities. The fish in the pond and the birds alongside, with the peacock in the garden, reinforce this impression. The drawing is constructed so as to show the sunken court of the open-air theatre in the garden, with its adjacent cooling pond, in relation to the building's elevations, and the striking concrete barrel-vaulted roofs coated in broken fragments of white porcelain. These long structures housed Doshi's architectural studio, as well as the Vastu Shilpa Foundation for environmental research and education. The garden is an essential component of the complex, protecting it from the heat and pollution of the surrounding city, where the temperature can reach 45 degrees Celsius, and acting as a permeable buffer to the floods of monsoon rain. This shaded realm, with its abundance of different kinds of trees, each of which is given its own character in the drawing, also functions as an extension of the internal accommodation. The stepped court is used for lectures, discussions and concerts on cooler evenings, and the entrance is sited at the rear of the building, requiring a *promenade architecturale* to be completed before entering inside.

**ADLER & SULLIVAN**

**Mercantile Club Building, 1891**

Pencil on paper

33 × 25 cm, 13 × 9¾ in

In 1891, a competition was held to find an architect for the Mercantile Club Building in St Louis, for which the firm Adler & Sullivan submitted an unsuccessful entry. In this project, Louis Sullivan experimented in a practical sense with the issues later resolved in his 1896 essay 'The Tall Office Building Artistically Considered' – here, seeking to create a domestic rather than commercial appearance. Using the top-floor banqueting hall as a device for reconfiguring the balance of the composition, he manipulated the scale of the whole as seen within an urban context. This massive crowning element, expressed as a box-like colonnade around the whole building, seems to be supported by two curved bays on each elevation that rise like giant, fenestrated pilasters from the decorative frame of the ground-floor base. Above, a steep pitched roof reinforces the unity of the whole, echoing a grand hunting lodge rather than the simpler, palazzo-like block of Adler & Sullivan's Wainwright Building in the same city, with its projecting cornice. Sullivan's Mercantile Club project was important in the development of his formal approach to the unprecedented high structures that were becoming possible thanks to new materials and technologies, and the increasing scale of commerce requiring accommodation in the late-nineteenth-century industrial city. In his 1896 essay, this design problem was approached from first principles. 'What is the chief characteristic of the tall office building?' he asked. And the answer was, 'It is lofty.' It is in this essay that the infamous phrase 'Form ever follows function' was first articulated, which would be used to justify later, far inferior, functionalist architecture. The intended appeal, however, was to a cultural and even poetic interpretation of the character of form, and not the articulation of a mass-produced system, expediently modified to fit different uses.

**BALDASSARE PERUZZI (1481–1536)**

**Basilica of San Petronio, c.1522**

Pen and brown ink with a brown wash over black chalk on paper

93.1 × 53.3 cm, 36¾ × 21 in

Between the sixteenth and nineteenth centuries, many proposals were made to complete the unfinished facade of the Basilica of San Petronio, including projects by Andrea Palladio and Giulio Romano. Italy's third-largest religious building after the cathedrals in Milan and Florence, its main elevation facing Bologna's Piazza Maggiore, bears little resemblance today to this drawing by Italian painter and architect Baldassare Peruzzi. The drawing is a composite of several conjoined sheets, which reflects its quasi-archaeological character – not simply in representing material continuity with the existing church but also in the complex narratives carved into its facade. These are told in this detailed drawing through a combination of fine-line drawing in brown ink and washes used to enhance the effect of three-dimensional modelling in the drawings of the reliefs, as well as augmenting the sense of space behind the façades, whose modelled surface is punctuated with the inky shadows of the doorways and arched windows above. Today, the top half of the facade remains an unfinished, naked brick wall with one simple, central arched window, near Peruzzi's rose window in this drawing. The section below the first cornice is similar although not identical to Peruzzi's final, unexecuted design, which embodies a modified version of the then-existing marble facade. This comprised late-fourteenth-century works by Antonio di Vincenzo and, later, Alfonso Lombardi and Jacopo della Quercia. Peruzzi is known to have been an early promoter of axonometric drawing, which he used in studies of antique buildings. In these, he developed an extensive knowledge through analysis of building materials and construction. These studies influenced his scheme for San Petronio, which has the character of a grand sculptural portico, with the dynamic three-dimensional qualities of its projecting Corinthian pilasters and recessed doorways clearly evident, despite the rich tapestry of detail at play in between.

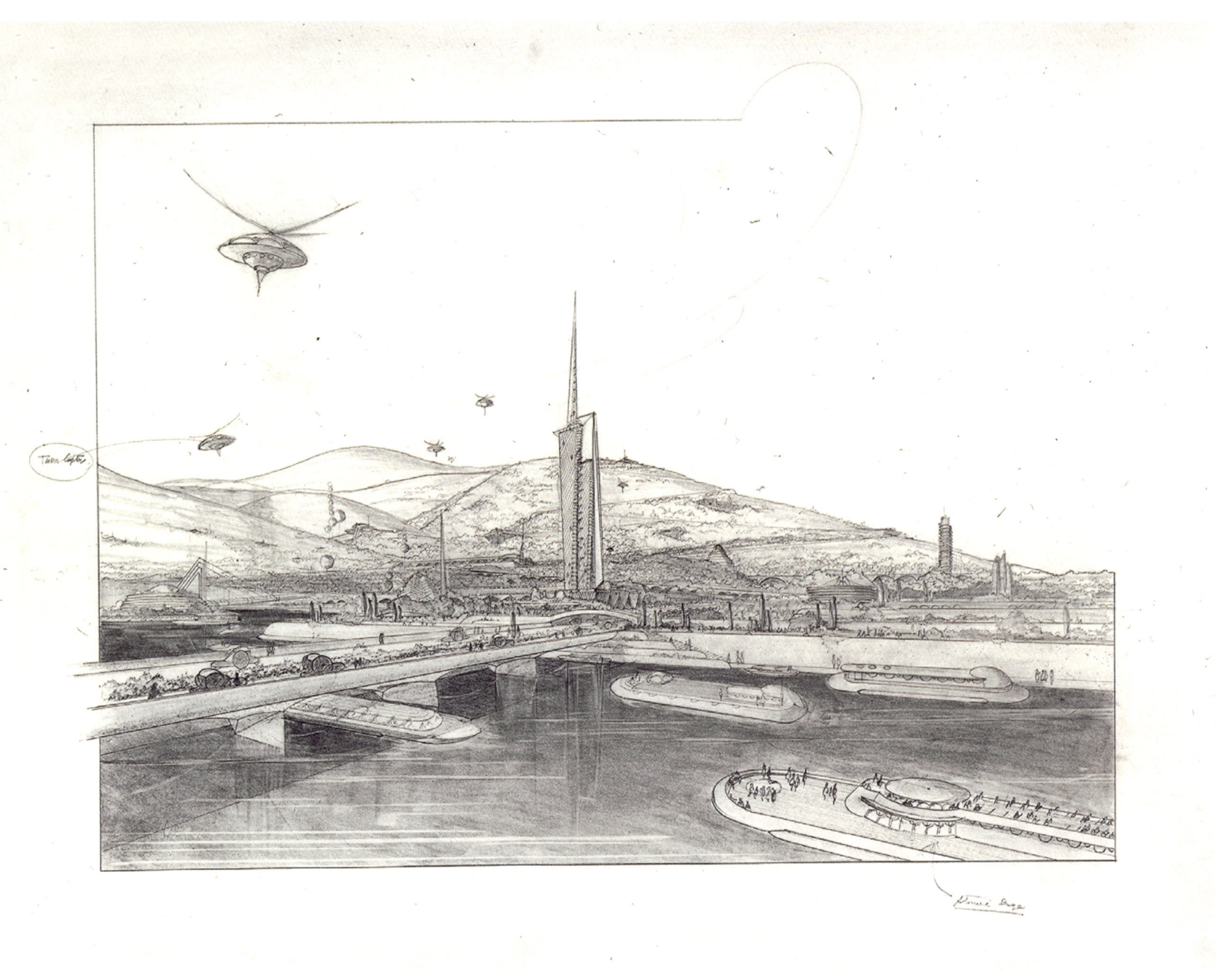

**FRANK LLOYD WRIGHT (1867–1959)**

**The Living City, 1958**

Pencil on tracing paper

82 × 106.7 cm, 32¼ × 42 in

In 1958, the ageing Frank Lloyd Wright published a book called *The Living City* – from which this detailed pencil perspective of a central zone is taken – describing the final iteration of his philosophy for an American urban landscape. In his architecture and ideas about the city, Wright proposed a cultural alternative drawn from Mayan ruins and Pueblo architecture but also influenced by Japanese culture. The results of this vision can be seen here in the pyramid structures emerging from clusters of trees. Individual transportation was the key; the circular flying vehicles seen in this drawing were already apparent in his work by the 1930s, their form reappearing in later Wright projects such as the Huntington Hartford Country Club, 1947, and the Guggenheim Museum, 1959. This perspective image, seen from above as if flying in one of these aerial transport pods, is unusual in depicting a relatively urban centre within Wright's decentralized agrarian proposal, which was dependent on the self-sufficient homestead. The tension between his fascination with transportation and communication technologies and Arts and Crafts-based, agrarian idealism is played out here. A tall building marks the centre of the composition, in a waterside leisure parkland. Large boats glide by, and snail-like cars join pedestrians on a wide causeway. In the distant hills, widely dispersed residences enjoy views across this fantasy landscape. For Wright, this utopian dreaming involved reimagining the city as spreading over and transforming the continent's vast open spaces, defined by a modified rural landscape rather than the high-density metropolis of skyscraper and skyline. This approach had begun thirty years earlier with his concept of 'Usonia', a word describing the egalitarian culture that Wright thought would spontaneously emerge in the United States.

**MOON HOON (1968–)**

**Seoul Prizone, 2009**

Red brush pen, gold pencil and black pen on paper

21 × 30 cm, 8¼ × 11¾ in

Seoul-based architect Moon Hoon's drawing practice is formulated in a succession of diaries, which he calls *magic books*, and, in his own words, stems from a life of excessive doodling. Despite this humble premise, the drawings consolidate a sophisticated range of visual references, from 1960s Radical Futurism to Russian Constructivism, and established architectural figures such as Le Corbusier, Lebbeus Woods and Tadao Ando to Japanese animation and the notebooks of Leonardo Da Vinci. His compositions and use of colour – notably the red ink seen in this drawing – rely on associational depth as well as formal ingenuity for their appeal. Biomorphic structures and strange mechanical objects often populate the drawings – which are sometimes, but not always, inhabited by tiny figures. The shell form – a recurring leitmotif in Hoon's work – has been transformed into a giant building in his drawing *Seoul Prizone*, which presents two parallel worlds: that of the red Dongho Bridge, which corresponds to the familiar and commonplace built environment, and that of an alternative fantasy realm defined by a parasitic, amorphic surface. This clings to the bridge, anchoring the huge shell structure and forming a constructed ground plane that supersedes the river's banks, sometimes sinking beneath the surface of the water. The term *Prizone* is a neologism invented by Hoon that synthesizes the words *Prison* and *Free Zone*. Hoon deliberately maintains the uncertainty of the hand-drawn line in these drawings, so that they have a playful, accidentally human quality. They are challenges to the orthodox architectural world that come directly from the imagination, moving architecture beyond its limits through what Hoon calls acts of creative terrorism.

**FRANÇOIS-JOSEPH BÉLANGER (1744–1818)**

**Design for a Wall Elevation at the Hôtel Dervieux, c.1789**

Pen and ink over graphite with coloured washes and gouache on paper

30.6 × 28.5 cm, 12 × 11¼ in

Admitted to the prestigious Académie Royale d'Architecture at the age of twenty, François-Joseph Bélanger became a well-connected architect and designer of entertainments for the French court. Despite his royal connections, he was only briefly imprisoned during the French Revolution, in Saint-Lazare jail in 1794. Upon his release, he married his mistress, dancer Anne-Victoire Dervieux, and renovated and extended her Parisian mansion. Starting in 1788, Bélanger enlarged the building, adding two new wings and decorating them in the latest Pompeian style, so that it became famous as an elegant and seductive *maison de plaisance*. Unlike many French Neo-Classical architects of the eighteenth century, Bélanger did not win the Prix de Rome or travel to Italy, and instead carried out his studies of antiquity at a remove from direct personal experience. This elaborate wall elevation drawing comes from an album of more than twenty alternative designs for a room in the mansion. Some of these are mere sketches, their line of thought abandoned early on. In this case, however, the whole scheme can be determined; the composition has been carefully set out using ruler and compass, and the fine detail carefully completed, obliterating the setting-out marks. An arch motif surrounds a niche whose presence can be determined by the divisions in the cornice line. Set into its yellow background, jewel-like frames surround portraits of figures barely discernible against their dark-blue backgrounds. A variety of decorative schemes are used: in the flat panel on the left a naturalistic rose briar curls, but the cornice is treated with a complex egg-and-dart motif. Within the arched frame, a fine scene is created that incorporates arcades, dancing figures, birds, griffins and swags in a scheme of Etruscan arabesques inspired by the archaeological excavations at Herculaneum and Pompeii.

**IVAN FOMIN (1897–1936)**

**Central hall of Teatralnaya Metro Station, 1936**

Paper, pencil, watercolour and ink

116 × 145 cm, 45¾ × 17¾ in

In June 1935, Joseph Stalin and Vyacheslav Molotov signed off the General Plan for the Reconstruction of Moscow, which proposed almost doubling its urban area, with the greatest densities at the centre, surrounded by a new Garden Ring of huge parks. Initial work on the Moscow metro system preceded this plan, with the first line being approved by the Central Committee of the USSR in 1932, when the larger urban plan was still in its preliminary stages. Located on the Zamoskvoretskaya line, near to Teatralnaya Square in central Moscow, which is the location of numerous theatres including the Bolshoi, the Teatralnaya Metro Station, designed by Ivan Fomin, illustrates how this approach was effected. This perspective drawing of its main hall shows the escalators at the end, ascending the 34 m (111.5 ft) to ground level directly from the excavated, cave-like space of the station. This is the most glamorous of caves, however, and the fluted pilasters that line it, interleaved by walls and marble benches with vaulted access-ways to the platforms, are faced with labradorite and white marble taken from the Cathedral of Christ the Saviour, which Stalin had demolished to make way for the Palace of the Soviets. Complementing the chequerboard floor pattern, whose grid neatly lines up with the escalators, the vaulted ceiling is decorated with diamond-patterned coffering. This is interspersed with majolica bas-reliefs by Natalya Danko, whose various figures refer to theatrical arts in the USSR, drawn from the ethnic traditions of nationalities incorporated into the Soviet Union. Although work on the metro was carried out by Soviet labourers, much expert advice came from British engineers trained on the London Underground – they advocated escalators as opposed to lifts, and tunnelling rather than a cut-and-cover approach.

**SOU FUJIMOTO (1971–)**

**Serpentine Pavilion, 2013**

Pen on paper

6 × 9 cm, 2½ × 3½ in

'I tried to make something melting into the green,' said Sou Fujimoto of his project for the ephemeral pavilion that he designed for the small, flat, tree-lined lawn outside the Serpentine Gallery in London. The fine translucency of the structure that he proposed in order to achieve this ambition is depicted in this sketch. It is typical of all his work, which refines the structural elements of his built works down to a minimal, cloud-like presence. Within a mat of red lines drawn lightly on to the cream-coloured paper, many having been made with a continuous up-and-down or side-to-side motion, the architectural form is crystallized by the figures captured within the drawing, who are dispersed in small groups or alone. Sketching is an important part of Fujimoto's design process, which he has described as a procedure of trial-and-error, an internal dialogue made present, which eventually gives form to vague architectural ideas. In his conceptual sketches, he maintains a deliberate ambiguity that is often transferred to the material reality, although not always in the same form. For this reason, he creates his drawings with loose and fluid lines, without applying explicit rules or formulae. As the sketch suggests, the Serpentine Pavilion was designed to combine the exterior atmosphere with its interior environment by creating a transparency interrupted only by the lines of the structural elements, which eventually resolved themselves into a white, three-dimensional grid. This had the interesting effect of placing visitors to the pavilion within a powerful perspective grid, their presence making colourful dynamic interventions. This is a development from the drawing, where the figures are trapped below the surface of the lines and drawn in the same colour and medium, so that they appear as extensions to the pavilion, or as accidental occurrences.

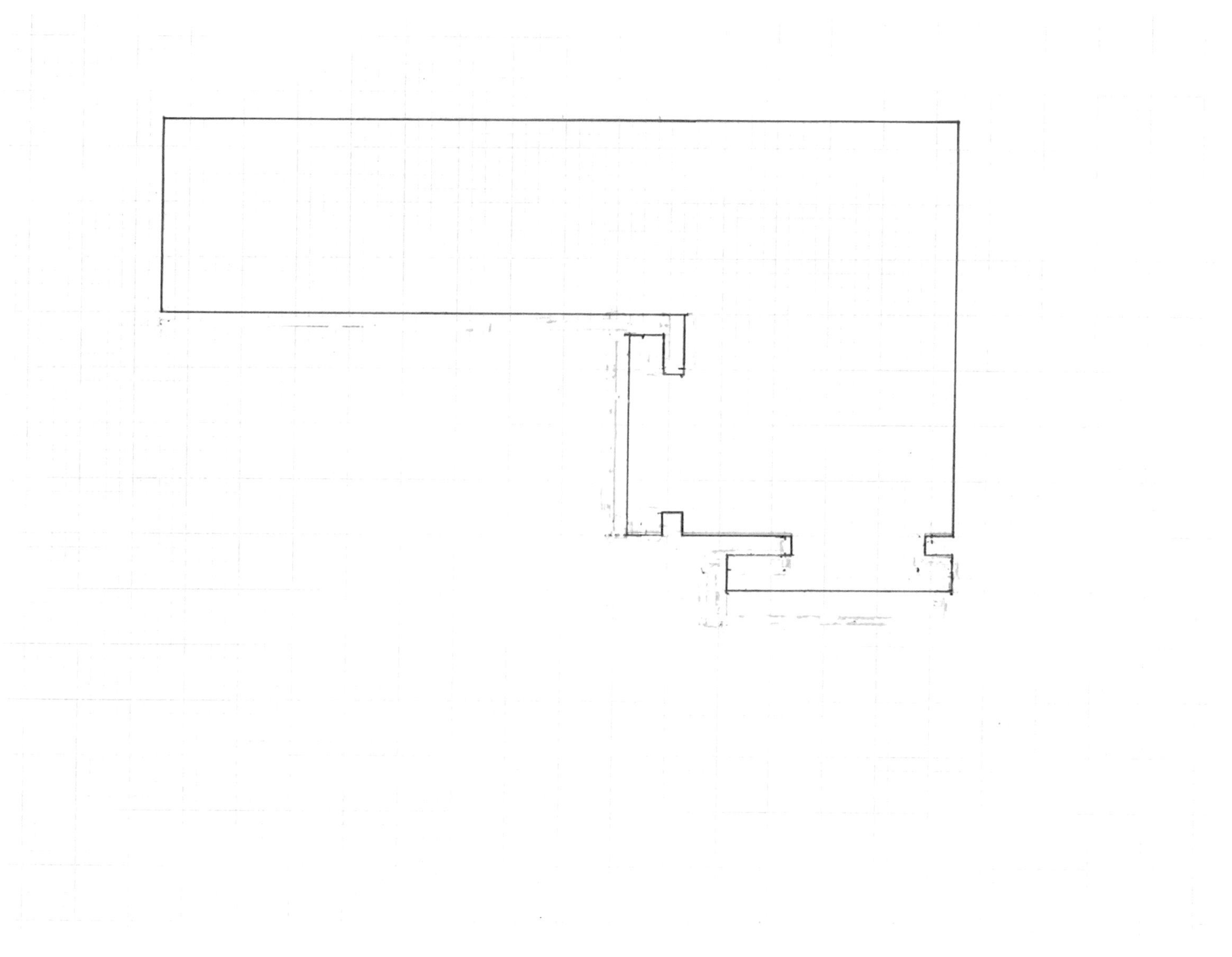

**JULIA FISH (1950–)**

**Working Drawing for Living Rooms, SouthEast-one, 2002**

Ink and correction tape on graph paper

45.7 × 60.3 cm, 18 × 23¾ in

In 2002, artist Julia Fish made a sequence of preparatory works for a series of ten paintings called *Living Rooms*. This drawing is one from a collection of working drawings, in which she analysed the different rooms of the first-floor living area of her residence in Chicago. Their titles refer to their location in the rectangular apartment plan, and they also give a sense of its orientation; the limits of the walls shown on the graph paper are based on a typical survey plan – here, at a scale of 1:12 in. Intended to inscribe Fish's own direct and sustained experience of inhabiting the space, their edges reference an objective relationship to reality, as the deliberate correction marks make clear. The purpose of the graph paper is ambiguous – it could be about keeping the lines straight or orthogonally related to each other, but the hand that drew them seems to have been guided by conventional draughting tools, such as a ruler and set square. The tiny grid could be providing a sense of scale, but the abstract nature of the lines gives no clue as to what this might be. The only figurative hint is a sense of wall thickness where the corners bend round, but the nature of the slivers of space at this point – perhaps they are doorways or niches – brings them into question. These drawings marked a turning point in Fish's observations about her interactions with the surrounding physical environment. Where prior she had made representations of fragments of everyday material surfaces, such as the tiled floors, asphalt siding and brick walls of home and studio, she now began to consider the thresholds of her domestic environment: staircases, landings and entrance ways. In this drawing, there are no explicit physical thresholds, however, and the line contains a singular, hermetic space.

**ALEXANDER DAXBÖCK (nd)**

**Tokyo Metropolis, 2016**

Computer software

82 × 42 cm, 32¼ × 16½ in

Composed like the page of a manga comic, this drawing shows a hybrid street in an urban environment, and is part of a triptych called *Tokyo Metropolis*. Each panel shows a tall building amid the complex detail of a typical Japanese street scene. The main perspective looks down a street towards but past the building, and two smaller drawings below show much shallower spaces – a close-up glimpse of the facade through a train window, and a view from its undercroft looking back at the train. Its author, Alexander Daxböck, experiments with the device of the manga, drawn digitally rather than by hand, but without using a three-dimensional model. Rendering decisions about shadow are therefore intuitive, as with a hand drawing. A manga, comprising a sequence of images in which a narrative unfolds, contains a blending of background with characters and action; the setting is important, and much thought and care is given to its invention and consistency. In an architectural drawing, which is usually a single image, the context is a static setting for the building subject that stands out as the principal compositional element. In manga drawings, scenes from real cities and urban places are often fused to construct such sets. In this triptych, locations in Tokyo are used – a simulacrum of which surrounds the tall building, seen from various angles. Daxböck sees it as something peculiar within its surroundings and uses the nature of the manga as a local Japanese manifestation of a globalized mediascape for the mass circulation of images to communicate this. The tall building itself is a synthesis of different buildings seen in magazines and on websites – an image of early twenty-first-century Dutch architecture transposed to Japan. Daxböck cites OMA, MVRDV and NL Architects as influences, but there are also echoes here of Japanese-architects, such as SANAA.

**JOHN RUSKIN (1819–1900)**

**The Exterior of the Ducal Palace, 1845**

Watercolour over graphite on paper

36.2 × 50.2 cm, 14¼ × 19¾ in

John Ruskin captures the microclimate of Venice in this image of the right-hand half of the Ducal Palace, viewed from a place where the waters of the Grand Canal and the lagoon merge. The mist that accumulates over the water disperses almost immediately beyond the boundary with the built-up ground, so that details are revealed in an intense light. Watercolour washes blend into the sky above the Ponte della Paglia, sketching out the shape of the bridge and the shadows beneath it in a technique echoed on the other side, where the arched fenestration of the palace and its arcade are ghostly voids. Only in the centre of the image does the detail of the facade come into focus, the arches with their individual characters animated by the play of light and shadow over intricate carving and giving depth to the openings. The decorative plane of the palace contrasts with the deep space created by the return of the canal, where a part of the Bridge of Sighs and the prisons behind are visible. For Ruskin, the Ducal Palace embodied the essence of Venetian Gothic, and also served as an allegory of the history of the city itself. He referred to the building extensively in his writings, especially in *The Stones of Venice*, 1851–53, and he described the whole book as being a kind of moral of the Ducal Palace. Ruskin himself was uncertain about this drawing's date, but scholarly commentators determine that it was made when he had moved away from the picturesque influence of Samuel Prout towards a more rigorous measurement, as indicated by the ruled lines and inscription, showing the tracery in analytical detail rather than as an impressionistic effect. The accuracy of the drawing was important to Ruskin, who noted that it was sketched by measurement with extreme care.

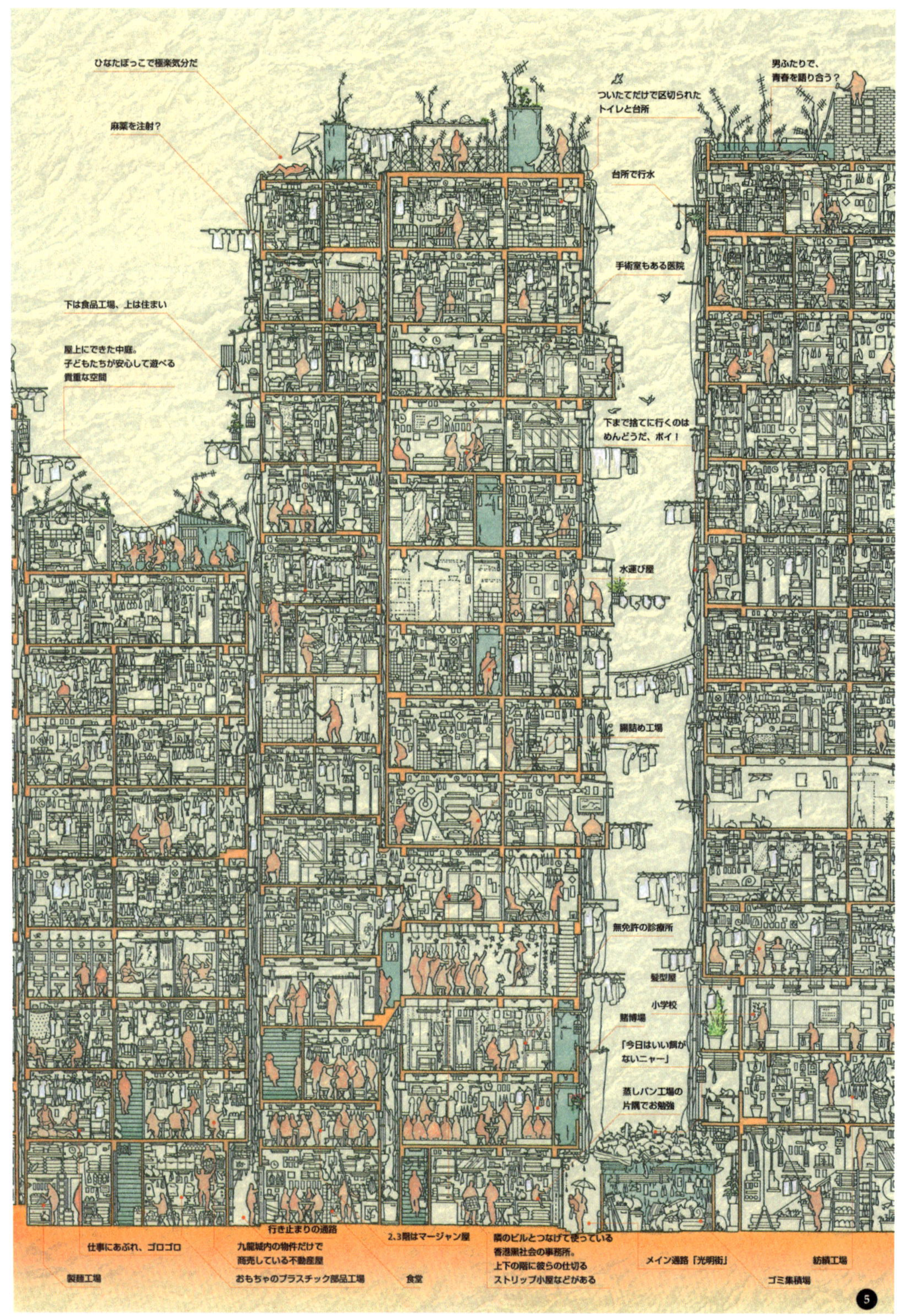


**HIROAKI KANI AND OTHERS**

**Kowloon Walled City, 1993**

Ink on paper

77 × 51 cm, 30¼ × 20 in

Days before its 1993 demolition, a group of Japanese researchers visited Kowloon Walled City. Led by historian and cultural anthropologist Hiroaki Kani, these architects, engineers and planners recorded the physical and social reality of its final days. They produced a range of drawings, including an extremely detailed long section, a fragment of which is shown here, cut through the structure and lives of the dense urban block. The drawing uses a simple convention to depict its complex subject, with all the solid elements shown in section shaded bright orange – immediately conveying the extreme slenderness of the structure in relation to the density of inhabitation. The humans working and living in the tiny rooms are also coloured orange – as if they, too, have been dissected. The only substantial part of the section is the undulating ground surface. In its latter days, this Chinese squatter settlement was the most heavily populated place in the world; one infographic reported a density of 1,920,000 people per km$^2$ crammed into a block 126 × 213 m (413 × 698 ft) long and restricted to 14 storeys in height due to its proximity to Kai Tak Airport. The settlement was a feat of organic urban living – evident in this drawing in the tiny service ducts, impromptu steps bridging floor-level disparities and narrow passages allowing ingress into the labyrinths that led from the main alleys and central courtyard. The structure was built and extended ad hoc, according to demand, with no formal services such as rubbish collection, drainage, electricity or water supply – water was pumped from seventy-seven different city wells to tanks on rooftops that can be seen coloured green in the section. The incredible diversity of unregulated activities taking place within the city's boundaries – including food production, manufacturing, prostitution, shopping and family life – had created an unconventional and sometimes dangerous, but self-sufficient, community.

**MIES VAN DER ROHE (1886–1969)**

**Office Building on Friedrichstraße, Berlin, 1921**

Charcoal and graphite on paper

173.4 × 121.9 cm, 68¼ × 48 in

'Only skyscrapers under construction reveal bold constructive thoughts, and then the impression of the high-reaching steel skeletons is overpowering', said Mies van der Rohe of his entry for the Friedrichstraße Skyscraper Competition of 1921. His proposal for a crystal tower, sheathed in a translucent-glass surface, rather than a conventional monolithic and decorated cladding, preserved the magical potential of the seemingly unfinished building. Drawn here with the darkest of materials, charcoal and graphite, the city streets and buildings lining them create a sooty, shadowy frame around the twenty-storey structure, whose floor plates are clearly discernible behind their reflective veil. The abstract geometrical form comprising three triangular towers soars into the sky in this perspective drawing – one of three made by Mies for his competition entry, which went under the pseudonym Wabe, or Honeycomb in English. Contrasting with the figurative volumes suggested in the silhouettes of encircling buildings, the project is clustered on to an important triangular site bounded on its three sides by the Spree River, the local railway station and a shopping street. The competition for a new landmark attracted 140 entries and generated debate about the future of the city of Berlin after World War I. Transparent glass towers have become ubiquitous in contemporary cities, but this design for Berlin's first skyscraper was a radical departure at the time, and Mies was the first to imagine a building that exploited the potential of the steel skeleton to free exterior walls from their loadbearing function. Alongside these pragmatic and constructional innovations, he was also interested in the symbolic qualities of glass as a building material – an aspect that also fascinated Expressionists such as the poet Paul Scheerbart and fellow architect Bruno Taut, in whose Expressionist journal, *Frühlicht*, Mies published this drawing in 1922.

**HANNS SCHMUTTERMAYER (c.1450–1518)**

**Pinnacle and gablet, 1486**

Pen and ink on paper

20.9 × 15.2 cm, 8¼ × 6 in

The design books of medieval master craftsmen like Hanns Schmuttermayer, a goldsmith, and Mathes Roriczer, a mason, today supply essential evidence about the education and geometrical knowledge that enabled the construction of Gothic architecture during the fifteenth century. Previously, trade secrets had been passed on orally from one generation to the next and transmitted through a hierarchical system of apprenticeship. These booklets marked a turning point in the method of education and transmission of technique, and formed the basis for a tradition of instruction disseminated through print that would become widespread by the eighteenth century. In his design booklet, *Fialenbüchlein* (Little Book of Pinnacles), from which this drawing is taken, Schmuttermayer was concerned with passing on practical information, showing how to carry out specific tasks to a clearly defined formula. In the prologue to the book, he mentions the art of geometry – but for him, this meant the technique of calculation for measured work. The drawing shows a finished pinnacle and gablet, its profiles marked with strong lines and modelled with cross-hatching. The carved details of the ornamental projections are animated by shading and individuality of profile within their broadly regular forms. It is the second in a pair of diagrams that are accompanied by detailed written instructions depicting the pinnacle in different states. The first defined the profiles of the raw, uncarved elements and their relationship with each other. The instructions are written as if spoken in the present tense, guiding the craftsman with caution: 'Then you begin to make the gablet: notice that the gablet and the pinnacle are derived from the eight shoes or squares. Now first make two lines horizontally under the gablet with the thickness of the space between the two lines being the width of the b [one of the modules shown in plan].'

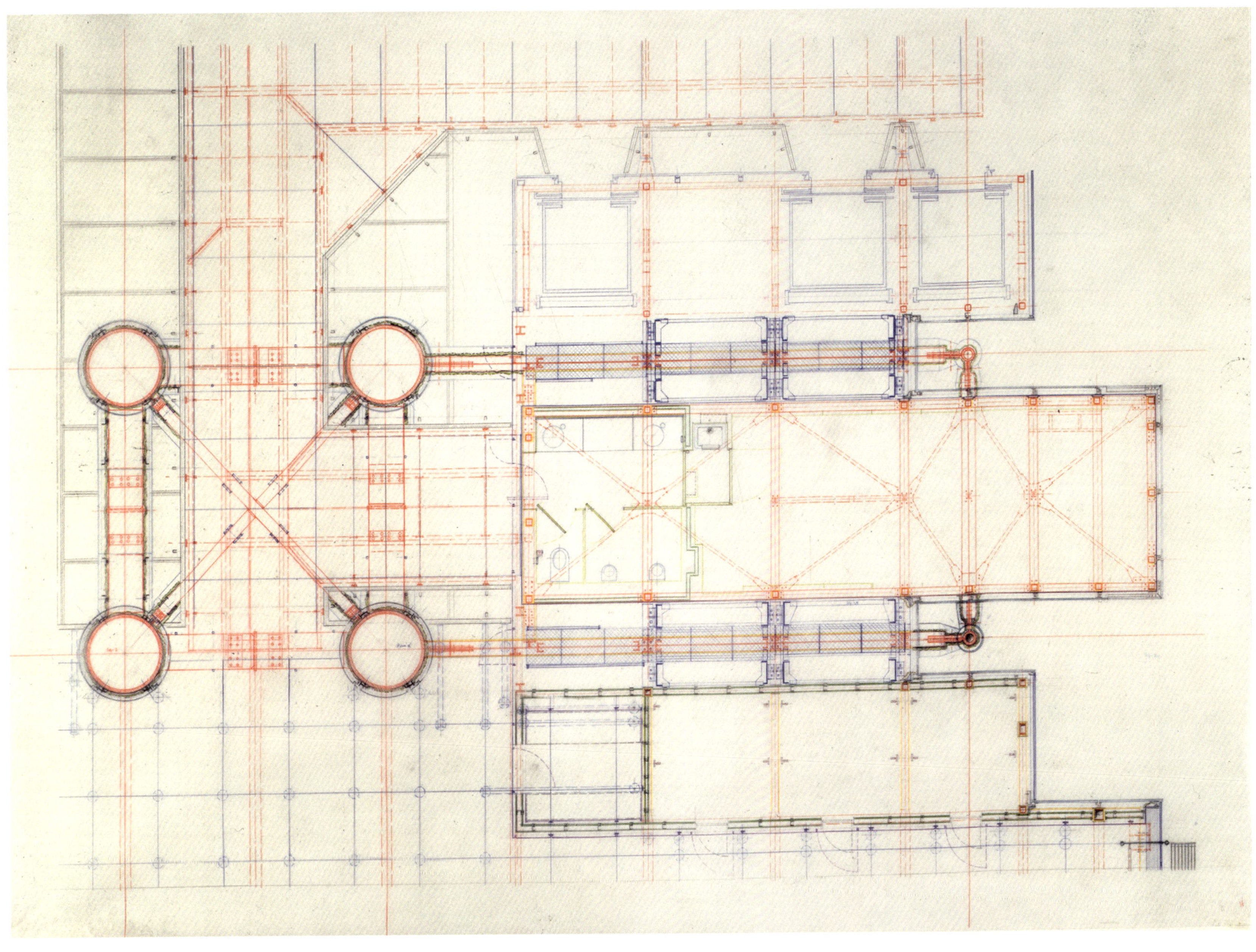

**FOSTER ASSOCIATES**

**Hongkong and Shanghai Bank, 1984**

Ink on paper

31 × 44 cm, 12¼ × 17¼ in

Showing the arrangement of core elements in one of the structural steel clusters for the headquarters of the Hongkong and Shanghai Banking Corporation in Hong Kong, this drawing reveals the complex relationship between structure and services within the building's construction. Hand-drawn – as evident in the uneven qualities of the dashed lines and the idiosyncratic nature of non-rectilinear elements, such as the yellow lagging around the columns – the detail is not the product of a single draughtsperson. In this case, it was developed and resolved over a short period of time by two of the principal architects overseeing aspects of the design and construction of the building: Ken Shuttleworth and David Nelson. The colour coding belongs to a drafting language particular to the office, and the two architects are speaking a shared and intimate language. Unlike design detail drawings made before construction starts on site, prepared so that the building can be understood and tendered for by prospective contractors, this drawing was made under pressure while the building was being constructed. The requirement to build almost 100,000 m$^2$ (1,076,391 sq ft) of floor space in a short timeframe demanded a high degree of prefabrication, including factory-finished modules. The three-dimensional intricacy of the many different structural and service systems coming together in this core element is being worked out in this drawing, which came out of the process of resolving complex coordination issues as they arose. In the plan, one of the eight principal steel masts can be seen rising as four huge columns bound into a vertical truss by the diagonal members shown crossing in the centre. These masts, from which the floors were hung, meant that the huge banking floors could be kept free of internal structure. The plan shows how the mast supports steel beams, within which is slotted one of the prefabricated modules for the lavatories and a large service void. The zones for the lifts are sketched in, lining up with the structural grid lines.

**ETTORE SOTTSASS (1917–2007)**

**Scenic Roadway, 1972**

Pencil on paper

31 × 25 cm, 12¼ × 9¾ in

Flowing down the centre of this drawing in voluptuous lines, its direction and name made clear by an arrow and label near the bottom of the sheet, is the Irrawaddy River. This huge waterway, referred to in a poem by Rudyard Kipling as 'the road to Mandalay', flows through Myanmar. As if to reinforce the symbolism of this jungle route, which is mentioned in the drawing's handwritten caption, Ettore Sottsass depicts a fantastic structure that he calls a gigantic Scenic Roadway for observation. Supported on legs with suckers at either end, the structure looks as though it is itself in motion. Like a giant centipede, it marches down the river valley, sinks under the water and rises up on to the bank in the foreground, where the nature of its enclosure becomes clear. Its bright yellow roof has a pneumatic quality, enhanced by the way it closes under water, and the winding structure seems able to bend in any way it wants in response to the landscape. The terrain over which it crosses takes on two scales: the human scale, depicted in a light grey and crisscrossed by tiny paths and roadways negotiating stands of trees; and the giant scale of a different reality, which the scenic road inhabits. The drawing belongs to a series of works collectively known as *The Planet as a Festival*, depicting a utopian land where all humanity is free from work and social conditioning – including the trappings of modern urban life such as supermarkets, banks and public transport, which are replaced by super-instruments made for entertainment. These include the Scenic Roadway, but also a monolithic dispenser for incense, drugs and laughing gas; a temple for erotic dances; river-borne rafts for listening to chamber music; and a stadium from which to watch the stars.

**LI HAN (nd)**

**Xizhimen Metro Station, 2008**

Computer software

39 × 56 cm, 15½ × 22 in

Showing the full vertical extent of the world of Xizhimen Metro Station, this drawing reveals the complex spatial journeys possible in this interchange for two metro lines, which has the longest transfer distance in the Beijing Metro system. A combination of section and axonometric, with deep sections of the ground cut away at three different levels, as if to reveal a giant anthill, the drawing's narrative can be read from any point. On top, the ground surface of the twenty-first-century city is elusive. Three long white blocks press down on the secret underground world, but they are supported on lower buildings whose colourful facades suggest that they are also above ground. Somewhere between, the escalators and staircases into which pedestrians pour find their upper datum. As they move downwards, towards the basement of these surface structures, they reach the intermediate hall – here, crowded with tiny black figures. From this point, the tunnels and escalators enter their own, seemingly discontinuous, realm until they reach the columned, double-sided platform and the trains far below, at the bottom of the sheet. According to Li Han, the endlessness, crowdedness and chaos shown in this place, one of the busiest in Beijing, make it a typical example of how people's daily lives and urban space influence each other. The commuters travel alone in the crowd, everyone walking forwards, no one conversing. The drawing emphasizes, he says, how to express the continuousness of this complicated space. Using sectional cutting with an invisible knife, the elements with different spatial relationships are cut apart to reveal the whole space. Even during Li's time working on the drawing, a new metro line was completed, further complicating the transfer route. Some parts of the space shown here have now disappeared, and the image is already a historical record.

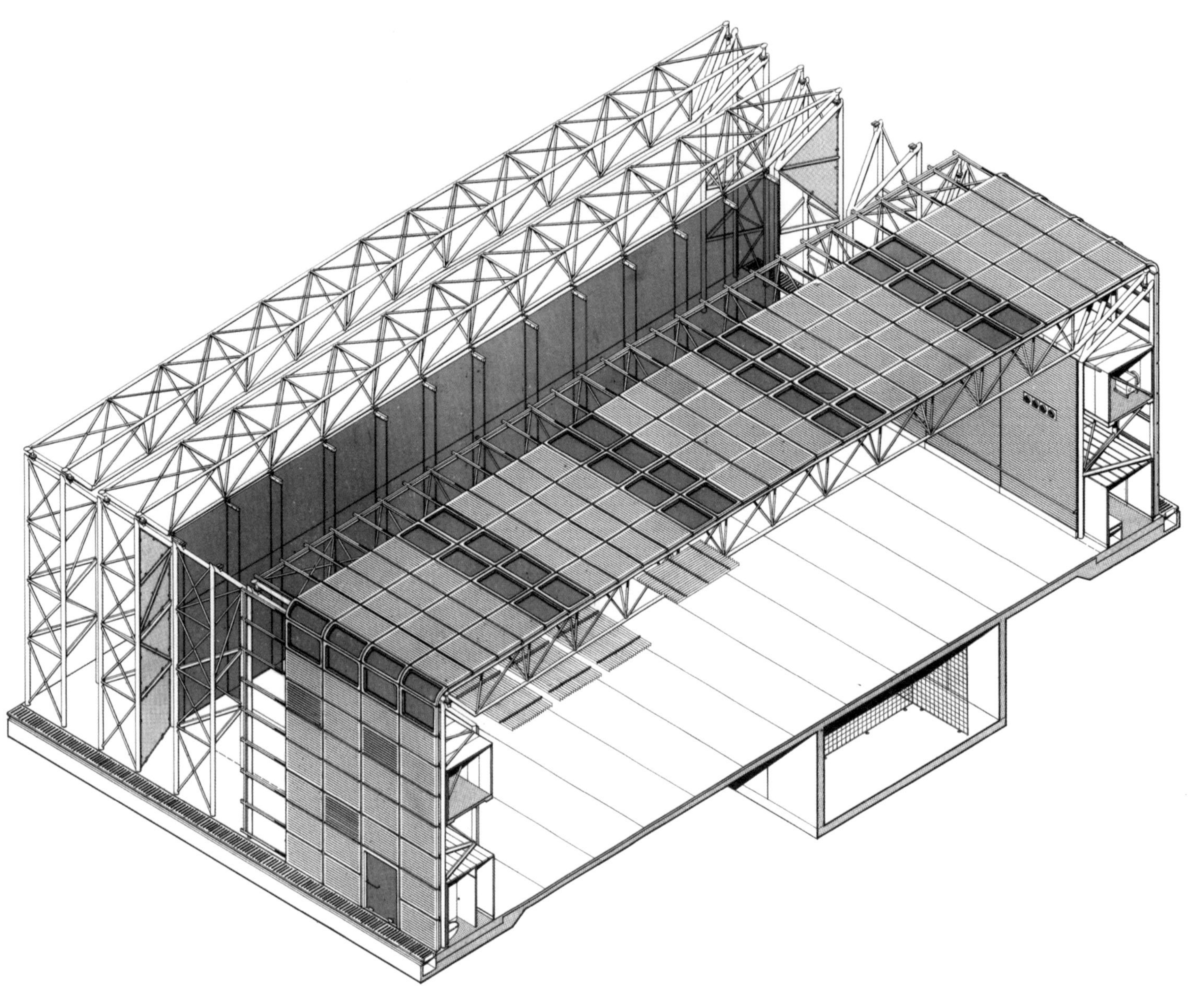

**FOSTER ASSOCIATES**

**Sainsbury Centre, 1978**

Pen and ink on paper

84 × 113 cm, 33 × 44½ in

This hand-drawn axonometric is sliced through at one end to reveal the sophisticated structural and constructional logic of the first building that Norman Foster designed for Sir Robert and Lady Sainsbury's art collection between 1974 and 1978. Located at the University of East Anglia, Norwich, on a greenfield site, its hangar-like interior contains an open-plan exhibition space that takes up the majority of the floor area, a restaurant, shop and offices. A floating, overhead, glass-sided walkway, not shown, provides high-level access, linking to the pedestrian street in the air of Denys Lasdun's university megastructure. This method of presentation was influenced by the cutaway drawings that appeared in the *Eagle*, a 1950s magazine for boys whose centre spread always featured an intricate analysis of modern architecture, such as the Festival of Britain's Dome of Discovery or Coventry Cathedral, or engineering marvels including nuclear-powered ships and futuristic, gas-powered cars. This axonometric similarly reveals the composition of the prefabricated structure. The front part of the drawing shows how silver-grey, insulated -aluminium panels clad the exterior of the tubular-steel trusses. The building is set out on a modular system, to which each of its parts corresponds. These trusses have uninterrupted spans of 28.8 m (94.5 ft) internally, and follow a proportional logic of 16:4:1 for length:width:height of the building, which is composed of 36 bays, each 3.6 m (11.8 ft) wide. Perforated aluminium louvres that temper the internal environment can be seen on the facade, slotted into the modular grid. The section reveals how all the plant and services needed to sustain the building's internal, conditioned microclimate are contained within the depth of its structural zone. The back part of the drawing shows the composition of the trusses with all their members revealed, and indicates how this extrapolated building ends – with a flat, glass wall overlooking a lawn.

**HENRI LABROUSTE (1801–75)**

**Reading Room, Sainte-Geneviève Library, 1842**

Lead pencil and ink pen on paper

45.5 × 58.5 cm, 17 × 23 in

This intricate drawing of Henri Labrouste's preliminary design for the reading room of the Sainte-Geneviève Library in Paris reveals the beauty of his innovative structural use of exposed cast iron. In this room, he invents a refined aesthetic language for use in a public interior, combining stylistic Classical elements derived from archaeological study, such as the Corinthian capitals of the slender metal columns and the references in plan to a temple at Paestum, with a mimicry of Gothic vaulting in the four arches that spring from each column. Two of these arches span lengthways, column-to-column, and support a central beam. In the other direction, arches span across the room from its centre to define the pitched roofs over the two aisles. Projected as a perspective skewed towards the left-hand side, so that the two aisles are displayed from different angles, the drawing also shows the depth of the monolithic external wall through its coffered reveals, while the composition of these walls is described in the end elevation. The decorative nature of the coffers is continued on the surface of ceiling planes, which become round vaults in the final design. In the drawing, these planes are seen behind a veil of fine wrought-iron details belonging to the arched trusses, so that a dynamic effect is generated by the three-dimensional depth of the decorative scheme.

This was the first large public reading room, and it occupies the whole of the upper level of the library building. Its large scale is not immediately apparent, for the bases of the columns are almost 4 m (13.1 ft) above the floor level, at the same height as a continuous upper gallery that give access to stacks of books between the piers, and supported by a deep wall of books below.

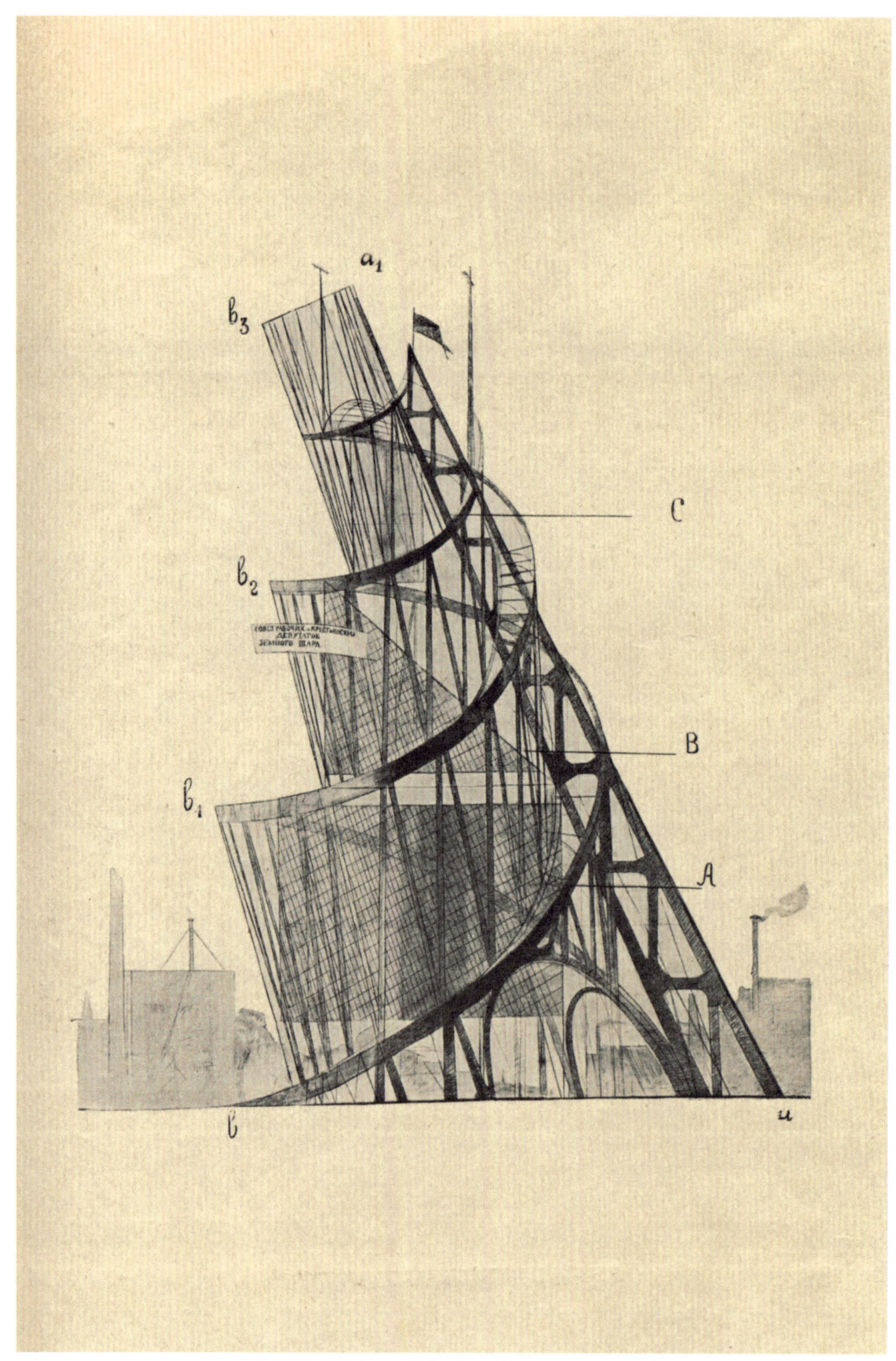


**VLADIMIR TATLIN (1885–1953)**

**Monument to the Third International, 1920**

Ink on paper

18 × 13 cm, 7 × 5 in

Artist and architect Vladimir Tatlin was charged with applying Lenin's plan to replace monuments of the tsarist period with new ones that communicated the ideologies of the new regime to the masses. The construction shown in this drawing is his most well-known scheme. Its subject – the Third International, or Comintern, which was an association of national communist parties that advocated world communism – is represented in it as a metaphor for a new social order. The elevation for the 303 m-high (994 ft) tower shown here illustrates it *in situ* at Petrograd in front of a non-descript skyline of industrial buildings in the misty distance. The tower itself is drawn in the manner of a scientific diagram, but the subject is an inherently symbolic rather than a utilitarian object. The dark ink rendering of the two intertwining lattice spirals, supported on and encircling a giant cantilevered iron beam that projects at an angle from the ground, shows the full trajectories of these delicate arms. Within their embrace are three great rooms contained in three platonic glass volumes: a cube, a pyramid and a cylinder, marked A, B and C. At the top is a small half-sphere housing a radio station. These elements are depicted in fine ink lines, and are given translucency with pale washes. Each rotates at a different speed – the lowest taking a year, the top taking just a day – symbolizing the harmonious coexistence of the different legislative and administrative arms of the Soviet state. Lenin's programme of monumental propaganda had, until this point, been manifest in figurative sculptures celebrating the heroes of the Russian Revolution. Tatlin's approach was aligned with the abstract, agitprop cultural agenda of artists such as El Lissitzky, and particularly the latter's notion of the Proun – an acronym for 'project for the affirmation of the new' in Russian.

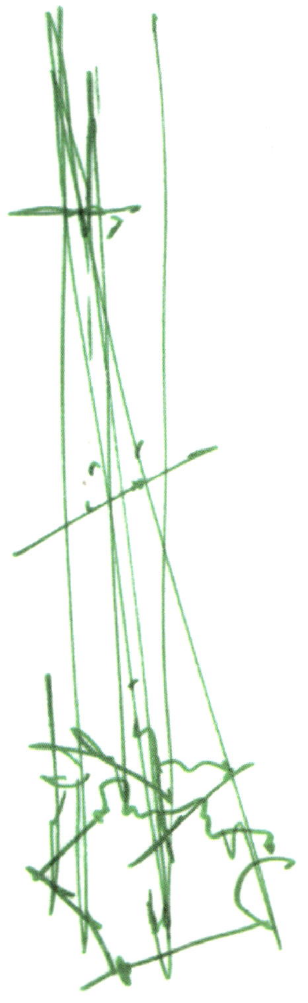

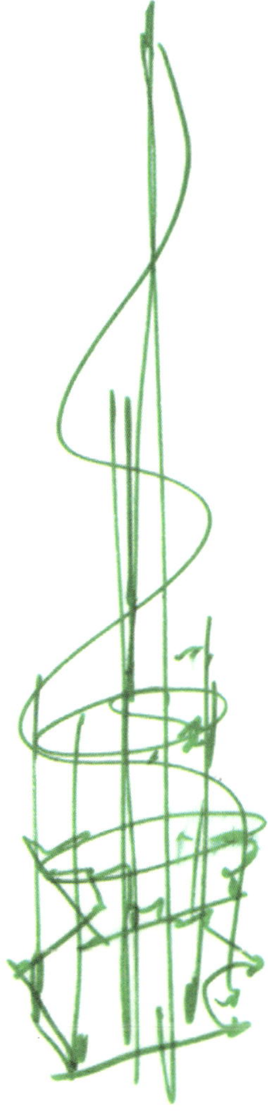

**RENZO PIANO (1937–)**

**The Shard, 2004**

Felt-tip pen on paper

20 × 29 cm, 7 × 11½ in

This series of three sketches in green ink by Renzo Piano is an example of his famous green drawings, made rapidly and often during a conversation, where a few simple lines capture the essence of a longer story. Sometimes the sheet will have a dedication to the conversant annotating it, but not in this case. These images show three ideas for the tallest building in London, officially called the Shard and designed by Piano. Each of the three figures depicts a slightly different formal solution for making the tall, slender tower, indicating where the roughly seven-sided plot at ground level is filled by the base of the structure, which reduces in size as it gets taller to culminate in a pointed apex. In the final, built version – and the first sketch is closest to this – the side elevation takes the form of a long triangle. As well as showing how the building tapers, it also illustrates how the facets never touch, and Piano has described the floating planes as flirting with each other. The evocative phrases that he uses, combined with the attractive sketches, have built up a mythology about the genesis of the building. This dates from a much earlier set of green sketches for the Shard, which Piano is said to have made on a restaurant serviette during a meeting with property developer Irvine Sellar, who initiated and carried through the project, in March 2000. Piano recalls the sketch taking shape very quickly, and Sellar now keeps the famous napkin in his offices. In an interview, Sellar recalled how Piano saw the beauty of the river and the railways and the way their energy blended, and began to sketch in green felt pen on a napkin what he saw as a giant sail or an iceberg.

**EUGENE HENRY FRICX (1633–1707)**

**Lille, 1709**

Ink on paper

39 × 39 cm, 15½ × 15½ in

One of the most celebrated eighteenth-century military engineers, Sébastien Le Prestre de Vauban led a victorious French siege of Lille – one of fifty such operations during his career – seizing it from the Spanish in August 1667. King Louis XIV ordered de Vauban, who became inspector-general of fortifications a year later, to design and construct a new fortress there. This plan was drawn soon after de Vauban's death in 1707 by Sieur Brüchman, under the direction of map-maker and printer Eugene Henry Fricx, and shows how de Vauban laid out the citadel as part of the city's northeastern defence system. He had perfected a logical sequence of twelve siege phases, requiring a maximum of forty-eight days to take a city, and an approach to planning that reached its pinnacle in this plan for Lille, a strategic site near the Belgian border. It takes the form of a star citadel: a pentagon that can survey the surrounding terrain from all angles, with no blind spots. The natural river course winds along the left-hand side of the drawing, and the grey-blue channels surrounding the citadel at the heart of the earthworks were filled with water and planted with thousands of piles, preventing ingress by boat. The marshy ground and the flood system thus created allowed the foot of the ramparts to be flooded, thwarting enemy attempts to mine them. The radiating concentric plan, its layout and construction, embody de Vauban's approach to fortified structures – surrounded by bastions and curtain walls, with a defensive slope, called a *glacis*, built around the entire site. In all his designs for fortifications, he used the landscape as a basic element, manipulating its characteristics – here, the marshy location – to his advantage. He would plant trees to hide the smoke of cannons, and reshape the ground to shelter troops.

**MARIE-JOSÉ VAN HEE (1950–)**

**Zuidzande House, 2007**

Pencil on paper

41.6 × 55.1 cm, 16½ × 21¾ in

Made from the very start of a project, Marie-José Van Hee's drawings begin with a consideration of the physical nature of the site: for example, the sizes of pre-existing buildings, surroundings and natural features; their materials and the construction culture of the region; and the quality of light and orientation. The Zuidzande House occupied a rural plot planted with many trees, making an island in the very flat agricultural plain near the border between the Netherlands and Belgium, close to the sea. A farmhouse and large barn already existed, and the sketch begins to address this collection of influences. Van Hee decided to make a new structure in the northwest corner of the site, and the sketch shows how a conventional core begins to dissolve towards the south, but also towards an open meadow surrounded by trees. The central core becomes a tower, its height matching that of the big barn – this decision is evident in the section of a staircase drawn near the bottom of the sheet. The feathery skirt surrounding it composes itself into a single-story element whose complex geometry embraces the garden, pulling it into the ground floor of the house, where it fractures around a double-sided fireplace deep into the living space. Van Hee explains that when she begins to think about a project, she draws continuously – first, sketching the contour or the plans of the new building in order to decide what is interesting enough to keep. The process of drawing is a way of making sense of the resulting whirlwind of ideas, she declares – adding that the drawing can be completely black by the end if the ideas don't emerge. These intense sketches comprise many images layered on top of each other; some parts may be erased, and a particular line or group of marks may predominate.

**ROGELIO SALMONA (1929–2007)**

**Torres del Parque, 1964**

Black ink on paper

29.5 × 20.5 cm, 11½ × 8 in

Rogelio Salmona began working on his first major project, the Torres del Parque residential complex in Bogotá, in 1964. As he developed his ideas in relation to the central urban site adjacent to the city's bullring and located in the abandoned Independence Park, the characteristics that would define his subsequent oeuvre took shape. This early sketch shows Salmona exploring the development's overall composition in a loosely made drawing that captures the essential qualities of the site and its setting. Seen against the dramatic backdrop of the Altiplano Cundiboyacense, to the east of Bogotá – a high plateau whose peaks form part of the eastern ranges of the Colombian Andes – two of the three towers are shown, both mimicking the mountainous forms but in different ways. The building on the left sits below the skyline, its vertical disposition defined by a strong core around which a spiralling cascade of terraces spills down to create a hill-like effect. The second building inhabits the centre of the drawing and projects above the horizon. The sweep of its terraces is much tighter, and flows down to join a stepped ground descending the hill upon which it sits. This transforms the man-made environment into a geographical feature – and on the right-hand side is mirrored by a formal garden. Two tall palm trees mimic the towers and confirm the equivalence of the park to which they belong with the paved route associated with the towers. To the far left, the circular bullring creates a counter curve, balancing the sketch's composition and implying continuity with the city fabric. This use of spirals, radial geometry and curves was important in Salmona's subsequent work, as was the distinctive red brick in which the towers were faced, which Salmona first encountered in the Moorish architecture of Granada.

**LUKE HIM SAU (1904–91)**

**Multi-use building on Des Voeux Road, 1962**

Watercolour and Ink on paper

30 × 22 cm, 11¾ × 8¾ in

This perspective rendering of a multi-use building on Hong Kong's busy Des Voeux Road illustrates in detail the character of Luke Him Sau's architecture. After completing his studies at the Architectural Association in London, he was commissioned by Tsuyee Pei, father of IM Pei, as chief architect of the Bank of China. In preparation for his new role, in 1930 he made an eleven-week European tour, followed by a return journey to China via the United States, during which he studied the bank buildings of Europe and America. Viewing the architecture with his characteristically analytical eye, he deemed European classicism to be unsuitable in an urban environment, where ornamentation gathered dirt and dust, and dismissed monumental planning as unscientific. He found the American approach to be more amenable to contemporary banking and the reality of the city. Through his work at the bank in Shanghai, which included not only banking halls and office buildings but also residences and warehouses, he developed an approach neither in thrall to Western Modernism nor based on Chinese tradition. As this image reveals, everything has its place. The block that he has designed stands out within its context, which echoes the rendering style of American artists such as Hugh Ferris. The volumes and proportions of the surrounding blocks and urban spaces are shown unadorned, communicating only their impact on light and shade, and compositional balance. The bottom three storeys of the building create a plinth-like element for accommodating the commercial aspects of the project. The street is populated with groups of figures approaching or crowded around the building, and a few cars add to the liveliness of the street. Above, the apartment accommodation is separated from the street by the plinth, and its facade articulated in a simple composition that responds to its surroundings in scale and disposition.

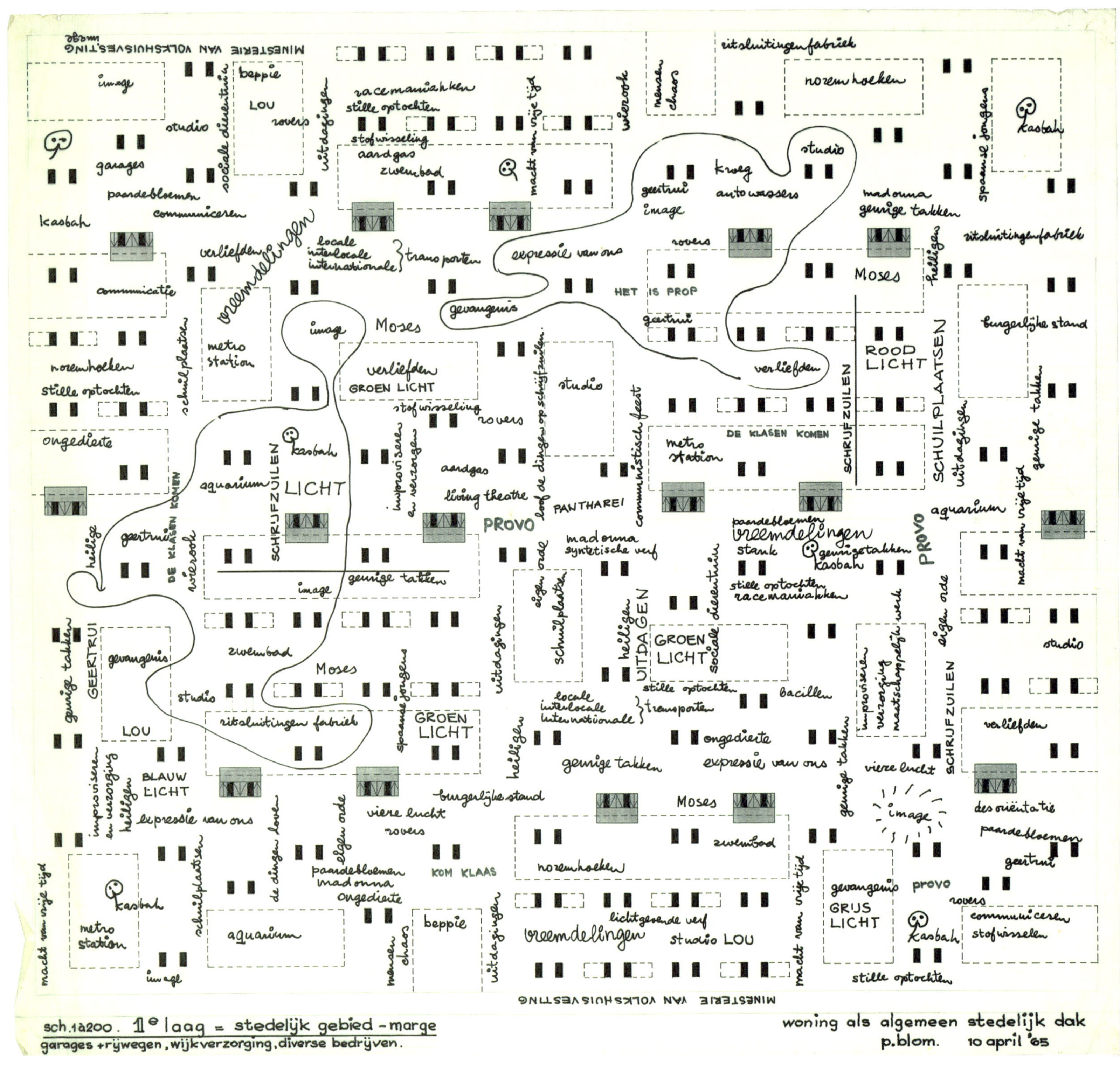


PIET BLOM (1934–99)

**Presentation drawing of the representation of various human functions such as 'sweet smelling twigs' and 'silent processions', 1965**

Ink on paper

49 × 53 cm, 19¼ × 20 in

This drawing by Dutch architect Piet Blom illustrates an anti-rational project, which he called *Kasbah*, for a new community model that integrates all the functions of urban living. Housing stands on pillars above the ground, and the black blocks depict the pillars of the elevated dwellings. Beneath is a collective space, and dotted lines mark voids for daylight. The curved lines punctuate the rigid structure with an irregular form, and the whole is covered in a field of words. Some of these words and phrases refer to qualities of light, or to obscure characters; others to unusual activities; while some are, on the face of it, nonsensical – 'the cocks that arrive', 'the silent parades that together make a wonderful chaos'. In 1959, Aldo van Eyck had written a provocative call to action in *Forum*, a magazine that he edited, calling for 'The Story of Another Idea'. This was a reaction to the divisive functionalism of Modernism and technocratic approaches to post-war reconstruction. Van Eyck was influenced by two early-twentieth-century art historians, Heinrich Wölfflin and Wilhelm Worringer, whose radical approach to historical time was based on formal and visual associations between contemporaneous and past art forms, replacing the diachronic vision of art or history moving forwards towards a utopian future with a synchronic view, whose subject is the structure of the present moment. This proposal for a more anthropological approach to design based on equivalence and simultaneity – called Structuralism in 1966 – was adopted by the core contributors to *Forum*, including Jaap Bakema, Herman Hertzberger, John Habraken and Blom. They formulated a poetic, humane alternative that considered the importance of human scale and the emotional impact of buildings. Their approach was concerned with issues of community, equal social relations and user-adaptability.

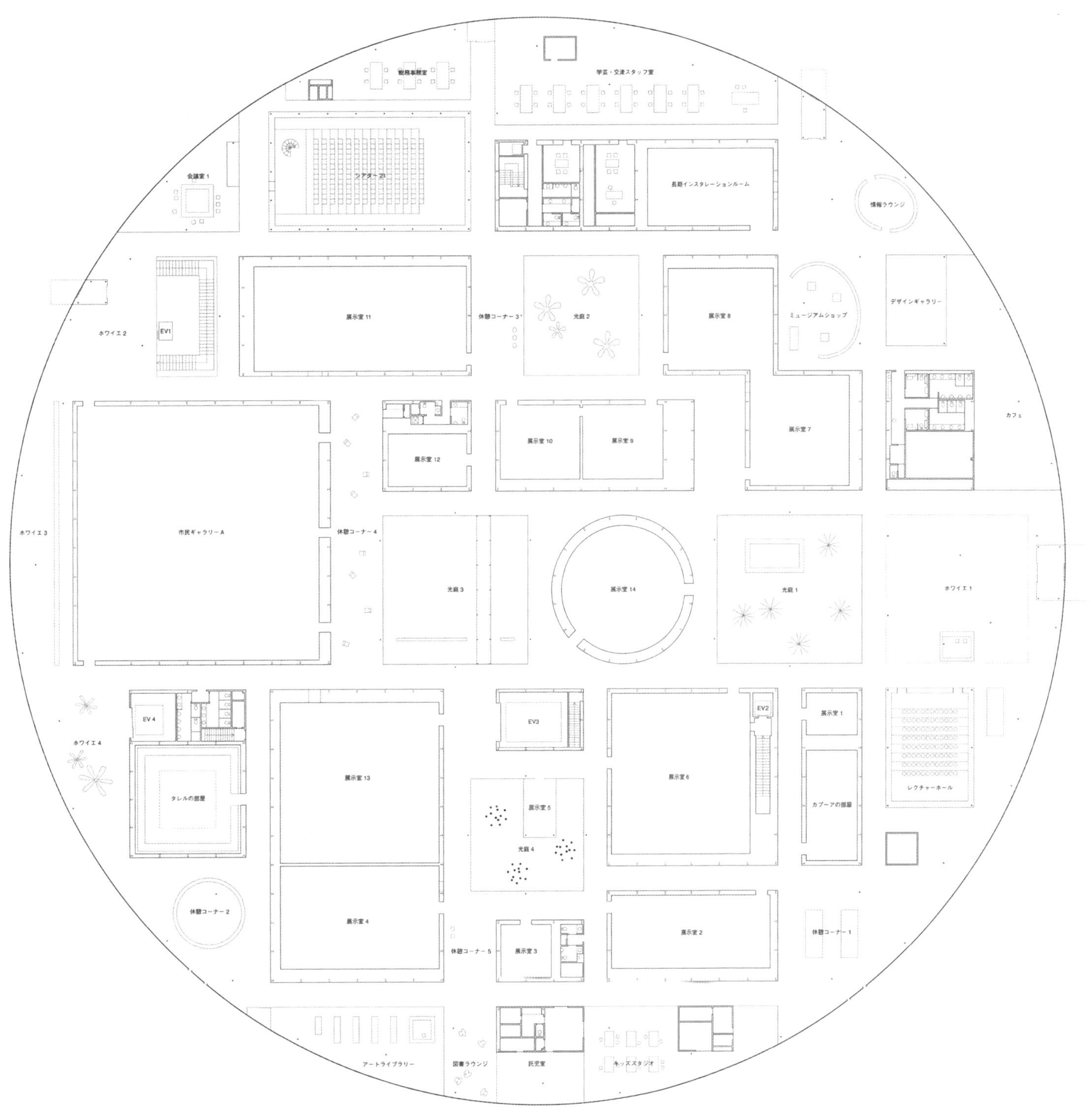


**SANAA**

**21st Century Museum of Contemporary Art, 2004**

Computer software

Drawn in pristine lines, this circular plan by SANAA's Kazuyo Sejima and Ryue Nishizawa for their 21st Century Museum of Contemporary Art defines a radical rethinking of the conventional museum's hierarchical spatial organization. The 1.4 km (0.9 mi) perimeter of the building encloses a labyrinthine maze of corridors that narrow to alleys and open up into small plazas. These form the ground to the figures within the space – a collection of white-cube galleries, offices, a shop, library, courtyard and restaurant, as well as more idiosyncratic spaces such as a Turrell Room and a People's Gallery. The thin roof slab covering the circular whole is punctured by the volumes of the different rooms; the highest, being 14.9 m (48.9 ft) tall, floats 4 m (13.1 ft) above the ground and is supported by thin white-painted steel columns. Above this flat plane, which mimics the floor plate, the different heights and proportions of the individual rooms are expressed as a landscape of white volumes – extrusions of the square, round and rectangular plan shapes seen here. In the finished building, the exterior glass wall dematerializes the boundary between the interior and the surrounding landscape, and is interrupted by multiple entry points – further disintegrating any sense of hierarchy. Solid walls with doorways enclose some of the rooms, but with other spaces the border is marked merely by a change in floor surface. Some boundaries are partially or fully glazed, with larger rooms extending upwards via internal staircases to an upper level and mezzanines, or downwards to two basement levels. The museum sits in the centre of the city of Kanazawa, in a municipal park and surrounded by a completely flat lawn dotted with trees. This banal landscape, which merges into the everyday urban fabric, is very different to the fragment of an autonomous city enclosed within its own fragile circular wall.

**KARL FRIEDRICH SCHINKEL (1781–1841)**

**Project for a Palace, 1838**

Pen and grey watercolour on paper

94.4 × 60.2 cm, 37¼ × 23¾ in

Dramatically depicting two different worlds separated by a deep but artificially constructed ground, this drawing uses two types of projection for emphasis. Karl Friedrich Schinkel's drawings often used asymmetrical compositions in order to encompass symmetrical Greek forms, as opposed to Imperial Roman references, but it is the theatrical, vertical separation that is most striking here. Above, an ethereal elevation of a simple Greek temple with Ionic columns is so flat that it seems to be made of the paper on to which the finest of pencil lines are traced. Only the lightest of washes suggests depth and an endless blue sky. The ground on which it sits gains substance with the tree roots that dig into it, and the drawing becomes a section. The earth that nurtures these strange foundations is held within niches in a deep beam that marks the drawing's transition to the grotto-like underworld. Supported on huge monolithic stone columns, a long polychromatic hallway lined with Ancient Greek sculpture, but otherwise uninhabited, is shown in a perspective that penetrates deeply into the picture plane, ending in a light-filled room. Despite its fantastic qualities, this project for a palace was for a real client, Alexandra Feodorovna, the Prussian wife of Tsar Nicholas I of Russia. The palace was to be built on a clifftop overlooking the Black Sea, on a site that Schinkel never visited, but he used historical reference to define what he considered the appropriate architectural language. Crimea had been colonized by Ancient Greece – hence, the Classical Greek form of the glass-faced structure above, which sits in its own special rooftop garden, guarding a substructure containing rooms designed to hold the tsarina's art collection.

**BERNARDO PREVEDARI (nd)**

**Interior of a ruined church or temple with figures, 1481**

Engraving on paper

70.8 × 51.2 cm, 27 × 20¼ in

This engraving, the largest from a single plate to have been made in the fifteenth century, was executed by the goldsmith Bernardo Prevedari, after a drawing by Donato Bramante. It continues to tantalize scholars with the complex nature of its construction, its style and its iconographic content. Its subject is unclear, and it seems to represent a pagan temple given over to Christian worship. This ambiguity is taken up in the detail of the scene. The cone-shaped shadow cast on the floor by the kneeling friar falls just short of the giant candlestick that he is facing, and disrupts the composition of the single-point perspective that is clearly indicated in the grid of the paving over which it falls. This unreal element represents the perspective pyramid, drawn as the shadow of a sundial tracing the passage of the hours and space, and evoking an overlapping of the temporal and spatial. This idea is continued in the jagged stonework of the side-chapel vault, which connects to the broken edge of an arch that touches the picture plane. Its ruined aspect suggests time passed, but also connects the interior to the exterior world. This relates to the debate about perspective that was happening when Bramante made the original drawing – between Filippo Brunelleschi, who had developed a system of linear perspective in the early fifteenth century, and Leon Battista Alberti, who codified the concept by substituting Brunelleschi's mirror with a gridded window. Bramante's perspective follows the more scientific, Albertian construction, and its vanishing point is off-centre so that the second perspective space of the side chapel can be revealed. The asymmetrical composition is consistent with the tension between order and chaos that pervades the image, and the mixing of sacred and profane that is objectified in the mysterious candlestick as a subject of veneration.

**LAKI SENANAYAKE (1937–2021)**

**Ena de Silva House, 1960**

Ink on paper

21 × 50 cm, 8¼ × 19¾ in

Drawn by the young Sri Lankan sculptor and painter Laki Senanayake, while working in the office of Geoffrey Bawa, this early elevation and section through the Ena de Silva House, designed for a young doctor, on the edge of Colombo, is a detailed rendition. Rather than the particulars of construction being depicted with lavish care, it is elements from the natural world and the imagined life of its inhabitants that capture the attention. The house's main volume centres on an open courtyard, where the mango tree spreads out around the eaves of a three-storey wing. Its strong character, like that of all the trees in the drawing – which were mostly brought in by elephant, aided by a tractor – influences the form of the architecture in its vicinity. The section is cut across the site so that the steep slope is not apparent, but from this space a long spine extends outside the field of the drawing and down the slope. It connects the house to the surgery in the garden at the front of the site. The house uses local materials and forms: stone columns can be seen in the section, supporting the eaves of the courtyard and the tall wing's upper floor. Passive cooling is encouraged by cross ventilation, enhanced by the stack effect, whereby warm air passes up through the open roof space above this double-height column. The fine detail of clay roof tiles and timber screens creates a horizontal band across the drawing. By the time Bawa was commissioned to build this house and surgery, Sri Lanka had been independent for eleven years. Bawa's work began to self-consciously reimagine the colonial legacy, and in the design of the de Silva House he reassembled the logic of the colonial bungalow, while blurring distinctions between external and internal spaces.

**GRAFTON ARCHITECTS**

**New Town House Building, Kingston University, 2013**

Computer software

Made to support planning drawings for an open, student-facing building, this section through Grafton Architects' New Town House Building conveys the playful, light and welcoming atmosphere of the structure embedded in its urban context. It sits lightly through the site and is most present in the layer of grey earth at the bottom of the sheet, which forms a firm ground for the rest of the drawing. The street side of the new building inhabits the right-hand edge, and the sections through the structural elements – the wall slabs and beams – are white rather than the conventional black or shaded. The elevation of the columns and wall surfaces shown behind creates a pale veil between the interior space and the misty treescape in the distance. A balance is found with the partial elevation of County Hall on the other side of the sheet across a wide street. The whole drawing is filled with colourful inhabitants – crowds of people at all levels, a red bus, a car, a crescent moon and trees of various sizes animate the scene. The digitally collaged image was created in a back-and-forth process, beginning with a hard-line Vectorworks base section and then transferring to Photoshop. The choice and application of colours were inspired by the paintings of David Hockney and Edward Hopper, the architectural drawings of Erik Gunnar Asplund and Sigurd Lewerentz, and the children's books of Miroslav Šašek. Photographs of some elements, such as County Hall, were used to describe material surfaces; for the sky, different colours, textures and masks achieve a painted look. The trees give a sense of urban scale to the project and link it to the human. As they fade out, the curve of the road disappearing into the distance is evoked, creating a feeling of space without recourse to perspective.

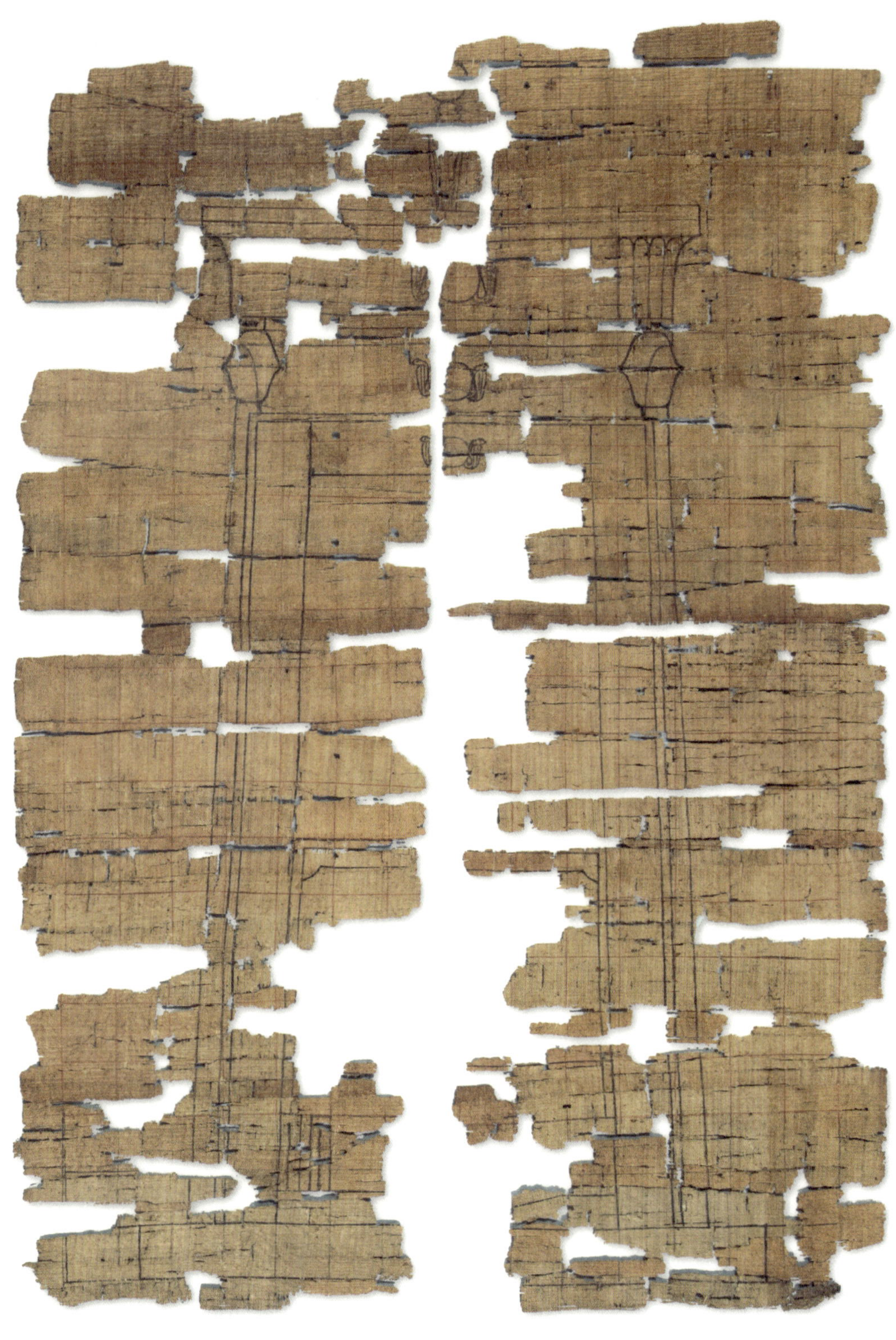

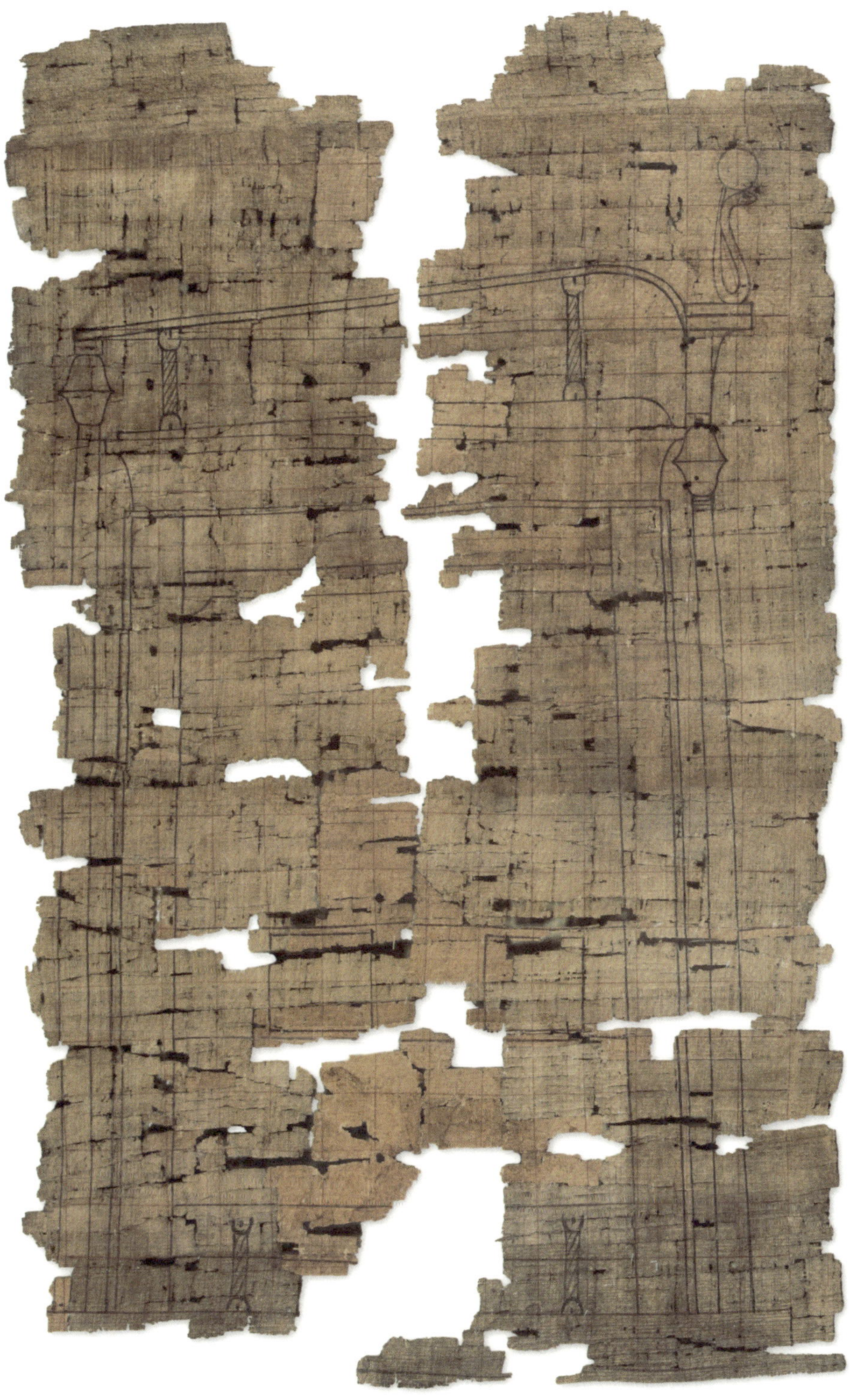

**ANON**

**Gurob Shrine Papyrus, c.1350 BC**

Ink on papyrus

53.5 × 28 cm, 21 × 11 in

These drawings are from the tallest papyrus sheet in existence. It comes from the archaeological site of Gurob, situated in the Al-Fayyum region of Egypt. Once an important town with a palace complex and a necropolis, the site was discovered by veteran British Egyptologist Sir Flinders Petrie. Papyrus sheets were made from overlapping layers of stripped papyrus stems that were dried and then polished with stone, seashell or hardwood to create a smooth surface. As was customary, this sheet was once part of a roll that has been broken across the middle and is therefore a pair of images, now made up of many fragments that were finally restored and reassembled in 1980. A grid of red lines drawn over the surface of the sheet underlies the design, drawn in black ink, for the side elevation of a portable wooden temple shrine made to contain a cult statue. The counterpart drawing, shown on the opposite page, depicts the shrine's front elevation. The shrine is shown as suspended by short ropes at the top and anchored at the bottom within a lightweight frame that could be transported using carrying poles. The underlying grid would have enabled a degree of accurate scaling by the draughtsman, and the drawing, thought to be at a scale of 1:3, was probably used during construction. It is known that carpenters in ancient Egypt were familiar with orthographic projections – which they used to determine the size, proportions and layout of timber elements – although another theory is that the drawing was used as a template for depicting shrines in wall paintings.

**HEINRICH TESSENOW (1876–1950)**

**Interior perspective, 1908**

Ink on paper

56 × 53 cm, 22 × 20 in

The frame around this drawing of a simple room captures a fragment of calm domestic space, everything in it a refined response to the art of everyday life. The room is not completely tidy, but every detail has been drawn in a simple and delicate line without shading. The image is luminous, and light is everywhere. On the table lie the remains of a household task, and a small doll has been flung so that its leg hangs down casually. The window curtains are drawn back around an open casement, and the bare stalk of a plant on the sill breathes in the fresh air. Another partially open curtain in the dresser reveals books and objects meant to be neatly concealed. The composition of the image looks into the corner of the room, and the carpet and dresser are unceremoniously cropped by the frame. The sense of their presence beyond the picture plane is enhanced by the embroidery-like pattern covering the walls and ceiling to make a seamless and encompassing field that could seemingly extend indefinitely. The recording and intellectualization of these instances of unconscious-but-perfect design through drawings such as this was an essential element of the work and teaching of Heinrich Tessenow, one of the founders of the Deutscher Werkbund, established in 1907. In 1909, he published his first book, *Der Wohnhausbau* (The Construction of Dwellings), full of such drawings, in which he proposes that the main purpose of domestic architecture is satisfying the basic needs of life. He was simultaneously working on designs for prototype row housing for workers, into which these observations fed. In addition to conventional plans, sections and elevations, he made drawings that envisioned how gardens and rooms would be inhabited, with thriving vegetable patches and interior scenes such as this one.

**KATSUSHIKA HOKUSAI (1760–1849)**

**Princess Shikishi, 1830**

Colour woodcut

36.8 × 25 cm, 14½ × 9¾ in

Artist Katsushika Hokusai's drawing depicts a lady who has fallen asleep waiting for her lover, seated on a raised platform and surrounded by screens covered in delicate calligraphy. Below, in the courtyard, two servants also sleep in front of the fire pit. Their environment is completely enclosed and internal; only the tiled roof and overlapping eaves in the left-hand foreground and the right-hand opening in the screens, which could be a threshold, suggest an exterior realm. Similarly, the natural world is not present and is instead represented by a painting of a lively horse, whose red mane and tail echo the abundant blossom of the branch under which it prances. Red is also used to depict material textures on some of the screens. Underneath the picture of the horse, a timber grain is shown, and two different red grids fill the area enclosed by the delicate timber frames surrounding the sleeping figures. The spaces that these frames define overlap, so that no clear boundary confines the figures, and even the opacity of the blank screens is not apparent. This woodcut's title refers to the writer of a classical Japanese *waka* poem, around which the image is based. An imperial princess and author, Shikishi died in 1201 and one of her *waka* is included in a famous anthology interpreted by Hokusai as *One Hundred Poets, One Poem Each as Explained by the Old Nurse*, in which he made a visual exploration of each poem in relation to his personal interpretation of it. Shikishi became the Kamo Shrine priestess at Ise in 1159, and the poem that she contributed to the anthology refers to a secret love affair that may have drawn on her own experiences in her isolated home in the centre of The Forest Where No Lies Can Remain Concealed.

**JUAN O'GORMAN (1905–82)**

**Landscape of the City of Mexico, 1949**

Tempera on masonite

66 × 122 cm, 26 × 48 in

Architect and painter Juan O'Gorman made many drawings and paintings of Mexico City – most more surreal than this one, but all containing the same intense sense of overlaid histories. This version won first prize in a competition run by the Mexico City newspaper *Excelsior* in 1949 for 'The City of Mexico Interpreted by its Artists'. An initial reading seems to show the rational and progressive evolution of Mexico City from its mythical Aztec past, symbolized by the flying serpent god Quetzalcóatl, and the presence of pre-Columbian building materials – the volcanic rock still used today. The colonial period is depicted in the sixteenth-century map of the Aztec capital, Tenochtitlan, which every year contributes new archaeological remains to the present as its lake bed shrinks and shifts. The caption reads: 'Represented here is the heart of the city of Mexico, as seen from above the Monument to the Revolution, looking towards the east.' O'Gorman's later work has been described as fantastic realism, in which simultaneous realities subvert traditional landscape genres to critique the present day. In this case, the present comprised the rapidly expanding city under 1940s and 50s President Miguel Alemán, whose opening of the economy to foreign investment and heavy industrialization promoted a modernity that many Mexican intellectuals found problematic. The hands in the foreground holding the map belong to the painter, the architect, mimicking an ex-voto painting connecting the real to the miraculous. A modernity that is a palimpsest embodying the past is evident in the presence of the steel skeleton under construction and in the blueprint held by the mestizo builder, which contrasts with the old map. Both cities are grids: one is a symbolic landscape, while the other, generated from the colonial grid, defines property values. In this sense, the painting presents a retroactive manifesto for Mexico City.

**ROB KRIER (1938–2023)**

**Altona-Nord, 1977**

Coloured pencil on paper

47 × 47 cm, 18½ × 18½ in

In 1979, Rob Krier published an analytical study of the typological and morphological elements that comprised European cities – specifically, Stuttgart in Germany – that had been devastated by World War II bombing. This animated hand drawing made for a commission to restructure the Altona-Nord district of Hamburg, a city almost obliterated during the war, reveals many of his preoccupations in its composition and subject matter. At the bottom of the drawing, a hole has been smashed in the picture plane that is rendered as a slab of stone, which shows a simple figure-ground plan of the space in which the children of the main perspective are playing. Low, tree-lined embankments surround this long urban square, which betrays no hint of vehicular traffic. Lining its upper levels are four-storey residential blocks articulated by double- and triple-height colonnades and a pared-down expression similar to that of the Tendenza architecture simultaneously being proposed in Italy. The heart of the drawing is occupied by a round communal building rendered in darker lines that resonates with more ancient references – a circular Greek temple or medieval Roman church, for example. Krier opposed Modernist ideas of tabula rasa city planning in which a new order would replace the old, finding them too close to the destructive impulses of wartime Europe. In the 1970s, debates about reconstruction and the role of historical and existing morphologies peaked, and Krier's alternative to Modernism was resolved through housing. The quality of life for the alienated urban inhabitant; the atmosphere of the environment; and the potential for individual expression, communal cooperation and moments of delight are all engaged with in this seemingly naïve portrayal of city life.

**LUIS BARRAGÁN (1902–88)**

**Las Arboledas, 1957**

Ink and coloured pencil on transparent paper

30 × 45 cm, 11¾ × 17¾ in

This is one of few existing sketches by Luis Barragán himself, drawn with a confident and expressive line. Characteristically, it emphasizes layers of foliage, crashing like huge breakers in a green ocean on to the pristine landscape of one of his property developments. Las Arboledas, and its associated country clubs, was a later Barragán project, begun in 1958 for an upper-class settlement. Located north of Mexico City in what was then a rural landscape, it included large parks and extensive sports facilities, which would enable the leisured lifestyle aspired to by prospective residents. Barragán's drawing of the first architectural intervention at the geographical centre of the *site – called the* Muro Rojo, or red wall – shows how the surfaces of its routes were organized and constructed. The grid of the paved road traversed by a 1950s-style car is simply described in black lines, with no coloured rendering to animate it. Alongside, a narrow pavement allocated to pedestrians is drawn in the same way, and two figures are shown approaching a shallow stairway protected by the red wall, left colourless in the drawing, which runs alongside the road. Between the pathway and a bright green fence bordering the neat lawn of a private garden lies a sandy bridle path, coloured a vivid orange. Here, three figures on horses cut elegant shapes, including two riders emerging down a gentle slope from the wild woodlands into a more ordered world. Like many Barragán works, Las Arboledas is symbolized by a beautiful photographic image – in this case, of the Bebedero fountain, a long water trough for horses ending in freestanding blue and white walls set among an avenue of ancient trees, called the Paseo de los Gigantes. This formed the project's historical heart, and is easily accessible from a main road, the Arboleda de la Hacienda.

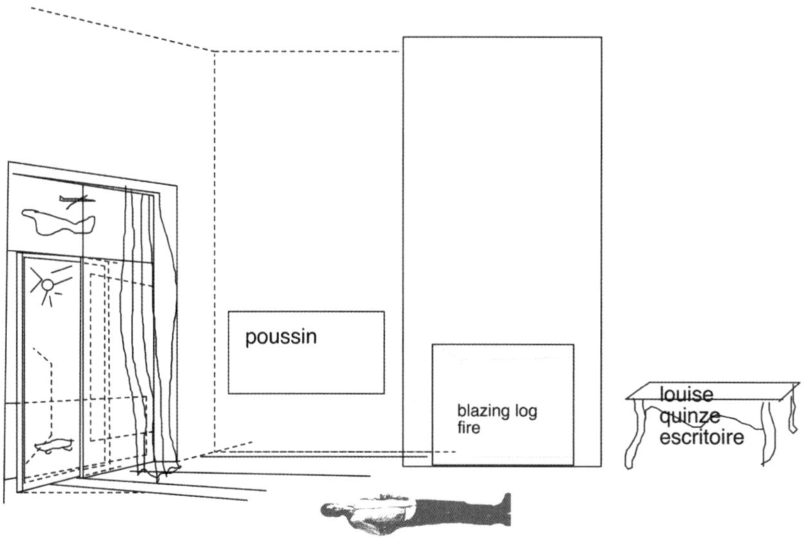

**TONY FRETTON (1945–)**

**Red House, 1999**

Computer software

20.85 × 50.8 cm, 8¼ × 20 in

Exhibited in 2016 alongside conceptual and observational sketches made by Tony Fretton on various different devices over the years, from the PalmPilot of the 1990s through various hand-held tools to the iPad, this enigmatic computer drawing was made at the turn of the millennium. Transcending the problem of obsolete programming that has made many digital drawing files from this period difficult to access and reproduce, these two images were printed out as a limited edition for the exhibition. At face value, they show in simple line drawings two interiors of the Red House that Fretton built in Chelsea, which was completed in 2001. On the left, a man lies on the ground of the spacious first-floor lounge; on the right, he leans against an armchair in a living room next to the garden. The same image of this man inhabits both spaces, replicated as if standardized and doll-like in its frozen state, his rigid standing posture is reinterpreted into positions of repose within the comfortable environment of his home. Reflecting Fretton's interest in the ways in which social forces are embedded within buildings, and the relationships between humans and the material world, these deliberately uncomfortable figures create the sense that the rooms are really stages for performance. Upstairs the explicit luxury of the room's trappings is manifest in symbols: the Poussin painting, the Louis Quinze escritoire and the blazing log fire, their material presence replaced by labels. Nevertheless, the outside world encroaches. An open balcony door lets the breeze flow into the room and a sketch of the sun in the corner means that the floor must be flooded with warm light. Downstairs, more desirable qualities are implied rather than named. Drifting vistas evoke spaces beyond. Lying on a rug over a wooden floor, a newspaper and discarded spectacles suggest time to spare.

**GEORGE AITCHISON (1825–1910)**

**Arab Hall, Leighton House, 1891**

Watercolour and ink on paper

28 × 21 cm, 11 × 8¼ in

This watercolour is a perfect miniature representation by George Aitchison of the Arab Hall that he designed for the painter Frederic, Lord Leighton. The edges of the finely detailed figure reveal the sectional cut, any tiny mistakes repaired with an opaque whitewash, with the skirting and cornice projecting in from the sides and the form of the beams and cupola above sharply defined. Aitchison designed the house, with its huge studio spaces upstairs and suite of reception rooms, for Leighton's extensive entertaining. The Arab Hall was a later addition, and showcased his collection of Middle Eastern treasures, which were acquired during travels through Turkey, Egypt and Algeria. This drawing shows the entrance into the hall bounded by Corinthian columns to mark the transition between the Orient and the Western Classical world, represented as a mysterious grey cloud, a device often used in archaeological drawings of doorways. Above the blue lintel, bearing Arabic script, is an intricate latticed screen, or *jali*, through which women would traditionally have looked down into the street; here, it sits in a niche in one of the hallways above. A golden dome reflects light back down into the dimly lit but glittering hall, whose small central fountain increases its sensual atmosphere. The lower walls are covered with blue-patterned tiles painted in minute detail by Aitchison himself, a task that would have taken many hours to complete. This is remarkable given that he had a well-rounded public life, belonging to an artistic milieu centred on Leighton and being a founding member of the Society for the Protection of Ancient Buildings, a professor at the Royal Academy and president of the Royal Institute of British Architects from 1896–99. This devotion suggests that drawing, for Aitchison, offered an escape from the increasing intensity of Victorian life into a private world.

**ANON**

**Medal showing St Peter's Basilica, 1506**

Dronze

5.7 cm diameter, 2¼ in diameter

The image embossed on the back of this foundation medal shows the only existing representation of Donato Bramante's design for the facade of St Peter's Basilica in Rome. The medal celebrated the laying of the cornerstone for the new basilica, which is located on the site of the original but now-demolished basilica erected by Emperor Constantine in the fourth century. Bramante proposed a centrally planned church in the shape of a Greek cross set within a square. The enormous dome, seen here obscuring the sky, would have been at the centre, with smaller domes and half-domes radiating out in a symmetrical pattern, and sitting on a rocky ground. One of these half-domes can be seen over the portico to the basilica, with two small domes visible between the corner towers and the building's central volume. Despite the flatness of its minimal relief, the image cast into the bronze surface reveals the complex spatial hierarchy of the design. The doorway with its pediment in the centre of the facade, which seems tiny in comparison with the whole, leads into the half-domed vestibule of one of the four aisles that progress in a series of expanding spaces. On the front of the foundation medal is cast a bust of Pope Julius II facing right, tonsured and wearing a cope with incised ornament. An important patron of Bramante, who became his principal architect and city planner, Julius II had ambitions to recreate the grandeur of ancient Rome, and decided to demolish the old basilica on the assumed burial site of St Peter. At the time of Bramante's death in 1514, construction of the new basilica was still far from completion, and work on it would continue for more than one hundred years, the final outcome bearing little relation to Bramante's original plan.

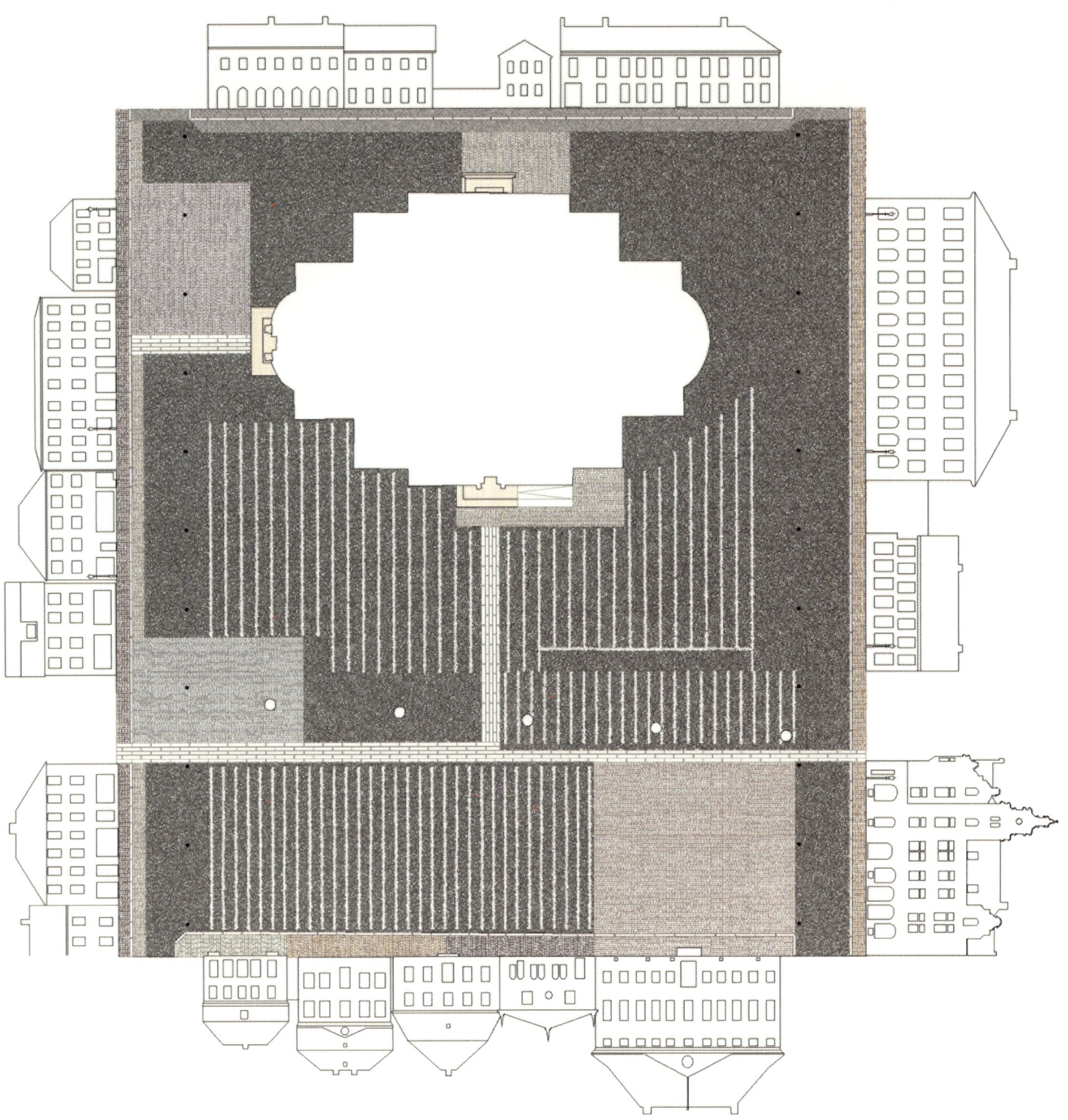

**CARUSO ST JOHN**

**Stortorget, Kalmar, 1999**

Computer software

Depicted in meticulous detail, the plan of the 98 × 107 m (321 × 351 ft) square surrounding, but mostly in front of, Kalmar's Baroque cathedral gives every one of the thousands of stones it contains an individual identity. Or at least this is how it looks in an image made at the transition between ink drawing and CAD technologies. This image is a hybrid combining a simple line drawing generated in a purely digital environment with elements drawn by hand, either on the computer or physically onto paper, and then scanned. Either way, the patterns are replicated like a sophisticated version of Letraset to create the fields of differently sized and textured stone surfaces of which Stortorget is composed.

The main material of the square is rounded glacial stones gathered from the fields around the town. These were removed to make that land suitable for agriculture and instead used to make the dry-stone divisions between fields. Within the surface of Stortorget the stones are structured into bands with lines of larger, found stones. The stones that have been *in situ* for three hundred years are joined by new stones to form a part of the new pattern for the square. These are given formal structure by the relaying of large, cut stones, *kattskallar*, which have been organized into smooth carpets in front of the town hall and the cathedral entrance. Large precast concrete slabs, with an aggregate made of local glacial stone, provide smooth paths across the square for pedestrians and cyclists. Scattered over the surface are the contributions of collaborating artist Eva Löfdahl, represented in plan. Small black dots indicate the sites of stainless-steel masts with red hand-blown glass lanterns at their tips; and circular covers indicate the five wells that act as echo chambers for the sound of gurgling running water. Enclosing facades enhance the sense of the square as a vast civic room, its floor cosily overlaid with carpets.

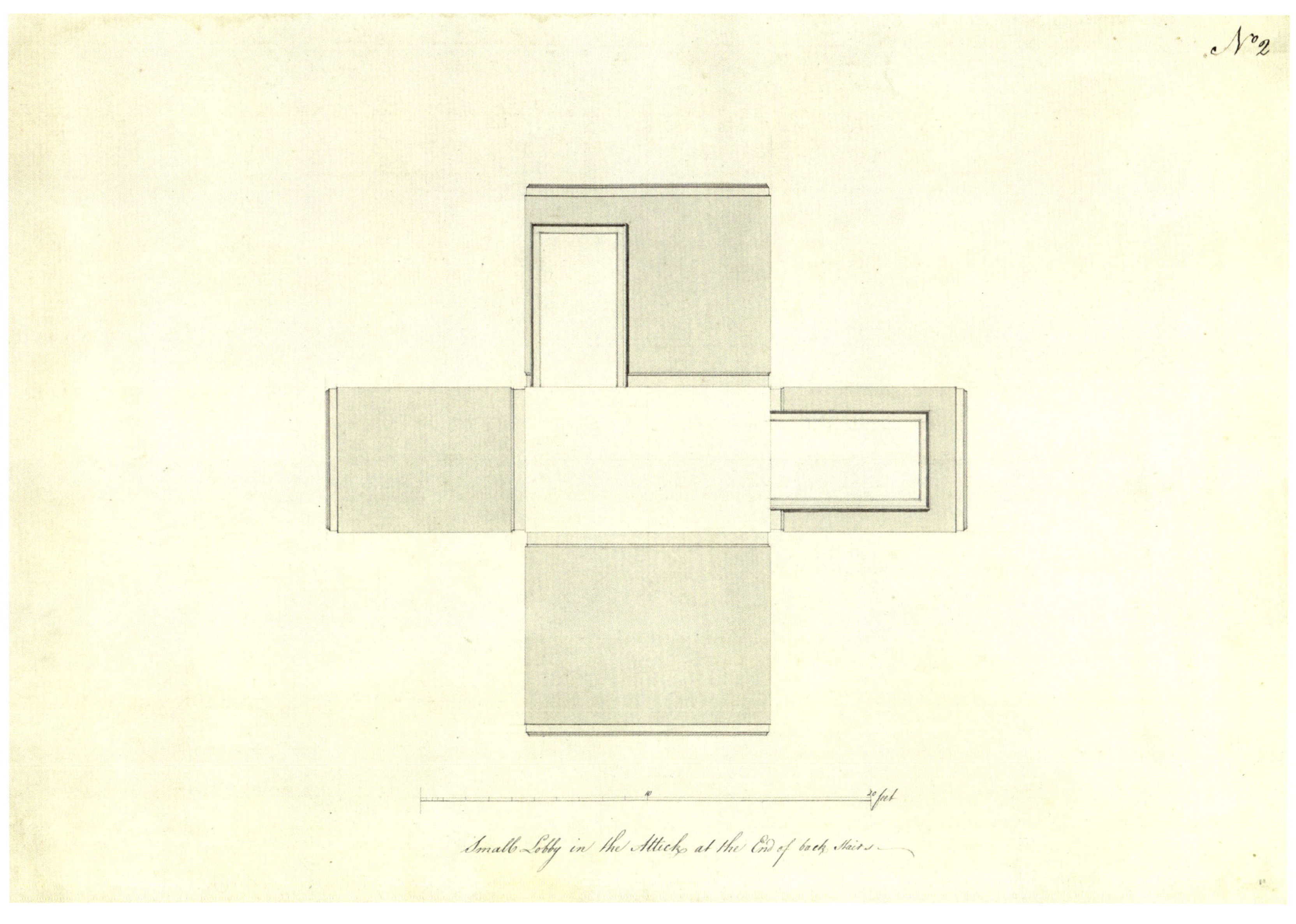


**LANCELOT 'CAPABILITY' BROWN (1716–83)**

**Claremont House, 1770**

Pencil on paper

21.2 × 30.5 cm, 8¼ × 12 in

Sometimes, Lancelot 'Capability' Brown would be commissioned to reconfigure a house as well as its garden, which was the case at Claremont, where he was employed by Robert, Lord Clive of India, who purchased the estate in 1768. John Vanbrugh had been the architect of the original house of 1708, which Clive had demolished, and Brown designed a Palladian mansion on a higher site within the grounds. This modest drawing showing the laid-out elevations of a small lobby in the house's attic reveals the simplicity manifest in the design of the Classical facades of the house itself. The mystery is why such a simple space should be represented so fully. It had no adornment or complexity in the modulation of its walls, save for the sparest of skirtings and cornices, and no furniture but two simple doorways set into plain walls depicted with neutral-coloured ink washes. This device was more commonly used for much grander rooms – to show, for example, the composition of their ornamental schemes or the location of works of art – and Brown did design such spaces at Claremont, including a Great Room, a Gothic Library and an Eating Room, none of which were adopted by Clive. In his 1803 book, *Observations on the Theory and Practice of Landscape Gardening*, Humphry Repton astutely observed that 'Brown's fame as an architect seems to have been eclipsed by his celebrity as a landscape gardener'. Indeed, this is how he is known today. In this capacity, he created around 170 romantic English landscapes, including gardens for the estates of Blenheim and Stowe, with a picturesque, informal approach influenced by Italian landscape painters. These naturalistic compositions were designed as settings for the Neo-Classicism that became fashionable during the eighteenth century, and in Brown's gardens took the form of pavilions and bridges.

**RICARDO BOFILL (1939–2022)**

**Study for the City in Space, 1970**

Pencil, ink and watercolour

18.9 × 30 cm, 7½ × 11¾ in

This colourful collage composed of fragments cut out of magazines and orthogonal drawings, filled with fields of reds and blues, communicates the intense liveliness of an imaginary city. The outside facade of this megastructural environment is presented as a cliff-face edge adjoining a densely inhabited foreground. It is hard to know whether this open space – inhabited variously by a crowd of people, cars driving by, loitering pedestrians and even the bare bones of a shattered tree – is part of the plan, or the contrasting problem. The drawing shows a version of the City in Space project developed by Ricardo Bofill Taller de Arquitectura (RBTA) in 1970, a development idea for a major housing complex that sought to house all the functions of a small town in a modular system that could be added to and manipulated as required. It established the physical and social structures of the development, while simultaneously being capable of rapidly assimilating and facilitating change, by virtue of its complexity and flexibility. The basic cubic module is readily discernible in the image, where square windows look out from rectilinear shapes marked in different hues, over which finer structures have accreted, and the shops at the base bear advertising signs. Evidence of streets, squares and arcades can be seen on several elevated levels, while the ground floor is occupied by services and parking spaces. The idea was that the complex would provide a mixture of functions on all levels and would be managed by a sort of collective cooperative. This theoretical study was made just before RBTA began designing and constructing huge housing complexes in reality – such as Walden 7 in Barcelona, completed in 1975, which inhabited and extended a former cement factory, and the Abraxas Spaces in Marne-la-Vallée in 1982 – and testing possibilities.

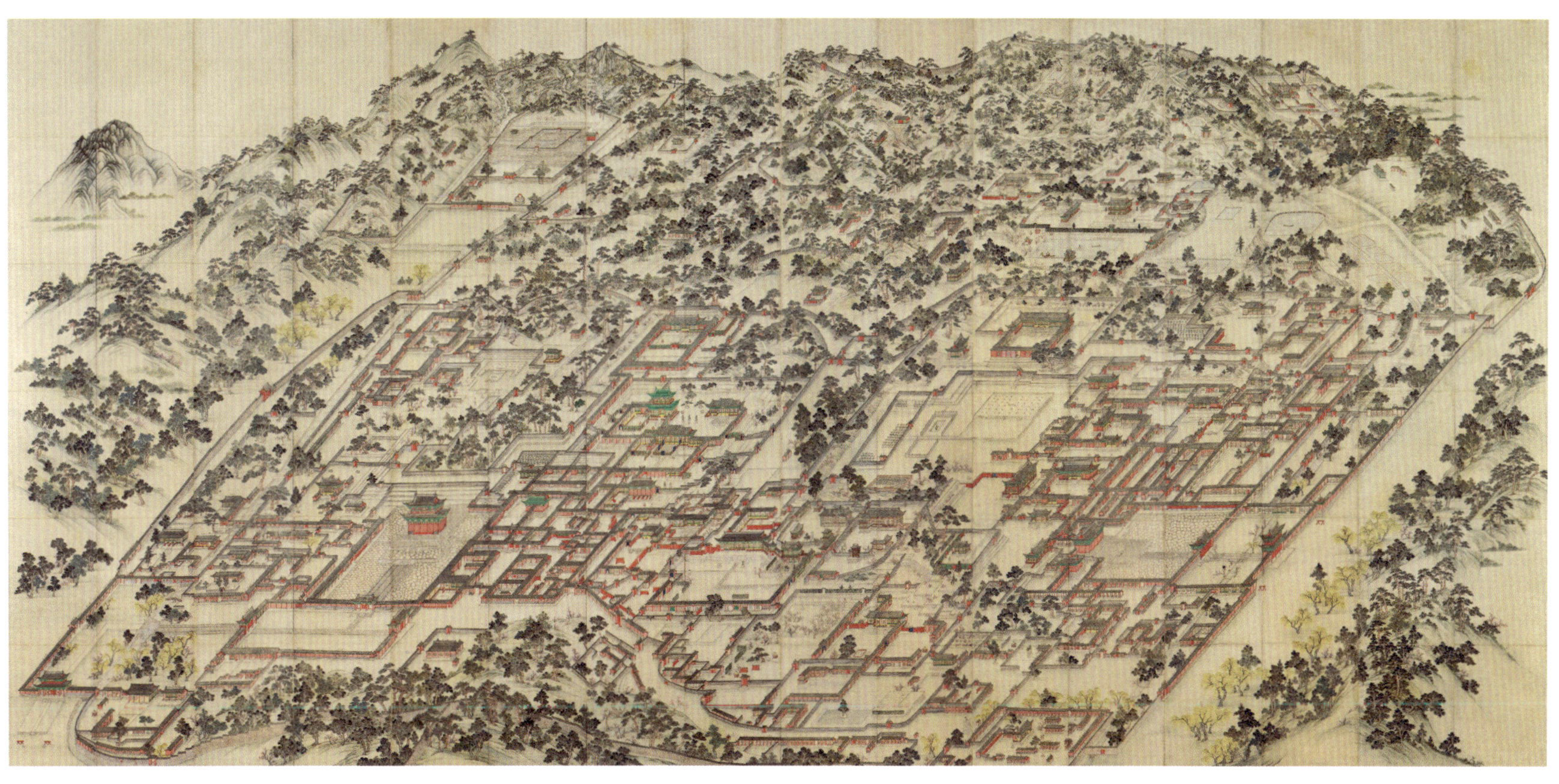

**ANON**

**Donggwaldo, 1830**

Ink on paper and silk

274 × 583 cm, 107 × 229½ in

Depicting the Eastern Palaces – two huge precincts called Changdeokgung and Changgyeonggung – *Donggwaldo* is a record of Korean courtly architecture and gardens. Seen from above, it is clear that the wooded hills and mountains surrounding the site also intermittently interrupt the formal landscape of the palaces; picturesque tracts meander across the complex field of courts and wide enclosures that make up the palaces. Celebrated for its depiction of the refined relationship between nature and man-made landscapes that is particular to the long Joseon dynasty (1392–1897), when society was organized around Confucian principles, the painting is also important for its detailed and accurate depiction of buildings. The fine brushwork of *Donggwaldo* describes not only the material quality and disposition of every pavilion, hall, gate and wall of the palace but also reveals intricate, and sometimes ephemeral, details such as building sites, trees and flowers, streams and ponds, potted plants, astronomical sites and bridges. Special places – like the two-storey Juhamnu Pavilion, raised up in its large precinct and entered through a special gate, and the Buyongji Pond – encapsulate the lie of the land. Here, the natural lay of the land is used to bring the architecture and landscape into unison, enhanced by the principle of *chagyeong*, or borrowed scenery, which is based on the framing of views. The image spreads over a folding screen composed of sixteen panels made of paper, silk and wood. Together with the vertical lines of their joints, a series of horizontal lines on the image create an orientating grid over the surface, becoming less discernible at the heart of the painting. The name of the artist who made the screen is unknown, but would have been employed by the Dohwaseo, the administrative office that commissioned official drawings and paintings during the Joseon period.

**PIERRE-FRANÇOIS-LÉONARD FONTAINE (1762–1853)**

**Drawing Model for a Music Room, 1803**

Pen, ink and watercolour on paper

12 × 18.5 × 14.4 cm, 4¾ × 7¼ × 5¾ in

Sometimes, architectural drawings are made to appeal to a sense of playfulness. Although they follow the conventions of traditional drawings, they subvert them into a simple and direct communication of the spatial idea. Pierre-François-Léonard Fontaine was a French architect and early creator of the influential Beaux-Arts tradition. He espoused a process of design proceeding from the disposition of regular architectural elements, defined by specific geometric configurations within precise limits. The fundamental element for Fontaine was the room, and for him the architectural project developed from its individual rooms and the ways in which they were linked and combined into series or sequences, in order to produce symmetrical ensembles. Here, Fontaine has isolated a single room, possibly a design for the Empress Josephine's bedroom at the Château de Fontainebleau, which he and his associate, Charles Percier, refurbished for Napoleon at the start of the nineteenth century. The drawing model follows the design of a common method of representing a room and its decorative schema used by the Neo-Classical architects of the previous century, in which the plan would be surrounded by wall elevations projecting from it. Each of the architectural elements is drawn to fit a formula – there is a way of drawing a window, a door and a language of decoration that was followed by architects and understood by their clients. Fontaine takes this one step further and, as the brightly painted wall surfaces fold up to make a jewel-box-like enclosure, the object comes to life. The niche of the window opposite the bed pops out, the yellow drapes enfold it on either side and the enclosing safety of the bed in its alcove, protected by layers of fabric and space, becomes apparent. Interacting with the object draws the viewer in, and its persuasive intent is achieved.

**THEO VAN DOESBURG (1883–1931)**

**Counter-Construction, 1923**

Gouache and heliography on paper

57.2 × 57 cm, 22½ × 22½ in

Dutch De Stijl artist Theo van Doesburg joined the Bauhaus in 1921, and his work proposed a radically different concept of space and its representation to the traditional one- or two-point perspective – an approach that proved popular with his students. He developed his ideas in a series of *Counter-Constructions*, such as the one shown here, in which the conventions of architectural representation – the presence of recognizable elements such as floors, windows and doors, and a sense of human scale, become irrelevant. Instead, coloured planes suggest relationships of interlocking spaces without defining their purpose. In this drawing, the construction floats on a generous golden ground reminiscent of the pre-Renaissance flowing space in paintings by Giotto di Bondone, which contained rather than dispersed its subjects within a spatial field. For van Doesburg, the aim was to situate the viewer within the painting rather than in front of it. These models of projects, such as the Private House and the Artist's House designed in collaboration with fellow Dutch architect and planner Cornelis van Eesteren, were drawn in the increasingly common isometric mode of projection and intended to communicate a sense of spatial dynamism, evoking the fourth dimension by way of colour and form. They received influential exposure through being exhibited at Galerie L'Effort Moderne in Paris in October 1923. As abstract, coloured analyses of load-bearing and dividing planes, they encapsulated van Doesburg's aim of creating an anti-individualistic, non-hierarchical architecture devoid of ornament and with no distinction between top and bottom, front or back. The house was conceived not as a cube closed in on itself, but as an open space that created no boundary between the inside and the outside of the structure. The point was not to live in the construction but within the atmosphere generated by the surfaces.

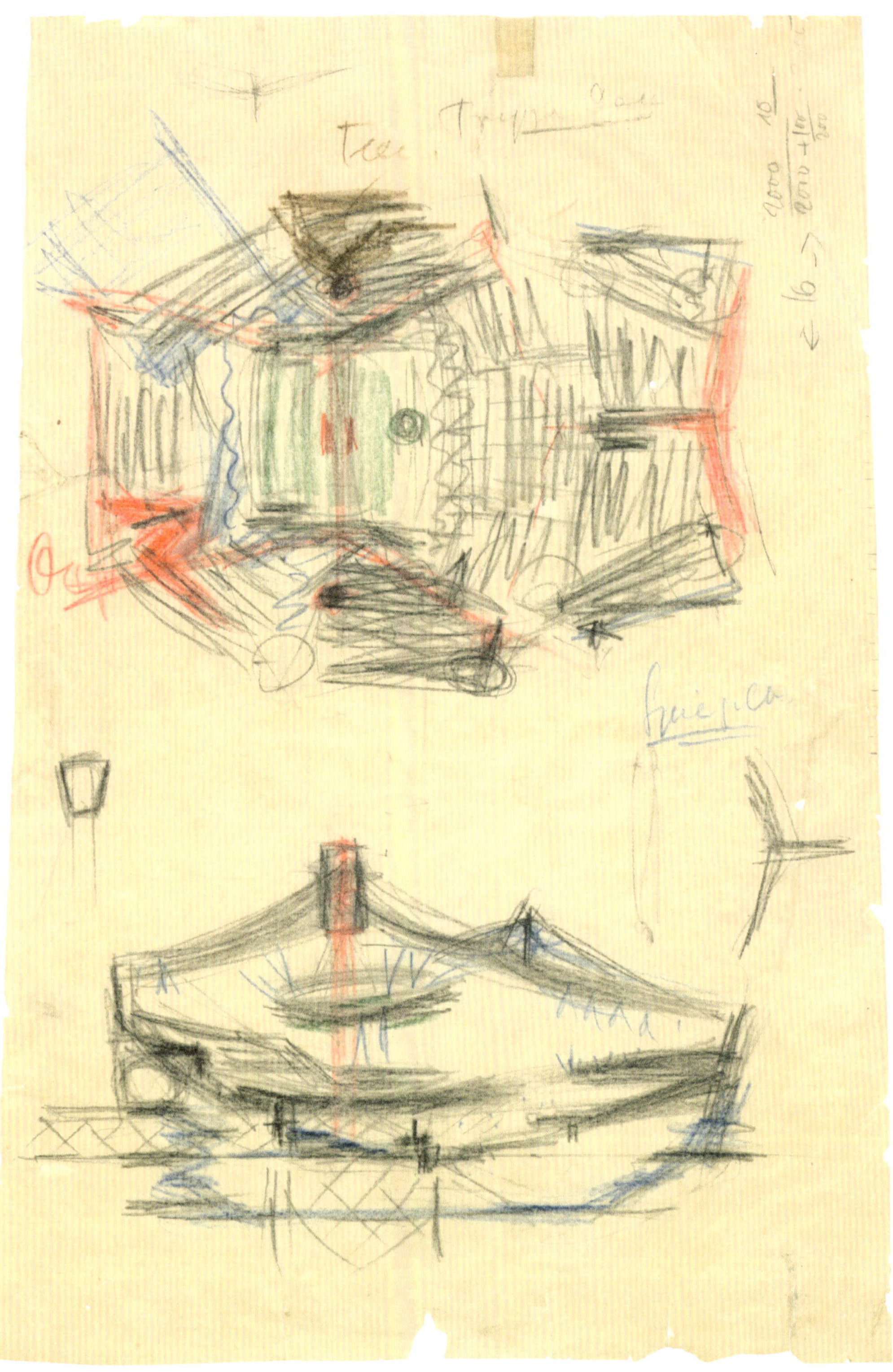

**HANS SCHAROUN (1893–1972)**

**Philharmonie, 1956**

Ink and coloured pencil on paper

29.7 × 21 cm, 11½ × 8¼ in

This early sketch for Hans Scharoun's masterpiece, the concert hall for the Philharmonie that was completed in 1963 in Berlin, shows how he was thinking simultaneously in plan and section. He imagined the huge, tent-like interior of the hall encrusted with its ancillary spaces, which in the final building are sited in response to its physical context and orientation. These are still almost non-existent in the sketch plan, where red and blue markings around the edges suggest break-out spaces and circulation. The foyer spaces that cradle the hall's scooped volume are hinted at in the section's sketchy blue lines, which seem to dig below the ground surface, their zigzag nature reinforcing their role as circulation routes. As in all of Scharoun's concert-hall designs, the building is designed from the inside outwards – from its heart. In this drawing, the design emanates from a circle in the plan where the conductor stands in front of the green field of the orchestra, and the section is defined by a huge, hanging element reflecting sound towards the longer part of the auditorium. This floats below a chimney breaking through the roof plane, within which series of red lines could indicate daylight coming into the space and penetrating deep into the hall, or rising hot air. The terraced landscape of the auditorium, which seats over 2,200 people within 32 m (104.9 ft) of the stage, is already clear, flowing downwards in a bowl shape and overlapping in a way that spreads the audience out vertically so that distance from the orchestra is never too great, and taking advantage of the radiating waves of sound that spread out in all directions. The plan is almost a diagram of this phenomenon, and the terraces encircling the stage take on the rhythm of crashing waves captured within the hall's faceted walls.

**HANS POELZIG (1869–1936)**

**Salzburg Festival Hall, 1920**

Charcoal on paper

68.8 × 84.3 cm, 27 × 33¼ in

The shadowy, prismatic cavern that Hans Poelzig reveals in this first design for an unbuilt Festival Hall for Hellbrunn, in Salzburg, has all the attributes of his distinctive style. The freehand charcoal lines pulse with energy – both when they are dark and heavy, and when they are light and feathery. The crowd of seats clustering in a semicircle round the stage makes a heavy base to the drawing, with only their tops highlighted by the glow from the stage. This contrasts with the delicate centre of the image, which shows an extravagant stage set glowing with light that radiates out over cloud-like balconies. Their interiors form shadowy caves, depicted by rapidly drawn marks that merge like feathered wings into the ziggurat-effect ceiling. The cavern in the drawing was the nucleus of a monumental complex of buildings that was designed to merge with the topography of the site, like a giant hillock in the town. Poelzig had trained as a painter and set designer as well as an architect, and this gave him the ability to transcend functional and technological concerns in his form-making. For him, the expression of emotional and symbolic content was equally important.

His belief in a *Kunstwollen*, an artistic will to form specific to the times, aligned him with the Expressionists and the artists and architects associated with the Glass Chain group, such as Hans Scharoun and Bruno Taut. Despite his great skill as a draughtsman, Poelzig did not regard sketching as an end in itself, as was taught in schools of architecture at the time, but as an essential tool of the imagination, bent towards realization. In this drawing, he manipulates the representation of space so that it becomes alive and plant-like as it encompasses the romantic, rococo grotto of the stage at its heart.

**RAPHAEL (1483–1520)**

**Pantheon, 1506**

Pen and brown ink on paper

27.8 × 40.4 cm, 10 × 15 in

This interior drawing of the Pantheon in Rome shows how Raffaello Sanzio da Urbino, known as Raphael, transformed the perspectival representation of architectural space. He diverged from the more familiar technique formalized by Leon Battista Alberti whereby the perspective was projected from a single viewpoint, producing a pictorial view of a scene. Instead, the viewer of Raphael's drawing perceives the space as if from the inside. In this applied perspective, the vantage point is situated approximately in the centre of the room. As the space is circular, the perspective could not be drawn according to Alberti's precepts, as if seen through a window, while still representing its three-dimensionality. The drawing does not reveal the impression received from a single glance, but presents multiple vanishing points that imply a sustained gaze captured over time. Raphael believed that the art of drawing buildings comprised three separate forms – plans, elevations and interiors – a discipline that he insisted upon during his time working on St Peter's Basilica. This drawing is almost an orthogonal drawing, and spatially it resembles what might be seen through a wide-angle lens. The flattening effect allows the detail of the wall surfaces and the decoration to be shown in a diagrammatic form that explains their rhythm and order. Cross-hatched shading indicates deep spaces behind the wall plane, as well as the modelling of columns and pilasters, which creates a sequence of light and dark, shallow relief and deep spatial modelling that draws the eye around the curved perimeter and gives a sense of the building's corporeal nature. The selection of a central, rather than distant, vantage point allowed the drawing to encompass a space in which the viewer is included, thus reversing the conventional relationship between observer and observed in the single-point perspective.

**PEZO VON ELLRICHSHAUSEN**

**Rode House, 2016**

Oil on canvas

30 × 30 cm, 11¾ × 11¾ in

Drawing and painting form an important part of the Chilean architectural practice of Mauricio Pezo and Sofia von Ellrichshausen. These forms of expression are used to inform and describe their built constructions, but are also developed as an autonomous practice in many different media, which they call architectonic art. This project for a single-family house alone is described in watercolour and monotone gouache, and in various other formats in addition to this intense axonometric painting, shown from a worm's-eye perspective. This technique of projection isolates the geometrical logic of the object, which floats in a depthless field of olive green. The house is constructed entirely of timber, and the semicircular shell of the building, with its steeply pitched roof plane angled towards the circle's centre, is lit here by an imaginary light source that colours it bright red. Where shadow falls, a brown hue is used. This defines the rectangular volumes inside that line up around two corners of a square bounded in plan by the circle. Containing cupboards, lavatories, a kitchen and other services in reality, in this abstract scheme they reinforce the defining geometry, crossing at one corner to project outside the circle. This move breaks the symmetry of the composition and creates a special cabinet room. Deep overhangs between the inner curve and the square create protected outdoor spaces looking towards the inner sea of Chiloé Island across the evergreen meadow in which the house is sited. The use of a single material enhances the pure geometry of the design but also responds to the artisanal carpentry traditions of the island, which developed through church and boat building. In Rode House, this extends from the structural framework as far as the cladding of all the internal surfaces with timber boards and the use of thin wooden shingles to cover the roof.

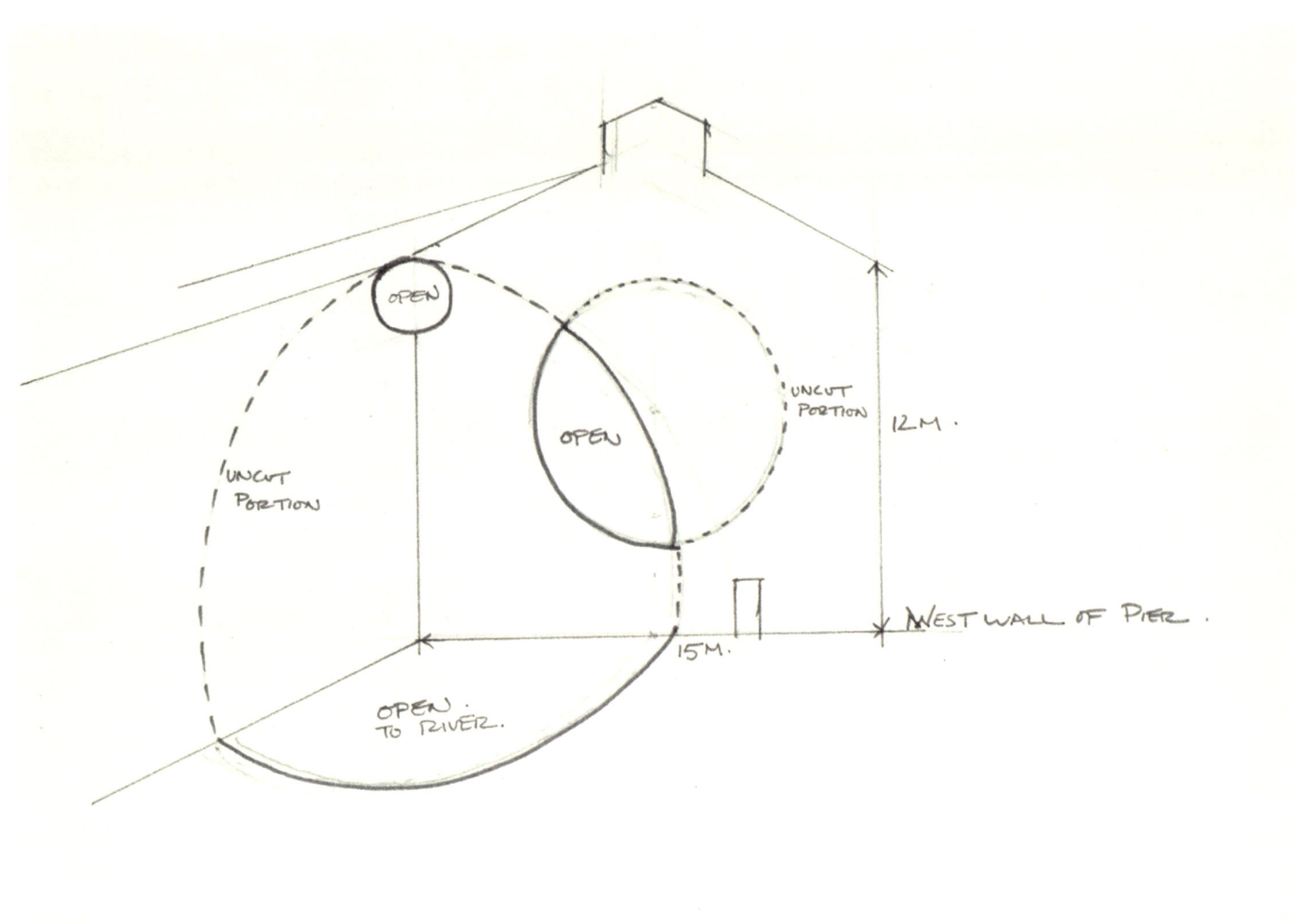


**GORDON MATTA-CLARK (1943–78)**

**Day's End, Pier 52, 1975**

Pencil and black ink on paper

23 × 28 cm, 9 × 11 in

During the summer of 1975, Gordon Matta-Clark discovered a derelict turn-of-the-century warehouse building on the wharf of Pier 52, on the Hudson River next to Greenwich Village. With some assistance, he spent two months furtively cutting and removing sections of dock, roof, wall and steel truss work from the site, only to be found out when one of the team applied for a permit to film the project. This drawing explains how 60 m (196.8 ft) to the front, a large oval penetration in the corrugated facade of the structure loomed over the river, and the steel web supports upon which the corrugated facade hangs had also been neatly removed, as Matta-Clark's collaborator Gerry Hovagimyan described the intervention. Another interpretation was made by the head of the docks, who asked what lunatic would cut out the structural steel beams from the underside of a pier. On the page the edge of this void is marked by a dark line on the floor and empty space labelled 'open to river'. Each end touches a point on the lines indicating the angle between wall and ground, the gable end drawn in elevation, the long facade in parallel lines that fade away as they become irrelevant, as does the line indicating the plane of the pitched roof above. The drawing's economy means that only the essential elements are annotated, such as key dimensions, the orientation, the lines of severance. Curved lines describe the geometry of the concept and the cuts that were made to represent it, without fully revealing the whole design. This logic is described in the drawing, though, where what is cut and evident in the dismantled planes of the building is marked in a solid line, with a dotted line indicating the thinking behind it all. The spaces that emerged took on figurative qualities when seen from a distance - resembling a sail, a rose window, or a quarter circle whose edges changed throughout the day.

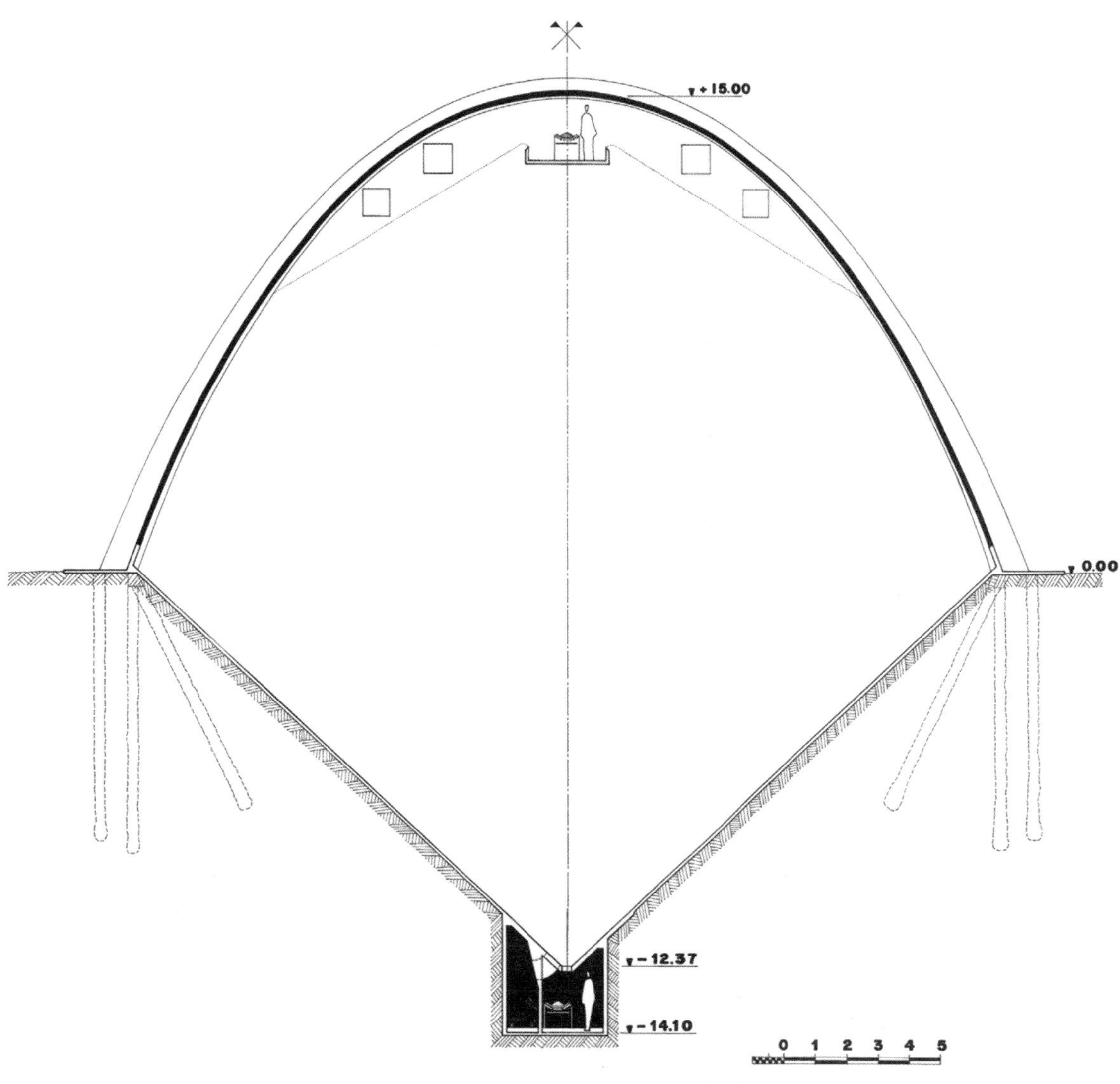


**ELADIO DIESTE (1917–2000)**

**Section through horizontal silos, 1974**

Ink on paper

76.5 × 85 cm, 30 × 33½ in

The building depicted here is a storage silo on the outskirts of the small eastern Uruguayan city of Vergara. Cutting crossways through a long extrapolated parabolic-arched structure, this section by engineer Eladio Dieste explains how its foundations are constructed so as to absorb the arch's downward and lateral forces. Below the ground-level datum, deep concrete piles can be seen on either side where the arch meets the ground. Here, two of the circular piles, which penetrate deep into the ground, are set at an angle to counteract the arch's tendency to push outwards; the remainder of the pile foundations carry vertical forces downwards. The large section drawing shows a deep, reinforced-concrete-lined triangular pit that sinks below ground and is designed to hold rice. Access to the silo is shown both below – in a long, dark pit asymmetrically located at the point of the triangular pit, occupied in the drawing by a lone figure – and above, where another figure shows the tight clearance of a gangway along the curved ridge of the roof. Dieste's structures usually comprise extremely thin, parabolic vaults made of hollow clay tiles, giving their surfaces a lively material expression and a warm, earthy colour. This readily available and cheap building material is made to work in structurally challenging situations like this one by inserting a grid of reinforcing bars into the mortar joints between the tiles. These strengthen the vault considerably, but it is the sinusoidal corrugations that make this structure highly resistant to deformation under the shifting pressures of external winds and internal piles of rice.

**QIU YING (1494–1552)**

**Spring Morning in the Han Palace, 1536**

Hand scroll, ink and colour on silk

30.6 × 574.1 cm, 12 × 226 in

The continuous scene shown in this hand scroll reveals everyday activities unfolding on a spring morning around the edges of a palace. Court ladies enjoy refined pursuits – strolling in the garden, playing musical instruments or reading – and in the centre of the composition an artist, possibly Qiu Ying himself, paints the portrait of one of the imperial concubines. This imaginary moment of court life during the Han period (206 BC–AD 220) was painted in the sixteenth century. Qiu Ying was a master of *gongbi*, or boundary painting, using a highly controlled technique and intense colour, in contrast to the freehand *xieyi*, or sketching of thoughts. *Gongbi* required the accurate depiction of architectural forms using a ruler and a meticulous brush technique. Qiu Ying sought to reveal the architectural detail of the palace, and the women's activities take place against and within a representation of its platforms, pillars, screens and open windows. Only a partial view is given, however; the roof is omitted so that the focus is on the gardens and the raised floor of the palace, whose depth is revealed not perspectivally but through the vertical projection of the elevations that skirt its edges, shown as if seen from the left. These vertical elevations trace a plan whose bays and projections create a variety of rooms along the facade intended for different activities: some are narrow and corridor-like; others, like the portrait room, have a depth that is enhanced by screens and columns. Other parts of the scene develop natural-world images that contrast with the artificial architectural lines. Here, this is represented by the bright blue, flame-like plant, tree bark or rock – but other sections of the scroll are enhanced, and sometimes obscured, by flowing branches of majestic trees or feathery bunches of fragrant pines.

**MICHELANGELO BUONARROTI (1474–1564)**

**Modano for a cornice for an unidentified location, 1530**

Pen, brown ink and red chalk

22.3 × 28 cm, 8¾ × 11 in

The word *modani*, or *modano* in the singular, was used during the fifteenth and sixteenth centuries in Italy to designate drawings for full-size, cut-out templates made on paper and used by stonecutters to carve building details. The *modano* shown here may have survived because it was never used, and therefore remained in the workshop. This would also account for the fact that it does not match any specific part of Michelangelo's built ornamental schemes, although there is some resemblance to the decoration of the Laurentian Library in Florence, where it may have been intended to transition from the doorway's complex trabeation to the simpler cornice of the reading room. The drawing was first set out in red chalk, and includes several ruled, vertical and horizontal lines as well as an incised line. These were drawn over in pen and brown ink, and then cut out. A discrepancy between pen line and cut edge suggests that the template was already being used to test ideas before being disregarded. The technique developed from the earlier template designs, or *paradeigma*, drawn or inscribed on the limestone surfaces of walls or floors of a building site to define the form of construction. Some of these are still visible today, such as those on the pavement in front of the Mausoleum of Augustus in Rome. Until the Renaissance, *modani* were the principal drawings required for building construction, and were also jealously guarded repositories of an architect's knowledge and evidence of his creativity. Michelangelo's brilliance was communicated through the many moulding and profile permutations that were invented in his workshop. *Modani* were experimental as well as instructional; in their role as tracing devices, they made it possible for architects to alter and adjust cornice details and column bases while a profile was under construction.

**BIJOY JAIN (1965–)**

**Saastrata-Mahindra Tape Drawing, 2013**

Pencil and tape on wood

83 × 185 × 1.5 cm, 32¾ × 72¾ × ½ in

Bijoy Jain's Saastrata is a low-density housing complex, with individual units designed around separate courtyards and a large, communal external space at its heart. This ambiguous room type, with the outside equal to the interior, is natural in a city like Mumbai where the idea of a tempered environment does not really apply. Deep overhangs are important in these spaces, creating shade when the sunlight and heat are especially intense and directing the drenching rains of the five-month monsoon period far away from the walls. This full-scale detail depicts the section through one of these eaves, and shows the gentle slope of the roof sailing over the vertical plane of the external wall. Made of masking tape stuck on to a cheap plywood board that is drawn over in parts with pencil lines and patterns, it is a representation of a special kind of drawing called a setting-out rod. Made by craftspeople, usually carpenters, this is a thin piece of plywood or board often painted white so that the drawing on top can be easily read; when repainted, it can be used repeatedly. On to this surface, the full-size form and measurements of an item are drawn by the craftsperson making it. According to Jain, these robust objects, of which the tape drawing is a representation, emerged spontaneously on site during construction. Paper drawings made for determining the size and joining of carpentry elements disintegrated rapidly in the humid atmosphere. One day, the carpenter came with a rough version copied from the architect's drawing, for him and the team to measure and compare the teakwood frame and fascia elements being prepared for the eaves construction. Instead of a conventional setting-out rod's white surface, the veneer is left dark and the supporting tape also functions as a drawn element.

**ELIEL SAARINEN (1873–1950)**

**Hvitträsk, 1901**

Ink and watercolour on paper

22 × 22 cm, 8½ × 8½ in

In 1901, Saarinen and his associates in architectural practice, Herman Gesellius and Armas Lindgren, bought a rural woodland site outside Helsinki. The name they gave their collective project, which combined a studio and office with the Saarinens' domestic accommodation, Lindgren's family apartment and a small separate structure for Gesellius, was Hvitträsk. This means White Lake, and refers to the wide expanse of water that it overlooks from its location on a hill crest. Direct and reflected light from the lake floods through the large window at the end of the hall in this interior perspective, illuminating the bright colours of the fabrics and painted surfaces. Responsible for the building's interior, Saarinen used this vignette to illustrate the totality of his designed environment, developing the final composition through a series of preliminary rough pencil sketches. As seen in the drawing, Hvitträsk is built from local natural materials such as granite and pine, from which the timber ceiling and wall panelling are made, combined with decorative glazed brick used for the capitals of columns around fireplaces and other interior features. These hard surfaces are relieved by fabrics, whose colours and patterns are enhanced by wall murals. A spatial complexity is created by the overlapping of rooms, using alcoves and stairways, bespoke pieces of furniture, screens and even carpets to connect and define functions within undefined locations – Saarinen depicts a fragment of this effect here. Before emigrating to the United States in 1923 to continue his architectural career in a very different context, Saarinen was an important contributor to the Finnish iteration of the National Romanticism that influenced Nordic countries during the late nineteenth and early twentieth centuries. Seeing the house as a total work of art, its design and decoration were interpretations of traditional crafts, materials and construction techniques.

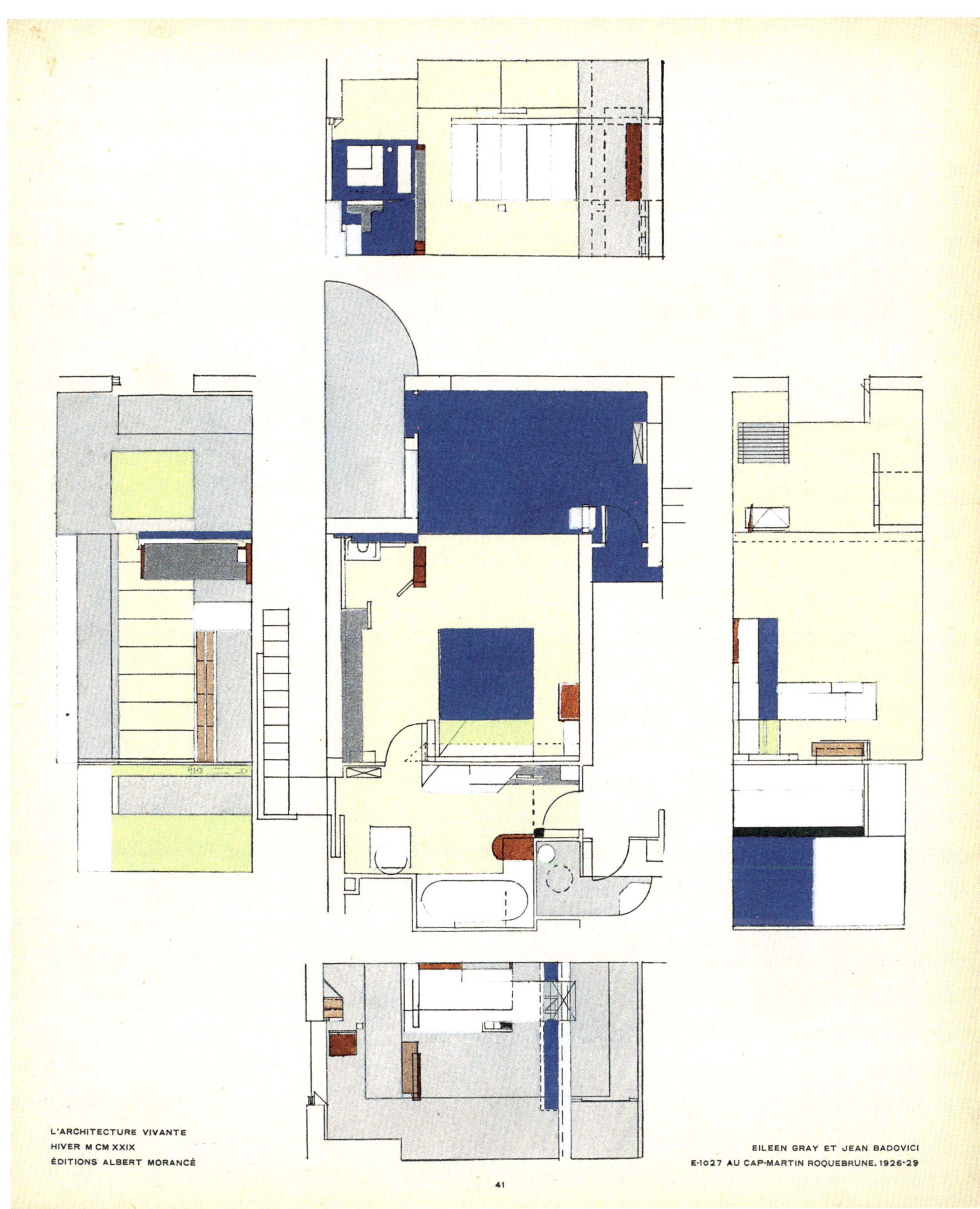


**EILEEN GRAY (1878–1976) AND JEAN BADOVICI (1893–1956)**

**E-1027, 1929**

Pencil and ink on paper

26.8 × 22.4 cm, 10½ × 8¾ in

This presentation drawing appeared in the Winter 1929 issue of the influential avante-garde architecture magazine *L'architecture vivante*, which was dedicated to architecture critic Jean Badovici's summer house overlooking the Mediterranean at Roquebrune-Cap-Martin. Designed by Eileen Gray, the dwelling's cryptic title derives from her name combined with that of her client and intimate friend: 'E' stands for Eileen; '10' for Jean, J being the tenth letter of the alphabet; '2' for Badovici; and '7' for Gray. The front of the house faces seawards, and the facades are designed to open out so as to inhale the atmosphere of the seaside setting, but also to close up. Its principal storey has an L-shaped floor plan, with a smaller basement level below and a flat roof above. The enclosed volume is quite small, so the house is designed to maximize the potential of the walls and screens between its separate rooms to serve as furniture as well as enclosure – principally as storage elements. The centre of this drawing depicts a fragment of E-1027's floor plan. The spaces shown are the two zones of the main bedroom, with the bathroom and lavatory behind. A small, projecting balcony, in pale blue, projects from the front of the dwelling towards the sea. Each intricate, built-in or specially designed piece of furniture is delineated on the four room elevations surrounding the plan. The windows are not shown on the plan, which has a completely enclosed feeling – even the door to the bedroom balcony is not visible from the bed. On the surrounding internal elevations, however, long strips of window stretch across almost the full widths of the exterior walls. The plan colours bear no relation to the decorative schema of the house in reality, but instead represent the relationships between the various wall and floor planes.

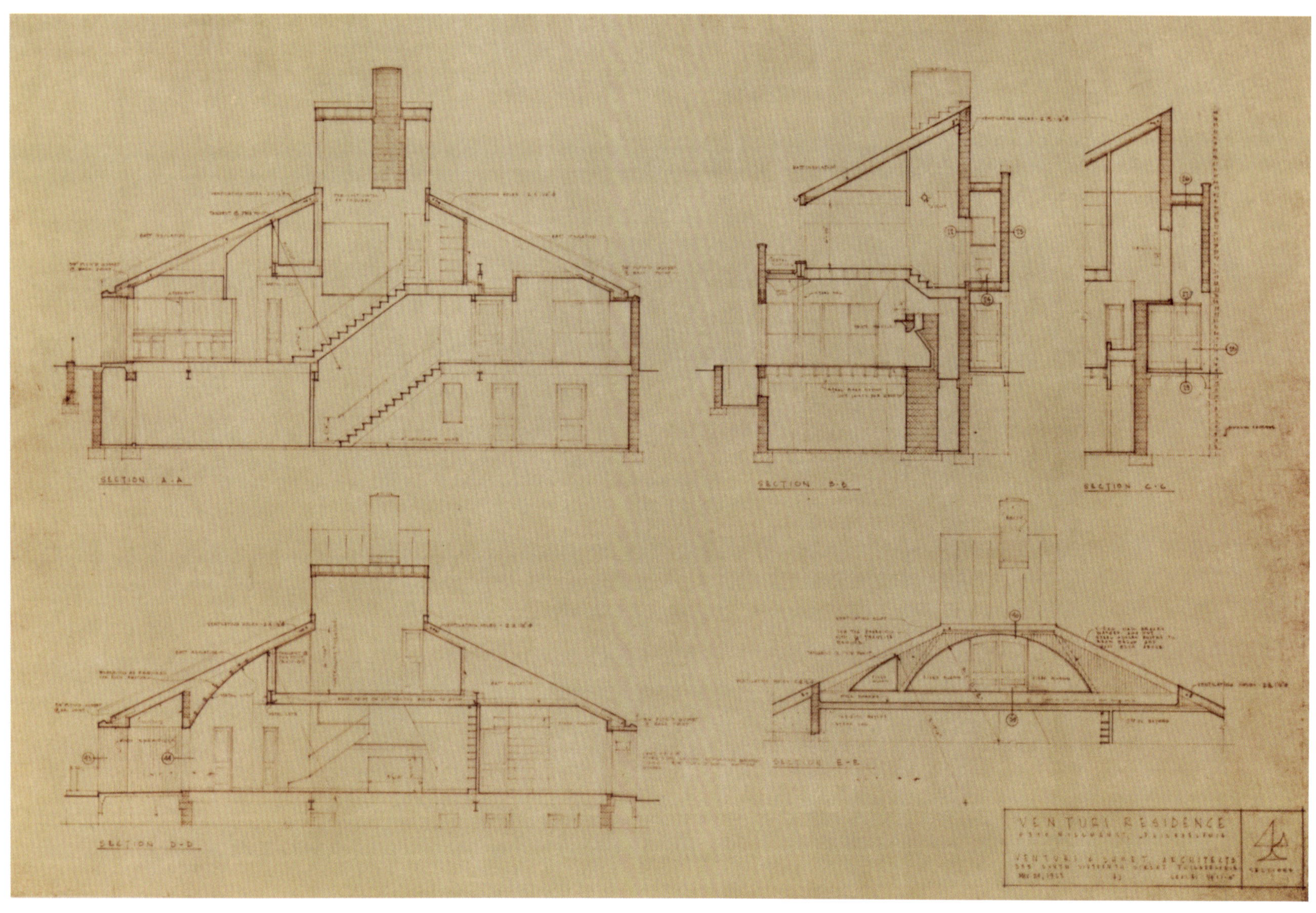


**ROBERT VENTURI (1925–2018)**

**Vanna Venturi House, 1962**

Ink and coloured pencil on paper

61 × 91.2 cm, 24 × 35 in

The home that Robert Venturi built for his mother in Chestnut Hill, Pennsylvania, between 1962 and 1964, and labelled by some the first postmodern house, became one of the stars of his 1966 book *Complexity and Contradiction in Architecture*. This series of construction sections reveals both its relatively straightforward materials and processes, and their relationship to the interior spaces. Without engaging with the narrative of the book or the reality of the house, the other layer of information that the drawing communicates is more difficult to discern. 'I like complexity and contradiction in architecture,' stated Venturi at the start of his 'gentle manifesto' against the reductionism, even moralism, of orthodox Modernist architecture. These qualities came from the richness and ambiguity of modern experience that feeds into and emerges from his design. Two vertical elements – the fireplace chimney, a solid; and the stair, a void – are both evident in section, and they compete for centre stage. In Section A-A, the staircase wins, although the chimney pokes out at the top. In Section B-B, the chimney takes over, and the stair has to contract and distort to negotiate it. Echoes of the house's elevational motifs and the shape-shifting volume of the whole emerge in parts of these sections: the curved ceiling in Section D-D, for example; and the segmented circle in the attic in Section E-E, expressed as an eye-shaped window under the eaves at the rear of the dwelling. The result is a little house with a big scale, which counter-acts the complexity and achieves tension. 'Less is more', a famous Modernist trope, was reinvented by Venturi here, for whom 'less is a bore'. The house has three storeys: the bottom one, a basement; the top one, a small attic guest bedroom within the pitched roof; and the main accommodation on the ground floor.

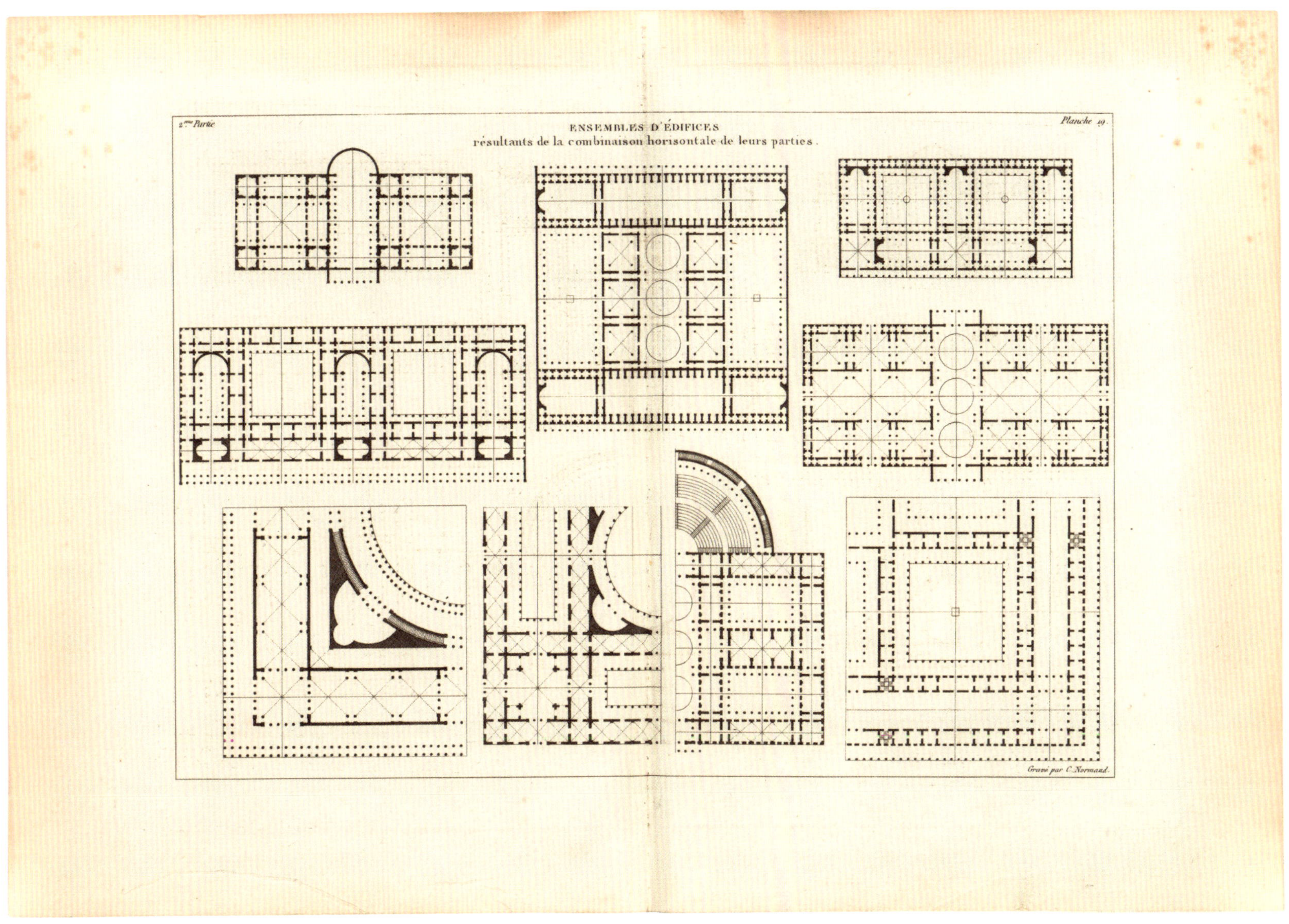


**JEAN-NICOLAS-LOUIS DURAND (1760–1834)**

**Ensemble d'edifice, 1819**

Ink on paper

27 × 39.5 cm, 10½ × 15½ in

The legacy of architectural thought of the eighteenth century was contained in two books published at the turn of the nineteenth century: *Traité théorique et pratique de l'art de bâtir*, 1802–3, by Jean-Baptiste Rondelet, dealing with the art of construction; and *Précis des leçons d'architecture*, a summary of lectures given by Jean-Nicolas-Louis Durand between 1802 and 1805 at Paris' École Polytechnique. This page, taken from *Précis des leçons*, is entitled *Ensemble d'edifice*, or groups of buildings resulting from the horizontal combination of their parts. Each group is shown in plan, the starting point of composition for Durand and always generated from a square. For him, the circle and sphere were the finest figures because they enclosed the maximum area or volume for the minimum circumference or surface area. But, accepting the impracticability of their constant use in building design, the next best solution is the square and cube. This figure is then transformed into a grid with main and subsidiary axes linking rooms, shown as faint lines on the plans here. Upon this grid, the architectural elements are imposed: walls and columns, and negative components such as window openings and doorways. The sections and elevations are arrived at by vertically projecting the plan. Form and volume are defined by rules, with symmetry and regularity, in an architecture that is the product of reason – the purpose of which is to create solutions to practical problems. Rondelet and Durand's books remained standard texts for over fifty years, providing the formulae for a doctrinaire orthodoxy. Durand's teachings arguably extended further, and it is possible to detect them within the precepts of twentieth-century Modernism in its response to industrialization – the ascendance of economical design, the eradication of decoration and the idiosyncratic historical styles.

**PETER MÄRKLI (1953–)**

**Language Drawing, Untitled 2115, 2012**

Pencil on paper

29.7 × 21 cm, 11¾ × 8¼ in

From the outside, it is often difficult to tell the intention or place of any one drawing within Peter Märkli's prolific output, which appears in sketchbooks but also on loose sheets of varying sizes such as this one. Mid-page, a fragment of an elevational grid has been hand-drawn within a square frame. Although there is evidence of erasure, and blurred testing lines make a haze in some parts of the drawing, the final result is very definite. Only the bottom line, possibly representing the ground, is tentative. This pencil stroke, broken in one place, connects the bases of three principal vertical elements belonging to a grand order, and two smaller intermediary ones co-planar with two horizontal elements equal in size and importance. The grey-coloured grid does not produce a regular series of square voids, but rather a rhythm that emerges from the systematic use of a proportional module, the effects of which are explored in the drawing. The grid is articulated by red knots. Often, in reality, these occur as small projections on the facades of Märkli's buildings at the intersection of precast concrete elements. Here, they mark the bottom and top of the grand order like subdued bases and capitals, and bosses at the intersections of the secondary grid, where they take on a slightly bluer shade. Dominating the composition are three orange squares that transcend the boundaries of the vertical elements within which they lie. These mark a moment of transition unrelated to the grid behind, where the vertical course of the monumental order changes in width from a thick Doric-like trunk to a larger, more slender strip above. These larger squares do not seem like knots or bosses, but more like powerful capitals holding up something that cannot be discerned with the naked eye.

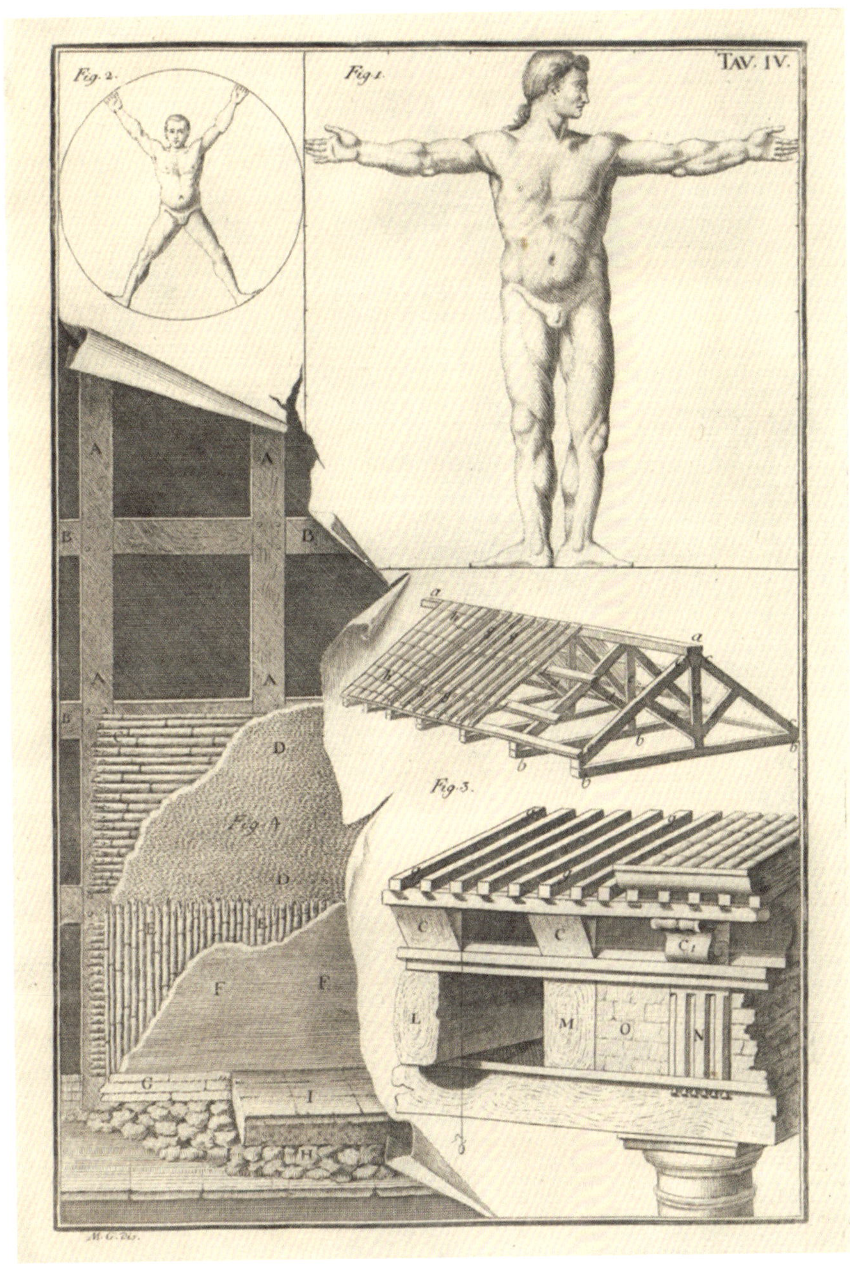


**BERARDO GALIANI (1724–74)**

**Table IV, from *L'architettura di Marco Vitruvio Pollione*, 1758**

Ink on paper

35.5 × 24.8 cm, 14 × 9¾ in

Concerned with the proportions of the human body and its defining relationship to the man-made world of architecture, which the original author of the work – a shadowy historical figure known as Vitruvius (Marcus Vitruvius Pollione) – regarded as the basis of the Classical orders, this plate shows as its primary image, Fig. 1, a man confined within a square. In Fig. 2, the same figure appears with arms and legs extended within a circle. This is one of twenty-five plates, etched in copper by Francesco Cepparuli, included in the thirteenth edition of Vitruvius' *Libri decem* (Ten Books) known as *De architectura*, published in 1758 and translated by Berardo Galiani. Galiani's edition was the first to explore the archaeological implications of Vitruvius' writings in relation to Enlightenment scholarship – as is apparent from his detailed drawing for Table IV of a roof structure and the definition of the different parts of its construction. These two aspects are organized in the drawing's composition using the device of a rent paper sheet, upon which the analytical drawing is made, and which peels back to reveal a realistic rendition, like an archaeological copy, of a layered wall construction. In this way, two separate parts are in dialogue. The top sheet contains a speculation about the relationship of the proportions of the structural elements – the carefully coded and labelled beams, rafters and struts of the pitched roof and the names of the eave components such as the triglyph and metope. Below, this is compared to the material reality of framed wall construction – layers of timber, reeds, plaster, rubble and stone that make up the building. This engagement with Vitruvius' text included the inventing of the drawings for the edition, following in a tradition of interpretative illustrations that began with *De architectura*'s fourth edition in 1511.

**WALTER GROPIUS (1883–1969)**

**Törten housing estate, 1926**

Ink, spatter paint and gouache on paperboard

107.3 × 88.8 cm, 42¼ × 34½ in

The pragmatic reality of an interwar housing estate built during a period of housing shortage in Weimar Republic Germany is transformed into a beautiful abstraction in this isometric image. The projection is cast so that the roofscape of the buildings is displayed in this fragmentary view of the streets and terraces comprising the arrangement of 314 houses that Walter Gropius designed between 1926 and 1928. The flat roofs of these modern dwellings are coloured black; the fin walls projecting slightly above their datum, coloured in red or blue, are strongly defined. These determine the party wall between each two-storey house, and are echoed in the thin lines over an earth-coloured ground that denote the garden plots for each unit. The composition's strength lies in the relationship between the diagonal of the projection and the geometry of the streets and pathways, which are perpendicular to each other. This enhances the subordinate relationship of the individual housing module to the whole, and where this strict typology is broken – specifically, in the semi-detached houses set back to make small squares – the divergence is clearly anomalous. Nevertheless, the estate did include a diversity of housing, constructed as a trial investigating the time-and-cost efficiency of the rational manufacture of housing. This meant organizing the building site like an industrial production line, using predominantly pre-constructed elements. The regularity of these repeated elements – the concrete party walls, glazing and roofing components, projecting extensions and even the doorsteps – make the composition of the drawing compelling. The only variable factor is the colour of the party walls and the extension exteriors, which is used at an urban scale to painterly effect and to bind the individual units into a homogeneous whole.

**THOM MAYNE (1944–)**

**Sixth Street House, 1990**

Screenprint with metal foil on paper

101.6 × 76.2 cm, 40 × 30 in

Dead tech was the kind of architecture that high tech would become in the world after the nuclear bomb or an ecological disaster, according to Thom Mayne of architectural practice Morphosis. The Sixth Street House project in Santa Monica, California, was an articulation of this challenge to the Modernist faith in industrial and social progress, and the role that technology plays in its inevitable failure and resolution. As the premise for the house project, it was enacted as the insertion of ten found and reworked objects retrofitted into the structure of the generic frame house. Each of these was to be made in Cor-Ten steel, the material that encapsulated the spirit of dead tech, to serve a conventional function: a staircase, a fireplace, a column and beam, or a light monitor, for example. The project was originally intended to be built, but without funding this became impossible. As an alternative, Mayne worked collaboratively with Andrew Zago to develop a set of drawings that would describe it. This was in keeping with Mayne's belief that drawing is always autonomous, and a set of drawings is itself the work, invested with its own life. The Sixth Street House drawings are representations specific to the project, and combine two innovations. The elevations and sections are drawn as oblique views rather than seen as parallel to a facade, so that the internal relationships between the objects are given equal status with the compositional elements of the facades. In this drawing, a composite of different views is brought together on one sheet – and different, interrelated treatments characterize all the images. Zago, who drafted the drawings, was influenced by Daniel Libeskind's *Micromegas* series, and Mayne by James Stirling, especially the mechanical precision and literalness of the latter's axonometric of the Leicester Engineering building.

**LOUIS KAHN (1901–74)**

**Salk Institute, 1959**

Charcoal on paper

38 × 19 cm, 15 × 7½ in

Of all orthographic projections, plans were, for Louis Kahn, the most important tool for thinking about space – from the earliest sketch making sense of a site, to detailed layouts depicting the location of every element. The plan-as-generator came from a Beaux-Arts training, in which the resolution of a project emerges through consideration of the spatial relationships between different functions, their orientation and organization. This sketch plan of the Salk Institute, a biological-science research centre in La Jolla, California, shows a fragment of Kahn's original solution for orchestrating the complex arrangement of laboratories, conference facilities and residential units that the brief required. He split it into three: the meeting house, or conference centre; the village, providing living quarters; and laboratories, the only part of the project to be built, whose disposition is described in this plan. Drawn in a soft charcoal that in places is partly erased, smudged so that its intention is not clear, but in other places making a hard, dark line, the drawing has a provisional quality. This is belied by the precision of the design decisions that it communicates, which, although drawn freehand, are precisely marked out and clearly legible. Two long blocks containing the laboratories mirror each other across a central courtyard. Along the edges of this space, ten towers containing small studies connect to the laboratory blocks by bridges alternating with sunken courts. The distinctive angles created by the towers – which twist westwards, facing the ocean – are already evident here. A steep cliff is indicated by contour lines at the bottom of the sheet, beyond the edge of the plaza. The space is shown filled with symmetrically arranged foliage that was removed on the advice of Luis Barragán, who introduced a simple water channel running down the centre of a flat, radiantly white pavement.

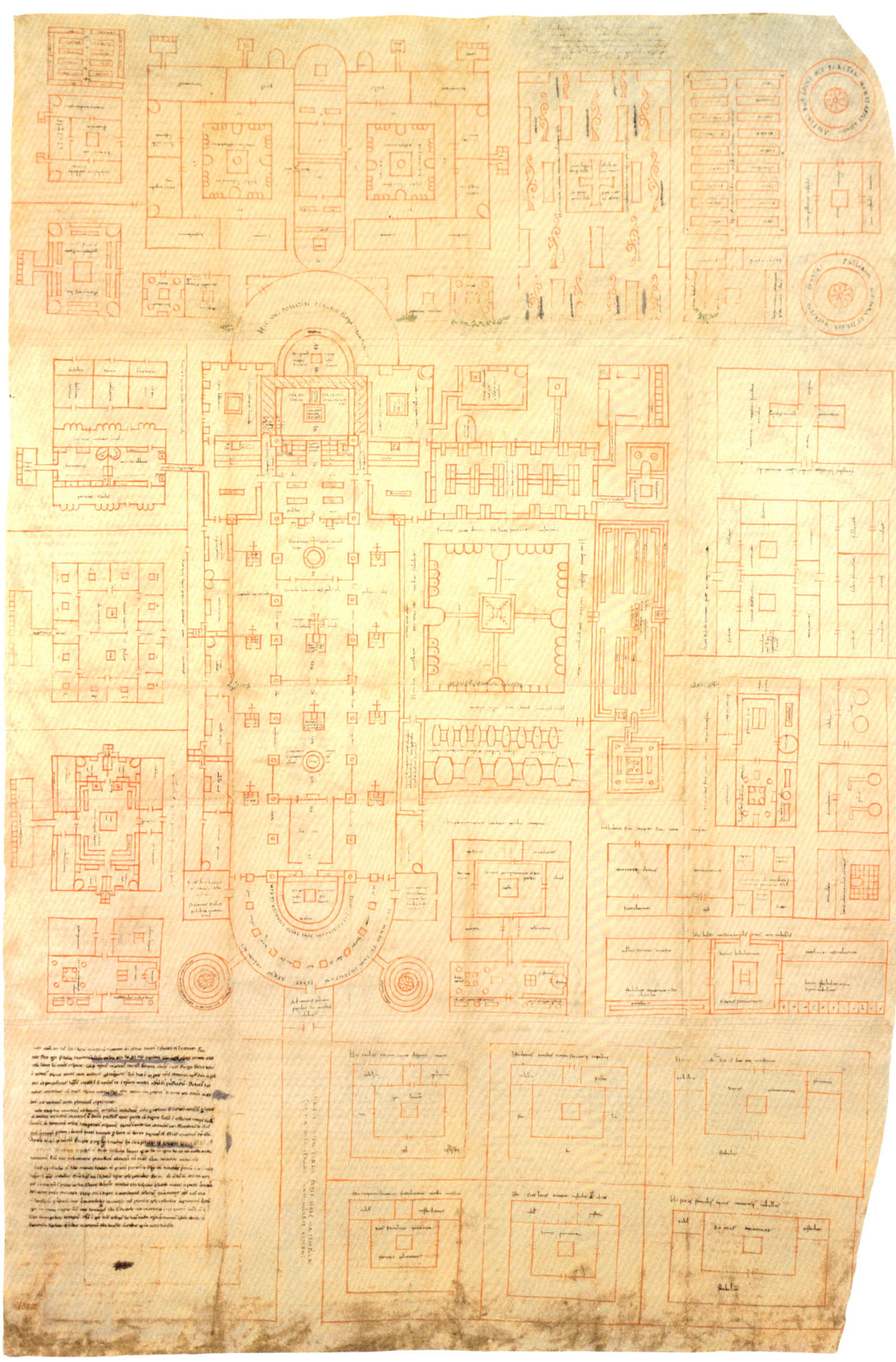

**ANON**

**Monastery of St Gall, AD 820**

Red and brown ink on parchment

113 × 78 cm, 44½ × 30¾ in

The reason for creating this rare visualization of a building complex, made during the Middle Ages, remains a mystery, although its content is easily interpreted through the 333 Latin inscriptions in brown ink that cover its surface. These describe the functions of the various buildings and gardens of a Carolingian monastery. One of very few surviving architectural drawings from the period between the fall of the Roman Empire in the mid-fifth century AD and the thirteenth century, the drawing consists of five pieces of parchment sewn together. Over this surface, an anonymous draughtsman has used a single line weight to create a fine network of lines in red ink that delineate the ground plans of over forty structures. At the heart of the walled community lies the monks' cloister, enclosed by the refectory, dormitory, warming room, kitchen cellar and larder that made up their collective living quarters. To the north of the cloister, the basilica dominates. Radiating out from this centre, the supporting functions of the self-sufficient, enclosed world of the medieval monastery are strictly organized. In addition to the abbot's house, school and guest quarters these include a bakery and brewery, quarters for servants and farm animals, workshops, an infirmary adjacent to a herb garden, and a cemetery set in an orchard. The notation at the bottom left-hand corner reveals that the design was made for Gozbert, abbot of Saint Gall (AD 816–837), and suggests that rather than being a design for a real monastery it was an idealized proposal to guide monastic planning. In reality, the design does not conform to the terrain of St Gall's river valley site, and the Carolingian church of Saint Gall does not correspond with the design of the church on the plan.

**CEDRIC PRICE (1934–2003)**

**Battersea Power Station, 1990**

Felt-tip pen and crayon on a sketchbook sheet

20.3 × 25.3 cm, 8 × 10 in

A competition was held in 1984, the first of many over the years, to find a solution for the empty but iconic Battersea Power Station, which had fallen into disuse only a year earlier while acquiring listed status. The brick building had housed a coal-fired power station that generated up to twenty per cent of London's electricity supply until it was decommissioned. Its second half, which introduced two more striking chimneys to the ensemble, was completed in the 1950s. Cedric Price was one of seven architects invited to submit a scheme, and his characteristically radical counter-proposal for creative, as opposed to painstaking, conservation of the existing structure demolishes the monolithic pile of bricks beneath the famous chimneys. This released the ground for development suitable for a multiplicity of uses, which was one of the consistent themes of projects such as the Fun Palace that Price developed with theatre director Joan Littlewood in 1961. He called his entry Bathat, and in his later sketchbooks he revisited his idea for the site, making a rapid sketch in soft orange-red crayon, the Victorian terraces of south London appearing as purple blocks – tiny in comparison with the volume of the power station. They are seen behind a veil of tenuous structure, ostensibly the existing steel structure laid bare, which Price has drawn in red felt-tip pen. The unpredictable results of this medium cause some elements to be more pronounced than others. The skinny, braced structures seem to tether rather than support the floating platform, whose weight has vanished with the wall but which retains the symbolic and landmark qualities of the original scheme – particularly the four towers, which appear as gesturing fingers in the sketch.

**ALDO ROSSI (1931–97)**

**San Cataldo Cemetery, 1971**

Coloured pencil on paper

41 × 59 cm, 16 × 23¼ in

This coloured rendering by Aldo Rossi of his scheme for the San Cataldo Cemetery in Modena is one of several iterations originating from a design drawing, and its colour palette is relatively subdued. It is not an accurate depiction, either, of the finished design or the fragment that was eventually built, but rather a symbolic representation of ideas about urban form that Rossi had developed in his book *Architecture of the City*, published in 1961. The composition shows a complex combination of different kinds of orthographic projection. These include plan forms, whose depth is sometimes, but not always, accentuated by a heavy shadow line; elevations, given form through the use of single-point perspectives with two different vanishing points; and other small vignettes, including a section through the conical tower shown in plan at the top of the drawing, which marks a communal grave, and a perspective view of the same tower. The site for this cemetery is adjacent to the grounds of a nineteenth-century cemetery that contains carved statues and tombstones marking graves, whose landscape forms the foreground of this House of the Dead. The drawing shows the enclosing wall of the cemetery creating deep shadows around the edge of the sheet, with the ossuary building, cubic in volume, near an entrance and flanked by the elevations of the perimeter buildings. In this project, Rossi is experimenting with the use of pure signs – the cone, the cube, the parallelepiped – to represent basic architectural types such as the factory, the house and the street. This formal language is reduced to its minimum in order to discover an expression for the personal nostalgia and collective memory that a cemetery naturally embodies.

**ERIK GUNNAR ASPLUND (1885–1940)**

**Woodland Chapel, 1920**

Graphite, crayon and colour crayon on tracing paper

21 × 26.7 cm, 8¼ × 10¾ in

Deceptively simple, this sketch by Erik Gunnar Asplund reveals much about the design by Asplund and Sigurd Lewerentz for Stockholm's Woodland Cemetery – on which they began their lengthy, twenty-five-year engagement after winning a competition in 1915. Constructed in layers, the drawing shows the front elevation of the small chapel in perspective so that the soffit of its deep portico is slightly visible, communicating a sense of shelter among the ordered columns of the porch that echo the surrounding tree trunks. A carefully drawn, wrought-iron doorway signifies the entrance to a different realm, whose presence is also marked by the heart-shaped plaque above. The porch columns sit lightly on the thinly-paved plinth that marks out the building's territory, its paving slabs given depth by two shallow steps and material substance by being faintly sketched out. This platform is barely larger than the chapel's footprint within the pine forest and, in the completed building, is reached via a narrow woodland path. The drawing's foremost figure is a tall pine tree, whose dark-green foliage provides the most intense colour in its monochrome palette, while the shadows of the woodland closing in behind are shaded in lightly sketched yellow-green or grey pencil. The cemetery design by Asplund and Lewerentz articulated the site's natural qualities, remodelled through excavation work to enhance its soft valleys, in the circulation layout and the disposition of its buildings. The design of the chapel was directly assigned to Asplund, however, and while it reflects these intentions by being embedded in its site it also embodies complex cultural references. It reflects the influence of Swedish Romanticism in its synthesis of Classical temple and indigenous hut – having been inspired by a vernacular cottage in Liselund, Denmark – and the dominant form is the steeply pitched black roof, echoing the darkness of the forest.

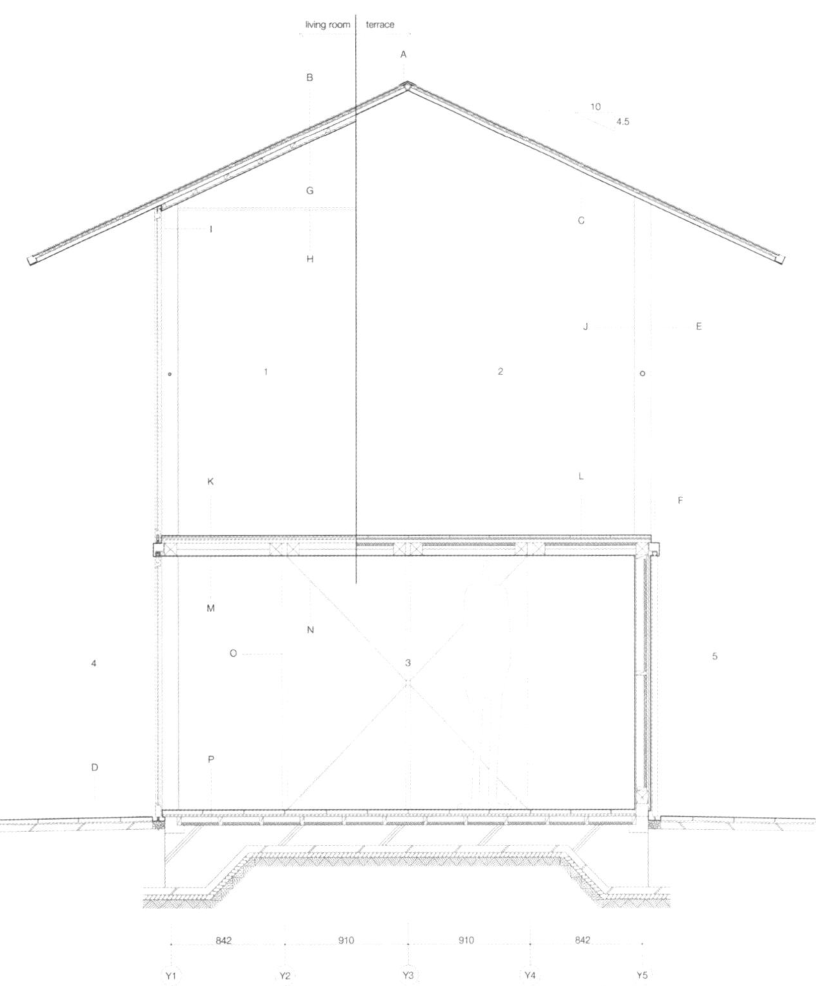


**GO HASEGAWA (1977–)**

**House in Kyodo, 2011**

Computer software

32.6 × 26.6 cm, 12¾ × 10½ in

Cut through a small house in the Tokyo district of Kyodo, this section captures the essence of domestic space in the majority of dwellings in Japan's largest city. At the ground-floor level, ceiling height almost matches that of a tall man at 180 cm (70¾ in), and it is evident that an extreme economy is at work. This is matched by the simplicity of the building materials and the slenderness and refinement of each element of the section, which has been reduced to a bare minimum. The rectangular plan measures 70 m² (753 sq ft) spread over two floors, and the intimate, enclosed ground floor contrasts with the tall upper space, containing an open, undivided room housing the kitchen and living areas. With views over gardens and across the low-rise neighbourhood, long, single-glazed perimeter walls are protected by the deep overhang of the roof, which comprises 6 cm-thick (2½ in) steel sandwich panels. There are no gutters or overlaps; the roof surfaces are smooth, and the structural elements supporting it barely visible. The underside of the eaves is a shiny silver, reflecting light gathered from the gap between the roof apex and the top of the gable wall, whose line is just discernible, echoed on the drawing in the line of the screen between terrace and living room labelled 'H'. The ground floor is enclosed by sliding panels that can be opened up as necessary to the outside world. The private spaces are on this floor, interspersed between the bookshelves of the publisher-clients' library, clustered under a warm-grained, timber-lined ceiling and placed over a floor of square, grey-clay tiles. The section shows that these are laid over a concrete raft foundation, under which the main insulation is located, with a tiny channel running around the edges of the house to disperse any rainwater running down its sides.

**ANON**

**Tahmina Comes into Rustam's Chamber, c.1434**

Opaque watercolour and gold on paper

20.8 × 10.5 cm, 8¼ × 4 in

This image of a scene from the *Shahnameh* epic by the Persian poet Abu 'l-Qasim Ferdowsi Tusi, written between 977 and 1010, shows the new direction that manuscript painting took in the Timurid court workshops of the fifteenth century. Although no text is preserved, later compositions based on this painting confirm that it illustrates an episode in which Tahmina, daughter of the king of Samangan, comes at night to Rustam's chamber. Its jewel-like details reveal the long-lost splendour of Timurid palace interiors. The picture plane is flattened so that the horizontal elements, such as Rustam's bed and the floor of the niche beyond, appear as elevations contiguous with the tower doorway through which Tahmina enters; they are fields of luscious pattern, existing on the same plane. Rustam's bed is situated within an *iwan* – a vaulted space walled on three sides with one end, where the viewer is positioned, entirely open. The outer *pishtaq*, or frame, around the *iwan* is supported on the side walls of the rectangular space where Rustam's bedding is spread. Three long windows, echoed by arched panels above, pierce the walls of the space beyond, which exhibits a perspectival logic in its construction, while below, the floor of the chamber extends the full width of the painting to tie the composition together. Produced in a workshop in Herat, Afghanistan, using the highest-quality materials, its exquisite draughtsmanship is the work of a master illustrator following the strict form of such paintings while simultaneously introducing subtle innovations. Mystery surrounds its date and purpose, for its proportions – twice as high as wide – are unusual and preclude its belonging to any surviving *Shahnameh* manuscript. It was once mounted in an album together with text and other illuminations, but now lacks context.

**DOGMA**

**A Field of Walls, 2012**

Computer software

11.7 × 13.5 cm, 4½ × 5¼ in

This curious section-elevation belongs to a set of drawings accompanying a white model of an imaginary Rome made by the architectural collaborative Dogma, led by Pier Vittorio Aureli and Martino Tattara, for the Venice Architecture Biennale in 2012. In the model, and with different aspects revealed in the drawings, the city's topography is dominated by fifteen rows of very long multi-storey inhabited walls. The project responded to a design brief by Peter Eisenman called Piranesi Variations, which asked for a reimagining of Giovanni Battista Piranesi's *Campo Marzio* etching from 1792. In Dogma's interpretation, Piranesi's image shows a space from which all the familiar types and forms of buildings normally found in a city are excluded, and so architecture becomes simply walls enclosing spaces. The walls in the model are what Dogma describe as non-typological, in that they are not specific buildings with a hierarchy of use, position and visual expression, but generic structures. Formally, in their nakedness and with their repetitive colonnades and square windows, they are similar to earlier Italian experiments in creating architectural form from the 1960s, such as those of Aldo Rossi and Superstudio. The walls in this section-elevation drawing, however, are very characterful. Its many layers suggest an archaeological intent, and some of the walls still seem to be underground but on the brink of exposure – as were the ruins at Pompeii at the time of Piranesi – then only accessible by narrow tunnels and visible as dark fragments. The section through a tower-like element that cannot be climbed divides the composition in two, and on the other side a stone wall embedded with closed-off round arches acts also as a foundation for the tall section. Behind, a whole crowd of buildings is layered in elevation, huddled between two huge non-typological structures shown in perspective.

**ETTORE SOTTSASS (1917–2007)**

**Progetto di architettura monumentale per la conservazione delle memorie nazional-popolari, 1976**

Colour gouache and India ink on paper

47.2 × 34.5 cm, 18½ × 13½ in

Austrian architect Hans Hollein compares the drawings of Ettore Sottsass to the vase – a leitmotif of his work and vision, embodying his attitude and philosophy. The drawing, as the vase, is a metaphor but also an intrinsically useless object that finds its use activated by the imagination. Theorist, writer, designer and architect, and one of the founders of the design collective Memphis, Sottsass produced many different kinds of drawing. This is an example of his architectural images, in which the volumetric is accentuated and colour plays a key role. In this drawing, the colours are relatively muted, dominated by black and a neutral blue. In this axonometric projection, the fields of colour are solid and dense, the blue fading to white on the floor of the plinth the only intimation of modelling by directed light. The dominant, subdued colours contrast with yellow and red details – animating the fluttering flags, for example, and colouring the archaeological fragments that lie scattered on the excavated ground and emerging plinth. Yellow is used to highlight the round arches on the top level and, along with red, defines the stepped motifs painted on the walls of the main volume that are reminiscent of Mayan decoration. Sottsass is playing with the nationalist overtones in the title of the drawing, poking fun at the earlier Novecento movement's preoccupation with Imperial Rome and the continuity of the Classical tradition, which was reflected in the autonomous architectural language proposed by the Tendenza architects. Sottsass suggests that other traditions can be as relevant to national and popular memory as those springing from Italian soil, and in this he locates himself within a relativist, post-modern tradition.

**ROBERT BRAY (1940–)**

**Living Area, 1970**

Gouache on board

39.3 × 57.7 cm, 15½ × 22¾ in

This interior perspective of an idealized living room featured in the January 1970 issue of *Playboy* magazine, and is one of a set of six room vignettes for a Playboy Duplex Penthouse. This design was the second in a series of Playboy Pads for the urban bachelor; the first was published in 1956. The imaginary inhabitant of the apartment, according to the accompanying narrative, believed that a man's home is not only his castle but also an outward reflection of his inner self – a place where he can live, love and be merry; entertain his friends; play poker with cronies from the office; or relax with a fond companion. The image of the room reflects the magazine's projected psyche of affluent male consumers of the period, giving insight into their aspirations. The double-height space of the living area is enclosed within the world of the apartment itself, with views to internal patios – one in the distance, and another behind a screen – and to other hidden places suggested by the two staircases, the long corridor and the internal balcony. While the sunken pit of the central seating area is brightly lit from above, the dark ceilings, floors and deep water of the pool, combined with the shady interiors in the distance, give a sense that this is one of a series of settings for secret selves. Seen from the foyer of the apartment, a slew of expensive designer furniture is on display in the space – including leather Domino and spun-aluminium Torino chairs, and a lacquered Knoll cocktail table, as well as an array of audio and video apparatus. The panel behind the dining niche is decorated with a colourful abstract graphic, and other small touches of pattern animate an otherwise cool, monochrome interior.

**HEINRICH TESSENOW (1876–1950)**

**Sepulchre in the Forest, 1905**

Pencil on paper

39 × 27 cm, 15½ × 10½ in

Heinrich Tessenow's mysterious drawing of a sepulchre hidden deep in the woods was made for an unbuilt project about which little is known. He worked on it during a prolific period of his early professional life when his deep interest in the vernacular, derived from observations of everyday forms of living, was being translated into modest housing projects. These were also informed by his knowledge of traditional materials – especially wood, for his father was a carpenter, and Tessenow himself apprenticed in the craft before studying architecture. The power of natural materials permeates this drawing, removed here from the commonplace into the mystical realm of the forest, from where the origins of the Germanic culture were believed to have emerged, and which still play a central role in the German psyche. The frame of the drawing is filled with the trunks of trees, the foremost of which spans its full height, but with no visible canopy. The only hints of life are black twigs attached to the trunks. Although the trunks are densely packed, the fine lines recording the bumps and ridges of their bark are lightly drawn, so that instead of lying in ominous darkness that deepens with perspective depth, the forest floor is pale. Against this bright ground, the dark form of the alien object, the sepulchre, is disconcertingly black and present. A rectangular form inscribed with a black grid is seen in elevation. Springing from the top, the branches of a much smaller tree, still leafless, are the darkest elements of the composition. They form a small canopy that defines a circular clearing in the woods. In this drawing, Tessenow's feeling for the monumental is forming, and soon he would become interested in the possibilities of Classical architecture. Connected to an innate Germanness, the simple symbolic image in this drawing belongs to no style or time.

**JOHANN BERNHARD FISCHER VON ERLACH (1656–1723)**

**Basilica Cistern**, 1721

Engraving

18 × 27 cm, 7 × 10½ in

Johann Bernhard Fischer von Erlach's image of the Basilica Cistern was constructed from his artistic imagination but using a wide array of archaeological and historical evidence, in keeping with his method. As architect, sculptor and architectural historian at the imperial court at Vienna, he had access to the large number of unpublished drawings held in the imperial collections, which included drawings of the Great Cistern at Constantinople as well as other structures that he included in his influential, comparative, seven-volume *Entwurf einer historischen Architektur*, first published in 1721 – and later in English, as *A Plan of Civil and Historical Architecture*. This plate shows the Basilica Cistern in a centralized perspective that accentuates the relentless repetitiveness evident in the plan at the bottom of the sheet. It would have been informed by contemporary archaeology and a variety of written sources, often including ancient writers and travel writers, coins and drawings of ruins still standing, as with Fischer von Erlach's other reconstructions. An ambiguity about the location of ground level shows that it is an imaginative rather than an accurate image, for the grid of columns could be standing on, rather than situated below, the ground, more like a mosque structure than that of a cistern. It belongs to the third of his five volumes, which depicted important structures from Islam, medieval and modern Persia and China. The first deals with the seven wonders of the world, and the last and fifth, his own work. His history of architecture searches for the origins of the architectural orders – which, in keeping with contemporaneous beliefs – he found in Solomon's Temple. His extensive built oeuvre harmonized heterogeneous parts into a unified whole as he sought the most successful solution for each individual task. In this, he was influenced by the ideas of his friend Gottfried Wilhelm Leibniz.

**ALVAR AALTO (1898–1976)**

**Finlandia Hall, 1970**

Pencil on paper

32 × 23.7 cm, 12½ × 9 in

This freehand sketch, made during the design phase of Finlandia Hall, shows the main auditorium's timber-wall relief sculpture. It demonstrates that Alvar Aalto's concern to embody the forms and presence of the natural world within the man-made one that he was creating happened at every scale – from the large-scale city plan to the detailed design of furniture, fittings and decoration. Sketching was an important part of the design process for Aalto, allowing him to work freely, resolving and synthesizing ideas. In this pencil drawing, he combines a three-dimensional exploration of the wall relief with themes that constantly recur in his work, such as the shell-like, undulating forms that here respond to the acoustic requirements of the space. On the right-hand side of the sheet are studies for bent-plywood acoustic shells for the ceiling of the hall's chamber-music room, and the overall direction of his thinking is indicated in the loose plan at the bottom. Aalto's Helsinki Centre Plan, 1959–64, linked the Finnish capital's historic centre to Lake Töölö lying near its northern edge, so that a sense of the surrounding natural world close by became embedded in its heart. Served by the principal transport systems and dispersed around the lake, the plan identified settings for the city's important new cultural buildings, which included museums, an opera house and a congress hall. Aalto designed the Finlandia Hall, inaugurated in 1971, himself, his final great building that encompassed all the themes of his late architecture. Finlandia Hall was placed at a pivotal point in his urban plan, on the east bank of the lake where it is embedded into granite bedrock outcroppings by a long straight wall. It has a free-form plan composition and – in contrast to the grey, rocky ground – is clad in white Carrara marble.

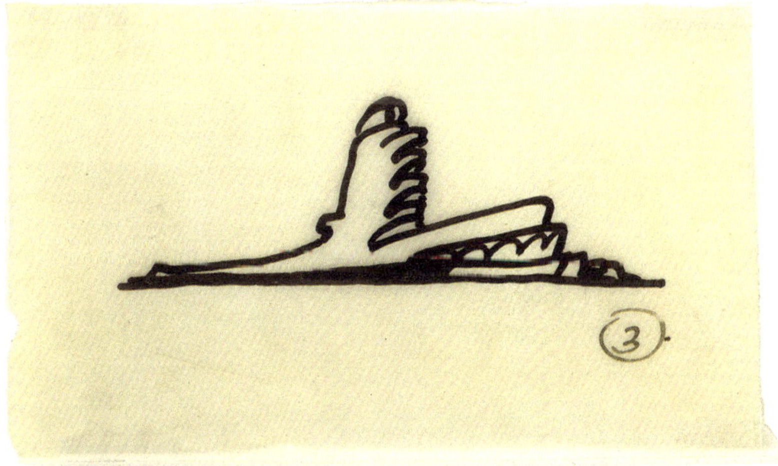


**ERICH MENDELSOHN (1887–1953)**

**Einstein Tower, 1920**

Ink on tracing paper

28.5 × 33 cm, 11 × 13 in

Erich Mendelsohn was a prolific designer, building up his practice during the 1920s to become the largest architects' office in Germany. During his lifetime, and in response to the different circumstances in which he found himself as an émigré, first in Britain and then in the United States, his oeuvre emerged as an eclectic sequence of Expressionism, Constructivism and Modernism – both in the sense of the soft Art Nouveau-inspired moderne and the International Style. When he designed the Observatory Tower in Potsdam for Albert Einstein, between 1917 and 1921, he was on the outskirts of various Expressionist groups. Following the ideological split articulated in the 1914 Cologne Werkbund exhibition, which pitted the normative approach to design of the industrializing state taken up by the Bauhaus against the expressive will to form, or *kunstwollen*, of the creative individual, Mendelsohn aligned himself with the latter. These three sketches of the Einstein Tower exemplify Mendelsohn's work at the time. Their rapid execution in sequence, as if walking around the building and looking at it from a distance, shows him exploring the formal idea of the structure as a sculptural object. The drawings numbered 2 and 3 seem to show the tower from the same viewpoint, but with a slight modification in the relationship of the swooping form of the lower roof and the two-storey structure beneath it. Mendelsohn is reworking the idea as he draws, using the sketch to consider modifications and then adjusting the viewpoint to test their implications. The tower was an experiment in the use of *in situ* reinforced concrete and a synthesis of various formal ideas circulating at the time in Expressionist architectural circles, combining the flowing lines of Henri van de Velde's Werkbund Theatre and Bruno Taut's Glass Pavilion – both Cologne, 1914 – with elements of Dutch Expressionism.

**LE CORBUSIER (1887–1965)**

**Letter to Mrs Meyer, 1925**

Indian ink on tracing paper

42 × 26 cm, 16½ × 10 in

In October 1925, Le Corbusier wrote to his client, Madame Meyer, with the first of four proposals for a house in Neuilly-sur-Seine, western Paris. The letter forms an illustrated narrative/storyboard in ten parts. He begins with an aerial view of the villa, a four-storey block surrounded by lush landscaping and crowned by a lively rooftop garden. A small balcony on the second floor and a bridge leading to a garden entrance at first-floor level further extend the house's influence outwards. The drawing is precise, the lines fine and single-thickness, in keeping with their illustrative nature. The second image shows the main entrance – controversially, on the side of the house: 'Would we be subject to the wrath of the academy?' he asks, before revealing the spacious vestibule inside. Below this, he shows the first-floor reception room – sparsely but stylishly furnished – before continuing through the principal spaces. The last two frames show an enticing and tranquil view of the lake outside his mother's house above a longer text on a sketch of a stone slab reiterating the poetry and rigour of his design. Throughout, Le Corbusier maintains a cajoling but humorous tone, explaining how the simple plan and structure will avoid the builder being too demanding and keep costs down. He points out how the sky and trees will be present through the wide expanses of glass, and highlights the sensuousness and privacy of the terrace, with its solarium and swimming pool shown in the seventh image, with grass surrounding the paving and only the sky above. This was his first project to incorporate the ideas of the free plan and free facade, which formed two of the Five Points of Architecture in his 1923 book *Vers une architecture* (Towards a New Architecture). Although unbuilt, the project was influential on his later work.

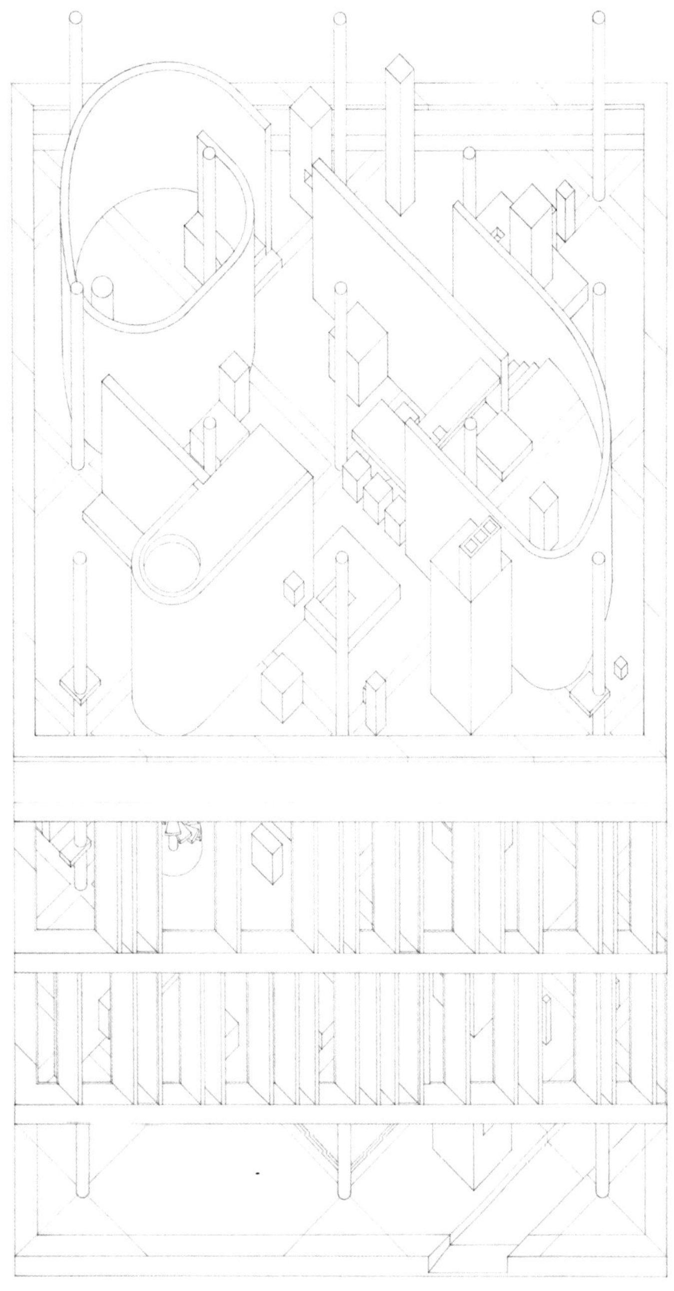

**JOHN HEJDUK (1929–2000)**

**Diamond House A: fourth floor with open-plan living area, 1963**

Graphite on translucent paper

68 × 68 cm, 26¾ × 26¾ in

In 1962, John Hejduk embarked on a six-year investigation into the architectural implications of a 45-degree rotation of the picture plane, which he called the diamond configuration. In his *Diamond Houses*, he developed three types, each concerned with the rotation's effect on a different element. In House A, the project to which this drawing belongs, he looked at columns. In House B, it was planes; and in House C, biomorphic shapes. As opposed to a perspective, which would locate the viewer as a participant in the scene, it is an axonometric, which maintains separation of the object being represented from the viewer – who is invited only to observe, not participate. It sits on a square sheet presented conventionally upright, with the composition boundaries parallel to the edges of the paper. The underlying setting-out plan – organized around a ten-square grid, the intersections of which are marked by thirteen circular columns – has been turned 45 degrees, with one column marking the centre of the drawing. An internal logic unfolds within the space of the house itself, the curved screens and platforms appearing to enclose comprehensible space. The disposition of the flat elevation at the bottom of the drawing, whose depth is shown in the perspective rendition of deep louvres, brings an ambiguity to the volume as a whole and its orientation within a larger context. According to Hejduk, his starting point for this investigation lay in abstract questions raised about composition and meaning of form by the diamond, or *losangique*, canvases of Piet Mondrian. For Hejduk, architecture was an autonomous, semiotic system separate from other cultural and social disciplines, and based upon a formal language for which he developed his own semiotic theory. For him, structural forms or compositions arose not from spatial organization but from the modulation of elements as linguistic signs.

**YAKOV CHERNIKHOV (1889–1951)**

**Architectural Fantasy, 1933**

Gouache, ink, ruling pen and pencil on paper

30 × 24 cm, 11¾ × 9½ in

This axonometric by Yakov Chernikhov contemplates the theme of industrial construction, focusing on the idea of repeated, prefabricated metal elements. There is no natural world. Seen from a vertiginous point in the sky, the landscape completely comprises man-made components against an absolute void. But its presence is subdued by the airy, beige paper surface, rather than the black-ink substance of fellow Constructivist Ivan Leonidov's drawings. The foreground is thickly populated with constructions, which form a kind of ground to the composition. Semicircular trusses that suggest barrel vaults surmount four long blocks on stilts. These are bounded by taller blocks, which play the role of uban-scaled walls enclosing a vast City Room. Two tall, dark pylons connect this potential site of human activity with the sky. No longer the realm of weather, clouds have been replaced by wires that cross the drawing in groups set at slightly different angles, and on various levels between smaller pylons of varying height, or floating, horizontal beams that extend into the composition from other parts of the city. During the 1920s, Chernikhov produced a series of conceptual images intended for teaching, which were published in a 1933 book called *Architectural Fantasies: 101 Compositions in Colour*. This name exploited the ambiguity of *fantaziya* in Russian and fantasy in English to mean both 'capacity for inventiveness' and 'power of the imagination', whereby the architect is liberated from convention to freely invent new rules and forms for the future – specifically, that of the Soviet Union. The essential precondition for creating an architectural fantasy was, for Chernikhov, the desire to present by various depictive, compositional and technical means all those ideas to which the architect's mind can give birth, to inspire the viewer to further develop them. The drawing was thus part of a collective inventive process.

**TONY GARNIER (1869–1948)**

**Smelting furnaces, 1917**

Colour lithograph

86 × 115 cm, 33¾ × 45¼ in

Tony Garnier came from Lyon, one of the most progressive nineteenth-century industrial centres in France, based around silk manufacture and metallurgy. His imaginary Industrial City was based in the region – its location defined by proximity to raw materials, a natural force capable of being used for energy, or the convenience of transportation methods. He imagined a site set on a river escarpment in a mountainous landscape, designed for 35,000 inhabitants and organized along socialist principles – without walls or private property, church or barracks, police station or law courts, its unbuilt surfaces devoted to public parkland. This perspective drawing is one of the few images depicting industry in the collection made for exhibition in 1904, and then collected to illustrate his 1917 publication *Une Cité Industrielle, Etude pour la construction des villes*. In the background, the hydroelectric plant that Garnier envisioned distributing energy to the city is visible as a huge dam spanning a distant valley. As with all collective amenities – including train services, hospitals, food supplies and refuse recycling – it was to belong to the public domain. The clarity and realism of the drawing reflect the rationality of the plan, and the metallurgical plant shown here is reduced to its bare bones. Not only is there no superfluous ornament, there is no wasted material in the design of the building. The drawing illustrates the manufacturing process rather than hiding it inside sheds. Storage silos, chimneys and tower-like structures for overseeing the work create a landscape of vertical elements that defines the factory precinct, which is flanked by two-storey administrative buildings. The natural environment that surrounds the city is represented by the hills around the dam, which are coloured in the style of old-fashioned postcards, reinforcing their picturesque quality.

**EL LISSITZKY (1890–1941)**

**Iron Clouds on Nikitsky Square, 1924**

Pencil and watercolour on paper

27.2 × 20.4 cm, 10¾ × 8 in

The *Wolkenbügel on the square by the Nikitsky Gate* was the full name given to this project by Lazar Markovich Lissitzky, better known as El Lissitzky. The drawing's annotation describes the towers as the Wolkenbügel for Moscow, looking towards the Kremlin. This term is often translated as Iron Clouds, but Bügel means hanger or T-bar, which is more evocative of the unusual horizontal disposition of the inhabited parts of the building that cantilever over the untidy reality of the old city, and hook, rather than soar, into the sky. Drawn in pencil below the black-ink lines and dense ink fields, the setting-out marks of this powerful one-point perspective disappear into an infinity where the sky and the road's surface leak into each other; there is no evidence of the Kremlin, or any other monumental building apart from Lissitzky's. The image presents the city as a grid of four-storey blocks conforming to an unreal concept of order, and is very different to a photomontage that he made of the project showing the paraphernalia of the actual busy transport junction. The location was to be the intersection of two main radial routes around the city, and the long, horizontal office blocks were to be supported on three vertical shafts containing lifts designed so as not to obstruct the traffic. Two lonely figures stand on the corner of the pavement looking into an empty roadway – one at the base of one of the Wolkenbügel's three huge columns, the other staring across the road in the foreground, suggesting the role and scale of a human in this imaginary world. This was to be Lissitzky's first built work, and technical drawings exist, along with a Proun painting – Proun being an acronym for 'project for the affirmation of the new' in Russian – and views of the skyscraper from key points in Moscow, but his designs never reached fruition.

**OPEN PLATFORM FOR ARCHITECTURE**

**Casa Brutale, 2015**

Computer software

In July 2015, a computer rendering of a fictional house for an imaginary clifftop site on the Aegean Sea was published online. It very quickly went viral, being cited by non-architectural news outlets within a week. One of the interesting aspects of the process was that the life-like quality of the rendering suggested a fantastic reality that, despite appearances, was evidently possible, and very desirable. According to its designers, Open Platform for Architecture (OPA), this was a deliberate move. After discovering that property developers were not interested in talking to them, they decided to generate interest in their work by creating a seemingly impossible but alluring artificial image, comprising references to the most glamorous lifestyle tropes that they could find. Features include a glass swimming pool, which is also the roof structure, over a glamorous bedroom illuminated by refracted light from above. A huge glass wall looks out over the horizon of the bright blue sea, and the unconfined cliff edge represents the image of freedom that infinity pools generate against the sky. The house is barely visible from land; only the presence of a car and two figures would suggest to anyone in the vicinity that anything was there. However, from the water – in a private boat, for example – it would be a very bold intervention in the cliff. Its presence thus becomes a matter of social perspective, and this secretive exclusivity is another desirable quality of the project. OPA claim sophisticated precedents for their project, including the Casa Malaparte, but especially the Brutalist architecture that has been increasing in fashionable cachet since 2010. This is referenced in the name of the project, Casa Brutale, and the designers cite the use of exposed-concrete surfaces combined with glass and steel, and a lack of ornamental surfaces, as justification.

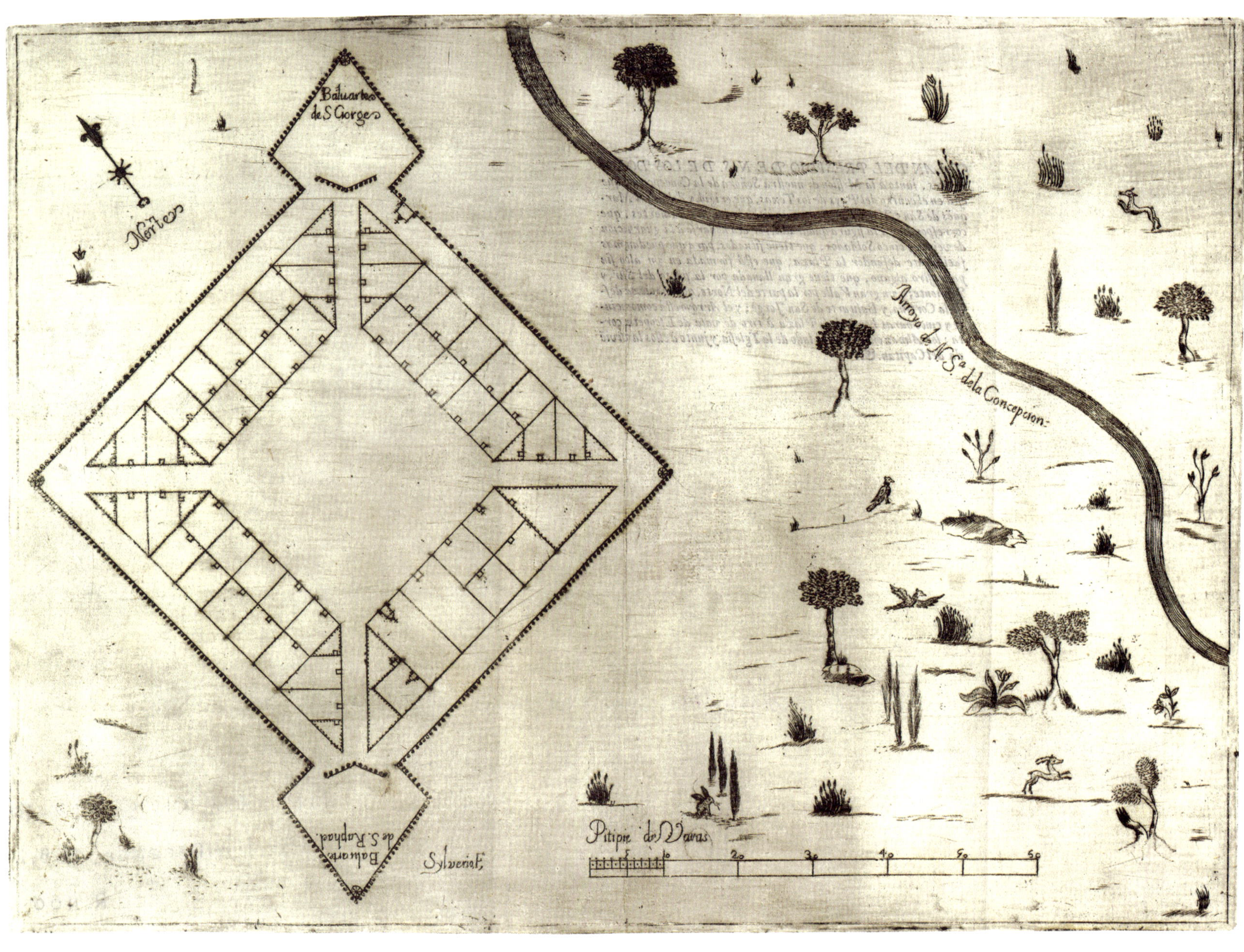


**JUAN ANTONIO DE LA PEÑA Y REYES (nd)**

**Presidio of Los Dolores de Los Tejas, 1722**

Ink on paper

29.7 × 42.6 cm, 11¾ × 16¾ in

This drawing was made during Spain's official colonization drive northwards into Texas during the eighteenth century. The Spanish system of town founding was initiated by itinerant Catholic priests or soldiers, who would first set up a mission or a *presidio* – derived from the Latin *praesidium*, meaning protection or defence – a fortified base, with an often temporary status, to protect its newly arrived inhabitants, who had no knowledge of the surrounding geography. The plan shows the form that the initial structures of a Spanish *presidio* would take, with its standard square arrangement comprising four wedges of inward-facing building looking on to a square. These are surrounded by wooden stockades, with each round trunk indicated in the drawing, and two corner bastions – here, facing northeast and southwest. The presidios would only be accessible to the Spanish military, whose role it was to establish ownership of a territory. The indigenous trees and animals shown in elevation between the fort and the river suggest that this drawing was used to indicate the potential of the land, as well as the location and disposition of the presidio. The drawing is not set up as a map with the north point at the top of the sheet; if it were, the fort would appear not as a diamond with the bastions at its end points but as an asymmetrical square. This fort would have been located on or near El Camino Real de los Tejas, the Royal Road to the land of the Tejas Indians, an eighteenth-century transportation corridor connecting the easternmost portions of the Province of Texas to Mexico City. The *presidio* in this drawing was established in 1716 on the east bank of the Neches River, labelled the 'Arroyo de Nuestra Señora de la Concepcion' on the plan, and protected four nearby missions.

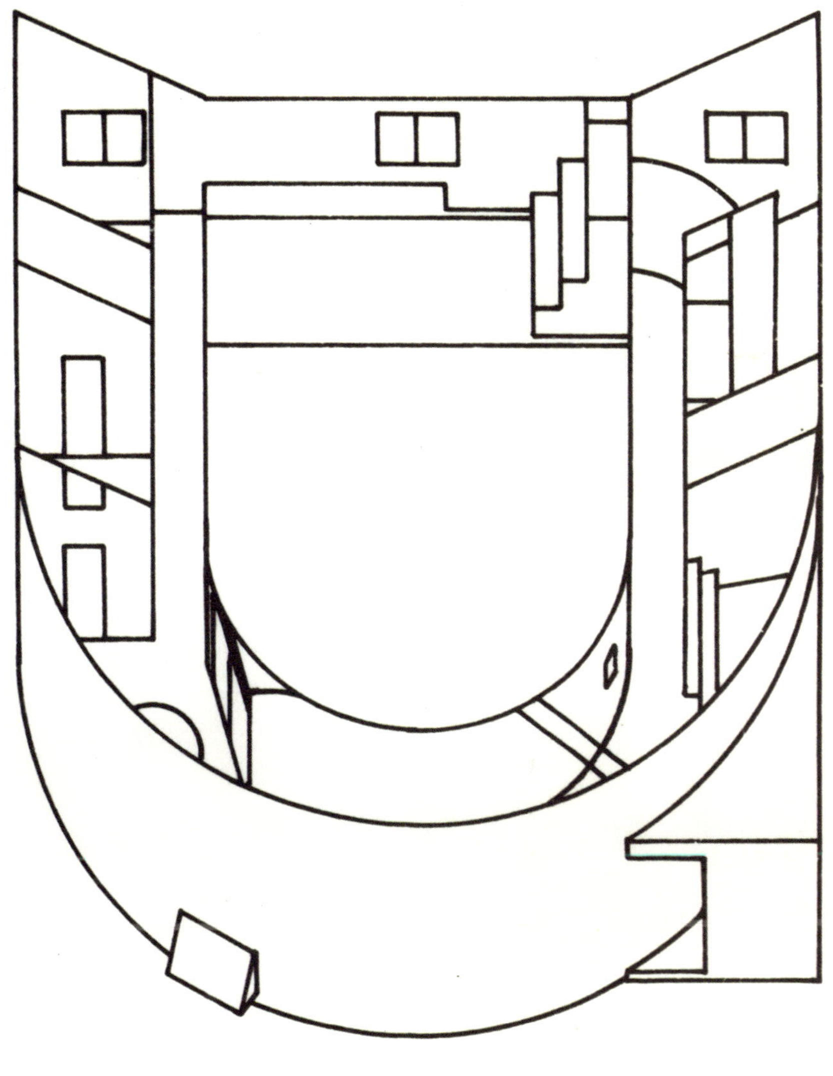

**TOYO ITO (1941–)**

**U-House, 1976**

Pencil on tracing paper

462 × 50 cm, 24½ × 19½ in

Toyo Ito designed the U-House for his bereaved sister and her children in 1976, locating it next door to his own house. The spaces outlined in this isometric drawing contained the world of the family; Ito categorizes it as a cave house, like an underground chamber. Connecting the bedrooms at either end, an enclosed U-shaped corridor widens centrally into a communal space. This strange room formed the boundary of a desolate internal patio, whose black-hole-like energy apparently precluded even the family pets from staying there alone. The lines depicting the walls are projected upwards from the plan at the same scale. The plan is not set at an angle, which in traditional isometric drawing is usually 30 degrees or 45 degrees to the horizontal, so that the orthogonal walls of rooms are shown in straight elevation. These are visible because Ito has chosen to leave the roof off the drawing so as to reveal the spaces in the single-storey building. The house was demolished in 1997 and remains as a myth – a sealed, abstract version of itself recorded only in drawings and photographs. As such, it is a metaphor for an immutable, enclosed world that is nevertheless a world almost fully open to itself within its enclosing walls – like Jorge Luis Borges' *The Aleph*, which contains all the universe in one sign. On the other hand, the emblematic character of both house and image associates them with Aldo Rossi's idea of Autonomous Architecture, in which the architecture of the European city provided 'a repository of accumulated "labour of our hands" ... of existing solutions through a reduced, "boiled-down" rendering of information of individual architectural objects into types'.

**PIETRO LINGERI (1894–1968)**

**Danteum, 1938**

Watercolour, ink and pencil on paper

15.2 × 20.6 cm, 8 × 6 in

Although the design of the Danteum has long been attributed to the Italian Rationalist architect Giuseppe Terragni, the drawings prepared for it are located in the archive of Pietro Lingeri. The project does not appear in a complete list of works included in the catalogue for the first commemorative exhibition of Terragni's work, published with an introduction by Le Corbusier in 1949. Showing a single space within a sequence, this is a view of paradise. It is the final destination within the Danteum – a museum, library and homage to the Italian poet, which took his *Divine Comedy* as its organizing concept.
A labyrinthine spatial sequence through Dante's three poems, or states, of 'Inferno', 'Purgatory' and 'Paradise' is played out, and this perspective drawing shows the last of the rooms to be reached – both in Dante's allegorical text and in Lingeri's visual and constructed interpretation of it in symbolic form. This space represents the lucid state of paradise, and Lingeri's fascination with architectural transparency – made apparent in the building's entrance portico, with its one hundred travertine columns – here becomes physically manifest. Watercolour washes indicate the changeable sky through a grid of glass beams that is echoed in the precisely drawn, square glass blocks of the floor below. The opaque container is uniform in colour, monolithic and immutable, in contrast to its thirty-three glass columns (the number of cantos in Dante's third poem). In the drawing, there is a tension between the ceiling, where the top of the columns coincide with the structure, and the columns' apparent misalignment with the perspectival grid of the floor. The project was proposed to Benito Mussolini in 1938, for Rome's upcoming Esposizione Universale. Sited on the Via dell'Impero, this conceptual scheme encapsulated Lingeri's belief in the ideological role of art and artistic thought. Overall, the Danteum comprises a rectangular precinct enclosed by a high wall, which opens at an entrance portico. The proportions of its plan are defined by the square and the golden rectangle.

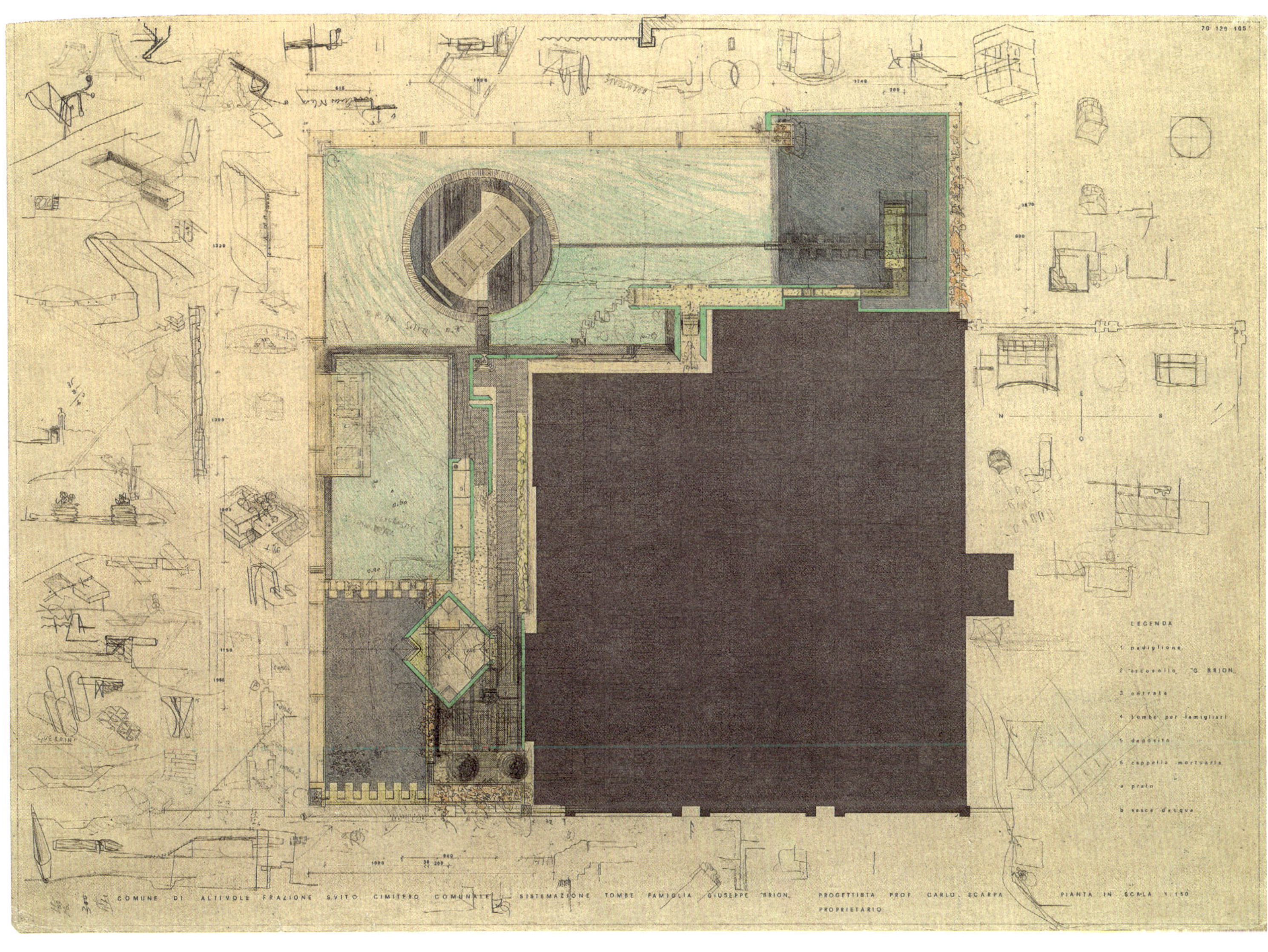


**CARLO SCARPA (1906–78)**

**Brion Cemetery, 1970**

Graphite, pen and coloured pencil on brownline copy

59.3 × 83.9 cm, 23¼ × 33 in

This animated, orthographic projection is typical of a Carlo Scarpa drawing. It depicts his early thinking for an extension to the municipal cemetery of the village of San Vito d'Altivole on the Asolo Plain. The family of wealthy businessman Giuseppe Brion purchased a 2,200 m² (23,680 sq ft) L-shaped plot around the existing cemetery, within which Scarpa's remarkable funerary landscape unfolds. The existing cemetery forms the dark heart of the drawing, and the narrow but grand gateway, known as the *propylaeum*, to the Brion precinct can be seen in the middle of the top, or east side, of the cemetery, leading to a ceremonial pond to the right, and the mausoleum to the left, with a meditation pavilion at the end. The plan uses coloured fields to indicate two pools of water and planes of lawn, the largest of which contains the mausoleum itself. The small sketches deal with minute issues of drainage, changing and interlocking ground levels, and ways of making boundaries that indicate that these were all held in Scarpa's imagination as he drew. For Scarpa, the architectural drawing was never a surrogate for building or an alternative to the construction itself; it was always a tool used in the realization of a design problem. He habitually worked through a sequence of plans, starting from an original idea and developing the design over the top of this base, constantly experimenting with – and testing through small drawings – the proportional and geometrical forms and relationships of individual elements. Later, Scarpa would move on to more detailed sections and elevations of specific parts, which again would be surrounded by less formal detailed studies. He gave priority to how his projects would be constructed above all else, and rarely used three-dimensional perspectives or isometrics to test out views of his designs, or for three-dimensional resolution.

**ZAHA HADID (1950–2016)**

**Leisure Club, 1982**

Coloured pencil and paint on paper

129.5 × 182.9 cm, 60 × 72 in

Zaha Hadid was famous for her drawings and paintings long before she built her first structure. Her immediately recognizable and original approach to constructing an architectural image was developed during her student days, when she immersed herself in the imagery of Russian Constructivist painting – especially that of Malevich, El Lissitzky and Rodchenko – and the articulation of complex geometries and calligraphy. Hadid used abstract painting as an imaginative design tool as well as a means of communication, and this hand-drawn and painted image was made following a competition held five years after she graduated. The brief was for a health club and spa in the hills of Kowloon, Hong Kong. Hadid proposed creating an architectural landmark on the steep slopes high above the congestion and intensity of the city, the central structure of which would take the form of a horizontal skyscraper teetering on a man-made topography of polished granite. The imaginary ravines of this night-time scene are painted in dark browns and blacks, often appearing as thin, jagged leaves of stone rather than solid volumes. The highlighting of these in pale grey and white defines the painting's composition as exploding outwards from a vortex point in the lower left-hand corner, where a road makes a sharp bend. This fragmented quality led to Hadid's inclusion within a group of architects labelled Deconstructivist in a 1988 show held at the Museum of Modern Art in New York. The meandering road in the painting traverses treacherous ground, connecting Hadid's design with the real world of the city below. The building itself is rendered in bright colours – green, yellow, red and blue – with dazzling white walls bounding its long, narrow bundle of cantilevered volumes. The inaccessible remoteness of these structures, floating above excavated subterranean voids, belonged to what she termed a unique geology, symbolizing the high life.

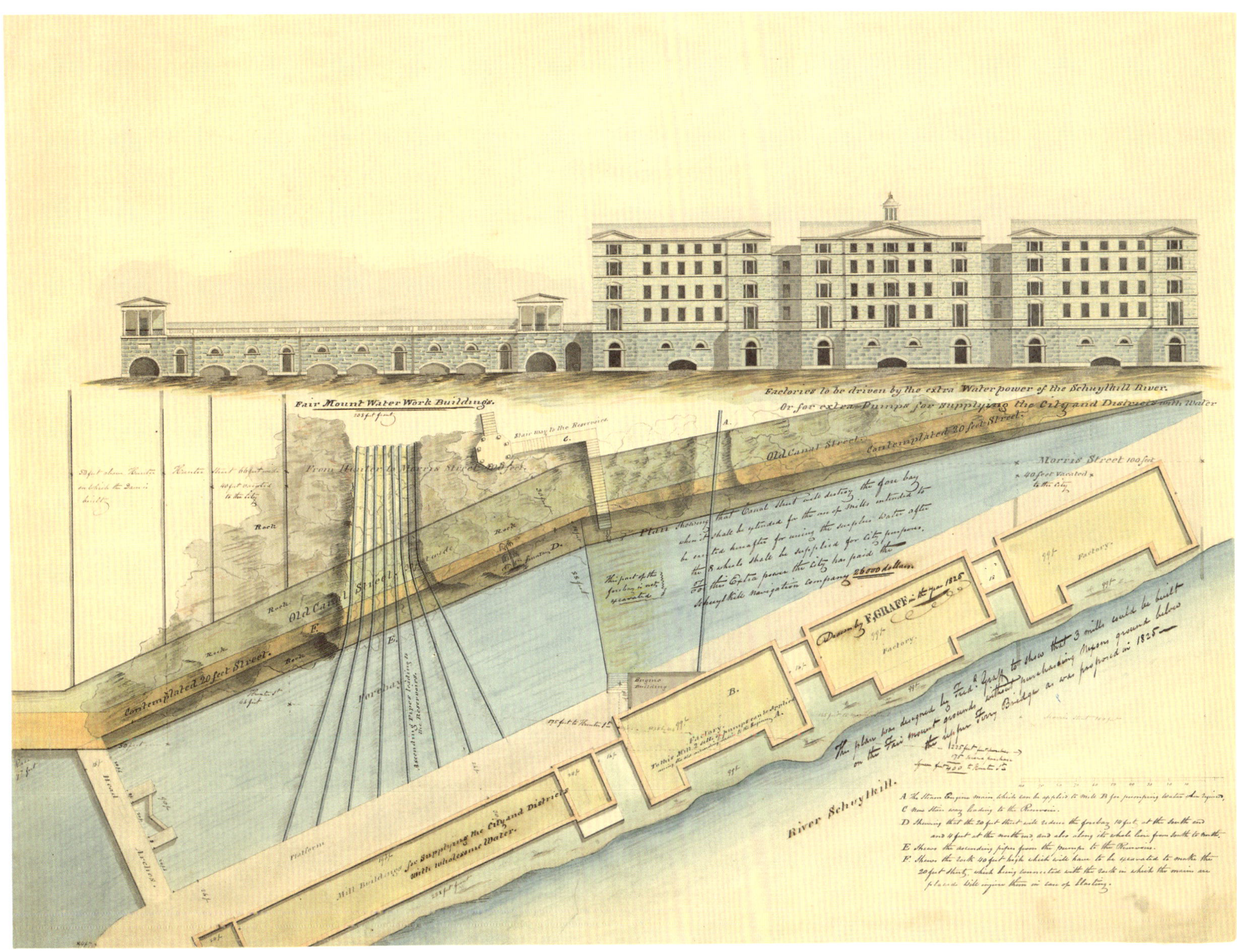


**FREDERICK GRAFF (1775–1847)**

**Fairmount Waterworks, 1825**

Pen, ink and watercolour on laid brown paper

56.5 × 76.8 cm, 22¼ × 30¼ in

Frederick Graff was a builder's son who began as a carpenter but, after meeting the Neo-Classical architect Benjamin Henry Latrobe, moved into architecture. He assisted Latrobe with working drawings for the Bank of Pennsylvania and the Philadelphia Waterworks, developing an interest in Palladianism. His reputation was founded on his engineering skills, however, and he was put in charge of the waterworks associated with Philadelphia's Fairmount reservoirs and their steam-powered hydroelectricity works, in which he developed his skill at combining man-made and natural landscapes. The drawing shown here is composed of a site plan and front elevation, with an accompanying ground plan for factories within the Fairmount complex. Although not built, it was designed to accompany his picturesque ensemble of the mill house and waterworks, and the dam can be seen crossing a water channel that flows into the river. It takes the form of a long stone plinth that continues along the banks of the Schuylkill River to form the water-level storey of the factory complex. At either end of the dam are two small, temple-like structures, which contribute to the sensitive juxtaposition of the scenic and the industrial. Their small scale contrasts with the four-storey factories, but their pediments are echoed in the skyline of the taller blocks. The collective volume of these structures is mitigated in elevation by their separation into a symmetrical composition of three connected blocks, whose disposition is visible in the ground plan. The use of stone added to the monumentality of the elevations seen from the river, which were designed as structures to appeal to prospective investors in the project. The careful rendering of the drawing, with its didactic colour washes clearly indicating the elements of water, ground and stone, suggests that it was made for presentation purposes rather than as a working document for construction.

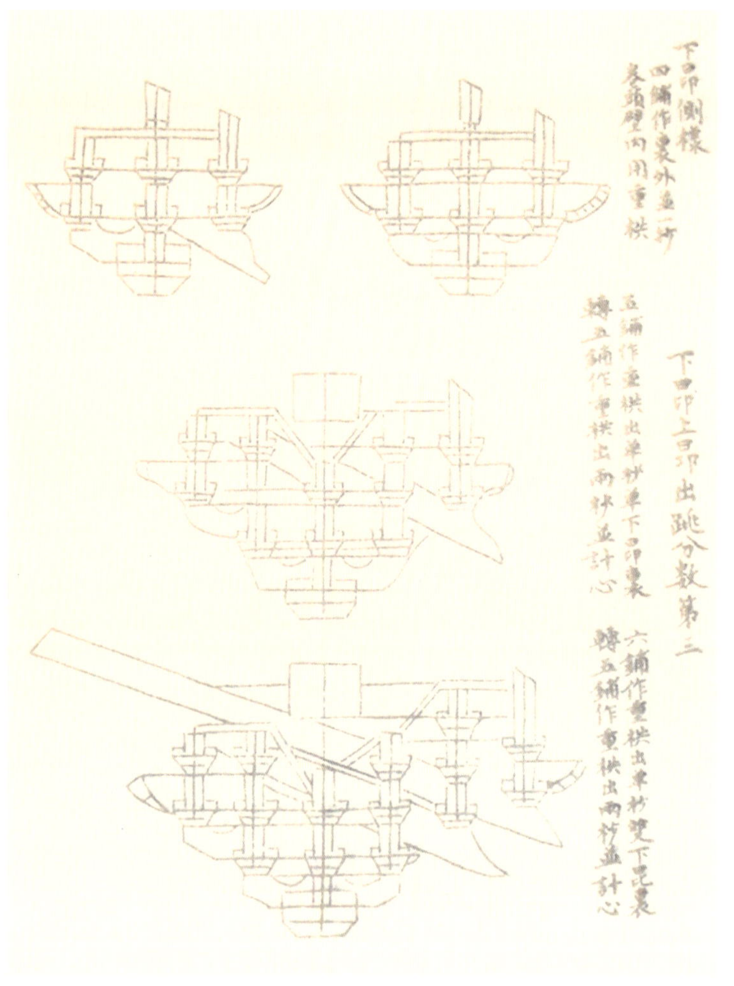

**LI JIE (1035–1110)**

**Bracket arm clusters, 1103**

Ink on paper

15.5 × 11.5 cm, 6 × 4½ in

The *Yingzao Fashi* (State Building Standard), published during the Song dynasty in AD 1103, is the oldest extant Chinese technical manual for building construction. The production of a manual that defined the standardization of building and unit measurement across China's vast terrain was significant. It formalized building codes already embedded in the *Yingshan Ling* (National Building Law), in alignment with other systems of communication and commerce – all of which had been subject to a centralized, universal system since the unification of China in 221 BC. The thirty-four-chapter volume begins with a concise glossary of terms, and includes specifications for paint mixes and estimates for labour expenditure, as well as design standards and construction principles, illustrated in drawings such as this. The page incorporates written instructions running down its right-hand side, with diagrams simply drawn in lines of equal weight and with great economy. Four examples of how to compose bracket arm clusters containing cantilevers progress, with increasing complexity, to the intricate boss at the bottom of the page. This drawing belongs to the section devoted to structural carpentry, in the fifth and last part of the book, comprising drawn illustrations explaining the practical details of carpentry and joinery, including jointing of elements, forms of structures and patterns of decoration. Chinese carpentry had developed over time within a secretive, state-registered family-guild system that had guarded its techniques. A series of social reforms that impacted on building and city planning during the eleventh century led to the loosening of this hegemony, and in 1097, Li Jie, Superintendent for State Buildings in the Ministry for Works, was commissioned by Emperor Zhe Zong to research and define the new code. He carried out his work partly through studying historical documents, but principally by gathering personal knowledge of these inherited methods and established practices.

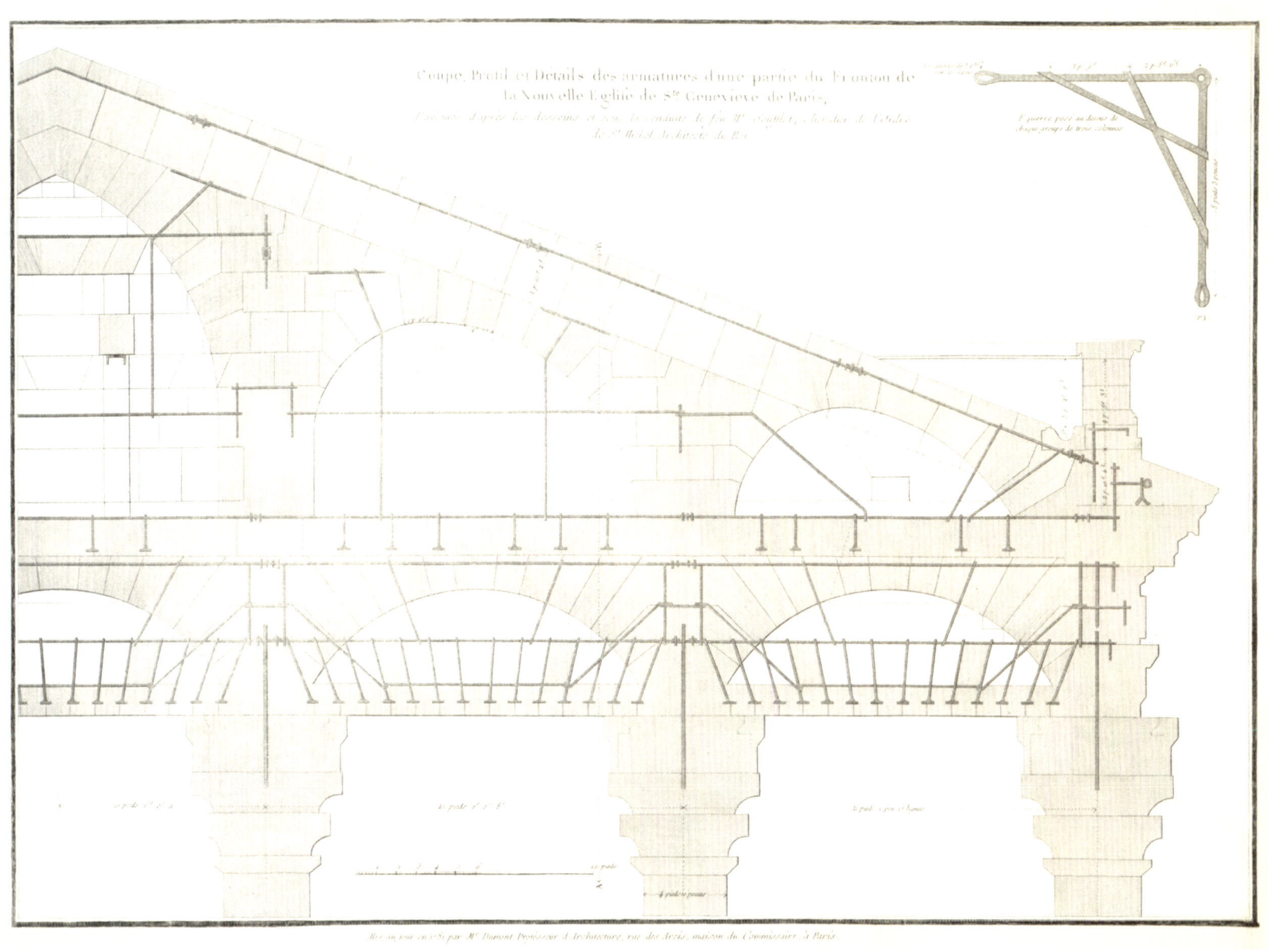


**JACQUES-GERMAIN SOUFFLOT (1713–80)**

**Detail of the armature of part of the pediment, 1781**

Etching

41.2 × 56.7 cm, 16¼ × 22¼ in

This etching by Gabriel Pierre Martin Dumont records an analysis made by Jacques-Germain Soufflot for reinforcing the grand pediment on the front facade of the church of Sainte-Geneviève in Paris, also known as the Panthéon. It reveals the secret side of the triangular portico: seen from within, the drawing shows the economy and elegance of the plain structure, as opposed to the public, decorative surface of the monumental temple portico, with its colossal Corinthian order. This portico led into the church's nave, and a dome with two cupolas was to rise above the transept crossing, where the shrine containing the saint's relics was located. For this to be visible from all corners of the church, the number of masonry pillars and arcades had to be minimized, and to contain the thrust of the dome and vaults, flying buttresses were hidden behind the attic storey of the facades. Soufflot also devised a system of reinforced stone by fastening the blocks together using the metal framework depicted in this section. A tint has been used to show where the structure is cut through, and the system of metal straps can be seen grounded in long, vertical elements extending towards the capitals of the columns. The joints between the stone blocks are also drawn, and the response of the reinforcement to the pattern of the stonework is clear. Arched vaults are cut into the structure, saving material but also making it lighter. The inside face of the portico is shown in elevation, unshaded, beyond. After Soufflot's death, his nephew, Soufflot le Romain, took over the works, accompanied by engineer Jean-Baptiste Rondelet, both of whom had to resolve cracking in the drums of the crossing caused by Soufflot's ambitious structural ideas. Rondolet extended the network of iron rods, in part to alleviate these problems.

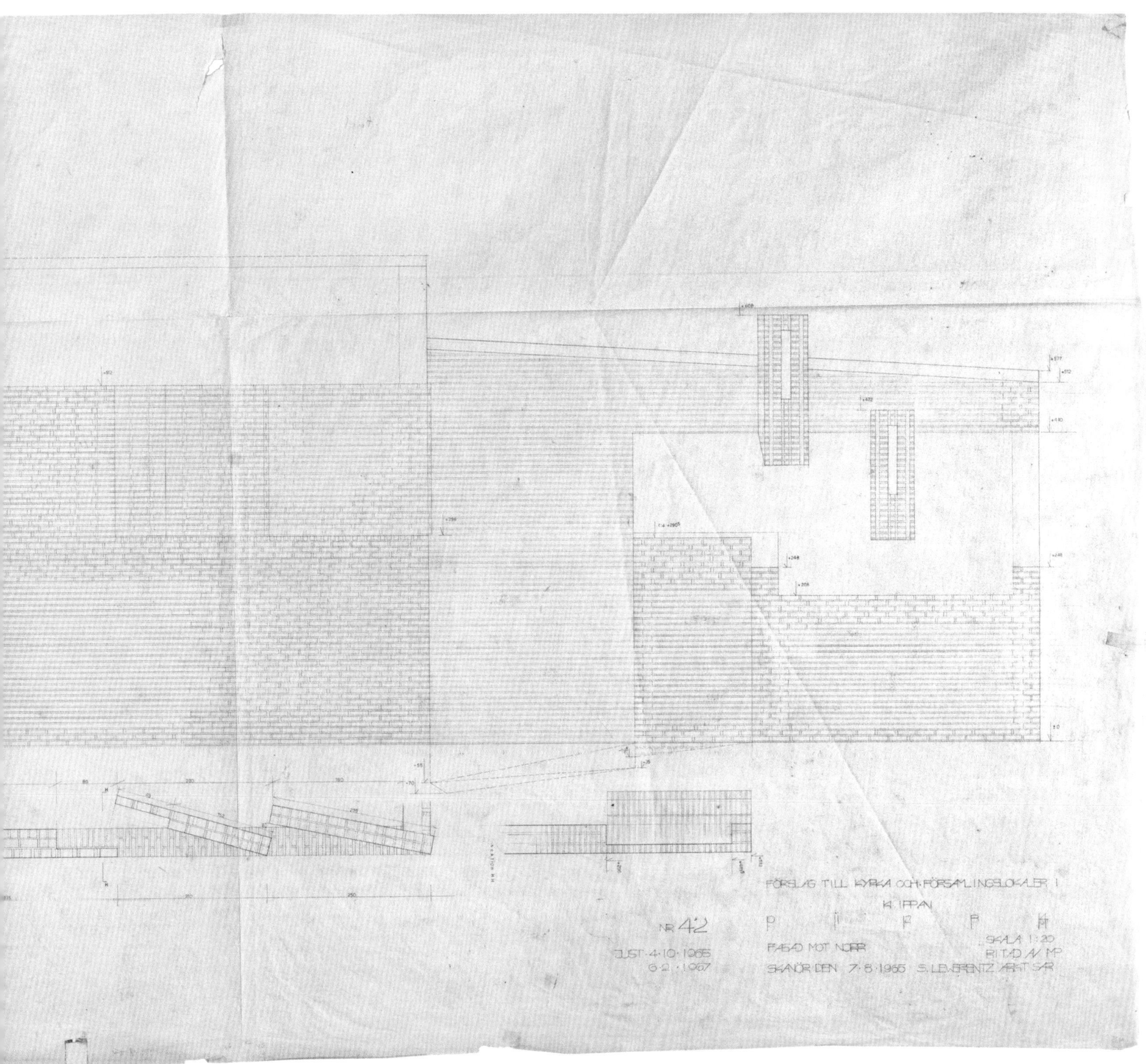


**SIGURD LEWERENTZ (1885–1975)**

**St Petri Church, 1965**

Pencil on tracing paper

74.6 × 171.3 cm, 29¼ × 67½ in

The finely drawn plans and details that Sigurd Lewerentz made to guide the construction of his brick churches hold within them the qualities of the material surfaces for which these late-career buildings are known. St Petri sits near the centre of Klippan, a small industrial town in southern Sweden, sited in a corner of the town park separated from the street by an embankment and a deep row of trees. Lewerentz was then living in the same province, Scania, and it was felt that he would be suited to design a church in that flat landscape. Its simple plan comprises two long wings at right angles to each other, creating a space sheltered from the wind. This is where the church is sited, its square plan elongated to the north by an addition containing the vestry and a bell enclosure, and a smaller, rectangular wing containing the vestibule. Lewerentz was seventy-seven when he started working on the design. During a short spell in hospital the wrong bricks of a different size were delivered to site, and he had to recalculate the setting out of the modular runs. Resolving the problems led to the distinctive thick mortar layers that are scraped along the surface of the walls, for example, contrasting with the dark grey-brown bricks. Many revisions and explanatory drawings were made for the contractor, who was a mason, but they were not easy to understand and often further instructions on how to read them were necessary. Inside, bricks line the sanctuary floor and the shallow barrel vaults above, making a warm unified surface. This drawing shows two fragments of the external elevation of the church. On the left, the wall steps inwards to make space for four freestanding brick piers that act as light scoops. On the right, the north elevation of the church shows the entrance vestibule, with a pair of tall brick chimneys also capturing light for the interior and animating its sloping roof. On the other side of the elevation is the wing containing the vestry and bell tower, with the strange brick piers visible in elevation from the side.

**ANON**

**Mausoleum of Itimad-ud-daula, 1828**

Pen and watercolour with applied gold paint

53.5 × 75 cm, 21 × 29½ in

*Pietra dura*, or *parchin kara*, is a technique of cut-and-fitted stonework used to create a pictorial mosaic using semi-precious stones. Its laying is highly skilled, since each piece is grooved so as to interlock with its neighbours, and a binding frame holds the intricate puzzle together. In this perspective interior of a mausoleum, these frames can be seen making an intricate geometric pattern over its vaulted ceiling, forming stars and pointed chevrons orientated towards the crowning blue, red and gold cupola. The section line that makes the frame of the drawing defines its shape but does not accurately depict the edges of the ceiling, instead forming a pleasing curve. Intense colours – scarlet, blue, green and gold – are used to represent the rare inlaid stones of onyx, cornelian, topaz and jasper in the parchin kara panels, and in the decorative treatment of the pierced screens and patterned floor. The cenotaphs of Itimad-ud-daula, a title that translates as Support of the State, and his wife can be seen in the centre of the mausoleum, which had been built in 1626 by Nur Jahan, wife of the Emperor Jahangir. Originally constructed for her father, Mirza Ghiyas Beg, the building is located near Agra in Uttar Pradesh. Thought to have been made by a Delhi or Agra artist, the drawing is one of many produced during the early nineteenth century for a market generated by British officials in India, who collected representations of the picturesque ruins of the Mughal Empire. The local artists who made the paintings would have been shown examples of European architectural drawings to inspire them, and evidence of this can be seen in this drawing through, for example, the European convention of perspective.

**CARUSO ST JOHN**

**Citroën Cultural Centre, 2018**

Inkjet print on coated paper

26.5 × 39.5 cm, 10½ × 15½ in

This composite image belongs to a competition entry for a large cultural centre, and illustrates the transformation of one of the sheds of the Citroën Garage in Brussels into an art space. Its purpose is to communicate the atmosphere generated by an architectural concept. A diaphanous curtain of glass covers the found shell of the existing structure, which is enhanced by new structural elements, lighting and temperature modifiers. This loose overcoat captures a volume of the museum's space and provides a controlled environment for the potentially delicate and valuable objects that will inhabit it, as if the room becomes a giant vitrine. In order to communicate these intentions for radical but almost invisible transformation, the first step was to create a white image, like a plaster model, through rendering light and soft shadows with no detailed structures, colours or textures. The decision to add roughness to the floor was made during this process, and a central perspective in this oval space was chosen to create a bala-nced and calm symmetry. This provided an even field that could easily be modified by elements balancing each other: the doorway, the yellow car, and the person cleaning. Behind the veil of the new structure, the ghost of a staircase and spectators on the balcony form a subtle counterpoint to the car's powerful presence. The final step in the image's construction adds a textural layer that represents the dispersal of light, achieving a vanishing behind the reflective layers of glass. The opacity of the glass and this almost indefinable, subtle, varnish-like layer is delicately modified so that the disparate parts of the drawing cohere without becoming too stable or abstract. After the first rendering in a drawing program – of the basic geometry and cast of light – the painterly effects are implemented using Photoshop.

**BRUNO TAUT (1880–1938)**

**Mountain Architecture, 1919**

Ink on paper

27 × 19.5 cm, 10½ × 7¾ in

In 1919, marking the end of World War I, Bruno Taut published this drawing as Plate 7 in a book called *Alpine Architektur*, a five-part treatise on utopian architecture illustrated with over thirty plates. The symbolic material for this ideal city was glass, and the second section of the book, which includes this scene, deals with the refashioning of the Alpine mountain ranges according to the principles of Paul Scheerbart – an author of fantastic fiction and architectural theory – which he described in his book *Glass Architecture*, 1914. The same year, Taut's Glass Pavilion at the German Werkbund exhibition in Cologne demonstrated the potential of different types of glass for architecture in a prismatic structure of concrete and glass. Its message was contrasted with that of the predominant materialist and utilitarian culture, expressed through brick construction. For Taut, it embodied a spiritual, pacifist utopia expressed in crystal architecture, in which glass represented purity and innocence. Taut's drawing of his fantasy glass city develops these ideas and manifests Scheerbart's dreams of a sublime, technocratic civilization, which he includes in the inscription at the bottom of the sheet that describes the content of the drawing. Above the vegetation line, the rock is hewn and smoothed into manifold crystalline shapes. The snowy summits in the distance are surmounted with glass arches, and in the foothills there are pyramids of crystal needles. Across the abyss in the foreground is a glass bridge made of cube-shaped glass forms, which is accompanied by the inscription and title *Der Kristallberg* (Crystal Mountain). The style of the drawing uses the strong, flowing lines of Expressionism, with their intent to convey meaning or emotional experience rather than physical reality. Here, the monolithic quality of the traditional city is replaced by the escapism of an imaginary, ethereal realm.

**FRANCESCO BORROMINI (1599–1667)**

**Facade of the Oratorio dei Filippini, c.1660**

Graphite on paper

43 × 30.3 cm, 17 × 12 in

This representation of Francesco Borromini's front facade of the Oratorio dei Filippini in Rome, which fronts the Piazza della Chiesa Nuova in a radically different form to that of the drawing, is divided into two parts. On the left, the basic frame of the composition is visible, drawn as a flat plane with the proportions of the main elements measured out. Below is a plan drawn conventionally, with structural material shaded in faint pencil lines behind a darker outline. The other side of this plan takes on the nature of the dramatic drawing above, with darker and more expressive lines depicting the architectural sense of the design – the steps, shadows, and points of tension. The three-dimensional modelling of the facade in the right-hand image above this plan reveals Borromini's facility with graphite pencil, his preferred drawing medium. A great variety of line is evident, achieved through modifying the pressure of the hand or the application of drawing instruments, using the point or the edge, for example, to make lines – some precise, but many overlapping – and to create shading through hatching, blurring and smudging. For Borromini, the pursuit of form is realized through drawing, where the marks overlap each other in search of a definitive configuration. Minute detail is as relevant as the whole composition – a point emphasized by the partial nature and ambiguity of the ultimate solution for the edge of the facade. Borromini described the entrance to the oratory as being like a man stretching out his arms, and the dynamic effect of the mixtilinear forms of the facade is repeated in the interior spaces. He borrows elements from the past, which are integrated into his personal poetic, rather than reinforcing academic rules of composition and form. He identified exceptions, and incorporated them into his fluid, dynamic spatial ensembles.

**BRUCE NAUMAN (1941–)**

**Crossed Stadiums, 1984**

Synthetic polymer paint, watercolour, charcoal and pastel on paper

134.7 × 184.2, 53 × 72½ in

Artist Bruce Nauman works in every conceivable artistic medium, but still uses drawing as a pragmatic part of his working process. This drawing utilizes various media – charcoal, which he usually uses to set out a scheme, with watercolour and polymer paint applied on top of this framework. How these marks are read and what they mean is not straightforward, but follows a strong material and conceptual logic full of deliberate contradictions. The overlaid frames for two different intersecting roof systems inhabit the centre of the page and reach almost to its edges. They are shown in axonometric, and are seemingly transparent. A surrounding dense, pale field of layers of paint creates a solid ground, within which the emptiness of these attic voids is heightened. Structural elements are depicted with charcoal lines; some are dark – those at the eaves and the roof ridges – while others are more lightly sketched – the rafters and studs that connect them. Sometimes, where seen through the space of the attic, the frame is represented by faint watercolour marks. The drawing could be about the practical problems that occur when these two different orders meet – the simple extrapolated triangle of the pitched roof and the more complex inversion of the butterfly roof crossing it. One has been extracted from the other, however, and in this move they have become autonomous. They will not enmesh themselves with each other, despite the various diagonal lines trying to make this happen. Two of the junctions have been partially obliterated by smudges of paint – a cancelling out that only makes them stronger – and another floats awkwardly, connecting only the ridge and eaves of the simple pitch. Tabs of thick, strong colour, red over yellow, mark the ridges and look like samples for the whole surface – suggestions of colour planes or a code for cladding layers.

**OSCAR NIEMEYER (1907–2012)**

**House at Canoas, 1953**

Ink on tracing paper

34.9 × 53 cm, 13¾ × 20¾ in

Oscar Niemeyer designed the house at Canoas, in Barra de Tijuca, a suburb of Rio de Janeiro, as his family home. Although best known for the government buildings of Brasília, in collaboration with his teacher and colleague Lúcio Costa, and his earlier large-scale works in Rio and Belo Horizonte, Niemeyer also built several accomplished houses during his long career. He worked until the end of his life, and was 105 when he died. This simple sketch of the house at Canoas reveals qualities about its architecture that were important to him, especially the embodiment of the natural world within the man-made form, and the relationship between these two seeming opposites. In his own words, he admitted that his work was not about form follows function, but form follows beauty. Not attracted to straight angles or to the straight line, which he described as hard and inflexible and created by man, he was attached to free-flowing sensual curves – the curves of Brazil's mountains, the sinuousness of its rivers, the waves of the ocean or the body of a beloved woman. The house is built on the slope of a hill overlooking Rio's bay, and at the top of the drawing a single straight line, the only one in the drawing, depicts the distant ocean horizon with one lonely ship traversing it. Below, the undulating curve of the thin concrete roof slab is shown almost in plan, from above, cantilevering out to swoop over the dense tropical vegetation that crowds in from both sides. The open interior of the house is inhabited by two comical figures sheltering under the roof and looking out over the circular pond and a rock that tie the man-made structure to the natural world.

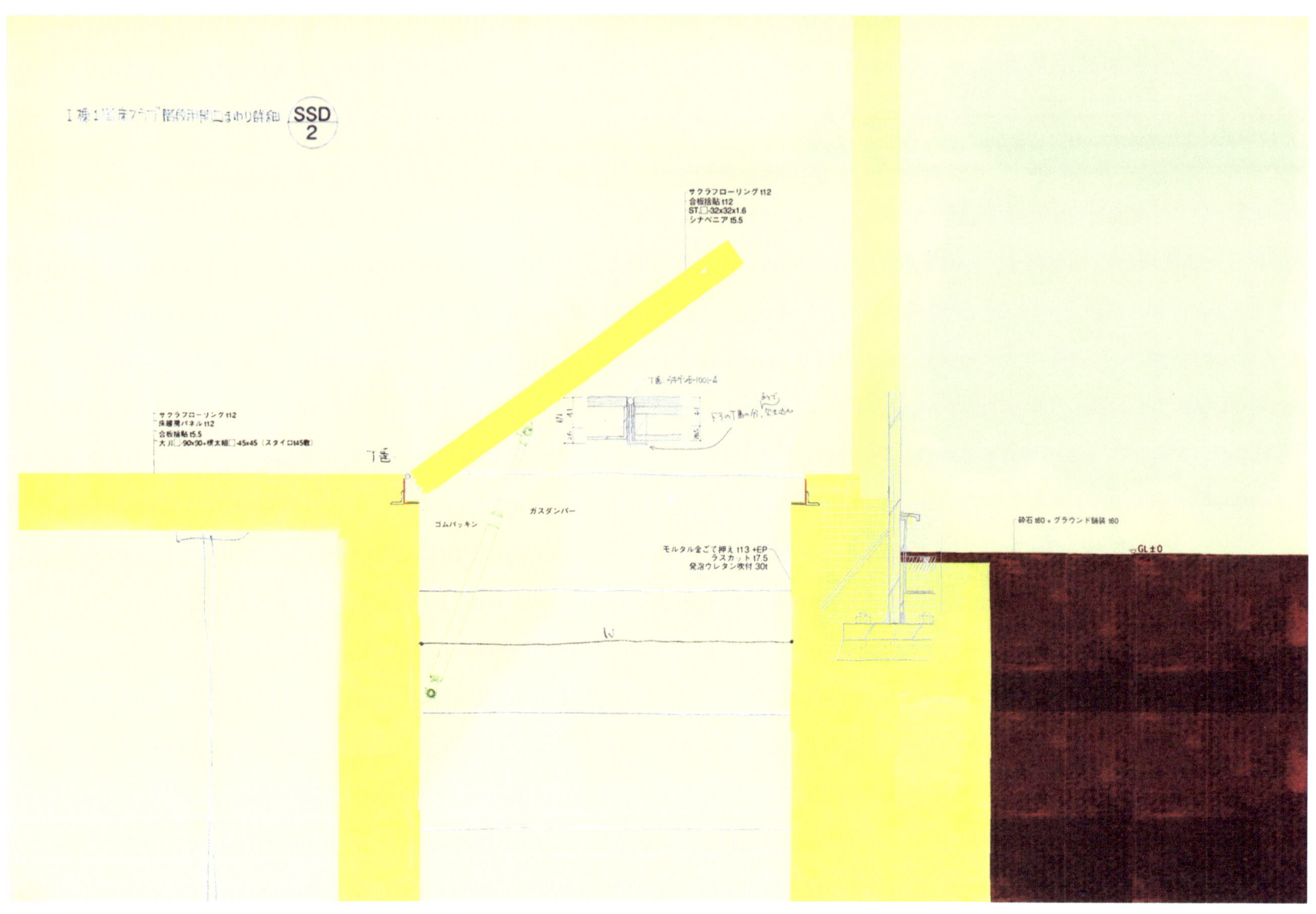


**RYUE NISHIZAWA (1966–)**

**Moriyama House, 2005**

Pigmented inkjet print

30.5 × 41.9 cm, 12 × 16.5 in

In 2017, a full-size model of Ryue Nishizawa's Moriyama House was constructed for a major exhibition, *The Japanese House*, at the Barbican, London. Dispersed over a rectangular plot, the dwellings comprising the house occupy ten boxes of different sizes in plan and height, ranging from one to three storeys. A myriad of shared garden rooms flows between them – comprising tiny patios, narrow alleys and a central courtyard – and the floors of the enclosures float just above the flat surface of the brown earth. This colourful detail reveals how simple the envelope of these structures is. Over a diagram of colour fields indicating a sectional cut, in which a dark-brown area represents the earth and yellow the construction material, the finer detail of how specific junctions and elements work is drawn in a variety of ways. An extending strut is depicted with orthographic precision in elevation, for example, but at the other extreme a vertical support is crudely drawn, perhaps indicating provisional status. Other details are neatly sketched, such as the hinge where the floor and a hatch panel make a flush surface, the panel's end fitting precisely into a small steel section. A similar drawing describes the elegant solution for throwing rainwater away from the external wall surface, showing Nishizawa's skill for construction with a minimum of effort. In the exhibition, the replica of the house was made of thin layers of white-painted wooden board, its purpose being to reveal the consequences and atmosphere of the unusually intimate disposition of the small living spaces inhabited by the owner and his tenants. Animated in a long film of daily life enacted in this living arrangement, it revealed the artful disarray of the many small but essential objects belonging to the people living in a place where very little space is assigned for storage.

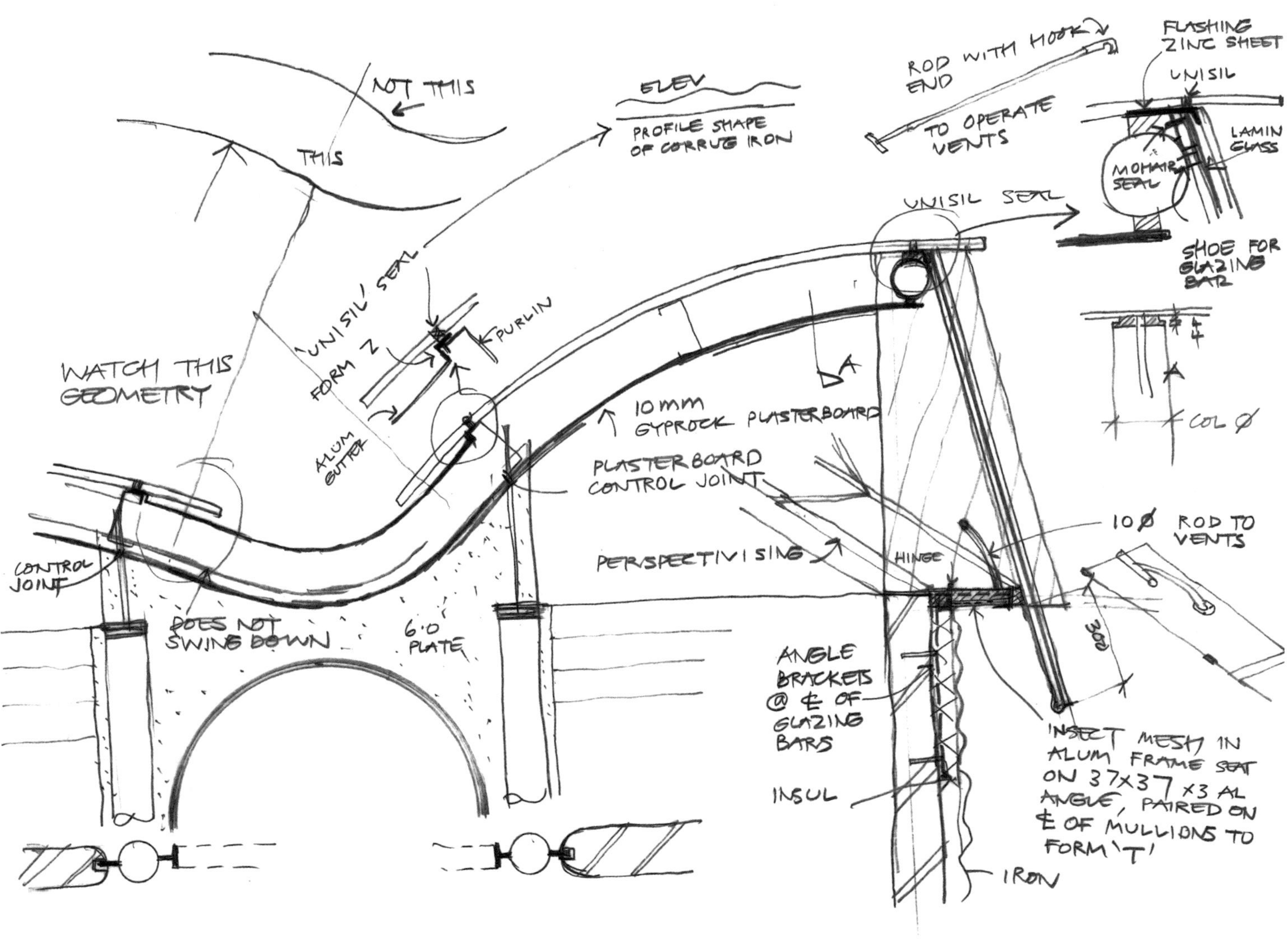


**GLENN MURCUTT (1936–)**

**Magney House, 1982**

Ink on paper

22 × 30 cm, 8¾ × 11¾ in

Altitude: 50 m above sea level; temperate climate with coastal influence; rainfall approximately 1,000 mm per year. This kind of information about the environment of a building's site is important to Glenn Murcutt. The Magney House in Bingie Bingie Point, Australia, the first of his houses for private clients, was designed as a lightweight shelter for holidays, and is no exception. This lively sketch detail communicates Murcutt's response to these conditions in a direct and informative way, both formally and through the logic of construction. The dynamic swoop of the roof, the form of which is defined by the sun's varying position throughout the seasons, is immediately apparent, with the important gutter for draining rainwater shown in section. Its gentle line is carefully specified 'watch this geometry' – 'not this', but 'this' – with a special sketch to show how the galvanized-iron sheet meets the aluminium gutter. Below the gutter detail is the principal metal structure, and through its arch runs the central circulation passage of the house. This sectional detail also reveals the resolution at its eaves of the south elevation, which in the southern hemisphere faces away from the sun and on this site braces against cold winds. A brick wall is seen emerging from the bottom of the drawing, clad in galvanized corrugated iron over a layer of insulation. Above this, a sloped plane of patent glazing rests on an ingenious system of adjustable horizontal vents at door-head height that allow cross ventilation in the summer. A system of vertical fins dividing them is made apparent through a curious device, whereby the shape of the space between the roof and the vents is shown in the continuation of the line of the wall and the vents with their insect screen. This is labelled 'perspectivizing', to distinguish it from the sectional information.

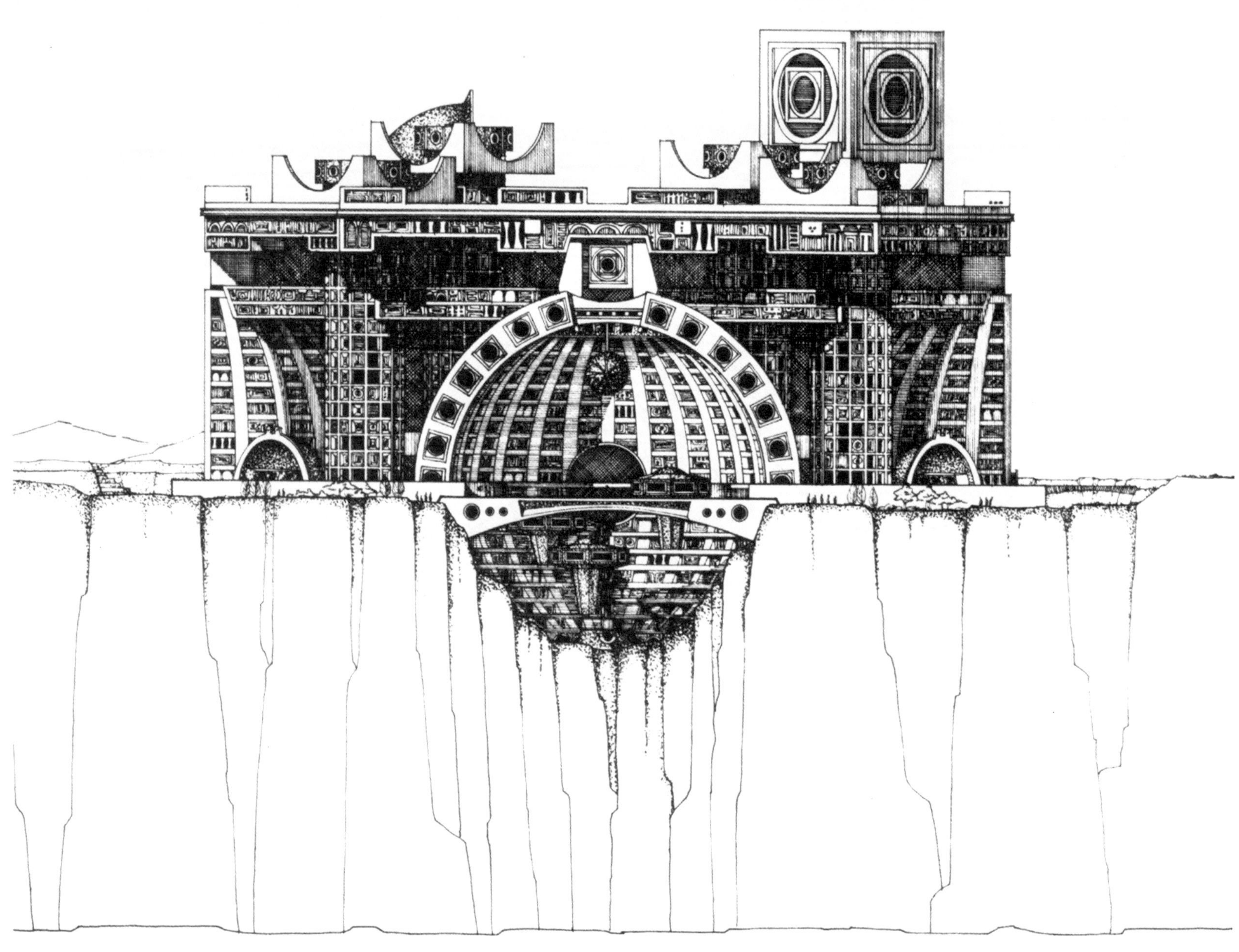

**PAOLO SOLERI (1919–2013)**

**Arcosanti, 1970**

Black ink on paper

89.6 cm × 76.2 cm, 35¼ × 30 in

Although born in Turin, Paolo Soleri spent most of his life living and working in the Arizona desert. The name Arcosanti, which was intended to become the physical manifestation of his ideas, is a melding of arcology – Soleri's proposed combination of architecture and ecology – and Cosanti, which translates from Italian as 'before things' and was the name of his studio near Phoenix. In the mid-1960s, a site further north in Arizona, near the Agua Fria River, was found, and construction of Arcosanti began in 1970. During this time, Soleri made many compelling drawings of his visionary plan, of which only a fragment was actually built. The drawings contributed to the fame of his project, which attracted celebrities including George Lucas, Francis Ford Coppola and Julius Shulman, along with the hundreds of volunteers who laboured on the site while taking part in workshops organized by the Cosanti Foundation. This section reveals many of the key motifs of the Arcosanti project. The depths of the earth beneath the rocky desert take up half of the sheet. Mossy accretions creep over the deep fracture lines, and where the central dome is echoed by a deep well cut into the rock, these take on a theatrical quality. The kasbah-like world above is constructed of huge semicircular elements within a more conventional grid. As well as forming the ribs of the central dome, these mark huge gateways into the complex, and open structures on the roof. Beginning in the late 1960s, Soleri's arcology took the form of a densely populated city that expanded vertically rather than spreading over the ground, reducing the need for cars and the impact on the natural landscape. The whole environment would be contained within a single structure that, as can be seen at Arcosanti, burrowed downwards as well as growing upwards.

**ÉTIENNE-LOUIS BOULLÉE (1728–99)**

**Metropolitan cathedral, 1782**

Pen, ink and wash on paper

33 × 63 cm, 13 × 24¾ in

This axial perspective shows a view through an immense imaginary building, originally intended as a project for a metropolitan cathedral on the Montmartre site now occupied by the Sacré-Coeur Basilica. Its vast space reveals a series of barrel-vaulted naves and aisles animated by a rigidly ordered system of coffers. This decorated surface enhances the two principal emotive effects of the drawing – the depiction of light and the perspectival effect. The coffers' relentless pattern breaks in the middle of the nave, where light floods in, suggesting the dome at the centre of a Greek-cross plan. It gradually becomes fainter as the coffered vaults recede into the distance, the final arch framing a bright but misty exterior lined by the rows of Corinthian columns that flank the aisles. The depths of the aisles are similarly enhanced by corresponding shadows, whose darkness suggests the coldness of the microclimate that such a huge volume can create for itself. Four-deep In the space between nave and aisle, the Corinthian columns support wide cornices that accommodate a higher level of galleries. The architectural style reveals Boullée's preference for a pared-down Classical language as opposed to the then-fashionable Rococo idiom, and his visionary Neo-Classical schemes were influential to the avant-garde at that time. This drawing, although made earlier, served as a precursor to a group of projects for individual buildings designed by Boullée that he made to illustrate his treatise *Architecture, essai sur l'art* (Essay on the Art of Architecture), which he completed in 1794 but which was not published until 1953. These included all the major structures for an ideal city: theatres, libraries, museums, courthouses – even city walls and gates. Drawn in pen with fine, pale washes, the drawing is similar in technique to the others in the set, in which pink, black and grey predominate.

**ANON**

**Mount Wutai Monasteries, Cave 61, c. AD 950**

Mural painting in a cave

15.5 × 35 cm, 6 × 137¾ in

The Mogao Caves, where this mural is to be found, are situated near the oasis city of Dunhuang, a major stop on the ancient southern Silk Road dating from the Han Dynasty (206 BC–AD 220), which also lies at its crossing with the principal route between India and Mongolia. The site contains a system of almost 500 temples, and one of the largest of its caverns, 14.1 m (45.9 ft) deep and 13.6 m (44.6 ft) wide, is completely covered in murals. The cave is also known as the Hall of Mañjuśrī, because it was devoted to an important bodhisattva – someone able to reach nirvana but who delays doing so out of compassion for others – the Bodhisattva of Wisdom. The most important mural is situated on the upper west wall, behind the altar that originally supported his statue. A panorama unfolds of his home, Mount Wutai, which is one of the four sacred mountains in Chinese Buddhism and lies over 2,000 km (1,242 mi) to the east. The mural is unusual in that it depicts the buildings of the region – principally monasteries, but also pilgrimage stations and hostels – within their geographical and social setting, in a bird's-eye-view panorama, with the ground plane tilted at about 45 degrees. It takes the form of a topographic map showing the relationships and routes between pilgrimage sites – a characteristic that makes it an important historical record, since it corresponds with the actual site – while depicting the experience of its tenth-century inhabitation. The painting contains many short inscriptions that identify details such as the names of individual buildings – including a dozen large temple complexes, as well as halls, pavilions and stupas. The temple complexes are portrayed as walled enclosures with corner towers and a two-storey structure by the entrance, sometimes with a central pagoda, set among the five peaks of the region.

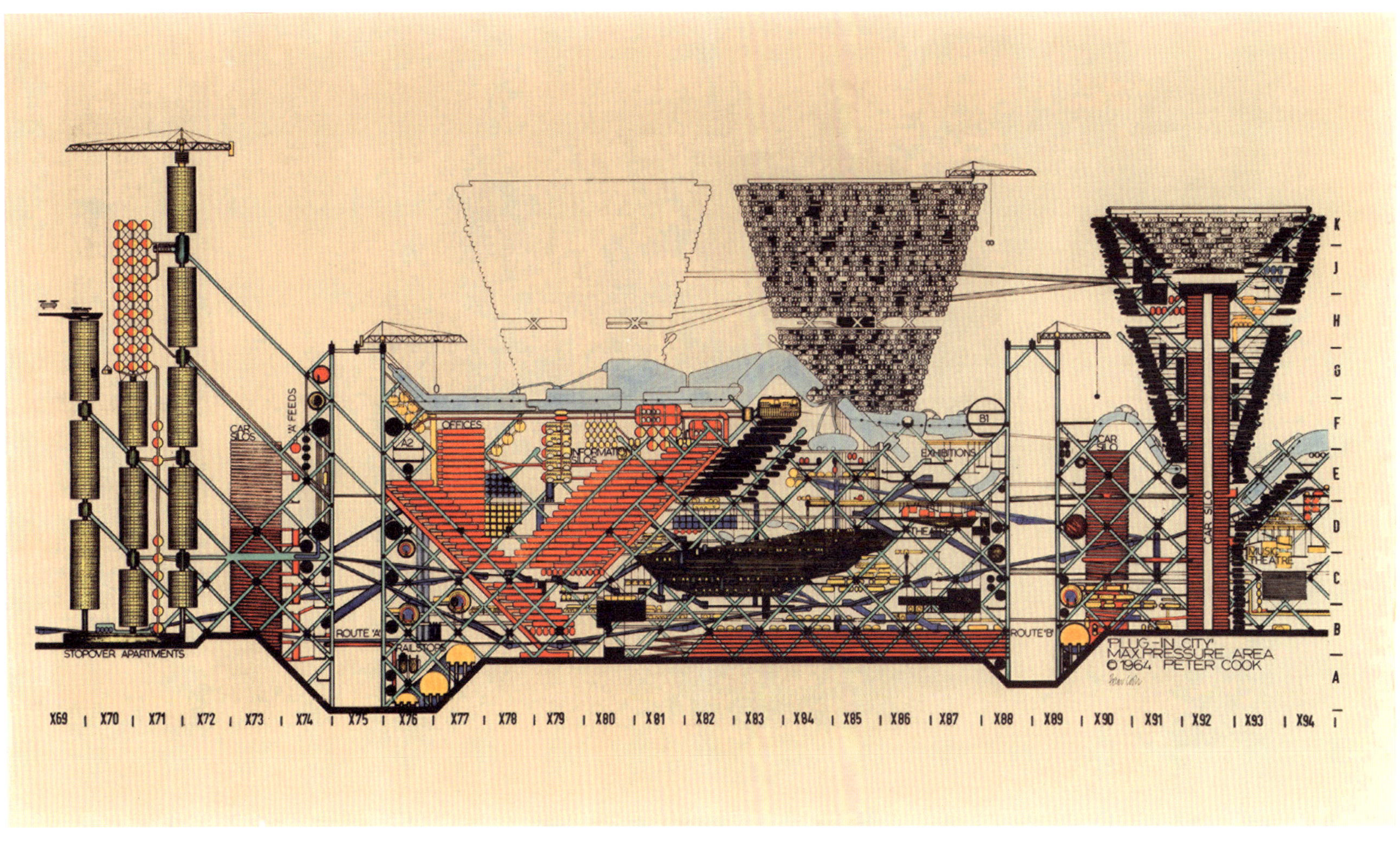


**PETER COOK (1936–)**

**Plug-in City: Maximum Pressure Area, 1964**

Ink and gouache on photomechanical print

83.5 × 146.5 cm, 33 × 57¾ in

The presence of X- and Y-axes at the edges of this drawing suggests that this fragment, designated the Maximum Pressure Area, belongs to a much larger, potentially endless, environment. It is possible only to imagine, rather than to know, what occurs in the zones preceding X69 and beyond X94. This speculation introduces a sense of time into the drawing – a sequence moving forwards, like progress itself, always in transformation. Responsiveness to the present was an essential aspect of Peter Cook's, and his Archigram group's, fantastic, visionary ideas for the late-twentieth-century metropolis, and Plug-in City was a constantly evolving mega-structure designed to encourage change through obsolescence. The principal structure, around which the functions of the imaginary city coalesce – the residences, services, industrial plants, business areas, cultural activities and circulation – takes the form of a pale-green grid. In this section of the city, X69–94, vertical chimneys containing thoroughfares – Route 'A' and Route 'B' – interrupt the grid and burrow down below what is nominally the ground surface in the drawing. Floating within it is a dense, three-dimensional world of escalators, ramps and variously shaped pods formed around different functions, which in the drawing are labelled 'offices', 'information silos', 'theatre', 'exhibitions' and 'rail stop'. Adjacent to the through routes are tall car silos, as well as other mysterious places, such as B1, 'A' Feeds and Stopover Apartments. Behind the frenzy of the Maximum Pressure Area, the outlines of three huge, inverted triangles provide an infrastructure for plug-in living capsules. On top of one of them, a crane is modifying the composition by either adding or subtracting one of the modules, indicating the continual rebuilding that generates the Plug-in City, and the nomadic alternatives to traditional ways of living with which members of the Archigram group were fascinated.

**ÉTIENNE-LOUIS BOULLÉE (1728–99)**

**Cenotaph for Sir Isaac Newton, 1784**

Black ink and grey wash with hues of brown

40 × 66 cm, 15¾ × 26 in

Étienne-Louis Boullée was a reluctant architect who had wanted to be a painter, and so it was as a theorist and teacher at the Académie Royale d'Architecture that he produced his spectacular, visionary later work. Like many intellectuals of his time, he was influenced by the work of Sir Isaac Newton and its radical transformation of our understanding of the Earth and its place in the cosmos. This striking section of his project for an imaginary cenotaph for Newton, who had died in 1762, belongs to a set of six drawings depicting this huge funerary monument, which also includes a plan, elevation and a section at night that shows the sphere lit internally, as if by daylight. This drawing shows the daytime aspect of the cenotaph, with its 150 m-high (490 ft) sphere filled with vast and sublime darkness, the tiny sarcophagus being illuminated by apparent starlight entering through holes in the vaulting. Outside, clouds depicted in fine ink washes suggest the less predictable atmosphere of reality. The section reveals both the abstract form of the monument, based on pure geometry – a sphere embedded in a circular base – and the dramatic, deliberately sensational spatial intention, with its immense, inhuman scale. This is a universe within the world, accessed through underground tunnels, like an ancient Egyptian tomb, and surrounded by inaccessible cypress terraces inspired by the Mausoleum of Augustus in Rome. As an intellectual exercise, the design is an interpretation of French Enlightenment thought in architectural form. This is manifest in its articulation of accepted forms of knowledge as properly classified evidence of scientific progress, such as the references to Greek and Roman archaeology, specimens of which were then being excavated; the symmetry and use of platonic form; and the symbolizing of abstract reasoning accompanied by individual freedom.

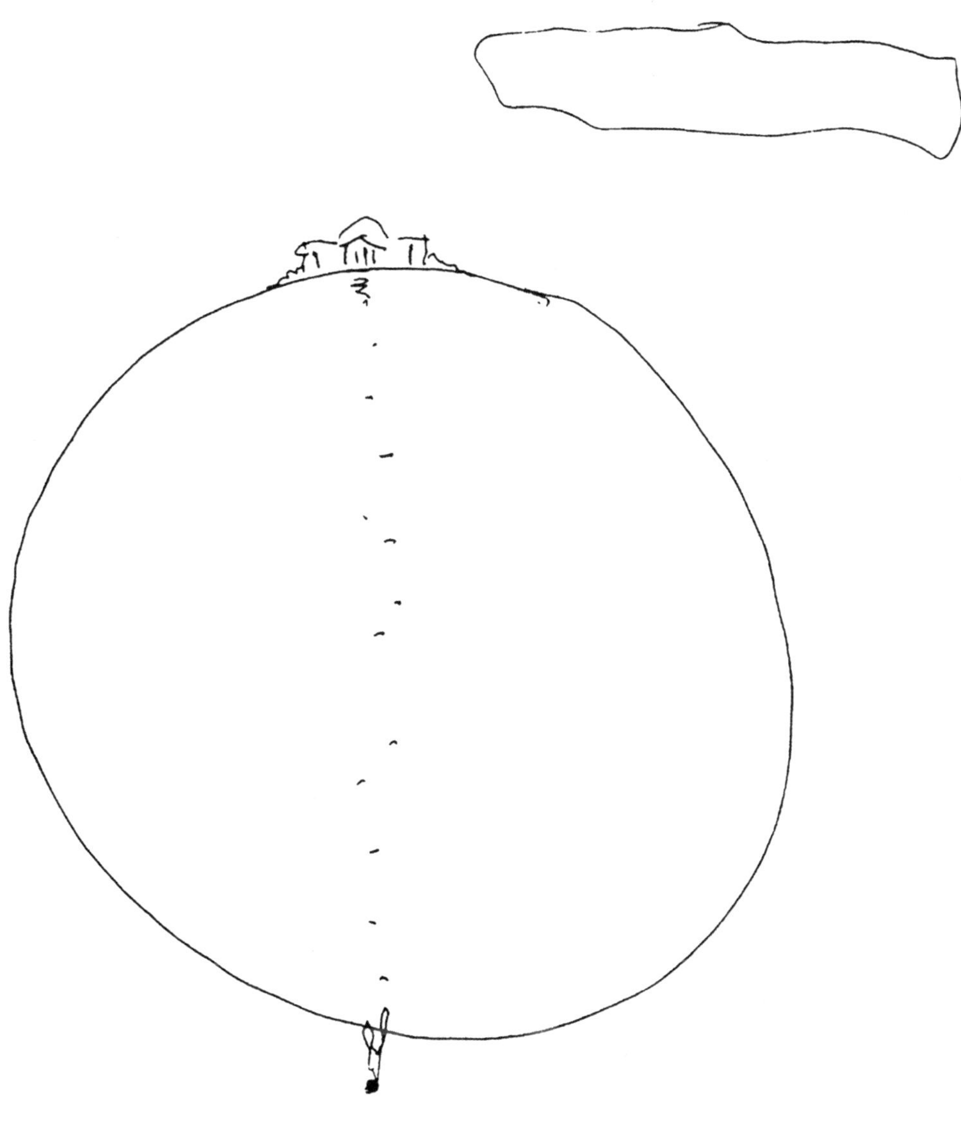

**SVERRE FEHN (1924–2009)**

**Villa Norrköping, 1963**

Ink on paper

22.2 × 14.4 cm, 8¾ × 5¾ in

In 1963, Sverre Fehn was one of five Nordic architects invited to design an ideal house for a family of four, 150 m² (1,614 sq ft) in size, to be sited in the *Norrköpingsutstillingen*, a housing exhibition held in 1964. This rapid sketch made in response, which led to a building that in 2001 became a listed monument, was a subtle joke of Fehn's concerning the loss of mystery. This came about when it was discovered that the world was round, he has explained, and so the perception of the horizon as its edge was superseded and the Earth became a finite sphere that could be scientifically measured. As a young man, Fehn had lived in Morocco, and from the vernacular houses in which he had lived and studied he gained a respect for simple, flexible structures made of natural materials. His design for Villa Norrköping was not made in response to a specific site, and the drawing gives the sense of it being on top of the world, perhaps in the Nordic realm, but also questioning its location – it could be anywhere. A large cloud looming in from the right changes the scale of the image, and relates to the presence of the building outlined there. Although swiftly drawn with a minimum of lines, its essential detail is discernible. The house Fehn designed is a maze with four identical facades, intellectually influenced by Andrea Palladio, and especially his Villa La Rotonda in the Veneto. One of the corners of this symmetrical volume projects outwards, and two of the other wings flank it on either side. Solid brick walls encase the ends of a cross within a square plan, whose glazed inset corners dematerialize the interior space while at the same time reinforce the strongly geometrical basis of the design.

**DIETER URBACH (1937–)**

**Interior view of the TV Tower, 1964**

Multiple media

73 × 105 cm, 28¾ × 41¼ in

During the 1960s and 70s, Dieter Urbach was commissioned by the leading German Democratic Republic (GDR) architects of the time, including Joseph Kaiser and Hermann Henselmann, to make glamorous images of their designs to present to representatives of the government for approval. Urbach created a collection of photomontage perspectives of these ambitious International Style architectural projects, and he often showed them in their urban contexts, which included vast open plazas surrounded by the surviving historic structures of East Berlin, to which they formed a utopian counterpoint. This image shows an interior view of the Fernsehturm, or Television Tower, for which Urbach made several promotional collages, also including it in commissions for other clients, such as the proposed Headquarters of the GDR state news agency. In his collages, he combined multiple media and techniques, including cuttings from magazines and photographic fragments, drawings in ink and pencil, airbrushing and the application of opaque white paint, which he employs here. The foreground is composed of layers of photographic cut outs depicting figurative elements – plants and women – pasted over more abstract elements made of shiny squares of material and snippets of paper where the correction marks are clearly evident, which are made to represent furniture. Beyond, a loose perspective is composed using cleverly selected photographic images juxtaposed together. The winding lines of the strata-like balconies that descend to ground level tie together all these different parts. Their balustrades are created from a simple white band that stands out against the detail, which is defined in parts by a ruled drawn line. The animating foliage reduces in scale towards the back of the room, enhancing both the sense of perspective and the surreal atmosphere of this clever simulation.

**PERCIER (1764–1838) AND FONTAINE (1762–1853)**

**Bedroom of citoyen V. in Paris, 1812**

Etching on laid paper

27.3 × 40 cm, 10¾ × 15¾ in

Charles Percier and Pierre-François-Léonard Fontaine met around 1779 while studying art and architecture in Paris; after a long journey to Rome, they began a lifelong friendship and working partnership. From 1798, they regularly published books disseminating their designs in all genres – the most influential being the *Recueil de décoration intérieures* (Collection of Interior Decorations), its seventy-two plates released as twelve issues of six plates each, the first published in 1801. Completed by 1812, the entire set of plates was bound in a volume with a preface describing their views about the total, unified control of interior decoration down to the last detail and placement of every element, as well as their wish to combine beauty with function. This perspective view is Plate 13 and, like its companions, it is made as an outline engraving in a style popularized by the English pottery designer and artist John Flaxman, a close friend of Percier. Its title includes the revolutionary word *citoyen*, meaning citizen, instead of the more conventional monsieur, despite the fact that citoyen V. was one of Percier and Fontaine's plutocratic clients. Their description for Plate 13 details the luxurious interior. Its ornamental elements to be painted in oil on plaster and designed without any fixed theme. Among them are still lifes of fruit and details of everyday objects painted in grisaille on light grounds. The furniture – the bed and the table facing it, a washstand, and a mantelpiece – is clad with bronzes, paintings on enamel and inlays of various kinds of wood. The tall pedestal in the foreground is a closet for night-time clothing. Percier and Fontaine perfected the version of neo-classicism known as Empire Style after Napoleon, who made himself emperor in 1804. They became the official government architects and decorators, but many of their interiors have since been destroyed.

**ANON**

**Life in a farm, c. AD 300**

Limestone and marble

21 × 29.7 cm, 8 × 11 in

This tribolate floor mosaic depicts a traditional Mediterranean house from around AD 300. The panel comes from Tabarka, a small coastal town in Tunisia, close to the border with Algeria, which was a Roman colony between the fall of Carthage in 146 BC and the Muslim conquest in AD 698. Even at that time, it was the seat of an ancient bishopric, with a monastery for men and convent for women, established during the Roman occupation. In the picture, the large villa is located in the centre of a beautiful garden with a profusion of trees and trained shrubs. The grounds are inhabited by birds – perhaps ducks or pigeons – which, together with the trees, give an impression of natural abundance. The farmyard is clasped between two structures that run horizontally across the composition. In the foreground, a more defensive building with its castellated rhythm suggests an outer protective boundary. The profusion of fenestration suggests that this structure contains a number of dwellings. The large building behind, a simple villa with barns attached, is depicted in elevation. Spatial depth is created by revealing a curved side elevation that pushes into the garden, but which has no perspective effect. The wealth of Roman Africa was based on farming, and the region supplied luxury items such as olive oil, gold and even wild animals for the Colosseum in Rome. Mosaics were commissioned by wealthy families and constructed by teams of craftsmen, using the abundant coloured limestone and marble of the region, resulting in compositions that resonated with more vibrant colours than their Italian counterparts. This idyllic image of the master's house on a rural farm illustrates the comfortable lifestyle of the expatriate Roman.

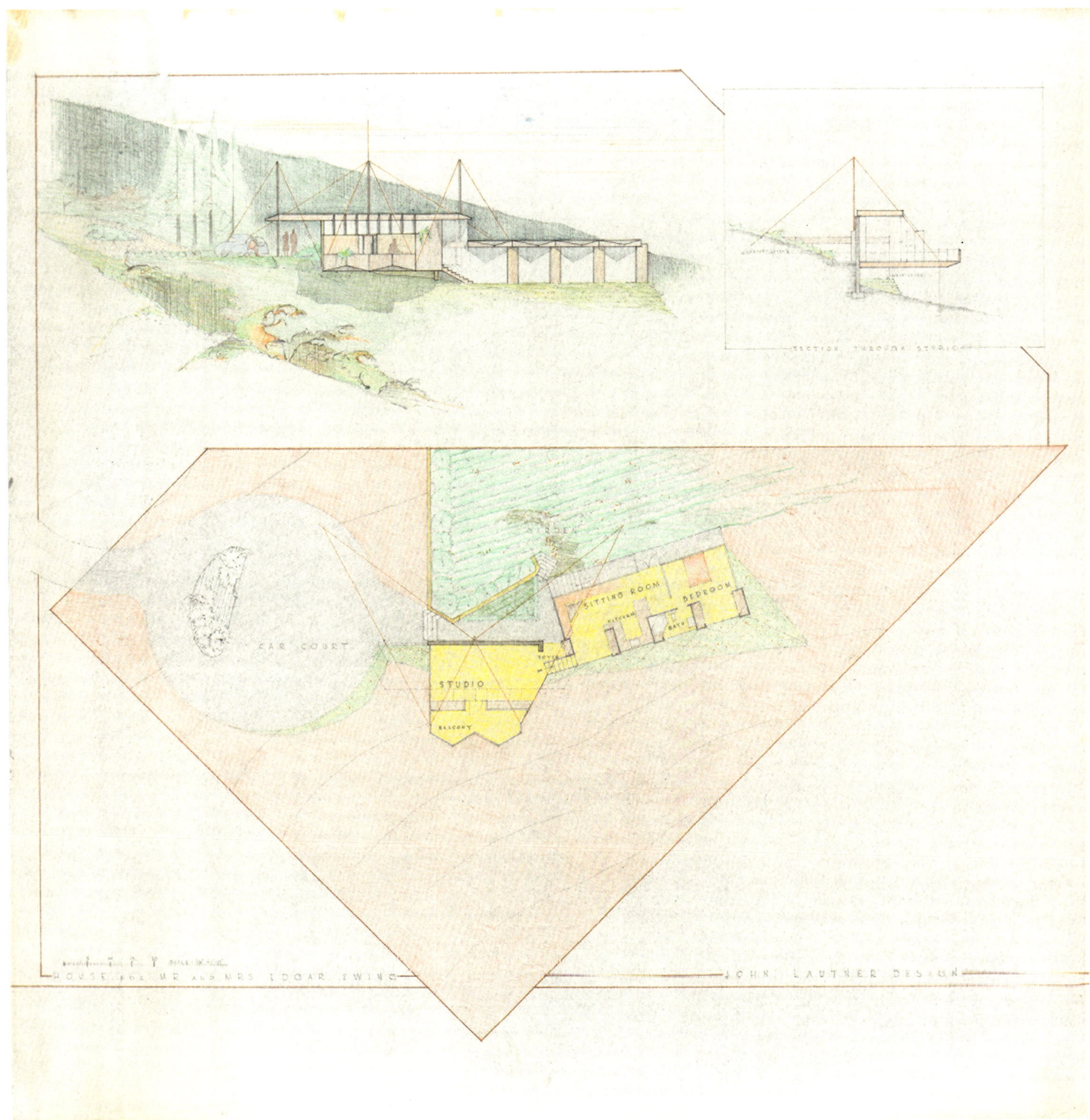


**JOHN LAUTNER (1911–94)**

**Suspended Scheme for House and Studio, 1952**

Print with colour wash, pencil and crayon

78 × 78 cm, 30¾ × 30¾ in

Encapsulating all the key plans needed to describe this preliminary design for a house and studio for the painter Edgar Ewing, the composition of this drawing echoes essential qualities of the building. The economy of presenting the site plan, section and principal elevation of the house bound together by a spiralling red line that also marks the site's boundaries echoes the economy of means of the building's construction. Built at a time of material shortage during a construction boom, the design takes advantage of the surplus materials of the local aerospace industry, and is made so that these prefabricated elements can be rapidly put together with a minimum of labour. The sloping plot is described both as contour lines in plan and as craggy foliage, among which nestle human figures and a car. This is the last in a series of houses by John Lautner that uses a suspension system supported by masts, two in this case, thereby reducing the extent of foundations, which are complicated to lay in unstable, hilly locations such as this. Coloured pencil is used to create a figural impression of the project, and especially its place within an atmospheric, wild landscape and the implied views. The multiple diagonal lines of the drawing – the cables, the slope of the ground, the encircling red border – resonate with each other and act as a foil to the horizontal planes of the dwelling itself. Colour is also used diagrammatically, to highlight the spatial disposition of the plan. A bright yellow field delineates the distinct functions of studio, sitting room and bedroom, which nevertheless intertwine, connected together by the domestic garden behind. Lautner designed over two hundred architectural projects during his successful forty-five-year career, which began at Taliesin as an apprentice to Frank Lloyd Wright, but many, including this one, were never realized.

**BENEDETTO BORDONE (1460–1531)**

**Ruins of Polyandrion, 1499**

Woodcut

29.5 × 22 cm, 11½ × 8¾ in

Written by Francesco Colonna and produced by the Venetian publisher Aldus Manutius, the *Hypnerotomachia Poliphili* is impossible to define within the genres that exist today. Sometimes it is referred to as the second Renaissance treatise on architecture, but it has a fictional narrative centred around a love story that takes place in a dream. This introduces the erotic not only into the literary form, but also into the essence of the abandoned spaces in waiting. Combining text and images in an original composition that was definitive for subsequent architectural publications, this narrative is used in an imaginative way to explore complex archaeological and linguistic questions. Colonna's designs were reproduced in woodcuts by Benedetto Bordone, but some scholars propose that they were originally drawn by artists such as Andrea Mantegna and Gentile Bellini. These depict both invented scenes and places more closely related to ancient and Renaissance sites in Italy, Greece and Asia Minor. Even the typeface is based on ancient Roman inscriptions. The drawing of the Ruins of Polyandrion reveals Colonna's taste for the ruin as integral in itself – a melancholic symbol of impermanence, as opposed to the more usual approach to ruins at the time, which saw them as evidence from which a complete original could be extrapolated. The text accompanying the scene talks about the heap of fragments of rough and humpy stone that lies in the middle ground of the drawing. This is neatly contained within the low stone wall of the foreground, where Poliphili, the hero, stands, having arrived at this point in a fantasy journey in which he searches for his beloved. Behind, a temple-like structure is shown as a partial ruin, with its curved niches depicted in a sketchy perspective. Alongside, two phallic elements – the palm tree and the obelisk emerge from a bushy copse, behind which another ruined structure screens the horizon.

**PETER EISENMAN (1932–)**

**House II, 1968**

Ink on paper

29 × 10.2 cm, 11½ × 4 in

This sketch is an unusual drawing in Peter Eisenman's published oeuvre, which normally consists of hard-line, axonometric drawings and paintings coloured with neat, even fields that express this process in a controlled, precise format. The constructions themselves mimic this diagram-like form, and Eisenman compares House II to model that sheds its scale specificity by employing conventions of the architectural maquette in the actual object – the house looks like, and is constructed like, a model. Built of plywood, veneer and paint, it lacks traditional details associated with conventional houses. In contrast to this stated intention to make a house like a model, this drawing unfolds down the page, nowhere revealing the full square of the plan or the whole volume of the house. Instead, the wobbly, hand-drawn lines in ink, possibly made using a fountain pen, suggest invention rather than completion. At the top, the drawing investigates the properties of solid walls making frames for doorways and windows, voids and ceilings, with shadows revealing spatial depth. Further down, they break up to become colonnades and frames, some twisted round so that the plan of these structural elements is shown as dark squares and rectangles. At the very bottom, the drawing descends into arches, with gutter-like forms between them – shapes that certainly did not make the final cut.

Designed and constructed between 1969 and 1970, for Mr and Mrs Richard Falk, House II was situated on a barren hilltop near Hardwick, Vermont, with broad, panoramic views. This was the second in a series of ten houses built between 1967 and 1975, in which Eisenman explored the geometry of the square plan, and the different ways in which it could be deconstructed. In House II, he manipulated rectangular elements defined as a series of lines and planes – columns and walls that create volumes converging in a complex but open-plan spatial arrangement.

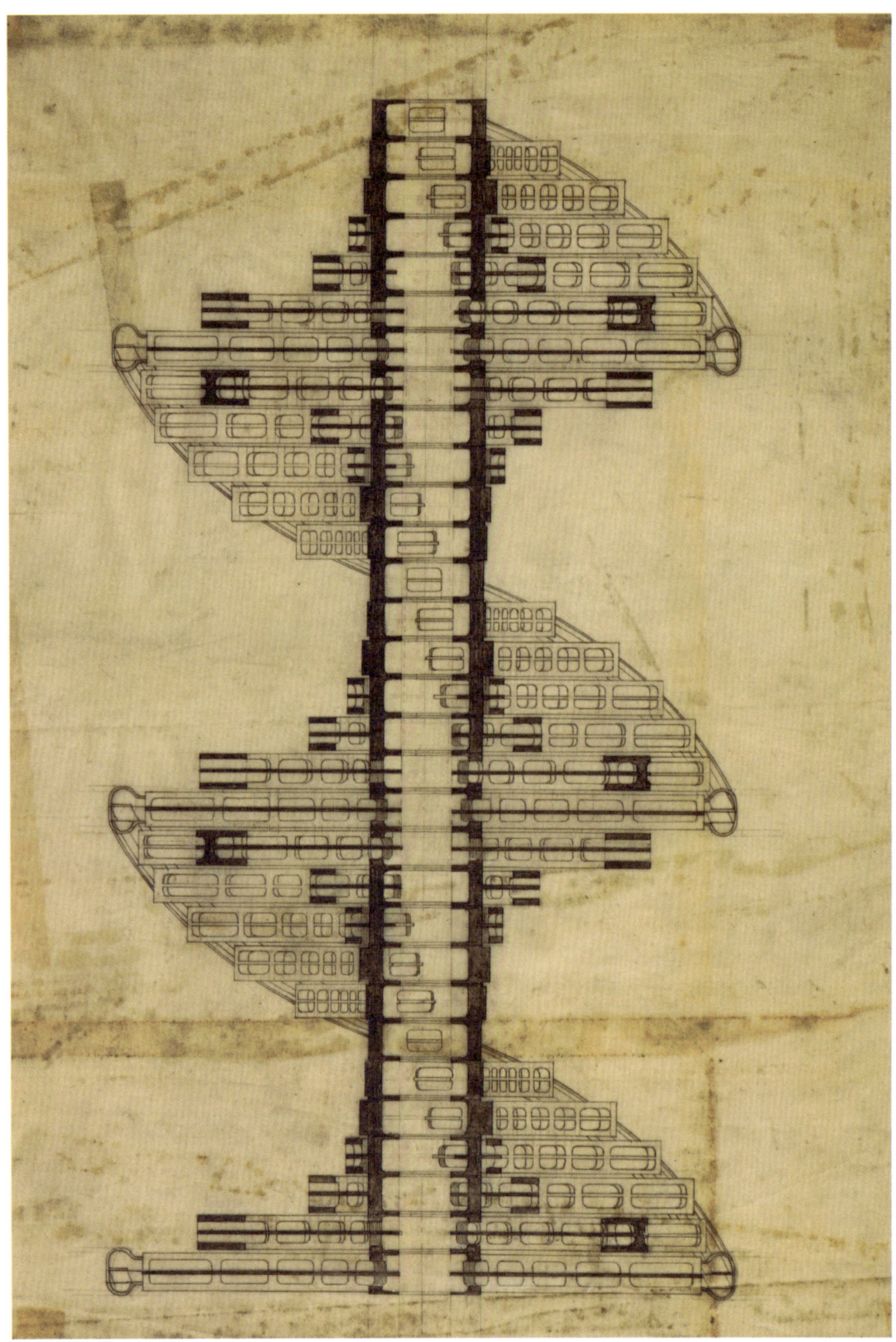

**KISHO KUROKAWA (1934–2007)**

**Helix structure, 1961**

Lead pencil on tracing paper

46 × 32 cm, 18 × 12½ in

Kisho Kurokawa's Helix City Project envisioned an organic city structure that, once initiated, would transform itself in response to the requirements of the contemporary world, and the opportunities afforded by technological progress. Some parts would flourish and grow; others would wither and become obsolete, in cycles that would maintain this self-supporting, artificial construct. This section reveals the helix-like double spiral of this huge structure that in plan extended over a large area, and which at this point is thirty-one storeys high. It comprised service and residential towers connected by an infrastructure of bridges crossing both land and sea. Here, a residential tower is cut through to show the relationship between a peripheral, curving structural element and a stable central core. The space between these two is filled with parking spaces for capsules. Kurokawa would later develop this idea in his Capsule House, exhibited at Osaka's Expo '70, and then in the Nakagin Capsule Tower, built in Tokyo in 1972. A similar logic underpinned many megastructural projects – not only those invented as a post-war reaction to Modernist planning in Japan, but also in Europe and North America. The megastructure was intended to respond to the self-perpetuating logic of capitalism as a natural manifestation. Kurokawa was a leading member of the Metabolist movement in 1960s Japan, whose proponents believed that cities could be designed according to organic paradigms. He had worked with Kenzō Tange on the latter's Plan for Tokyo, 1960, which introduced him to urban-design issues. In a practical sense, the Helix City Project was a response to the extreme housing shortage in Japanese cities, but his solution follows an organic analogy. Kurokawa described it as being like the spiral structure of DNA, which had been discovered in the early 1950s – both in its formal appearance and as a space frame for data transmission.

**ALBRECHT DÜRER (1471–1528)**

**The Triumphal Arch of Maximilian I, 1515**

Woodcut on 195 conjoined sheets

357 × 295 cm, 140½ × 116 in

Albrecht Dürer's *Triumphal Arch* is the largest woodcut ever made. Maximilian I commissioned two monumental woodcuts to evoke his rule among the far-flung administrators and subordinates of his empire – *The Triumphal Procession* and *The Triumphal Arch*. To maintain authority within the vast, culturally diverse territory of the Holy Roman Empire – which then included modern-day Germany and Austria as well as parts of Italy, France, Holland and central Europe – the emperor's achievements and dynastic ambitions were represented in these transportable monuments, circulated for display in libraries, archives and galleries. *The Triumphal Arch* took three years to cut and print. This huge endeavour was a collective production, carried out in the print workshop in Dürer's house in Nuremberg under his supervision, with form-cutter Hieronymous Andrea coordinating a team of artists. The subject is not a building but an imaginary structure designed to be shown as a perspectival elevation, and is a composite of various artists' inventions. Albrecht Altdorfer designed the outer towers, for example, and the central tower was by Dürer himself. The architectural frame of the tripartite arch lends the monument substance, and the three gates represent Honour, Praise and Nobility. Unlike a built monument, which uses its presence within a specific site to communicate its symbolic message, this paper monument with no fixed site has to rely entirely on representation. The densely detailed image communicates a great deal of information to the viewer, which would have required great skilfulness to convey. It is organized into seven scenes glorifying Maximilian's military achievements and the splendour of his House of Habsburg. The historical events of his reign are depicted over the side gates, for example, and Maximilian himself sits in the niche of the cupola above the Hapsburg family tree, surrounded by symbols of power: the lion, the bull and the eagle.

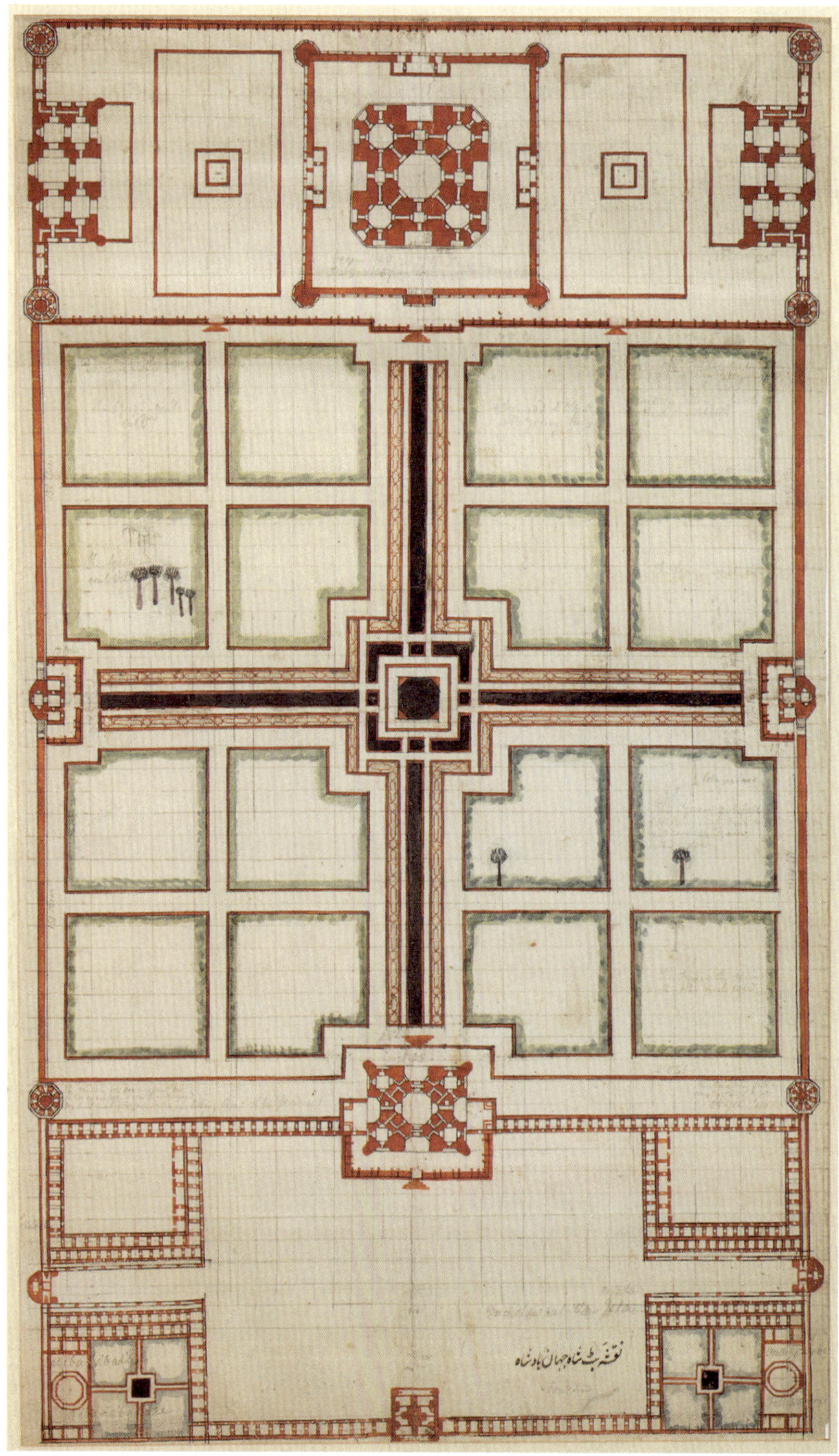

**ANON**

**Gardens of the Taj Mahal, 1805**

Pencil, ink and opaque pigments on paper

70 × 41.2 cm, 27½ × 16 in

This ink drawing is set out over a light pencil grid that indicates the modular planning of the Taj Mahal complex. Although its principal purpose is to delineate the geometry and disposition of the pathways and boundaries of the parterres in relation to the buildings on raised plinths at the top and the bottom of the sheet, some planting is also indicated in the smudgy green edges of the square beds and the little clump of trees painted in elevation, with their two lonely companions below. These are accompanied by written descriptions and identifications of different plants in each flower bed, and indicate a relationship with the plan made by Thomas and William Daniell in 1789, which was published in 1801. The earliest existing plan showing the gardens, or *chahar bagh*, meaning a four-fold garden, in relation to the Taj's mausoleum, mosque, assembly hall and caravanserai, set within a much wider context, is the map of Agra made for the Maharajah of Jaipur in the 1720s. That layout is echoed in this drawing, where the riverfront terrace is shown to the north, at the top. Sitting on this plinth, the structural walls of the mausoleum are depicted in red ink. This is flanked by the mosque on the left and the *mihman khana*, meaning guest house, on the right. The use of red ink to depict monolithic structural elements continues with the garden walls surrounding the *chahar bagh*. These are interrupted on each side by entrance pavilions at either end of the transverse axis. The principal entrance is from the south, through the great gate from the *jilaukhana*, meaning forecourt, which houses two smaller tombs and quarters for tomb attendants. This space serves as a transition between the funerary zone, entered through the monumental gate, and the worldly zone of the caravanserai and bazaar.

**OFFICE KERSTEN GEERS DAVID VAN SEVEREN**

**Border Crossing, USA-Mexico Border, 2005**

Computer drawing

The typological simplification and semiotic complexity that imbues the work of Kerstin Geers and David van Severen is already evident in this collage made early in their partnership. Constructed for an international design competition for a US-Mexico Border Crossing, which they worked on with Wonne Ickx, this image of their winning entry belongs to an oeuvre developed through collaboration with photographer Bas Princen. Conscious references are made also to the collages of Mies van der Rohe, and the early work of David Hockney, and in this project there is an echo of Pietro Lingeri's Danteum. The desert landscape of the photographic background slips underneath their proposal like a tablecloth, and shows a fragment of the border territory where there is no discernible difference between the two sides. Tracks approach then swerve abruptly away from the fence, which is depicted as a net-like strip, the regularity of its rendition suggesting an applied rather than hand-drawn technique. The lines defining the white walls of the box-like enclosure have a different quality, some darker than others, but tiny gaps around them give them a provisional air. The box is projected in a single-point perspective that veers towards a pass in the mountain range behind, rather than towards the centre of the horizon. Within it a distended but rectilinear no man's land takes the form of a large, shaded garden, or an oasis that becomes a point of reference in the vast Tex-Mex desert. It is hidden within the open landscape by its walls, and, according to Geers and van Severen, raises questions about the desire for the promised land. Situated within a grid of palm trees, four strategically dispersed pavilions and associated clearings, not visible here, provide accommodation for administration and passport control.

**LE CORBUSIER (1887–1965)**

**Dom-Ino House, 1914**

Ink on paper

22.4 × 27 cm, 8¾ × 10½ in

Extremely simple yet very influential, the structure depicted by Le Corbusier is the prototype for a standardized housing system along Fordist lines. Inspired by the efficiency and success of the mechanized production lines of the Ford car factories in Detroit, and prompted by devastating housing shortages in Flanders, Belgium, at the beginning of World War I, Le Corbusier proposed a housing solution that could be mass-produced and readily assembled by a relatively unskilled labour force. Although recognizable now as the skeleton underlying a multitude of housing solutions across the world, at the time it was an unprecedented and radical proposal that the twenty-seven-year-old architect wanted to patent. The essence of the idea is expressed in the name that he assigned to the project: Dom-Ino, describing a system that could be repeated end-to-end like a row of dominoes, but also a composite of the ambitious combination of 'domus' and 'innovation'. Pared down to the absolute minimum – *in situ* concrete floor slabs supported on a grid of concrete columns and connected by a concrete staircase – the design incorporates no walls and no rooms. The house was designed as a basic framework, open to interpretation. The drawing itself is constructed as a simple perspective, with the viewpoint almost at ground level. This gives the drawing a human scale, while at the same time clearly revealing all the elements of the structure and how they work together – from the foundations to the columns that support the floors. Although the structure is entirely open, a sense of enclosure is produced by the soffit of the concrete slabs, and the staircase positioned at the rear of the composition.

**CHARLES DE WAILLY (1730–98)**

**La Comédie Française, 1776**

Ink wash and bistre

59.5 × 93.5 cm, 23½ × 36¾ in

This magnificent section through architects Marie-Joseph Peyre and Charles de Wailly's proposal for a new Comédie Française theatre in Paris was made to enchant and inspire the public, displayed in a 1781 exhibition held one year before the completion of the building itself. Developing the Renaissance device of a section combined with an interior perspective, the drawing is populated inside and out, to suggest the experience of moving through the sequence of spaces that a visit to the theatre would have entailed. From the tiny characters in the street outside, dwarfed by the Neo-Classical Doric colonnade, to the figures dispersed throughout the grand interiors that become ever more embellished, the social spectacle of this imaginative realism brings the drawing to life. It also describes the various innovations that this important theatre introduced, such as seating in the pit; continuous, uninterrupted galleries supported by iron structures; and the unity of stage and auditorium within a single, circular sweep. Originally, de Wailly wanted the columns on the stage shown in the drawing to continue this unbroken line, but caryatids were substituted when the building was constructed. The section's dramatic effect is enhanced by the contrast between the huge shed-like structure and the delicate interior shell that it contains. Its complex, shallow domes, niches, vaults and distant perspectives into a magical world are flooded with light, while the cavern of the attic, with its pulleys and ropes, is cast in dark shadows that only occasionally inhabit the mysterious corridors of the theatre. Like many accomplished draughtsmen of the late eighteenth century, de Wailly was influenced by the drawings and etchings of Giovanni Battista Piranesi's fantasy constructions, with their powerful, chiaroscuro-defined atmospheres. None of the original interiors survive now, but this drawing enables the viewer to explore what must have been a spatial and sensual tour de force.

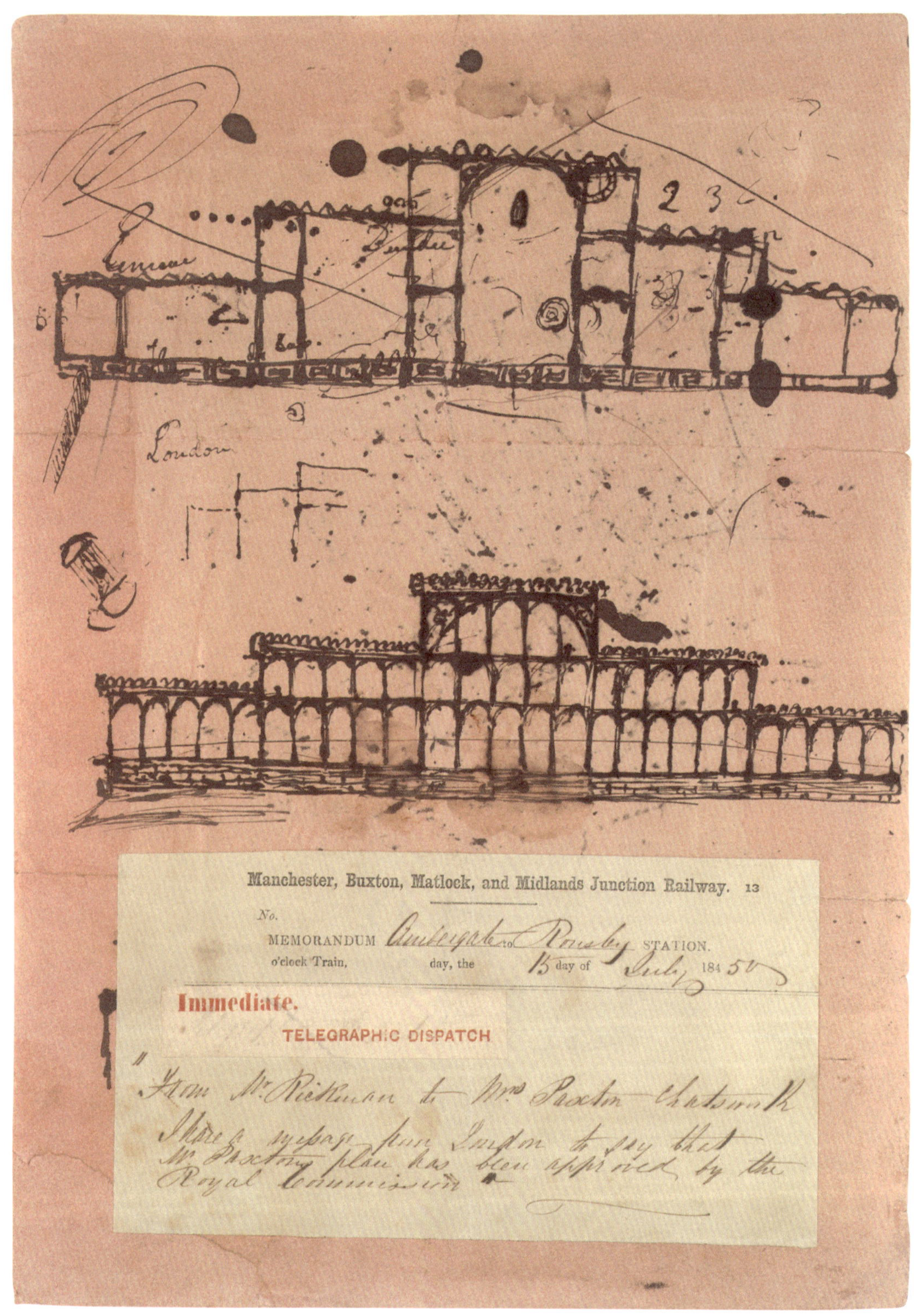


**JOSEPH PAXTON (1803–65)**

**Great Exhibition building, 1850**

Pen and ink on blotting paper with a telegram form

39.1 × 28 cm, 15¼ × 11 in

Drawn rapidly on to a sheet of blotting paper, when Joseph Paxton was attending a Midland Railway board meeting in Derby, these sketches encapsulate, with great economy of line and form, the iron structure of the Great Exhibition buidling. At the meeting were key members of the building committee for the World's Fair – Isambard Kingdom Brunel, John Scott Russell and Robert Stephenson – and the two sketches – an elevation and section accompanied by miscellaneous small explanatory jottings and blots – are mounted with a telegram to Mrs Paxton, informing her that the design had been approved by the Royal Commission. An architectural competition had been held previously, but it had produced only proposals that would take too long to build, be too expensive and consume a vast amount of material. Paxton's elegant and unprecedented solution, which emerged from his experience building extensive greenhouses for the Duke of Devonshire at Chatsworth, proposed a vast prefabricated structure of cast-iron and glass. Within a week, his first sketches had been converted into engineering drawings, and the economy and speed encapsulated in the sketch permeated the process of design and construction. Designed around the 2.44 m (8 ft), cladding module, a kit of parts including the cast-iron columns and girders was prefabricated in Birmingham. These – along with more than 300,000 sheets of plate glass, a material technology recently perfected by the Chance Brothers – were transported by water and steam from the Midlands to London. The timber glazing bars and guttering were cut by steam engines on site, and the newly invented telegraph network enabled the necessary swift communication between off-site manufacturers and the construction team. The grand structure took less than nine months to build, and became an influential symbol of the industrial age, as a building process made manifest in a most spectacular way.

**BARTHÉLEMY PROSPER ENFANTIN (1796–1864)**

**Proposal for a Cité Militaire, 1849**

Watercolour, ink and pencil on paper

29.5 × 35 cm, 11½ × 13¾ in

This flat, decorative image depicts a proposal for a military town or complex in North Africa – possibly for a specific Algerian location, but equally likely a generic solution – designed by French economist and political theorist Barthélemy Prosper Enfantin in 1849. After the death of Henri de Saint-Simon, he had become the leader of a group of intellectuals called the Saint-Simonians, who proposed a system of utopian socialism to resolve the social and political changes wrought by industrialization. In France, this corresponded with expansion into Algeria and, following a visit to North Africa, Enfantin had published a treatise called *Colonisation de l'Algérie* (Colonization of Algeria) in 1843. In it, he proposed that state lands recently expropriated from the Algerians could be used to create complete villages, comprising many smallholdings, rather than being under the jurisdiction of large property owners. In the first instance, the military would establish a prototype: the *école normale de la colonisation*. In the proposal for a military settlement shown here, Enfantin's response to the harsh desert landscape and climate is the impractical construction of huge glass structures within a familiar, colonial, gridded urban plan, its roads marked out by pink-coloured strips, and the design of two central urban blocks shown in greater detail. The elevations above their plans give some clue as to their nature and purpose. To the left is a glasshouse, and the plan suggests that this could be a garden subdivided into smaller grids that do not, however, correspond to the structural layout of the elevation. Across the road, and filling the right-hand block, a sister building looks like a market in plan. The elevation shows it to be similar in form, if not in material, to the glasshouse, above which a very tall pole seems to focus and disperse the sun's rays.

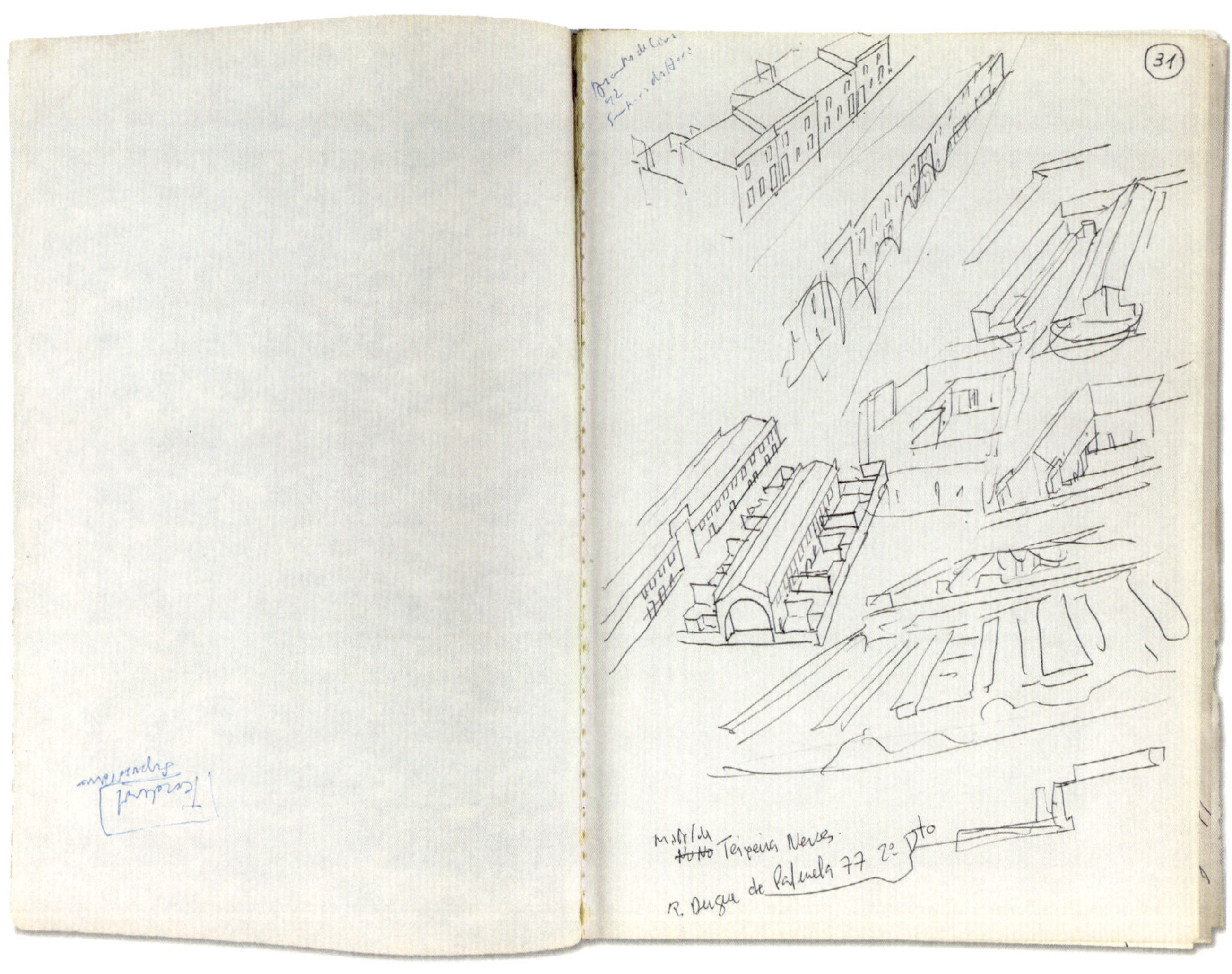

**ÁLVARO SIZA (1933–)**

**Page from a sketchbook, Vila Viçosa, 1979**

Ink and pencil on paper

21 × 29.7 cm, 8¼ × 11¾ in

Álvaro Siza began carrying a sketchbook in March 1977. Before that, his habit of constantly drawing the world around him and in his head had been carried out on loose sheets and scraps of paper. These drawings inhabit the first page of a black-bound, plain A4 sketchbook that he carried during February 1979. Compared with many of the drawings that follow – which include portraits of friends and family, angels, torsos, furniture, annotations and memoranda, lighting for a Bank in Vila do Conde and self-portraits, some even of himself, drawing – this series is clearly of a specific architectural project. Made at the beginning of the design process for the Cooperativa Florbela Espanca housing project in Vila Viçosa, in eastern Portugal, they explore the urban presence of terraces. At the top of the sheet, is a conventional terrace of small, low-cost houses that could appear in many cities around Europe. Their facades are pressed right up to the roadway and behind are small, enclosed back yards. A first iteration alongside it, in which individual units have been merged and brought together by a single grand portal, has been scribbled over. Below this is a more successful sketch, in which the terrace and portal are given purpose by a parapet and pitched roof. Opposite this is a block in which the back yards have switched over to the front of the dwellings. The private, open spaces have become visible to the community and adjacent to the shared space of the cooperative. This spatializing of the community – a making room for social engagement that ranges from chance encounter to mass gathering – is a fundamental move by Siza. His more architectural sketches were often made alongside the production of larger-scale work. Others were made less self-consciously – at meetings, or during social and private occasions.

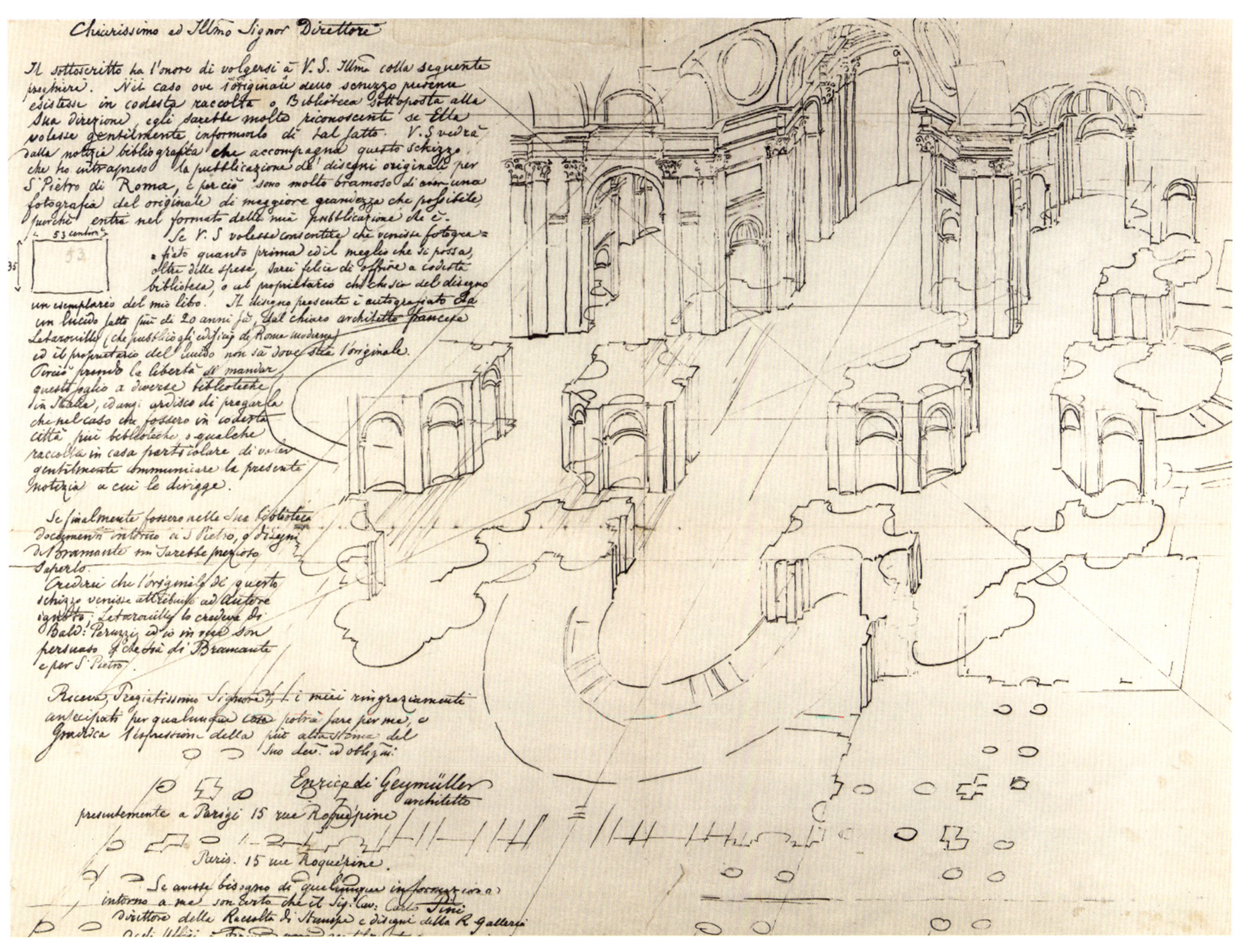


**BALDASSARE PERUZZI (1481–1536)**

**St Peter's Basilica, 1535**

Pen and ink on paper

34.5 × 46.4 cm, 13½ × 18 in

This ink drawing grows from the building plan, which is drafted in sanguine – a reddish-brown chalk. This allows the plan as a diagram of the building to remain distinct from the three-dimensional perspective without disrupting the composition's overall clarity. The perspective at the rear, where the discontinuous line of the sectional cut winds its way around the curves of the domes and vaults, is connected to the foreground plan by means of an intermediate zone drawn in perspective, where the piers terminate just above their niches. Made using a ruler and compass but with freehand additions, this perspective interior shows part of the Basilica of St Peter. Drawn by Baldassare Peruzzi, who became its architect after the death of Bramante in 1514, it was made to convince Pope Paul III, who had recently ascended to the chair of St Peter, of the beauty of Peruzzi's preferred volumetric approach – the quincunx system. This is a geometric pattern comprising five squares in a cross formation, four of them forming the corners of a large square, with the fifth at its centre. In plan, this produces nine bays – the central one and four angular ones covered with domes. The remaining four bays are surmounted by barrel vaults; one is shown in section in the centre of the drawing. Peruzzi was the first of his peers to use this composite projection type. The piers, shown in the horizontal, represent the plan form but also the solidity of the masonry. The drawing presents the interior so that it is possible to understand how the space would appear while standing under the central dome. This differentiates it from the bird's-eye views of Leonardo da Vinci, for example, which give an impression of the building as a whole but do not give a sense of the space within.

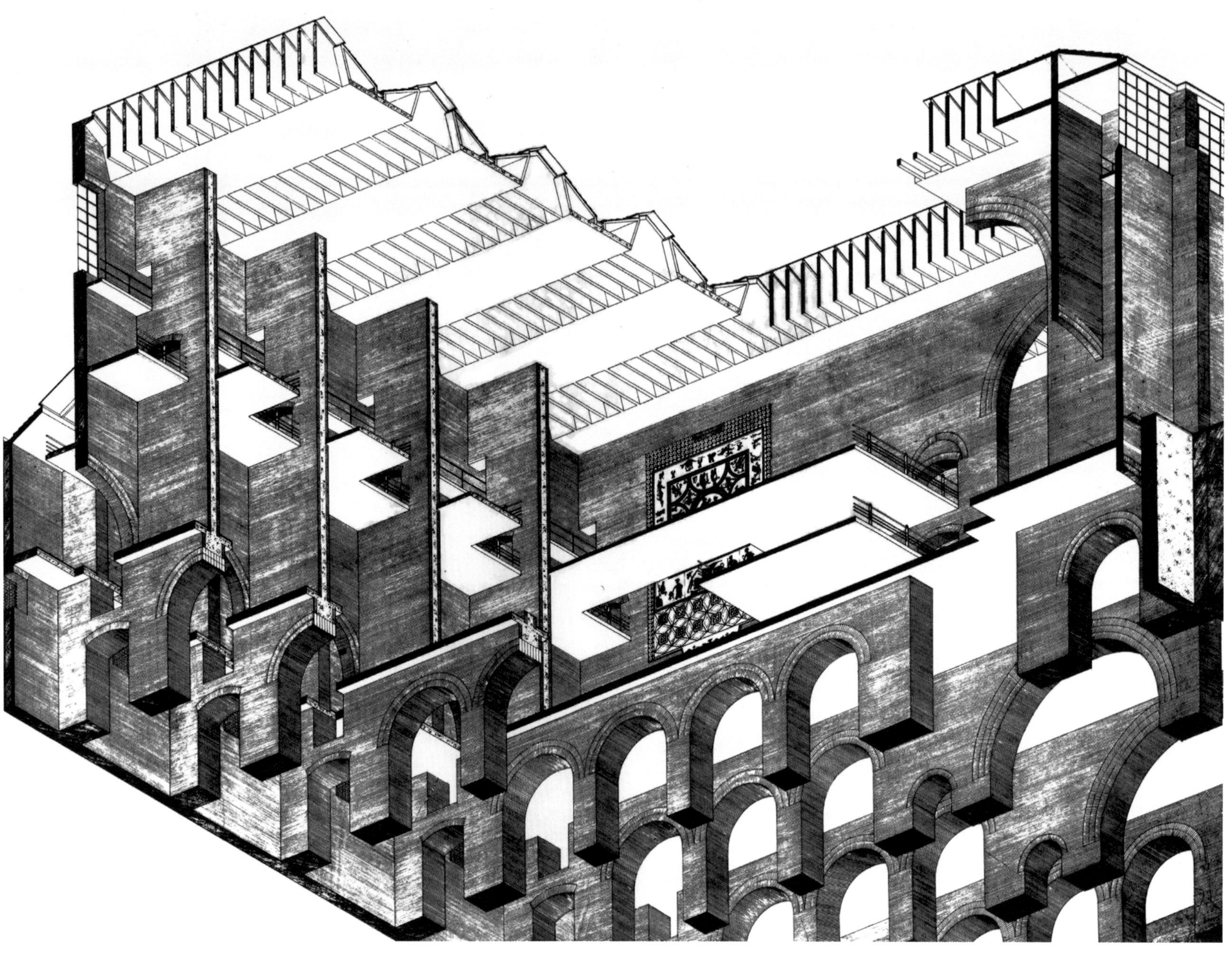

**RAFAEL MONEO (1937–)**

**National Museum of Roman Art, 1986**

Pencil on sketching paper

107.6 × 130.1 cm, 42¼ × 51¼ in

This axonometric drawing showing the principal structural elements of Rafael Moneo's Museum of Roman Art in Mérida is viewed from an unusual, low viewpoint, often termed a worm's-eye view. Here, the structural system of transverse walls that defines the basement and upper plans is immediately apparent, but these arched walls have been cut away in the centre to reveal the various levels of the building. These appear as the white soffits of the floor slabs surrounding the void of a central hall, the floor of which is supported by the arched walls. These create a crypt containing the archaeological remains of the old Roman Mérida – its almost-intact, ancient theatre and amphitheatre lie just across the road from the museum. A single artefact appears on one of the upper walls in the drawing, at the end of a series of deep brick fins buttressing the tall outer wall. This is a mosaic floor that spans two storeys and has its own viewing platform. The section continues throughout the whole height of the building to show the glazed roof above, with its multiple pitched roofs that follow the rhythm of the structural system below and bring daylight deep into the building to dance around the sculptures on display. The worm's-eye projection is difficult to read at first because it is so artificial, but the process of working out what the drawing is revealing compels the viewer to make their own sense of the building as a formal object. In this presentation drawing, Moneo has used this contemplative method to show the brick structure of his museum, allowing time for reflection on the references he makes and the memories he evokes. The way in which the structure has been broken is reminiscent of an archaeological ruin, for example, and semi-circular arches were a common motif in Roman architecture and engineering.

**AUGUSTE CHOISY (1841–1909)**

**Palatin, 1873**

Etching

51 × 33.4 cm, 20 × 13½ in

Engineer Auguste Choisy analysed the construction arts of ancient civilizations, making brilliant illustrations that reduced the complexities of architecture to simple, almost aphoristic line drawings. This axonometric, represented as an etching by J Bury in Choisy's book *L'art de bâtir chez le romaine* (The Art of Roman Building) demonstrates what he called the determining structural concept of a late Roman building. Much of his research in this field attempted to prove that the economics of construction were influential in regards to the monumentality of Roman structural systems – requiring an interest in both the material and formal qualities of these structures. In order to explain the relationship between the quantities and surface qualities of construction materials, and their interface with structural systems, Choisy developed a technique of parallel projection called the worm's-eye view – an isometric drawing extrapolated upwards from a rotated plan. At the bottom of the drawing, a scale with three axes indicates how effectively this technique could communicate three-dimensional information, and also reveals the angle of the plan's rotation. The rotational space of this approach meant that internal material surfaces could be understood as essential components – here of a vault's spatio-tectonic form. The white, exposed plan forms, cut at different heights, show the variety of different compositions of the pillars of stone, and possibly concrete, which support the vaults – from these spring the arches of the vaults. The wall surfaces and curved planes of the vaults are all clothed in a variety of brick patterns. Although technical in intent, the drawing is rendered with shadow that enhances its three-dimensional quality, and the underside of the structure contrasts with the brightly lit external wall and the blustery spring sky above.

**PETER CELSING (1920–74)**

**The Bank of Sweden, 1970**

Gouache painted on a photograph of the model

37.5 × 38.7 cm, 14¾ × 15½ in

Encapsulating the layering of forms of representation that architects use to imagine solutions, this hybrid image of a painting over a model photograph depicts the main facade of the Bank of Sweden in Stockholm. Designed by Peter Celsing in collaboration with Jan Henriksson, over a period of eleven years, the building was a response to Brunkebergstorg – the long, triangular, paved plaza shown in the foreground of this image. The painting transforms the immutability of a plain model – expressive only of the proposal's volume, with its stable and solid formal presence reinforced by the repetitive grid – into a scene with a sense of immediacy. The fresh sky is reflected in the fluttering blue-and-white Swedish flags in front of the facade. The impression of a windy day is reinforced by the fluttering blue dabs of colour that at first seem to represent reflections in windows, but which continue into the street to give the image a festive air. The triangular space presents as an irregular precinct, with the cars on busy Malmtorgsgatan – which runs along the longest, west edge of the triangle – crowded into the bottom left of the image to give a sense of urgency, and the speed of urban life. The brown trees that break up the grid of the plaza's surface suggest autumn. The facade's eight-storey grid is made of hewn black granite or diabase – split slabs from southern Sweden's Hägghult mine – echoing Stockholm's own bedrock, which emerges in bare outcrops around the city. Its irregular surface, barely shown in this painting, creates a pattern of shadow and light that animates the rigid grid, behind which the main banking hall sits on the ground floor with the main public areas. This liveliness of the rusticated stone surface is embodied in the image in a different way.

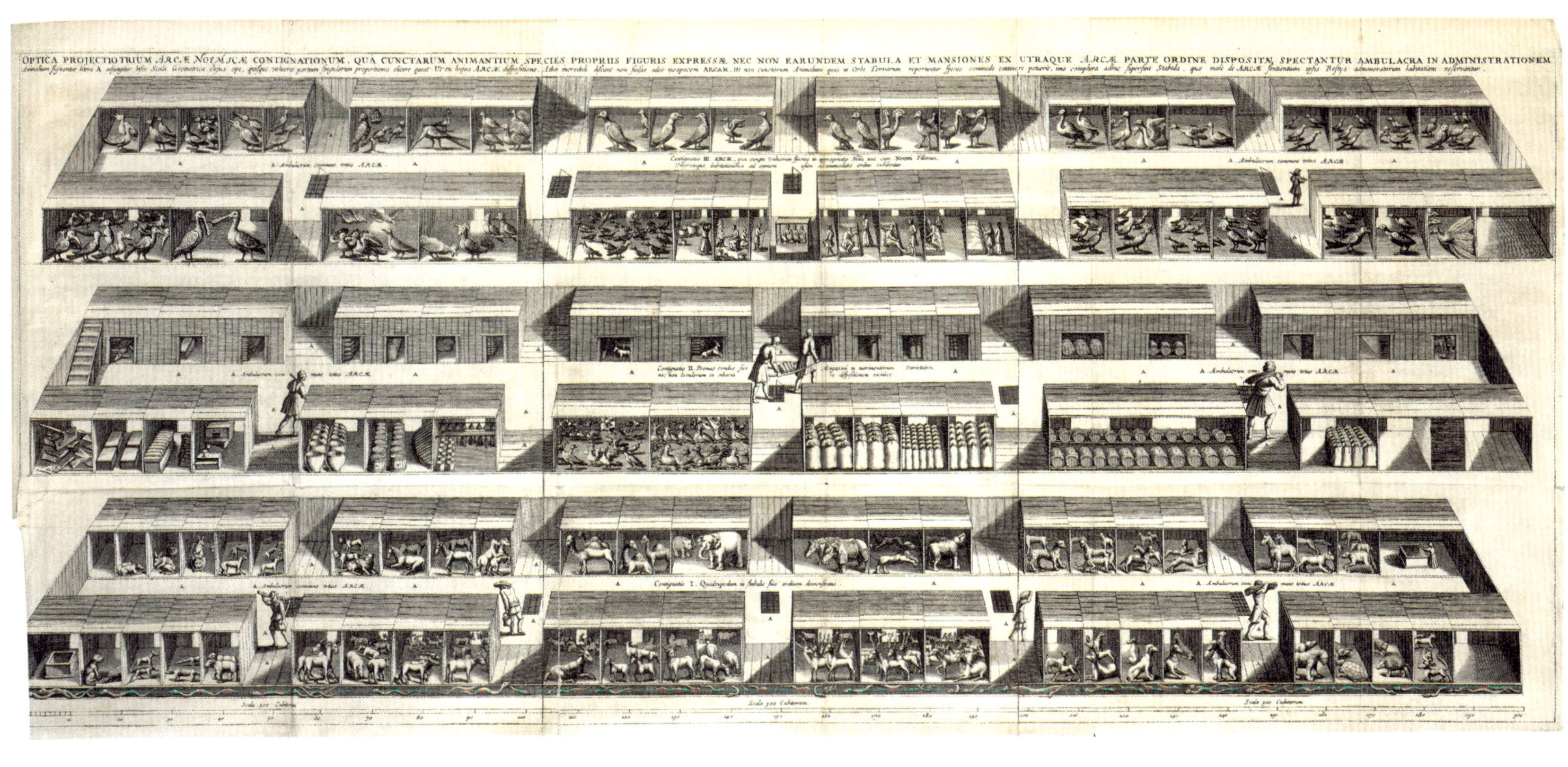


**ATHANASIUS KIRCHER (1602–80)**

**Arca Noë, 1675**

Engraving on three plates

99 × 44.5 cm, 39 × 17½ in

This long drawing, represented in an engraving made on three separate plates, shows the disposition of the inside of the biblical Ark of Noah, as defined by seventeenth-century Jesuit scholar Athanasius Kircher. It belongs to a book that he published in 1675 entitled *Arca Nöe*, in which he collected his research on this biblical construction, and to which various artists contributed illustrations and diagrams such as this. In response to the Protestant Reformation that began in 1517, the Catholic Counter-Reformation (1545–1648) introduced a new conservatism into theological research, and study of the Old Testament as literal truth replaced a looser allegorical interpretation. In line with this, Kircher's analysis involved the calculation of what he perceived to have been an objective reality, based on information available in the book of Genesis, with assumptions deduced from the scientific knowledge of the day. According to the Bible, the Ark was made of wood and reeds and coated with pitch inside and out, but in Kircher's version the whole internal construction is of timber boards. The dimensions were given as 300 cubits long, 50 wide and 30 high, and encompass three floors. Despite the apparent clarity of these sizes and proportions even measurements were subject to a hermeneutic, and the definition of a cubit was a subject of debate. The description at the top of the page defines the image as an optical projection of the three storeys of the Ark, whereby all the animal species are shown, as well as their stables and pens, which are arranged in order on either side of the Ark. Kircher organized his layout to suit the number of species known to him, and in relation to their maintenance throughout the water-bound hiatus they were bound for. This included consideration of livestock for feeding carnivores, as well as the supply of grain and potable liquids that can be seen filling some of the stalls on the middle deck.

**FRANCESCO BARTOLOMEO RASTRELLI (1700–71)**

**Stone Embankment Opposite the New Winter Palace, 1760**

India ink and watercolour on paper

49.5 × 37.2 cm, 19½ × 14½ in

The Winter Palace was designed on the banks of the Neva in St Petersburg for Empress Elizabeth, daughter of Peter the Great, by Italian-born architect Francesco Bartolomeo Rastreslli. Its monumental, colonnaded north facade looks towards the river across an embankment, and is flanked by other eighteenth-century riverside palaces and villas, for which it was necessary to build up, strengthen and regularize the banks of the Neva. By the mid-1710s, the embankment's wooden walls had been shored up with sand and stones, but for his palace Rastrelli had to significantly improve this situation. This drawing, a section through the embankment, shows a far more robust solution, with oak piles driven stake-like into the earth. Further reinforcement is created through layers of log walls holding huge granite boulders that fill in a deep, lead-lined cut in the bank below the water. Above the water level, the final stage of embankment construction comprised granite blocks that formed picturesque slopes into the water, their joints reinforced by iron straps. This pictorial quality animates the drawing, whose technical nature is offset by the colourful rendering of the materials, which are given character in their irregularity. The huge boulders contrast with the thin layer of cobbles lying over the ground; their heavy weight is felt pushing against the piles and the river's depths, which become paler further below the surface to provide more contrast with the dark embankment. The Winter Palace played an almost-theatrical role within St Petersburg's urban planning, but was also the administrative and ceremonial centre of the Russian state, and today it houses the Hermitage Museum. The palace itself was built in a grand Baroque style, influenced by Francesco Borromini and Gian Lorenzo Bernini – its construction was a huge undertaking, requiring the labour of over 4,000 people.

**AMANCIO WILLIAMS (1913–89)**

**Bridge House, 1943**

Ink on paper

58 × 92 cm, 22¾ × 36¼ in

The Bridge House, or Casa del Arroyo, is set within a large garden of great beauty near Mar del Plata, a coastal city southeast of Buenos Aires. Crossing a stream called the Arroyo las Chacras, the form of this simple dwelling that Amancio Williams designed and built between 1943 and 1945 for his father, the composer Alberto Williams, is defined by two architectural concerns: to reduce intervention in the natural environment by making a simple bridge across the shallow valley to support a single-storey dwelling; and to reveal the structural means of this reinforced-concrete building. The viewer of this perspective looks from a low angle, as if standing on the grassy left-hand riverbank, which wends its way up the centre of the composition to disappear into an increasingly dense thicket of overarching trees. On either bank, the slender trunks of leafless trees make an informal colonnade with zigzag branches that screen but do not hide the facade of the house. The underneath of the flat plane of the elliptical arch that spans the water is a strong element in the drawing, and emphasizes its important role in a way that would not be apparent in a flat elevation. Williams made another drawing depicting bathers swimming beneath its cave-like roof. Above, vertical planes support the concrete tray of the house, and the frames of the windows between this and the flat roof slab have been omitted from the drawing, so that it floats like a magic carpet, some 6 m (19.6 ft) above the level of the river's banks. Embedded into monumental columns on either side are its two entrances. These can be seen in the passage from the terraces on the riverbank to the staircases that rise over the flanks of the arch and into the cosy, timber-lined interior of this Modernist dwelling.

**ANTONIO DA SANGALLO THE YOUNGER (1484–1546)**

**St Peter's Basilica, 1519**

Pen and ink on paper

30.4 × 46.2 cm, 12 × 18¼ in

When this drawing was made, the design of the Basilica of St Peter had become a palimpsest of work by different architects including Rafael; Antonio Sangallo the Younger's uncle, Giuliano; and Baldassare Peruzzi, who added to and transformed Donato Bramante's original plans for a Greek-cross form with a dome inspired by the Pantheon. Constructed partly with a straight edge and compass and partly sketched freehand, this drawing was made by da Sangallo, who had started as Bramante's assistant, simultaneously with other exploratory designs for the facades. Principally a line drawing, the spare use of shading, utilizing hatching rather than washes to model the facade and interior sketches, shows that the three-dimensional character of the surface was as important as its geometrical composition. At the centre of the sheet is a layered rendition of the facade of the basilica, accompanied by a sketch of the dome above and explorations of different internal design problems. Combined, these reveal da Sangallo's complex layering of different ideas, showing how the thought process about one building element was interconnected spatially and formally with many other parts. This proposal shows the elevation of the cathedral in flux – with the large, central portico supported by groups of double columns flanked by an indeterminate solution, with one proposal for a new, tall order overlaying another for a low colonnade. In the sketch of the dome above, da Sangallo moved away from the Pantheon-like designs of Bramante and Rafael to propose a structure inspired by Florence Cathedral. Discussions of drawings from this period often use archaic forms of measurement, with terms like *palmi* – a measurement based on the palm of the hand, and *braccio* – equivalent to the forearm and equal to two *palmi*. These were, in fact, different in Rome, Florence and Milan – as well as varying between professions.

**ALDO ROSSI (1931–97)**

**Urban Scene: scene for il Teatrino, 1978**

Magic marker and paint on board

73 × 107.3 cm, 28¾ × 42¼ in

Aldo Rossi was fascinated by the word *theatre*, and the private and repetitive character of the fictional world that it encompasses, both as a place and as an idea. Preceding his Theatre of the World, or Teatro del Mondo, which he made for the first Venice Architecture Biennale in 1980, the Teatrino Scientifico explored the simple and provisional nature of the *teatrino*. The term is the diminutive for theatre, and these structures were traditionally made for temporary summer shows or puppet theatres, for example. This image of an empty urban landscape composed of forms taken from Rossi's language of architectural typologies – such as the chimneys in the background, or the stretched pediment or triangular roof form balanced on a thick column – is a proposal for a scene within the space of the Teatrino structure. This was composed of a simple wooden frame that was enclosed on three sides and open at the front so that the stage inside would be visible to an audience. A simple pediment with a clock and a flag signified the proscenium, and the project was devised with two collaborators – Gianni Braghieri and Roberto Freno. Various stage sets were designed to go into the Teatrino: sometimes they comprised flat scenes exploring compositions of basic architectural forms, such as this one. These would have a minimal set laid out in front of them, while others constituted complex three-dimensional constructions. The provisional quality of the Teatrino was developed in the Teatro del Mondo, which was celebrated as an event, and recorded by photographs and a film that was made to chart its journey during the summer of 1980 northwards up the Adriatic Sea. A ghostly precursor of the structure that he designed for the Teatro del Mondo – a floating, enclosed tower – sits on the horizon line of this drawing.

**HASSAN FATHY (1900–89)**

**Ismaïl Abdel-Razeq Villa, 1941**

Ink and watercolour on paper

69.4 × 45 cm, 27¼ × 17¾ in

This elevation drawing completely flattens the building and its site into a single plane. The lush garden with its fishpond, the long path to the entrance lined with formal shady trees, and its almost symmetrical background of striated, brown earth are at one with the ochre wall of the house. The only sense of depth is given by the shadow of the seat adjoining the door, on which a solitary figure rests, and the setback of the wing above it. Here, the house wall merges with the sky, and is almost the same colour, but the ground encloses it within the high horizon of a cultivated landscape. The drawing is an idealized version of the house that Hassan Fathy built early in his career for Ismaïl Abdel-Razeq, in the desert landscape of Abu Girg in Egypt. Its design marked a change in Fathy's work that would be developed in his later, much larger, projects such as the New Gourna village, 1946; the High Institute for Popular Arts, 1962; and the Menia Village of 1980. These developments derived from vernacular Egyptian architecture, and were material and spatial responses to the intense desert climate and geography, as well as economic circumstances. Fathy is known for re-establishing the use of mud brick and adobe as opposed to Western building materials like reinforced concrete, which had been used for Modernist architectural interventions in North Africa earlier in the century. In this house, he also introduced a different spatial approach to plan disposition, using an exterior courtyard space to create a distinction between the public rooms adjoining it and the private areas adjacent to the dwelling's periphery. He also began using domes to control the internal environment. They are not shown in this drawing, but might at this stage of design development have been hidden behind a parapet.

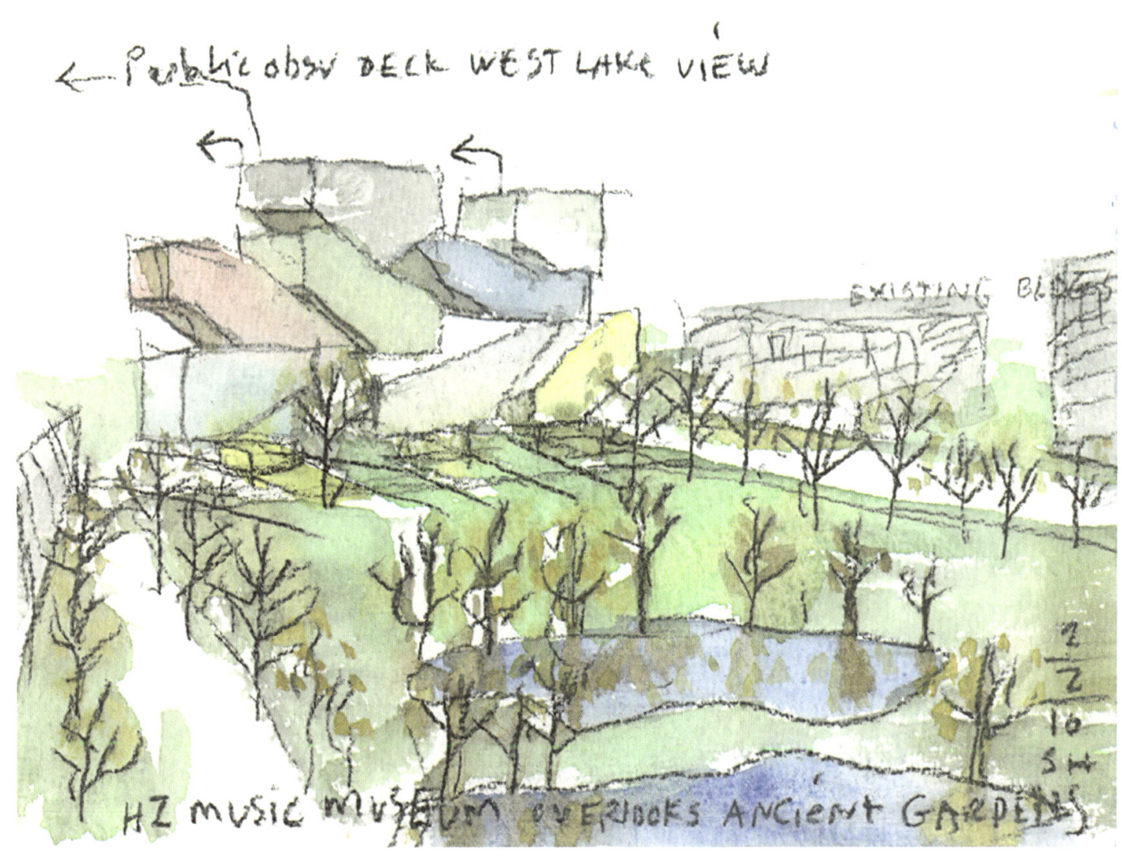


**STEVEN HOLL (1947–)**

**Hangzhou Music Museum, 2008**

Watercolour on paper

12.7 × 17.8 cm, 5 × 7 in

Making watercolour paintings and sketches of his work – from simple, abstract moments to more complex images such as this – forms an important part of Steven Holl's work. This image shows Holl's project, designed in collaboration with Li Hu and Chris McVoy, for the Hangzhou Music Museum in China, which won a competition in 2008. The museum's main structure sits at the north end of a beautiful wooded garden; the lower caption confirms this. The fields of watercolour have been allowed to overlap and blend, so that the foliage, the grass and the reflections in the water make a mottled field articulated by the edges of the water and the dark strokes of the tree branches. In the distance, paler strokes outline existing buildings on the wider campus. The timber-clad surfaces of the new structure mimic but do not copy the blended colours of the natural environment. Their varied hues define the irregularly stacked volumes of the eight small performance halls, which are based on the Eight Sounds of traditional Chinese music: silk, bamboo, wood, stone, metal, clay, gourd and hide. A further annotation at the top of the drawing directs attention away from the ancient garden, telling the viewer that there is an observation deck looking west towards the city's West Lake, which is not visible here. For Holl, drawings are an outlet for intuition, and this exploratory sketch is evidence of an important process allowing conceptual underpinning – which often eludes the conscious, problem-solving mind – to drive a design. This image was made in one of the small sketchbooks that he keeps for this purpose, making rapid exploratory sketches to investigate and define his thinking. Alongside this sketchbook, Holl keeps a record of written conceptual aims in order to clarify the intuitive drawn work, and to create a word/drawing/word cycle.

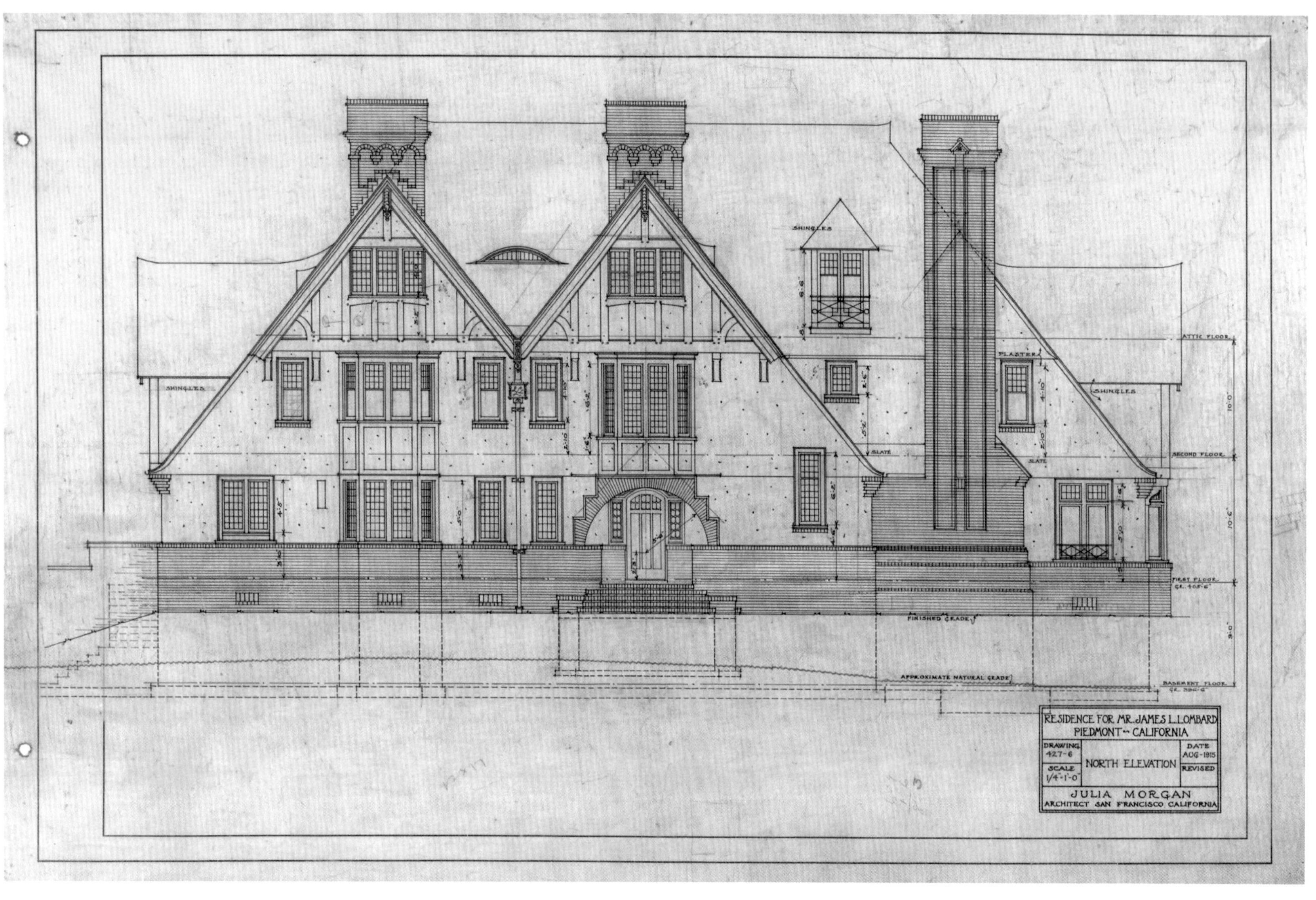


**JULIA MORGAN (1872–1957)**

**Lombard House, 1915**

Red and black ink on linen

28 × 43 cm, 11 × 17 in

Julia Morgan was a native of San Francisco who trained as an engineer at the University of California before becoming the first woman ever accepted at the École des Beaux-Arts in Paris in 1896. She established her own practice in 1904, and over the following 46 years she designed nearly 800 buildings, including the Asilomar Conference Centre, 1913–29 and Hearst Castle, 1919–39. Her work was influenced by her Beaux-Arts training, but also by a deep knowledge of California's landscape and history. Apparently inspired by a watercolour of a manor house in Croydon shown to her by her client James Lombard, Morgan's north elevation of the house that she designed for him in 1914 and built in 1915 depicts the front facade of a four-story Tudor Revival mansion. This street elevation extends the length of a city block and, guided by the desires of the client and the unique experience of responding to the mysteries of a painting, breaks away from the Classical models of symmetry and rigorous formal control of the Beaux-Arts system under which Morgan trained. Instead, she incorporates a range of romantic detailing, including high-peaked gables; brick corbelling; a third-storey overhang embellished with half-timbering; an arched brick porch, which is situated at the centre of the elevation; and the tiny scale of lead-lattice windows. Despite this, the whole composition maintains a strong balance, its tripartite definition articulated by the powerful brick-chimney structures. The whole building is raised above the existing ground level, seen as a dotted line labelled 'approximate natural grade', its lowest point marking the floor level of the basement. Further raising of the house's main volume is created by the brick band that runs across the front at ground level, which incorporates the grand staircase up to the entrance and small windows into the basement.

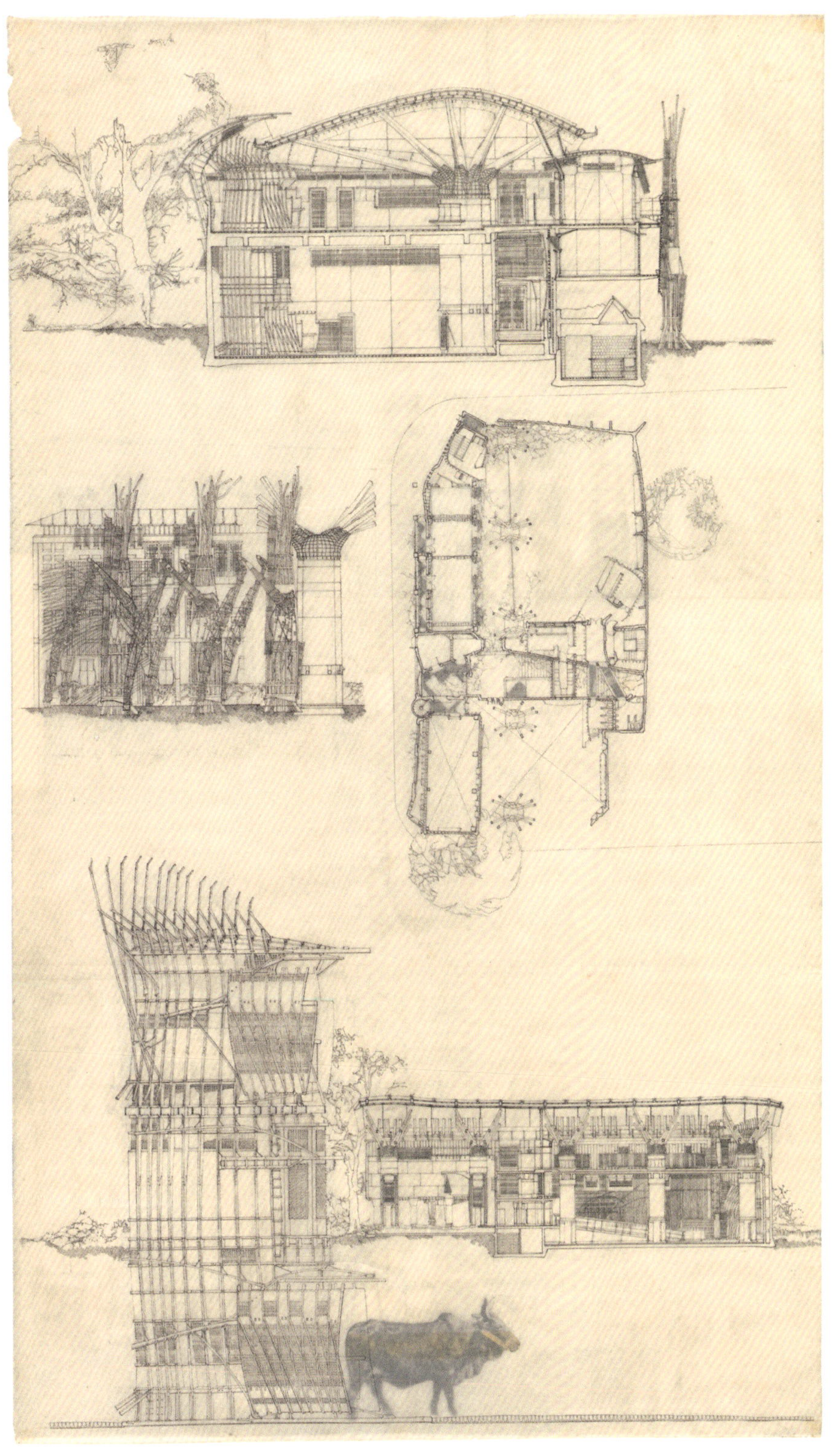

**MACDONALD + SALTER**

**ICI Trade Pavilion at the Royal Agricultural Showground, 1983**

Ink on paper

136.5 x 92 cm, 53¾ × 36 in

In the 1980s, Chris Macdonald and Peter Salter established an architectural practice, Macdonald + Salter, that never built anything but fully intended to. Their description of this project for the ICI Trade Pavilion at the Royal Agricultural Showground records the visceral reality of a day at the show: 'Prize bulls called by name over the tannoy and often as not calling back. Stomach overwhelmed by meat pies, milky tea and everywhere the crowd's exuberance. An armful of special offers: looking up and thinking that storm will surely be here soon. A day to remember.' The intensity of the experience is carried through into this drawing of the west elevation of their refreshments and entertainment pavilion. The crafted nature of the image is apparent: neat, ruled lines that are the product of parallel motion and adjustable set square are accompanied by deliberate wavers – not only in the naturalistic treatment of the heaped-up ground around the edges and the branches of surrounding trees, but also in the thin lines of the intricate window grilles and the elaborate columns. Places where mistakes have been scratched out with a razor blade and redrawn, tiny smudges and marks, all attest to the concentration and labour required to make such a drawing. Both architects taught at London's Architectural Association, with its strong workshop and making culture, and their drawings produced in response to this were influential. Macdonald and Salter's work was grounded in reality, depicting an attitude towards the elements of construction and a proliferation of details that bordered on a romantic fetishization of the art of building and inhabiting. Their work celebrated the complexities and difficulties of drawing with ink on paper: the compositions are deliberately complex; the line weights carefully chosen, and proliferating into an intensity of detail.

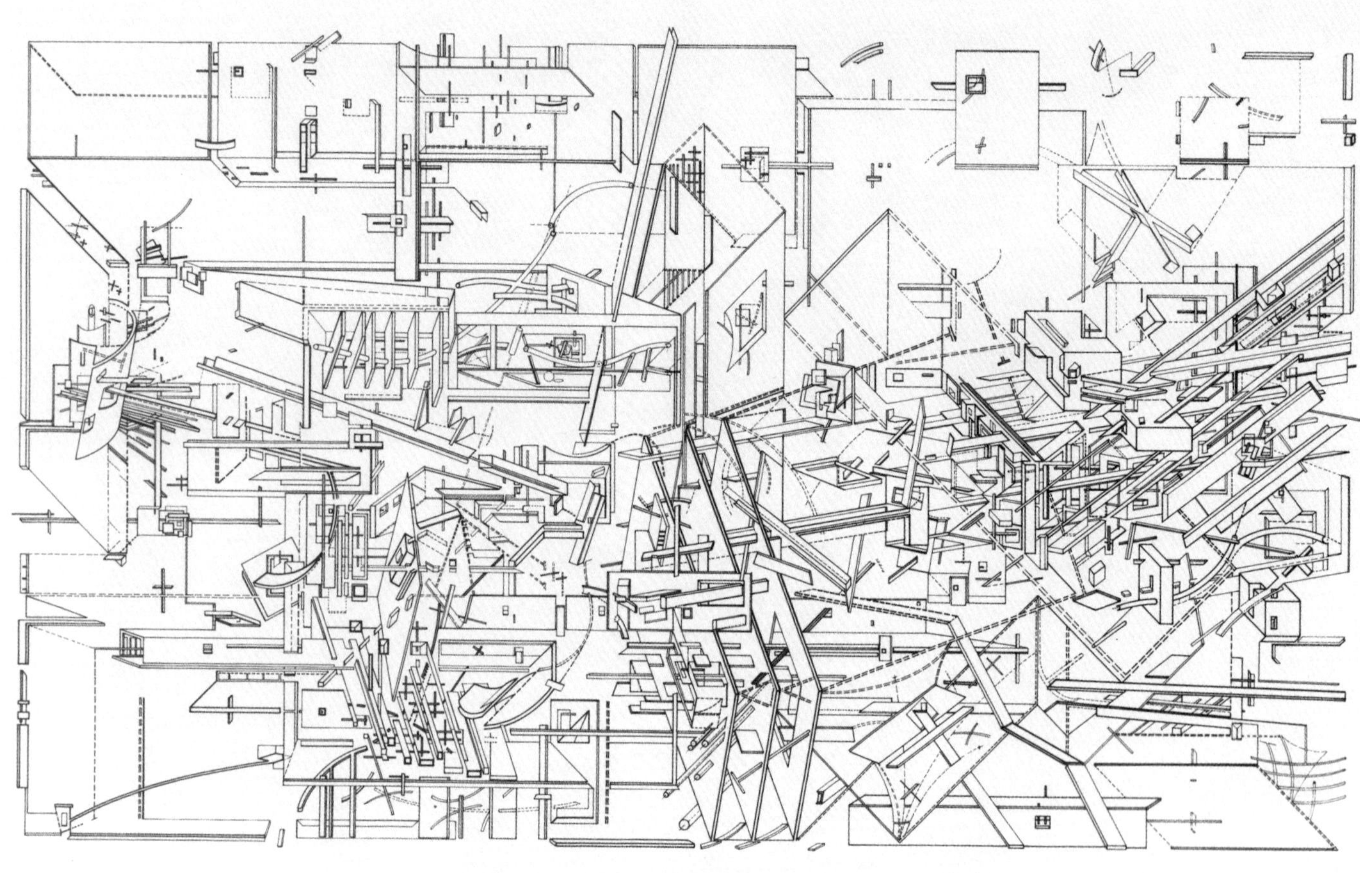

**DANIEL LIBESKIND (1946–)**

**Time Sections, 1979**

Silkscreen on paper

66 × 91.8 cm, 26 × 31 in

The career of Daniel Libeskind has two distinct parts. The latter part began with the completion of his first built project, Berlin's Jewish Museum, in 2001, and has produced numerous buildings. The first part, however, was entirely theoretical and concerned with the nature of architectural space and the fragmentation resulting from the subjective perception of inhabitation. In this, he was challenging architectural ideas that emerged during the Enlightenment, one of the results of which was the classification of knowledge that placed everything within a seemingly objective system. This rational approach became the basis of Modernist architecture, which in its attempts to assimilate the industrial world, subsumed the individual as a subject for architecture, unless they were rich, within the collective. These explorations were enacted through drawings, the majority belonging to two series: *Micromegas*, 1979 and *Chamber Works*, 1983. The *Micromegas* project, named after a short story by Voltaire, began with eleven pencil drawings that served as studies for a series of twelve prints. *Time Sections* is one of these prints, and its name reveals one of Libeskind's principal concerns about the nature and purpose of architectural drawings, which he saw not simply as graphic devices but 'as much a prospective unfolding of future possibilities as … a recovery of a particular history'. The rectangular drawing is almost completely framed by architectural elements drawn in axonometric, but within this frame the direction of their projection is inconsistent – some lean to the left, others to the right and a few of them are ambiguously flat. This variety of projections suggests the passage of time through movement, in the same way that Cubist paintings tried to show all sides of an ensemble of objects at once. Similarly, the drawing does not depict a single physical space or familiar architectural form but intends to define an architectural concept internal to itself, which Libeskind describes as 'more than a shadow of an object, more than a pile of lines, more than a resignation to the inertia of convention'.

**ANON**

**Headless statue of Gudea, c.2130 BC**

Carving into diorite stone

93 × 41 × 61 cm, 37 × 16 × 24 in

The earliest recognizable architectural plan is carved into the diorite-stone lap of a headless statue known as the *Architect with a Plan*. This material speaks of the importance of the statue, for diorite was known as a noble material for its durability and value. The figure was one of several excavated during the 1880s by French archaeologist Ernest de Sarzec from the Palace of Adad-nadin-ahhe in the modern-day Iraqi location of Telloh, also the modern Arabic name for the ancient Sumerian city of Girsu. Depicting the southern Mesopotamian ruler Gudea, it is one of a large number of statues that he commissioned in which he is shown either standing or sitting in front of the gods of his kingdom, Lagash. Gudea is shown here as the architect of the temple, or *Eninnu*, dedicated to his personal god, Ningirsu – one of the religious monuments that he built or restored during his twenty-year reign, c.2145–25 BC. The drawing is depicted on a stone tablet, and consists of an orthogonal projection of the windowless wall around Ningirsu's shrine, which would have been made of clay and brick. The smooth inner plane of the interior is supported by a regular rhythm of pilasters that act as buttresses and it is pierced by six narrow entrances, which attest to the fortified nature of the wall. The figure itself is covered with the longest known inscription in Sumerian; it reveals an account of the construction of the temple, including the geographical sources of the building materials – stones from northern Syria, cedars from Amanus and treasure confiscated in Elam, the two last-named locations in modern-day Turkey and Iran respectively.

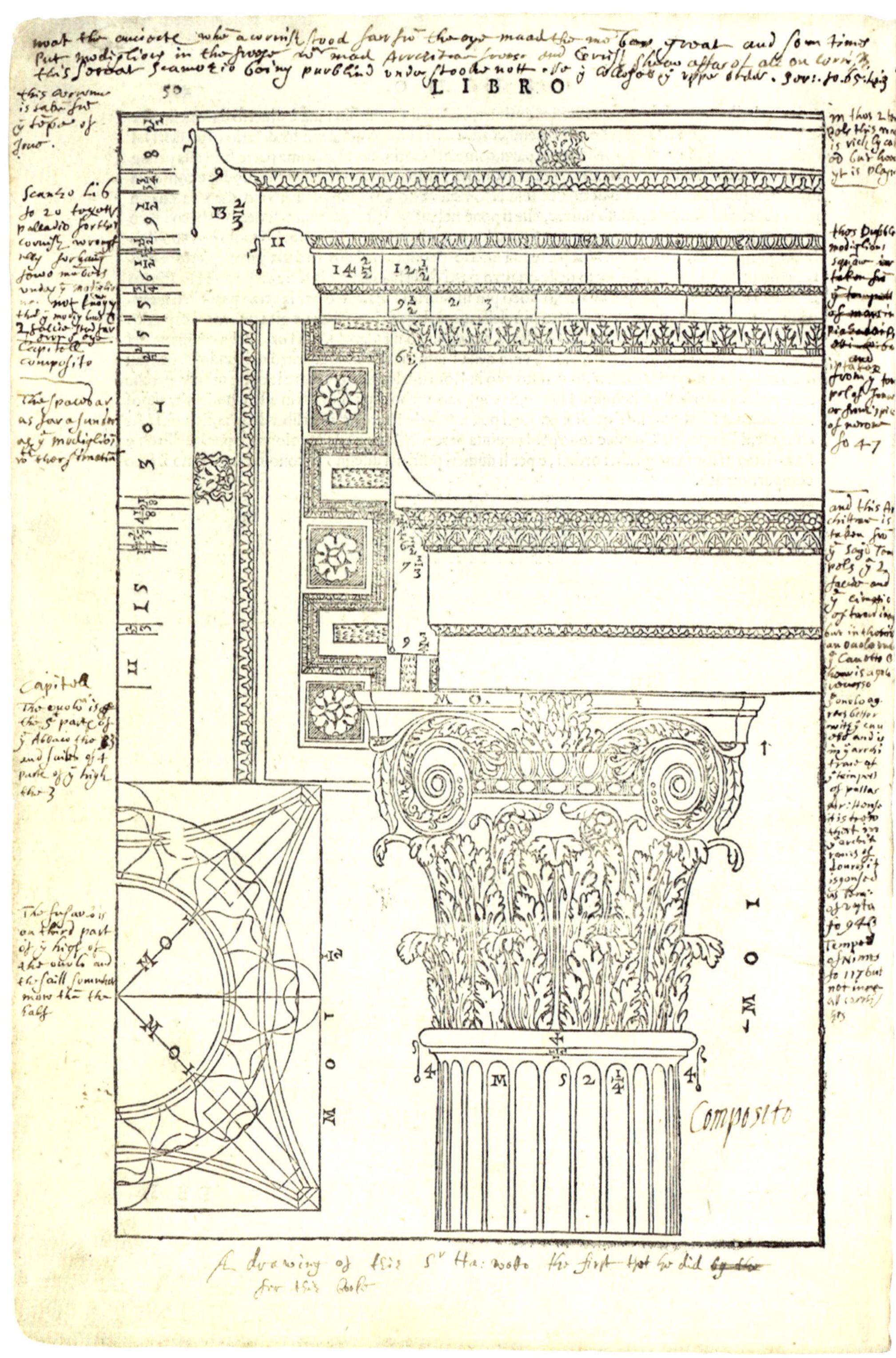


**INIGO JONES (1573–1652) AND ANDREA PALLADIO (1508–80)**

**Annotations on the Corinthian order, 1601**

Ink on paper

32 × 21 cm, 12½ × 8¼ in

Throughout his working life, beginning when he was still designing masques for the royal court, Inigo Jones maintained an intimate relationship with his copies of Andrea Palladio's *I quattro libri dell'architettura*, which was first published in 1570, three years before he was born. Since it was not translated into English, as *The Four Books of Architecture*, until the eighteenth century, Jones owned one of the early Italian versions – probably acquired on a trip to Italy after 1597 – which were printed in dark black ink and illustrated with fine woodcuts made after Palladio's own drawings on thin vellum. This page is taken from the first book's exploration of the five orders of architecture – in this case, the Corinthian – and around the edges are examples of the extensive marginalia that Jones added to Palladio's text. Here, the notes are fairly close to the subject illustrated, but as a whole they include doodles, translations, medical recipes and remedies, travel jottings and commentary. The second book discusses private town houses and country estates, almost all designed by Palladio and presented in plan, section and uprights or elevations. The third book illustrates streets, bridges, piazzas and basilicas, most of ancient Roman origin, and the fourth analyzes ancient Roman temples, including the Pantheon. Palladio's treatise on architecture was disseminated throughout Europe, reaching America by the end of the eighteenth century and introducing architects and patrons to Palladianism, which formed a compelling basis for subsequent Classical revivals. In Britain, Jones was the first architect to formally introduce the Classical architecture of Rome and the Italian Renaissance, inspired by Palladio and his own travels in Italy.

**THOMAS JEFFERSON (1743–1826)**

**Monticello, 1771**

Brown ink on laid paper

35.6 × 48.9 cm, 14 × 19.3 in

Thomas Jefferson, third president of the United States, spent over forty years experimenting with architectural ideas through the construction and reconstruction of his Neo-Classical house on a hilltop site called Monticello, on his family estate in Charlottesville, Virginia. This conventional drawing shows the final elevation of the house's first version, begun in 1769 when he was twenty-six and had not yet visited Europe. Jefferson was a self-taught architect, and this design is influenced by his reading on Neo-Classicism and the work of Andrea Palladio – whose *Four Books of Architecture*, via the influence of British Neo-Classicist James Gibbs – were a primary source of inspiration for Monticello. Showing Jefferson's attention to detail, this elevation is drawn precisely to scale. Composed around a central, two-storey portico, it is topped by a pediment, which was never finished. Two curious chimneys are placed at either side of the pediment, which although symmetrical present a challenge to the Classical design. The four columns – Ionic above, Doric below – divide the entrance into three bays. While the doors and windows, with their triangular motifs on the first floor, echo the porch's pediment, the lintels over the doorway and ground-floor windows reflect the continuous entablature above. The flanking bays are simple, and the drawing does not show the semi-octagonal bays of the plan, drawn at the same time, which were a characteristic Jeffersonian motif. Jefferson embraced Neo-Classicism as an appropriate architectural style for the new American nation. Between 1785 and 1789, he was located in Paris as United States Minister to France, and took the opportunity to visit buildings that he had previously only seen in books. Seven years after returning, he began radical alterations to the house, testing new ideas that were carried through in projects such as the University of Virginia at Charlottesville, whose library had a domed rotunda based on the Pantheon in Rome.

**ANON**

**Stark von Röckenhof Town House, c.1530**

Pen, ink and watercolour

55.8 × 42.3 cm, 22 × 16¾ in

Vibrant with colour, this unusual elevation drawing accurately employs the sophisticated technique of single-point perspective to suggest another world beyond the plane of the facade, one that does not correspond with the everyday reality suggested by the heavy, wooden street door at ground level. It shows the fantastical effect seen in trompe-l'oeil murals called *Lüftlmalerei* that were typical in southern Germany and Austria at the time. This mural was commissioned by Ulrich Stark III, of the aristocratic Stark von Röckenhof family, between 1521 and 1528. Their multi-storey town house was located in Weinmarkt, Nuremberg, close to the Church of Saint Sebaldus, and the murals were inspired by the paintings of Albrecht Dürer on the city's town hall, completed in 1521. It is not easy, however, to distinguish between the real and the fictional. The street facade here is divided into four by square stone pillars, and two red columns with Corinthian capitals flank the doorway. Blank walls pierced by small and mysterious windows span the other spaces between the piers that are topped by a cornice line upon which lions prowl and Neptune slaughters a sea monster. A flat and inky blackness permeates the space behind. Above, a detailed rendition of inscrutable bottle-glass windows hides the transition from this terrible realm to the sunny landscape that unfolds above the pink and blue, panelled balustrade – along which pairs of young men, one of whom is Holy Roman Emperor Maximilian I, and one woman are engaged in discourse. This is terminated at the top by another strip of windows alternating with small balconies, and the timber underside of this narrow gallery that belongs firmly to the world of the street anchors the frame to the magical scene behind. Glimpses of hybrid structures, part-Classical and reminiscent of large church furniture, are bathed in a lucid Mediterranean light.

**PAUL KLEE (1879–1940)**

**Architecture, 1923**

Oil painting on burlap

58 × 39 cm, 22¾ × 15¼ in

Paul Klee's *Magic Squares* series was inspired by a 1914 visit to Tunisia, where he began to abstract the landscapes that he saw, with his stranger's eyes, into compositions broken down into squares of different hues. At the time he wrote, 'The colour possesses me. There is no need to try to grasp it. It possesses me ... the colour and I are one.' Representing mosaics, the reduction of the painterly surface into the basic element of the square allowed the close juxtaposition of discrete colour fields that were given equivalence in size and position, whereas in a conventional image they would be blended and proportioned according to an interpretation of reality. Colour theory became the basis of Klee's teaching at the Bauhaus in Weimar and Dessau between 1920 and 1931, and in the *Magic Squares* series he experimented with the dynamic transitions identified in his colour wheel. An analogy has been made between the *Magic Squares* and the system of twelve tones invented by Arnold Schönberg in 1923, the same year that Klee painted *Architecture*, based on the numbering system that he used to define proportions of colour intensity and hue. In *Architecture*, Klee reinterprets the application of chiaroscuro into a fractured approach, using the rhythmic repetition of the squares to gradually create the sense of light penetrating into a dark urban space. A strong vertical rhythm is created by a faceting of the lower rows, so that light appears to reflect off one side, with shadow cast on the other. Towards the top, these implied structures smooth out into a flatter field, like a facade, and culminate in bright triangles – one yellow and one white, which seem to glow. Other rows terminate less strongly, petering out towards the horizon and suggesting a far distance as their size decreases.

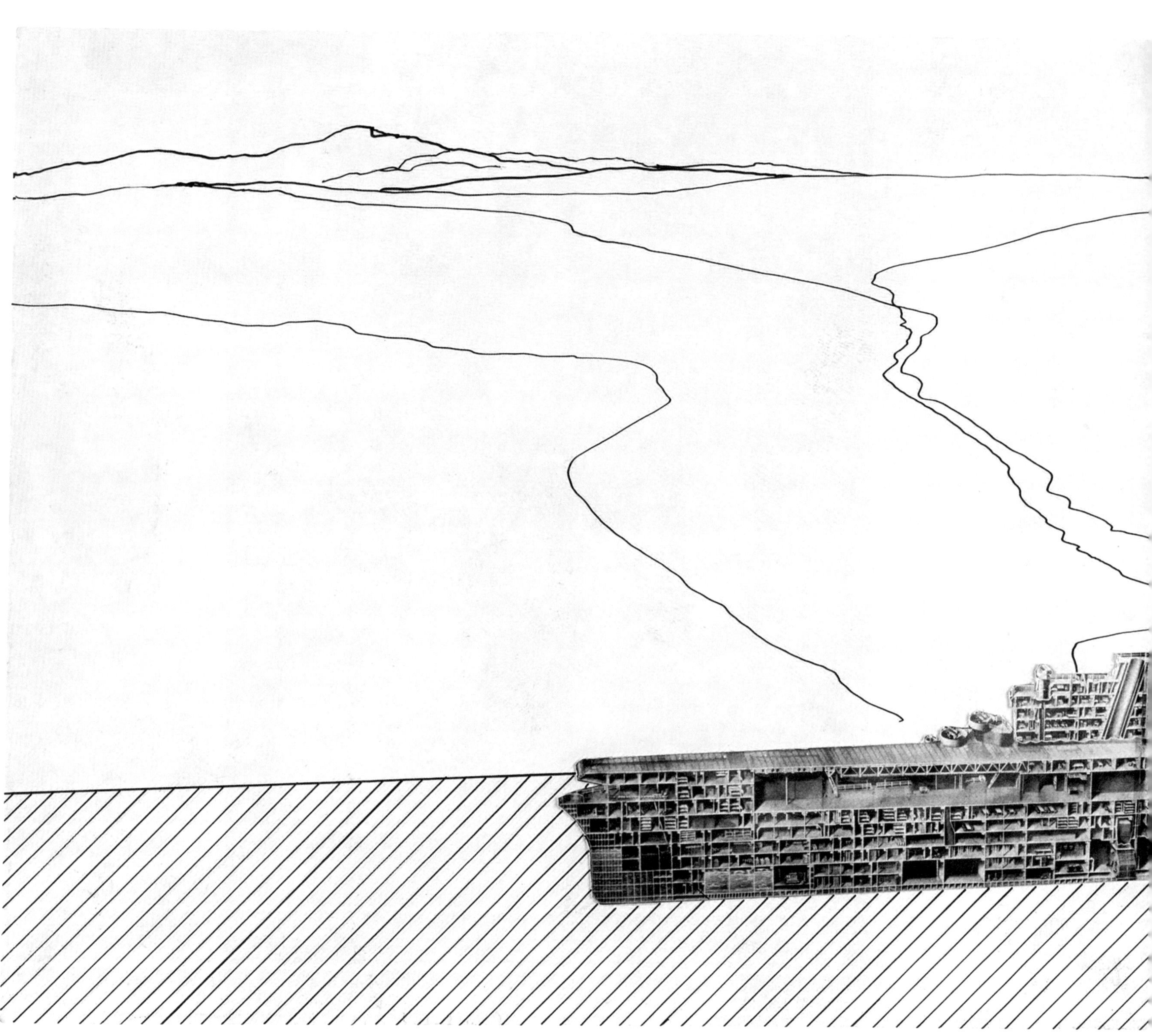

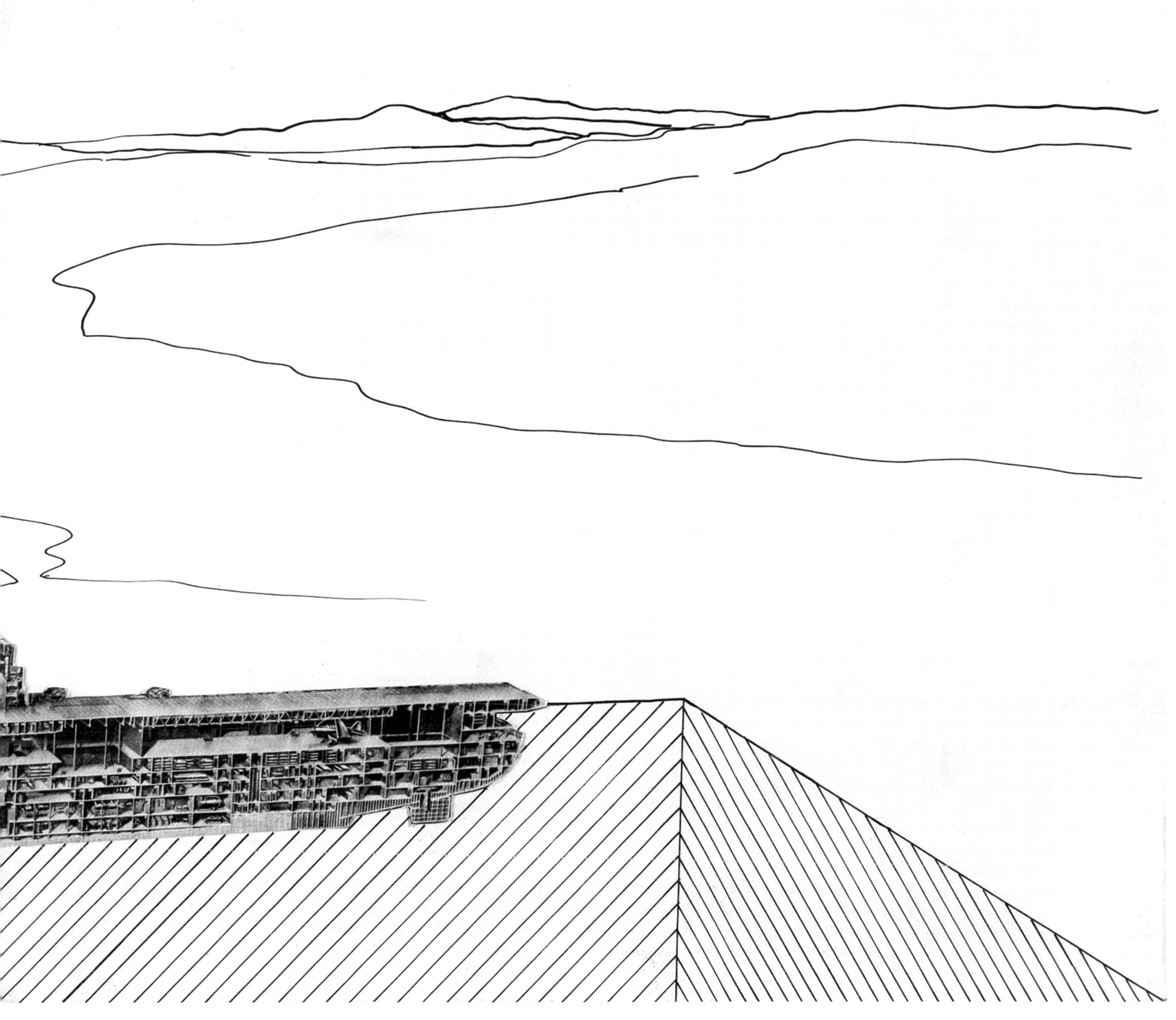

**HANS HOLLEIN (1934–2014)**

**Aircraft Carrier in Landscape, 1964**

Cut-and-pasted reproduction and ink on glazed paper

21.6 × 100 cm, 8½ × 39 in

The young Hans Hollein proposed that 'everything is architecture', and made his mark with a series of avant-garde photomontages called *Transformations*, completed between 1963 and 1968. In these, he used images of machined objects, such as sparkplugs, an aircraft carrier and a car grille – all products of twentieth-century technology – as symbols of a pure, absolute architecture. This section combines a line drawing in ink with a cut-out photographic image of an aircraft carrier the size of, and analogous to, a village – its scale and intention sympathetic with the megastructural ideas of Hollein's Metabolist contemporaries in Japan. In both countries, large expanses of urban territory had been devastated by wartime bombing, and here Hollein treats the rural landscape as a place for action. The land is seen as barren, empty and unused – an aesthetic condition that could exist anywhere – rather than a useful agricultural resource. The aircraft carrier is situated at the front of the drawing and embedded into the ground so that its deck is the datum. The cut-through earth is represented with neat diagonal lines and becomes the ocean, but the edge of the ship lies on the banks of a wide river that makes a sweeping curve as it flows by. The edges of the river's wide valley are marked by low hills on the horizon. The vast, exposed internal volume of the monumental object is subdivided into small, cellular spaces, with long, communal spaces just below ground level serving the role of village square, church and town hall combined. Hollein is making a critique of Modernist architecture and the consequences of twentieth-century technology on various levels. By using a ship, he refers to Le Corbusier's advocacy of the cruise liner as architecture par excellence – siteless, autonomous and nomadic.

**MASSIMO SCOLARI (1943–)**

**Addio Melampo, 1975**

Coloured ink, watercolour and graphite on board

30.2 × 25.4 cm, 12 × 10 in

In this drawing, a cluster of fantasy architectural forms emerges from a transparent pyramid, but their nature is obscure – either they have each been projected at different angles or they are strangely aligned. Some of the longer forms seem distorted by perspective, but this must be their actual shape. This mysterious quality could be explained by the title – *Addio Melampo*, or goodbye Melampus – with its cultural references cited as a dog in a nineteenth-century Italian poem or a character in Greek mythology. Massimo Scolari belies this careful, imaginative forethought, however, when he extols the medium of watercolour for the way it responds to speed of thought and to sudden afterthoughts. The colour spreads over the paper, he says, as the light is progressively extinguished. This perfectly rendered image of an imaginary landscape, with the natural and the archaeological blending into each other, is made using his characteristic ink and watercolour. The white, which here shines through in the carved pyramids of the middle ground, comes from the paper, he says, and the glimmers of light not preserved disappear in subsequent washes. In this work he has manipulated these layers to explore the pale light of a winter's day. According to Scolari, his watercolours are deliberately small, allowing maximum control of the images as they develop. Designed for publication, they are conceived as pages of a book, intended for life-sized or slightly reduced reproduction. Scolari was also fascinated by the practice of oblique drawing. More commonly described as isometric, this employs a vertical plane measured up from a plan, usually to the same scale, which is set at an angle so as to reveal the three-dimensionality of a volume or building.

**MARION MAHONY GRIFFIN (1871–1961)**

**Section B-A Northerly Side of Water Axis, 1912**

Ink, watercolour, gouache and gold oil paint on linen

One of 4 drawings forming a 6 m-long (13 ft) panorama

Architect Marion Mahony Griffin worked for fifteen years in the office of Frank Lloyd Wright from 1895, and during that time produced over half of the drawings that helped to make Wright famous in Europe when they were reproduced in the Berlin-published *Wasmuth Portfolio*, 1910. Traces of the techniques of these drawings can be seen in the watercolour perspectives that she prepared for an international competition to design the new Australian capital of Canberra with her partner Walter Burley Griffin. Influenced by Japanese woodblock painting, their controlled and intricate lines trace foliage and buildings that coexist together; the natural is defined by a freehand outline, and the man-made by orthogonal construction. The dramatic and stylized depictions of landscapes that she developed in Wright's studio influenced her approach to these huge drawings, in which the natural world dominates. Set against a deep, horizontal band blocked out in gold oil paint that runs along the whole length of the panorama, the silhouette of Black Mountain fills the centre of the composition and pierces the band of gold to rise above the line of inhabitation. The hill forms the backdrop for the new city's buildings, which are strung out along the shores of one of the urban lakes that the Griffins incorporated into their plan in order to temper its powerful geometries. Buildings and foliage are drawn with an equivalent fine line, and the buildings are washed with the white ground that can be seen on some of Wright's Prairie School drawings, giving them a ghostly appearance but allowing the detail of their facades to stand out. The city's reflection gives the composition a stabilizing symmetry as it melts into the waters of the lake, in which an echo of the golden horizon faintly shimmers.

**LEBBEUS WOODS (1940–2012)**

**Terrain, 1999**

Electrostatic print with felt-tipped pen, ink and coloured pencil on paper with sanding

49.2 × 59.4 cm, 19½ × 23½ in

This drawing, called *Terrain*, relates to a group of intricate models of the same name that Lebbeus Woods made in 2003 in collaboration with Dwayne Oyler, which translated his two-dimensional explorations into a three-dimensional installation, taking the form of a dense construction of tiny polystyrene planes that were confined within vitrine-like frames. In his practice, Woods chose to eschew the practical task of constructing buildings, concentrating instead on the dissemination of his distinctive drawings through architectural publications and pamphlets, in order to communicate his reimagining of the modern world and its environments. Often concerned with the destructive forces at work in the world, and with reinterpreting their creative potential, his work framed critiques of the destruction of Sarajevo in *War and Architecture*, 1993, for example, or the project *San Francisco: Inhabiting the Quake*, from 1995. The *Terrain* project grew out of Woods' sketchbooks and drawings, and this image is an electrostatic print of one of these, enhanced with felt-tipped pen, ink and coloured pencil. Split in two, its top half contains a framed line drawing showing many splintered planes writhing together as if part of a cataclysmic geology that nevertheless has an underlying, hierarchical system – like a tree or a crystal. Connecting the top with the bottom half of the sheet, an inset box frames a detail, seemingly of a different drawing, in which an architecture of posts and platforms emerges from the chaos. Below, a carefully ruled zone contains an overlapping composition of conventional text; two rectangular frames, out of which various doodles spring; and a grid of numbers that melts into the text. Together, these form a characteristic Woodsian accumulation that transmits the sense of a mutating dynamic form following a mysterious logic, in order to create a provocative landscape of the imagination.

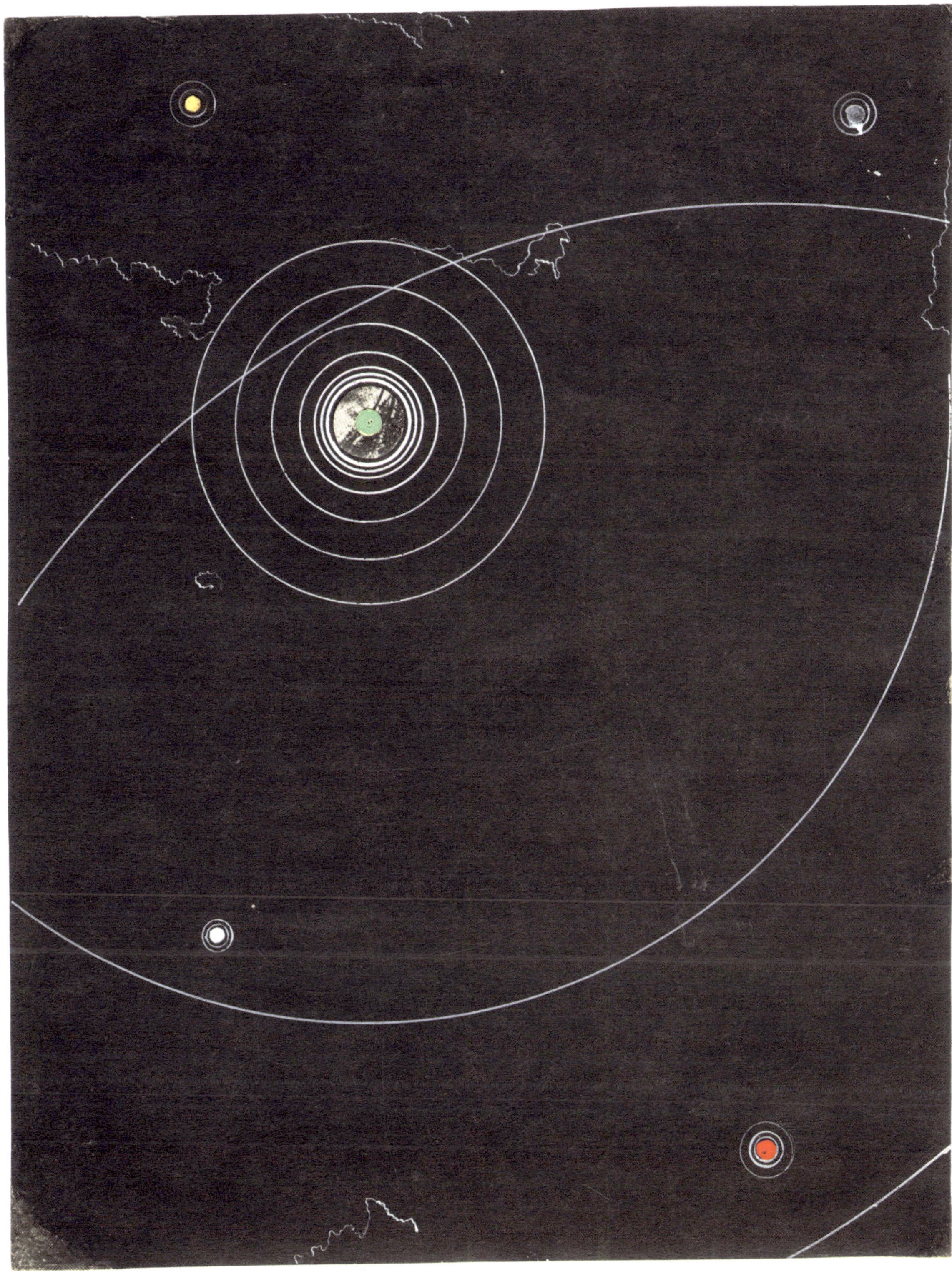

**IVAN LEONIDOV (1902–59)**

**Schema of Spatial Culture-Organization, 1928**

Ink on paper

48.5 × 38 cm, 19 × 15 in

This mysterious drawing, which Russian architect Ivan Leonidov presented as illustrating his workers' club design, caused ripples when it was shown at the First Congress of Constructivist Architects in Moscow in 1929. Formally, it challenged the conventions of Constructivist architectural and artistic practice in its lack of functional specificity; programmatically, it raised provocative questions about the role of Soviet cultural life within the regime. It did not look like architecture at all. At this early stage of his career, in which he built very little but produced many theoretical projects and competition entries, Leonidov's work was strictly defined by two characteristics – a reduced visual palette of monochrome graphics using ink on paper, and the circle as a formal generator. For Leonidov, this device could both sustain iconographic and conceptual power and generate the planar and volumetric geometries that concerned him. His project for a Club of a New Social Type comprised a pair of parabolic domes, a wide plinth and a series of cubic volumes in what was essentially a park-like arrangement that would contain various cultural and educational facilities – including a planetarium instead of a theatre, thereby elevating science above dramatic entertainment. This drawing, which is difficult to read in any conventional terms, shows a scheme for social organization and media infrastructure, rather than an architectural composition. The diagram of segmental arcs that radiate across an almost blank landscape represent electromagnetic radio waves, and an absolute idea about space and distance is replaced by the abstract idea of signal strength. The buildings appear as nodes on the black plane, each one given a significance equal to its potential for dissemination – but the representation of a material reality was not the point; these were orientation points within a vast realm, rather than buildings.

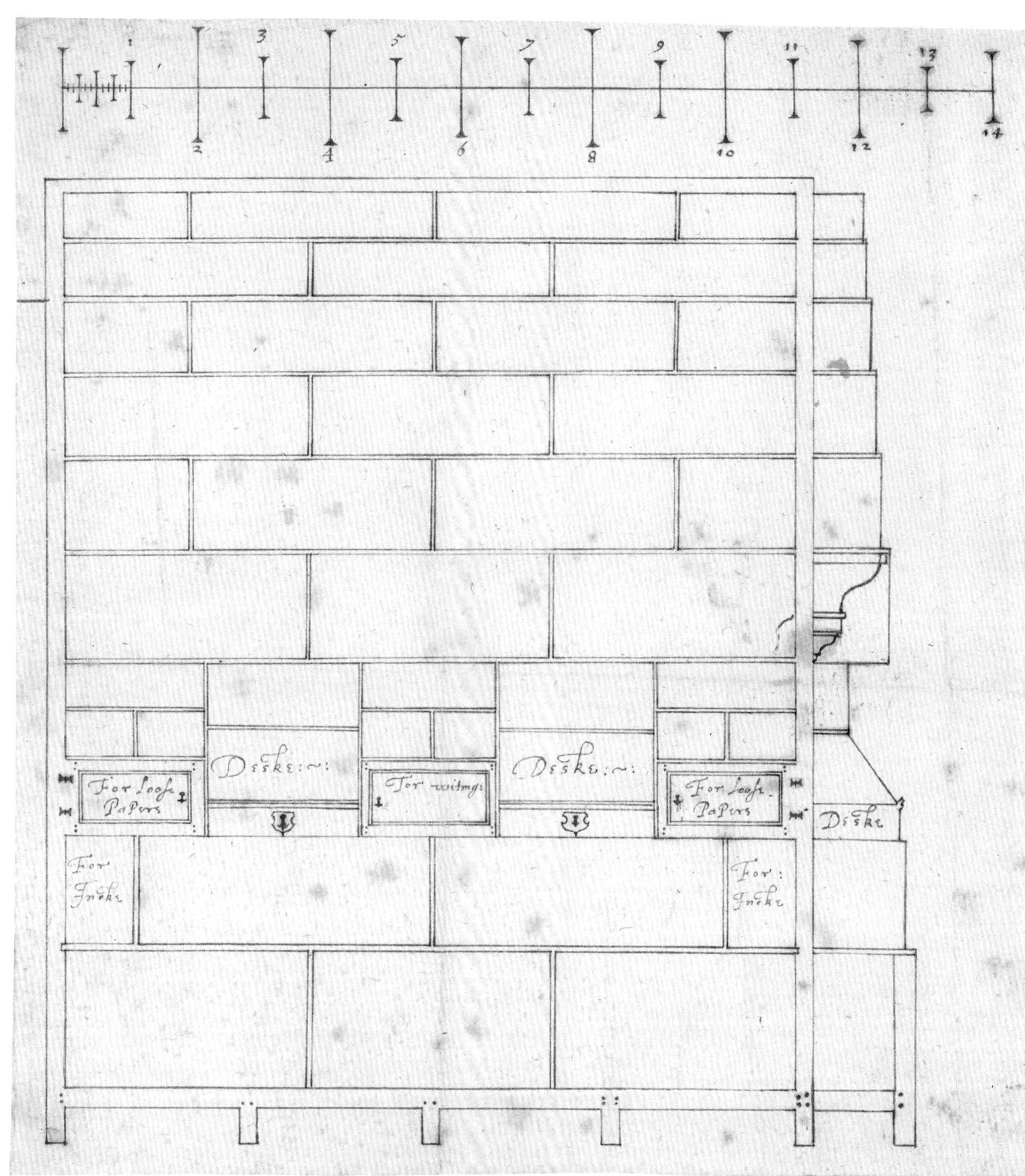


**ROBERT SMYTHSON (c.1535–1614)**

**Design for a closet, 1580**

Ink on paper

21 × 29.7 cm, 8 × 11 in

Detailed building drawings such as this are unusual survivors from the Elizabethan era. At that time, large commissions for religious buildings and great houses were undertaken by hierarchical teams of peripatetic craftsmen. Made by skilled masons and carpenters, the drawings showed details like balustrades or formed elevations – uprights, as they were called – for stone or timber constructions. Robert Smythson was a master mason, leading one such team. Having learnt his trade at Longleat House, 1568, he supervised design and construction at Wollaton Hall, 1580–88, and other houses, interpreting the spreading influence of Italian Renaissance architecture through a consumate knowledge of his craft, his gift for order and a sense of rhythm. His upright of a closet – a small room for estate business or a study – is a setting-out drawing to coordinate the different elements of a relatively complex construction where the trades of carpentry and masonry coincided. It is drawn accurately, to a scale shown at the top of the sheet – but its units, although probably feet, are not immediately apparent. Similarly, the drawing's conventions make its information ambiguous. The upright is contained by a frame that looks to be made from timber, with joists under floorboards supporting it, but there is no section line confirming this. Outside this frame, on the right-hand side, is a profile corresponding to the elevation, which could also be a section. The elevation incorporates two inset writing desks, and the section appears to be cut through one of the desks. The lip of its drawer is elaborated, but the lintel above is not shown in elevation. These inconsistencies call into question the construction material itself. The divisions between blocks are probably mortar joints; their equivalence to the carpentry of the desks, however, suggests that this could be an elaborate carpentry-shelf system lining the room.

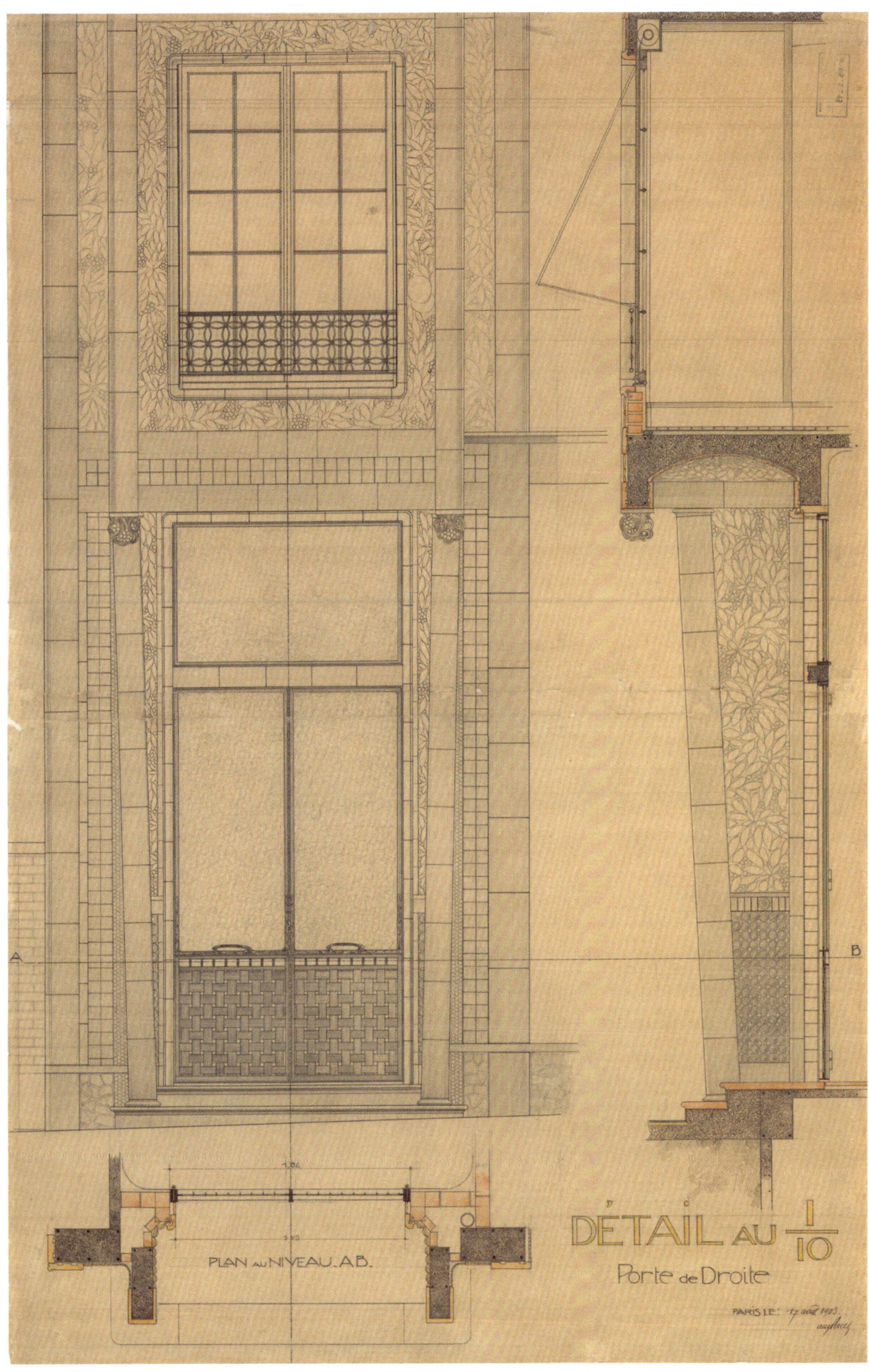


**AUGUSTE PERRET (1874–1954)**

**25 bis rue Franklin, 1903**

Ink and pencil on paper

50.5 × 32.5 cm, 20 × 12¾ in

This drawing illustrates how, by the start of the twentieth century, patented construction systems were being used by talented architects like Auguste Perret. The apartment block on rue Franklin was Perret's first work to fully express its concrete frame, which can be seen in this illustrative detail of a window bay on the front facade. Showing, at the same scale, an elevation alongside a section through the window, as well as a plan underneath the elevation and aligned with it, the sheet illustrates the bay's full construction. Reinforced-concrete elements are shaded black, and the projecting columns around the windowsill are clear in plan.

In section, a coffered beam supports the projecting floor above, and the concrete sill projects below. The expression of the frame on the facade is representational: a distinction is made between the plain terracotta tiles that clad its surface and the flamboyant sunflower-pattern infill, with a more robust studded surface below. The articulation of the frame shown in this drawing has the characteristics of timber construction, an impression reinforced by the addition of a boss applied to the cantilever, visible on both the elevation and the section, which reveals how Perret's formal interpretation of the concrete frame drew on existing constructional traditions. By 1897, French engineer François Hennebique had patented a system of reinforced-concrete construction that greatly increased the possible heights of buildings, spans of beams and flexibility of structural systems. Contemporaneously, new materials such as Alexandre Bigot's patent ceramic tiles – used by Perret to clad the facades of 25 bis rue Franklin – were meeting the requirements of stringent building regulations. Perret's accomplished experiments with these innovative techniques influenced his student Le Corbusier and provided the model for many Modernist concrete buildings.

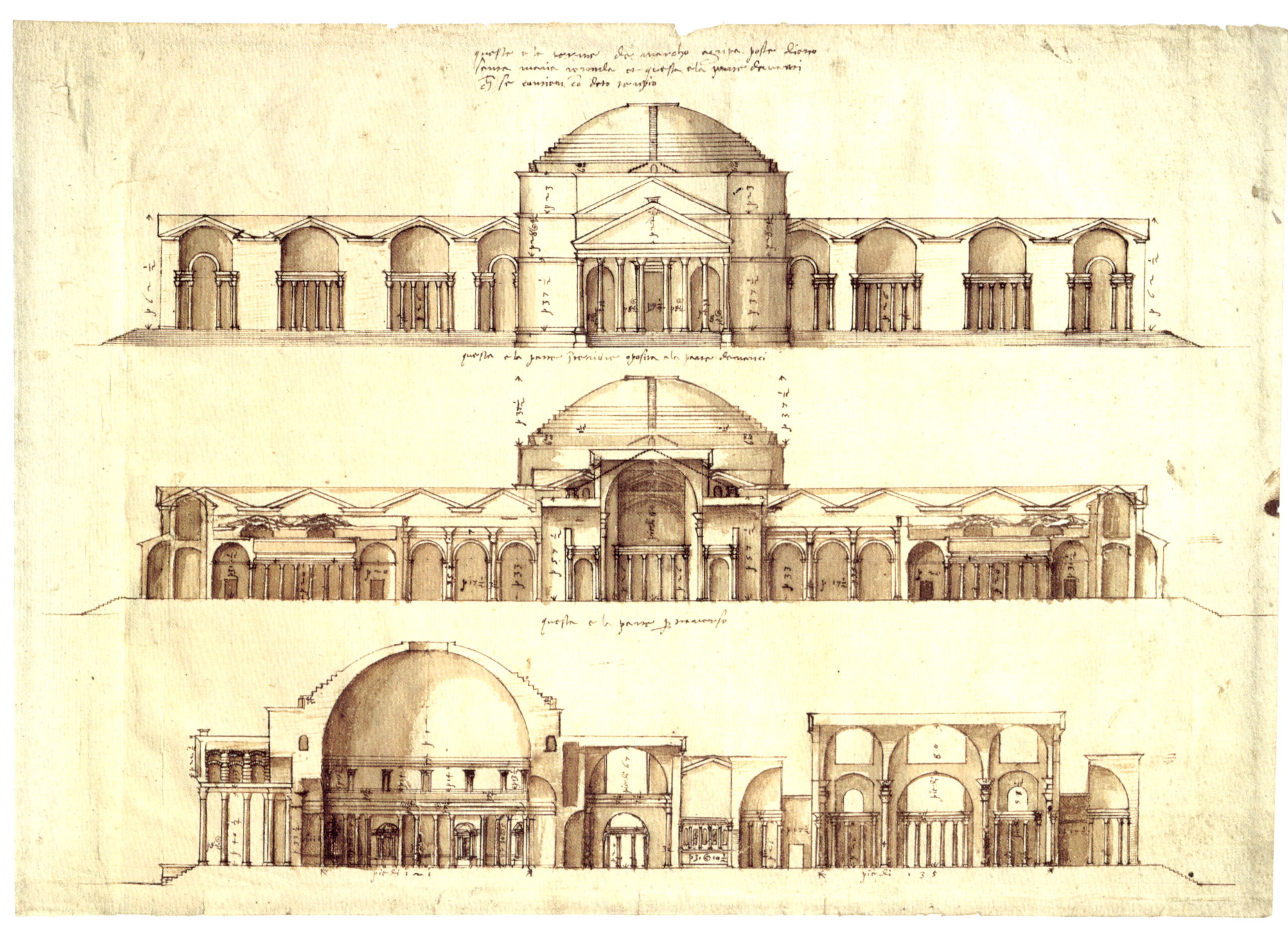

**ANDREA PALLADIO (1508–80)**

**Baths of Agrippa, c.1550**

Ink and coloured pencil on paper

28.6 × 41.8 cm, 11¼ × 16½ in

The elevation and sections of Andrea Palladio's imaginative, idealized reconstruction of the Baths of Agrippa are emboldened by strong contrasts of colour, light and shade created through the skilful use of ink washes. This both increases the spatial depth of the flat planes and enhances the rhythmic sequences of the north facade's portico and niches, and the interior rooms and colonnades. The Roman Baths of Agrippa, which were destroyed by fire in AD 80, had been constructed around 25–12 BC, to the south of the original Agrippan Pantheon and Basilica of Neptune, and had been influential in the development of the Classical imperial bath systems. Although invented, Palladio's reconstruction is based on a deep knowledge of the archaeological site gained through making a large and accurate survey plan during a visit to Rome. In the upper two drawings, the compositions are symmetrical, but in the lower section, a harmonious relationship between the different parts is maintained through balancing two equal but different volumes. On the right is an interpretation of the Pantheon of Hadrian; on the left is the Basilica of Neptune. Above the elevation, Palladio writes that these are the Baths of Marcus Agrippa behind Santa Maria Rotonda (the Pantheon). In his proposal, wide lateral wings with suites of changing rooms flank the Pantheon. The section from the south, the middle drawing, shows small heated rooms at the edges, with two courtyards containing open pools. The bottom section shows the relationship between the entrance portico, seen on the elevation leading into the Pantheon that is connected by a high hall to the Basilica behind, and its auxiliary bays and vaulted niches, influenced by the Baths of Diocletian and Caracalla. The composition of the whole complex is unified by the building being placed on a high platform.

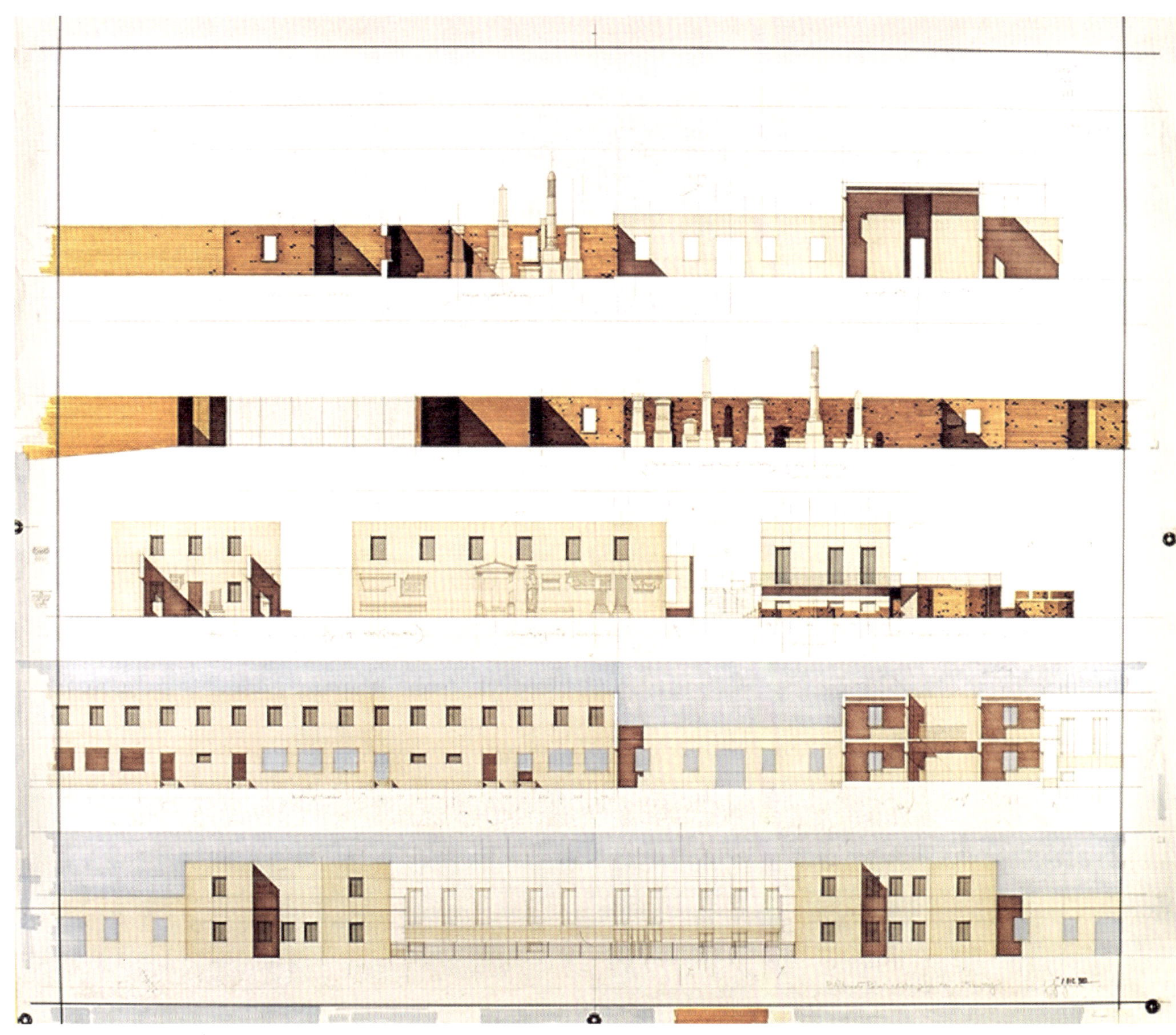

**GIORGIO GRASSI (1935–)**

**Prinz Albrecht Palais, 1984**

Pencil and colour washes on paper

16 × 19 cm, 6¼ × 7½ in

This sheet is one of several containing a series of study sketches in elevation by Giorgio Grassi for the Prinz Albrecht Palais, 1737–39, located in Kreuzberg, Berlin. The three-storey Prinz Albrecht Palais complex, with its large courtyard and extensive gardens, had been destroyed in an air strike in November 1944. Involving both the reconstruction of the complex and the recomposition of the ruins inside the perimeter of the block, the challenge of this project was to address a principal preoccupation of post-war German architecture: how to rebuild. For the Italian Grassi – a member of the Neo-Rationalist Tendenza movement, and a theorist as much as a practising architect – this project was an opportunity to test out ideas about authenticity and artificiality in the relationship between antiquity and the past, the pre-existing and the present, which permeated his work. In these elevational studies – drawn not freehand but meticulously, in hard line pencil, with the proportion lines set out underneath the frame of the drawing – vivid colour washes make apparent the relationship between void and solid. Severe shadow lines indicate the modulation of the facades. Only the existing archaeology – the crumbling brickwork of the walls, and the shapes of monumental tombs and obelisks – deviates in representation from the unadorned lines of the rest of the drawing. Delicate railings are the only proposed elements to be drawn with finely repeated lines. The new additions introduce a new density of construction, which is reduced to two storeys in order to maintain a close link to the park inside the perimeter.

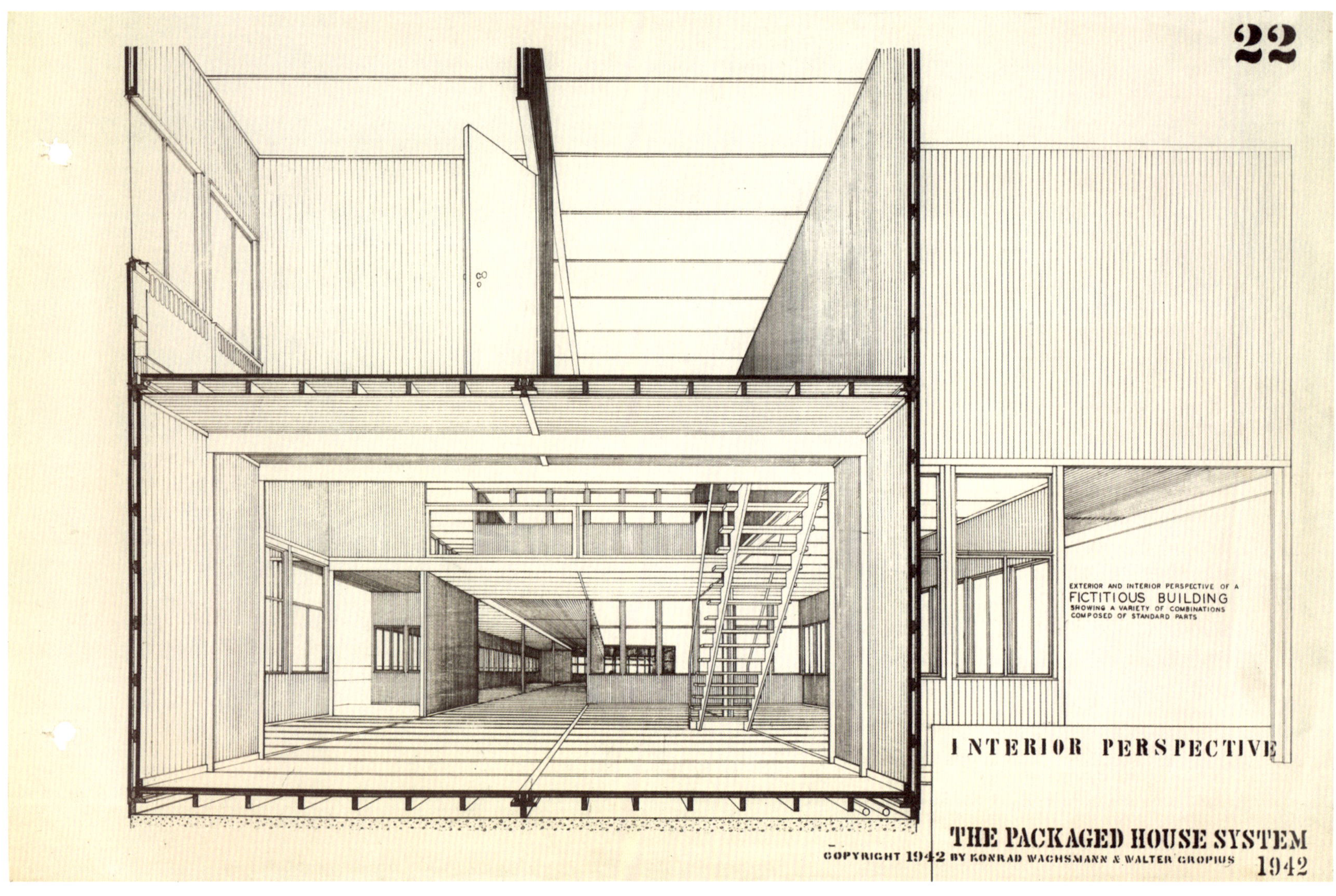


**WALTER GROPIUS (1883–1969)**

**The Packaged House System, 1942**

Ink and pencil on paper

21 × 29.7 cm, 8 × 11 in

Walter Gropius and Konrad Wachsmann, both recently exiled from Germany to America, began collaborating at the end of 1941 on a project for industrialized, modular housing that became known as the Packaged House System. Although their scheme for a factory-built, flexible system was widely promoted in the contemporary architectural press, and funding was forthcoming, the venture collapsed in the 1950s after producing only a small number of houses. This single-point, sectional perspective shows a splendidly spacious individual house composed from the prefabricated system, its accommodation burrowing deep into the surface of the picture plane and framed by the meticulously drawn structural section. The sectional cut projects beyond the elevation of a wing that is visible on the right-hand side of the drawing, and a note describes it as a fictional building showing a variety of combinations composed of standard parts. This illustrates the modular nature of the system, which allowed accommodation to be added as required to the periphery of a long, timber-framed rectangular volume. The drawing emphasizes the slenderness of the structural elements and the screen-like nature of the internal and external walls. Their lightness and refined proportions, combined with the deliberate transparency of the ladder-like stair and the screens between the open-plan spaces, evoke the elegance of a Japanese pavilion. Although shown on other plans of the system, no foundations are depicted for the house here, which is unconvincingly supported on a flat ground by small steel sections. Other factors suggest that the drawing was made for poetic rather than constructional effect: the building is uninsulated, both at ground level and within the walls, and the roof structure is vague, having the appearance of a flat, translucent surface rather than the robust, protective shelter that would be required against the often harsh climate of inland United States.

**JAMES GOWAN (1923–2015)**

**Housing at East Hanningfield, 1975**

Colour print

30.5 × 38.2 cm, 12 × 15 in

This presentation drawing, made by James Gowan, symbolizes and celebrates his interpretation of the prosaic in his 1978 project for ninety-eight council homes in the village of East Hanningfield. It is a section through one of the houses, dismantled to reveal all the different elements that go into its highly standardized construction – the most commonly used form of building for housing at the time. It flouts convention in depicting neither a coherent and continuous building envelope nor spatial qualities. Only fragments are revealed, and the logic underlying their inclusion is not clear – a lavatory seems to be located outside, for example. The explanation of the interior space hinges on the stove, which can be seen both beyond the stairs in section and located under two wide windows in an elevation alongside. The section comprises brightly coloured elements of red, yellow, green and blue that highlight the various assembly phases, which would have been carried out by different subcontractors. Each colour represents a building material with its trade: yellow for the carpentry of the roof trusses and the staircase, red for tiles or brick, blue for cast materials like steel and ceramic, and green for concrete. All of these material elements are prefabricated, apart from the ground slab that is shown in the garage, and so what is important is the process of their assembly. The section also transmits other information about the building – for example, the round window is one of the project's identifiable forms and a key compositional element of the drawing. It is echoed in the circular framed details, the radii of the door swings, and the movement of the windows in the roof and the attic hatch. The monopitched roof provides a loft for storage, and challenges the Modernist orthodoxy of the flat roof.

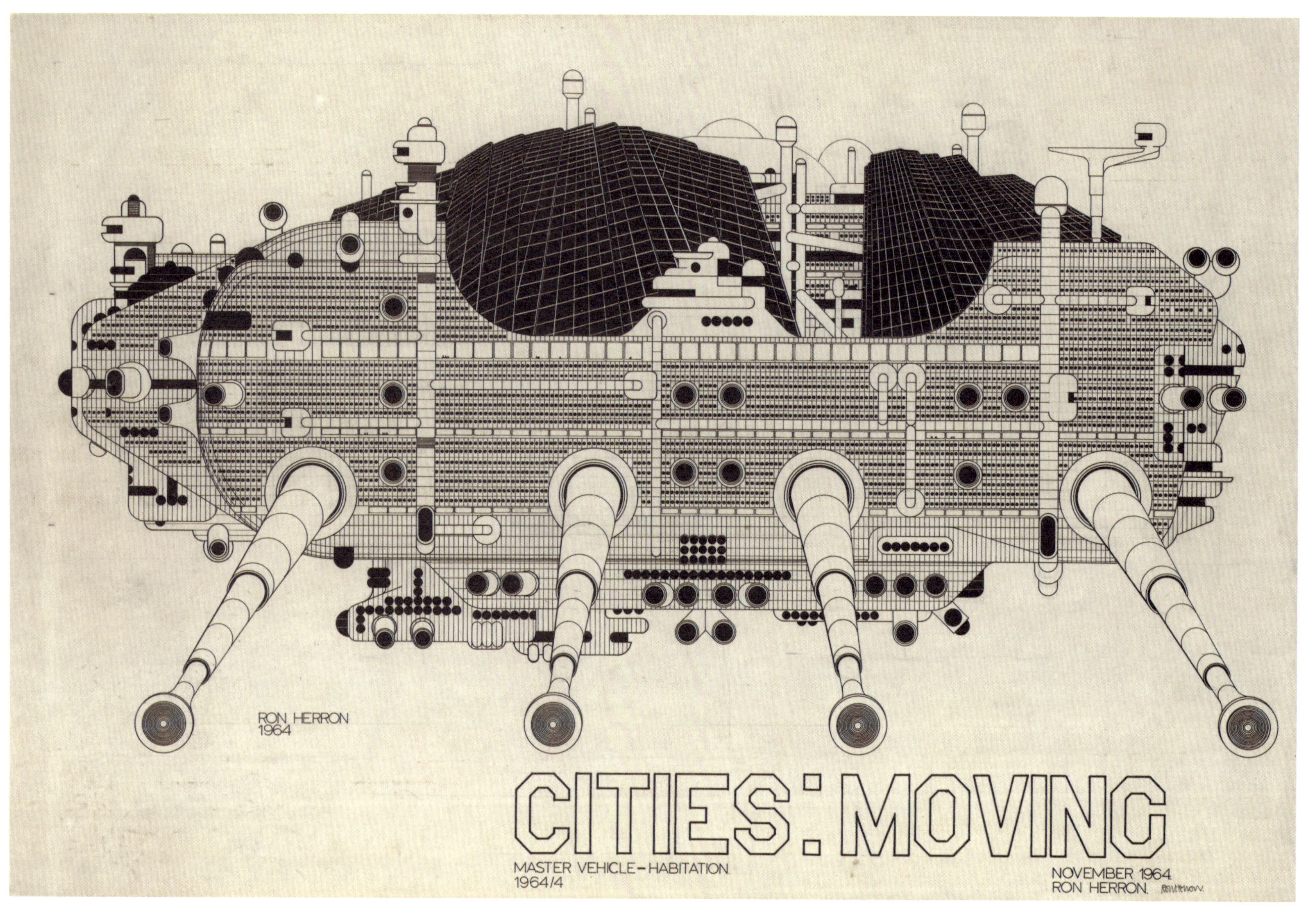


**RON HERRON (1930–94)**

**Cities: Moving, Master Vehicle-Habitation project, 1964**

Ink and graphite on tracing paper

55.2 × 83.2 cm, 21¾ × 32¾ in

Ron Herron's image of a Master Vehicle is presented as a portrait from an already existing reality – a fully resolved and functioning machine in a handbook of technical drawings. The title of this intricate line drawing clearly states that it belongs to a project called *Cities: Moving* that became known later as the *Walking City*, depicted stalking across the ruined post-nuclear landscapes that seemed always imminent at the time. Herron was a founding member of Archigram, an English group influenced by the technocratic ideology of Richard Buckminster Fuller, interpreted through the critic Reyner Banham in his 1960 book, *Theory and Design in the First Machine Age*. Archigram disseminated their ideas through an eponymous magazine, whose ten issues were published between 1961 and 1974. Herron's *Walking City* featured in the fourth issue of *Archigram* magazine in 1964, which was called Zoom and took its inspiration from sci-fi comics and Pop art references to popular culture – in terms of both content and presentation. It proposed an alternative to the conventional, static city that had been recently modified by Modernist planning and housing strategies. The project consisted of giant roaming pods containing different urban and residential functions within them. In this drawing, the telescopic legs, designed to traverse the roughest of terrains, are clearly visible, with their round footpads shown in plan. The scale of the object is ambiguous. At first sight, the circular openings in the body of the machine resemble portholes in a ship, but the internal structure that sits between the black, insect-eye-like roof membranes has the appearance of a multi-storey housing block. The individual pods could be connected by retractable corridors to form a conglomerate metropolis in a solution that was more an ironic critique of the present than a workable solution that could be realized by society.

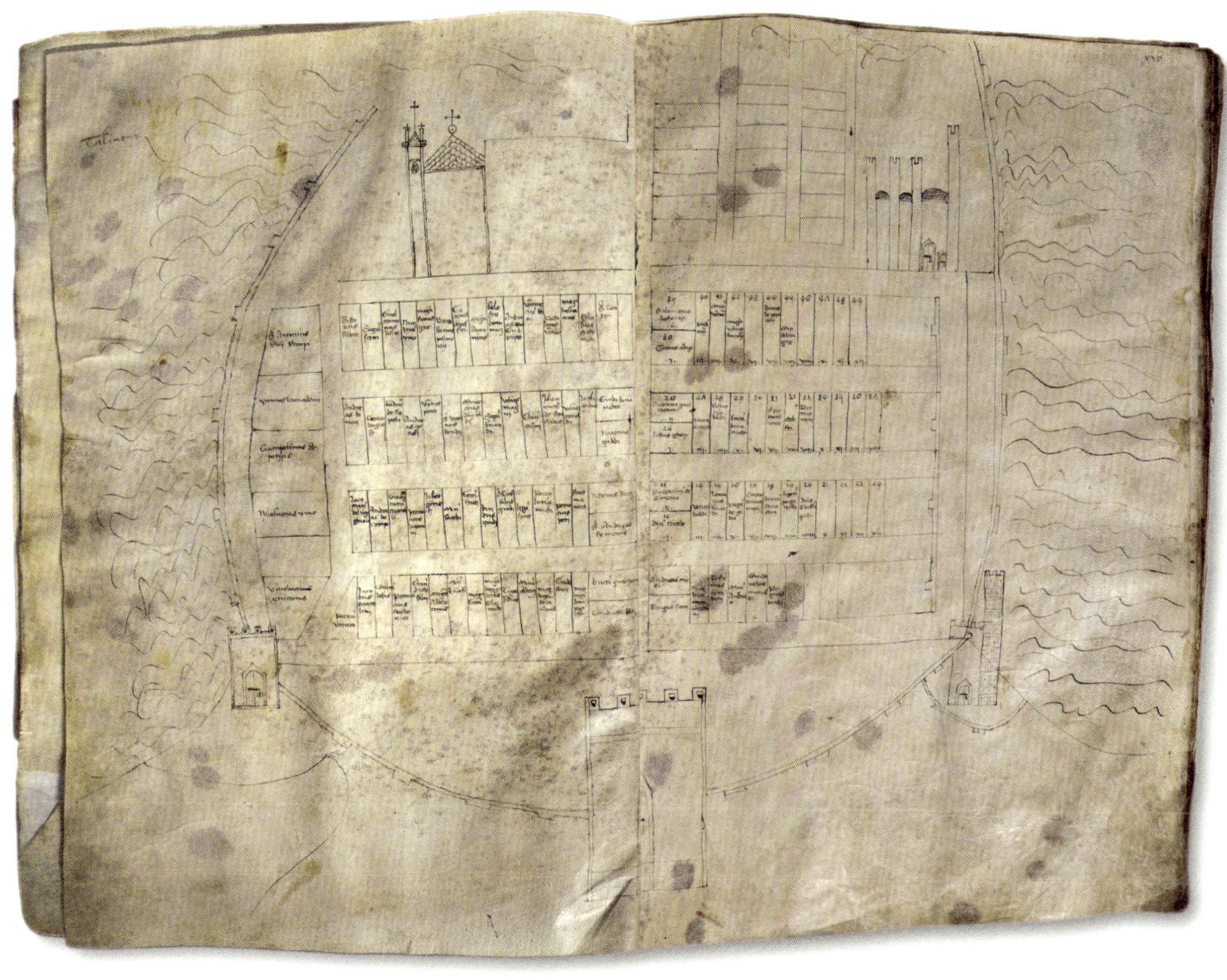

**ANON**

**Plan project for the town of Talamone, 1306**

Brown ink on parchment

44.2 × 59.6 cm , 7½ × 23½ in

This is considered the earliest example of a European town plan still in existence. In 1303, the abbot of the monastery of San Salvatore of Monte Amiata sold the fishing town of Talamone in Tuscany to the administration of Siena, which hoped to create a major seaport within its territories. Crude, undulating lines represent the water surrounding the town on three sides in the drawing. The drafting technique is inexpert, and the perimeter wall, towers, churches, streets and town gates at the bottom, or landward, section of the drawing are all depicted with great simplicity in brown ink lines. The town was scheduled to be rebuilt and repopulated, so this drawing was made as a settlement plan or future proposal rather than an accurate record of existing streets and urban spaces. The plan shows an urban fabric defined by rectilinear streets that traverse the ground inside the town walls in rows, almost entirely filling the space with buildings. Each settler would have had a site for a house and a kitchen garden within the walls, and territory for a vineyard and a patch of land for sowing grain outside. The urban plots marked with the future owner's name are indicated in plan, while the public or civic buildings – including the towers, gates and churches – are shown in elevation, in order to give an idea of their size and importance relative to each other. There is thus a distinction between the technical assignment of land and the pictorial depiction of the townscape and its surrounding context. Talamone's repopulation never reached fruition, despite substantial investment by Siena, but the morphology of the medieval town that grew on the site shows a relationship with this plan, with an axis crossing in a north–south direction and the existence of city gates and towers.

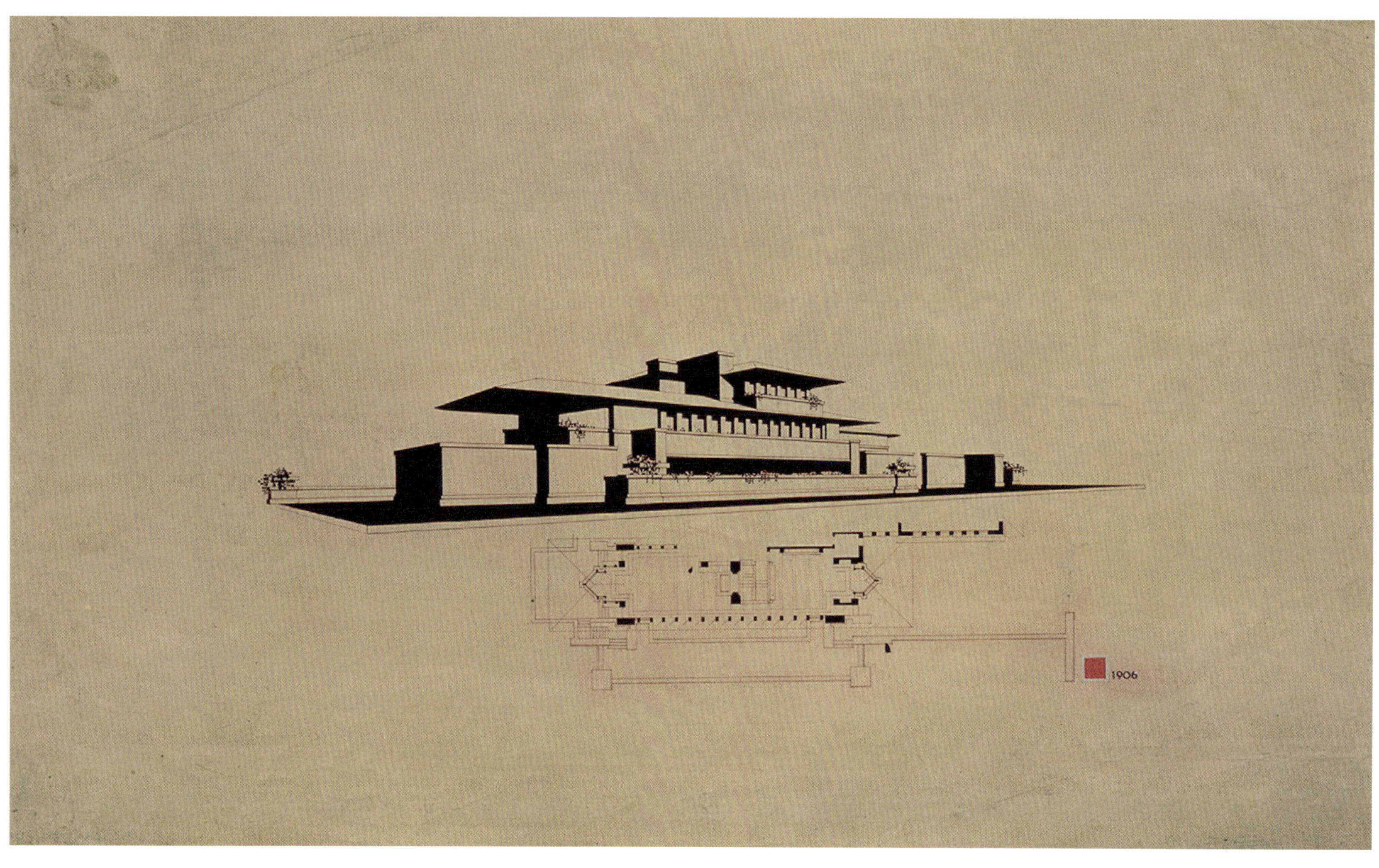


**FRANK LLOYD WRIGHT (1867–1959)**

**Robie House, 1909**

Ink on paper

22 × 35 cm, 8½ × 13¾ in

Influenced by the flat and seemingly infinite expanse of the prairie landscapes of the American Midwest, Frank Lloyd Wright's Prairie Houses, as they came to be known, are exemplified in the last of them – the home for Frederick C Robie and his family, located in an affluent and spacious suburb of Chicago. This striking monochrome rendition of the building's exterior as seen from the street, with its heavy shadows and exaggerated perspective, emphasizes the horizontal qualities of the composition. This mimics the dominant horizon in the landscapes of Illinois, and responds to the reality of its climate and geography. Externally, this is manifest in gently sloping roofs that appear to be almost flat here, which contribute to a gradually ascending skyline that accrues in layers of heavy, brick volumes modified by rhythmic rows of piers. Deep overhangs suggest shelter and shade over protected terraces, while monolithic chimney structures intimate the nature of the interior landscape. This is made clearer in the plan that is situated in the lower part of the sheet, which reveals the section of the ground floor that is depicted in the perspective. This constitutes a huge reception area, split into two parts – living and dining – by a central staircase and a large fireplace in the living room, denoting the heart of the dwelling. Around this core are disposed a series of external spaces – a private terrace, a long balcony that separates the interior from the street, and a porch protected by a deep cantilever – all evident in the perspective above.

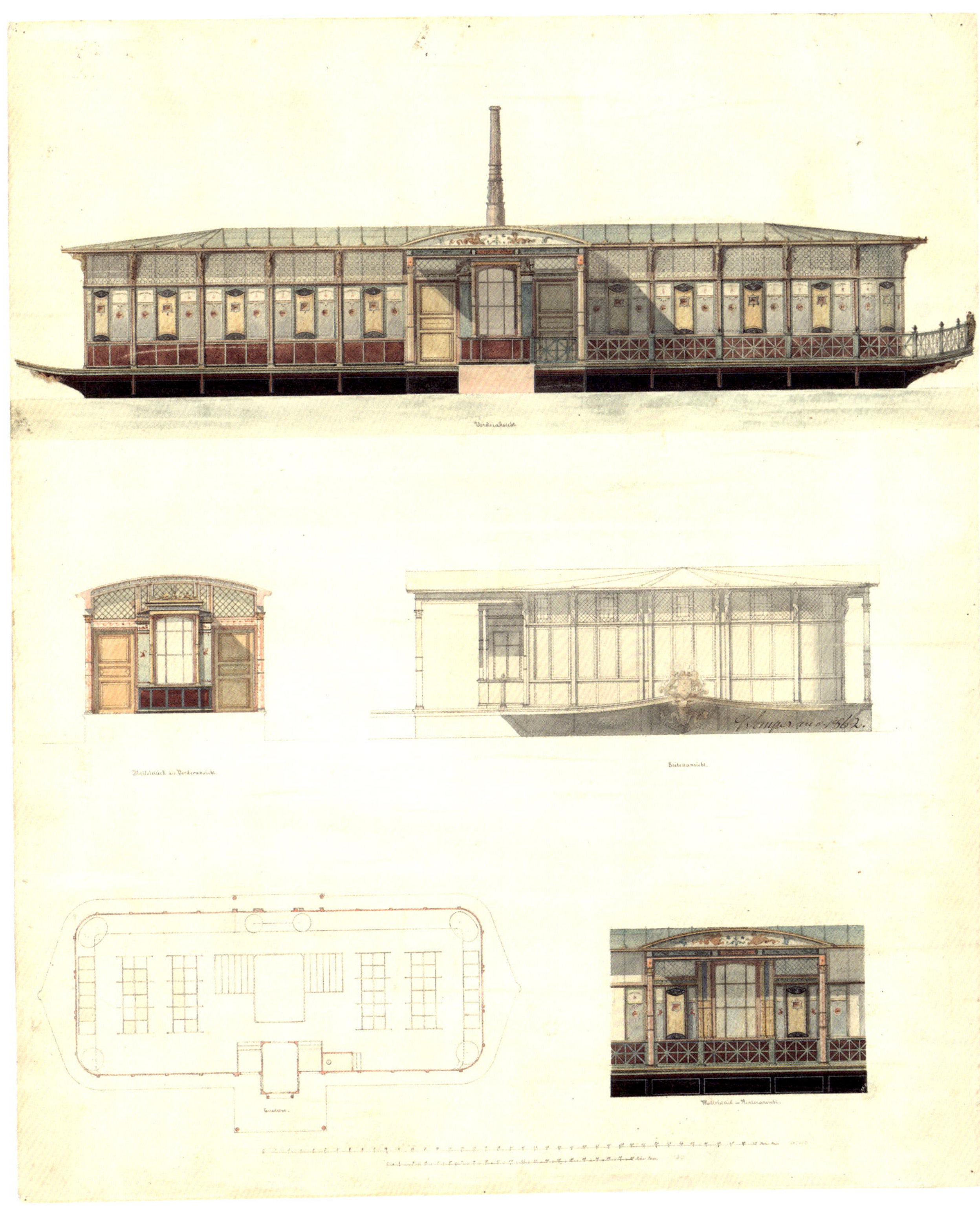

**GOTTFRIED SEMPER (1803–79)**

**Design for the laundry ship Treichler, 1862**

Ink and watercolour on paper

69.3 × 58.3 cm, 27 × 23 in

From the Middle Ages, public laundry ships had operated along the shores of Swiss river cities, and Gottfried Semper self-consciously revived this tradition for Swiss entrepreneur Heinrich Treichler. In many ways, his design deviated from the conventional laundry ship – especially in the internalization of the washing process, evident in the plan at the bottom left-hand side. Its festive facade is supported by a steel frame and composed of painted metal panels depicting Pompeiian domestic scenes; a tall, central chimney is the only evidence of the activity within. Between 1830 and 1833, when the excavation of Pompeii was slowly moving forward, Semper had travelled to Italy and Greece to study the architecture of antiquity. One outcome of his travels was his book *The Four Elements of Architecture*, published in 1851. In this, he reveals an anthropological and archaeological, as opposed to typological, approach to the origins of architecture. This was based on the creation of four symbolic domestic places, in which corresponding constructional technologies developed: the communal hearth, with its material technologies such as metallurgy and ceramics; the roof, with its carpentry structure; the enclosure made by the use of textile formed through weaving; and the mound, composed of earthworks. The *Treichler*'s panels are the cladding, the clothing, which masks the interior. Ambiguity is created by the transposition on to a facade of apparently three-dimensional but actually two-dimensional paintings taken from private interiors. The ship takes a domestic function and makes it civic, while at the same time making it private. Semper also makes a commentary on the symbolic transfer and continuous evolution of traditional forms of ornamentation that accompanies technological advances, as they respond to the possibilities of new materials and functions.

**MICHELANGELO BUONARROTI (1913–89)**

**Study for Porta Pia, 1560**

Pencil, pen and watercolour on brown paper

42 × 28 cm, 18½ × 11 in

When Pius IV ascended to the papacy in 1559, he began a series of urban improvements that included straightening and levelling some of Rome's streets. The resulting via Pia led out of the city through a suburban landscape of luxurious villas surrounding the Aurelian walls, and replaced the existing via Nomentana. In 1560, Pius IV commissioned Michelangelo Buonarroti to design a new gate, the Porta Pia, to replace the closed Porta Nomentana. Michelangelo prepared three different sketches for this gate and, according to Giorgio Vasari, the Pope chose the least expensive. Many preliminary sketches have survived, and Michelangelo's design process can be traced through them: this orthogonal elevation is a presentation or working drawing. It has been carefully set out in pencil, with its proportions measured out by a workshop assistant, and then possibly reworked by Michelangelo. Although the final design is defined in the strong modelling of light and shadow, created using ink washes, underlying layers showing different possibilities can be detected. There are vestiges in pencil of a triangular pediment beneath the ink, and a ghostly figure flees in a burst of white light from the opening towards the viewer. Drawings directly attributed to Michelangelo in the series include schematic tools for working out ideas and details, made in black chalk and not as precise as this one. This drawing, known as Dussler 134 recto', shows the doorway with broken segmental pediments and with enclosing shells above the opening, an anti-Classical approach that is characteristic of Michelangelo's later work. The cornerstone was laid in June 1561, but there is inconclusive evidence to show that the gateway was completed to Michelangelo's design after his death in 1564.

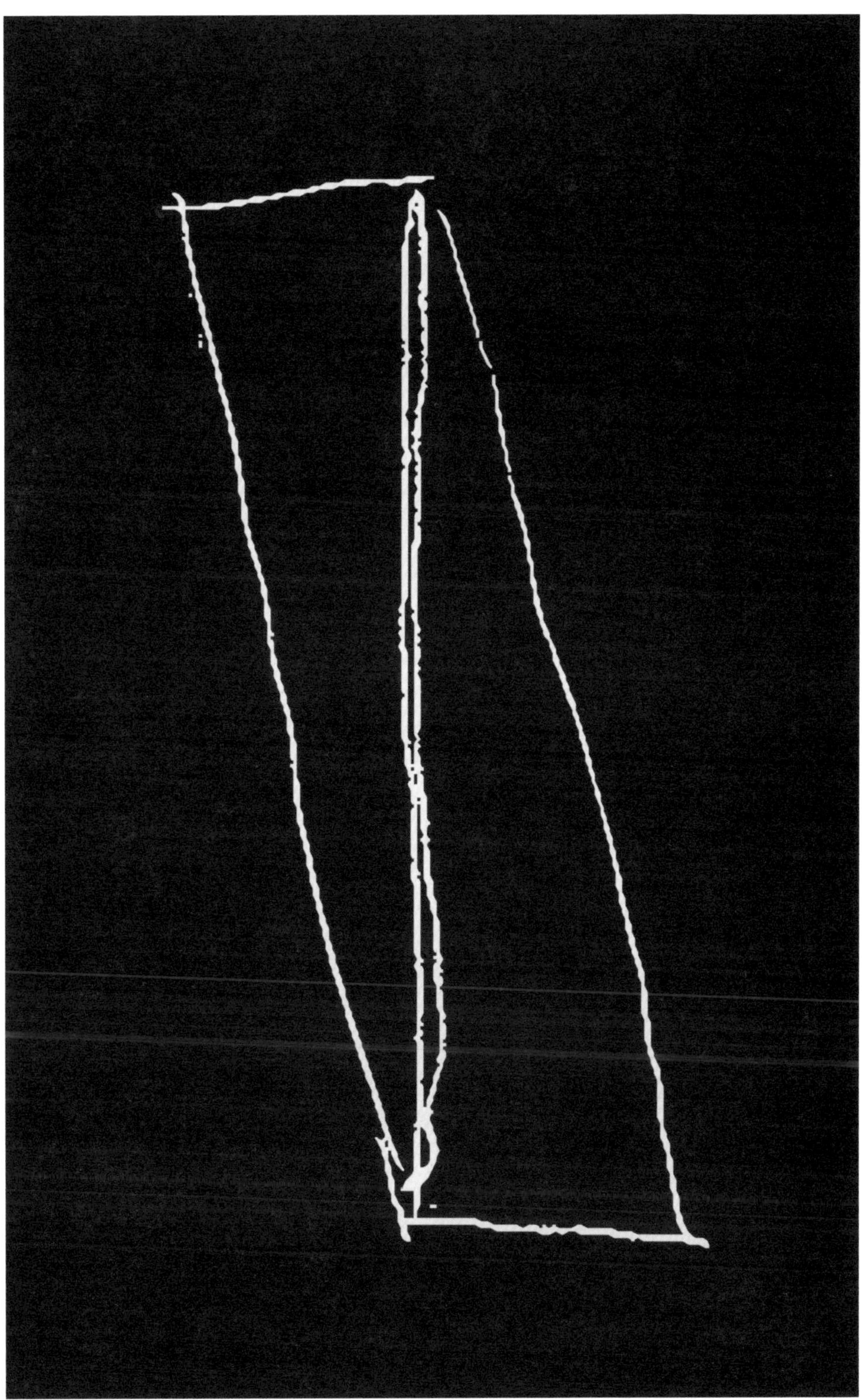

**PHILIP JOHNSON (1906–2005)**

**Puerta de Europa, 1995**

Ink on paper

30 × 25 cm, 12 × 10 in

The Puerta de Europa comprises two leaning towers that suggest but do not complete a gateway to the grand Madrid boulevard called Paseo de Castellana, at the point where it joins the north side of the circular Plaza de Castilla. It was designed as a collaborative project between John Burgee architects and Philip Johnson – who, as design consultant, generated the primary, iconic image for the project that is captured in this quick sketch. It is one of Johnson's trademark simple phrases, so pared down that only one side of the symmetrical composition needs to be drawn. The sketch is composed of two right-angled triangles, the base of one sitting firmly on the horizontal plane and connecting the building to the ground. The second triangle hangs off the vertical side of the first, and this strong perpendicular double line defines its presence as a tower. Looming over the street, the second triangle seems to cantilever from the first, creating a tension and a question about where the great forces generated by this turning motion are counteracted, and why this situation is created in the first place. The answer is that the towers sit either side of an underground rail interchange, making it impossible for them to stand near the street. The forces are reined in by post-tensioning the outer wall of the building and countered by deep pile foundations. Johnson's long career in the world of architecture, in the course of which he formulated some of its most influential art-historical categories, spanned over seventy years. Beginning with the invention of the International Style, a concept which he developed with Henry Russell Hitchcock and Alfred H Barr Jr in the eponymous exhibition at the Museum of Modern Art in New York in 1932, he then went on to produce many self-consciously iconic buildings.

**ANDREA POZZO (1475–1564)**

**Illusionistic Architecture for the Vault of Sant'Ignazio, 1685**

Pen and ink with grey wash on two joined sheets of laid paper

50.4 × 91.2 cm, 19¾ × 36 in

Andrea Pozzo began work on his most famous work, the illusionistic trompe-l'oeil fresco on the vaulted ceiling of Sant'Ignazio, Rome, in 1685. Saint Ignatius founded the Jesuit order, of which Pozzo was a lay brother, and the scene shows him welcomed into Paradise by Christ and the Virgin Mary, surrounded by allegorical representations of the known continents. This grey-and-brown ink drawing bears none of this narrative, but describes Pozzo's bold use of *quadratura* perspective – a complex technique based on linear perspective manipulated geometrically to respond to a vault's curved surface, its images of architectural features painted on walls or ceilings so that they seem to extend the real architecture of the room into an imaginary space beyond its physical confines. Merged into a magical whole, some parts of the drawing depict elements that have a physical manifestation while others form the painting's fictive architectural framework. The edge is outlined by a solid dark field that depicts a section cut through the thick masonry wall of the church, showing the plan of its nave at the level of a proposed but unbuilt upper balcony, which can be seen floating just in front of the profile of the inner elevation. Beyond this, the realms merge. The windows belong to reality, as does the wide arch leading to the domed crossing of the nave and side aisles. In the painting, the curved projections between the windows that look so solid here are already the site of writhing figures that touch the meniscus between the two worlds. The area above, where Corinthian columns support another cornice, from which spring arched gateways into the sky, belong to the fictive realm. A marble disc set into the middle of the church's nave floor marks the ideal spot from which observers might fully experience the illusion.

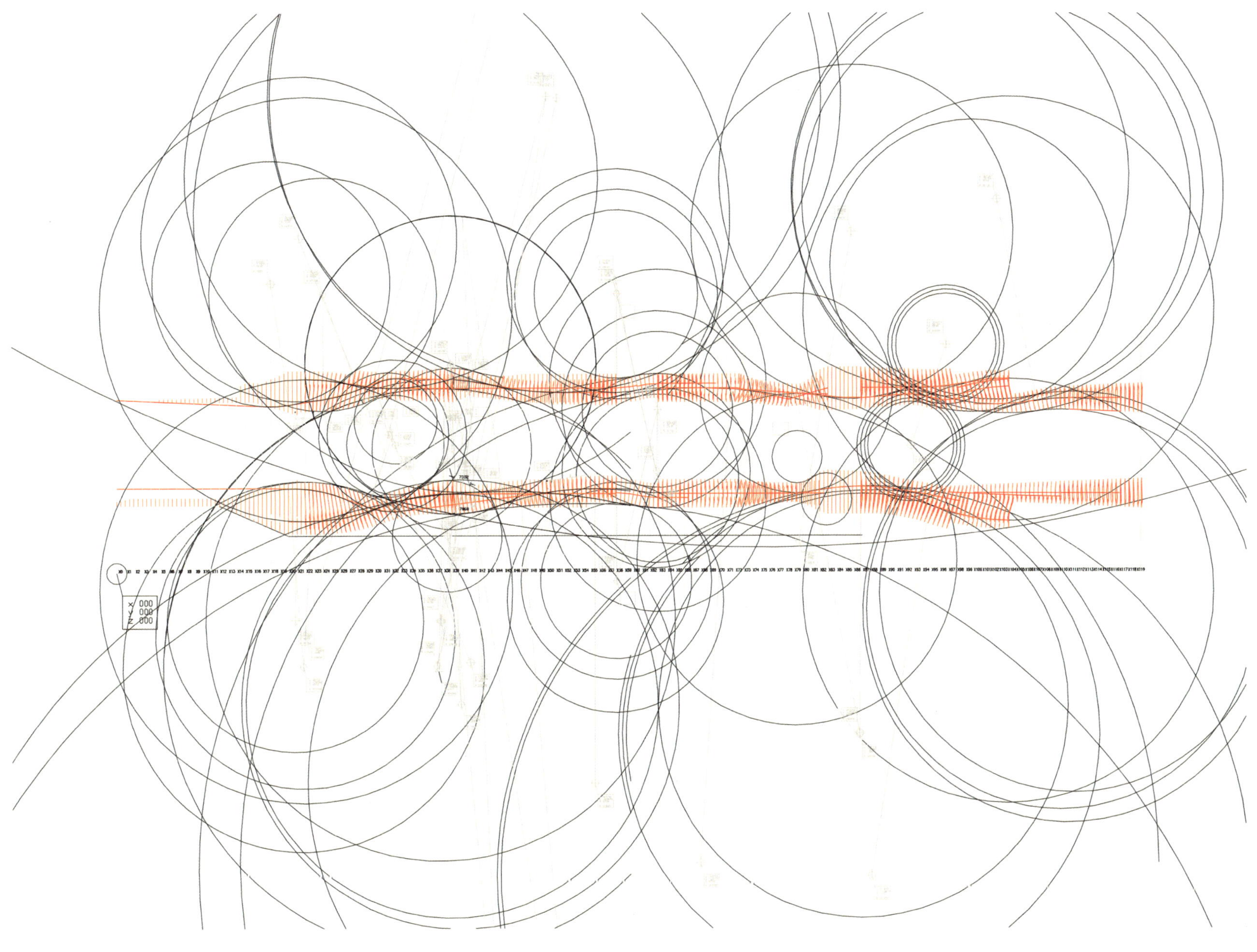

**FOREIGN OFFICE ARCHITECTS**

**Yokohama Ferry Terminal, 2002**

Ink on paper

18 × 26 cm, 7¼ × 10¼ in

When it was constructed, the Yokohama Ferry Terminal seemed to inaugurate a new kind of architecture. Not only did it introduce a novel means of generating form, but it also redefined the relationship of that form to urban morphology. The designers of the building, Farshid Moussavi and Alejandro Zaera-Polo, of Foreign Office Architects, described this phenomenon as phylogenesis, a process for creating form via constantly mutating and proliferating computer programs. These generate, or evolve, into solutions that take the form of undulating planes, or new landscapes, rather than discrete, volumetric structures. This new kind of architecture would be categorized not according to functional typologies but by species – morphological aspects that are adaptable through time and space. Before winning the competition to design the terminal, Moussavi and Zaera-Polo had been developing this approach through theoretical experiments enacted through eight years of teaching at the Architectural Association, where the method would develop and flourish as a subject known as parametric design. This intriguing diagram gives a sense of the process and physical reality of the ferry terminal; the edges of its structure emerge in the red lines, the orientation of which diverges from the horizontal in relation to the arcs of a multitude of circles that cover the sheet. This pattern has a recognizable correlation with the more traditional orthographic drawings that were made later, depicting the interconnecting levels of the three-storey building, which accommodates a huge range of functions – from car parking and office space to customs and immigration zones, restaurants, shops and waiting rooms. The top edge of its continuous surface, supported on a sophisticated system of folded steel plates and girders, forms an undulating timber-boarded observation deck that projects 430 m (1,410 ft) out over the water.

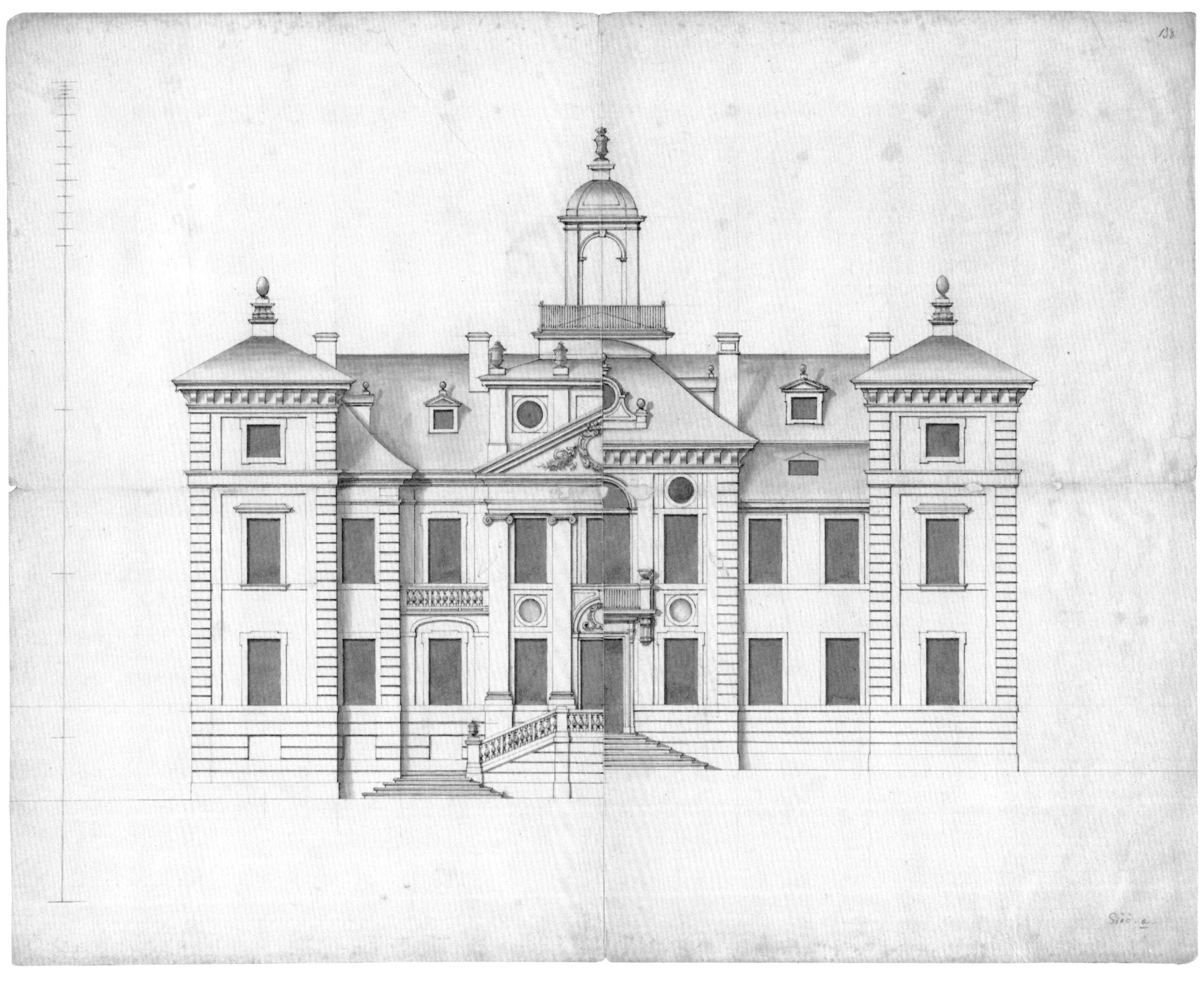

**NICODEMUS TESSIN THE ELDER (1615–81)**

**Swedish mansion house, 1670**

Ink on paper

45 × 57 cm, 17 × 22½ in

The two faces presented in this elevation of a prototypical design for a country mansion are sometimes associated with Sjöö Castle, an estate dating from the Middle Ages and located in Swedish Uppland. Designed by Nicodemus Tessin the Elder, with Mathias Spieler, the front facade of the seventeenth-century manor house resembles this drawing, with its slightly projecting wings at either end of a long, rectangular body within which a central bay defines the entrance and reinforces the symmetrical arrangement. It is more likely, however, that Tessin was experimenting within his own architectural language in a more generic way. Having trained as a military engineer, he travelled and studied extensively in Germany, France, the Netherlands and Italy, where he remained between 1651 and 1655, bringing ideas back to Sweden that he put into play, developing a compositional style that can be seen at Sjöö and in the many other aristocratic and royal mansions he was commissioned to design. The composition of this drawing shows Tessin trying out various configurations of this formula based on a compact central body flanked by tower-like corner projections and compact wings. The central fold of the paper marks the line of symmetry, with the tower elements, including the central tower, acting as the constants on both sides so as to maintain a compositional balance across this central line.

The horizontal cornice and eaves line is used as a datum to connect the various components of the elevation's arrangement in different ways on either side of the fold, so that two quite different facades emerge. The ground level of the version on the left drops substantially lower to create an entrance level raised over a functioning lower floor, reached by a grand staircase. Ionic pilasters and a triangular pediment define the central portico on this side, in contrast to the more locally inspired resolution of the right-hand elevation.

**ARCHITECTEN DE VYLDER VINCK TAILLIEU**

**Les Ballets C de la B and LOD, 2008**

Pen, pencil, aluminium foil and Tipp-Ex on tracing paper

12.1 × 26.7 cm, 4¾ × 10½ in

Jan de Vylder defines architectural drawings as preparation for an approaching reality; once ideas and projects are realized, they become redundant. This drawing, made by him with Inge Vinck, is an object constructed from various different media that range from conventional pen and pencil to materials, such as aluminium foil and Tipp-Ex, which add additional texture to the paper's surface. This character releases it as an object from de Vylder's definition: it exists beyond the production stage of the building, and is included in a three-volume collection, two of which describe the work of the Architecten De Vylder Vinck Taillieu practice purely through images. This representation of a facade is for a building designed for two performing-arts companies in Ghent. Drawn on tracing paper, by hand and sometimes with ruled edges, the influence of Sol LeWitt is evident in the fine hatched lines revealing the hand's movement as they are made in their trajectories. Tipp-Ex, usually used to cover over mistakes, gives a luminous quality to the ceilings and diagrammatic undersides of staircases that form strong diagonal rhythms across the elevation. The spindly lines of fenestration mingle with those of internal partitions, handrails and opening planes in the elevation, outlining blank and opaque panels immediately behind them and enhancing an ambiguity of surface caused by the layered construction of the building. The facade frames deliberate conflicts and juxtapositions – between the glass surface and the blank panels, for example, or in the chaotic pattern created by the different elements in contrasting shades. This can be seen as a commentary on the chaos of the constantly changing urban fabric of a capitalist city, or as an expression of the stage-like role of the building – both in its purpose as production studios, and in its wider role within the city landscape.

**GERRIT RIETVELD (1888–1964)**

**Schröder House, 1924**

Pencil, ink and watercolour on collotype

83.5 × 86.8 cm, 33 × 35 in

The experimental dwelling that Gerrit Rietveld designed for his unconventional client Truus Schröder-Schräder was the first truly open-plan house. Overturning conventional distinctions between public and private life, it responded instead to the specific daily rituals of her single-parent family. Rietveld's design is the most complete architectural interpretation of De Stijl principles, which were based on the idea that the purpose of art is to express the absolutes of life reduced to essentials of form and colour – here pared down to a palette of black, white and primary colours. This isometric drawing, unlike a perspective, gives equal importance to each part of the plan of this first-floor space where the family lived, and most clearly describes its complex spatial strategy. It shows the whole living area, which could be either entirely open or separated into up to six rooms by a series of sliding and folding screens. The house responded organically to the needs of its occupants as these changed throughout the day. Each space could be inhabited in many different ways, unlike the restrictive traditional house with its fixed, cellular rooms. It could be part of a greater whole for communal living, or closed into a private retreat defined by its furniture – piano, bath, divan – rather than a preconceived function. Historical decorative traditions were replaced by a different aesthetic approach, influenced by the De Stijl painter Piet Mondrian, in which Rietveld transformed the role of art in the domestic realm from its hitherto decorative function into one that was utilitarian and spatial. Bright planes of colour express the structural elements of the building, and define the key objects around which daily life is enacted.

**JOHN SMYTHSON (nd–1634)**

**Design for a house with a castellated wing, 1600**

Ink on paper

26 × 48 cm, 10¾ × 19 in

Like a stage set, with its paper-thin facades, this drawing depicts an unusual ensemble of disparate parts, and has been made in order to consider how they will fit together. The ruled brown-ink design traces the outlines of four different volumes. These are gathered in an experiment with perspective in which the usual intent to bind the whole into a single spatial schema gives way to an idiosyncratic diversity. One of the two vanishing points is off centre down a passageway between two buildings, ending not in a spectacular view or a distant horizon, but at a modest one-storey elevation. The scene, with its empty ground and sky, is viewed from above as if by a floating observer, which increases the dreamlike and abstract quality of the drawing. Made by master stonemason John Smythson, the design reveals an especially English attitude to architectural style. John was trained by his more famous father, Robert, who is sometimes identified as the first British architect, and learnt his trade at Wollaton Hall in Nottinghamshire. Their collective works are known for their coherence, symmetry and light, but this drawing brings together an eclectic combination of Gothic, Classical and vernacular forms and references in a picturesque assembly. As a stonemason, Smythson would have been trained to conceptualize the total composition of an architectural project as well as the details of its individual parts. This drawing shows how he employed this facility to tease out formal problems. The clarity of the heavy ink lines that he used here brings the unresolved juxtaposition of the new, castellated, three-storey wing with the two-storey existing manor house into focus. Later, Smythson would go on to work on much larger projects like Bolsover Castle in Derbyshire, where the interest that he is experimenting with here – in disturbing the balance and creating an uneven, topographical composition of volumes – was brought to fruition.

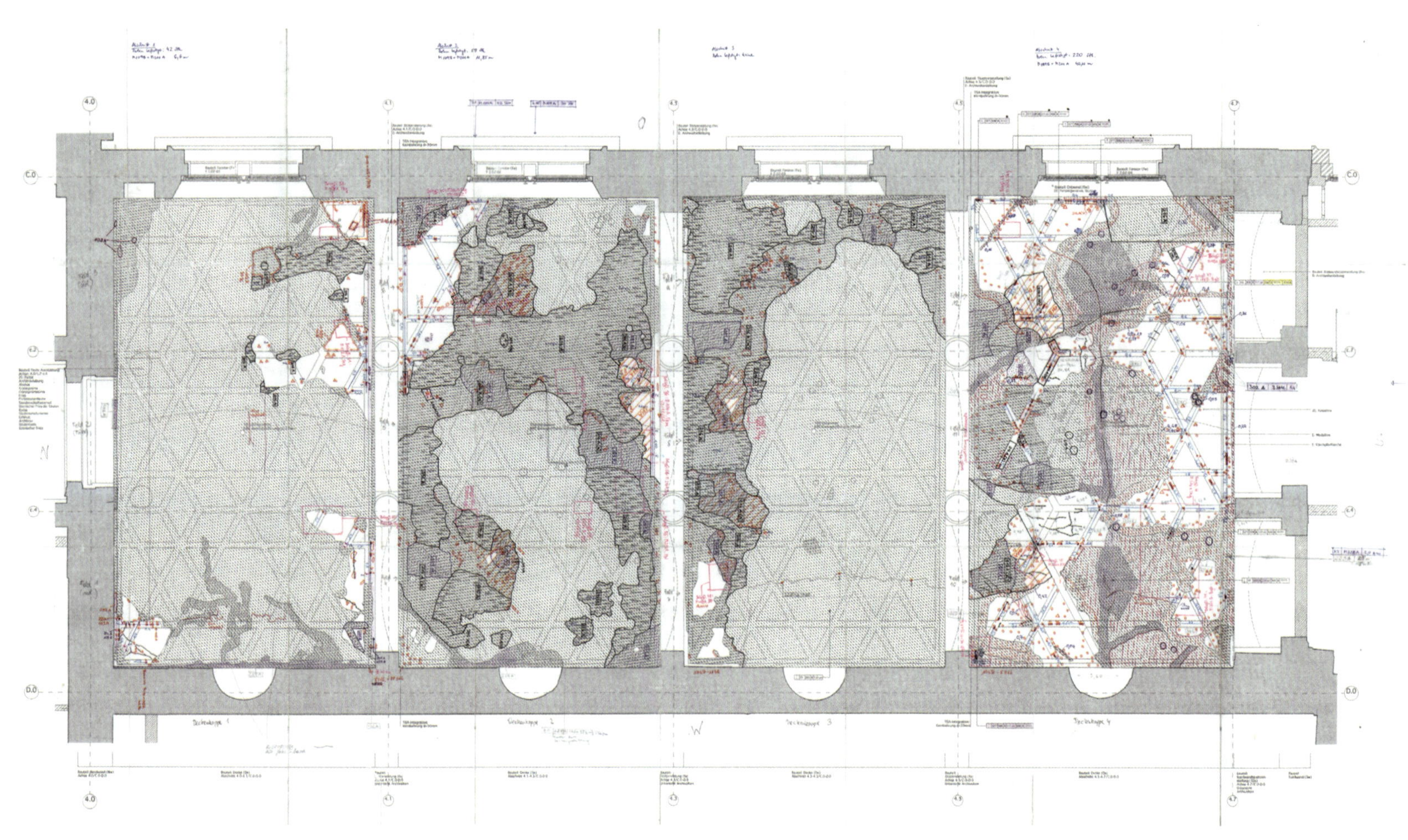

**DAVID CHIPPERFIELD ARCHITECTS**

**Roman Room, Neues Museum, 2009**

CAD drawing with hand annotations in pencil

After lying in ruins for more than fifty years following World War II, the nineteenth-century Neues Museum in Berlin was remade from fragments by David Chipperfield Architects, who needed to transform it into a functioning museum without losing the material quality and patina acquired through its traumatic history. This working drawing maps out the restoration process for the ceiling of one of the temporally – and culturally – specific exhibition rooms of the original museum, which were decorated in the style of the objects that they contained. This is the Roman Room, which was originally covered with painted murals and colourful mosaics, and the geometric grid of the original painted pattern can be seen as a guiding structure below representations of the layers of remaining material. The surrounding thick layer of masonry walls shows that the ceiling comprises four rectangular panels, aligned with four windows along one wall that face a corresponding niche opposite. The room is a terminal space as opposed to part of an enfilade, and opposite its entrance is another window. The drawing reveals the strategy for retaining and restoring, as far as possible, the remaining fragments of this fragile layer. Many separate procedures were necessary, and the drawing captures three distinct layers of information. First is the printout of a CAD drawing, a reproduction of a survey of the existing conditions prior to restoration. This shows the damage, cracks, structural faults and areas where the room's surface has come away. Following set conventions, various codes and hatches added to this drawing guide the conservators on how to treat the building surfaces; some of the instructions are technical and others are annotations related to aesthetic issues. The annotations were added on-site by the conservators, who used different-coloured pencils to record the various stages of the work or condition of the fabric.

**JOSEPH MICHAEL GANDY (1771–1843)**

**A Bird's-eye View of the Bank of England, 1830**

Watercolour on paper

84.5 × 140 cm, 33¼ × 55 in

The artist and architect Joseph Michael Gandy enjoyed a long and fruitful collaboration with Sir John Soane, producing many paintings to illustrate Soane's principal works and visions. As in this watercolour depicting Soane's design for the Bank of England, Gandy frequently used two-point perspective, with twin vanishing points along two perpendicular facades, to impart drama and power to his renderings. However, this image, chosen by Soane for exhibition at the Royal Academy in 1830, was also accompanied by a caption describing it as a meat pie with its crust cut off. Although subsequently called *The Bank in Ruins*, it is clear that the intention behind it was far more complex, and it is more analogous to a project model combining plan with elevations. The painting draws from traditions of architectural representation such as references to Renaissance cutaway, aerial perspectives and the romantic dishevelment and spectacle of Giovanni Battista Piranesi's archaeological landscapes. The atmospheric effect of this magical image comes from Gandy's technique of painting light, which highlights the unusual setting for the building. A wall of radiant cloud creates a veil between the exposed spatial and constructional workings of the huge, city-like building and the cramped streets and offices of the City of London that press inwards towards it. Some of the bank's interior is in shadow, but the foreground, in contrast, is depicted with great clarity. The halls and domes of this part of the building, which appears to be set on a rocky plinth, belong to a pre-existing archaeological landscape. Gandy evokes the Roman ruins upon which London and this new imperial monument sit, and with which he and Soane shared a fascination. The street alongside the intact facade has crumbled away, and between the viewer and the ground ancient fragments nestle amongst Arcadian shrubs, framing the scene.

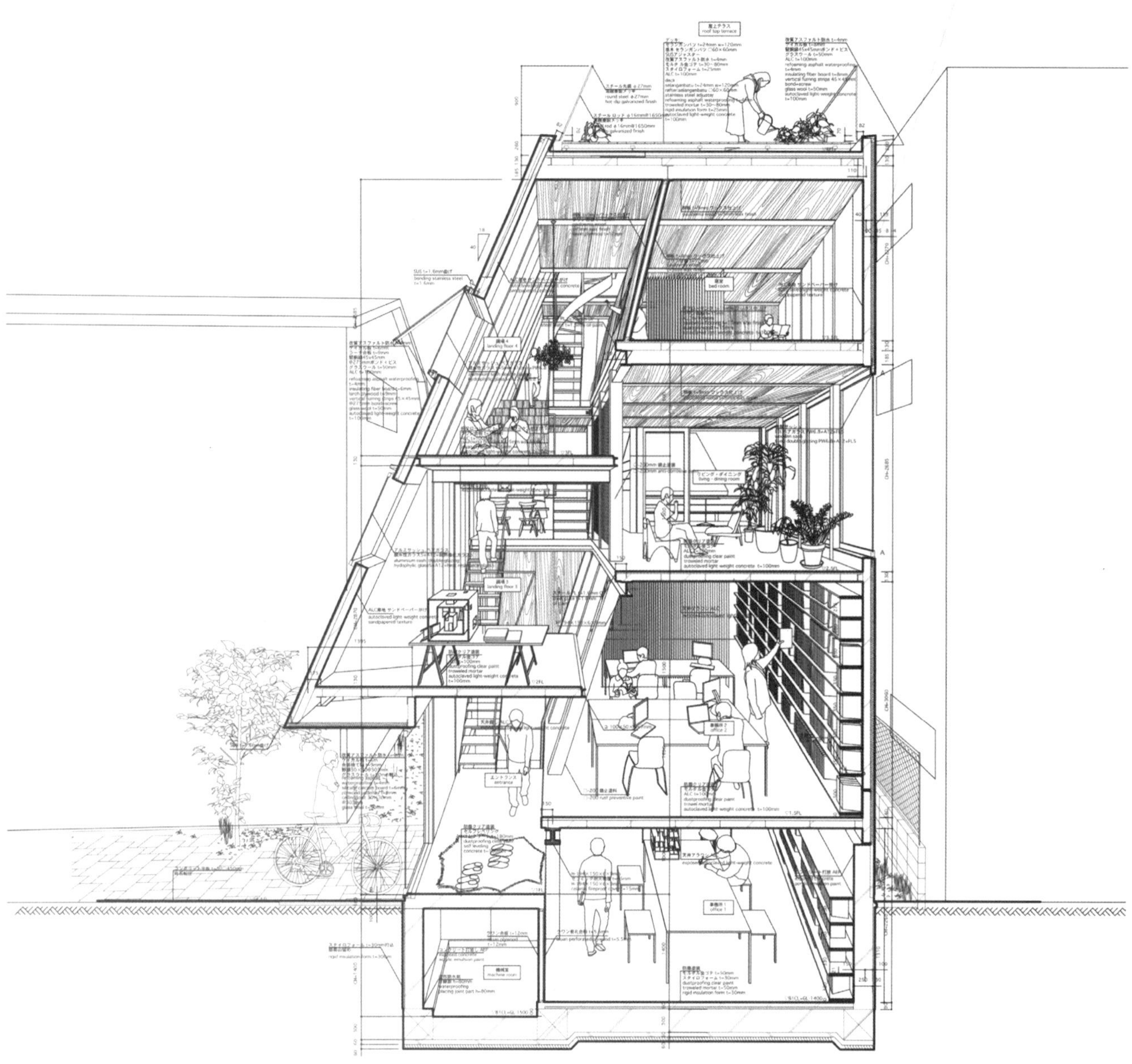

**ATELIER BOW-WOW**

**House and Atelier Bow-Wow, 2005**

Ink on paper

52 × 26 cm, 20½ × 10¼ in

Yoshiharu Tsukamoto and Momoyo Kaijima of Atelier Bow-Wow compare architectural drawings to the scientific diagrams of plants and human bodies made by anatomists and botanists. Their conventions both reduce the transmission of the personal into the drawing, and give it a compelling realism. This perspective-section of their own house and office in the centre of Tokyo is one of a catalogue of detailed drawings that they prepared for an exhibition and a book – thus, presentation rather than construction documents. These images describe their buildings in the manner of anatomical drawings in the way that architects always do, using and developing the rules of orthogonal drawing. Many layers of information are presented in the section of the Bow-Wow House that, although quite technical, can be understood by non-architects. The strong narrative sense of the drawing is created through the presence of the clutter of everyday objects, such as stools and chairs, a bookshelf and a bicycle, and dining surfaces littered with model buildings. These are drawn as representative of the many people inhabiting the house, who, in going about their lives, give scale and sense to window heights, stair locations and the waterproofing for the flat roof, which is both depicted in detail and described in the annotations. The building is explained by showing how it works as a system. This includes the thick concrete slab that seals the basement off from the damp ground and the slope of the long mansard, with its alternating solid and glazed sections, which throws off the rainwater, and also defines the spaces within. The textures of the materials – the grain of timber, the smoothness of steel and the softness of fur – all contribute to this story of a building.

**CLORINDO TESTA**
**(1923–2013)**

**Banco de Londres y América del Sur, 1995**

Ink on paper

43.8 × 31.8 cm, 17¼ × 12½ in

Covering the whole sheet of paper, the black-ink brush strokes of this rapidly made drawing create an atmosphere of movement and energy. This fills a space barely defined by the three structural elements that represent the building in the sketch. Clorindo Testa, the architect of the headquarters of the London and South America Bank in Buenos Aires, made the drawing many years after the building's completion, and so it has a curious status. In part it is a memory and represents an idea of the building, but it is also a keepsake that enhances the presence of the building beyond its physical site. The bank, completed in 1966, is an exposed-concrete structure with a powerful presence in the heart of the city. Its expressive street elevation comprises thin and deep columns connected laterally in a striking composition. A glazed facade is set back behind this structure, and at the corner a huge cantilever marked by a hanging concrete slab defines an open urban room that creates a covered square at the crossing of two streets. The sketch depicts its counterpart, the interior atrium that houses the main banking space on the ground floor, which was envisioned as a covered public plaza. Two additional levels of public space cantilever over the banking floor, supported by discrete structural cores that stand like short trees within the huge room. One of these looms like a dark shadow in the background of the sketch, with the high-level, enclosed rooms on the floors above depicted at the top of the drawing in elevation, and tiny figures at work behind the tinted glass. The diagonal lines at the side of the sketch depict the curves of the concrete facade, with the vertical plane of glazing behind. On the street, smudges of black ink portray pedestrians in motion.

**JOSEF FRANK (1885–1967)**

**New York, Slum Clearance, 1942**

Pencil and watercolour

55 × 65 cm, 21¾ × 4¼ in

Between 1941 and 1946, Austrian-born Josef Frank lived and worked in New York, during which time his design and architectural practice principally took the form of teaching at the New York School for Social Research and writing unpublished novels. One of these was *The Four Freedoms*, a satire of American society based on President Franklin Roosevelt's State of the Union Address, 1941, in which he proposed four fundamental freedoms that everyone in the world should enjoy. This design could be seen as a continuation of that critique, produced in response to a south-Manhattan slum-clearance project called Stuyvesant Town. The bird's-eye perspective is projected from the plan of a city block that has been developed along Modernist planning principles: tall, high-density housing blocks are set in a green and communal landscape that flows around the base of the towers. This is reminiscent of a romantic English garden or a fragment of Central Park, with its tree-lined avenues and unfenced perimeter, meandering paths and pond. At the bottom left-hand corner, Frank positions figure-ground plans of four old-fashioned city blocks, which can be seen underneath painted in dingy browns and greys. He contrasts these plans – in which continuous, low facades surround a slum-block perimeter, leaving space only for dark courts at its centre – with the brightly coloured proposal, with its yellow, red and blue towers. The slum-clearance area is equivalent to four city blocks and its plan is shown in the top right-hand corner, with the floor plates of the building coloured bright blue. Their fanciful shapes form creative, decorative elements at the corners of the site, with two smaller cross-shaped plans in the middle of the garden. The city fascinated Frank so much that he also designed the Manhattan textile print, comprising snapshots in plan of various fragments of the island.

**DUARTE DE ARMAS (1465–nd)**

**Olivença with Badajoz in the distance, 1510**

Pencil on paper

36.5 × 52 cm, 14¼ × 20½ in

The hilltop town of Olivença is depicted in this early sixteenth-century drawing by Duarte de Armas, a royal clerk and *debuxador*, meaning draughtsman, commissioned by King Manuel I of Portugal to record fifty-six fortifications lying on his kingdom's border with Castile. Manuel's reign was an important cultural and political period in Portuguese history, producing a late-Gothic architectural style called the Manueline, which benefited from the extensive voyages of discovery undertaken during his rule. De Armas' more than one hundred survey drawings were gathered together in the two volumes of *The Book of Fortresses*, and constitute plans accompanied by measurements, cartographic annotations and explanatory notes. Scenes such as this one were not drawn as formal perspectives, but a sense of distance is created in the relative sizes of their different parts, and the overlaying of the hills and undulating paths. To this day, Olivença still lies on disputed territory on the Spanish–Portuguese border, and the presence of the watchtowers in the drawing show that this was also the case for this strategic site in the 1500s, with the towers of Spanish Badajoz within view in the distance. This drawing does not reveal the intricacies of Manueline architecture but rather suggests the character of a hybrid, fortified hill town, with its combination of medieval and vernacular forms. The castle shown in de Armas' depiction was erected by the Templars after the Christian reconquest of the Iberian Peninsula, but early in his reign Manuel had ordered the building of further fortifications and a bridge over the Guadiana River in the valley beyond the town. The new fence, constructed using the stone of the old, appears in the drawing. Its fortified walls can be seen enclosing a densely packed town of simple, pitched-roofed dwellings, which spills out over the slope of a nearby hill.

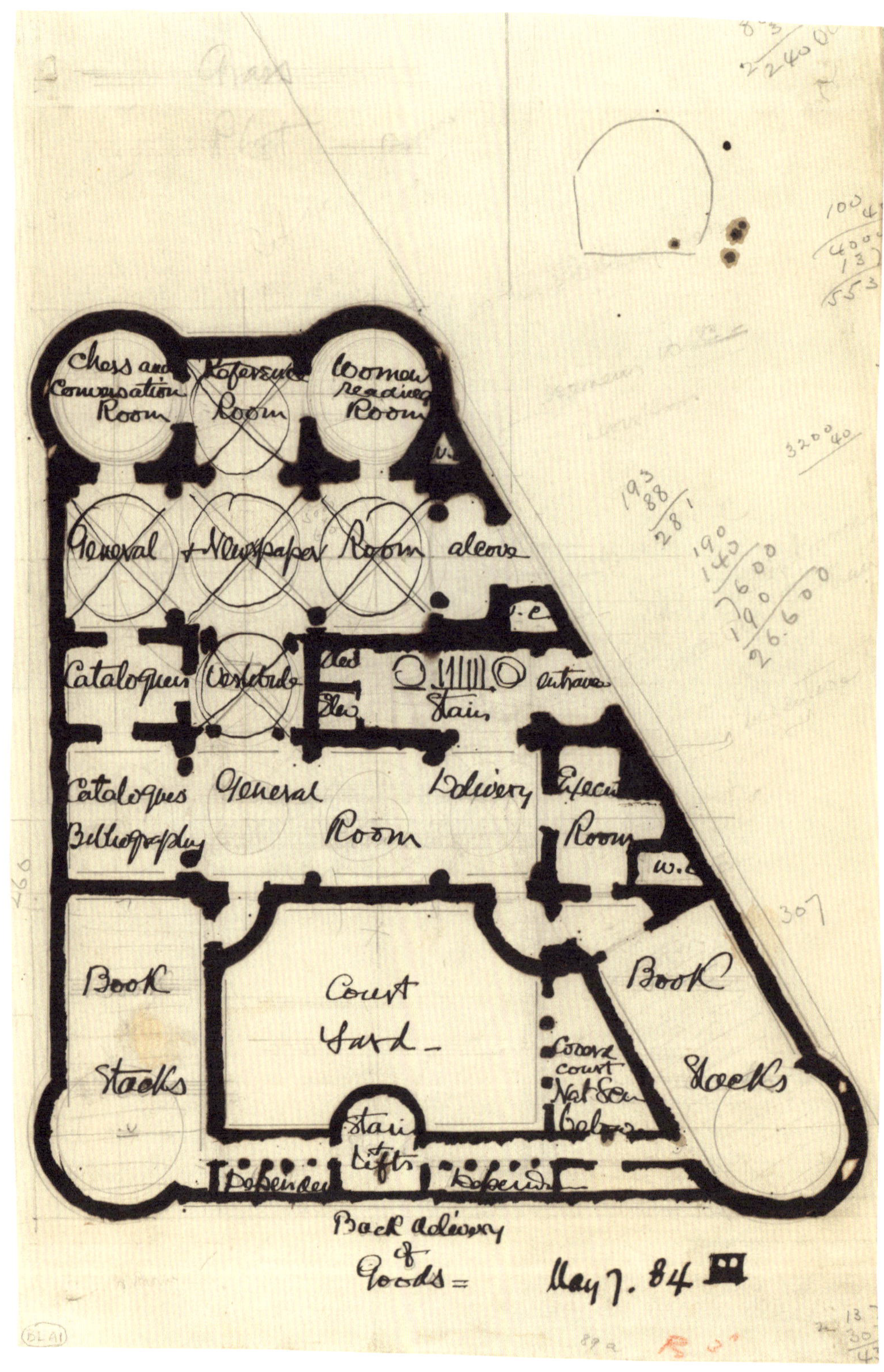


**HENRY HOBSON RICHARDSON (1838–86)**

**Plan of Young Men's Association Library, 1884**

Indian ink and pencil on stiff white paper

41.5 × 29.9 cm, 16½ × 11¾ in

Henry Hobson Richardson was one of the first American architects to design large-scale structures for the new types of building that were coming into being in the industrializing, urbanizing landscapes of the nineteenth century. His means of defining these unprecedented forms was to look backwards in time, and interpret liberally from European precedent. His foundation, however, lay in the Beaux-Arts tradition, its design process founded on the conceptual sketch, or *esquisse*, defining all the principal elements and the terms on which the scheme would be developed. Following this tradition, almost every drawing for Richardson's buildings known to be by his own hand is a sketch – like the drawing shown here – that captures the essence of the proposal. The entry for this library competition in Buffalo, which was unsuccessful, was made during the last period of his life. Richardson's mature designs centred on two new building types – public libraries and railway stations. The approach in this sketch is typical of his libraries, with a paring down to the Norman, or Romanesque, as a vehicle of formal expression, tempered by his powerful, idiosyncratic approach, which untethered it from its European origins. The plan – drawn in thick, black Indian-ink lines – is annotated, and Richardson uses more delicate pencil lines to set out marks indicating the locations of vaults and a staircase. Its principal intent is to show the disposition of the rooms, which at first appears complex. The arrangement of the main reading rooms around a cross axis at the top of the plan, and the stacks and offices around a courtyard with the large general room between continues the Beaux-Arts logic. The external wall shows no openings except for space in an alcove near to the entrance, which suggests a massive, monolithic stone or brick enclosure articulated by large, elemental corner turrets.

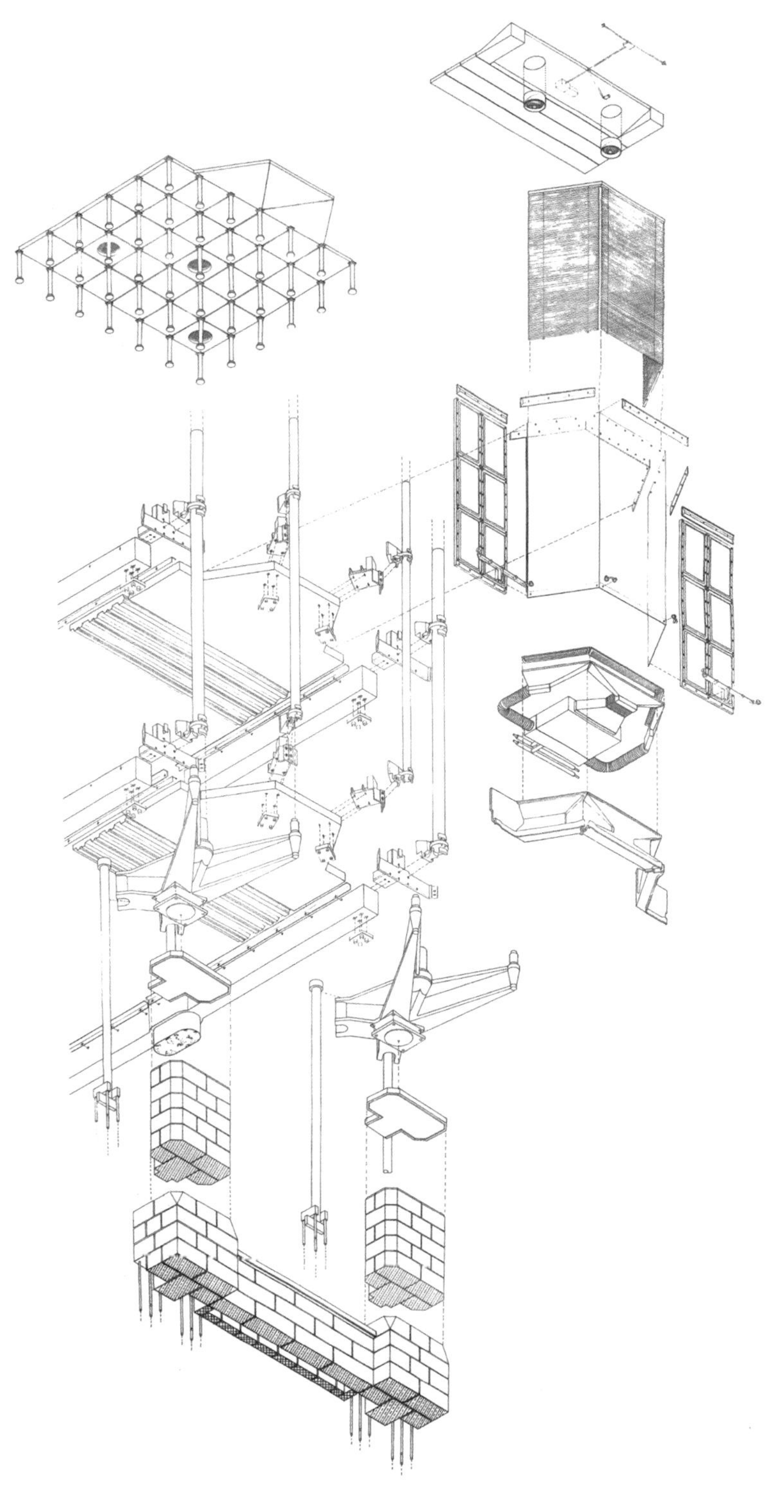

**HOPKINS ARCHITECTS**

**Bracken House, 1992**

Ink on tracing paper

64.5 × 34 cm, 25¼ × 13¼ in

Exploded axonometric diagrams are useful for showing multiple layers of information and how individual elements relate to each other spatially. This example, showing how the different parts of the facade of Bracken House in London go together, was made by hand, and the final ink-on-tracing-paper version shown here would have been traced over a base drawing set up in pencil. Here, the breathing space between the parts is clear, and is easiest to understand if the drawing is examined from the bottom upwards. Two stone piers rise from the masonry base, whose plan can be seen from below. These are separated from the lower structure and moved upwards as shown by the dotted, vertical lines connecting them. Above, the tripartite, cast-bronze elements that support the facade structure, on one side, and the floor beams, on the other, are isolated within their own realms. This junction forms the most complex part of the drawing, and each of its multiple fixings is drawn in three dimensions, with the dotted axes of the screws corresponding with their sockets. Flying outwards horizontally, the air-conditioning unit – in reality, hidden behind the specially designed facade element to which it is connected – is fully displayed. The shape of the gunmetal structural bays is articulated, from which the frameless windows hang. At the top is the suspended floor, with its multiple supports that correspond with the corners of the tiles, the under-floor zone showing how new office buildings of this period were responding to emerging requirements for servicing computers. The most common method of creating exploded axonometrics is to use a layered plan, which permits the various, stacked sections of the diagram to be shown in different planes. These planes allow the whole to explode in two directions – the elements separate vertically from each other, at the same time moving forwards.

**LOUIS KAHN (1901–74)**

**Sher-e-Bangla Nagar, 1963**

Charcoal and crayon on tracing paper

45.7 × 50.8 cm, 18 × 20 in

Sher-e-Bangla Nagar translates as City of the Tiger of Bengal, and is a zone in Dhaka designated for Bangladesh's National Parliament, designed by Louis Kahn. Its national assembly building and three hostels were grouped together and described as the Citadel of the Assembly. This perspective sketch shows a view through huge, arched openings from the enclosed garden of the hostels' dining and lounge courts. The long facade disappearing into the distance was drawn to try out the composition of the three-storey hostel facades. The strong light of the region was of concern to Kahn, and the notes he wrote at the bottom of the sheet address this: 'Alternate designs for wall openings of the hostels. Glare greatly modified as walls against the light receive light themselves'. These annotations accompany further small sketches of differently arranged motifs – repetitive, semicircular arches mimicking those of the garden enclosure, and a more varied motif comprising circular and triangular shapes. In the tiny sketches of human silhouettes shown against triangular openings, Kahn investigates the effect of reflecting light off the wall behind the openings in controlling glare. A section at the bottom right of the sheet bakes under a fierce sun, beating down on a stepped-back facade, in which the openings create an intermediate zone between the inner rooms and the outside. This was tested in the pyramidal section of the assembly building, which can be seen in the far distance in the perspective and which ultimately became a far more complex structure, with a central, circular assembly space encased in a layered shell whose outer casing consists of chapel-like blocks containing offices and various meeting spaces. The motifs that Kahn experiments with in this drawing repeat, however, in the final, monumental scheme for the National Parliament building.

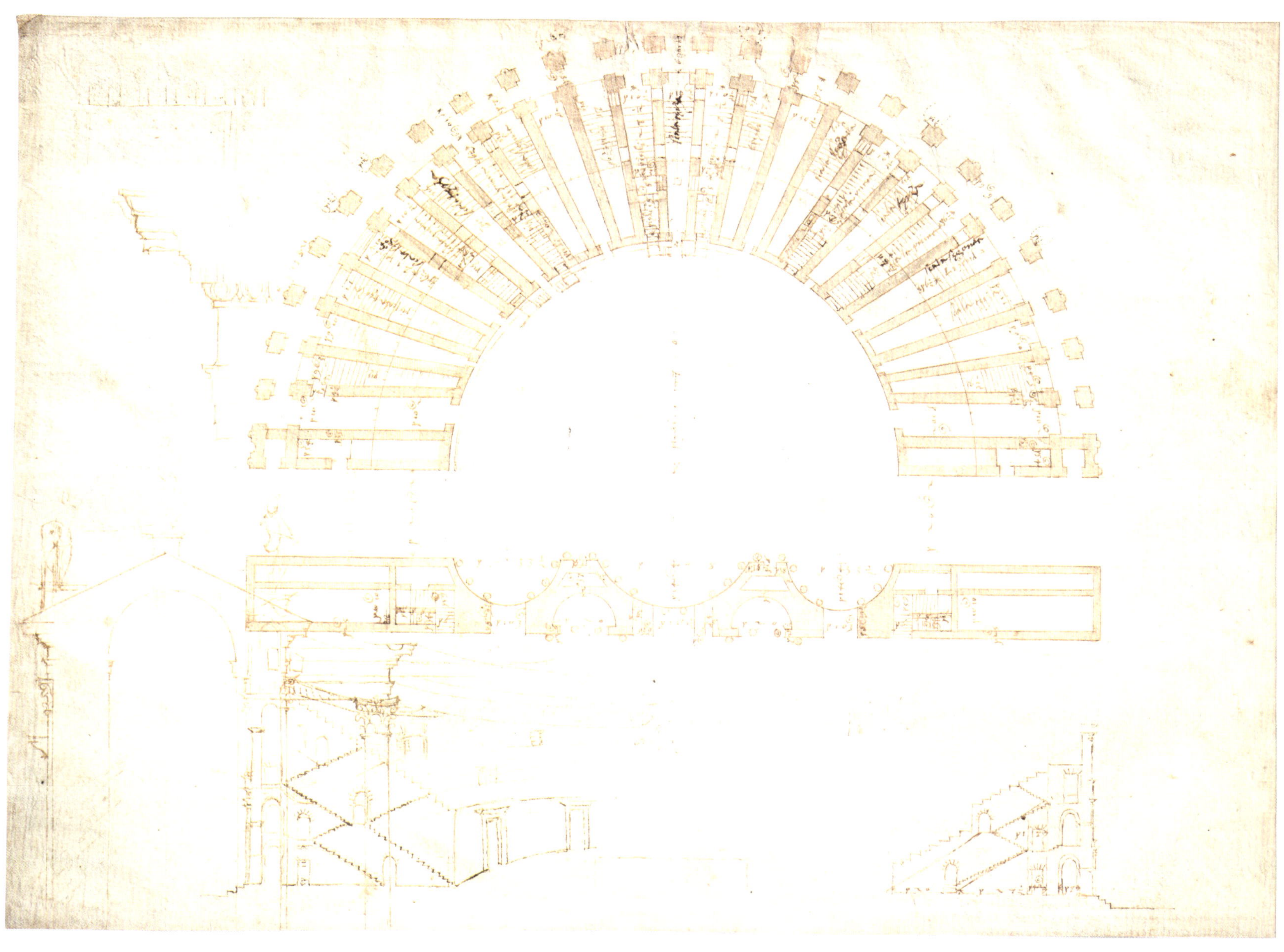

**ANDREA PALLADIO (1508–80)**

**Berga Theatre, 1536**

Ink on paper

28.7 × 41.1 cm, 11¼ × 16 in

This early Andrea Palladio drawing belongs to an interpretation of the ruins of the ancient Berga Theatre on the outskirts of Vicenza, Italy, which both he and his fellow architect and patron Daniele Barbaro considered a prototype. An interest in the theatre reflected the privileged status of Vicenza's aristocracy, and was a symbol of their power. In response, Palladio's project invented a new form – a departure from convention and an attempt to restore the idea of classical theatre. The reconstructed plan form, not entirely accurate in its reproduction of the site's archaeological reality, is accompanied by various sketches – three sections below, one extended into perspective, and a cornice profile to the left of the plan. The themes and forms of these small drawings recur and develop in sketchbooks and other drawings by Palladio. The divergence of this idealized plan from the original theatre structure lies in the fact that Palladio reconstructed its geometry using a Vitruvian diagram. This was based on the larger circle derived from the perimeter of the *cavea*, or seating sections, rather than the smaller one of its internal face, and the *cavea* itself is a semicircular, steeply sloping volume accessed by straight flights of steps visible in the sections. The proscenium faces the *cavea*, and is arranged around three large open niches, the central one wider than the others, with doorways for scene changes. In introducing the motif of the large, curving colonnade, the drawing has been influential in architectural history, revolutionizing late Renaissance, Baroque and Neo-Classical planning. It becomes transferred almost immediately in a sketch project for a villa at Dolo, where Palladio interprets it for the first time as a frame to the entrance court. The design itself can also be considered as a precursor to Palladio's Teatro Olimpico, still extant in Vicenza, which was begun in 1580.

**WILLIAM HARVEY (1883–1962)**

**Dome of the Rock, 1909**

Pen, watercolour, Indian ink and gold

90.8 × 121.3 cm, 35¾ × 47¾ in

A measured drawing is an accurate, scaled representation in orthogonal format of an existing building – usually a basis for additions or changes to it, or perhaps illustrating it as an archaeological artefact. This section through the building in Jerusalem known as the Dome of the Rock – looking south, drawn at a scale of 0.6 cm (¼ in) to 30.5 cm (1 ft)– is, as a measured drawing, unusual in its extravagant use of colour and intricate detail. Its striking black background includes plans of the ground floor and cave under the rock, along with a section of the cave, outlined in gold. The whole composition covers seven sheets that have been joined together, and an inscription states that it was measured and drawn on the spot. No representations of the building existed before 1833, when Frederick Catherwood spent six weeks surveying and drawing it, paving the way for engineer William Harvey to make this drawing of the medieval structure. The section shows three levels: the dome; the drum of the dome; and the arcade level that supports the drum and extends outwards to the peripheral walls, which are octagonal in plan. The dome's double-layered construction can be seen in the section, and its inner surface is decorated with plaster ornamentation that includes inscriptions from the Qur'an in various styles. The drum is decorated with original mosaics, and pierced by sixteen windows, eight of which are shown in the drawing. The detailed depiction of the arcade reveals the colours of the different marbles used in construction. The shrine was built by Umayyad Caliph Abd al-Malik in 691 upon the rock from which the Prophet Muhammad ascended to heaven on horseback, and is therefore one of Islam's holiest buildings. For Jews, it is revered as the place where Abraham offered his son Isaac as a sacrifice.

**VICTOR LOUIS (1731–1800)**

**Grand Théâtre, 1773**

Ink and pencil on paper

34.7 × 48 cm, 13½ × 19 in

Bordeaux's Grand Théâtre was the most magnificent and largest auditorium constructed in pre-Revolutionary France, at a time of prolific theatre building, and would become a model for subsequent constructions. Louis-Nicolas Victoire Louis was one of the first representatives in late-eighteenth-century France of the revised Classical style, which permeates his design. Inside, the Neo-Classical vestibule is adorned by a grand but plain symmetrical staircase that leads from the rusticated ground level to colonnaded balconies above, lit by a glass dome. The building is a long rectangular block with a portico of twelve giant Corinthian columns presenting a grand horizontal facade to the Place de la Comédie in the middle of the city. This section does not reveal its grand spaces, however, or its urban presence. It cuts across the middle of the building's rectangular volume, looking eastwards, to show how the structure of the theatre supports the imaginary world at its heart. This space is shown in perspective and the picturesque composition of the stage set, which winds along a vaulted arcade into the distance towards a brightly lit street, a small wing diverging off to the left, contrasts with the severity of the rest of the drawing. This shows a structure comprising two types of material: monolithic masonry, encasing two layers of space between the stage and the street; and prosaic timber struts and trusses, supporting the horizontal planes surrounding the stage. Neither of the street facades on either side is the monumental arcade of the front of the building, but together they make a symmetrical composition that is permeable to the street at ground level, with public rooms above. These lead into inner vestibules giving access to the balconies of the auditorium, acting as a buffer between the creative inner life of the city and the action of the street outside.

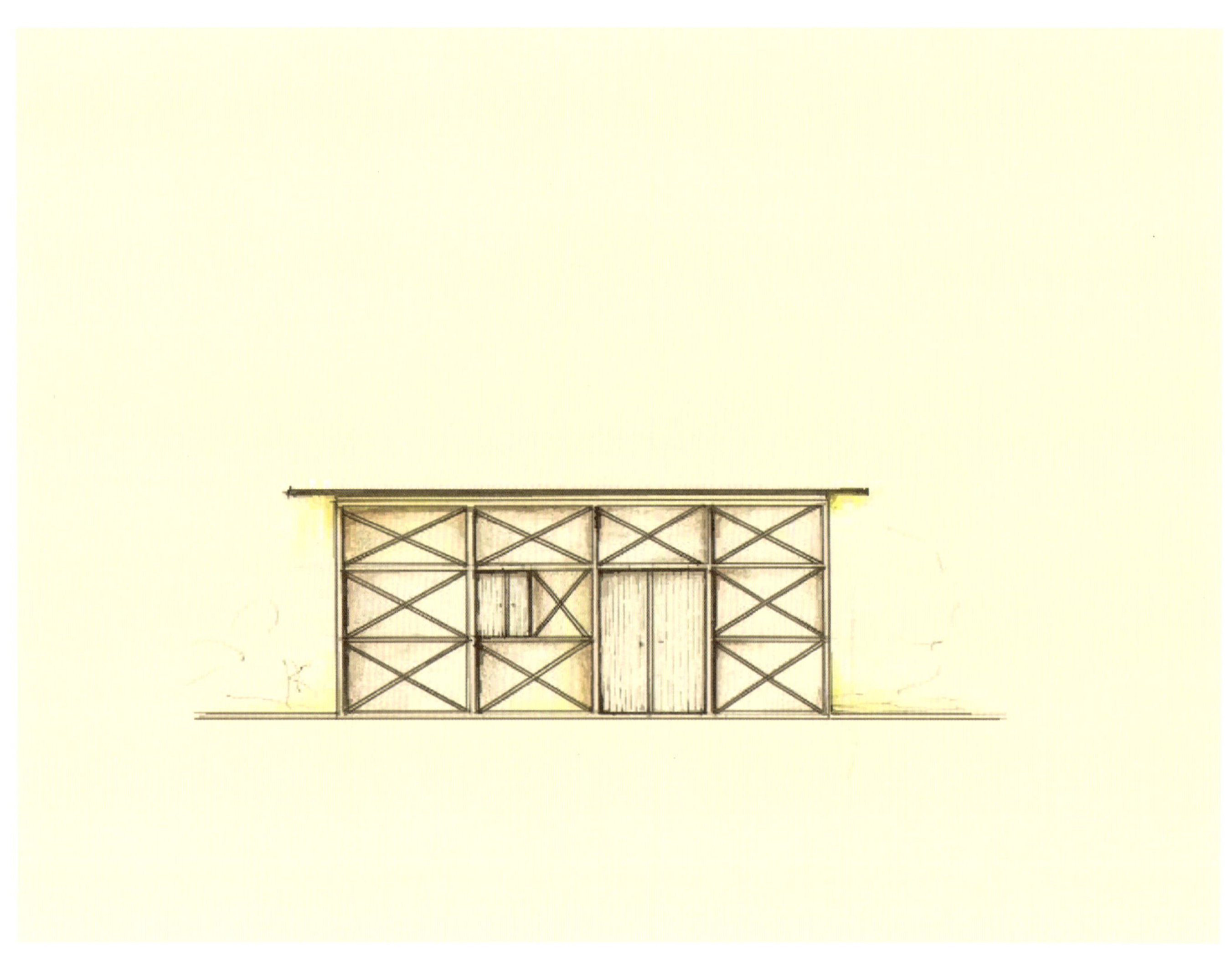

**YASMEEN LARI (1941–)**

**Emergency home, 2010**

Coloured pencil on paper

23.5 × 38 cm, 9 × 15 in

The economy of this solution for temporary homes is reflected in the economy of the drawing. From this elevation of emergency housing for victims of flooding in northern Pakistan's Swat Valley district, it would be possible to construct the simple, four-bay, flat-roofed structure that is depicted. The frame is constructed of bamboo stabilized on a basic platform of stone and compacted earth. Lime-mud is reinforced by the cross-braced frame to make the walls. The flat roof is formed of the same material over a simple woven frame, and soon after construction it sprouts grass and other weeds. Each one of these emergency homes, called Green Karavan Ghar, provides the basic means for dwelling, with a large room, a veranda, kitchen, lavatory and washroom. Although designed by architects, these structures are intended to be self-built, using materials both cheap and readily available in the surrounding environment. As temporary dwellings, they are designed to last for six months, until a more permanent solution can be created. The architect responsible for these houses is Yasmeen Lari, working in this instance in collaboration with the University of Glasgow and with inspiration from the Scottish Crofting Federation. Lari was one of the first architects in Pakistan; President of the Institute of Architects of Pakistan, 1980–83; and the first chairperson of the Pakistan Council of Architects and Town Planners. Her long and complex career has spanned all aspects of architectural practice – from designing concrete-and-steel, Brutalist structures for state-amenity buildings and corporate clients to the preservation of Pakistan's architectural heritage. Since 2005, Lari's focus has been on creating programmes for emergency housing across the country, and she has been responsible for the construction of over 36,000 disaster-relief dwellings via institutions that she has established: the Heritage Foundation, KaravanPakistan and the Karavan Programme for Indigenous Technology (KAPIT).

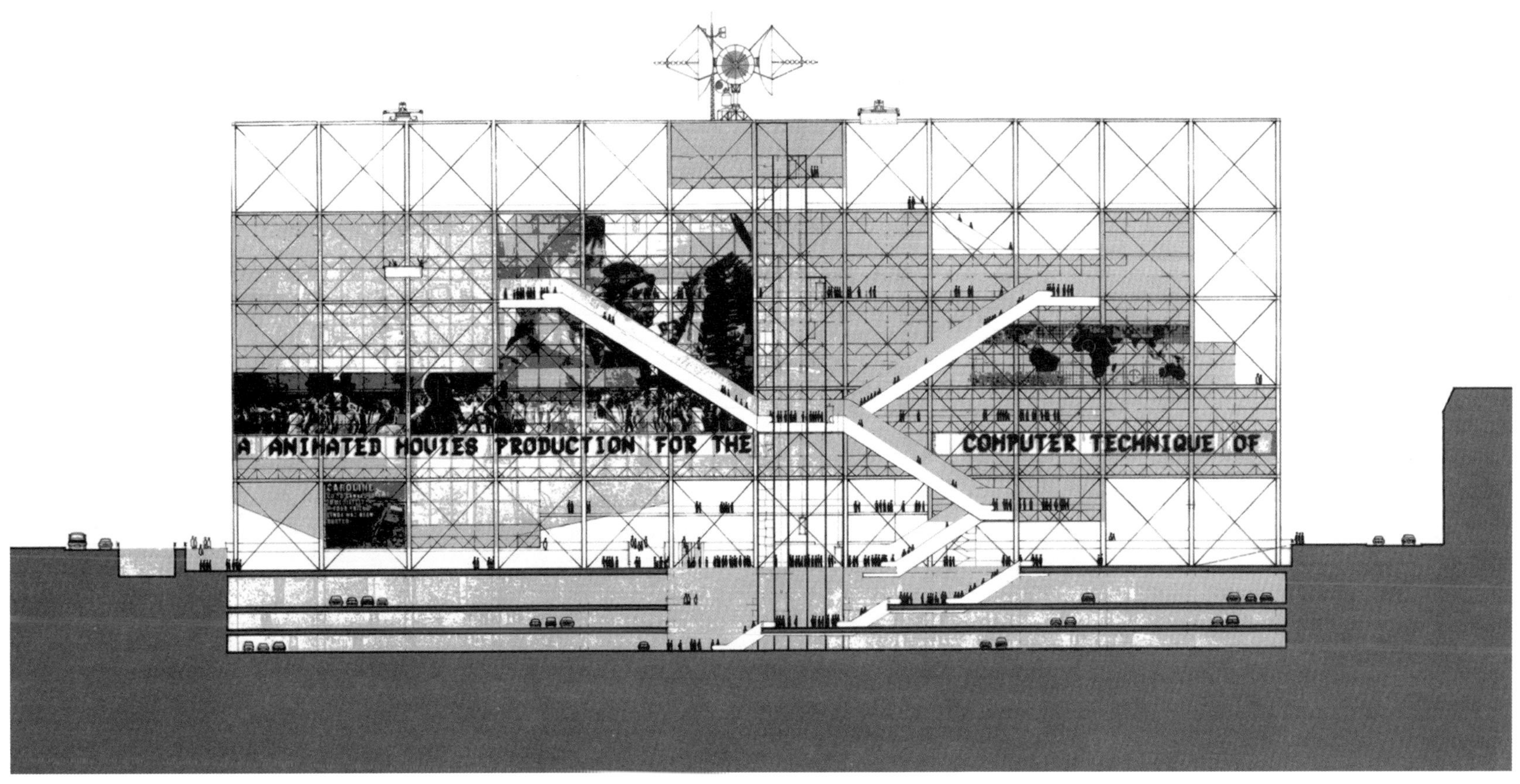


**RENZO PIANO (1937–) AND RICHARD ROGERS (1933–2021)**

**Pompidou Centre, 1971**

Pencil on paper

60 × 90 cm, 23½ × 35½ in

The protagonist of this cross-sectional drawing is the animated, interactive facade of what appears to be a huge shed. It was the centrepiece of Renzo Piano and Richard Rogers' entry for an international competition in 1970 to design a new, multidisciplinary cultural centre, which attracted 681 competitors from 49 countries. The facade seemed to symbolize technological progress in an explicit relationship with transparent social democracy – enacted through dynamic communications via the giant information screens of an accessible, contemporary cultural programme. Although the ambitious communication technologies envisaged here were not fully realized, the expression of services on the outside of the building – especially the transparent elevator tubes that give passengers fantastic views of the surrounding city – created a constantly changing backdrop. Precedents include Cedric Price and Joan Littlewood's Fun Palace, which advocated an indeterminate flexibility that could theoretically respond to the spatial and servicing requirements of any imaginable cultural manifestation. Strategically sited in the centre of Paris, between the redeveloped Les Halles markets and the then-run-down, historic Marais district, Piano and Rogers' huge, rectangular volume inhabited only half the city block designated as the competition site. The other half remained open as a public, pedestrianized square large enough for the facade to be appreciated from a distance – a symbolic space for public gathering within the dense urban fabric. Like the building itself, it has a different scale to the city around it, as shown in this drawing in the height of lower blocks of the Marais lining the adjoining street, and the relative narrowness of the surrounding thoroughfares. Named after the then-President of France, Georges Pompidou, the project was first conceptualized in 1969 in the wake of the anti-capitalist May 1968 riots that took place across the country, initiating a social revolution. The building itself was immediately embraced as a sensational popular monument.

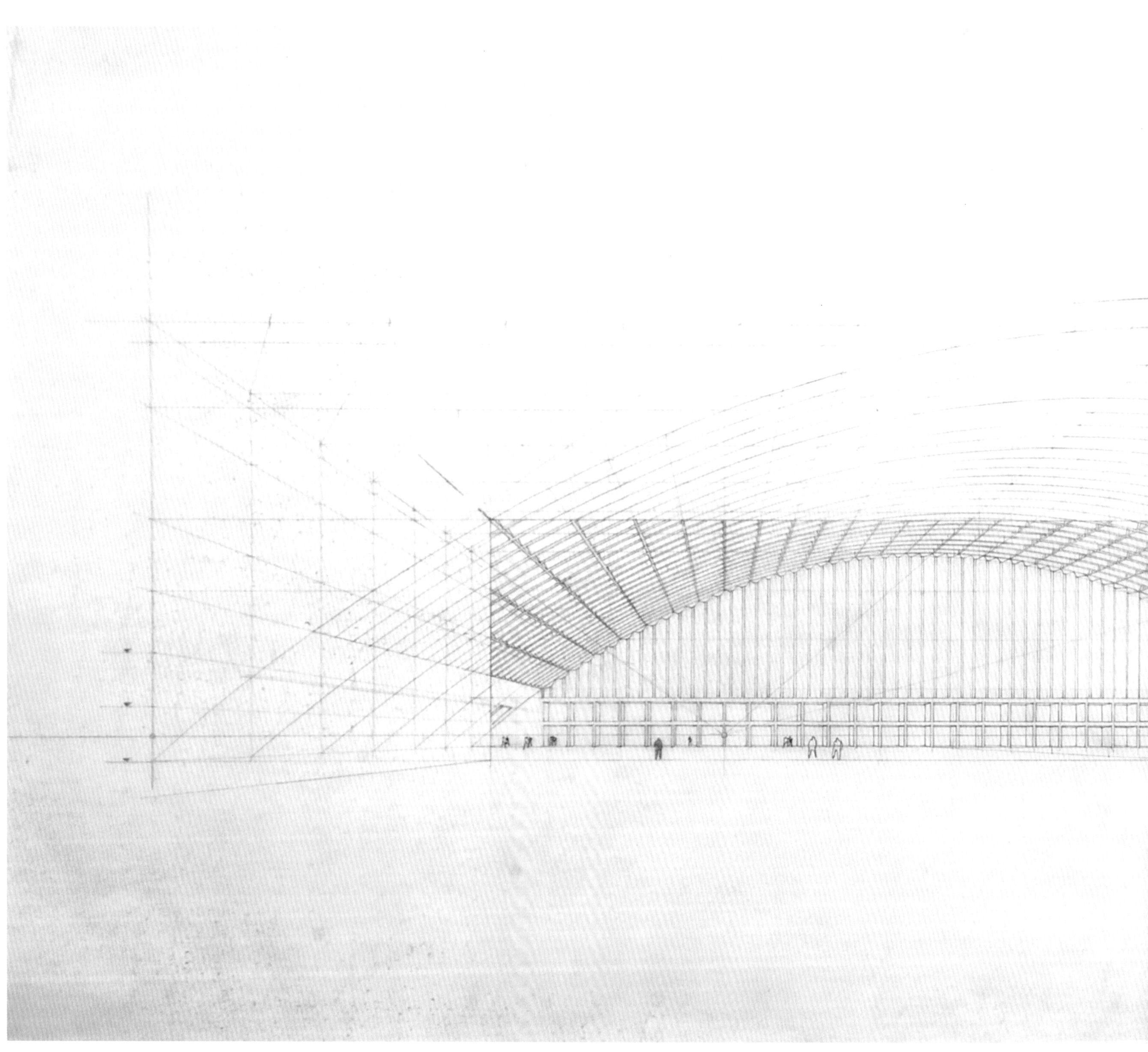

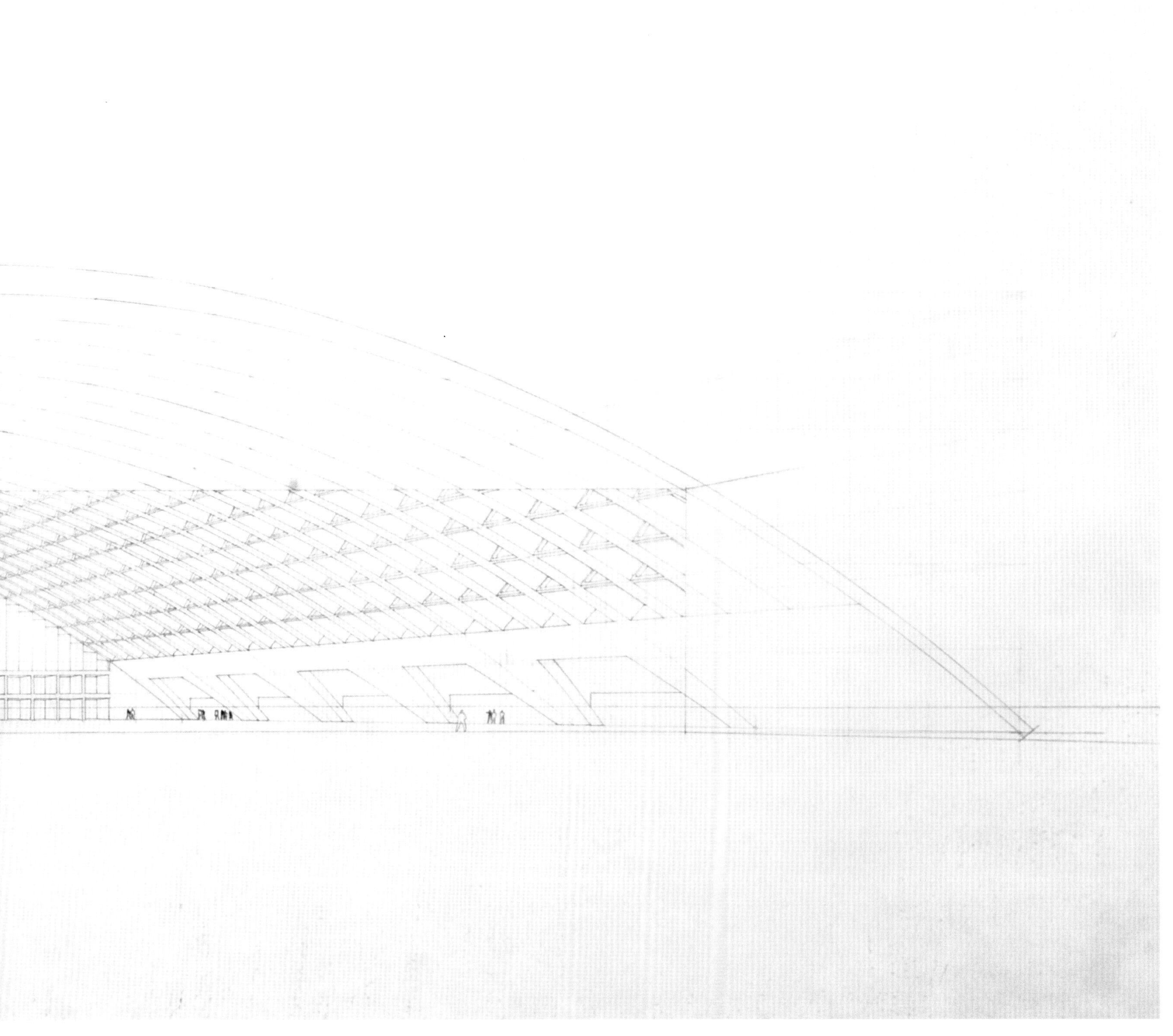

**PIER LUIGI NERVI (1891–1979)**

**Project for hangar, 1949**

Ink on paper

27 × 84 cm, 10½ × 33 in

This delicate structural perspective section by engineer Pier Luigi Nervi was made to describe an unbuilt project for an aeroplane hangar in Buenos Aires. Prefabricated, V-shaped reinforced-concrete elements form the coffer-like ceiling of the vast arched space, which spans 180 m (590 ft) and is almost 40 m (131 ft) high. The drawing highlights the beauty of the repeated rhythm and depth of these roof elements – not only through perspective projection, which increases in intensity in the depths of the image, but also by framing a second, rectangular picture plane in which this detail is elaborated. The rear wall of the hangar is composed of folded, precast units that provide rigid bracing. These rest on a horizontal, shelf-like concrete grid that projects back two bays beyond the vertical plane of the back wall in a more conventional columned structure. At the front of the hangar, not shown in the drawing, a deep concrete slab supports the vertical folded plane above, and frames large, sliding doors. Tiny figures populate the elaborated realm, revealing the huge scale of the structure. They contrast with the concrete abutments at ground level, which continue the elliptical line of the arches, resisting the pressure of their outward-pushing forces and weight, and carrying them down into the ground. No aeroplanes are shown in this drawing, perhaps because they would obscure and interrupt the structural rhythms set up in it. Outside the internal picture frame, the construction lines of the drawing create a ghostly pattern that blurs the edge of the image, suggesting that the structure could perhaps be extrapolated infinitely. The front of the building is not shown, and vertical planes on either side of the space are outlines that do not exist in the reality of the drawing but which are used to set up its perspectival lines.

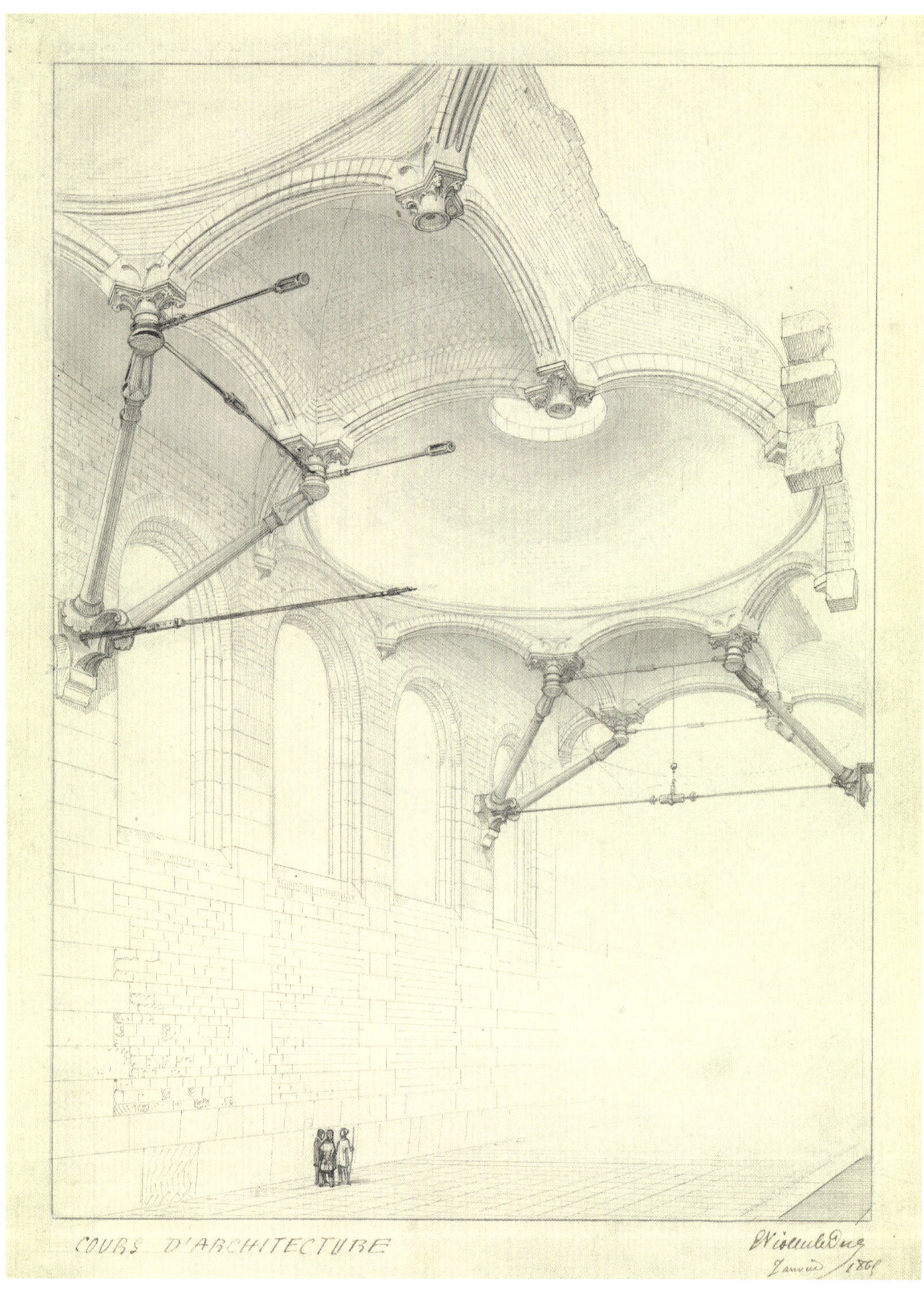


**EUGÈNE EMMANUEL VIOLLET-LE-DUC (1814–79)**

**Hall with a twenty-metre span, 1863**

Engraving

33.3 × 24.9 cm, 13 × 9¾ in

Eugène Emmanuel Viollet-le-Duc was a prolific and talented draughtsman who made many different types of drawings. This perspective drawing was made in response to his experiences as a founder of historical restoration and preservation, and emerged from his controversial thinking, based on Gothic rather than Classical principles. A copy of it was engraved by Claude Sauvageot to appear in the first volume of Viollet-le-Duc's *Entretiens sur l'architecture* (Discourses on Architecture), 1863, appearing as Plate 21 in the section 'Masonry'. This book constituted a direct challenge to the predominant methodologies of the École des Beaux-Arts, presenting radical solutions to architectural and structural issues. The drawing illustrates a fascinating hybrid structure that combines conventional, monolithic stone construction for the walls of a large hall, using centuries-old techniques, with the use of robust, diagonal iron struts and ties to support and brace the ring beams of a system of domed masonry roof vaults. It demonstrates how a medieval vault might have been made, had its builders had access to structural iron. This supporting structure is provocatively exposed to view, and demonstrates the use of a combination of materials – ancient and modern – in their various capacities, expressed separately rather than fused into a confusing and dishonest artifice. Each of the structure's diverse parts is designed to serve its purpose with efficiency, but not without decorative intent. The iron joints and brackets bear leafy flourishes, and the brickwork of the vaults is organized into different patterned textures that reflect the tectonic nature of their surfaces. The smooth circular vault is treated differently to the faceted dome, and the continuation of the window piers of the stone wall are articulated down to ground level.

**LÉON KRIER (1946–) AND JAMES STIRLING (1926–92)**

**Restaurant at the Olivetti Headquarters, 1970**

Ink, colored pencil and graphite on paper

41.6 × 55.1 cm, 16½ × 21¾ in

Drawings played an important role in James Stirling's office, but he was not always their author. Even at the early stages of a project, various staff members made small sketches for discussion and approval. This single-point perspective was made for publication by Léon Krier, who worked there between 1968 and 1971, and hand coloured later by Stirling. The interior depicted the restaurant for the British headquarters of Olivetti, in Milton Keynes, but it was never built, so the drawing has an aesthetic autonomy in which ideas about British design, taste and architectural reference are developed. Stirling himself is seated just outside the perspective frame, on an early-nineteenth-century Thomas Hope chair. In front of him, still outside the boundary but in the centre of the perspective, is a Neo-Classical Hope table bearing an open book. Stirling points across the perspective's heart, in discussion with another young staff member, Brian Riches, who, leaning on a matching Hope chair, is watched by Krier in the form of a classical bust. The realistic technique references drawings by Le Corbusier but also the simple line perspectives made by Hope to illustrate furniture settings in his book *Household Furniture*, 1807. Above this animated foreground, the dark ceiling is brought into the picture. This enhances perception of the glass wall separating the space from the hills beyond, reminiscent of work by Alvar Aalto. The presence of the ceiling also brings into play the yellow mushroom columns whose capitols allude to a nineteenth-century industrial heritage as well as a classical lineage: the broken column near Riches creates an archaeological fragment. The columns mark a conventional perspective, but in their relationship to the other elements – the spiral staircase, the mezzanine, the curved glass wall, and even the pot plant – they reveal a free-form space unconfined by strict geometry.

**FILIPPO JUVARRA (1678–1736)**

**Concorso Clementino, 1705**

Pen and watercolour on paper

130 × 100 cm, 51¼ × 39½ in

In 1705, the Accademia di San Luca in Rome, a select association of artists, held a competition calling for designs in the style of their recently introduced three-sided emblem – symbolizing the equality of the three arts: painting, sculpture and architecture. The young architect and stage-set designer Filippo Juvarra entered and won first prize, plus entry to the Accademia in 1706, with a proposal that caused a sensation – not only for the brilliance of his design and graphic facility but also for the size of its four sheets, which were the largest ever submitted for such a competition. This sheet shows the ground plans of the three villas that Juvarra set in the middle of a garden, reached by bridges over an encircling artificial lake. The ornamental gardens formed an idealized setting for the central structure. Its complex plan, set out around a hexagonal central court, lies within the frame of an imaginary insert sheet, whose curled edges are prevented from springing shut by decorative ties at the top and sides. Above this plan, an elevation shows the main facade of one of the villas, flanked by two wings with grand external staircases, whose semicircular projections are surmounted by domes with pointed lanterns. In elevation, the ensemble has the presence of a small citadel, with its variety of overlapping and undulating planes and its layered composition on a rusticated base bounded by double-height pilasters. The section above is cut through the apartments for one of the characters and their court on the left, which looks into a small, private court separated from the central space by a continuous colonnade. The rhythm of this two-storey cloister is shown in elevation, and the section ends on the right by revealing the volume of the grand, domed hall gracing each of the villas.

**OFFICE FOR METROPOLITAN ARCHITECTURE (OMA)**

**Renovation of a Panoptic Prison, 1978**

Colour pencil and watercolour on paper

68.6 × 113 cm, 27 × 44½

Rem Koolhaas, OMA's figurehead, rarely draws; all the images to come out of the office since its foundation in 1975 have been, in his words, made by OMA as a cooperative venture. This early presentation drawing for the renovation of a panopticon style prison in Arnhem is no exception, and the project appeared in a book in which OMA revealed its multimedia approach to architecture – *S,M,L,XL* (1995) – in the M (medium) section. The whole prison is seen from the air, not in perspective but drawn as an axonometric so that all parts are to scale, and the surrounding urban fabric is represented in plan. Unlike in traditional aerial or atmospheric perspectives, the density of the muted colours – varieties of grey and brown with cold blue and two small divergences to red and salmon pink – is consistent throughout. The separate world of the prison, surrounded by walls and entered through a curious castellated gateway, is luminous and spatial. The central space, a 56 m-diameter (183.7 ft) cylinder, had been built for solitary confinement, with an observation tower, the eye, at its centre. Over the years, the spatial relationship had been subverted and the centre of power abandoned. The guards' canteen ended up in the centre, observed by the unconfined inmates – among whom the guards circulated to effect their control. The project proposed adding two streets, which can be seen most clearly in the cylindrical space connecting this centre to the edges of the prison. They form an exit from the dome, and their intersection obliterates forever the Panopticon eye. All new facilities are accommodated along these streets as autonomous elements – some inside, but most outside. The project is an ideological critique of imprisonment, but also a celebration of the success of this spatial form – both as inmates' lived environment and metaphor for social organization.

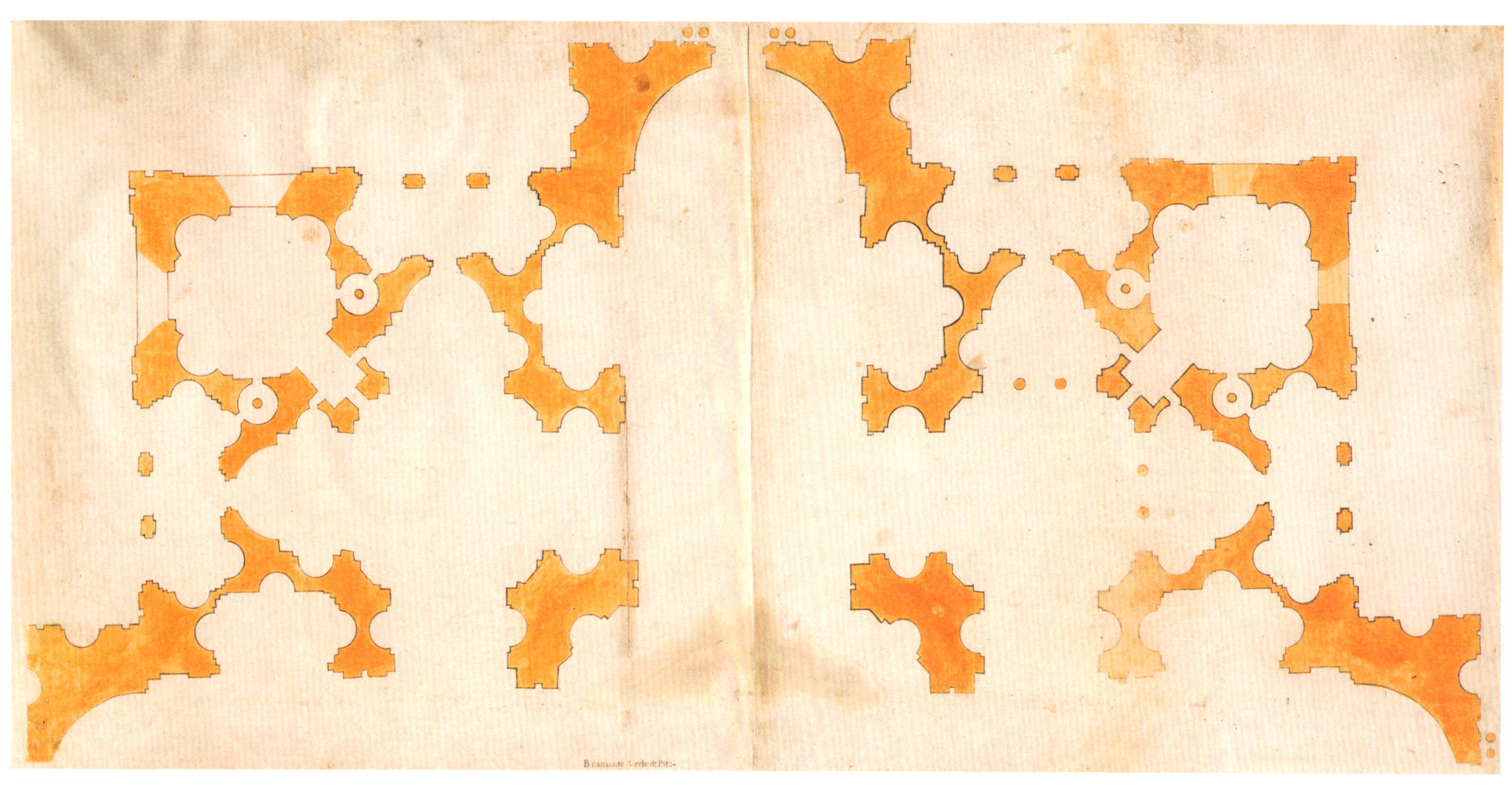

**DONATO BRAMANTE (1656–1723)**

**St Peter's Basilica, 1505**

Ink and watercolour on parchment

55.8 × 110.5 cm, 22 × 43½ in

The creation of a new St Peter's Basilica, which started at the beginning of the sixteenth century with Donato Bramante's designs, generated an exceptional quantity of fine drawings, many of which survive. It represented a shift in architectural practice: before the Renaissance, a building designer was typically a master craftsman engaged directly in both design and construction. Drawings of the new St Peter's were made by the architect to communicate the design to craftsmen, and a new separation between the theoretical and the constructional appeared. St Peter's in Rome is one of the earliest buildings for which an extensive record of preliminary, design-stage drawings exists, revealing the exploratory process that was carried out on paper. This famous drawing, the parchment plan of Bramante's original, unbuilt scheme, is one of the earliest architectural drawings of its type. It shows the western part of Bramante's first scheme, and the absence of a scale shows that it is a presentation drawing rather than a constructional one. Although it is unclear whether the whole plan is longitudinal or centralized, the drawing reveals the mathematical rigour of his solution for expanding the space. The density of the ink-filled columns, piers and walls, undisturbed by other lines or detail, transmits the power of the masonry work in a visceral way. This deceptive simplicity and clarity belies the difficult task of making room for the structure without disturbing the position of the obelisk or threatening the integrity of the Sistine Chapel, while maintaining a consistent, if complex, modular system. The plan shows how Bramante enlarged niches so that they appear to erode the wall masses that contain them – a move that emphasizes the symbolic shape of the Greek cross and provides an opportunity to enlarge the secondary domes and corner towers of the cathedral.

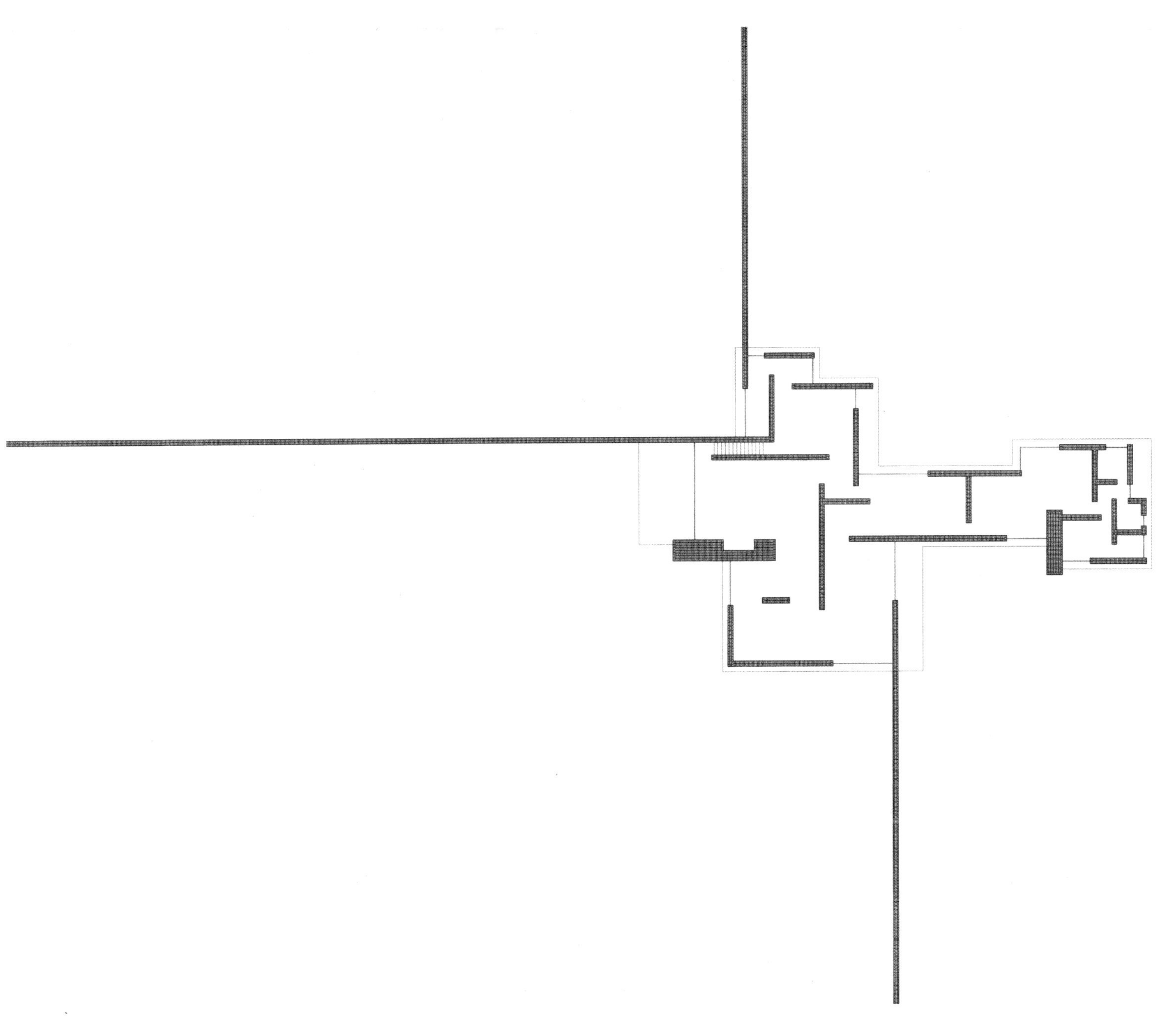

**MIES VAN DER ROHE (1886–1969)**

**Plan for a brick country house, 1923**

Ink on illustration board

76.2 × 101.6 cm, 30 × 40 in

This plan – made for the design of a brick house, possibly for the architect himself – was the last of a series of experiments with materials and building types, the drawings for which were lost when Mies emigrated to America. The design was shown in the *Neue Sachlichkeit* (New Objectivity) exhibition at Mannheim in 1925, which presented a reaction to Expressionism, with a new attitude towards the production of art and architecture that was sympathetic to the functional, the useful and the professional possibilities of the technological world. The plan accompanied a not-quite-matching perspective, and together they illustrated a low building with a flat roof set on a gently sloping site defined and divided by long garden walls, which in this drawing can be seen extending to the edges of the sheet and connecting the heart of the house with the boundary of its plot. The drawing has been compared with Theo van Doesburg's abstract compositions in its challenge to the idea of bounded and hierarchical space, or rooms in the domestic context, but for Mies the system of construction was as important as the definition of space. Here, the walls are linear planes of Flemish-bonded, load-bearing brickwork unified by projecting roof slabs. The uniform thickness of these uninterrupted walls, except for the volumes containing fireplaces and flues, makes the usual distinctions between inside and out, structure and partition, more ambiguous than usual. The plan reveals a fundamental transformation of traditional residential space, with doors and windows reduced to sheer openings between wall slabs. Instead of a conventional, axial progression of reception rooms, these larger spaces interlock and merge with each other in a matrix of wall fragments that circle around an empty core. A service wing is discernible by its smaller and more defined rooms.

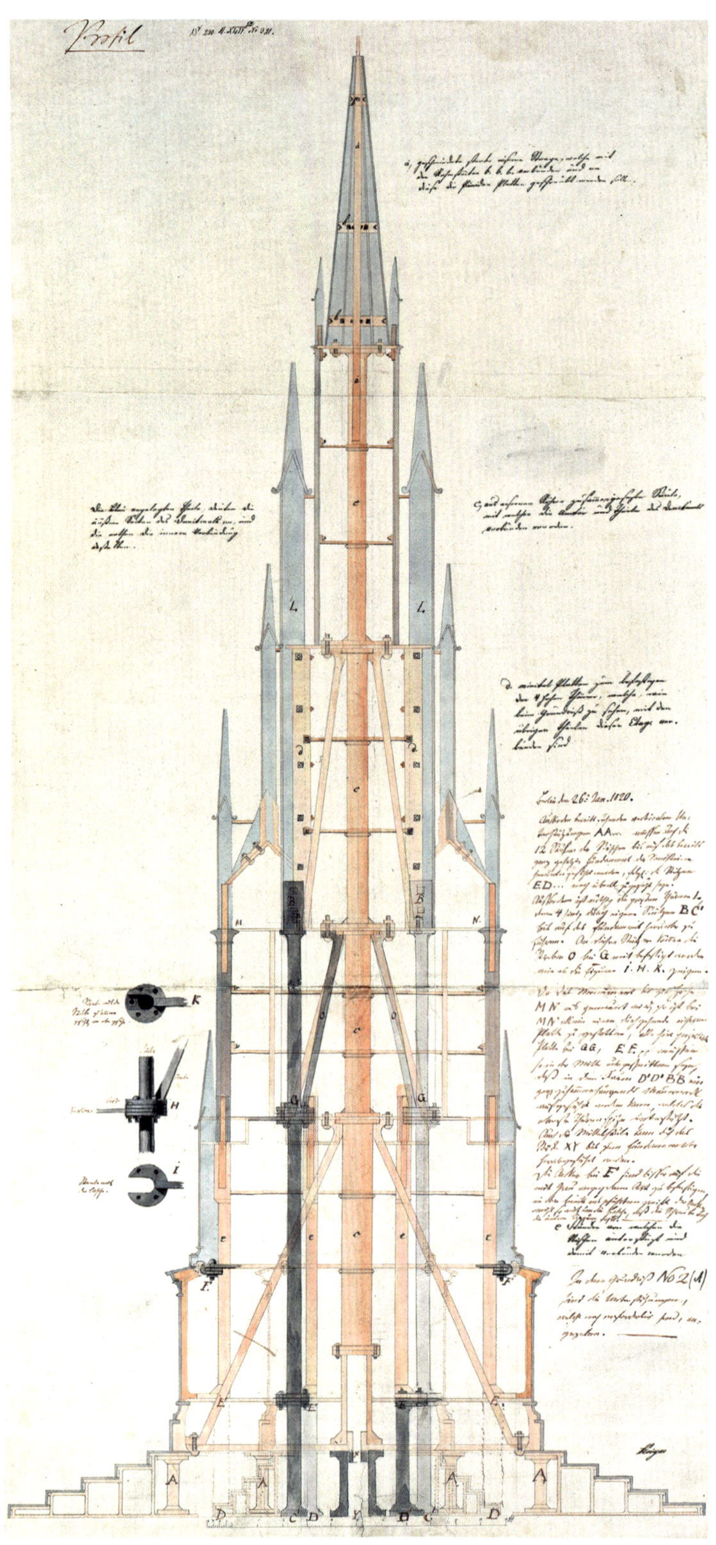

**KARL FRIEDRICH SCHINKEL (1781–1841)**

**Kreuzberg Monument, c.1820**

Pen and watercolour over graphite on paper

105 × 50.4 cm, 41¼ × 19¾ in

Cast iron was an important and symbolic material in early-nineteenth-century Prussia. It was associated with the modernization campaigns of Friedrich Wilhelm III, in the context of an emerging German national consciousness in response to French invasion. In 1796, the Prussian king established a royal ironworks in the mining district of Silesia. Karl Friedrich Schinkel played a leading role in promoting the new construction material, and the National Monument of the Fallen that he designed at Kreuzberg in Berlin to remember those killed during the 1813 War of Liberation is an interesting example of his relationship with the material. This finely coloured section through the tall and slender, 20 m-high (65.5 ft) tower, with its Gothic pinnacles and screens, is cut through a structure entirely formed out of cast iron. All of the parts of the monument were produced at the Royal Ironworks. The decorative external elements are coloured in a light grey, and support only themselves. In the drawing, they are shown as smooth and pointed, and the decoration encrusting the finished object has been omitted. A hidden, cast-iron core, revealed in the void of the section, supports these decorative cast-iron panels and pinnacles. The central and principal structural core is coloured red; it takes the form of a central pillar that becomes more slender towards the top, through a series of elements that decrease in diameter. Each of these, apart from the very top, is supported by a diagonal strut system, also in iron and painted red. A secondary structure is painted black, and supports the buttressing of the lower level and some of the primary struts. This was Schinkel's last romantic Neo-Gothic design, a style which was associated with the medievalism underlying the construction of a new national culture; his later work is defined by Greek Classicism.

**LYONEL FEININGER (1871–1956)**

**Zukunftskathedrale, 1919**

Woodcut

41.0 × 30.5 cm, 16 × 12 in

This black-and-white woodcut by Lyonel Feininger adorned the cover of the first Bauhaus manifesto, the *Programm des Staatlichen Bauhauses in Weimar* (Programme of the State Building School in Weimar), published to define the aims of this revolutionary art and design school founded by Walter Gropius. Also in 1919, the newly formed Arbeitsrat für Kunst (Workers' Council for Art), to which both Gropius and Feininger belonged, published a manifesto. In sympathy with the Bauhaus, it stated that '[a]rt and people must form an entity. Art shall no longer be a luxury of the few, but should be enjoyed and experience by the broad masses. The aim is the alliance of the arts under the wing of a great architecture.' The image of a cathedral – a symbol of the old, hierarchical order – might seem at odds with this ambition, but this was a *Zukunftskathedrale*, a utopian cathedral of socialism. The early Bauhaus was inspired by the structure and community of medieval guilds in its desire for a new unity of craftsmanship and art, and it was structured around crafts-based workshops that included the printing studio run by Feininger between 1919 and 1925, when the Bauhaus moved to Dessau. In 1919, however, it was the manifesto of the Workers' Council that Gropius and his team were inspired by, and it was the total work of art, created with the active participation of the people and embodying popular and decorative traditions within the definition of the arts, that they aspired to. In this woodcut, Feininger has purposefully used the Gothic cathedral to reference the communal effort and joint vision of artists and artisans. The prismatic light refracted within the sky around its spire recalls Bruno Taut's utopian dreams for a glass architecture, while the primitive quality of the woodcut process underlines the hand-rendered craftsmanship of its production.

**FRANK LLOYD WRIGHT (1867–1959) AND JOHN H HOWE (1913–97)**

**Fallingwater, 1937**

Pencil and coloured pencil on tracing paper

39 × 69.2 cm, 15.4 × 27.2 in

Landscape as a tangible experience was integral to Frank Lloyd Wright's idea of architecture. In this perspective of Fallingwater, the holiday house that Wright designed for wealthy businessman Edgar J Kaufmann in the heart of the Bear Run Nature Reserve, the landscape seems to have been made and revealed by the house, which has the same colour as the rocks. The building inhabits the top half of the drawing, with the view from below – an infrequent device in drawings from Wright's studio, which were usually drawn from conventional eye height, or from above. This has a powerful effect on how the scene is perceived. Firstly, it makes the picture plane relatively shallow: only the recesses of the structure contain depth and shadow. The rocks, trees and bushes all inhabit the same plane surrounding the house, and are made lively by skilful rendering in Wright's beloved coloured pencils and by texture. This flattening enhances the powerful presence of the balconies over the 9 m-high (29.5 ft) waterfall, whose vertical drop is framed by the horizontal cantilevers looming over it. Compared to iconic photographs of the house, the position of the water's edge seems modified to intensify the sensation of the rushing water, the steep banks and the wild vegetation. John H Howe was chief draughtsman at the Taliesin Fellowship at the time, and would have made the drawing under Wright's supervision as the final presentation drawing for the scheme. Perspectival drawings were important in Wright's design process, and were set out using mechanical projection so accurately that they were more true representations of proportion and scale than subsequent photographs. This is the case here, where the viewer has been lifted from the ground in order to control the convergence of horizontal planes evident in earlier sketches, and to give the sheet of water a longer drop.

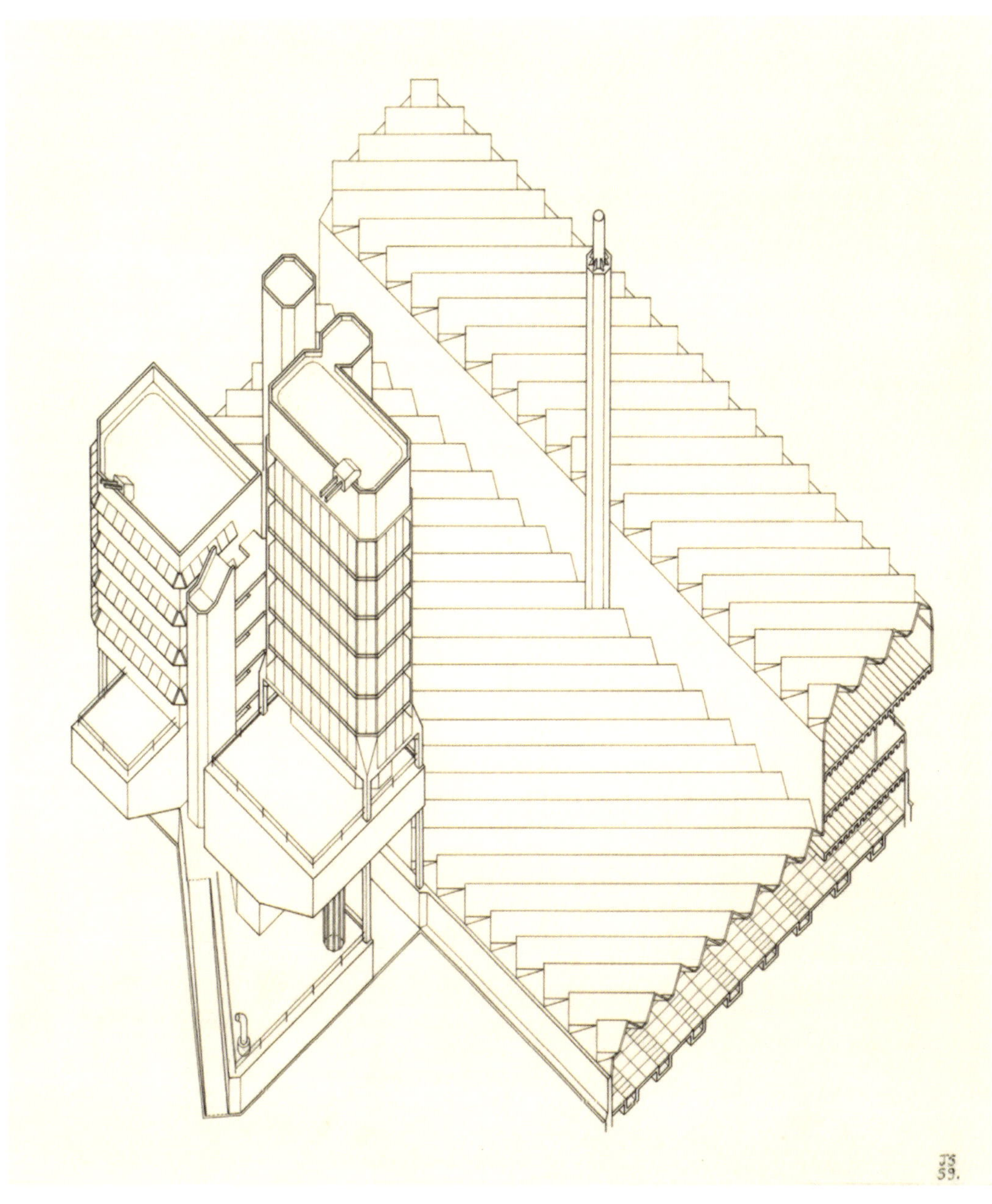


**JAMES STIRLING (1926–92)**

**Leicester Engineering Building, 1963**

Ink and graphite on paper

43.7 × 34.2 cm, 17¼ × 13½ in

The Leicester Engineering Building is like a built diagram, said Léon Krier, held together by a mysterious system, more like a three-dimensional diagram than a building structure. This axonometric drawing of the whole complex – including workshops, laboratories, lecture theatres, staff rooms and offices – was drafted by James Stirling, who initialled and dated it in the bottom right-hand corner. Echoing Krier's words, the building is presented as a volumetric collection of forms: a complex and contradictory object, devoid of physical context. Its collage of disparate volumes somehow coheres, its collection of references from architectural history extending outside the limited Modernist orthodoxy. In addition to Russian Constructivism – specifically, Konstantin Melnikov's Rusakov Workers' Club – critics have identified echoes of the Crystal Palace, Antonio Sant'Elia's Città Nuova, Frank Lloyd Wright and English industrial-vernacular buildings, but about these Stirling was mute. Sited on a flat ground, a convenient tabula rasa, the laboratory slab's external walls define a plinth-like element supporting the entrance level of the administrative towers, into which the lecture halls are embedded. This is reached by a ramp not visible in this drawing. Stirling has used a single line weight, giving no emphasis to sectional cuts or structural elements, so that everything is equivalently drawn, but some components are explained in more detail. The mullions of the tower windows are shown, for example, as are the precast-concrete elements of the floors, the cranes for cleaning, the chimney and the vents. The corrugated glazing forming the roof over the large slab of the workshops and the raised, four-storey wing of laboratories that this steps up to is comparatively undefined. It is presented as a simple, folded plane but is far from that in reality – being an extraordinary crystalline structure, whose presence, according to myth, was only conceived when the design was projected in an axonometric such as this.

**JOHN HEJDUK (1929–2000)**

**The Voided Centre and Death House, 1980**

Grey, green and brown pencil over graphite on paper

86.4 × 110.2 cm, 34 × 43½ in

This elevation belongs to a group of forty-nine images made by John Hejduk between 1980 and 1982 for exhibition and publication in *The Lancaster/Hanover Masque*, 1982. It is No. 4 of the nine large final drawings that illustrate sixty-eight structures defining a dramatized, imaginary rural farm community, and it shows two of the central elements: the Voided Centre and the Death House. The placing of these structures within his fantasy world relates to themes of death, and the mystery of the drawing is enhanced by their relationship with the ground. A horizontal datum runs along the bottom of the sheet, upon which sits a series of small cubicles next to the triangular volume of the Death House. Fine pencil lines depict an ensemble of flat shapes representing volumes, some adhering to the datum while others appear to float in a kind of pre-perspectival space. Although some elements belong to a familiar architectural language – the window grid, metal panels and tall chimneys – their scale is not apparent and the group seems to exist in a void. Hejduk was Dean of Architecture at the Cooper Union in New York, 1964–2000, and his architectural practice was largely a theoretical challenge to conventional architecture. His work lay on the boundaries between architecture, scenography, sculpture and poetry, and contributed to the increasing influence of theory in architectural education during the 1970s and 80s. *The Lancaster/Hanover Masque* makes reference to other farm communities, such as the Roanoke Colony, and to Claude-Nicolas Ledoux's ideal farm structures. Consistent with Hejduk's interest in ritualistic performance, the project is described as a masque – a type of seventeenth-century theatrical production whose structure is not determined by a linear narrative. Its roots lie in medieval mime, and its internal logic is made apparent through repetition.

**HUGH FERRISS (1889–1962)**

**Buildings in the Modeling, 1924**

Conté crayon on board

31.8 × 81.3 cm, 12½ × 32 in

In 1929, Hugh Ferriss published an influential book called *The Metropolis of Tomorrow*, and this two-point aerial perspective, peering into the ravines of the city's upper realm, belongs to a series called *Buildings in the Modeling* that appeared in it. It presents an image of how tall buildings could be shaped, or modelled, in order to retain the maximum mass and rentable volume while complying with New York's recently introduced zoning regulations. Ferriss used a soft Conté crayon to depict this ensemble of faceted towers, defined by the chiaroscuro of an artificially lit landscape. The play of shadow and light across their surfaces reveals solid but seemingly translucent masses. For Ferriss and his clients, the dense metropolis was the future for modern humanity, and he used his skill to envision the power and beauty, as well as the psychological impact, of the city's new Giant Order. In 1916, a pioneering series of laws had come into force in New York City called the Zoning Ordinance, which regulated the use, area and height of new buildings. It prescribed maximum heights and setbacks, and defined the physical qualities of different urban zones, such as residential and industrial. In 1922, Ferriss had been commissioned by skyscraper architect Harvey Wiley Corbett to create a series of drawings exploring how these laws impacted on the formal massing of tall buildings. These became known as The Four Stages or Evolution of the Set-back Building, laying out the formal principles for a new kind of skyscraper. Ferriss had trained as an architect before coming to New York to work as a delineator for Cass Gilbert, later setting up an independent practice. By 1920, he had developed an atmospheric style of drawing night-time cityscapes that attracted many architects, and his work began to appear in newspapers and magazines.

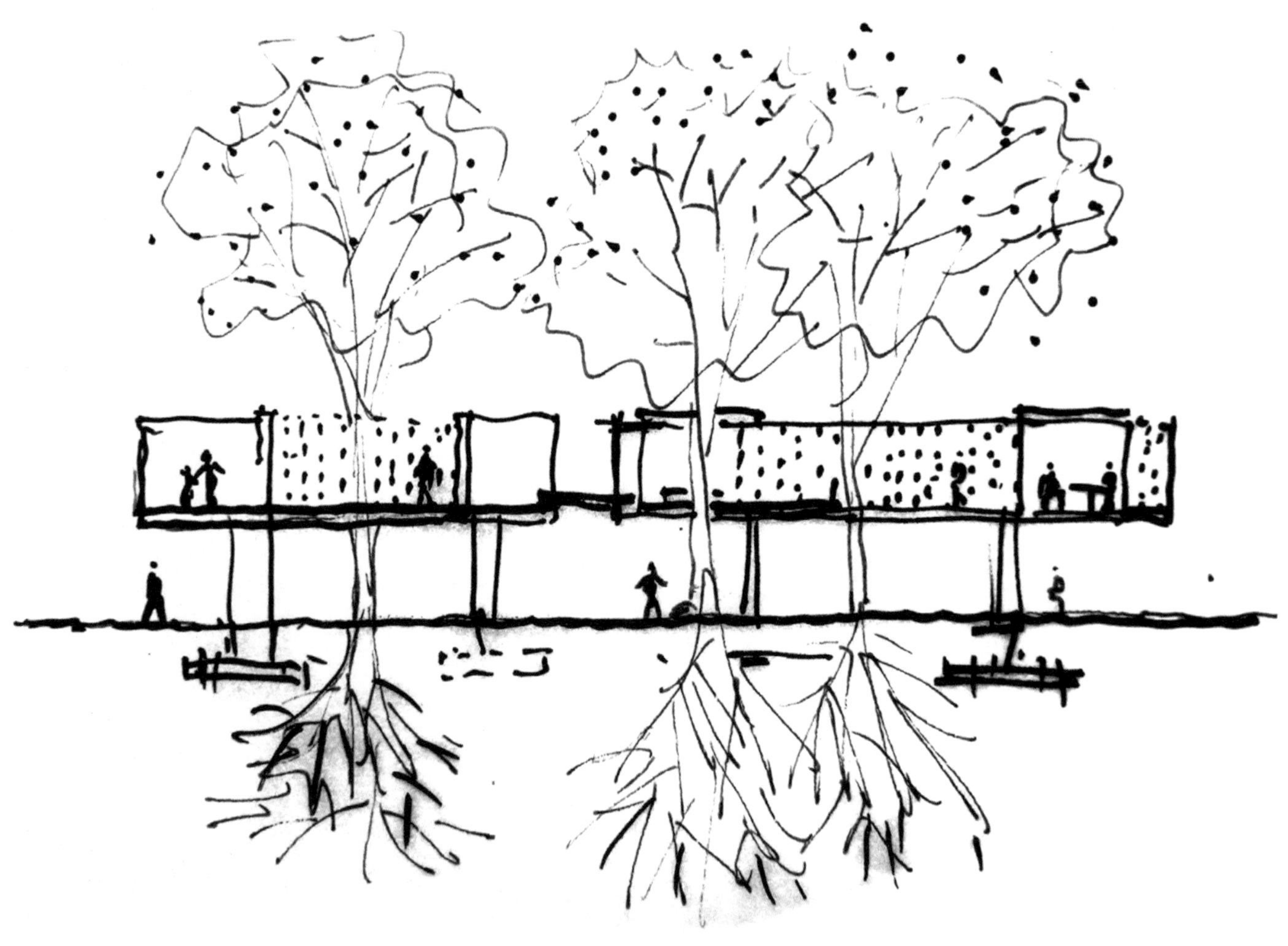

**SCENIC ARCHITECTURE**

**Huaxin Business Centre, 2012**

Ink on paper

25 × 18 cm, 9¾ × 7 in

The difference between the natural world and the man-made is immediately communicated in this section through the floating world of Huaxin Business Centre in Shanghai. Reflecting the ambitions of the project through the name of the practice designing it – Scenic Architecture, founded by Zhu Xiaofeng in 2004 – the scheme contemplates the relationship between the ephemeral but fixed presence of man-made architecture and the enduring but changing natural environment. The roots of the six tall camphor trees, three of which are shown here, sink deep within the ground, characterizing the building's flat site, which in reality is covered with a layer of grey asphalt. Darker, finger-like marks reinforce their subterranean presence and, as they grow up towards the canopy that reaches over the roof of the single-storey raised building, tiny dots of the same quality signify the airy dispersal of their leaves. Drawn in a thicker, blacker line, the section of the business centre sketched out in this drawing shows the foundations for the slender piloti upon which the building is raised, barely more substantial than the tree roots, far less extensive and probably more short-lived. Two of the four independent business centre structures are shown here, and in plan they create an interconnected diagram of rectangular spaces that sit at angles to each other, merging and diverging. They are embraced by screens composed of twisted and pre-stressed aluminium strips, the resultant surfaces of the spaces translucent rather than solid, reflecting light off them in unpredictable ways that mimic the filtering effect of the branches and leaves surrounding them. This is represented by tiny dots in the drawing, in sections that span between enclosed spaces inhabited by tiny figures, one even sitting at a desk, and spaces requiring privacy, such as meeting rooms or executive offices.

**TECTON ARCHITECTS**

**Air raid shelter, 1939**

Ink and wash on paper

18 × 30.5 cm, 7 × 12 in

Between the world wars, various influential émigré architects arrived in Britain from Germany. One of these was Berthold Lubetkin, who in 1931 reached London from Georgia, via Germany and Paris. He met British engineer Ove Arup in 1933, when he was seeking structural advice for his Gorilla House design for London Zoo. During the war, they worked together on various public air-raid-shelter projects such as the one shown in section here. Arup was on the Air Raid Precautions Committee for Finsbury Borough Council, and the Georgian terrace shown sitting above ground, seemingly grand, is typical of the housing stock in this part of North London. The shelter needed to provide protection for up to 7,600 people – the entire population of Finsbury – against a direct hit from a half-ton bomb. Prohibited from building in the borough's Georgian squares, the only solution was to excavate downwards, and the majority of the drawing depicts the underground realm of London, its layers of clay and chalk loosely represented in the different colours of the painted ground. The shelter is protected by a thick and heavily reinforced concrete slab labelled ① in the section, and lies between the entrances at ① and ③. Below this, a six-storey structure taking the form of a large, spiral ramp drills into the ground, sized so as to be useful as car parking when the need for the shelter had passed. Despite government opposition to large shelters, Finsbury Council pursued funding for the structure, which, in the end, was never built. Both Lubetkin and Arup were members of MARS (Modern Architecture Research), a left-wing group affiliated with CIAM (Congrès Internationaux d'Architecture Moderne), and they also collaborated on other experimental, reinforced-concrete structures, including London Zoo's Penguin Pool, the Highpoint apartment buildings, and the Highgate and Finsbury Health Centres.

**DILLER + SCOFIDIO**

**Slow House project, 1989**

Computer-generated print on frosted polymer sheet with graphite and coloured ink, mounted on painted wood with metal

121 × 92.7 × 3.8 cm, 47½ × 36½ × 1½ in

This drawing challenges the conventions of architectural representation, and questions the process of its production and the role of the draughtsman in it. A wooden board serves as support for the image, which sits over two roughly painted zones on the board – each showing a different level of the two-storey house. Printed on to a transparent polymer sheet, the computer-generated drawing has an intimate relationship with the equipment attached to the board. This suggests the hand-drawn quality of the traditional orthographic rendering – a fiction belied by the nature of the lines. Two straight lines form a quadrant, marking the limits of the drawing, upon which lie two photographic fragments. One of these takes the form of a rear-view mirror, symbolizing travel away from the city. The unbuilt Slow House was designed for an art collector and entrepreneur, and the project explored the physical and conceptual distance between this holiday home, with its slow-paced Long Island seaside surroundings, and the intensity of city life. The drawing shows a curving series of transverse sections through the structure of the house, with the plan clearly visible. This series represents the trajectory seen through the car's rear-view mirror, evoking the journey from city to waterfront. This is mimicked within the house, which arcs from the entrance facade, barely more than the front door, to the double-height picture window framing the view that is the subject of the second image. Elizabeth Diller and Ricardo Scofidio describe the house as a passage, a door leading to a window. The journey within is deliberately slowed, using various architectural devices – the curved plan that widens out, for example, combined with a mediation of the experience in the form of a film of the seascape seen on a screen inside the house, relaying the view before it becomes a reality.

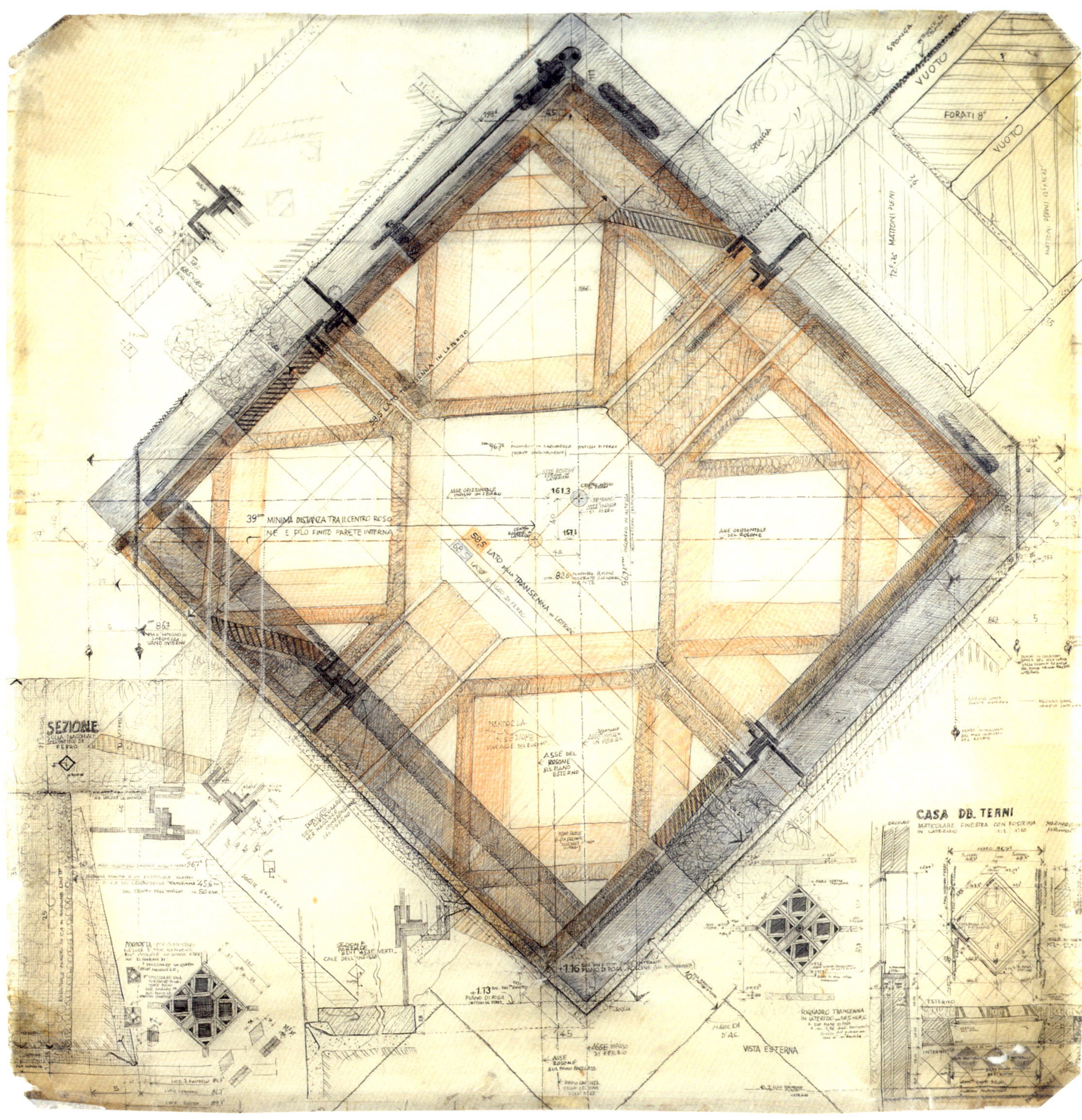


**MARIO RIDOLFI (1904–84)**

**Casa De Bonis, 1972**

Pencil and coloured pencil

106 × 107 cm, 41¾ × 42 in

The building shown in this detail drawing – a house that Mario Ridolfi designed for Pietro De Bonis, in Terni – belongs to the architect's Marmoro period, named after the village where he lived. Its design reveals Ridolfi's interest in the local vernacular construction, modified by a fascination with geometry that would become a defining principle in his architecture. Daylight plays an important role in the house, filtering down from the staircase and a patio, and there is a close relationship between the drawings of the details and the building's actual construction. This detail shows a square window set diagonally in an external wall and protected by deep eaves – a motif that Ridolfi used in several houses of this period. The drawing, made and coloured by hand in pencil, is dense with information. It communicates on many levels, explaining material qualities and the atmosphere that they generate, the context of the detail within the house construction, and the geometrical organization of the element. Around the central, full-size detail describing the timber joinery and opening mechanisms are smaller drawings and sketches at 1:10 scale. These show how the window is set within the cladding pattern in elevation and the effect of shadow on the perception of the framework. The house was constructed at a time when Ridolfi had moved away from his Italian Rationalist beginnings in Rome; he was exploring a neo-realist interpretation of architecture – first in Rome and then in Terni, in the Umbrian hills, where he retired after a serious accident. Detailing and construction were important aspects of architectural practice for Ridolfi, and in 1945–46 he contributed to a *Manuale dell'architetto* (Architects' Handbook), which explained his interpretation of the science of construction, as opposed to the craft of building that he would explore later in projects like the De Bonis house.

**VICTOR HUGO (1802–85)**

**The Eddystone Lighthouse, 1866**

Pen and brown-ink wash on vellum

89.5 × 47.7 cm, 35¼ × 18¾ in

Poet and novelist Victor Hugo was a prolific draughtsman, producing over 4,000 drawings in his lifetime. He often started with a tiny detail, according to an account by his son Charles, who described how he begins 'his forest with the branch of a tree, his town with a gable … and little by little, the entire composition will emerge'. This drawing was made when Hugo was living in political exile on the Channel Island of Guernsey. It depicts an image evoked by a passage he came across in a book called *The Delights of England* describing an extraordinary lighthouse, magnificent and extravagant, with balconies, balusters, turrets, little boxes, gazebos and weathercocks, figurines and cartouches with inscriptions. At the time, he was researching seventeenth-century England for his novel *The Man who Laughs*, and the drawing may possibly have been an illustration for the book. Although Hugo's drawings were often made at a small scale, this example is quite large – and the paper is almost filled by the picturesque form of the lighthouse with its intricately drawn, fantastical details that encrust the surface of the tower. He uses a characteristic brown-ink wash in layers in order to evoke a stormy sky that is indiscernible from the choppy waters below. The Eddystone Lighthouse is a real landmark that still exists today, calling out the presence of the dangerous, and sometimes submerged, Eddystone Rocks, at the entrance to Plymouth Sound. The first lighthouse was designed by Henry Winstanley and completed in 1698, but was washed away in a great storm five years later. A 1761 print shows a rendering of Winstanley's design that resembles Hugo's ink sketch in character and form.

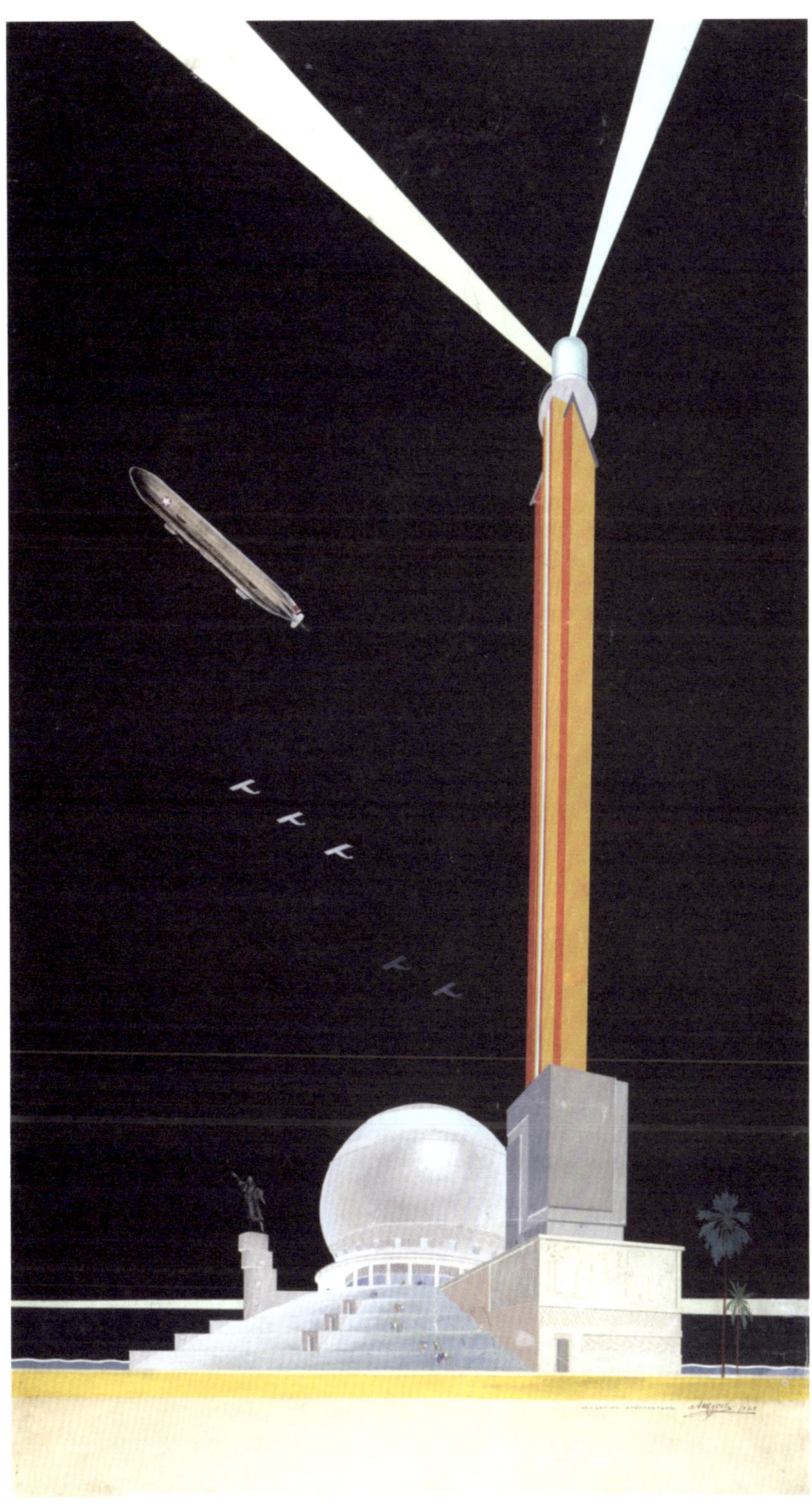

**ALEXEY SHCHUSEV**
**(1873–1949)**

**Entry for the Monument to Christopher Columbus Competition, 1920**

Ink, gouache and tempera on paper

142.7 × 79.3 cm, 56 × 31¼

In 1929, to celebrate Columbus Day, an international competition was launched for a Monument to Christopher Columbus, or the Columbus Memorial Lighthouse, in Santo Domingo, in the Dominican Republic. Initially, it drew most entries from the US; however, after much encouragement, it also saw 196 from Latin American countries – and 26 submissions from the various factions of the Russian avant-garde. These included Iakov Chernikov, Ivan Leonidov, Konstantin Melnikov, and this striking image from Alexey Shchusev, who entered the competition with two lesser-known colleagues – I.A. Francuz and G.K. Jakovlev. Their design for the lighthouse is presented as a perspective with a very small depth of field, so that it is almost an elevation. The majority of the image is filled with a black sky, against which the tall figure of the lighthouse and its diagonal beams of light stand out vividly. An airship and five aeroplanes also inhabit this sky. The ground takes up a very small area at the bottom of the drawing, depicted as a horizontal yellow stripe, and echoed in a wavy blue line for the sea and a white line on the horizon, which cuts across the plinth of the monument, where it meets a domed structure. The hybrid design reveals Shchusev's ability to practise in any architectural idiom requested, from Art Nouveau to Rococo, and is interesting in that it is what he, unfettered, chose to do. The aforementioned strong cohort of busy, productive Soviet architects considered competitions an important arena for developing conceptual and graphic ideas. Columbus Day would also have had significance in the Soviet consciousness after an 1847 speech by Friedrich Engels reflecting on the impossibility of envisioning the transformation of European society and institutions that Columbus's discovery would effect as the foundation for the liberation of all nations. Although this sentiment was not shared by all Americans, it would have resonated with post-Revolutionary Russians.

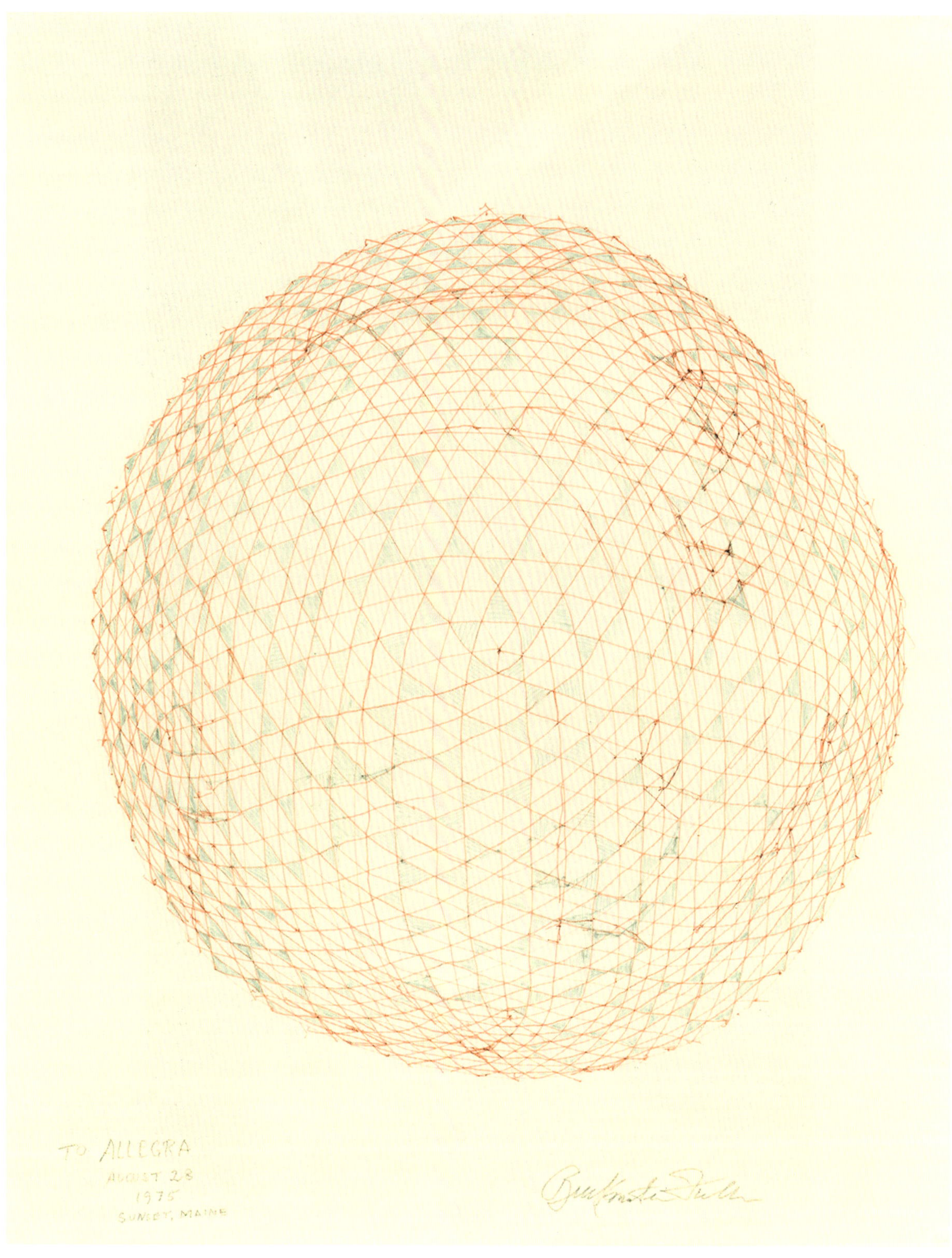


**RICHARD BUCKMINSTER FULLER (1895–1983)**

**Study Drawing for a Geodesic Sphere, 1975**

Pen and pencil on paper

61 × 48 cm, 24 × 19 in

Frail and delicate, Richard Buckminster Fuller's geodesic sphere floats, without context, in the paper space that it inhabits here. More than the form that it reveals, its net of thin red lines expresses the presence of the space within it. A perspective effect emanates from the central point of the image, the triangular modules growing increasingly compressed as the surface curves around, and this results in a greater density of material around the edges – specifically, of red ink and pale grey pencil lines. The centre seems to glow, pushed forward by a gentle pressure from the other side. Made in 1975, the drawing relates most directly to the geoscope that Fuller had described in his book *4D Time Lock*, which initially was a gigantic planetarium. From inside this sphere, it was possible to observe the moon and the stars but ultimately also to see them in relation to the Earth itself. Later, between 1965 and 1975, the geoscope was developed as part of the World Game, originally devised for the 1967 World Expo in Montreal. This interactive device constituted a huge sphere covered in coloured lights and connected to a computer so that it could display large-scale data patterns related, for example, to population, natural resources or means of communication in transformation around the globe. The clustering and tightening of the net in the drawing, and the places where lines are duplicated or errant, indicate these shadows of data-emotion moving over the face of the sphere. Fuller's impetus was utopian, and the interconnected parts of the drawing are like a model for his ideal society – where, in place of the selfish motives of a merciless society, he proposed an ethic of acting together for the common good – echoing the utilitarianism of Jeremy Bentham and interpreting it through technological and ecological filters.

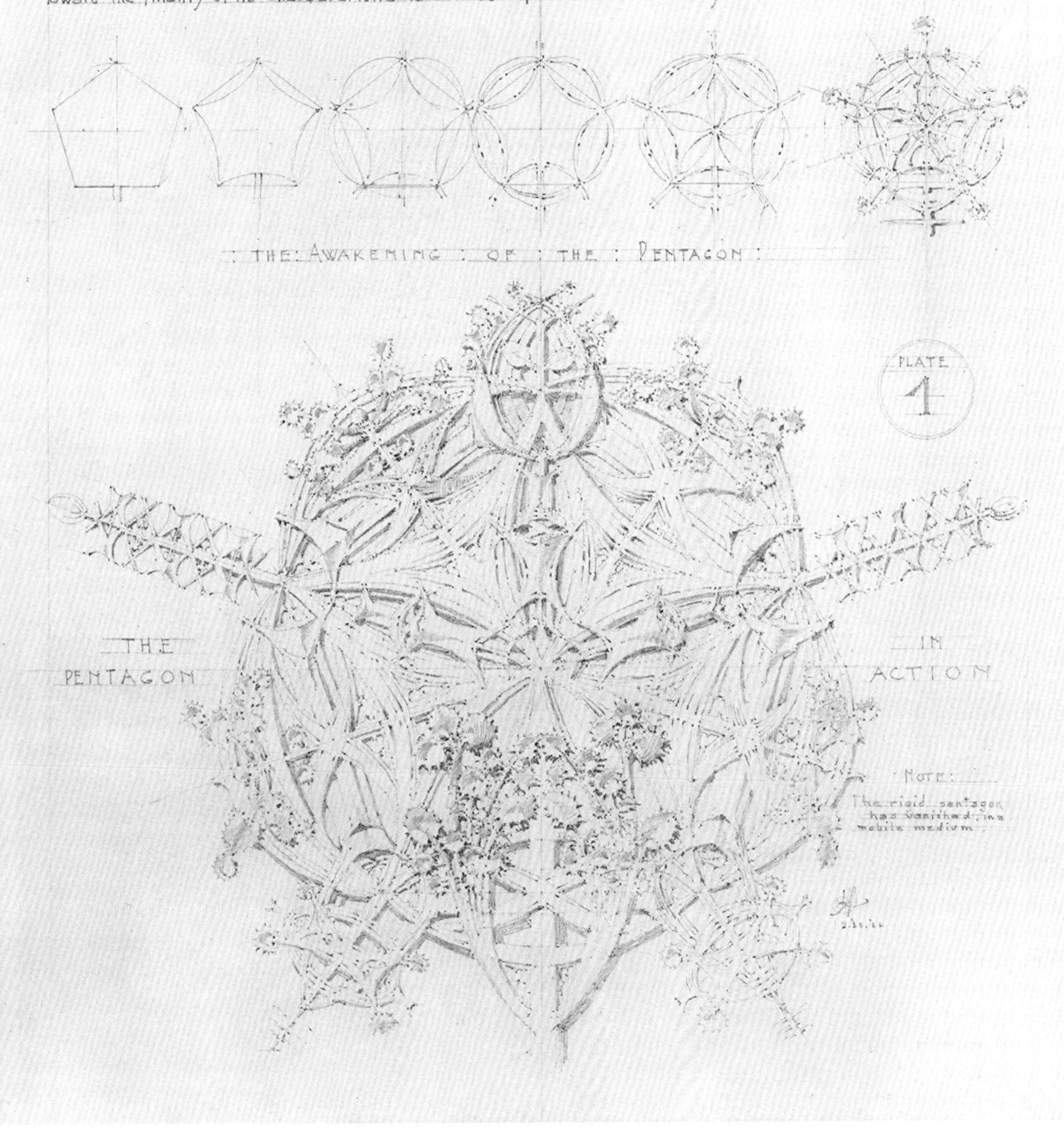


**LOUIS SULLIVAN (1856–1924)**

**Plate 4, Fluent Geometry, from System of Architectural Ornament, 1922**

Graphite on paper

57.7 × 73.5 cm, 22¾ × 30 in

Louis Sullivan's buildings are remarkable for their intense ornamental surfaces, created using cast terracotta. This drawing comes from Sullivan's final book, *System of Architectural Ornament*, 1922, commissioned by Chicago's Burnham Library of Architecture. It included twenty plates describing his approach, with titles like *Fantasy, a study of curves in three dimensions*. The designs provide insight into his interpretation of ornamental principles and their relationship with architecture and the natural world. Influenced by transcendentalists like Ralph Waldo Emerson, Sullivan made connections between the subjective and the organic, and the objective and the inorganic – a critique of incipient Modernism, and crucial for the thinking of his pupil, Frank Lloyd Wright. He also suggested practical and rational solutions for building design that were inspired by the American natural world, by demonstrating the underlying similarities between the simple geometries of science and the curvilinear configurations of nature. His terracotta ornaments were a product of the late nineteenth century, when Sullivan – with his partner, Dankmar Adler – had been most prolific. Both prefabricated and, with new mass-production techniques, easily replicated, they also reflected in their intricate character an earlier time of hand craftsmanship. Terracotta was also a fireproof material that could protect the vulnerable iron structures of tall buildings – an important characteristic in Sullivan's home city of Chicago after the fire of 1871. The use of terracotta units meant that an overall schema could comprise repeated elements. Individual motifs would sometimes be split over a group of tiles, and at other times composed through the rhythm of a repeated image. During his final years, Sullivan devoted himself to formalizing his ideas about these decorative elements into a language that was specifically American, as opposed to European, and responding to issues that he had previously addressed about architectural form and the new types of buildings required for the industrial city.

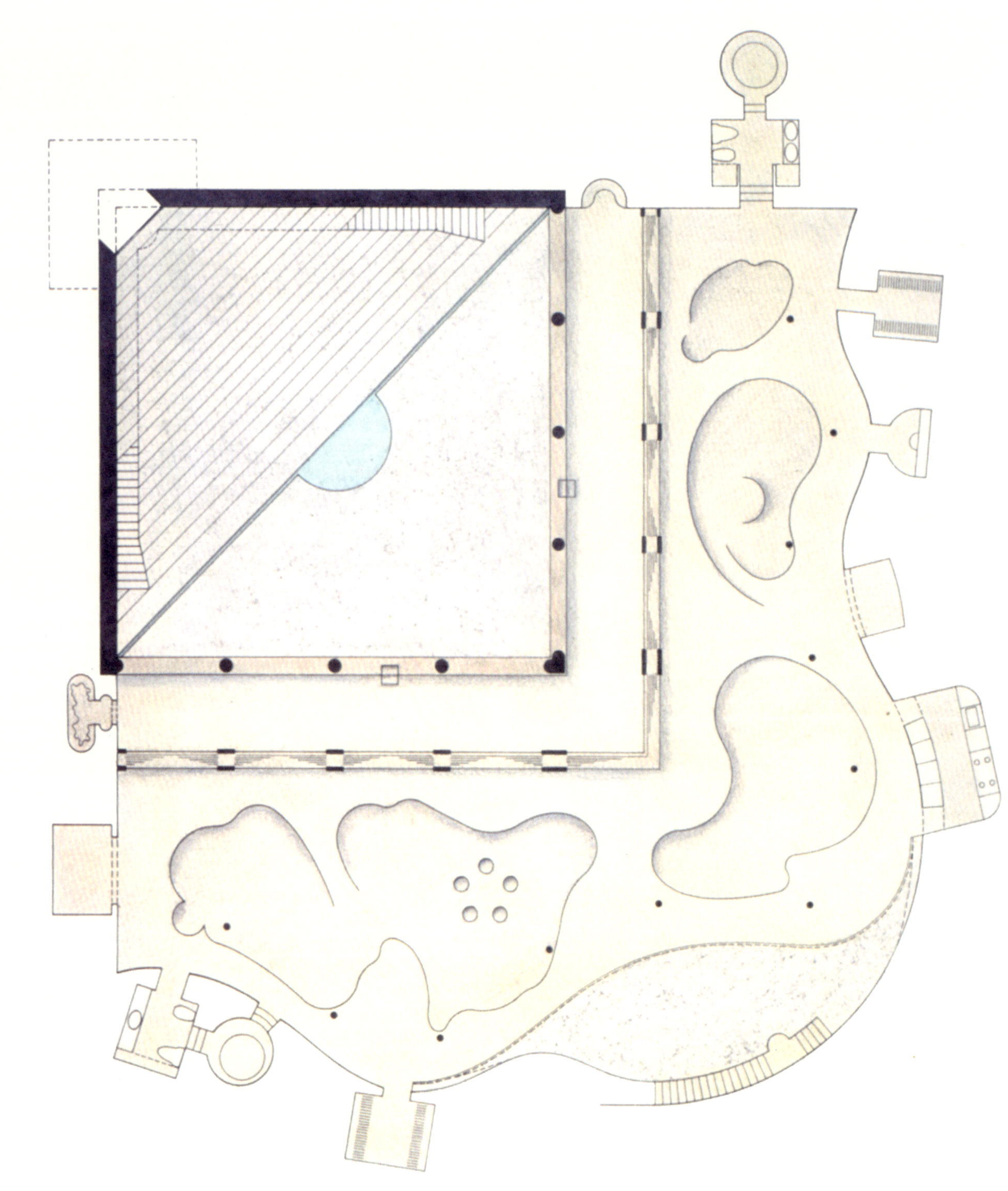

**EMILIO AMBASZ (1943–)**

**Plan of Casa de Retiro Espiritual, 1975**

Ink on coloured paper

40 × 32.4 cm, 15¾ × 12¾

The image of two white walls rising from a sea of green grass was much-circulated in the United States after Emilio Ambasz won the Progressive Architecture Project Award in 1980 for his theoretical project for a house of spiritual retreat near Cordoba. This plan explains the workings of his design, and the famous white walls are represented by two blacked-out lines broken at the corner where they meet to show the location of an opening high up the facade, reached by the two long staircases shown running up the inside of both walls. Celebrating the ritual of approach and entry, the plan's curvaceous and fragmented edges mark the boundaries of the site, showing a series of mysterious rooms hidden underground, beneath the lawn. Only the eye-shaped entrance patio, with a staircase leading downwards, is accessible from the surface, its white walls continuing to interrupt the greensward in intermittent, undulating shapes. A circular window set in the ground lies under one of these shapes, like a winking counterpart to the patio. The plan shown here informed the construction of the abstract project that Ambasz carried out thirty years later. Most of the house lies below ground, at the level of the small private rooms – a sequence of bedrooms and bathrooms lit from above by the winking oculus. The large hall within the curved perimeter that constitutes the living room is lined by thin columns, and the amoeba-like shape is an internal pool. Once this hall has been traversed, a colonnade is reached, through which the visitor passes into the main courtyard. Water trickles down runnels in the recessed handrails of the staircases leading to the high balcony, reminiscent of Moorish gardens but also essential in the scorching heat of the Andalusian plain in summer.

**ANON**

**Two seaside villas, Pompeii, c. AD 40**

Fresco

22 × 53 cm, 8¾ × 21 in

This panel consists of two frescoes from Pompeii, the Roman seaport that grew up in the shadow of Mount Vesuvius, which have been assembled in modern times into a single frame. The left-hand panel shows a garden with a tree in the foreground, and on either side a double-height structure frames the garden, in order to create a symmetrical image. The horizon is dominated by a majestic central hall with a hexastyle, or six-columned portico, and a *porticus* (portico) on either side. The right-hand panel shows two wings of a three-armed structure in perspective, and its central pavilion is analogous to the central hexastyle of the left-hand view. Other buildings are distinguishable in the background – including a *tholos*, or tomb. The frescoes are typical of the Third Style of Pompeian art, also called the ornate style, which is characterized by strict symmetry that divides compositions into three horizontal and three to five vertical planes. Other features are planes of colour and intricate architectural details. Here, these are represented in the antefixes – ornaments to hide the ends of the roof tiles, which can be seen along the roof pitch – and the rendering of the capitals for each column. These two frescoes are unique, notwithstanding the great quantity of scenery paintings surviving from the Vesuvian area, both for the rarity of their subject matter and for their intact architectural character and use of perspective. The paintings depict two opulent, maritime villas belonging to rich and powerful Romans, and designed as status symbols. Unlike the closed walls that the houses within the city of Pompeii offered to the street, these properties lined the coast, with the long, colonnaded walkways that are shown in these paintings providing sweeping sea views. Some of them even had private theatres, sports arenas and extensive baths.

**CLAUDE (1613–88) AND CHARLES (1628–1703) PERRAULT**

**Sainte-Geneviève, c.1680**

Ink on paper

19 × 17.5 cm, 8 × 7 in

The project for the vast church of Sainte-Geneviève in Paris was a collaboration between brothers Claude Perrault, an architect but also a physician and anatomist, and his brother Charles, a poet, storyteller and provocateur in the debate raging at the time in France between the Ancients and the Moderns. Claude Perrault was already known for his translation of *De Architectura* by Vitruvius into French, which influenced his design for the east wing of the Louvre, under construction between 1665 and 1680. This drawing reveals how the project for Sainte-Geneviève belonged to Claude's development of a French Neo-Classical architectural style, representative of the progressive Modern. The formal concept is traceable to an earlier 1511 edition of Vitruvius, through Rafael and the design of the entrance of the Palazzo Farnese in Rome, although at the time there was no church like this. Freestanding columns with Corinthian capitals line the long nave, carrying a deep horizontal entablature with a curved vault above. The sectional cut reveals the structural components of the design. The timber truss of the pitched roof far above the thick vault, whose weight is borne down through the entablature, acts as a long beam supported by the columns below. Two thick masonry walls define the outer boundaries of buttressing side aisles and the church itself. This structural system is described further by the central perspective that reveals the spatial plan of the nave, and the scheme of clerestory windows lighting the vault through deep semicircular openings that follow the rhythm of the columns. In the foreground, the drawing continues as a plan, with a single figure standing in the entrance dwarfed by the massive thickness of the structure, which is depicted in solid, black shading.

**FRANK FURNESS (1839–1912)**

**Provident Life and Trust Company, 1885**

Coloured ink on paper

41.6 × 55.1 cm, 8 × 11 in

This perspective elevation of Frank Furness' first building for the Provident Life and Trust Company in central Philadelphia appears on an illustrated plan of the city. Published just one year after the building was completed, a perspective map offers a bird's-eye view of the industrializing city, with images of its most important commercial buildings reproduced around its border. Furness' building occupies the top right-hand corner of the plan, its robust, idiosyncratic style standing out among its conventional neighbours as it did in real life. The L-shaped building had two formal facades – one for the insurance offices on Fourth Street and this one, at the front. It comprises an eclectic assemblage of architectural elements. At the lowest level, the central entrance is set within a shallow colonnade defined by four piers, each of which contains dense columns compressed between heavy masonry piers top and bottom. Although the building is the equivalent of six storeys in height, the elevation reads as having three levels, their scale mediating between the buildings on either side. Over the entrance arch, another arch is raised above in canopy, springing from a band of rustication. This is flanked by two pointed-arch windows under a triangular motif. These framing elements serve as a hierarchical centre, like Palladian half-pediments in a more conventional building. In this mutated composition, however, medievalizing elements take their place to create a new physical imagery that ruptures any Classical continuity of tradition. Such panoramic maps were a popular cartographic form during the late nineteenth century, celebrating the new urban architecture made possible by material and technological developments. Disseminating the self-images of rapidly expanding cities, they were often commissioned by local chambers of commerce or estate agencies.

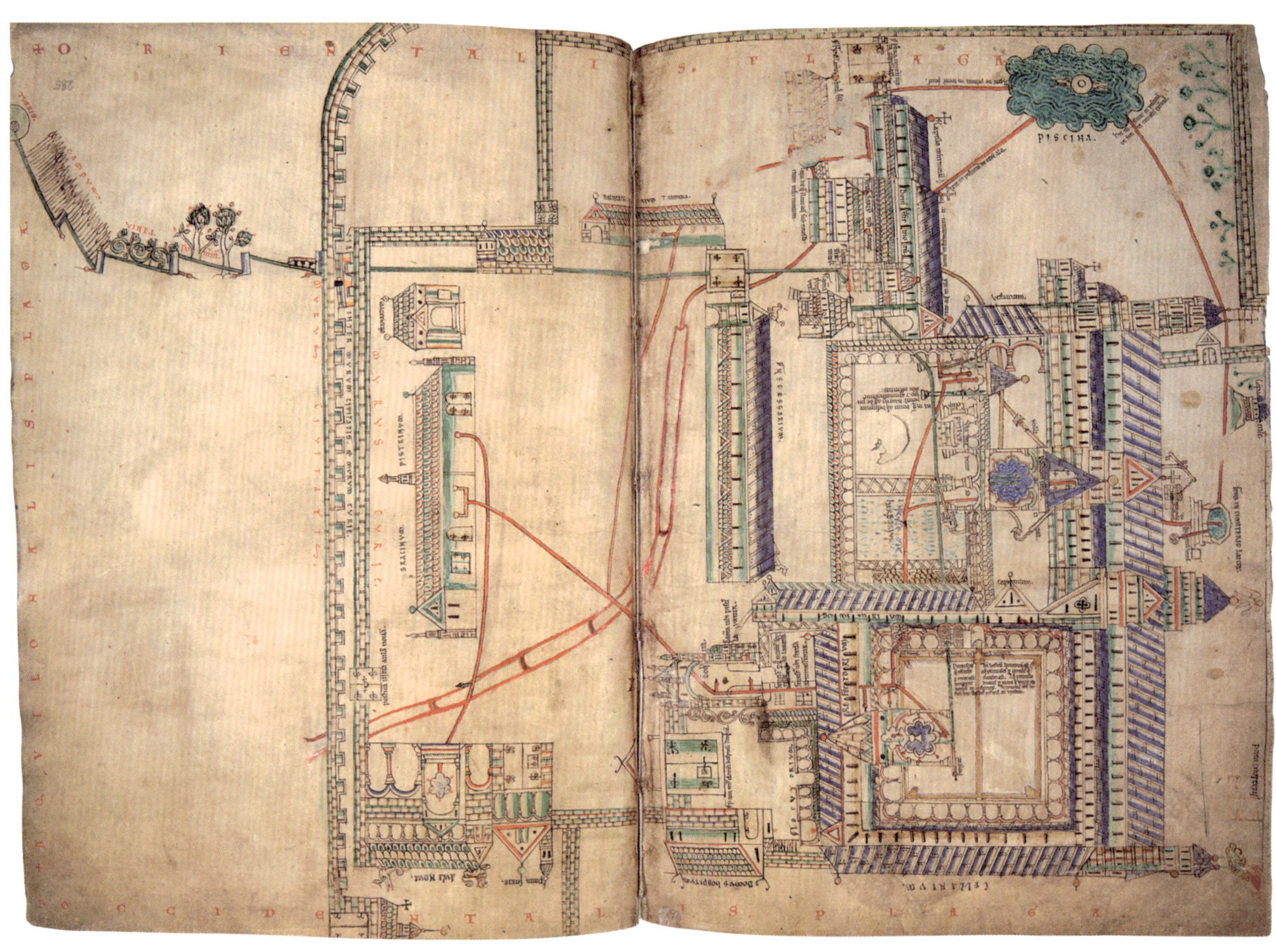


**EADWINE**

**Canterbury Cathedral waterworks, 1155**

Ink and colour wash on paper

33 × 46 cm, 13 × 18 in

The prosaic purpose and practical nature of this drawing, to describe hydraulic plumbing and sanitary arrangements, means that it provides a wealth of information about the great medieval Benedictine monastic complex of Christ Church at Canterbury, whose urban location presented particular sanitary problems. Rather than presenting an artistic or symbolic interpretation, the necessity to accurately show the location and function of the hydraulic system results in a depiction of the context and physical nature of the buildings, as opposed to a conventionally stylized view. Although restricted by the format of the page, there has been an attempt by the draughtsman to adhere to the proportional relationships between the major buildings. Covering and drawn onto an already-bound double page of the heavily illuminated *Eadwine Psalter* manuscript, named after the scribe and monk who oversaw the production of the work, this ink drawing with coloured washes reveals the reality of a walled Norman priory, with its surrounding fields of crops and orchards, and the importance that water played in everyday life. A bird's-eye view – a primitive site plan with east and west clearly indicated – shows the buildings as flat elevations orientated correctly on the ground, so that the destination of the water flow and its purpose are apparent. Four colours are used to indicate the condition of the supply: green for fresh water coming from a source about 1 km (0.6 mi) from the site and supplemented by two wells; orange-red for the clean supply pumped under pressure through the conduit house and settling tanks into the infirmary, lavatorium, kitchens and offices; and brown for rainwater. Finally, wastewater was used to feed the fishpond in the courtyard, and then carried back for the flushing and disposal of waste through the red pipes from the necessarium before being washed away to the city ditch.

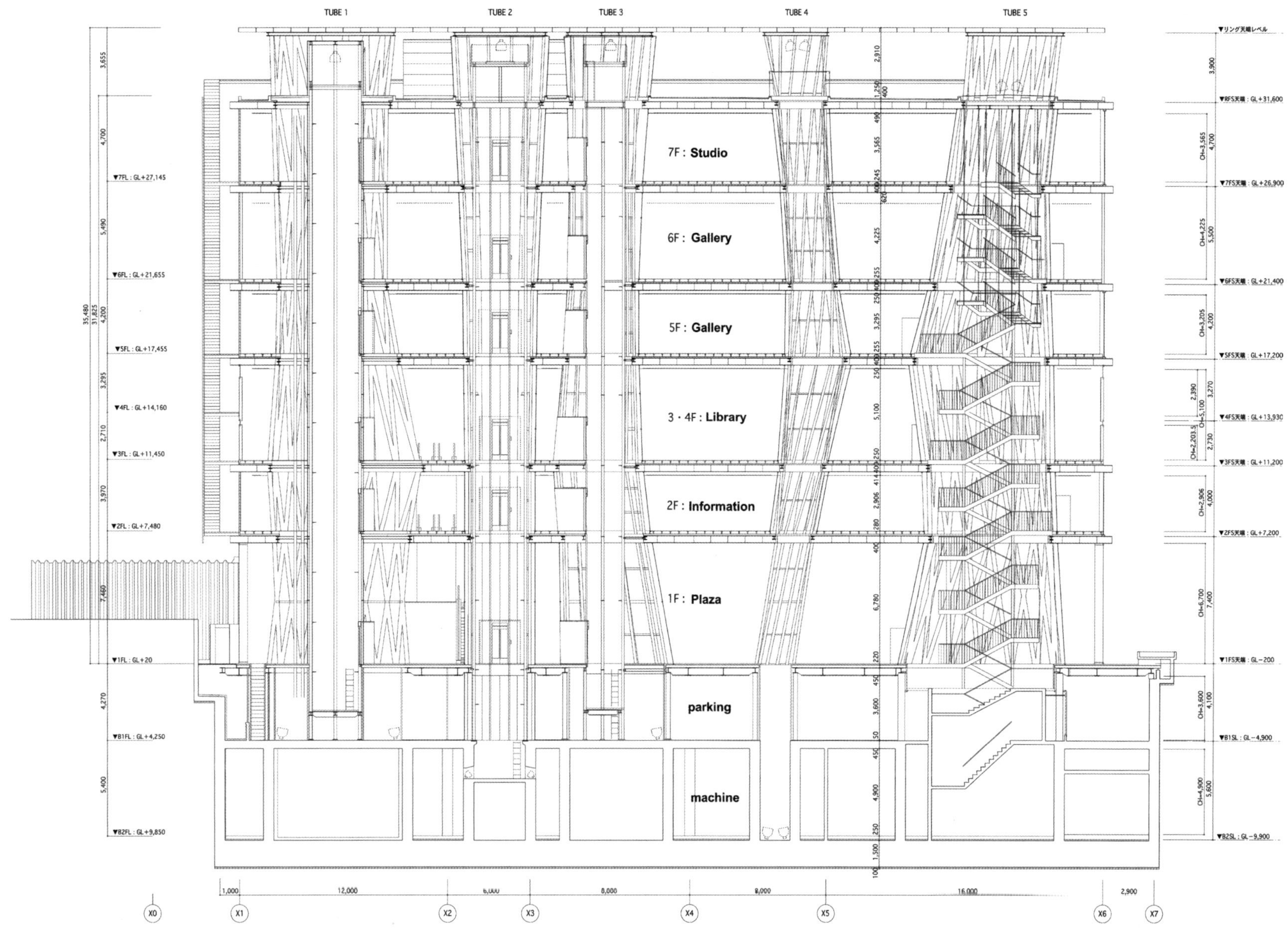


**TOYO ITO & ASSOCIATES**

**Sendai Mediatheque, 2001**

Ink on paper

30 × 38 cm, 11¾ × 15 in

This project aimed to make a simple prototype for a new sort of building, one that required a flexible system capable of meeting any and all programmatic conditions that might arise. This cross section reveals three of the Mediatheque's vertical-tube elements, and shows how each has its own special character. The large tube on the right contains a staircase for much of its height, while the other two smaller tubes serve as energy-core connectors, containing ducts and cables, air-supply and exhaust flues. They also act as light conductors, carrying natural light down into the lower levels. At night, the translucent skin of the building transforms the section into an elevation when the presence of the tubes and the interior activities become visible through the branches of the trees lining the street. The commission to design the Sendai Mediatheque was won in a competition by Toyo Ito's practice in 1995, and since then it has been an unusually mediated project. Various books and films about its design and erection are available, and the form and construction of the structural latticed tubes that run through the building from top to bottom so that the open-plan spaces weave around them has been a focus of attention. According to the architects' description, the building is structured by tubes and plates and covered by a translucent skin, providing a twenty-first-century alternative to Le Corbusier's Dom-Ino House. Where Le Corbusier's chosen material was concrete, the Mediatheque's floors are honeycomb slabs composed of twin steel plates with ribbing in between. The columns are circular, hollow bundles of steel pipes, each with its own tubular shape, with diameters ranging from 2 to 9 m (6.5 to 29.5 ft).

**ERNESTO BRUNO LA PADULA (1902–68)**

**Palace of Italian Civilization, 1939**

Tempera on wood

90 × 89.9 cm, 35½ × 35½ in

The Palazzo della Civiltà Italiana is shrouded in a lonely melancholy, reminiscent of the surreal, Neo-Classical paintings of Giorgio de Chirico. Ink washes create a darkened sky that only brightens on the horizon, giving the screen of arches an uncanny glow. Its four facades are covered with a grid of spare, unornamented arches, the only animation provided by twenty figures in rhetorical poses that inhabit the central twenty arches. At either side of the building's dark, high plinth, giant statues of horses are frozen in movement; in front, accentuating the perspective that reveals the depth of the arches in the facade, the building is reflected in a still pool of water. Its monumental character refers back to Imperial Roman architecture, but at the same time to the Italian vernacular tradition that had recently been the subject of the 1936 Rural Italian Architecture exhibition in Milan. Both Neo-Classical and modern, the Palazzo has been described as late-antique modern. The drawing also makes apparent the travertine cladding applied over a reinforced-concrete skeleton, in response to the policy of self-sufficiency necessitated by sanctions imposed on Italy after its invasion of Ethiopia in 1935, but also symbolizing the continuity of ancient history into the civilization of modern Italy. The building was designed by a team of Rationalist architects responding to an architectural-competition brief for the *Esposizione universale Roma* (EUR), to be held in 1942 just outside Rome. The EUR's permanent structures – museums, memorials and palaces – were designated by the then Fascist Prime Minister Benito Mussolini to become the core of a Third Rome. The Palace of Italian Civilization was to be the centrepiece of this extravagant ideological gesture, and, although the EUR was eventually cancelled, several buildings had already been constructed – including this one, which is now called the Palace of Labour.

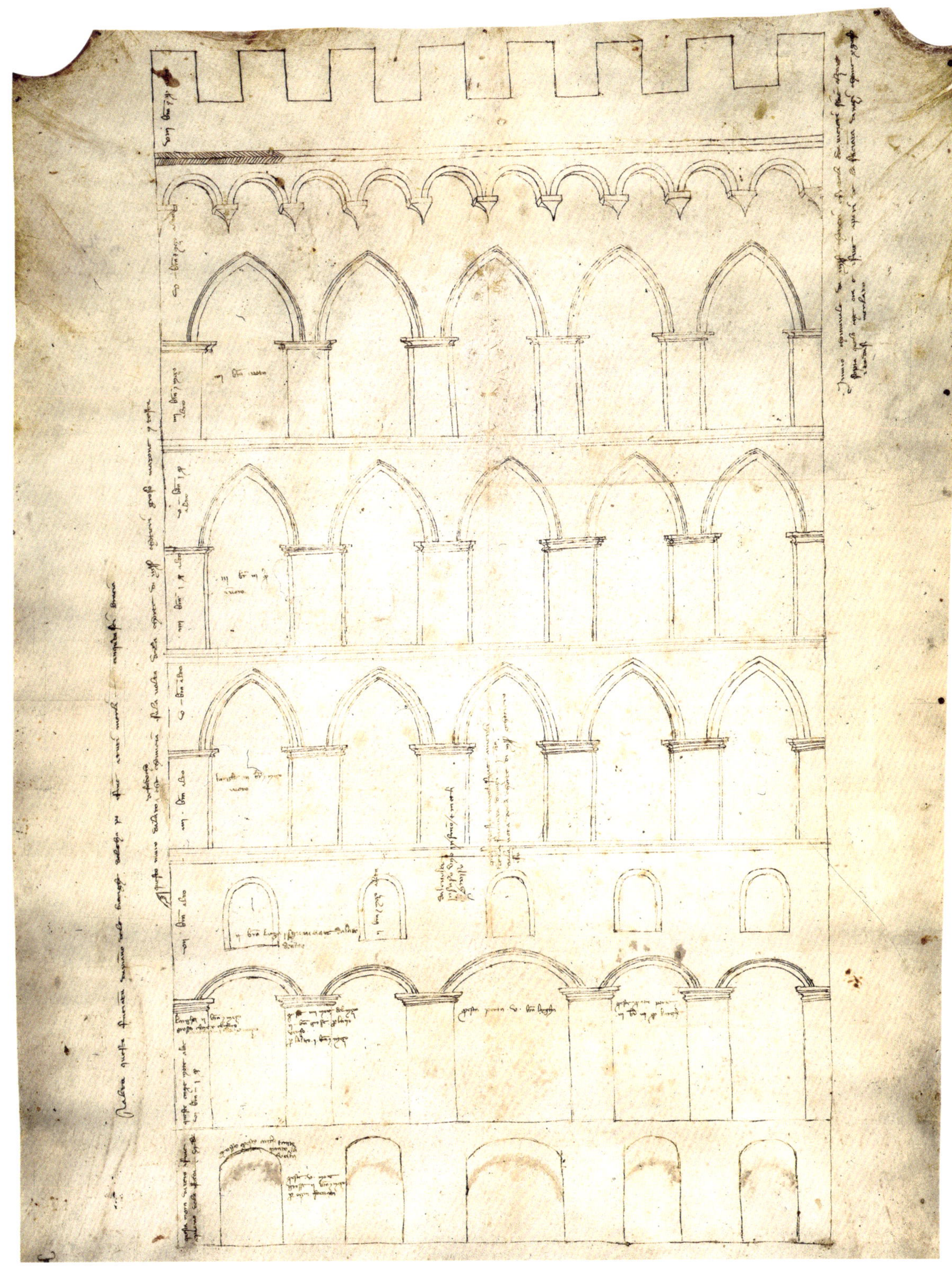

**AGOSTINO DI GIOVANNI (c.1310–70)**

**Facade of the Palazzo Sansedoni, Siena, 1340**

Brown ink on paper

122 × 58 cm, 48 × 22¾ in

This elevation is associated with a contract between Gontiero do Goro Sansedoni and Agostino di Giovanni; his son, Giovanni; Agostino di Rocco; and Cecco di Casino, for the construction of the Palazzo Sansedoni – a Gothic urban palace with a tower that is not shown in this drawing, which fused the households of five noble families. It is a mostly freehand copy of an original architect's drawing for an initial design proposal that no longer exists, and a disparity of technique between the confidently drawn upper windows and other more clumsily drafted sections below suggests this preliminary nature. This early measured drawing uses an archaic system, with dimensions noted in the vernacular Tuscan *braccia*, corresponding to the length of a forearm.

It has been argued that the dimensions of the facade were based on a standard medieval masons' design method know as *ad quadratum*, which depended on the relationship between the sides of a square and its diagonal.

The annotations are in the hand of Agostino di Giovanni, and specify that the building conforms to an Ordinance of 1297 stipulating that all palaces adjoining Siena's central Piazza del Campo should use windows with columns, in emulation of the city's Palazzo Publico. The long, concave facade of the Palazzo Sansedoni runs along the northern edge of the Campo, and faces directly towards the Palazzo Publico. When it was built, it closed one of the access points into the space. While the front facade of the palazzo has since been restored beyond recognition, fragments of the facade shown in this drawing, of the elevation onto the Banchi di Sotto, on the other side of the building, are still recognizable. These include the portals – of which only the central one remains, with its small window above – and the order of the larger window bays.

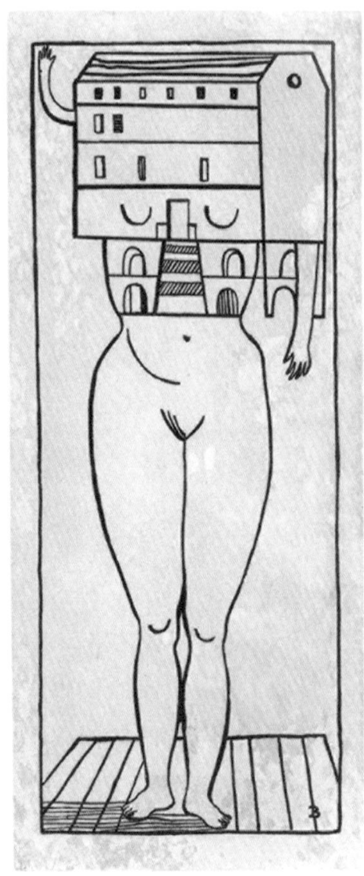

**LOUISE BOURGEOIS**

**Femme Maison, 1947**

Line block

23.3 × 9.3 cm, 9¼ × 3¾ in

During the 1940s, when American-French artist Louise Bourgeois made this drawing as part of a group of works called *Femme Maison*, she was bringing up three sons. This activity can keep a woman housebound unless she has the means to replace herself, and the house is suffocating the female figure depicted here. The woman is standing upright on a small wooden platform, or perhaps confined within the walls of a tiny room. The simple line drawing, with no shading or spatial modelling, uses the floorboards upon which she stands to create a basic perspective motif. The house itself shows two of its facades, but they are flattened into a single plane. The title is a pun, for *Femme Maison* can translate as housewife, or literally as woman house. The building replaces the head of the woman so that she becomes a woman house, and even her breasts appear as drooping eyelids or shuttered windows looking demurely downwards. Her small arms poke out of the sides, one waves hopefully and the other hangs passively. Bourgeois characterized this figure as someone who does not know that she is half naked and exposed within her domestic prison, and she does not know that she is trying to hide. When she made this drawing, Bourgeois herself would have been struggling with the mutually exclusive roles and realms of time and space necessary to the mother and the artist, which somehow had to be reconciled. These separate places that had to be compressed together would have been located within her domestic environment, and she used architecture as a motif in her work to symbolize her feelings, and as a repository of memory for those emotions and the circumstances that produced them. Architectural structures, like the structures of memory, were a refuge – an invention that could also be a trap.

**ROBERT VENTURI (1925–2018) AND DENISE SCOTT BROWN (1931–)**

**I am a Monument, 1972**

Ink on paper

15.2 × 22.9 cm, 6 × 9 in

During the autumn of 1968, architects Robert Venturi and Denise Scott Brown took a group of students from Yale to Nevada for ten days to make studies of urban sprawl and, specifically, the Las Vegas strip. The result of this trip to the desert was the influential and controversial book *Learning from Las Vegas*, 1972. Its polemical sketch of the shed that proclaims itself as a monument, with radiating lines suggesting flashing neon, is an extremely simple and memorable line drawing that symbolizes a complex concept. In the book, the term employed is the *decorated shed* – a simple structure that uses applied symbols to define itself. The image generates many challenges, such as the ordinary and ugly character of the neutral, box-like building in the drawing that contradicts any pretence to originality. Another aspect under attack is the assumption that an exterior expresses an interior, when contradiction between them is clearly possible. Channelling the influence of Pop art, which had permeated the American imagination by this time, the book's polemic transformed the art world's ironic critique of high culture by assimilating imagery from popular and mass culture to become a criticism on the tenets of high architecture. Equivalence was claimed, for example, between the prosaic structures represented in the sketches – which lined the Las Vegas strip, shouting out their presence and purpose with myriad roadside signs – and Baroque cathedrals covered in sculptural reliefs. The critical intent of the book, which includes much detailed, technical analysis, was to question the predominance and elitism of high architecture – specifically, ascendant heroic Modernism and its functionalist principles that elided the role of decoration altogether.

**PAUL RUDOLPH (1918–97)**

**Model Flap House for Grand Rapids housing exhibition, 1955**

Black and brown ink with pencil underdrawing

64.5 × 106 cm, 25½ × 41¾ in

This perspective elevation of Paul Rudolph's model house, representing the American Southeast, was an early proposal for a project called The Home Research Foundation, which, although short lived, was extensively promoted in the architectural press. The wooded, 32-hectare site was intended to showcase the creative ideas of the nation's leading designers, including Buckminster Fuller, Rudolf and Eliot Noyes. Rudolph's design engages with the flat, lakeside landscape outside Grand Rapids, Michigan, by embracing its tabula rasa qualities. His Japanese-pavilion-like house is shown raised on a simple platform above a perfect lawn traversed by a paved path. On either side of the plot, the plinths of neighbouring houses can be seen; below, a paved street informally planted with trees frames the plot. Above, the delicate canopy of these trees forms a lacy edge to the drawing and the house is seen against the horizon of the wide lake, whose distant wooded banks are just discernible. Although the drawing has great depth of field, the quality of line is always consistent – with thicker lines used to delineate the edges of structural elements and two thinner line-weights for depicting natural objects, furniture, paving and brick coursing. This is one of a pair of drawings. The two versions seen together emphasise Rudolph's approach to the issue of temporary inhabitation particular to this kind of weekend house. Designed for the warm climate of the Southeast, there are no windows and the wall panels surrounding the simple space are raised mechanically to expose the interior to the outdoors during the day and when the house is inhabited. In the drawing of the house opened up, it is possible to discern faint pencil marks where the position of tree branches was modified, suggesting that this was used as an underlay for setting out this predominantly closed version.

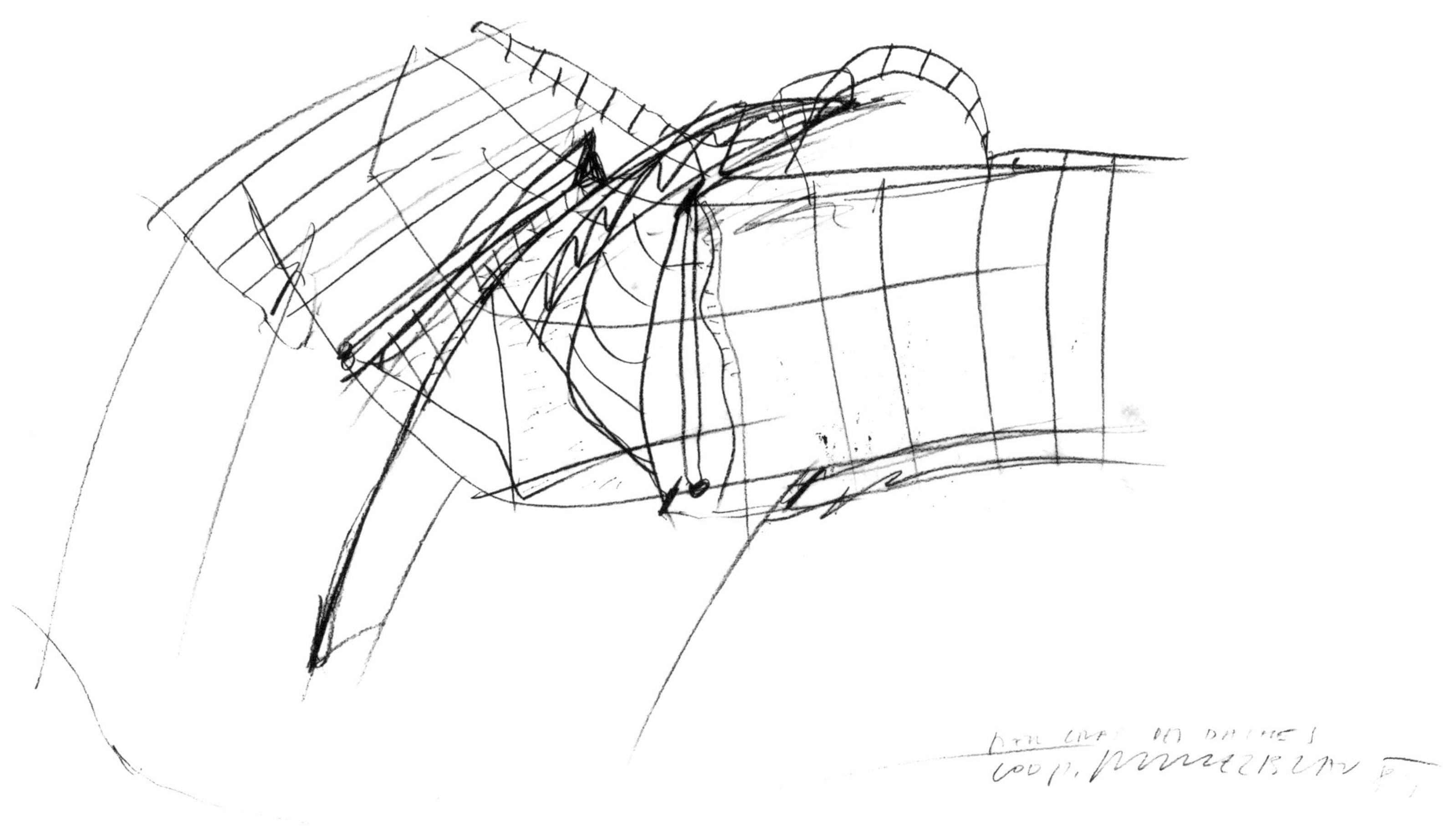

**COOP HIMMELBLAU**

**Rooftop remodelling Falkestraße, 1983**

Pencil on tracing paper

41.6 × 55.1 cm, 8 × 11 in

Coop Himmelblau describe their model for the generation of form as beginning with an explosive sketch drawn with the eyes closed in intense concentration, in a starting point reminiscent of the automatic drawing practice of Dada artists in the 1920s. Although the initial sketches and design for the rooftop remodelling at the corner of Falkestraße were made in 1983, this extension for a collection of office spaces for a Viennese law firm was not completed until 1988, just as their drawings were featuring in the *Deconstructivist Architecture* exhibition at the Museum of Modern Art in New York. This drawing is bursting with energy, and the lines are very swiftly drawn. Unlike other Coop Himmelblau sketches, this one has a recognizable form although it does not correspond exactly with the insect-like structure that peers over the parapet. While designing, they said, they envisioned a lightning bolt reversed and a taut arc. The differentiated and differentiating constructional system, which is a cross between a bridge and an aeroplane, translates this spatial energy into constructional reality. The sketch is structured by two opposing arcs – they could even be trusses, and the axis of one is extrapolated into a plane that descends like a sheet of water towards the street below. Coop Himmelblau's founding partners – Wolf Prix, Helmut Swiczinsky and Michael Holzer – had previously produced various ephemeral performance and installation pieces such as *House with a Flying Roof*, 1971, and *Blazing Wing*, 1980, which were responses to the idea of the unleashed emotional subconscious as a critique of urban reality. They explained the name of their collective, which translates as Blue Sky Cooperative, as evoking the architecture that they intended to produce: light and fluctuating like clouds, and dematerializing the orthogonal heaviness of conventional architecture through unexpected angles and complicated, illogical spatial solutions.

**OWEN JONES (1809–74)**

**Capitals of Columns, 1856**

Ink on paper

30 × 20.7 cm, 11¾ × 8 in

The first four plates in the Egyptian series for Owen Jones' book *The Grammar of Ornament*, originally published in 1856 but republished many times since, feature isolated decorative motifs such as the column heads shown here. The following five plates were more consistent with the remainder of the book, showing swatches of decoration. This illustration is entitled *Capitals of Columns*, and its eight intensely coloured drawings present a highly selective view of Egyptian ornament. In the composition of the page, Jones used horizontal and vertical lines to set up a visual harmony and symmetry, and colours are carefully combined. The two plates preceding this examine different iterations of the lotus and the papyrus, important sources of form and colour in Egyptian art, which are, in this and the following plate, applied to specific examples. The capitals are numbered, assigned a provenance and accompanied by lengthy captions describing, for example, the three stages of growth in the papyrus plant. Jones undertook extensive typological research in preparation for these pages, but omitted many of his classifications and findings – specifically of fauna, such as eagles and snakes, and other figurative elements – in order to present an aestheticized vision of Egyptian ornament as geometric and non-figurative. Jones also had another, more controversial, agenda, which was to challenge the prevailing museological practice of presenting unpainted marble and stone works with little interpretation of their original context, making it seem as if this was how they originally appeared. He first became concerned with archaeological polychromy when writing the handbooks for the Fine Arts Courts for London's Great Exhibition of 1851. He curated the Egyptian court with Egyptologist Joseph Bonomi, which formed a basis for *The Grammar of Ornament*. In his selection, Jones promoted awareness of polychromy in ancient art through an imaginative extension of Bonomi's research into colour.

**MARIO BOTTA (1943–)**

**Rotonda House, 1980**

Ink on paper

59.4 × 84.1 cm, 23½ × 33 in

In 1982, Mario Botta published a book called *Casa Rotonda*, about the house of that name he had designed and built in Ticino, Switzerland, between 1980 and 1982. Isometric projections played an important role in it, appearing in the section 'How the House was Built'. Their abstract, autonomous presence was ideal for explaining Botta's formal and conceptual concerns, as opposed to constructional and practical parameters. The dwelling is contained within a pure geometrical shape – a circle extrapolated upwards over three storeys to form a short tower. This avoids the need for facades, and the axonometric becomes one of the most expedient projections for communicating the formal composition of the building's continuous elevation. Botta has made various incisions into this form in response to specific aspects of the site and brief that also related to wider experiments with the matrices of pure form that he had been carrying out since the early 1960s. The two isometric drawings shown here depict the circular volume from a worm's-eye view, as if seen from below. This effect is enhanced by the figure walking away from the building as if on a sheet of glass. The plan of the lowest of the three floors is revealed at the base of the drawings. The dominant feature is the stairway that is encased in a curved masonry wall that ends in a tight semicircle. This reads as a massive Tuscan column on the exterior, as shown in the drawing on the right, surrounded by a stepped wall that at ground level creates a deep porch. The drawing on the left highlights the cleft cut into the facade along the north-south axis that lets light penetrate from above through the triangular skylight visible at the parapet level. From this apex, the cut in the facade widens and forms a flat plane that defines a balcony on the middle floor. The void of the window is echoed on the other side by the column-like presence of the staircase.

**CHARLES RENNIE MACKINTOSH (1868–1928)**

**Hill House, 1903**

Pen on paper

33.6 × 57.2, 13 × 22½ in

Hill House, Mackintosh's domestic masterpiece, was completed in 1904, five years after the opening of the first phase of his world-renowned Glasgow School of Art. Inspired by the latter, Glasgow publisher Walter Blackie commissioned Mackintosh to design a family house within commuting distance of the city. This two-point perspective would have been a presentation drawing for the client, but it shows the house almost as it appears today. Its siting above Helensburgh, with wide views south towards Gare Loch and the River Clyde, is only hinted at, and the house is contrasted with uncanny natural surroundings. Although the drawing is entirely composed of lines, the sky is a dark, striated field that merges into the roofs of the north wing and the turret, whose presence is made apparent through the different quality and direction of the shading. This darkness contrasts dramatically with the brightness of the house walls, bringing the composition of the variously proportioned windows that are strewn over their surfaces into focus. The building's features are depicted as simple outlines, with no shadow or texture; this is reserved for the stylized trees lining the path and in the foreground. The picturesque composition of the elevations reveals subtle relationships between the interiors and their expression on the exterior in their dynamic play: in the proportions of the windows; the projecting porches and bays; and the positions of chimneys, eaves and parapets. There is a tension between the austere Scottish vernacular and its deliberate stylization that resonated with architectural developments in Europe at the time.

**PAUL ROBBRECHT (1950–)**

**Archives Bordeaux Metropole, 2013**

Coloured ink on paper

84 × 119 cm, 33 × 47 in

The delicate marks of this red-ink sketch are organized into a veil-like drawing that, despite its implied depth, remains on the surface of the paper. Two factors effect this perception. Firstly, contrasting with the calligraphy of the lines, the presence of dark blots and marks – sometimes accidental, at others deliberate elements of the composition – creates another order on the sheet. Secondly, the sizes of things, especially the openings in the side facade, disrupt the image's scale. This sketch has a definite perspective structure holding it together: from the flat plane of the section at the front, it slides down the page in the direction of a distant vanishing point. This is unlike many of Robbrecht's sketches, in which a spatial sensibility more akin to Giotto di Bondone's early Renaissance depiction of relative space is created by the tension between objects whose size is determined by status rather than location. In this drawing, a pictorial space is implied in which each part belongs to a whole held together by a perspectival grid, but the projection is described as axonometry. An ambiguity is set up; perhaps the ground slopes upwards to eat the elevation from below, or maybe the roofline is not what it seems. The section shows clearly the relationship between an existing ruin, abandoned after the original warehouse was destroyed by fire in 2008, and the new roof structure that swoops over to follow the line of the old gable and then falls in a curtain of translucent glass that transforms it into a new version of itself. Inside, the thousands of objects belonging to the archive are represented by tiny, dark dots that crowd into a public consultation hall on the ground level and are contained on the rows of shelves that can be seen filling the upper floors.

**BORIS IOFAN (1891–1976)**

**Competition entry for the Palace of the Soviets, 1933**

Pencil and watercolour on paper

129 × 193.5 cm, 50¾ × 76 in

The huge international competition for a new Palace of the Soviets in Moscow, which took place between 1931 and 1933, marked a turning point for Russian architecture, and the end of the Constructivist period. The eventual winner was a Neo-Classical design by Russian architect Boris Iofan, which he revised in collaboration with Vladimir Shchuko and Vladimir Gelfriekh into a soaring 415 m-high (1,361 ft) skyscraper, including a 100 m-tall (328 ft) statue of Lenin – in what would have been, at that time, the world's tallest structure. The revised scheme is shown in this monumental perspective view, in which the tall structure sits in a vast empty plaza freed up by the demolition of the Cathedral of Christ the Saviour, a symbol of pre-Revolutionary Russia, ordered by Lenin in 1931. The Moskva River flows along the left-hand side of the composition to the south of the plaza, which is surrounded by the elegant Neo-Classical blocks and garden squares of the reimagined Soviet capital. A broad boulevard defies perspective to widen towards the periphery of the city and a riverside park in the far distance. Building started on the site in 1937, and by the outbreak of World War II the foundations and base had been completed and the construction of the steel frame of the tower begun. The scarcity of building materials and labour caused by the war halted its progress, and the steel frame was dismantled and redistributed for more prosaic but practical projects. Abandoned after the war, the ruins of the foundations were transformed into the vast outdoor Moskva Pool, eventually, and symbolically, replaced by a faithful reconstruction of the cathedral in 1995. Entries to accommodate this administrative centre and congressional complex came from designers as diverse as Auguste and Gustave Perret, Hans Poelzig, Naum Gabo and Le Corbusier, along with numerous Russian architects.

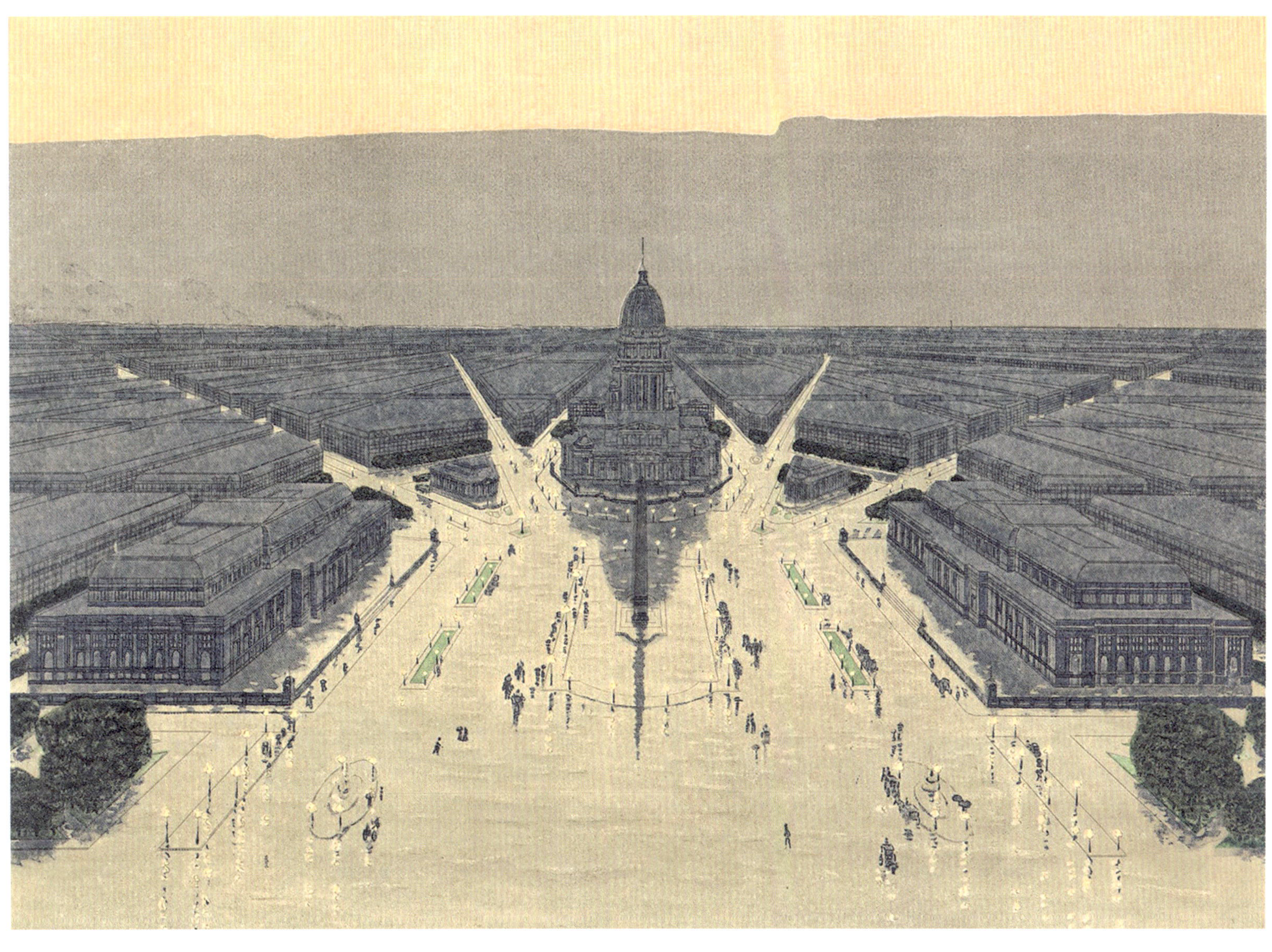

**DANIEL BURNHAM (1846–1912)**

**City Center Plaza, Plan of Chicago, 1909**

Ink and watercolour on paper

38 × 55 cm, 15 × 21¾ in

Looking west across the proposed civic-centre plaza, this aerial perspective fantasy for the rapidly expanding metropolis of Chicago, reincarnated as the *City Beautiful*, featured as Plate 132 in Daniel Burnham's *Plan of Chicago*, published in 1909. The vast urban space is captured in a moment of intense atmospheric effect that would have been familiar to inhabitants of the city, even if never seen in this way and from this height. Dark clouds roll away westwards after a storm, leaving a shimmering, watery veneer over the wide ground of the huge civic space. Street-light reflections burrow like poles of fire into the earth, clusters of people are magnified, and the reflected city hall's shadowy dome creeps down the page towards the viewer. The evenly proportioned city blocks are delineated in a blue wash that anticipates the night, and their edges bleed into the surrounding pavements. In contrast, their vertical lines of fenestration are sharply ruled, repeating into the distance. From the plaza, wide boulevards inspired by Haussmann's reconfiguring of Paris for Napoleon III lead towards the horizon, where the sun sets over the immense prairies surrounding the city. This space is the metropolitan heart, and the dome is the centre from which the radial circulation arteries diverge through the city and into the countryside beyond. The seeds for Burnham's transformational plans were sown at Chicago's World's Columbian Exposition, held in 1893, when he presented ideas for improving the waterfront. This led to him being commissioned to prepare the *Plan of Chicago* by local business leaders, who wanted to improve the city as a commercial, rather than a political, centre. Few of his ideas were implemented as such, but the plan influenced the development of the city's centre, resulting in vital thoroughfares; extensive waterfront parks; and, further out, regional forest preserves.

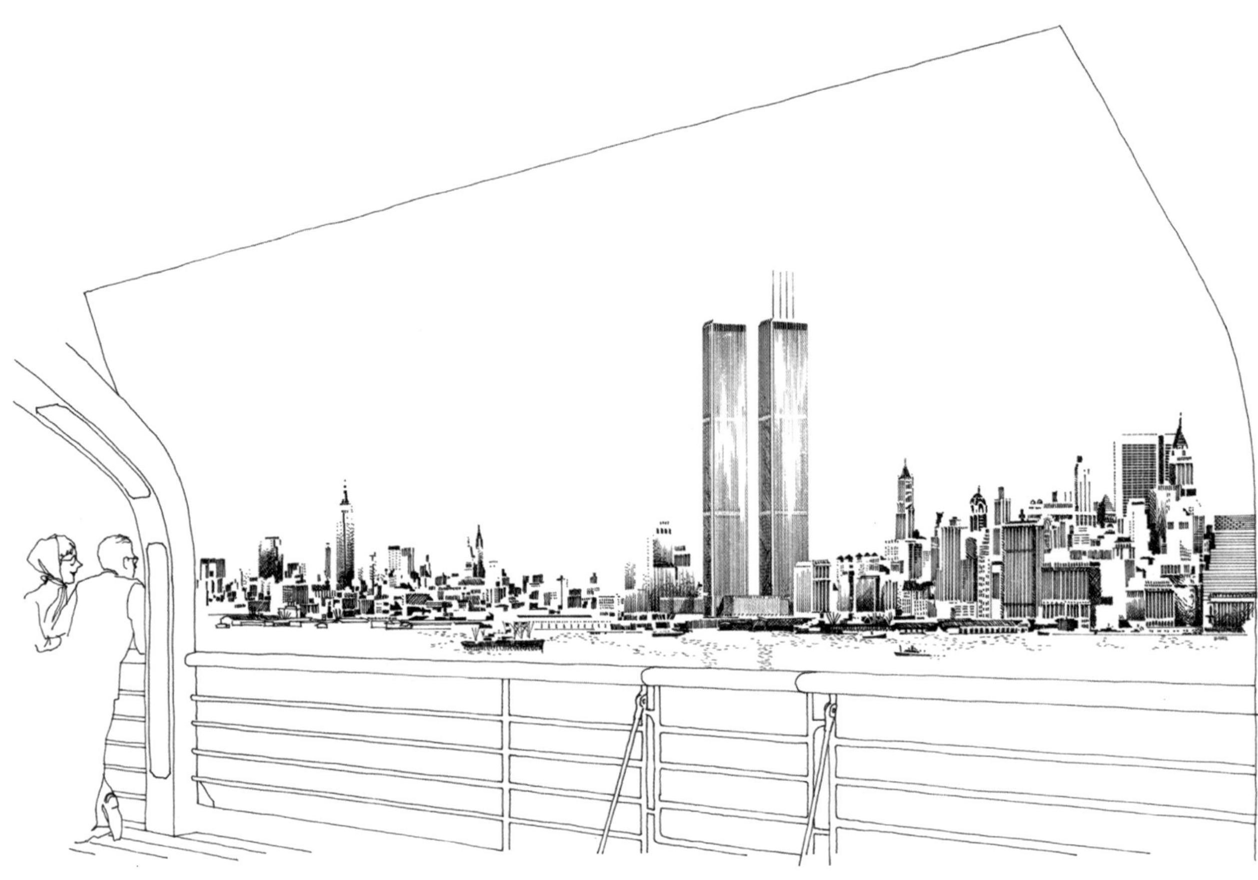

**CARLOS DINIZ (1926–2001)**

**View of the World Trade Center, 1963**

Pencil and ink on paper

23.7 × 32 cm, 9¼ × 12½ in

From 1957, the rendering studio of Carlos Diniz was employed by US architect Minoru Yamasaki, whose practice was commissioned to design New York's World Trade Center in 1962. For six years, Diniz' office produced images illustrating the evolving designs for the centre, introducing it to the public imagination and defining its powerful, iconic presence – Diniz recalled his first encounter with the project when he was shown a model so tall it pierced the ceiling of Yamasaki's studio and left him agog. This simple line drawing is unusual in that it solves the problem of revealing the full power of the whole complex, and its spectacular presence. With elegant economy, the twin towers are shown in their physical context at a completely different scale to the cluster of much shorter buildings around them, and are of a different order – their sleek, unadorned flanks contrasting with the jumble of vertical and horizontal lines used to depict the complexity of the city below. The drawing has two parts, which are separated by the expanse of the Hudson River seen from a ferry. The experience that every New Yorker and many tourists would have enjoyed is exploited to bring the reality of these alien buildings into the realm of everyday life. It is easy to imagine inhabiting the boat's deck in the foreground, leaning on the rail to gaze at the scene of Manhattan, shown in elevation from across the water. Over the years, a huge variety of drawings of the twin towers came out of Diniz' studio; they primarily engaged with the problem of how to make the the buildings work in scale with their surroundings – usually focusing on the street level and the plaza, with a partial view of the towers themselves.

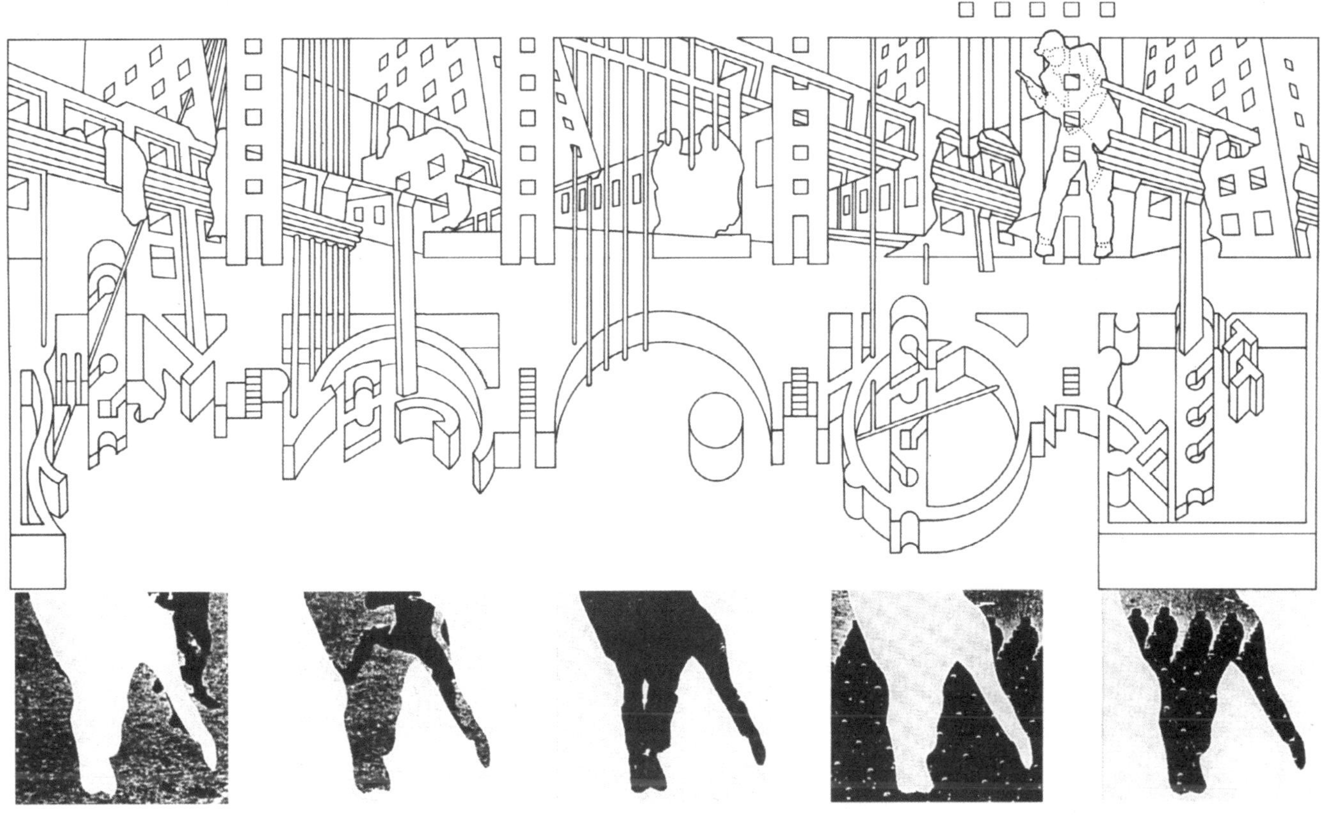

**BERNARD TSCHUMI (1944–)**

**Scene from The Block, 1981**

Ink on paper

45.7 × 76.2 cm, 18 × 30 in

Bernard Tschumi's *Manhattan Transcripts* were devised between 1977 and 1981, when they were published as a collection. They differ from most architectural drawings in not representing either real or imaginary construction, but rather the relationship of the city dweller to the architectural landscape of Manhattan. Displaying sequences of events analogous to the frames of a film, which incorporate the animated body within them, the Transcripts are organized into four episodes – The Park, The Street, The Tower and The Block. This page shows one of fifteen panels constituting The Block. The drawing is split into two sections. Below, five square photographic images repeat the same outline of two figures, cropped to show only their legs. There is something ominous about their disposition; they could be taking part in a riot, or perhaps they are dancing. The figure–ground relationship of their outline to the background is transformed in each frame, sometimes reversed. Above, a fragment of the city is depicted in a simple close-up line drawing, as if traced from a photograph, including the optical distortion of a tall building. It is repeated five times with the same rhythm as the photographs, but separated by a representation of the edge of a photographic negative. Recognizable elements confirm that it is the same place seen over and over again – an elevated rail track, an anonymous facade – but each time the view is different. The relative position of the viewer shifts, or perhaps it is the means of perceiving the scene that changes. The lower part of this scene is constituted of an isometric projection of an imaginary sequence of urban spaces, which flow into each other like the musical notation of a film score, enhancing the sense of time passing, in a life separated from reality.

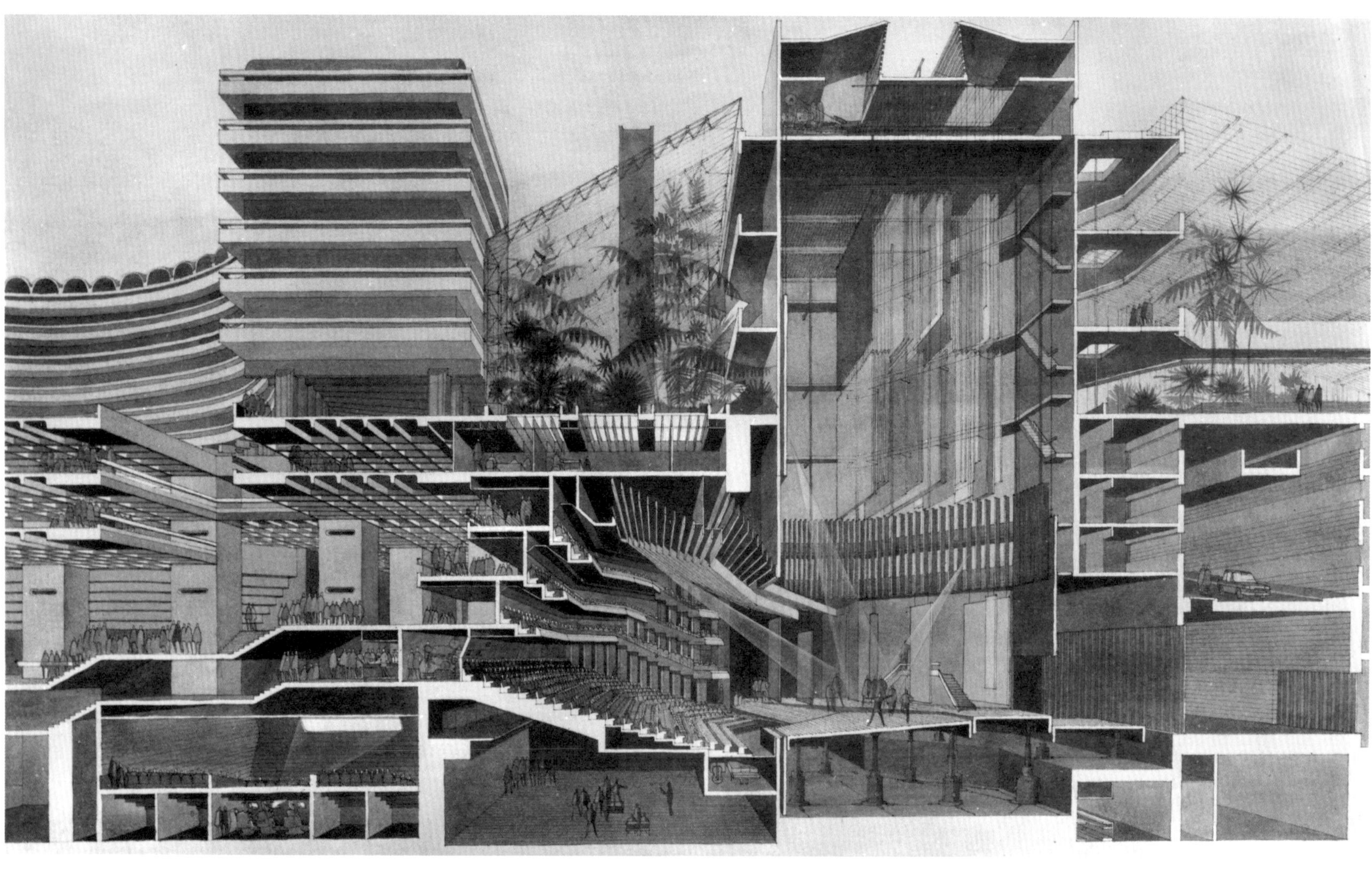

**CHAMBERLIN, POWELL & BON**

**Barbican Centre, 1970**

Pencil and ink on paper

50 × 42 cm, 19¾ × 16½ in

The incredible complexity of the interlocking volumes of the Barbican cultural centre, the surrounding residential estate of 2,000 apartments and the public realm that connects them is fully articulated in this perspective section. The purpose of the drawing is not to explain the construction of the building or its structural organization, but purely to give a sense of the symbiotic relationship between the theatre and the supporting spaces that make performance possible. The theatre inhabits the centre of the drawing, and the vanishing point of the perspective is located somewhere between the auditorium and the footlights, hovering in the shadowy region between the acoustic baffles and the ceiling. The soaring fly tower above the stage, with its rows of scenery hanging in waiting, is disguised on each side by a conservatory whose feathery trusses and exotic plants contrast with the powerful, concrete section. To one side, a car is seen descending a ramp into the depths of the car park, and it becomes clear that there is no longer a natural ground surface in this self-contained, utopian world. In the spaces below the auditorium, there is a small experimental theatre space called The Pit, and a cinema below the crowded foyers and suspended walkways. The architects – Chamberlin, Powell & Bon – worked on the Barbican project for nearly thirty years, from the mid-1950s until 1982, when the complex opened. Constructed on a large bomb site in the City of London, excavation for the project moved 190,000 $m^3$ (6,709,786 $ft^3$) of soil and, at its peak, employed 10,000 workers.

**GIOVANNI BATTISTA PIRANESI (1720–78)**

**The Well, c.1750**

Etching

15.3 × 21.8 cm, 6 × 8½ in

Giovanni Battista Piranesi's series of drawings and etchings of imaginary prisons, *Carceri d'Invenzioni*, have long been considered his most provocative works. The *Carceri* compositions are also mysterious, for they depict not features commonly associated with prisons but grand spaces of immense scale and splendour that could be fortresses or enormous warehouses. This image, called *The Well*, presents a complex scene inhabited by freely moving figures dispersed around a vast hall, the space of which is interrupted by a steep staircase but whose extent is suggested by a grid of high-level, arched bridges and huge timber structures. The surface of the image, with its deep spatial quality and intense atmosphere, was built up through a process of consecutive techniques. First came the sketching out of the block forms: here, the well and the frame of the monolithic structure surrounding it, the staircase with its strange dormers, and the overhanging beams. These would be filled in with broadly hatched lines interspersed with curlicue strokes. Acid smeared directly on to the etching plate would produce the blackness of the deepest shadows, which would be burnished away to create the illusion of misty beams of light. The process of cutting and burnishing would be selectively repeated, for aquatint was still to be invented, and the end result is not one of spontaneous passion but of meticulous work producing a carefully accrued effect. *The Well* is one of fourteen compositions from Piranesi's original series for the *Carceri*, whose plates he reworked for a second series published in 1761. All the copper plates were changed to produce darker, more detailed images, and to expand the space depicted. The vastly extended space in *The Well* opens up large, bright background areas that in this second version can be read as exterior rather than interior realms.

**ARATA ISOZAKI (1931–2022)**

**Incubation Process, 1962**

1990 silkscreen of a 1962 drawing

104.1 × 87.3 cm, 41 × 34½ in

When Arata Isozaki made this collage, part of a series in response to the ruins of Hiroshima, he wrote a poem as its caption: 'Incubated cities are destined to self-destruct / Ruins are the style of our future cities / Future cities are themselves ruins / Our contemporary cities, for this reason / are destined to live only a fleeting moment / Give up their energy and return to inert material / All of our proposals and efforts will be buried / And once again the incubation mechanism is / reconstituted / That will be the future.' Isozaki's drawing belongs to the Japanese Metabolist movement, whose vast architectural megastructures – both imagined and, to a certain extent, achieved in reality – were capable of accommodating whole urban populations. Their huge, repeating elements house all the associated functions of the metropolis, but their form and conceptualization was modified by an interest in the process of organic growth – incubated, as Isozaki said, rather than complete and instantaneous. The fractured nature of the collage and the poem together reveal the origins of this approach, and the world presented here has not come into being through a seamless cultural and material progression. Instead, the systems of each era have been layered, palimpsest-like, over the ruins of preceding civilizations. In this collage, the ruins are not Japanese but European. The scale of Greek columns that would have supported simple buildings within an ensemble has been exaggerated enormously. Now they form foundations for huge towers joined by continuous, horizontal megastructural elements belonging to a scheme that Isozaki developed separately called Prototype City in the Air. The ruined base of one of the Greek columns has become a geological feature, a hill in a flat landscape overlaid by a multi-lane highway that is populated with tiny cars rushing along. Minuscule figures crowd on to walkways or peruse the ruins – even those of the megastructural city itself.

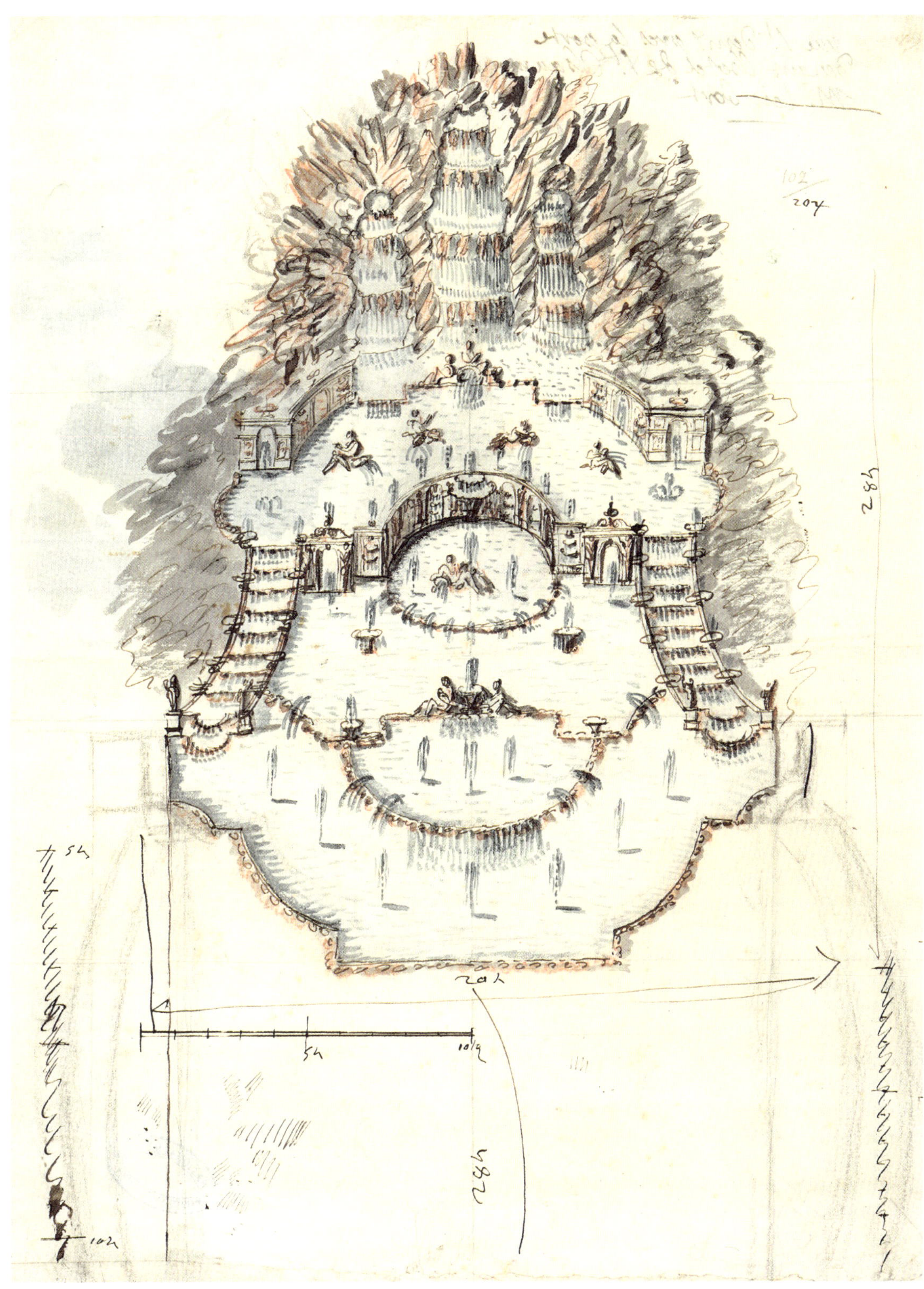

**ANDRÉ LE NÔTRE (1613–1700)**

**Project for Fountain with Cascades and Sculptures at Versailles, 1685**

Graphite, pen, ink, wash and watercolour on paper

41.8 × 32 cm, 16½ × 12½ in

André Le Nôtre created the gardens at Versailles over thirty years, beginning in 1661. In order to depict work for important clients, his studio produced many fine presentation drawings in which the design process and its graphic representation were separated, and the image constructed using codified elements to represent trelliswork, shrubs, trees, geometrical figures and water features. Le Nôtre was a skilful draughtsman; growing up in a house adjoining the Tuileries Gardens in Paris, where his father was chief gardener, he returned to gardening after studying painting. Some signed, rough, preliminary drawings – such as this one, for an unrealized project at Versailles – still exist, and reveal his painterly approach. The huge complex of water features is shown in a bird's-eye view – without perspectival distortion, but not in elevation. The three cascading fountains from which the water sources spring are sited in an artificial cliff, and the rough banks of the surrounding terrain that buttress this man-made hill are drawn in loose strokes of watercolour animated by brown-ink lines. These edges are lined with colonnaded wings that shore up the banks, transforming into shallow, stepped watercourses either side of the symmetrical composition, creating sites for the contemplation of sculpture and various water jets. His client Louis XIV, known as the Sun King, was especially fond of fountains, which were challenging to construct. Le Nôtre oversaw the work of thousands of soldier-labourers who transformed the swampy site at Versailles, moving vast quantities of soil and diverting and controlling natural watercourses to conform to his intricate, geometrical plans. On a flat site, Le Nôtre constructed a landscape animated by cleverly contrived vistas that manipulated perspective to create a sense of intimacy within the estate while, at other vantage points, giving a sense of infinite depth.

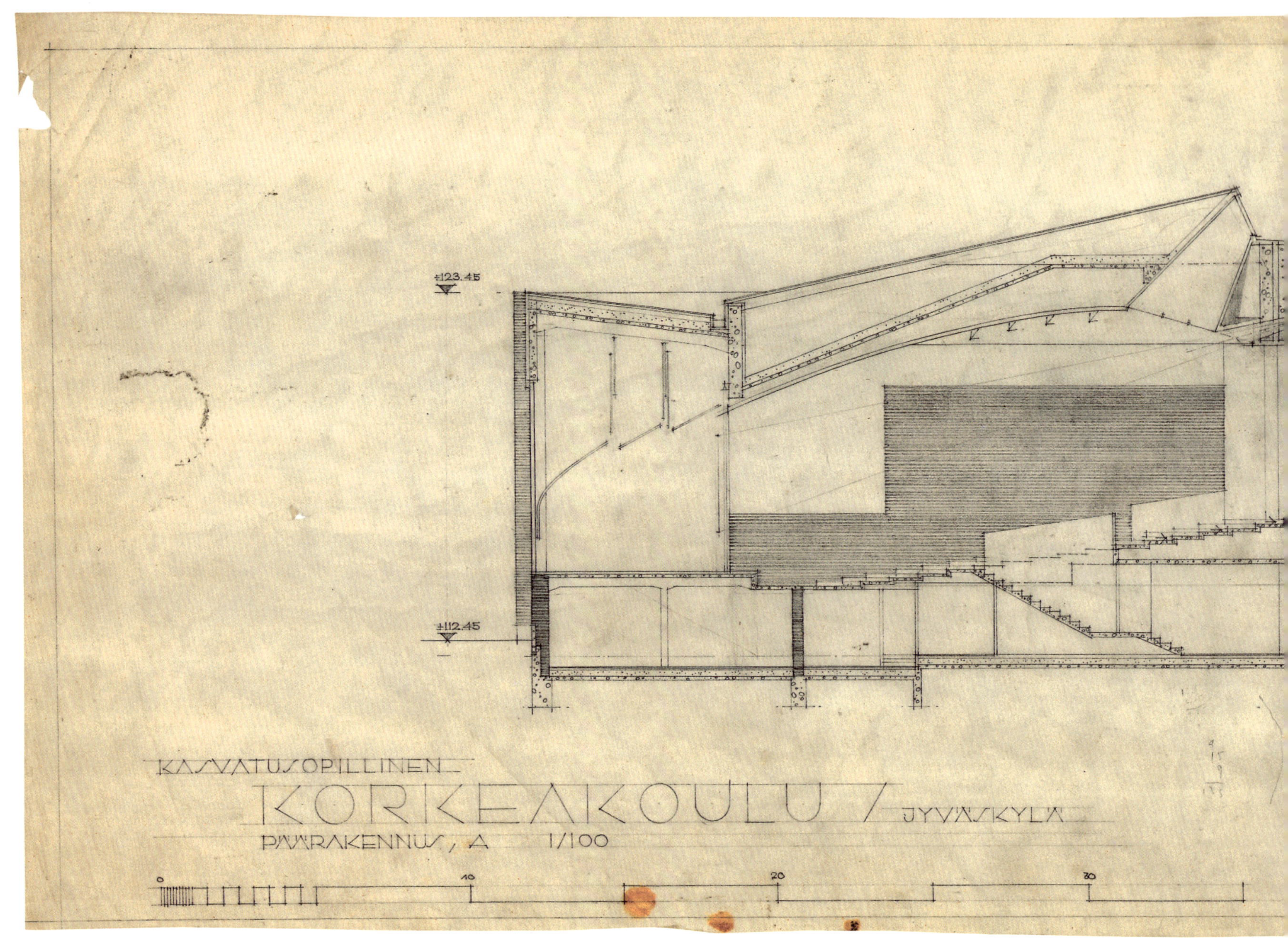

±123.45
±112.45
KASVATUSOPILLINEN
KORKEAKOULU / JYVÄSKYLÄ
PÄÄRAKENNUS, A 1/100
0
10
20
30

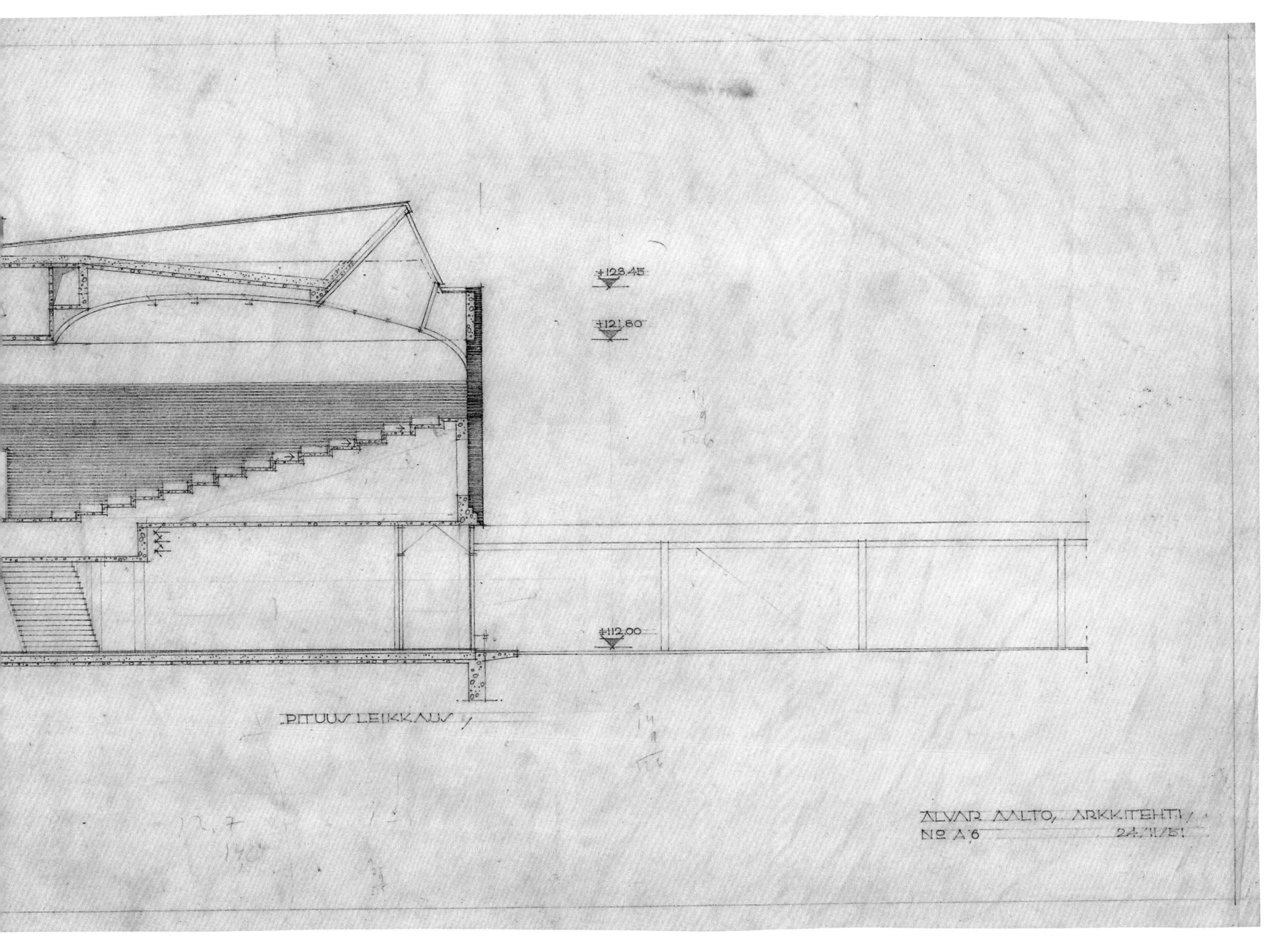


**ALVAR AALTO (1898–1976)**

**Festival Hall, Jyväskylä University, 1951**

Ink on tracing paper

30 × 86 cm, 11¾ × 34 in

The University of Jyväskylä is laid out on a campus that, when originally commissioned, was situated at the edge of this provincial city, surrounded by dense forest. This section cuts through Alvar Aalto's Festival Hall, which he designed to be a public gathering space that would mediate between, and be used by, the inhabitants of both city and academic centre. It constitutes a wing of the main building, a larger complex made in red brick that housed the library, various classrooms and administration offices. This section reveals the nature of the roofline that Aalto designed, with a series of complex, sloping surfaces culminating in an end wall looking over the entrance plaza at the front of the hall. The profile gradually rises up to the centre of the hall, culminating in one of two deep light scoops that bring Finland's changing seasons into the interior. The second element casts daylight over the seating at the back of the hall, bathing the hollowed-out shapes of the ceilings that are lined with reflective white slats. The hand-drawn section also shows how the space is divided by solid, sliding walls in the centre, which allow it to be used as two separate, acoustically independent halls, or opened up for a single audience of over 700 people. The structural concrete elements are easily discernible in section, their depth filled with the conventional symbol for the material, while the delicate, curved planes of the acoustic ceilings are drawn with simple pencil lines. In plan, the symmetrical hall comprises a series of fan shapes. The outermost consist of small projections from shorter elements flanking a deeper volume, and the articulated form is echoed in its dramatic roofline. The wing containing the hall has a different character to the administrative wing's subdued, rectilinear form.

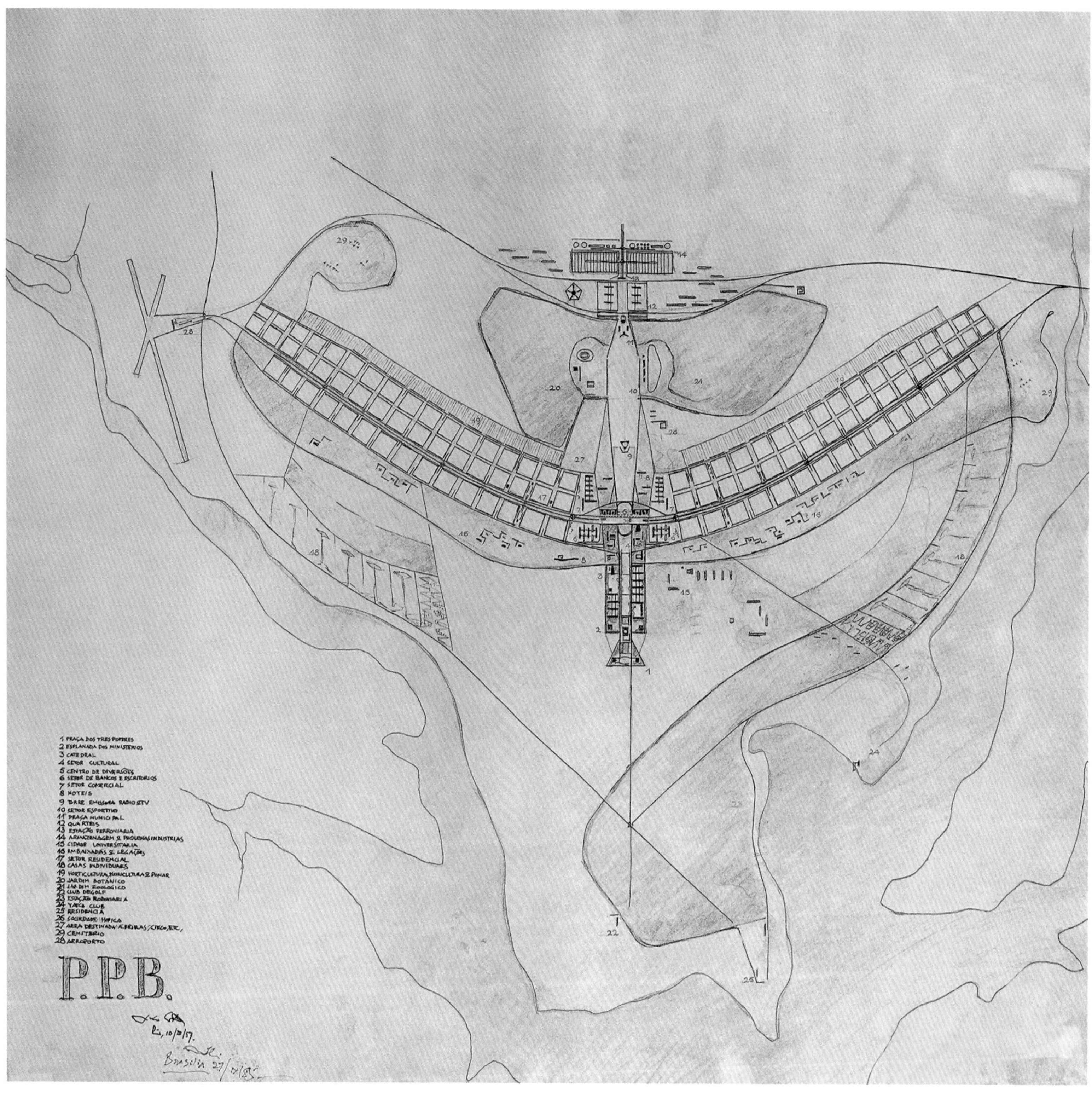


**LÚCIO COSTA (1902–98)**

**Pilot Plan of Brasilia, 1956**

Ink and coloured pencil on drafting paper

57 × 67 cm, 22½ × 26½ in

In 1955, the site for Brazil's new capital was determined at the confluence of two rivers deep in the vast country's interior. Newly elected president Juscelino Kubitschek saw the opportunity to symbolize a modern, industrializing country, and this ambition defined the competition brief for the city plan, to which 26 Brazilian teams responded in 1956. Oscar Niemeyer had already begun designing the presidential palace, defining Brasília's architectural character of lightness, grandeur, lyricism and power, as Kubitschek described it – but it was Lúcio Costa's striking plan that encapsulated the image of the city as archetypally modern. Contained within a notional equilateral triangle, its cross is orientated to the points of the compass, and is a primordial sign marking Brazil's conceptual heart. The curves of the arms transform the rigidity of the colonial-style grid and cross the east–west axis at the Esplanade of Ministries. The way that the unscaled plan is drawn has an interesting ambiguity: while being a clear and compelling diagram, it maintains a casual, hand-drawn quality that resonates with the loose sketches of the plan often seen alongside it, which isolate and exaggerate its symbolic, conceptual nature. Accompanied by a report articulating detailed guidelines in 23 points, ranging from the assignment of zones for civic functions such as entertainment, commerce and administration to traffic circulation, the provision of residential super-blocks along the north–south axis and the physical nature of the monumental heart, the plan was free to communicate the more symbolic aspects of the proposal. From above, it was an aeroplane in flight; at ground level, a crossroads for a new country – and in its organization, it was consummately efficient and ordered. For Costa it was a civitas rather than an urbs – not an organic, responsive entity but a predefined civic, administrative and monumental system.

**ANON**

**Carthaginian architecture, c.350 BC**

Red-ochre mural

39 × 69.2 cm, 15½ × 27¼ in

In 1952, the site of the Punic city of Kerkouane was discovered on the tip of Cap Bon in Tunisia. It is one of the most extensively excavated Carthaginian settlements, having survived as a relatively intact example of Phoenician town planning since no Roman city was built over it after its destruction in 146 BC. Its port, ramparts, residential districts and urban spaces remain as they were in the third century BC. This wall mural is located in an underground tomb chamber found in the necropolis near the city site, and is possibly a representation of the city of Carthage itself, whose site lies around 100 km to the west, within the Gulf of Tunis. The quality of the red-ochre line is very simple, and shows a crenellated, walled city with square buildings beside a niche with the symbol of Tanit – a Punic and Phoenician goddess, and one of the chief deities of Carthage – and a rooster, which was a symbol of the soul. Below, a frieze composed of red triangles continues around each wall of the rectangular tomb, underlining two drawings of lighthouses on the perpendicular walls. Shown as if from a bird's-eye perspective, seen from the south or the west looking towards the sea, the drawing is not expressive of town planning beyond its depiction of the surrounding fortified wall. The buildings within the wall are not shown in plan but in crude elevation, which reveals that the houses themselves were also fortified and tightly clustered together. At that time, these dwellings had flat roofs with access by stairs and ladders, and often had interior courtyards that were entered through narrow corridors from the street.

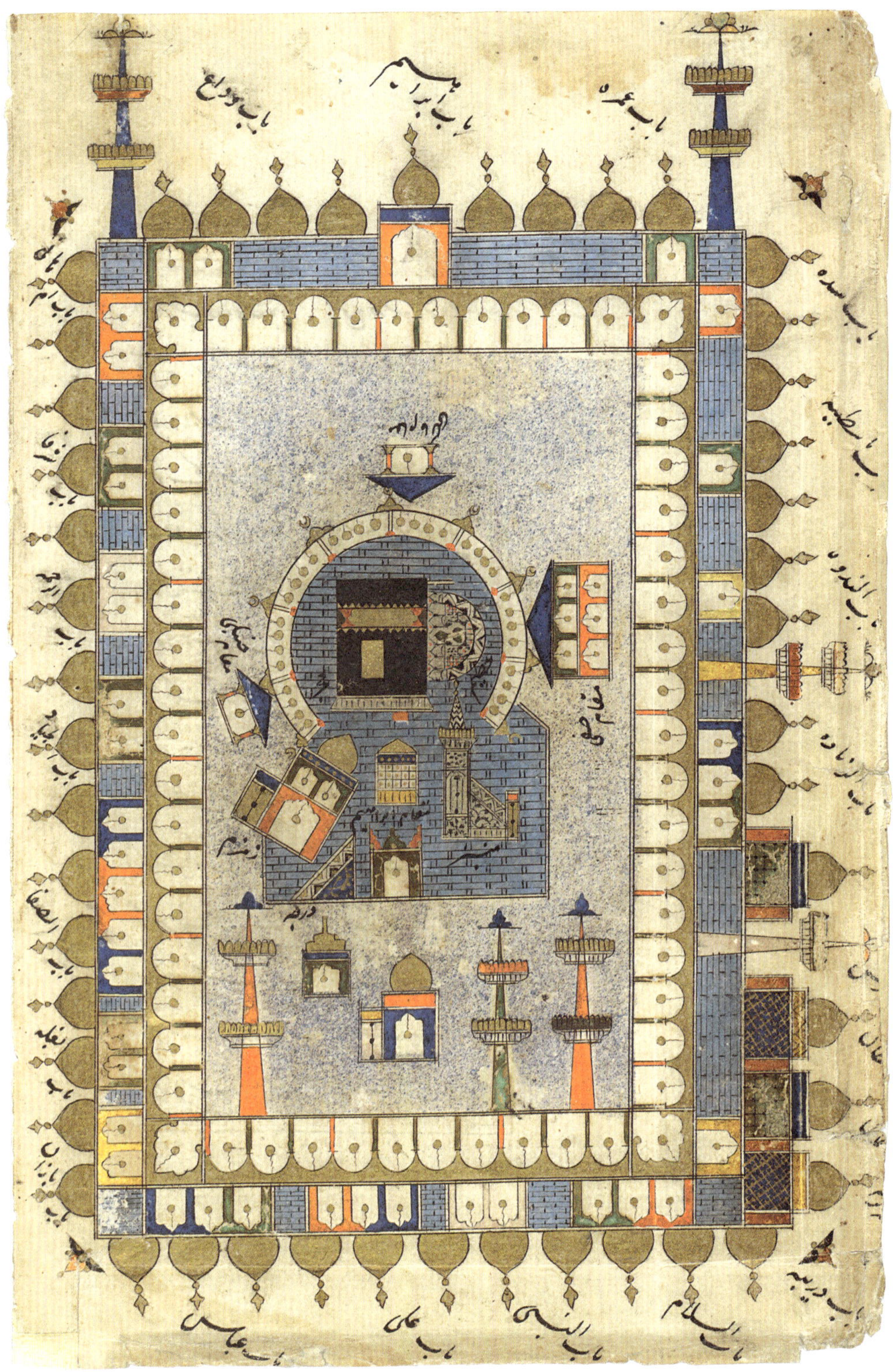

**ANON**

**The Kaaba, c.1550**

Ink, opaque watercolour and gold on paper

22.2 × 14.3 cm, 8½ × 5½ in

In this drawing, the Kaaba – a shrine made of granite that is the most sacred place on earth for Muslims – is shown in elevation, with the distinctive markings of the cloth of black brocade that usually covers it clearly visible. It is located near the centre of Islam's most important mosque, the Masjid Al-Haram, or Great Mosque, in Mecca. The Kaaba is shown surrounded by a field of blue, brick-shaped tiles and set within a representation of a semicircular low wall known as the Hateem, which in reality sits opposite just the northwestern wall of the Ka'ba and was originally part of it, almost touching its corners. Various religious structures are dispersed within the boundary of the blue floor and shown in elevation, including a highly decorated *minbar*, or pulpit, with a tower, and several small shrines. These are sited in the large courtyard of the mosque, which is shown in plan and fully enclosed by a regular rhythm of semicircular arches drawn in elevation, which still exist today. A second, upper level shows an irregular rhythm of arches within the wall, interspersed with the same blue brick as the floor of the space around the Kaaba. The illuminated sheet, painted in luxurious materials, is Folio 20 of a sixteenth-century illustrated-manuscript anthology, or *Majmu'ah*, that comes from the Hejaz region, the area of Saudi Arabia in which Mecca is located. The other sheets from the collection all contain text, and the image of the Kaaba is itself annotated, but they also include images of other religious sites, such as the Tomb of the Prophet at Medina, a cemetery and other mosque representations. During the period in which it was made, Hejaz was a province of the Ottoman Empire under Turkish rule, which began in 1517.

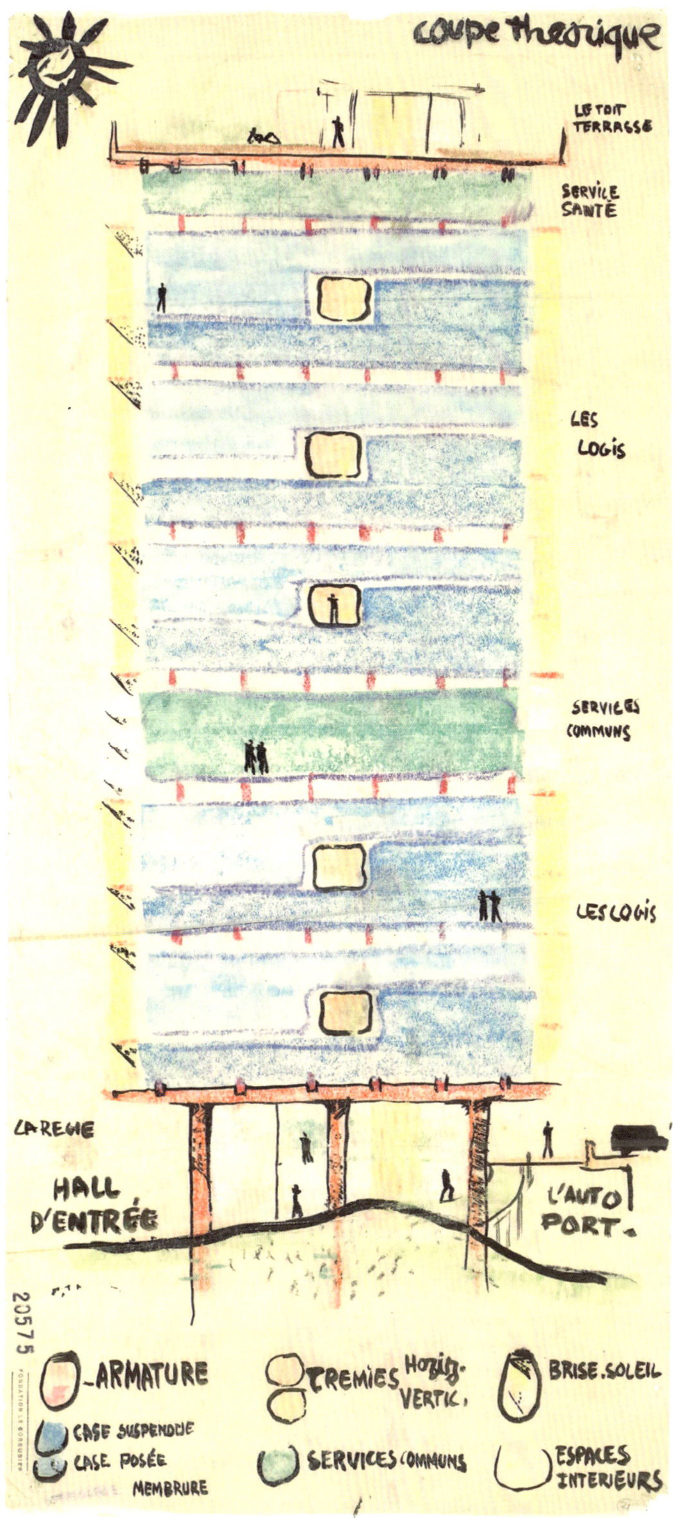


**LE CORBUSIER (1887–1965)**

**Unité d'Habitation, 1946**

Ink and coloured pencil on paper

48 × 22.5 cm, 19 × 9 in

Sunshine and daylight are elements as architectural as structure and cladding in this diagrammatic sketch made by Le Corbusier to describe the disposition of his eighteen-storey block of flats in Marseilles, known as the Unité d'Habitation. It shows a cross section through the long block, which was orientated north–south so that the principal elevations, the ones shown on this section, would face either east or west. Apartments would span the width of the building, allowing cross ventilation and also, ideally, east-facing bedrooms and west-facing living rooms. However, in this section only half the flats have this disposition. Very little is outlined in dark ink in the drawing. The thickest line delineates the ground, which is left in its natural state as an inconvenient undulation whose irregularity is resolved by the three piloti supporting the ground-floor slab. These are shaded brown and sink into the earth, giving them the primitive look of tree trunks. Beside one of them, a small, curved wall sketched in perspective suggests an underground car park. Above the new datum of the floor slab, the building rises like a cloud of zones shaded in pale and darker blue and green, where two flats share three floors so that double-height living rooms embrace the access corridors running down the centre of the block. These stand out because they are outlined in ink and coloured yellow. Communal spaces are coloured green, and do not benefit from the architectural treatment of the facades designed to respond to the sun. A jolly sun shines down on the west facade, the windows of which are protected by deep balconies and the *brise-soleil* noted in the key at the bottom, to provide shade. On the roof, tiny figures enjoy the sunshine, while scattered around the drawing their companions provide scale and animation.

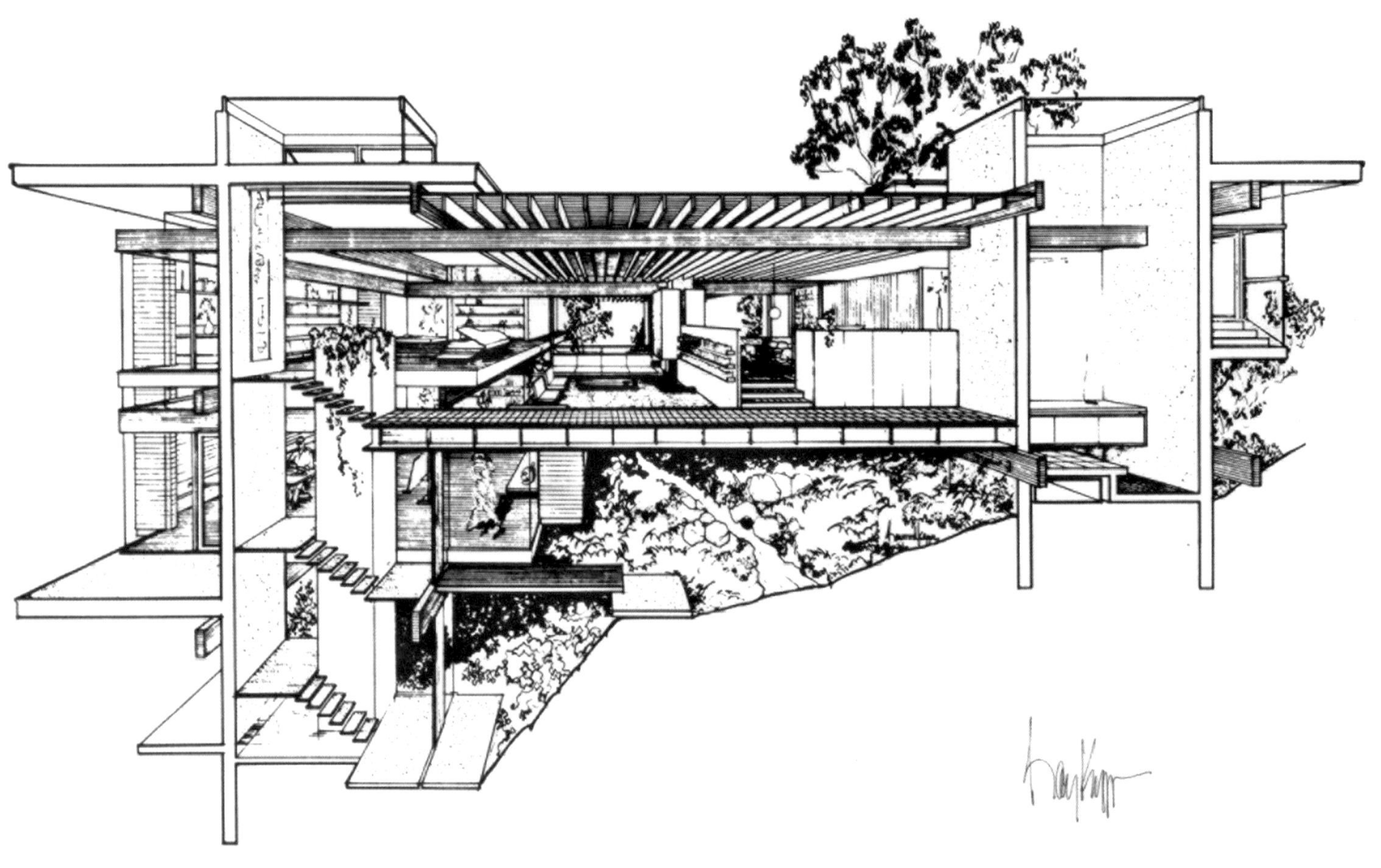

**RAY KAPPE (1927–2019)**

**Kappe Residence, 1967**

Ink on paper

21 × 25 cm, 8¼ × 9¾ in

Raymond Kappe experimented with the design of his own house, located on one of the hills of Pacific Palisades in California, as he sought a method to build on this difficult terrain that was made more problematic by the region's seismic activity. This perspective section shows how he resolved these issues in his prototype for hillside construction, while at the same time indicating through the animation of the interior how the house would feel as a home – Kappe himself can be seen working at a desk. Six concrete towers, two of which are shown in the drawing, bear the seismic load. One of them, on the south side, encompasses a staircase, and the other contains storage on the northern edge, at the top of the sloping site. Exposed, laminated-timber beams are placed in relation to the natural contours of the landscape. This means that as the seven levels of this open-plan house step down the hillside they take on different volumes and heights, so that each space has the character of a separate room. This spatial variety is echoed in the views from these rooms – some look over the wide expanse of the valley, others are internal connections to other parts of the house. The most unusual offer glimpses of the secret stream that runs underneath, which is shown in the section like a magical heart. Clerestories and skylights over the tower units illuminate every part of the house with daylight, which is tempered and animated by the surrounding trees. The flat roof provides the strongest sense of perspective through the delicate Douglas fir beams that run the full width of the central family areas. This level corresponds with the top of the site, and becomes an outside terrace that is reached by a laminated-wood bridge surrounded by trees.

**PAUL RUDOLPH (1918–97)**

**Lower Manhattan Expressway, 1970**

Print on mylar

97 × 122 cm, 38 × 48 in

In 1941, a visionary plan by US public official Robert Moses to connect the Manhattan and Williamsburg bridges to the Hudson River's Holland Tunnel was approved by the City Planning Department. This would link New Jersey to Brooklyn, Queens and Long Island via huge expressways that would cleave through Lower Manhattan, demolishing huge swathes of the city in its path. His proposals continued to develop over the next twenty years, but were eventually defeated in 1962 due to public opposition led by the campaigner Jane Jacobs. In 1967, the Ford Foundation commissioned Paul Rudolph to make a study of the project, which he worked on intermittently for the next five years, publishing his response as *The Evolving City: Urban Design Proposals by Ulrich Franzen and Paul Rudolph* in 1974. Over the period of study, Rudolph made many drawings that explored the expressway project at all scales. This coloured drawing is unusual in the set because it shows the infrastructure of the expressway in relation to the city around it, whose urban blocks are represented by simple line drawings that include few of the incidental details – the water towers, aerials and rooftop gardens – that animate the city skyline. The foreground consists of a section cut through the rocky ground of Manhattan Island, showing steep embankments leading down to the capsule train tracks and multi-lane motorway below. The route taken by the expressway can easily be traced in the perspective, the triangular form of its A-framed megastructure cutting away the traditional city blocks and rising above them, reaching a peak at the intersection of the two routes shown in the distance. Although the scale and geometry of the new structure are alien elements within the existing city, the local streets are maintained, crossing over from one side to another into tree-lined parks.

**ZAHA HADID (1950–2016)**

**Page from a sketchbook, 2001**

Ink on tracing paper

41.8 × 21 cm, 5¾ × 8¼ in

Taken from one of Zaha Hadid's many sketchbooks, this drawing does not have the polished finish of the paintings and other images that she produced for presentation and seduction. In her sketchbooks, Hadid explored many different aspects of her work – from the relationship of geometry to form, and the ways that this could be fragmented and distorted, to the effects of different techniques and mechanisms of drawing and painting. Over the faint, blue grid of the paper, which is completely disregarded, a series of hand-drawn ink lines change character as they flow. Sometimes, they take on the thickness of the edge of the pen; more often, they have the hard, precise character produced by its firmly controlled nib. Hadid has described how, growing up in Iraq, she was encouraged to play with maths problems as much as with pencils and pens – to draw no boundaries between the two. In this sketch, a complex template repeats many times, overlaid and displaced so that an intricate figure emerges on the page. The abstract, formal possibilities of the overlapping profiles have been drawn out by dissolving some ink strokes with water so that deposits of pigment seep inwards to fill some of the shapes created by the intersections. Mostly, these are controlled and even in tone, but in some places they have been allowed to fade out, giving a sense of reflected light. Elsewhere, the shapes have been filled in with intensely black ink, appearing as deep shadows or voids. The ink's shadowy presence is reminiscent of a story told by Madelon Vriesendorp, who taught Hadid in painting workshops when she was a student at the Architectural Association during the 1970s, of Hadid's habit of burning the edges of her drawings so that they looked like futuristic treasures dug up from the ground.

**MICHELE MARCHETTI (nd)**

**Villa Malaparte, 2013**

Ink on paper

57 × 45 cm, 22½ × 17¾ in

Between 2010 and 2017, the architectural magazine *San Rocco* always featured on its front cover a drawing by Michele Marchetti – an image created by lines between fields of glossy, black ink printed on a matt white surface without name or caption. The mysterious quality of these abandoned, or autonomous, buildings from all historical periods and locations was implied by the avoidance of classification or labelling. The drawings were set up in a form called *axonometry*, meaning an isometric drawn at the same vertical scale as the plan from which it was projected. The plan was placed not at an angle, as was conventional in isometric drawing, but with its edges parallel to the horizontal. An iconography of abstract architectural images resulted, always depicting buildings known to cognoscenti; in this case, the Villa Malaparte, by Italian Modernist Adalberto Libera, is the protagonist. It featured on the cover of *San Rocco*'s seventh issue, whose theme was Collaborations, and the famous house is not completely isolated but rather set within the immediate, natural context of the rocky peninsula, projecting off the island of Capri into the Tyrrhenian Sea, in which it is embedded. The bushy surroundings contrast with the house's smooth surfaces, and two kinds of line seep between the cracks of the black ink field – one depicts an architectural condition; the other, far less precise, outlines the trees that move in the wind, the rocks around which the water swells and an escaping bird, top left. Over time, Marchetti's method evolved: initially, a plan and sections were used to construct a simple three-dimensional computer model, from which the projection was generated. As Marchetti's process became more intuitive, he was able to set up a two-dimensional image straight away. The ink fields covered up construction lines, so that the drawing's messy entrails were hidden.

**MEISTER ARNOLD (nd–1308)**

**Cologne Cathedral, 1280**

Iron gall ink on parchment

406.5 × 166.5 cm, 160 × 65½ in

During the second half of the thirteenth century, the Rhineland emerged as one of the most dynamic centres of Gothic architectural culture, which was produced out of the cathedral workshops of Strasbourg, Cologne and Freiburg. This huge drawing, the parchment of which is composed of twenty differently sized sheets, was made by Meister Arnold, the second cathedral master builder at Cologne (1271–99). Depicting, in intricate and accurate detail, the screen of tracery for the whole of the cathedral's west elevation, this drawing is known as *Plan F* within a set of seven medieval drawings remaining at Cologne and made concurrently with the ground plan, *Plan A*.

*Plan F* actually played a significant part in the process of German emancipation from French Gothic influence – particularly, the conception of the harmonic west front, in which facade and towers were given more or less equal emphasis, such as at Notre-Dame in Paris, started in 1163, and Reims, started 1211. In *Plan F*, this grounded composition was superseded by a sublime verticality, encapsulated in the gigantic steeples, which were then unprecedented in Gothic architecture. These innovations would not have been possible without drawings such as this, which in addition to facilitating the rapid transition of ideas between neighbouring workshops also enabled, through their precision and detail, an understanding of how every stone embellishment was set out in relation to all other parts of a facade – a formidable feat of forward planning for the time. The physical reality of the drawing itself reveals this strategic intention, whereby the basic geometrical frame of the facade – a five-storey stack of octagonal modules corresponding to the footprints of the spire bases – is echoed in the trimming of the parchment sheets.

**HUGHSON HAWLEY (1850–1936)**

**Woolworth Building, 1911**

Gouache and graphite on board

180.9 × 81.3 cm, 71¼ × 32 in

When commissioned by the architect Cass Gilbert to make a presentation board for his design for the Woolworth Building, and the world's tallest skyscraper on its completion in 1913, Hughson Hawley was an artist at the peak of his powers. Hawley's watercolour portrait of Gilbert's tower became the definitive image in a public-relations campaign to draw worldwide attention to the Woolworth project; in May 1911, FW Woolworth copyrighted a version of the rendering to print as a giant chromolithographic trade card for wide distribution. Gilbert's Neo-Gothic design takes on a golden hue in the drawing, New York's spectacular light reflecting off the Hudson River and shimmering on the glass planes of its skyscrapers. The glow of the tower's facades gradually shades to a darker colour towards their edges, so that the intricate silhouette of the building is clearly visible against the bright sky, joining with the skyline of the tiny buildings at its base. The mottled blue and white of the sky provides a theatrical backdrop to the tower. The breaking up of this plane into a field of clouds that cast their shadows over the tower's facades brings the building into this sublime realm, which is completely different in scale to the tiny figures that crowd the street below. At the top, the tower's pinnacle belongs to the weather; even its base has a giant, three-storey order that gives it a monumental scale. Trained as a theatrical scene painter, Hawley became popular among leading New York architects such as Gilbert, creating the perspectives with which they enchanted their clients into building big. Unfazed by the scale of tall buildings made possible by construction innovations and the invention of the elevator, his experience in the theatre brought an aura of glamour to his architectural perspectives.

**LUDWIG KARL HILBERSEIMER (1885–1967)**

**High-rise City, 1924**

Ink and watercolour on paper

97.3 × 140 cm, 38¼ × 55 in

This large and powerful drawing needs to be experienced in real life to be fully appreciated; its reduction diminishes both its grandeur and pathos. Even in reproduction, however, it remains a compelling representation of the imagined world that Bauhaus architect and teacher Ludwig Hilberseimer published in his book *Großstadt Architektur* (Big City Architecture) in 1927, in which he set out his ideas for city planning and architecture. These joined a debate about how to control – especially socially, through form and aesthetics – the growing cities of the industrializing West. Hilberseimer's proposal for a high-rise city, which now seems spacious and modest in height compared to contemporary metropolises, brought together the principal activities of urban life – leisure, labour and circulation – into a vertically integrated system. The section through the earth in the drawing's foreground reveals underground services and train tracks neatly contained in tidy ducts. One track rumbles right across the drawing, meeting an upper-level walkway at one point and revealing the disparity in scale between the underground and aerial worlds: either the trains are tiny or the above-ground people are huge. The dramatic perspective, with its central vanishing point at the eye height, perhaps, of a low-flying pilot, highlights the wide north–south street that inhabits the lowest level of the above-ground world. This flows in an orderly grid between five-storey blocks of shops and offices. Above, the mass-produced human world, with not a speck of matter out of place, is carried on raised walkways. These are lined with buildings, whose dirty, grey surfaces suggest a residue of pollution. Their relentless window grids reinforce the perspective movement towards the distant vanishing point, giving the impression that this city could go on for ever.

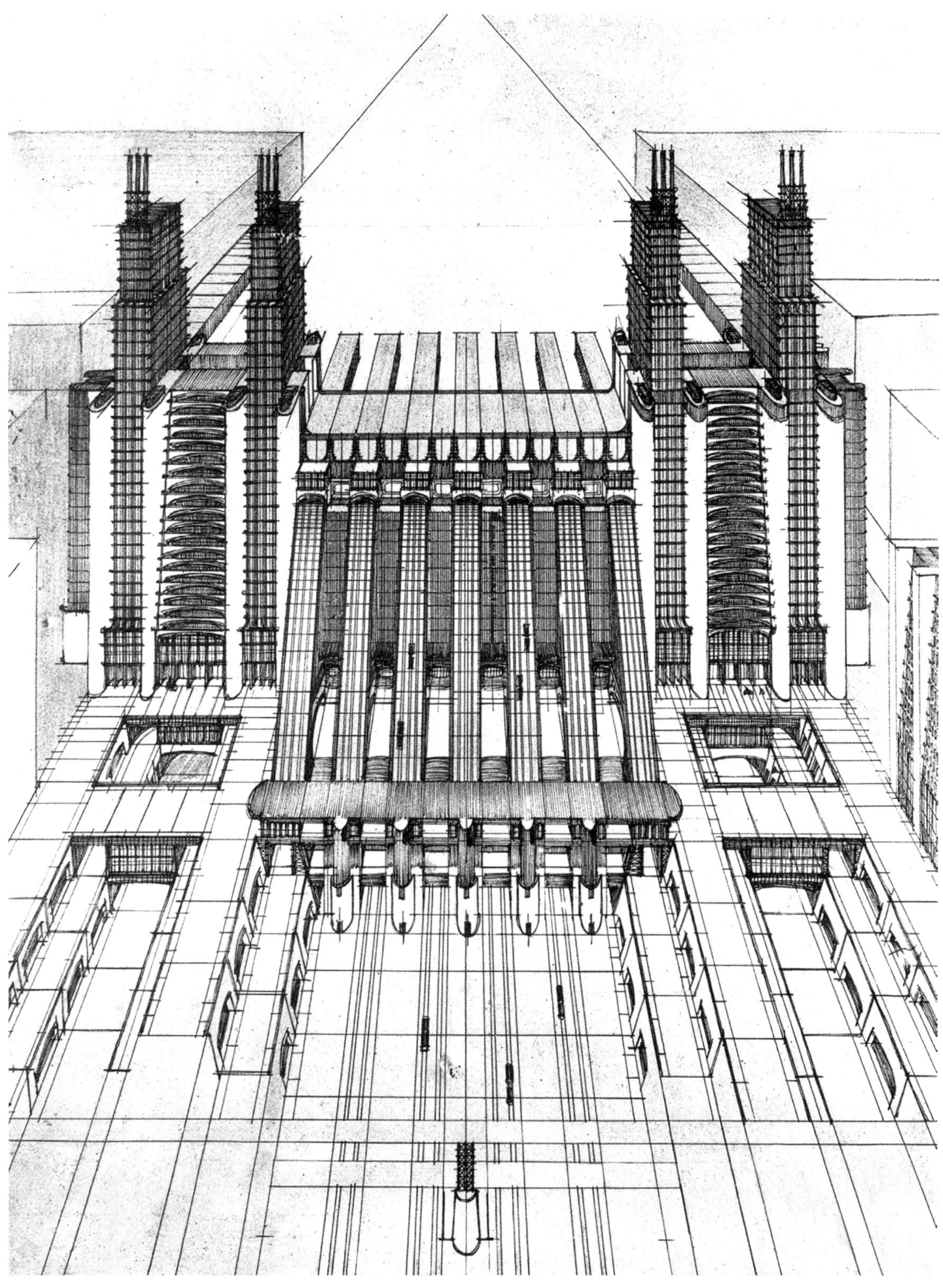

**ANTONIO SANT'ELIA (1888–1916)**

**Railway station and airport, 1914**

Black ink and grey pastel on paper

50.7 × 40.8 cm, 20 × 16 in

This monument celebrating the potential of rapid transport was designed by the Italian Futurist architect Antonio Sant'Elia as a centrepiece for his Città Nuova – a new city for a new society pre-World War I. The single-point perspective indicates the total control of the technocratic architect in this revolutionized world. Seen from above, and absolutely symmetrical, this transport interchange combines a railway station with a funicular that connects three distinct ground levels, and a long airport runway that reaches almost to the vanishing point of the drawing. Constructed of the materials of the industrial world – concrete, iron and glass – and eschewing traditional forms and ornamentation, this vision of a large-scale and mobile society was unprecedented. The building forms and even the way that it is drawn – with long, vertical lines, some by hand – and the curvilinear shapes belie Sant'Elia's earlier association with the decorative yet modern forms of the Stile Floreale, Italy's Art Nouveau movement. From around 1912, Sant'Elia joined the Futurists, who transformed the role of nature in art and architecture into one analogous to the man-made world. Futurism founder Filippo Marinetti stated that nothing was more beautiful than a great, humming power station holding back the hydraulic pressures of a whole mountain range, synthesized into control panels bristling with levers and gleaming commutations. Sant'Elia followed suit with his own architectural manifesto, his revolutionary *Messagio*, in which he defined his *dinamismo architettonico* (architectural dynamism). For him, the defining role of future architecture was to glean every benefit of science and technology, and to establish new forms, lines and reasons for existence out of the special conditions of modern living. 'We no longer feel ourselves to be men of the cathedrals and ancient moot halls,' he said, 'but men of the Grand Hotels, railway stations, giant roads and glittering arcades.'

**BUCKMINSTER FULLER (1895–1983)**

**4D Tower Garage, 1928**

Charcoal and coloured pencil on paper

32 × 24 cm, 12½ × 9½ in

The crazy, joyful practicality of this ramped structure, resembling a giant maypole, celebrates car ownership and seeks to resolve one of its key problems – where to keep a car when it is not being driven. By the 1920s, the automobile was a fixture of American cities, with 23 million passenger cars registered in the United States by 1929. The intention of Richard Buckminster Fuller's four-dimensional design – incorporating, he said, the fourth dimension of time in order to represent efficiency – is communicated in this playful drawing, complete with instructional annotations: 'Self parking – keep on up till you find a space', is written on the left-hand side. 'Up & down' and 'ramps never cross', the handwritten text explains, so that the double spiral of the structure becomes apparent. Tiny festive dots of red, blue, grey and black represent cars parked around the edges of the ramp. Faint ruled lines running down from the apex to the ground delineate the cables from which the ramps are suspended. These extremely long ramps, which wind around in ever-decreasing circles from the ground to a small platform at the top, are shown as super-thin, unbraced elements, and it is easy to imagine them undulating in Chicago's fierce winds. The peak from which they hang is supported by a central elevator shaft, and together they synthesize in an impossible structural solution. The concept of the spiral ramped car park was later realized in the two towers of Chicago's Marina City, 1968; however, that structure formed the lower nineteen floors of sixty-storey towers with apartments above. Fuller imagined his four-dimensional tower garage while working on designs for a four-dimensional residential tower made of plastic, again with a central mast containing all the services and a windmill at the top to produce electricity – but this time supporting hexagonal floor plates composed of inflatable flagstones.

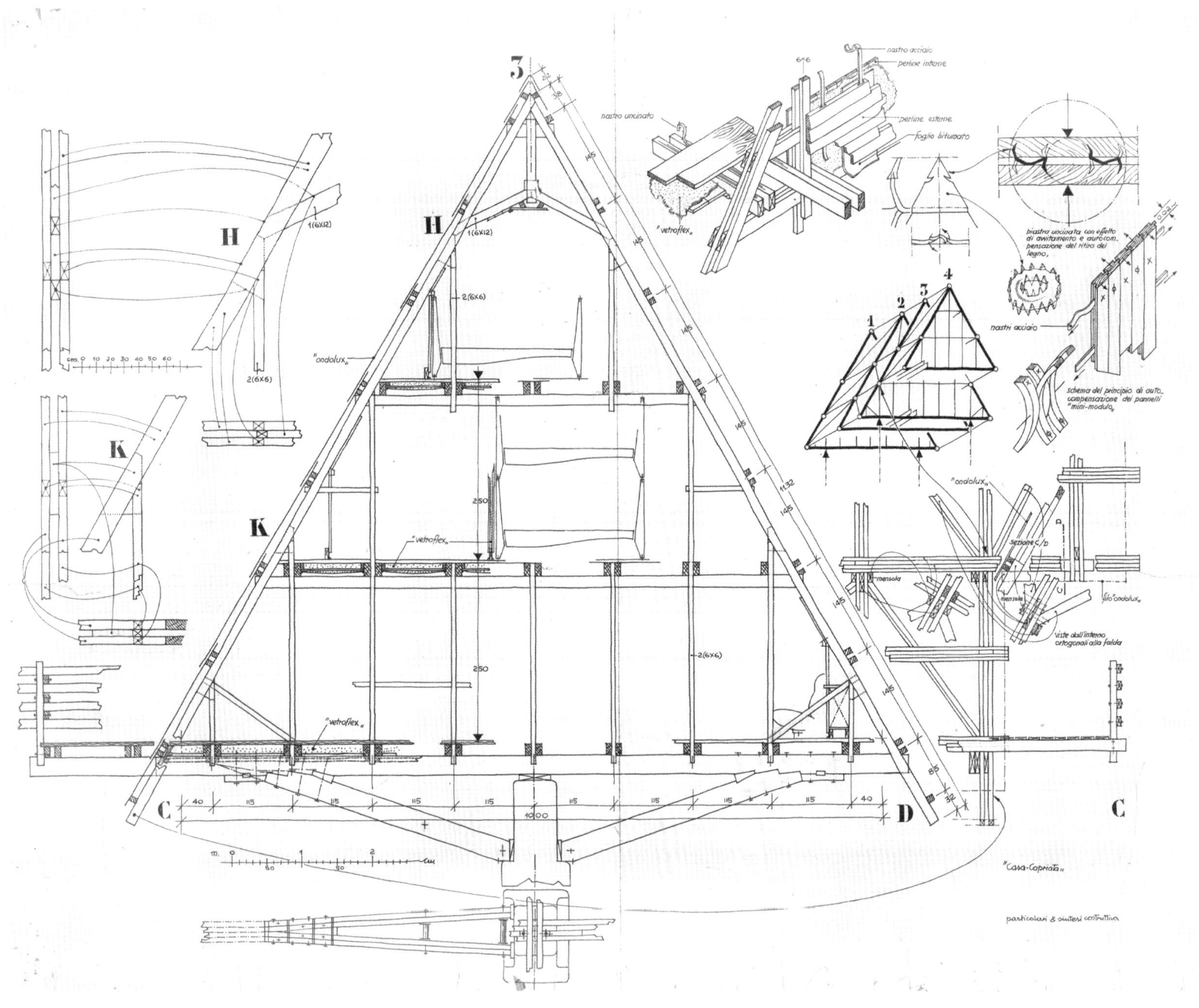


**CARLO MOLLINO (1905–73)**

**Casa Capriata ski lodge, 1954**

Black ink on paper

68 × 87 cm, 26¾ × 34 in

Although drawn to describe the construction of a simple A-framed structure built for the tenth Milan Triennale, this section also gives a sense of the inhabitable areas of the house. The middle and top floors are given a human scale by the beds shown in elevation, and a cosy armchair is placed in the corner of the bottom floor. One of the three principal A-shaped trusses that define the house's lateral walls is shown in section, dominating the middle of the sheet. The simple timber construction is clearly explained, with the wall studwork and cladding battens providing bracing. Struts from one of two central posts that were embedded in the hillside support the lowest floor, which forms the platform for the house and the main horizontal cross-element of the truss. The inclined external walls are weatherproofed by overlapping tiles, with larger-scale details elaborated in section to the side of the drawing. On the other side of the sheet, three-dimensional figures give further information about the layers of battening and insulation, as well as a description of how the three trusses work together. Inside, the various rooms are spread over three floors, with the living-dining room, kitchen, utility area and a small hallway for ski storage adjacent to the entrance all accommodated on the largest, bottom level; two bedrooms and a bathroom on the middle floor; and two further small bedrooms and storage units on the top floor. The simplicity of this mountain refuge, located in a small village in the Italian Alps, is at odds with the extravagant figure of architect and furniture designer Carlo Mollino, whose credo was that everything was permissible as long as it was fantastic. He loved the mountains, however, and was an enthusiastic skier who described this building as a house for extremist skiers.

**MICHAEL GRAVES (1934–2015)**

**Vacation House, 1978**

Black ink, pencil and colour crayon on tracing paper

28 × 35.5 cm, 8 × 13.9 in

Michael Graves has signed this elevation of a holiday house in the mountains at Aspen, Colorado, and labels it the entrance facade; it is the east elevation of a sprawling compound that was described at the time as a cross between a Classical mansion and a western corral. The Vacation House is set in a tamed wilderness that is intimated by the faint outline of peaks against the sky, the creek drawn in section with cypress trees lining its banks, and the dense green of the trees in the orchard and the shrubbery that forms part of the architecture. Here – along with the familiar lunettes, domes and columns – it is vernacular forms, not necessarily American, that Graves reinterprets; the entrance gates stand open in a protective wall made of logs that embraces a gazebo in the orchard. When they were made, and for a long while afterwards, Graves' drawings were influential for a generation of American, Canadian and British architecture students who coveted their fine papers, delicate colouring techniques, and characterful, hand-drawn lines in pencil and ink. Graves himself, in an article called 'Architecture and the Lost Art of Drawing', defines three types of drawing in his practice: the referential sketch, the preparatory study and the definitive drawing. This drawing belongs to the last category, which today, Graves says, would be produced on the computer even in his own office. The presentation drawings that he made in the 1970s and 80s were done by hand, however, and their clear, narrative style seemed appropriate to the reconfigured but very recognizable forms of postmodern architecture. They were drawn on translucent yellow or tracing paper, which allowed the final image to be traced freehand over a preparatory drawing that had often been drawn accurately to scale with hard lines on a drawing board.

**JACQUES ANDROUET DU CERCEAU (c.1520–86)**

**Château de Montargis, 1570**

Pen and black ink with grey wash on vellum

51.1 × 74.5 cm, 21 × 29¼ in

The meticulous survey drawings of Jacques Androuet du Cerceau were published in two volumes, in 1576 and 1579, documenting the 'most excellent buildings of France'. Included in them were drawings that he had made during his time at the twelfth-century Château de Montargis, as both religious refugee – a Huguenot in hostile Catholic France – and restorer of the partially ruined castle. This drawing has a pleasing dual quality. It is an accurate survey revealing the architectural character of the main hall of the castle. This houses two huge rooms for large gatherings: the first hall, above, with its grand space and decorated, vaulted ceiling; and the lower, second hall below. Despite its clarity, the relationship between the two gabled elevations is distorted. The line of the long side facade, partially removed to reveal the spaces within, meets the turret at one corner. The other gable-end facade projects farther out, however, despite having the same rhythm of fenestration, as if du Cerceau wanted to show this in more detail and so enlarged its proportions. In addition to this neat record of the hall, employing a perfect mechanical technique that initiated a tradition of fine rendering in French architectural drawing, another narrative is at play on the sheet. The upper hall is amply inhabited – some people are sitting in window alcoves, some are dancing. There are two shields with the French royal coat of arms at one end, and at the centre a painting above a fireplace showing a man wrestling with a dog. The caption below recounts the legend according to which the dog defeated the man, who then admitted to having killed the animal's master, and du Cerceau adds that the fight allegedly took place in the room depicted here. Three men are walking in the foreground, and a figure measuring the ground nearby is purported to be du Cerceau himself.

**LINA BO BARDI (1914–92)**

**Preliminary study for sculptures-cum-stage-props on Trianon Terrace, Museum of Art São Paulo, 1965**

Indian ink and watercolour on paper

56.2 × 76.5 cm, 22 × 30 in

This seemingly naïve and colourful drawing depicts a generous open plaza spread out in front of the north elevation of Lina Bo Bardi's Museum of Art São Paulo (MASP), one of her best-known buildings, which occupies an important site in the city. Originally a belvedere or terrace belonging to Trianon Park opposite, it is located halfway along the Avenida Paulista, at that time the financial heart of the city and an area lacking in public space, so the design endeavoured to maintain the open ground. To do this, the building is split horizontally in the middle so that the two larger lower floors are below ground, with their roof forming the plaza. The structure above ground comprises a pair of huge, prestressed-concrete beams, each 70 m (229.7 ft) long, from which hang two further floors containing offices and galleries for the collection. Although they are a subdued grey-brown colour in the drawing, they are in reality now the bright red of the slides, with a striking presence on the busy avenue to the south. Bo Bardi was an émigré in Brazil. Having trained with Gio Ponti in Milan, she arrived in 1946 and co-founded an art magazine called *Habitat*, which was closely bound up with the cultural intentions of MASP to challenge social inequality and elitist notions of culture. In keeping with these ambitions, the drawing shows the public plaza connecting to the street behind and extending under the building towards the north in order to create a place for collective social life. The view is from the north and shows planting around the edges of the terrace, which appears to connect with the park beyond. The gallery building is in the background, and the terrace is inhabited by tiny figures enjoying a playground filled with slides and carousels.

**THEO VAN DOESBURG (1883–1931)**

**Preliminary colour scheme for floor and long walls of dance hall in Café Aubette, 1927**

Ink, gouache and metallic gouache on paper

53.3 × 37.5 cm, 21 × 14¾ in

The graphic quality of this composite drawing for Café Aubette in Strasbourg is in some ways the opposite of Theo van Doesburg's spatial images, such as his *Counter-Construction* of 1923, which shows the arrangement of coloured planes forming the external boundaries of an imaginary building. Whereas that explored the possibility of boundless volume, this composition encloses the box-like café space and shows only its internal faces. The café is entered from the street through a 1767 Baroque facade, and is entirely separate from the outside world. The floor plan is marked out in the centre of the composition, flanked by elevations of the long side walls at the top and bottom. The only element recognizable as an architectural feature is the staircase leading to a walkway halfway up the back wall, which sails over two doorways and disrupts the Mondrian-like motif painted on the wall behind. This preliminary study's intention to transform the orthogonal interior space by the application of another geometrical and abstract system is the same in reality – in this drawing, it is set at 45 degrees to the horizontal datum. This irregular grid defines the fields of primary colour interspersed with white, black and grey that van Doesburg uses to activate the space. The walkway overlooks the rows of booths that can be seen on the plan, set within low walls that define a realm of intimacy for two people looking out towards the interior of the larger room. On the other side of a large open floor used for cabaret and dancing, with space to screen films on to the end wall, is an identical arrangement of booths. This is set in front of the four tall windows looking into the street, but these provide only light, not views, for the café turns its back to the street.

**ANON**

**Palace of Nur Adad, c.1865 BC**

Clay tablet engraving

12 × 8.8 cm, 4¾ × 3½ in

Larsa was a capital city of Babylonia, belonging to the ancient Sumerian civilization, and lying on the then banks of a branch of the Euphrates River. This ground plan depicts the Palace of Nur Adad, and is engraved into a tablet made of the purple-hued clay characteristic of the region's ancient riverbeds. The plan's purpose is unknown, and its ruled lines appear hastily drawn before the damp clay surface hardened. They sometimes cross and sometimes scarcely meet to make a corner, and the ends of the internal walls around the numerous doorways are rarely delineated. Nevertheless, the drawing is a fairly accurate depiction of the design and proportions of the excavated palace, and is the only known extant example of a plan of an identifiable building on a clay tablet. The palace would have been built in mud bricks and not fixed with mortar or cement, and so constant reconstruction would have been necessary to keep it intact. The plan has a large central courtyard at its heart, to which no direct access from the exterior is possible. Instead, a winding labyrinth of interconnecting rooms leads there from the only opening in the external wall – although the tablet is incomplete, so a secondary entrance cannot be ruled out. Adjoining the courtyard is a throne room, but the purpose of the other apartments and ante-chambers is unknown. Between 1932 and 1934, a French archaeological excavation led by André Parrot initiated discoveries at Larsa that continued sporadically during the 1970s and 80s, revealing a ziggurat, a temple and the remains of the Palace of Nur-Adad (1865–50 BC), who was briefly king of Larsa. Excavations show that the palace was not completed, perhaps due to Nur-Adad's short reign, and there is no evidence of the usual spaces associated with the day-to-day life of such a palace complex.

**SAUL STEINBERG (1914–99)**

**Graph Paper Building, 1950**

Ink and graph paper

30.5 × 23 cm, 12 × 9 in

American artist Saul Steinberg often used graph-paper and musical-score sheets as transformative supports for his drawings. This one is made in the margins of a sheet of graph paper, whose gridded surface becomes the subject of the title: the *Graph Paper Building*. 'Graph-paper architecture' became a derisive term, often used to describe the ubiquitous, International Style, curtain-wall skyscrapers that dominated post-war New York developments. This sketch – one of the earliest of a series of graph-paper buildings that Steinberg drew between 1950 and 1954 – is a witty critique of this architecture, and perhaps the progenitor of the phrase. It shows the gridded field of the graph paper surrounded by an ink rendering of older buildings, minuscule in comparison, that crowd into the margin, in contrast to the over-scaled intrusion of the huge apartment block next to them. Accentuating this sense of inappropriate enormity, tiny figures crowd the wide pavement, delineated by a single line that curves around the corner of the building, hinting that the volume of the structure could be as paper-thin as its presence on the street. The corner is marked by a fancy wrought-iron street lamp and at the bottom of the page, beyond the margin of the graph paper, cars drive by. A canopy that leads from an unmarked entrance on the building to the edge of the pavement, perhaps to meet one of these vehicles, also has the appearance of a cannon poised to shatter the fragile glass surface. This work is a variant of a drawing, the whereabouts of which are unknown, published in 1950, in the short-lived and extravagant magazine *Flair*, a glamorous showcase for the work of a diverse range of artists, writers and friends of its editor, Fleur Cowles, including Tenessee Williams, Jean Cocteau, Simone de Beauvoir, Gloria Swanson, Eleanor Roosevelt, the Duchess of Windsor, and Salvador Dalí.

**ADOLFO NATALINI (1941–2020)**

**The Continuous Monument reaches New York, 1969**

Pen, ink and blue crayon on thin wove paper

34 × 27.5 cm, 13½ × 10¼ in

The Continuous Monument was an anti-utopian riposte to the promise of technology by the Italian design collective Superstudio, formed in 1966. It was described by Adolfo Natalini, the group's leader, as demonstrating the absurdity of many theories of that period – particularly, that technology would solve everything and provide ever-greater possibilities for mankind. This page from Natalini's sketchbooks reveals one of the instances of the monument's presence. He described how important it was to lay it over real and beautiful landscapes. Here, it is Manhattan that has been captured by the monument, which forms a square enclosure around the irregularly shaped island that squeezes out at the edges into the Hudson River. Critiquing the American frontier mentality that made the most remote wildernesses – even the moon – seem accessible, Superstudio created a monumental symbol that would encapsulate and challenge it. The result was a vast, impenetrable and seamless megalith faced in mirror glass that travelled the globe. Whether it was inhabited or not was irrelevant – perhaps it was a continuous strip of urbanization or even an alien intervention. The collective produced many images of the Continuous Monument traversing and transforming iconic landscapes in what was imagined at the time as an image of disaster – a warning, not a proposal for the future. Some were collages of photographs with fields of gridded lines obliterating parts of the scene, others were simple line drawings with an equivalence between landscape and monument. Here, anything anomalous to the grid has been regularized into a vertical extrusion of man-made structures, but Natalini opted not to express the Monument's surface grid in this drawing. Instead, the reflection of a cloudy sky shaded in blue pencil is the only intimation of a natural world, and the curvature of the earth's surface is discernible as if from a great height.

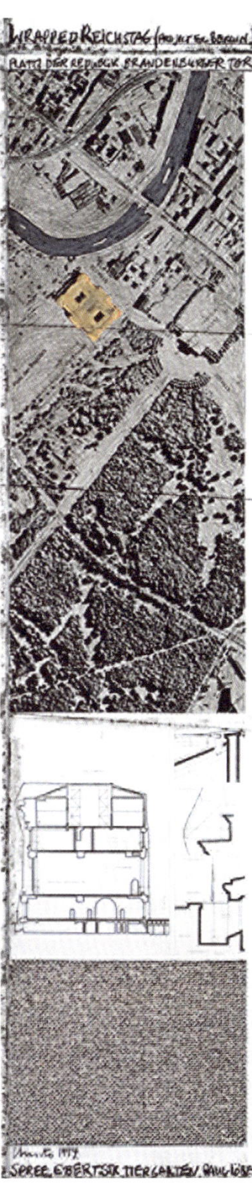

**CHRISTO (1935–2020)**

**Wrapped Reichstag (Project for Berlin), 1994**

Pencil, charcoal, pastel, wax crayon, fabric sample, aerial photograph and technical data

165 × 106.6 cm and 65 × 42 in (left), and 165 × 38 cm and 65 × 15 in (right)

The principal image on this pragmatically titled composite sheet shows the Reichstag in Berlin completely wrapped in fabric and surrounded by the Tiergarten. The River Spree winds past to the north, and the Brandenburg Gate is in the foreground. There is a tension here, enhanced by the seemingly bucolic setting: the two monuments – the Reichstag in the west, and the Brandenburg Gate in the east – lie either side of the Berlin Wall. In the column on the right, the position of the Reichstag in the city is further explained, but there is no evidence of the wall; instead, the ground is made even by a field of obscuring pencil marks and the Reichstag is highlighted in orange, as if locating it were the only purpose of the drawing. Below, two more frames seem to give additional objective information about the project. A diagrammatic section through the building shows the layer of fabric making a second envelope, with details in section showing how it is attached to the building. And a fabric sample at the bottom suggests the nature of the material used for the vast shroud shown in the main image. The shadows are darker in this larger drawing. Every crease in the fabric is rendered, and the scene is eerily uninhabited. This artifice was effected by drawing in thick layers of pencil and crayon over an aerial photograph of the site, and although made and signed by Christo, the project itself was conceived and enacted in collaboration with his partner Jeanne-Claude. Together, they had been making temporary installations in Germany inspired by its division. The Reichstag project was conceived in 1971, but it was not until after reunification in 1990 that the project was able to move forward, and in the summer of 1995 the building was finally covered for two weeks by 100,000 m$^2$ (1,076,391 sq ft) of silver-grey fabric, bound by 15 km (9.3 mi) of blue rope.

**WILLIAM KENT (1685–1748)**

**Decorative study: interior elevation, 1725**

Pen and black ink on paper

20 × 10 cm, 8 × 4 in

This elevation of the decorative schema for a wall, dado, cornice and ceiling detail in the Grotesque style belongs to a set of three studies exploring the effects of subtly different versions of this ornamental approach. William Kent's design shows the pattern covering the room – from the lower wall surface below dado level, over the main body of the room between the large windows and beyond, where its pattern is broken by the cornice to transform into a coffered design appearing to undulate over a curved ceiling. The illogical nature of the subject matter, which transformed man-made elements into natural forms – with reeds substituted for the columns, and fluted appendages with curly leaves and volutes taking the place of pediments – had, according to Vitruvius, the advantage of challenging the rigidity of trabeated Classical architecture, its only requirement that it fill the field defined by its frame while belonging to an antique tradition. As a concept rather than a language, being open to reinterpretation and invention, it was adaptable to change and development, and responsive to fashion and context. Kent's ornamental scheme includes fountains and urns, canopies and cornucopias. Among a structure of twisting foliage and arabesques are bells, putti, peacocks and swans. Kent's interpretation of the Grotesque belongs to the distinctive style based on first-century Roman models – most importantly, the painted interiors in the surviving wing of Nero's Golden House in Rome, built between AD 64 and 68, which lay buried in the substructure of the Baths of Titus before being rediscovered in the fifteenth century. Several generations of Italian decorators were inspired by this ancient painting, which formed the basis of European surface ornament until the nineteenth century, but by the time Kent was working the style had fallen out of fashion in Italy.

**JUNYA ISHIGAMI (1974–)**

**Extreme Nature: Landscape of Ambiguous Spaces, 2008**

Colored ink on paper

15.6 × 81 cm, 6 × 32 in

Commissioned to design the Japanese Pavilion for the Venice Architecture Biennale in 2008, Junya Ishigami decided to make an installation in the Giardini della Biennale, situated near the easternmost tip of the city, which questioned the traditional relationship between architecture and the landscape. Starting from the premise that they are often defined as small structures in vast surroundings, his intention was to create architecture and landscape as a single entity. He prepared a series of delicate conceptual sketches that describe the architectural object as being the scenery, rather than being located within it. This drawing shows a collection of different buildings of very varied heights, the smallest with the profiles of small rural dwellings alongside which two tiny figures converse. A thin boundary line describing the profile of other shapes of building with a more urban scale remains the only suggestion of architectural figure in the drawing. The elevations of these implied structures appear in overlapping layers, and their vertical fields are composed of plants. Sometimes the scale of their texture relates to the size of the elevational field that they cover – the large L-shaped block in the middle is covered with huge flowers supported on swaying fronds, while the smaller shapes in front appear as flowery bowers from a different garden. The central skyline follows a more conventional city pattern, but these towers are covered in tiny, delicate markings in green and purple that bear no relationship to the predictable glass grids with which such structures are usually clad. Ishigami designed four greenhouses with extremely slender structural elements at different scales in the garden encircling the Japanese Pavilion. Their proportions and sizes were in accordance with the trees and flowers of the pre-existing environment, responding to the way that they grow, their forms and their light requirements.

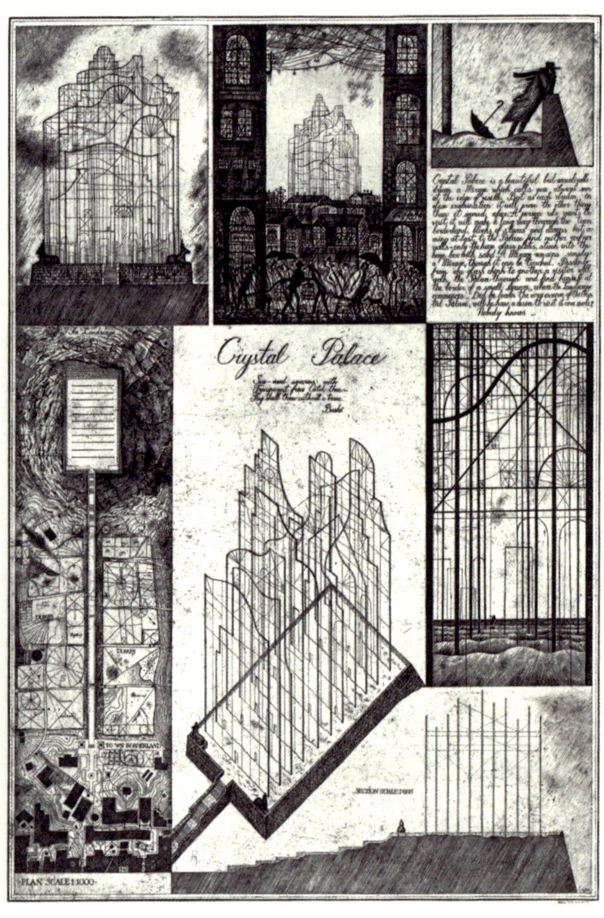


**ALEXANDER BRODSKY (1955–) AND ILYA UTKIN (1955–)**

**Crystal Palace, 1982**

Etching

83.5 × 58 cm, 33 × 22¾ in

Russian architects and artists Alexander Brodsky and Ilya Utkin produced a series of huge, copper-plate etchings depicting an imaginary world, the line density and spatial complexity of their compositions emulating the appearance and subject matter of antique prints. The centre of a group called the Paper Architects, their work provided a critique of Soviet utilitarianism and a commentary on Russia's depleted urban landscapes. This image, entitled *Crystal Palace*, won first prize in a 1982 Japanese competition, and marked an important turning point in their work. Divided into six parts, it reveals, in various guises, an impossible structure that evokes the rollercoaster landscape of a fairground. A plain elevation makes this proposal very clear; it is then seen framed by tall, sombre buildings, rising like a shining dream above a sea of roofs and bowed pedestrians. The third panel in the top register contains an English-language text below a solitary figure. Its poetic description explains that this is a beautiful yet unfeasible dream: a mirage beckoning, always at the edge of the visible beyond the city's boundary. A long plan shows the rows of glass plates that form the Crystal Palace, on a plinth reached by a long, stepped causeway atop a rocky outcrop above a strange ground covered with rune-like drawings. The text explains that the lonely visitor who passes from one glass plate to another will walk through the palace and find himself at the edge of a small site, beyond which the landscape begins. The name of the project refers to Joseph Paxton's Crystal Palace, 1851, and the optimistic dreams it inspired of a future enhanced by technology. This palace of commerce and invention, container of myriad cultures for sale, is reduced here to a mirage hovering behind the slums of a dilapidated and unloved city.

**FERDINANDO GALLI DA BIBIENA (1657–1743)**

**Plate 49, from Direzioni della prospettiva teorica..., 1732**

Etching

33.5 × 26 cm, 13¼ × 10¼ in

Painter, architect and theatre-set designer Ferdinando Galli da Bibiena belonged to a celebrated family of Italian scenic artists, including brother Francesco and son Giuseppe. This plate belongs to one of his publications, a book called *Direzioni della prospettiva teorica...*, published in 1732. It included a section on theatrical scenery, in which he presented the only detailed method for stage design published by a member of the family. In his explanations of how to set up perspectival scenes from a plan projection, the process is unconstrained by the physical form of the stage itself. Bibiena transformed the traditional seventeenth-century stage picture, in which a single, central vanishing point was presented as an extension of the theatre's main axis. He set up his scenes at a 45-degree angle, thereby creating an asymmetry that broke down the confining edges of the picture plane and admitted the mystery of potentially endless space. This was one of the Baroque theatre's greatest stage innovations, making a clear break with the axial space of the auditorium. The illustrations in *Direzioni della prospettiva teorica...* present two stage ground plans – one geometric version seen from above and the other set out with vanishing points, from which the two-point perspective of the scenery is projected upwards to scale and elaborated with Baroque exuberance. The stage is taken as a single line in elevation, and the horizon and ground lines coincide with the vanishing points located either side, in the wings. As well as his many successful scenic designs, Bibiena designed various buildings. These included an early villa and garden at Colorno, and the royal theatre of Mantua. Because Bibiena's theatrical work was necessarily ephemeral in character, its richness and splendour, as well as his personal skill as a draughtsman and perspective artist, can only be judged from the large number of drawings that survive.

**ANTONI GAUDÍ (1852–1926)**

**Casa Batlló, 1903**

Pencil on tracing paper

50 × 67.5 cm, 19½ × 26½ in

Although lightly drawn in hard pencil lines, this sketch of the facade of Antoni Gaudí's Casa Batlló in Barcelona shows various types of information that give clues to his early thinking about this strange and experimental work. The principal central drawing is applied over a regular framework depicting a conventional masonry structure with rectangular windows set in four equal bays over six storeys. Floor heights are indicated at the side, revealing that this lower drawing is a survey of the existing structure – which Gaudí gutted and transformed, having failed to obtain permission to demolish it. The accretions of Gaudí's applied facade, which eat into and embellish this frame, are drawn on top in darker pencil lines. More restrained than the final construction, the fantastical carved-stone columns, supporting a carapace that swells over the first two storeys and the edges of the third, are only ghosts here. Above the first floor, the drawing elaborates the billowing quality of the projecting gallery, framed by bone-like elements. Ground-floor intentions are shown in the facade plan at ground level, below the survey on the left-hand side. Its flat surface has been broken up, and the undulating profile of columns and balconies is sketched out. At the top, Gaudí depicts his ideas for an additional, asymmetrical storey that dissolves the eaves line of the street facade on the left-hand side to drop down and create a hollow in the volume of the building. Although showing the same plane as the elevation below, the curving vaults covering these spaces are shown in section because they project over the street; the irregular domes behind are drawn as modelled elevations, with various rooflines possible. Ultimately, the domed spaces were kept behind the eaves line, their tiled surfaces clutching the edge, and only the galleries and balconies below projected outwards.

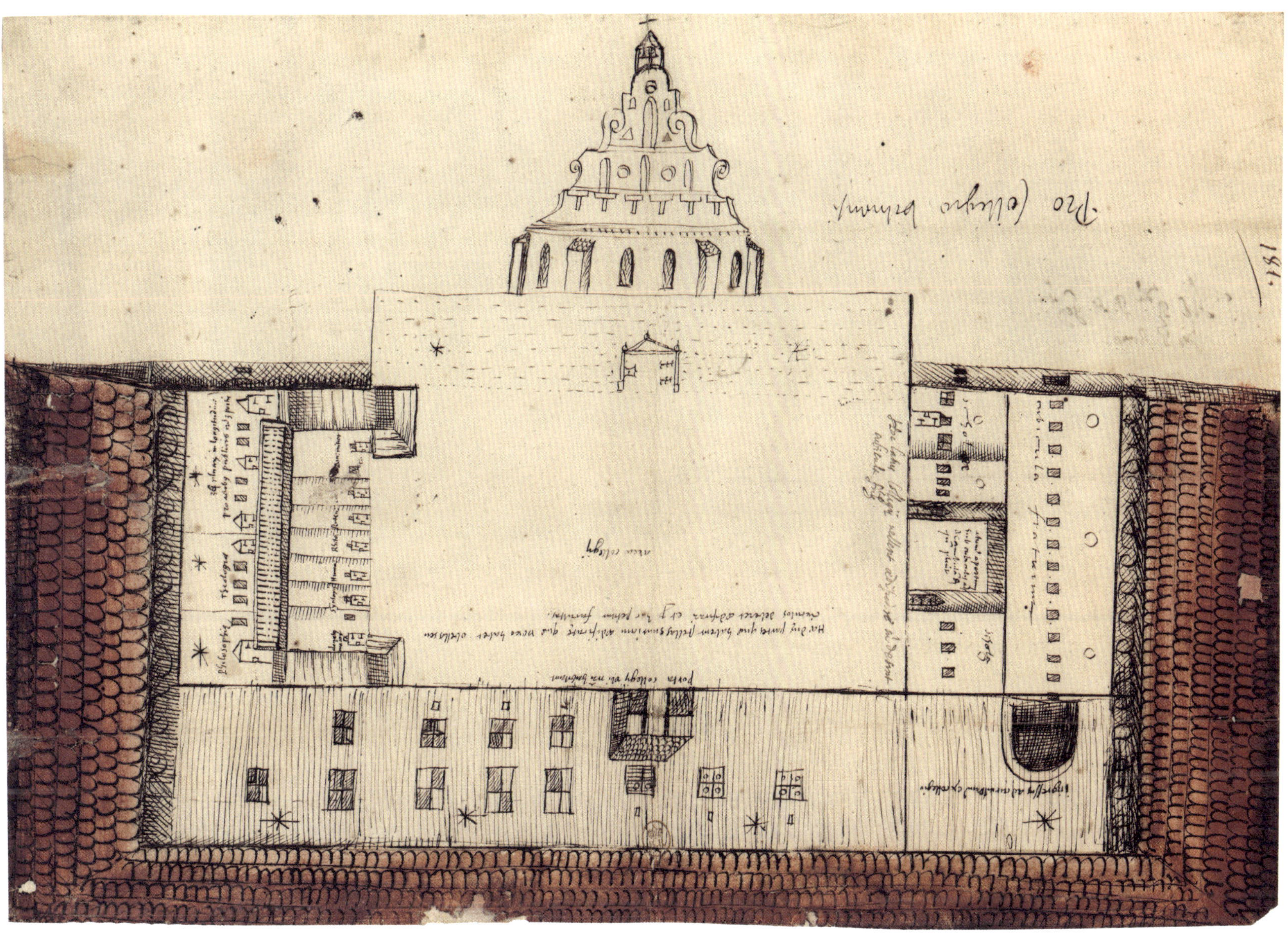

**PAUL BOXA (nd)**

**Old College of St John of Vilnius, c.1582**

Indian ink and red wash on paper

28 × 40 cm, 11 × 15¾ in

This drawing is the earliest architectural representation in a collection of records containing the plans of all houses and churches belonging to the Jesuit Order in Vilnius, Lithuania, before its abolition in 1773. It shows the site around St John's Church, the centre of the city's Jesuit University, at the start of its life at the heart of an educational establishment. Prepared by Brother Paul Boxa – the first vice-rector, and then rector, of the university – it records his plans for extending the existing accommodation. St John's Church is shown at the top of the drawing in an evocative, elevational sketch of its upper storeys, but the church was reconstructed during the sixteenth and seventeenth centuries and so its accuracy cannot be tested. Its base is disconnected from this flamboyant sketch, and takes the form of a high, plain wall with a closed doorway. The rectangular courtyard in front of the church is represented in plan, while the buildings surrounding this central space are shown as elevations, flattened out from the corresponding edge of the court. Boxa uses a system of stars to indicate the buildings that already exist and circles for proposed new buildings, for which permission is required. The treatment of these elevations is complex, and includes crude perspectival cuts into the flat planes that convey an intriguing sense of space – if not logical congruity – with the elevations of the courtyard. The existence of the Society of Jesus was approved by the Pope in 1540, and from that time grew rapidly. Foreign mission work was important; by 1556, Jesuits were working throughout Europe, Asia, Africa and the New World. Vilnius became an important centre for Jesuit education and ministry from Prussia to Russia. The first four Jesuits arrived in 1569, and St John's Church was entrusted to them in 1571.

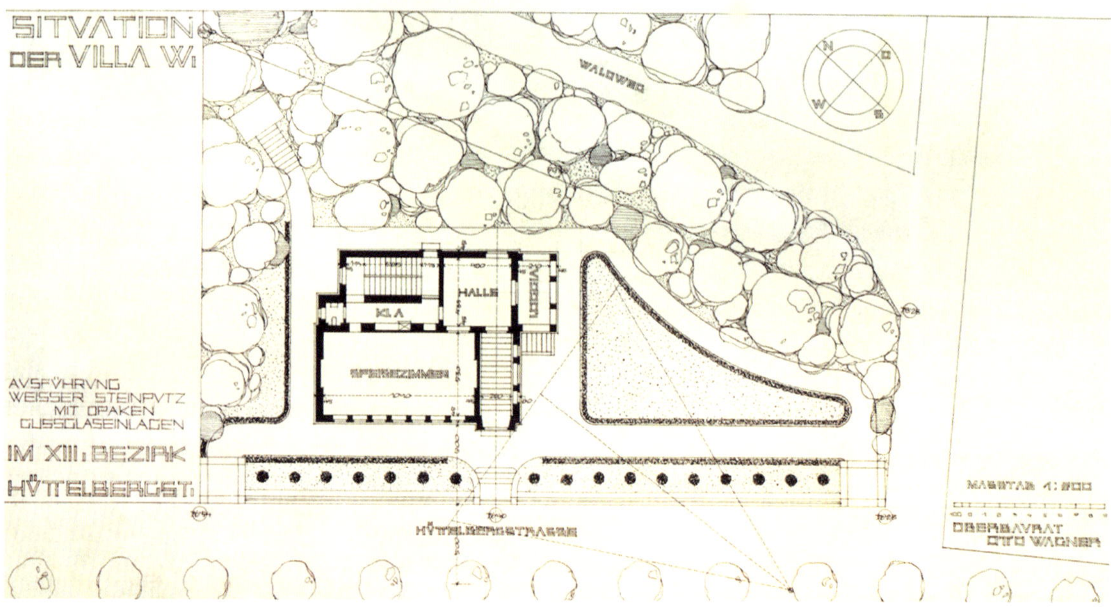


**OTTO WAGNER (1841–1918)**

**Villa Wagner, 1912**

Coloured pencil on paper

35.5 × 28cm, 14 × 11 in

Otto Wagner was a quintessential Viennese architect. His sophisticated architecture and urbanism responded to the complex identity of this centre of an empire on the cusp of disintegration, but also undergoing the transformations of the modern, industrialising world. In the designs that Wagner made for the second villa he designed for himself and his family, he used a very simple, basic shape – the rectangle – to define an intricate compositional system. In this way, he incorporated the reductionist, formal tendencies of mass production within a decorative schema that still belonged to the Jugendstil aesthetic. In this perspective of the Villa Wagner, in Vienna, the strong, simple geometrical volume of the building, with its rectangular plan and deep cornice, is enhanced by the sharply cut shrubs that adorn its garden. The house is placed close to the street with a loggia on one side. This asymmetry is continued in the internal spaces and echoed in the composition of the front facade, where the main entrance is placed on the right-hand side. The basic rectangular shape of the ground plan is repeated in deeply set, rectangular windows and is the main motif of the design, occurring in all aspects of decoration and detail. In 1897, Wagner had founded the Vienna Secession, along with Gustav Klimt, Joseph Maria Olbrich, Josef Hoffmann and Koloman Moser, who, through their journal *Ver Sacrum*, disseminated ideas relating to the aesthetic fusion of art and literature, graphic art and text. In keeping with their concept of the dwelling as a total work of art, the facades Villa Wagner are enhanced by works of decorative art, including a frieze of glazed blue and white tiles that runs all around above the rusticated ground floor, broken only by the frame of the grand entrance. Not shown in this drawing is a mosaic depicting a landscape above the entrance doors, and, overhead, a stained-glass window shows the goddess Athena carrying the head of Medusa, as well as a loggia decorated with mosaics by Moser.

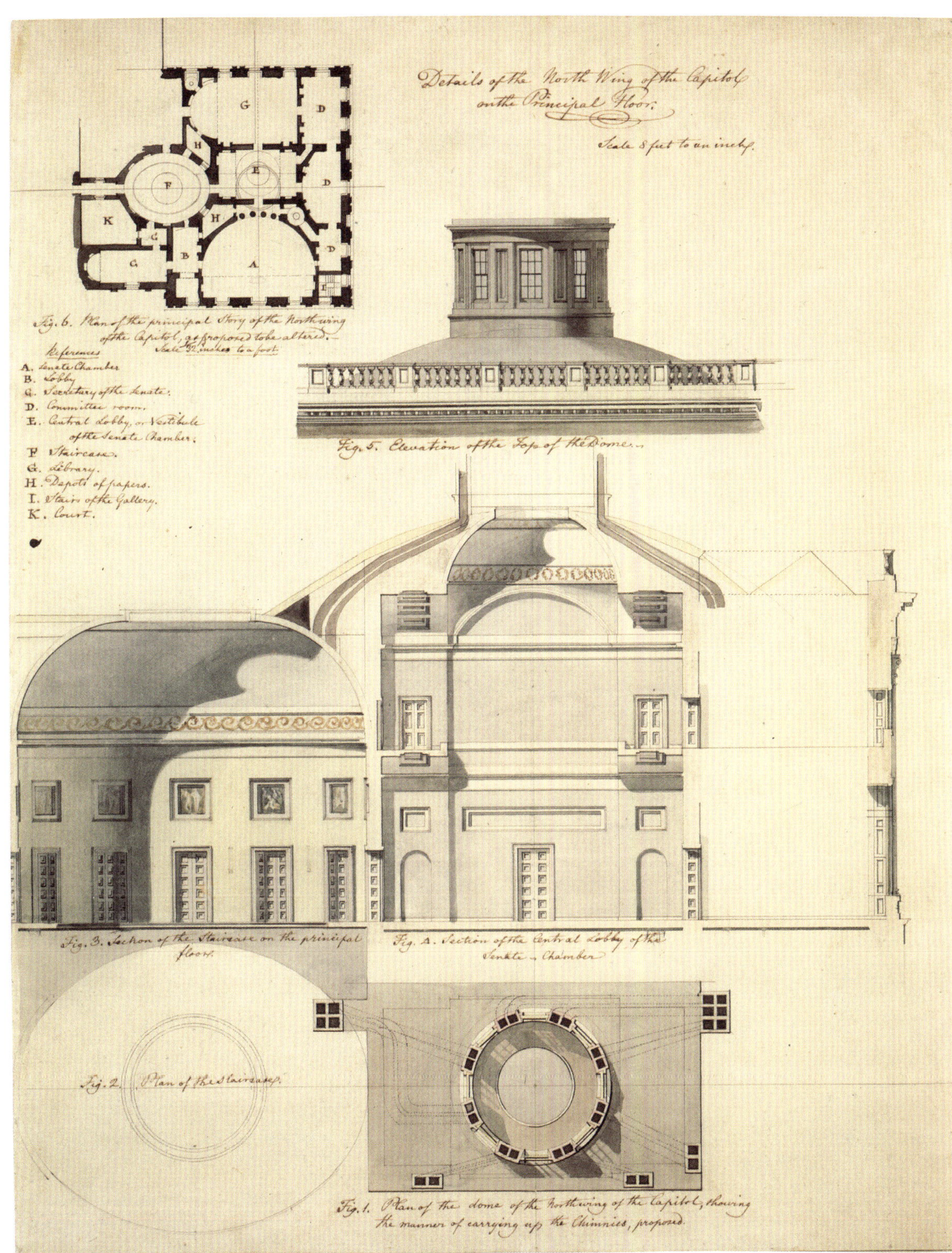


**BENJAMIN HENRY LATROBE (1764–1820)**

**North Wing of the United States Capitol, 1817**

Ink, watercolour, wash and graphite on paper

48.2 × 38.1 cm, 19 × 15 in

Benjamin Henry Latrobe was one of the first formally trained architects to practise in the United States, arriving from Britain with a Neo-Classical European education. He built important edifices in Philadelphia and Baltimore, but is best known for his work as the second architect of the United States Capitol in Washington, DC, which he carried out as Surveyor of Public Works. The North Wing, part of which is shown in this drawing, was the final part of the building that he worked on. The sober but grand decorative scheme and lofty series of rooms show that the wing was intended for occupation by the Senate. This sheet combines the orthogonal conventions of scaled plan, section and wall elevation in order to fully describe the Central Lobby in its place within the grand sequence of rooms at the end of the wing. It includes several layers of information, from the technical to the aesthetic, and the drawing techniques employed show how even the representation of details within the conventions of architectural drawing had become an art form by the late-eighteenth century. Skilful use of ink washes reveals the spatial qualities of the rooms, where the outlines of shadows give an atmospheric sense of the vaulted ceilings, arches and domes as if lit only from the lantern above. The fall of sunlight from the left is consistent in each part of the sheet. In the elevation of the clerestory lantern and dome, a dark shadow enhances its curves; in the section through the sequence of rooms below it describes the shape of the ceilings; and in the plan of the dome at the bottom, ghost-like projections of the windows are visible. This plan describes the routes for chimney flues from the rooms below that can also be traced in the section above.

**DIMITRIS PIKIONIS (1887–1968)**

**Aixoni settlement, 1951**

Pencil, coloured pencil and watercolor on a photocopy

28 × 74 cm, 11 × 29 in

Between 1951 and 1954, Dimitris Pikionis developed prototype housing for Aixoni, a coastal village south of Athens, which was never built. Pikionis was an accomplished draughtsman, as comfortable with freehand work in pencil, pastel and crayon as with ink and orthographic projection. He often combined both methods of communicating to produce atmospheric portraits of buildings within their landscapes, their character evident in the dishevelment and variety of their surroundings. This is shown in this elevation of a row of houses along an informal street, in which the facades of four buildings are drawn using orthographic conventions. Surrounding them is evidence of the rural landscape that they fit into – the stick fences, small enclosures and majestic trees animating the horizon are drawn in pencil and highlighted with a dense, white crayon that could be depicting shadow as much as light.
In the Aixoni project, Pikionis began to move away from explicit expression of his vernacular influences, which since his 1933 paper for the Congrès Internationaux d'Architecture Moderne had embodied references from Eastern architecture and philosophy – particularly of India and Japan. His prototype structures began to synthesize these influences into his own idiosyncratic formal language, which was responsive to the existing natural and informal topography of rural life while not seeking to change it to fit a preconceived idea of dwelling. His alternative was to seek a visual-poetic equivalence between the two worlds, using drawing to communicate this. In his paper, Pikionis had set out his definition for a Greek modern architecture that opened up Modernism's focus on generic types of buildings to encompass a vernacular that was as cultural as it was formal.

**GILLES-MARIE OPPENORDT (1672–1742)**

**Section of a staircase for Hôtel Gaudion, 1733**

Pen and black ink, grey and mauve wash, and highlights in white gouache

75.2 × 46.1 cm, 29½ × 18 in

This section and elevation shows a fragment of the opulent Rococo interior that Gilles-Marie Oppenordt designed for the apartments of the Duke of Orleans – an important record of this grand architectural decor, which has since been demolished. The drawing's full title indicates that this corner of the vast stair-hall is where one of the four entrances to the large enfilade apartments on the first floor is located. It forms an inventory of decorative tropes popular during the reign of Louis XV, which defined the origins of the Rococo style that emerged from Paris during the early eighteenth century in reaction to the heavy Classicism of the Palace of Versailles. The term derives from the French rocaille, used to describe the shell-covered rock carving decorating artificial grottoes. Oppenordt is, in fact, credited with inventing his own style of Italianate rocaille decoration. Described in delicate detail in the elevational parts of the drawing, these decorative features include the hybrid pilasters bordering the arched frame of a tall mirror and the intricate cast-ironwork of the balconies that is discontinued in parts to reveal the doorways behind, and reflected faintly, in contrast to the misty depths of the mirror. Asymmetry and picturesque diversity mimic the natural world and evoke the fantastic imagination, diverging from strict Classical rules. This approach is evident in the plasterwork figures above the doors and nestled in the cornices, which are modelled with ink washes, the definition of their form drawn in fine ink lines that illuminate their pattern rather than emphasizing their depth. The silhouette of the space follows the intricate surface of the modulated walls, fine cornices, curved vaults and oval dome, and the sectional cuts are drawn in fine black lines so that they form an absence of space rather than an assertion of volume.

**VILLARD DE HONNECOURT (1200–50)**

**Tower of Laon Cathedral, c.1230**

Ink on parchment

22 × 14 cm, 8¾ × 5½ in

The disparate collection of drawings on parchment that itinerant French draughtsman Villard de Honnecourt made during the early thirteenth century, bound together into a small leather portfolio, became influential during the nineteenth-century Gothic Revival when they were first published. Architects seeking the source of Gothic sensibility copied them, but there are theories that his drawings were themselves copies. The figure of Honnecourt, and the purpose of his drawings, are subjects of speculation among scholars, who debate his role as a travelling mason and discerning witness to thirteenth-century culture. His original drawings were accompanied by descriptive inscriptions, and for this drawing of the upper part of Laon Cathedral's west facade, his words attest to his having been there. 'In no place, ever, did I see a tower such as that at Laon,' he wrote, having also visited and made drawings at Reims and Chartres, as well as travelling into Hungary. He was concerned with the stylistic core of Gothic high architecture and correctly identified Laon Cathedral as special, since it manifested the earliest application of Gothic, linear articulation to any portion of a building exterior. Although the Laon elevation is an interpretation rather than an accurate representation, which suggests that Honnecourt knew little of stereotomy, or construction, its fixation on the richly articulated bar tracery captures the *manière*, or formal development, of the moment. The accompanying plan and description, although inconsistent, more accurately describe the facade's composition and structure, while this drawing includes elements that are surreal in their exaggerated scale: the oxen with their finely drawn, hair cloaks that reveal his skill at drawing drapery; and the Laon hand, which holds a jewel between its thumb and middle finger. It has been suggested that the placing of these elements describes the basic proportional relationships of the tower.

**TATIANA BILBAO (1972–)**

**Extract from Perspectives, 2017**

Collage

35.5 × 48.2 cm, 14 × 19 in

Tatiana Bilbao uses collage as a collaborative technique, as seen in the proposal for a tower that she developed as a response to her invitation to participate in the 2017 Chicago Architecture Biennial, for which she designed a tall, gridded framework called *(Not) Another Tower* that defined sites for 192 projects by fourteen Mexican architecture offices. Crowded together and cantilevering precipitously, the logic of conventional property values was reversed by the desirability of the bottom of the tower. The book that accompanied the exhibition is called *Perspectivas/Perspectives*, and this moment within its pages encapsulates some of Bilbao's preoccupations about how to represent three-dimensional space, and her conflicted feelings about enclosing it. With a book, enclosure happens by the action of closing it and putting it away. When the book is opened, as shown here, the mountainous landscape, the image of which covers the spread, becomes exposed – not as a flat plane, but as an embracing corner. The relationship between the two moving leaves of the adjacent pages makes a space within this corner in which the delicate leaves of three flights of steps open out to inhabit it, exposing the sloping quality of the site and leading to picture-plane entrances into imaginary worlds. In 2017, an exhibition called *Perspectivas: Tatiana Bilbao Estudio* presented nineteen projects designed within Bilbao's studio and organized into three themes: Espacio (space), Habitar (dwell), and Collage, and accompanied by a collection of books called *Biblioteca temática y en movimiento* (Thematic and Moving Library). Covering three sides of one of the rooms in the Collage area of the space, a mural consisting of a line drawing depicted a composite landscape, in which seventy-seven of Bilbao's projects were located. This represented her observation that every new piece of architecture contributes to an existing collage, whether urban or rural.

**ANON**

**Tale of Genji Scroll, c.1850**

Pigment and ink on Japanese paper

35.3 × 9 × 9 cm, 14 × 3½ × 3½ in

The *Genji Monogatari Emaki* (Tale of Genji Scroll) is a hand scroll illustrating scenes from the classic Japanese fictional work of the same name by lady-in-waiting Murasaki Shikibu, which was first published in the early tenth century; the earliest surviving painted scroll was made in the twelfth century during the Heian period. Many narrative scrolls depicting scenes from the fifty-four chapters of the book have been produced over the centuries, and this version, or monoscenic narrative, was made during the eighteenth century. This painting is from chapter 4, *Yugao*, which is the name of a flower called evening face, but also the name of a woman whom Genji is pursuing. The flowers adorn the outer screen of Yugao's residence, and at the entrance of the inner room, Genji's servant Koremitsu makes enquiries. The techniques used in the making of the image belong to the *yamato-e* genre, which follows specific conventions such as stylized and abbreviated facial features and the use of thick pigments and bright colours. Large bands of clouds obscure and divide space, and these can be seen as golden mist that frames the scene here, which appears as if seen from above through a parting in the cloud. Architectural elements were illustrated using a technique called *fukinuki yatai*, which means blown-off roof, a glimpse of which can be seen here, where the interior of Yugao's house is visible behind the flowers. The composition of the painting is formed as a series of screens that lie diagonally at 30 degrees across the page so that they are seen in elevation. Even the green carriage on the street follows this pattern, and in the empty spaces between these vertical planes the players in the scene enact their part. There is no perspective, and the fragmented nature of the image seen from above is enclosed by the clouds, which maintain a restricted spatial boundary that encompasses no great distance.

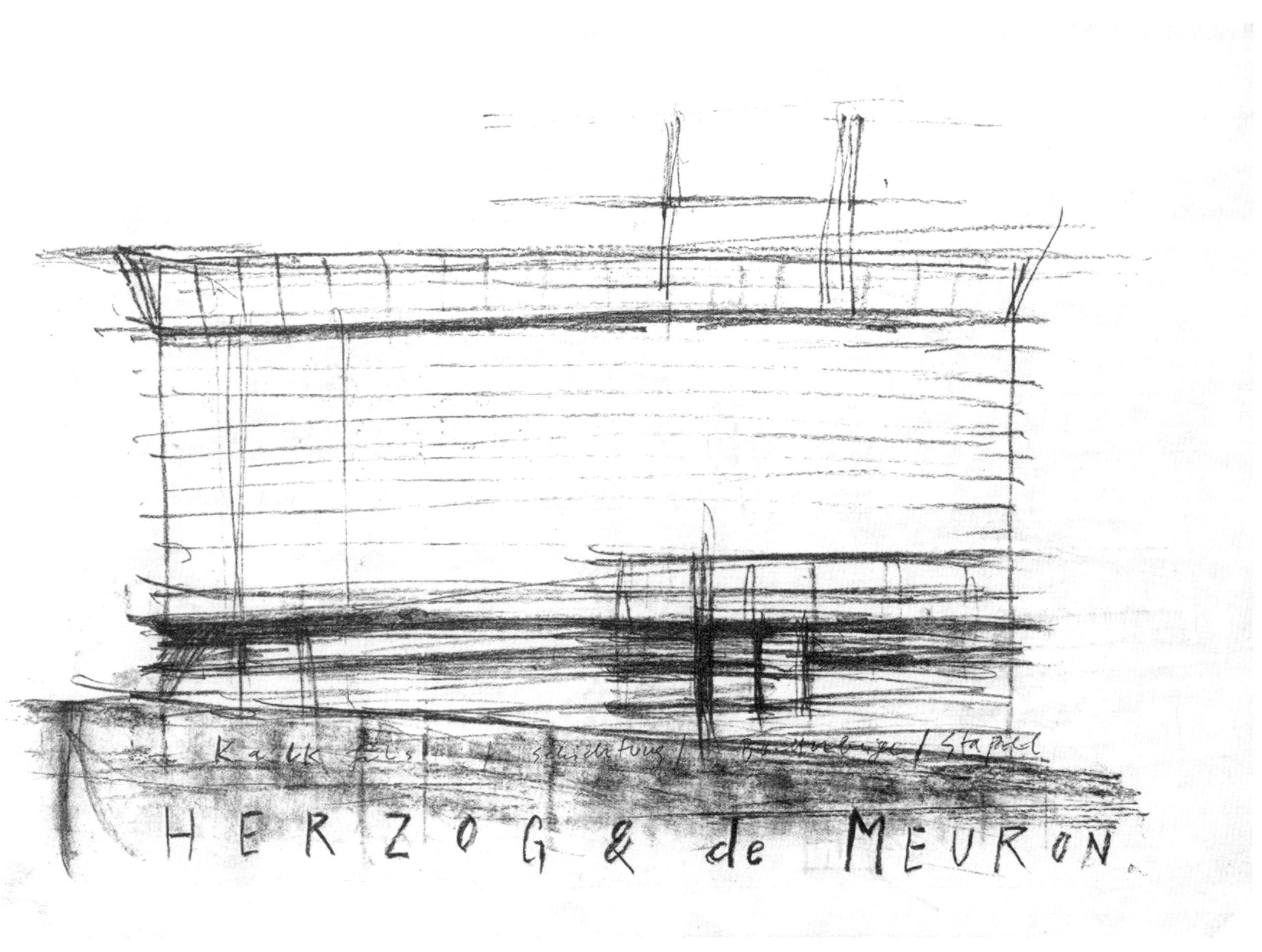


**HERZOG & DE MEURON**

**Ricola Storage Building, 1987**

Pencil and graphite on paper

21 × 29.8 cm, 8¼ × 11¾ in

Herzog & de Meuron has always used many different forms of representation, or by-products of the design process as they call them — from sketches on the back of old print-outs to refined models, conventional production drawings, manipulated material samples and video clips. This is an initial sketch made by Jacques Herzog for an early project, a warehouse building completed in 1987 and one of several for the Swiss herbal candy manufacturer Ricola. Economical in its expression and using a minimum of lines made with intense energy, the drawing captures the essential qualities of the external cladding of the windowless facade, and makes the conditions to which the building responds apparent. This is a side elevation of the building seen from the west, and this sketch investigates the figure that it will have. The swelling scale of the horizontal Eternit panels, narrow at the bottom but growing in size towards the eaves is not yet present in the sketch, but the sense of stacked layers is very strong. The line of the sloping chalk ground of the site against the vertical is marked by the rough shading from the side of a crayon or pencil, like a plinth that bears the title Herzog & de Meuron. Darker lines create a flat datum above this sloping ground, and mark the locations of doors for the loading bays, which are present as two rectangular shapes behind the horizontal strata. In the final construction these are framed by boxes, which interrupt the layers. At the top of the drawing, the exposure of the galvanised sheet metal box behind the layer of cladding supported on wooden battens fastened to the steel structure is apparent behind a row of struts that support the projecting eaves. Their diagonal disposition forms a volumetric element, a veil-like cornice that runs along each elevation, and a dark line marks the boundary where this transition occurs.

**KARL MOSER (1860–1936)**

**Church of St Anthony, view from the street, 1926**

Charcoal on paper

55 × 61.5 cm, 21½ × 4¼ in

Blending with the billowing foliage lining the street opposite, the plain facade of Karl Moser's St Anthony's church, drawn with smooth strokes from the side of a charcoal stick, takes on the same mottled texture – a blank canvas for the shadows of clouds. The bright sky, left un-rendered, contrasts with this effect, and the shaded roadway that reflects the church, its tower and framing trees indicates that the drawing depicts a sunny day in Basel. The bell tower dominates the drawing and is set off-centre; the emphasis of its vertical lines, formed by two huge offset concrete planes, is reminiscent of Futurist drawings. The composition of both drawing and facade is balanced by a monumental gateway at the other end of the church, comprising stepped frames that reduce in size from the scale of the tower to that of the street and, finally, to that of the human figure. The largest transcends the eaves line, the smallest defines a low passageway that cuts through the edge of the city block into an internal garden with access to the vicarage and the baptismal chapel. Halfway down the dim passageway is the church's principal entrance to the main axis of its brightly lit nave. The 60 × 22 m (196 × 72 ft) rectangular church is symmetrical in plan. It is built of, and celebrates, in-situ reinforced concrete; the concrete surface, including its shuttering marks, is exposed internally and externally. Eight slim columns highlight the structural capabilities of concrete. They define two side aisles and support a concrete, coffered barrel vault along the nave. Although not obvious in the drawing, large gridded fields of stained glass on the street facade create dynamic, colourful patterns over the plain concrete surfaces. Moser, architect of over six hundred buildings, was known as the father of Modernism in Switzerland.

**TADAO ANDO (1941–)**

**Church of the Light, 1989**

Lithograph with colour pencil

102.9 × 72.7 cm, 40½ × 28½ in

The Church of the Light, a renovation of an existing Christian compound in Ibaraki, Osaka, is one of Tadao Ando's best-known projects. This simple, abstracted plan drawing illustrates his fascination as an architect with the way that light defines a space, particularly as it shines across or onto a surface. As with many of his buildings, the smooth, even vertical surfaces in this case are of exposed in-situ reinforced concrete, poured to a very high standard so that the marking of the formwork makes a delicate pattern on the wall, in which shadows linger. The building's floor is laid with dark wooden board. In the drawing, the representation of the physical walls is equivalent to the pattern of the light as it is cast on the ground, and Ando's recurring theme of duality explored through a play between solid and void is made manifest. Where the walls have been cut to reveal their plan, they are shown in pale grey, making a broken rectangular shape pierced by the diagonal wall that defines the meandering entrance into the chapel. The rows of pews, made of the planks used for the building's scaffolding, adjust their length in relation to this diagonal wall, swelling out towards the space of the altar, and are delineated in black with their seating components in blue, like the floor below. Where the altar would usually be there is emptiness. The faint lines of the floorboards lightly disturb the darkness, which is bisected by a pale blue cross. This is the light falling through a cross cut into the east wall of the chapel, the only prominent Christian symbol in the unadorned space.

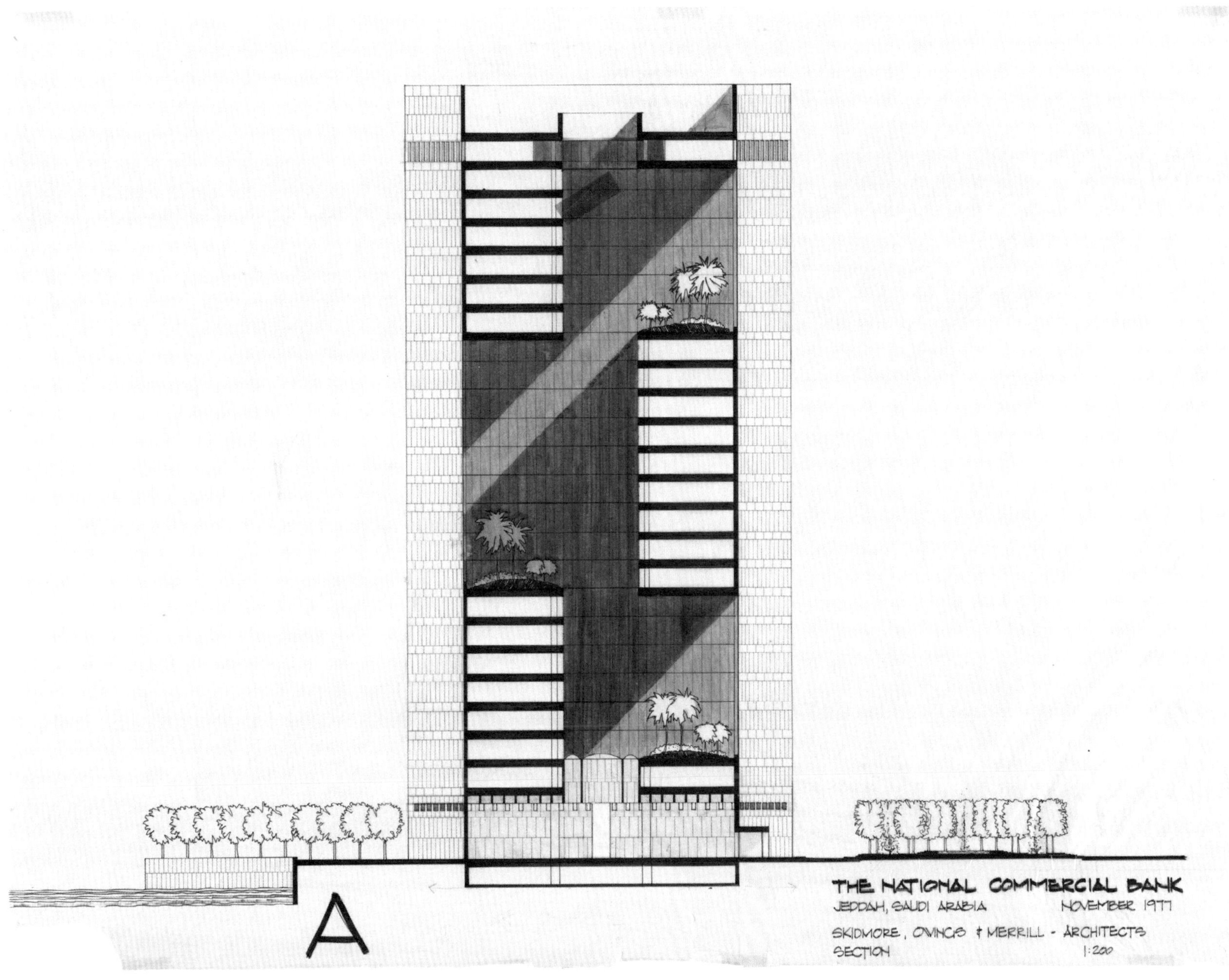


**GORDON BUNSHAFT, SKIDMORE, OWINGS & MERRILL**

**National Commercial Bank, 1977**

Ink on tracing paper

75.6 × 101 cm, 29¾ × 39¾ in

Wealth generated by the 1970s oil boom initiated the growth of the Saudi port city of Jeddah, transforming its character as a traditional Arabic settlement comprising of four- and five-storey buildings laid out along a maze of narrow streets and alleyways, into a modern centre. Its new buildings were designed by large international architectural practices such as the American firm Skidmore, Owings & Merrill, who brought their expertise in Western construction techniques and processes into this desert environment. Gordon Bunshaft, partner at SOM, designed the National Commercial Bank, and in this project refined his tendency towards dramatic form into an ingenious solution to the problem of making tall buildings cool in a hot, dry climate. He did this by placing huge, multi-storey openings within the otherwise blank facades of the building, which is triangular in plan and situated on a large open seafront plaza. This allowed partly cooled air to be drawn into a central atrium space, which is surrounded by the office floors with windows looking into it. This air rises as it is heated, to flow upwards and out of the top of the building, creating a cooling and ventilating current in the void. The section shows the presence of these voids on two of the facades: on the right-hand side, a single central opening nine storeys high is sandwiched by fourteen storeys of offices; opposite are two smaller openings at the top and bottom of the tower. The tower is visible for miles around, so that the structure itself generates the identity for the bank, rather than just signage.

**JAMES WINES (1932–)**

**Highrise of Homes project, 1981**

Charcoal and ink on paper

55.9 × 61 cm, 22 × 24 in

In 1970, an organization was established in New York called SITE (Sculpture In The Environment), with the intention of exploring the boundaries between architecture and environmental design through a process that they call 'environmental thinking'. This involves a fusion of approaches to a problem from the perspectives of building design, landscape and urban planning, the visual arts and environmental impact. This charcoal-and-ink perspective drawing, made by SITE founder James Wines, is for an imaginary project that nevertheless had a proposed site in Battery Park City, and which he described as a Highrise of Homes. Drawn in Wines' characteristic style, it is figurative and describes a discernible reality, but at the same time has a monolithic intangibility derived from the tiny monotone strokes from which it is made up. The object seems to be made from an insubstantial element – ash, perhaps, or dust – that calls its proposed reality into question. Wines describes this project as a 'vertical community', designed to 'accommodate people's conflicting desires to enjoy the cultural advantages of an urban centre, without sacrificing the private home identity and garden space associated with suburbia'. This is a formal and spatial merging of the oppositional environments of American suburb and metropolis. The steel-and-concrete frame that formed the skeleton of many twentieth-century urban housing blocks has been transformed in Wines' proposal into a real-estate scenario for a greenfield site where the three-dimensional grid takes the place of the subdivided plot of ground. Each site becomes available for the construction of a house and garden in a style selected by the buyer, the whole ideally coalescing into a village-like community on each floor. Wines' proposal allows individuals to express themselves as consumers and exercise their right to choice as a means of achieving personal identity.

**XU YANG (c.1712–nd)**

**Burgeoning Life in a Resplendent Age, 1759**

Coloured Ink on silk

35.8 × 1,225 cm, 14 × 482¼ in

Xu Yang was a native of the city of Suzhou, the subject of this 12 m-long hand scroll, which he made in his role as courtier and painter during the reign of the Qing dynasty's Qianlong Emperor (1735–96). Located on the Yangtze River, the city was a leading metropolis of the time – a market centre specializing in the silk trade – and this scene depicts the important river with its intricately built-up banks. The scroll's format is used to present a continuous, unfolding narrative of city life, enriched by the observational detail gathered by Xu Yang during the six years that he took to complete it. More that 4,600 figures, 2,140 houses, 40 bridges and 300 boats inhabit the painting.

The starting point for viewing the scroll is its far right end, looking at each section in sequence as if travelling through a landscape on a journey. Using a scattered perspective technique, which was influenced by European painting, enabling one scene to flow into another, Xu Yang combines a Western method of depicting space with Chinese compositional devices – including layering events in time and space, and reproducing specific representations of antiquities formalized by past masters. The scroll formed a visual record of a journey made by Emperor Qianlong in the spring of 1751, and evoked his memories of the city as a series of episodes. The extract shown here depicts the prefectural examinations, usually held in the fourth month of the year, so that the spring season is defined. This episode also symbolizes the harmony of the inhabitants, expressed in a formalized cultural event. In this traditional world, the young men seen here crowding into the cloisters and against the walls of the courts, and filling the commercial street that traverses the painting, would be waiting for their first assignment to government office.

**ANON**

**Topkapi Scroll, 1490**

Ink and dye on parchment

34 × 295 cm, 13 × 116 ft

The Topkapi Scroll was compiled in the late-medieval Iranian world by master builders, who recorded existing patterns and developed concepts for complex geometrical systems related to brick- and tile-based architecture rather than stone masonry. The scroll contains 114 illustrations in square or rectangular frames, defining the schema for the setting out of pattern on wall surfaces and vaults, or honeycomb-like muqarmas pendentives, but is too large for practical use as a set of working drawings. These two drawings, the 33rd and 34th on the scroll, would have been generated from un-inked, incised construction lines that appear on the paper as a dead drawing. Specific points on, or intersections of, these lines were connected, to generate the final visible pattern. The design of the right-hand image is described as a quarter repeat unit of a star-and-polygon pattern with two superimposed layers. Over a layer of invisible, incised lines that form a series of radial semi- and quarter-circular patterns, red-dotted grid lines define polygons whose sides are bisected by two crossed black lines meeting to form the star-and-polygon pattern. Lines extend from the black-ink large-star patterns to form an interlocking patter of star fragments and polygons. The left-hand drawing is considerably denser, its complexity generated by the concentric circles that define the structure of the 'dead drawing.' Its subject is a quarter repeat unit of a pattern featuring two superimposed layers, both based on five- and ten-pointed stars and polygons. The intersecting orange grid lines connect the radii of invisible circles to determine the centre of all the ten-pointed and some of the five-pointed stars in black ink, which interlock with various polygons. Such Timurid-Turkman architecture aimed for a geometrization of design that synthesized structure, ornament and space.

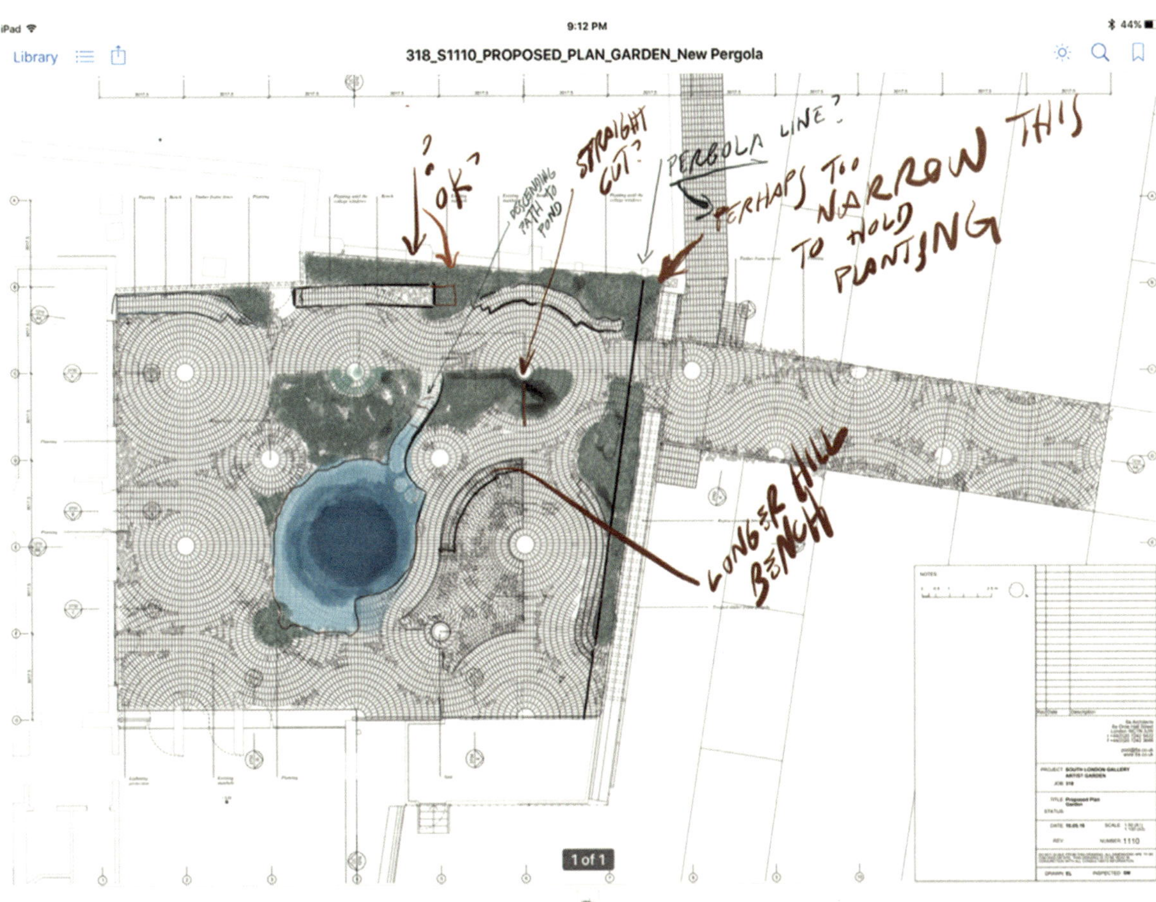


**GABRIEL OROZCO (1962–)**

**Annotated plan of the garden at the South London Gallery, 2016**

WhatsApp message

Belonging to a long series of drawings,like film stills, of an intense conversation that took place over several months in 2016, this image was sent as a WhatsApp message from artist Gabriel Orozco to Stephanie Macdonald of 6a Architects, and represents one moment within an oscillating collaborative process. The garden is a work of art by Orozco, made physically manifest through research and responsive action by 6a. The image shows a hand-drawn note about specific details, made during the final stages of design by Orozco on his iPad over an architectural drawing that clearly bears the marks of its palimpsest-like character. The underlying construction plan for the garden started out as hand drawings by Orozco that were reproduced in Autocad and redrawn by hand using watercolour on paper over several layers of prints. In this iteration, the complex pattern of Orozco's radiating circles covers the garden's surface. It is clear that many decisions have already been made and that the design is reaching completion. For example, the plan is set out using a single-brick dimension unit with York stone elements, the planting growing through this is more subtly ruinous than an earlier but impossible-to-enact concept for laying roughly shaped and graded stones from the quarry. All around the perimeter of the garden, beyond the wall shown in the plan, earlier notes now agreed are embedded, and they range in their practical-lyrical responses – the rainwater pipe that discharges into a channel on the ground, the stacked brick hill +1200, and the planting that allows the use of the door. At this moment in the proceedings, the stone cylinder containing a pond has been coloured blue, but the limits of the water's edge are ambiguous.

Timeline

2130 BC — p. 163
1865 BC — p. 272
c.1350 BC — p. 57
c.350 BC — p. 255
c. AD 40 — p. 229
c. AD 300 — p. 136
AD 820 — p. 91
AD 950 — p. 130
1103 — p. 116
1155 — p. 232
1230 — p. 287
1280 — p. 262
1306 — p. 181
1340 — p. 235
c.1434 — p. 96
1481 — p. 53
1486 — p. 38
1490 — p. 18, p. 296
1505 — p. 212
1506 — p. 65, p. 74
1510 — p. 197
1515 — p. 141
1519 — p. 156
c.1522 — p. 27
1530 — p. 80, p. 166
1535 — p. 149
1536 — p. 79, p. 201

**c.1550**

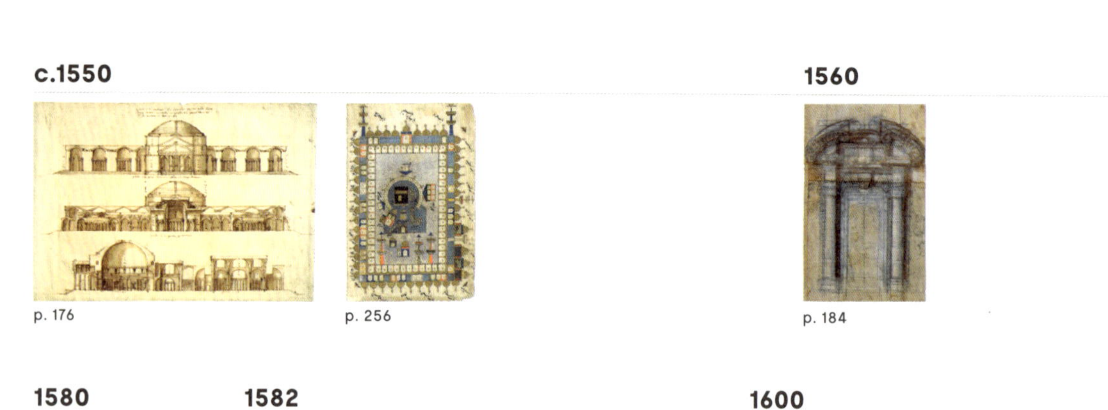

p. 176

p. 256

**1560**

p. 184

**1570**

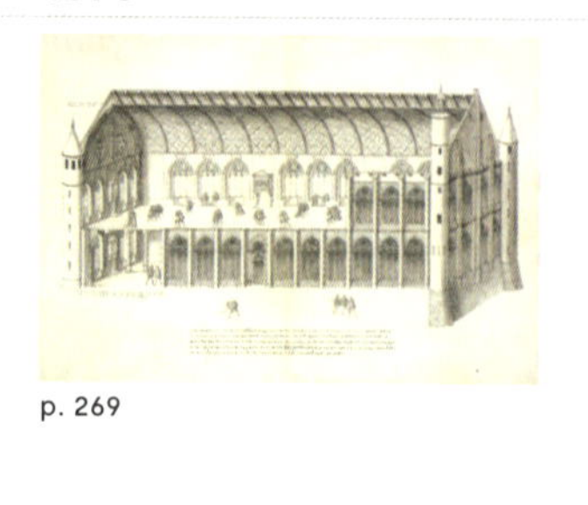

p. 269

**1580**

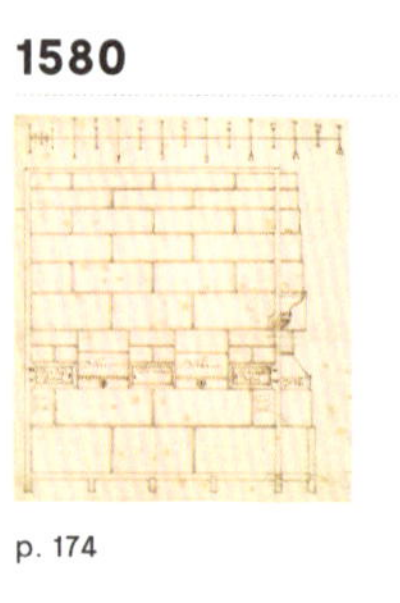

p. 174

**1582**

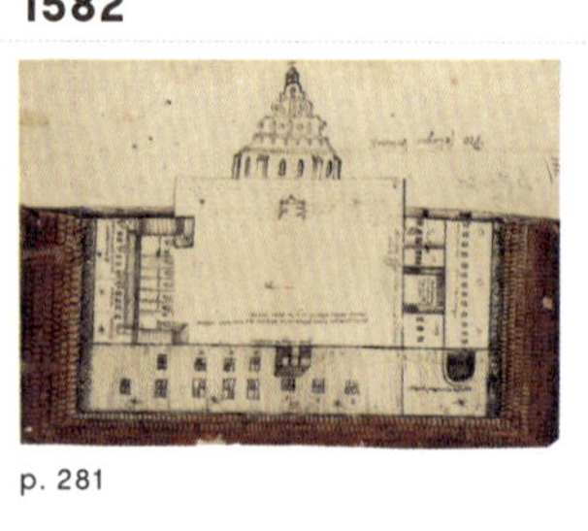

p. 281

**1600**

p. 191

**1601**

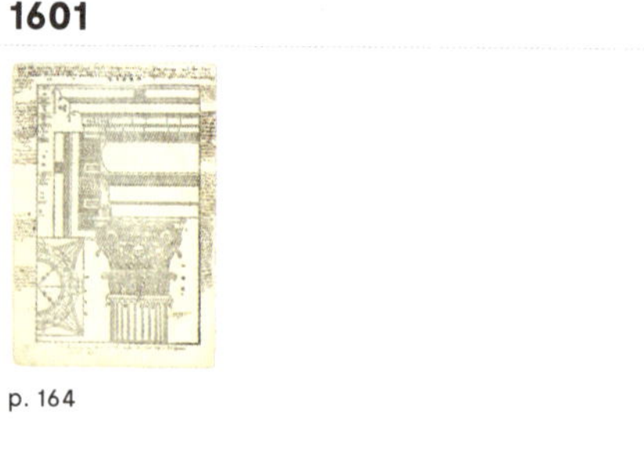

p. 164

**1653**

p. 21

**c.1660**

p. 123

**1664**

p. 13

**1670**

p. 188

**1675**

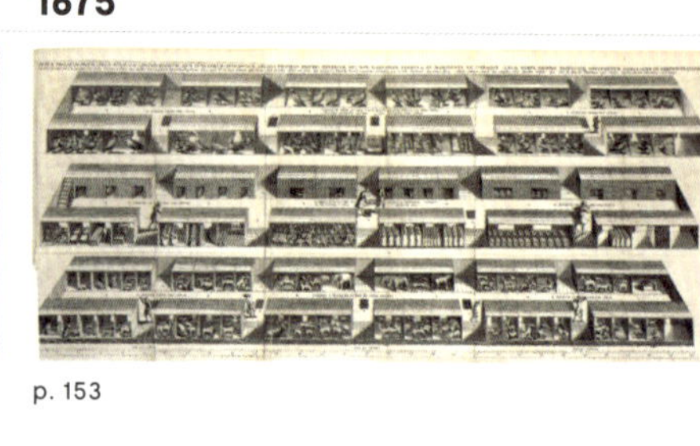

p. 153

**1680**

p. 230

**1685**

p. 186

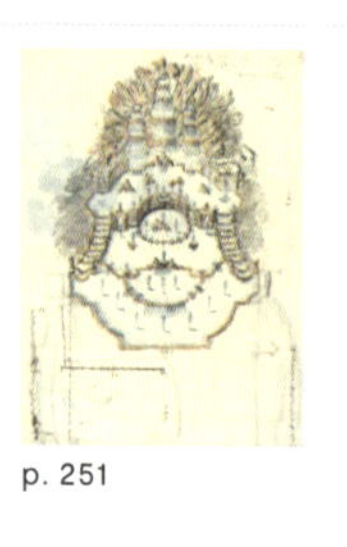

p. 251

**1705**

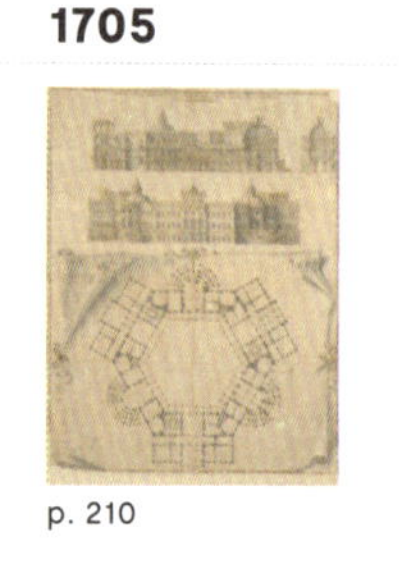

p. 210

**1709**

p. 46

**1721**

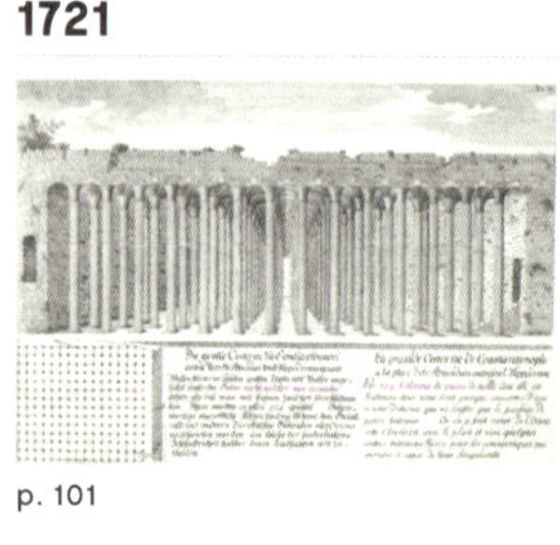

p. 101

**1722**

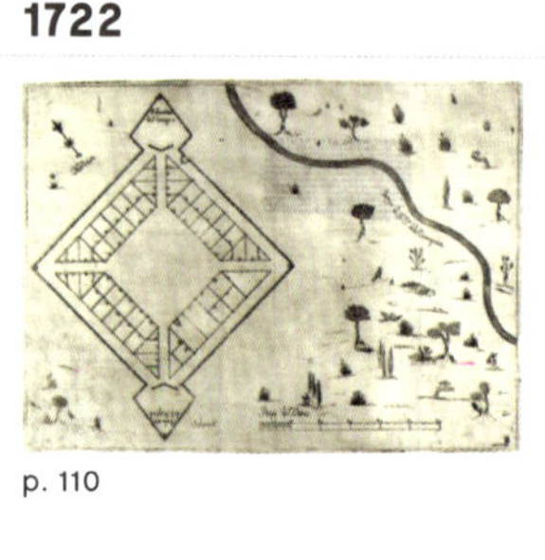

p. 110

**1725**

p. 276

**1732**

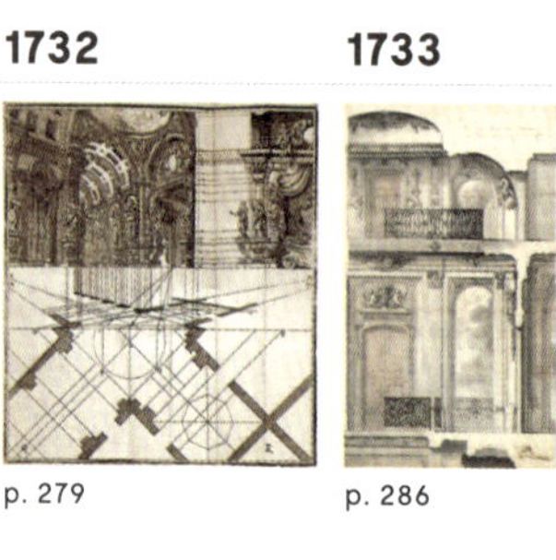

p. 279

**1733**

p. 286

**c.1750**

p. 249

**1758**

p. 87

**1759**

p. 295

**1760**

p. 154

**1770**

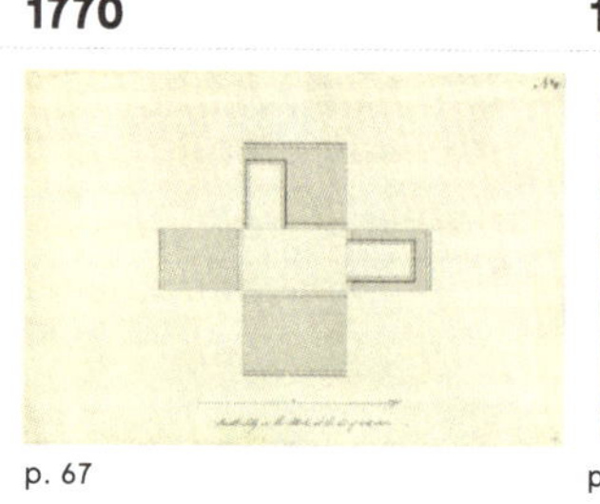

p. 67

**1771**

p. 165

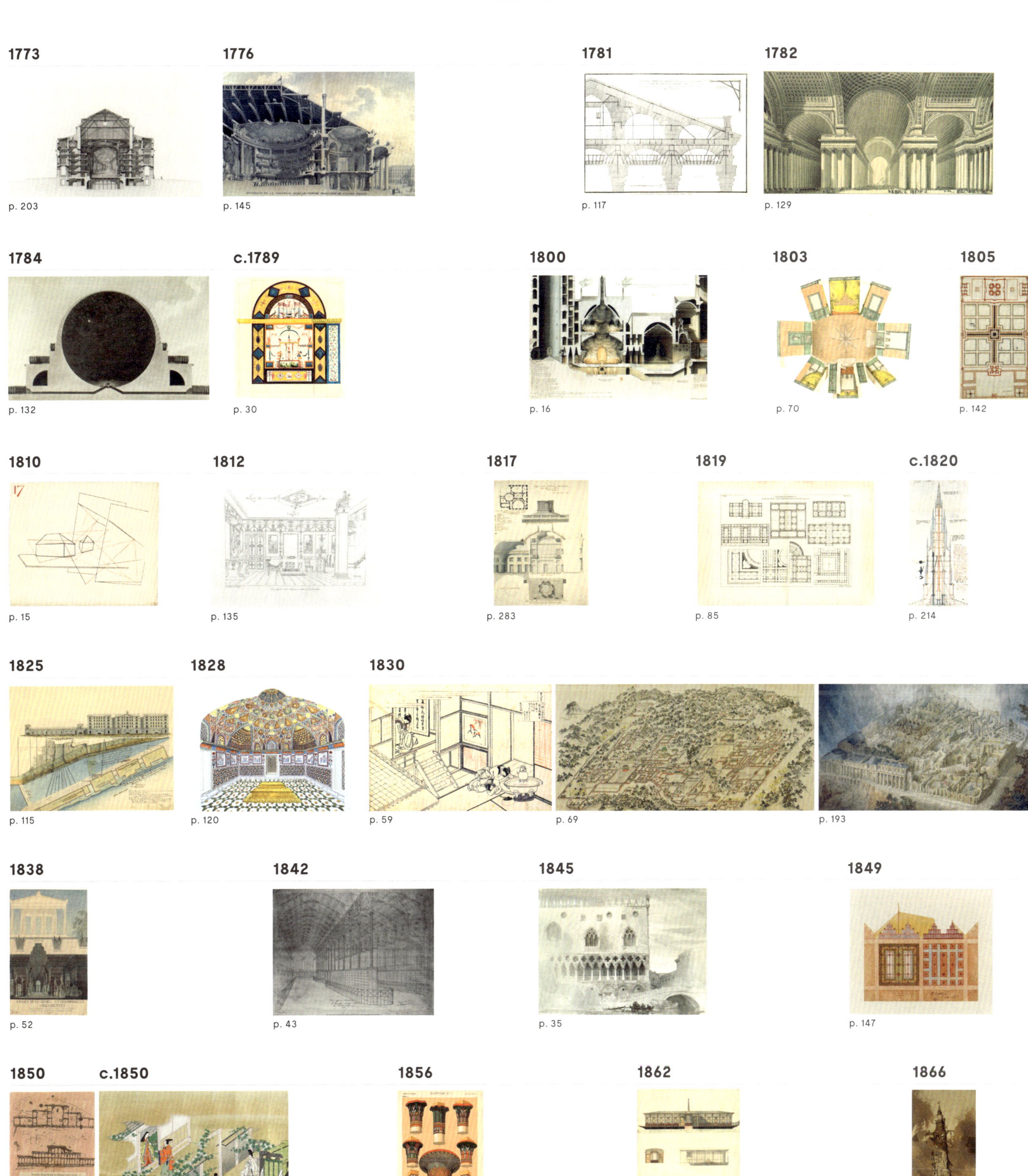

**1773** p. 203

**1776** p. 145

**1781** p. 117

**1782** p. 129

**1784** p. 132

**c.1789** p. 30

**1800** p. 16

**1803** p. 70

**1805** p. 142

**1810** p. 15

**1812** p. 135

**1817** p. 283

**1819** p. 85

**c.1820** p. 214

**1825** p. 115

**1828** p. 120

**1830** p. 59, p. 69, p. 193

**1838** p. 52

**1842** p. 43

**1845** p. 35

**1849** p. 147

**1850** p. 146

**c.1850** p. 289

**1856** p. 240

**1862** p. 183

**1866** p. 224

## c.1872

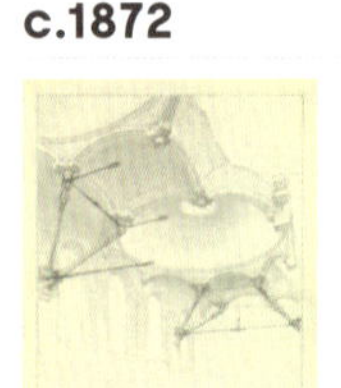
p. 208

## 1873

p. 151

## 1884

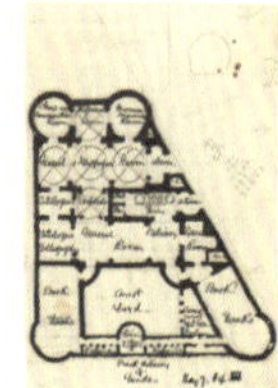
p. 198

## 1885

p. 231

## 1891

p. 26

p. 64

## 1901

p. 82

## 1903

p. 175

p. 242

p. 280

## 1905

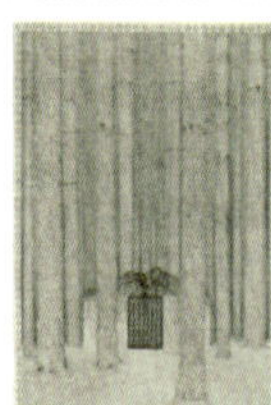
p. 100

## 1908

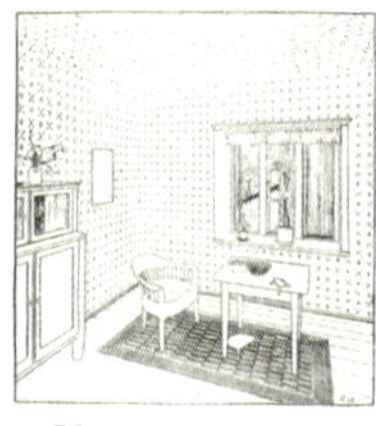
p. 58

## 1909

p. 182

p. 202

p. 245

## 1911

p. 263

## 1912

p. 171

p. 282

## 1914

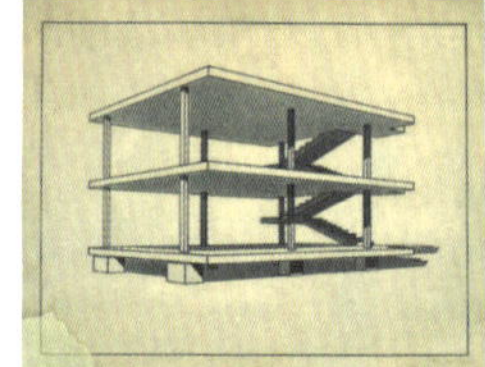
p. 144

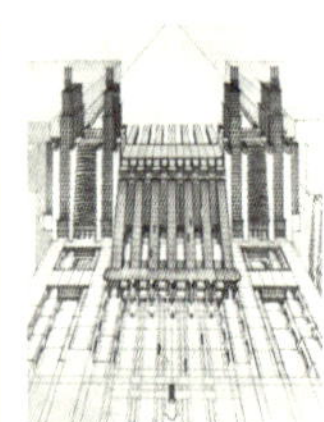
p. 265

## 1915

p. 160

## 1917

p. 107

## 1919

p. 122

p. 215

## 1920

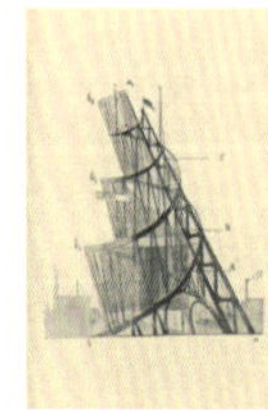
p. 44

p. 73

p. 94

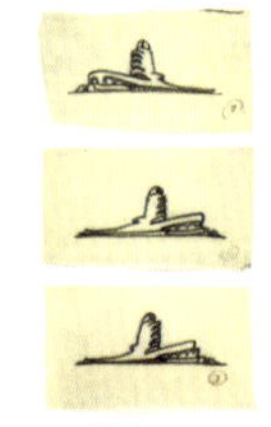
p. 103

## 1921

p. 37

## 1922

p. 227

## 1923

p. 71

p. 167

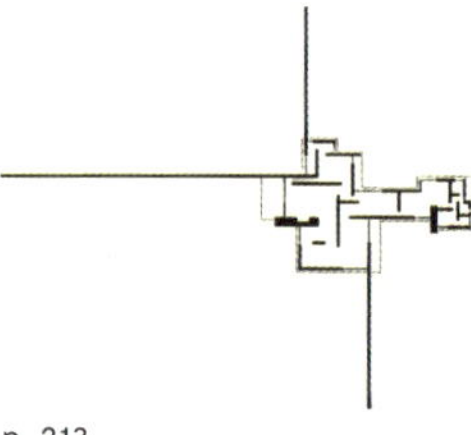
p. 213

## 1924

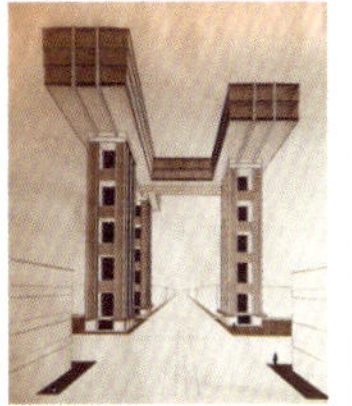
p. 108

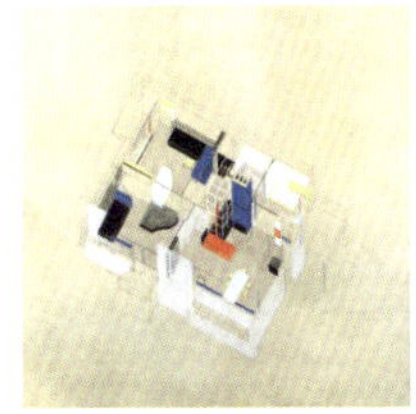
p. 190

p. 219

p. 264

## 1925

p. 104

## 1926

p. 88

p. 291

## 1927

p. 271

## 1928

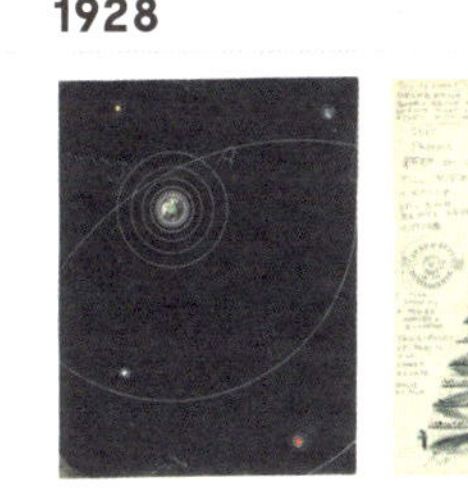
p. 173

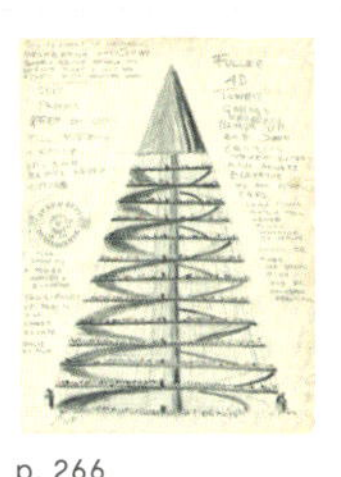
p. 266

## 1929

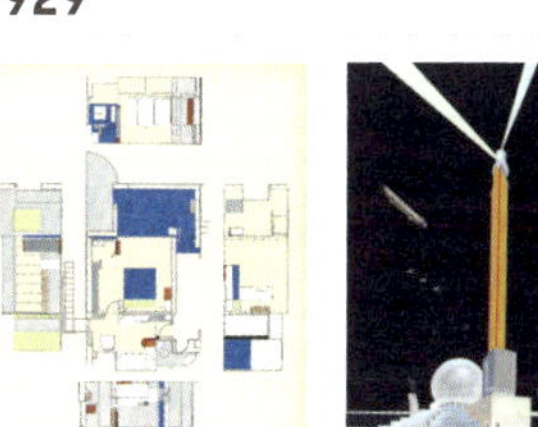
p. 83
p. 225

## 1933

p. 106

p. 244

## 1936

p. 31

## 1937

p. 216

## 1938

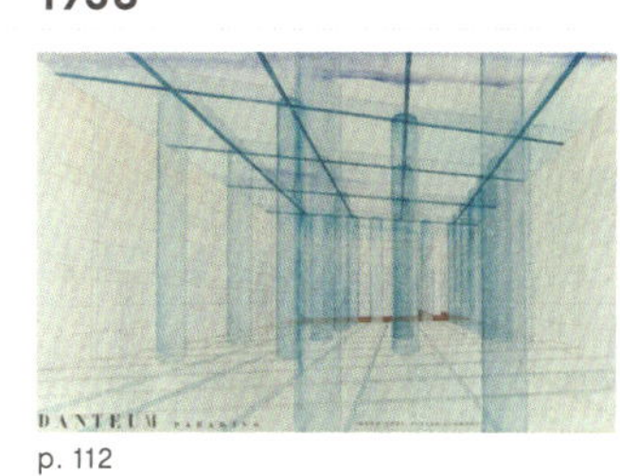

p. 112

## 1939

p. 221

p. 234

## 1941

p. 158

## 1942

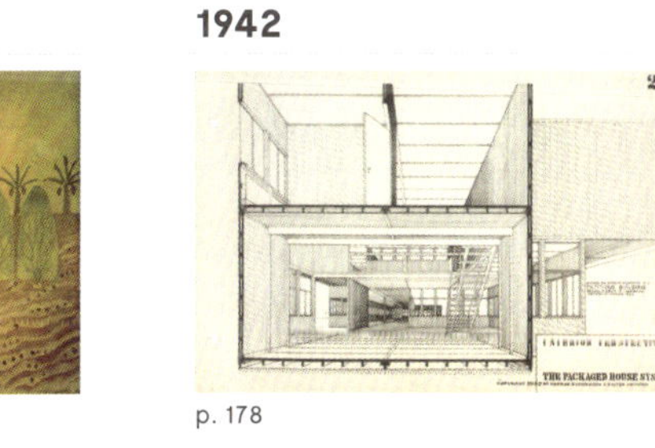

p. 178

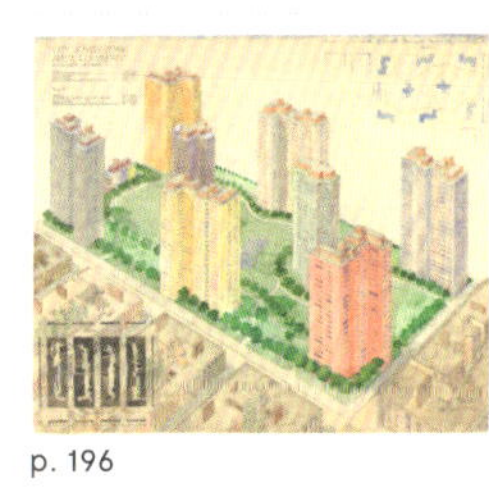
p. 196

## 1943

p. 155

## 1946

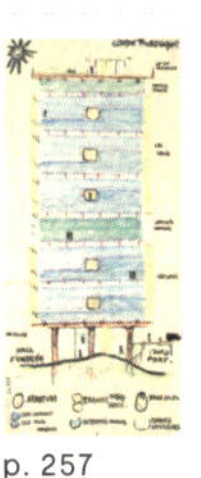
p. 257

## 1947

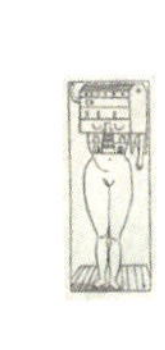
p. 236

## 1949

p. 60

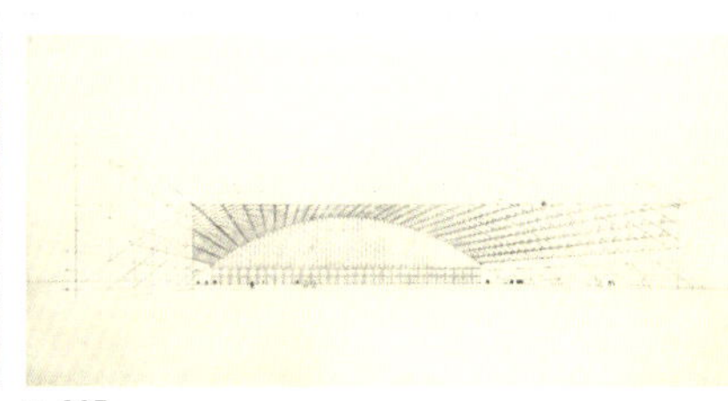
p. 207

## 1950

p. 273

## 1951

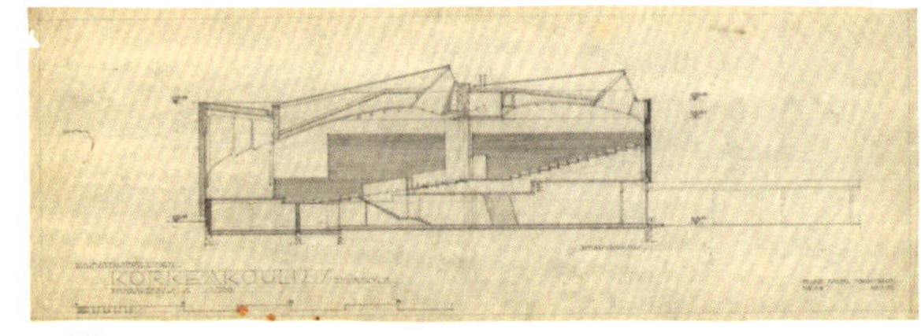
p. 253

p. 285

**1952**

p. 137

**1953**

p. 24
p. 125

**1954**

p. 267

**1955**

p. 238

**1956**

p. 72
p. 254

**1957**

p. 62

**1958**

p. 28

**1959**

p. 90

**1960**

p. 54

**1961**

p. 140

**1962**

p. 23
p. 49
p. 84
p. 250

**1963**

p. 105
p. 133
p. 200
p. 217
p. 246

**1964**

p. 14
p. 48
p. 131
p. 134
p. 169
p. 180

## 1965

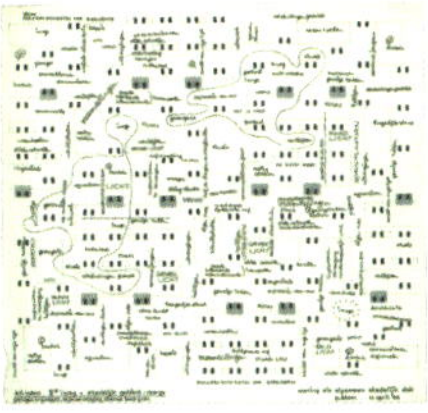

p. 50

p. 270

## 1967

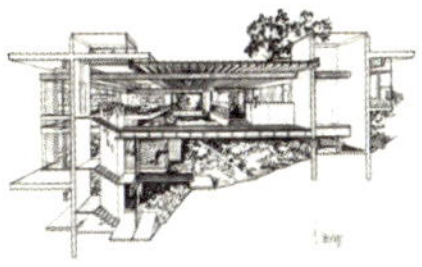

p. 258

## 1968

p. 139

## 1969

p. 128

p. 274

## 1970

p. 68

p. 99

p. 102

p. 113

p. 152

p. 209

p. 248

p. 259

## 1971

p. 93

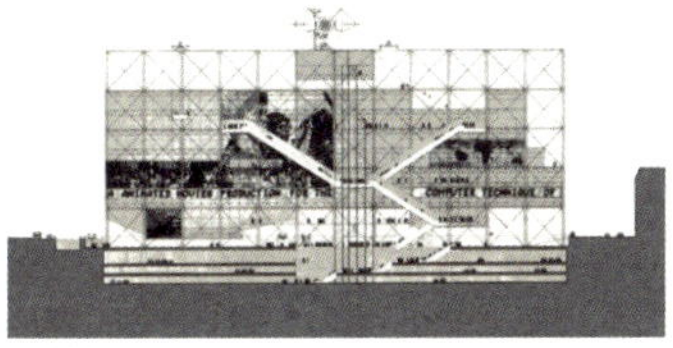

p. 205

## 1972

p. 40

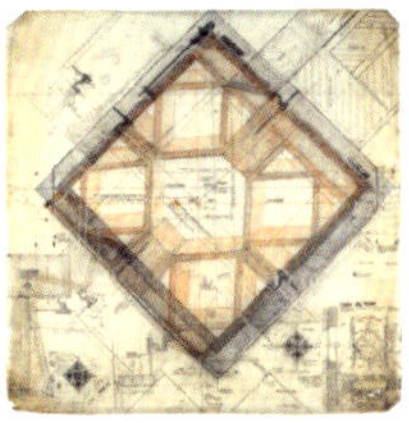

p. 223

p. 237

## 1974

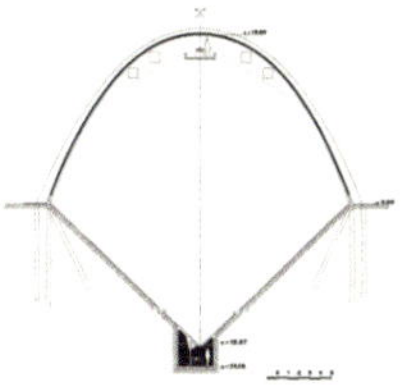

p. 77

## 1975

p. 12

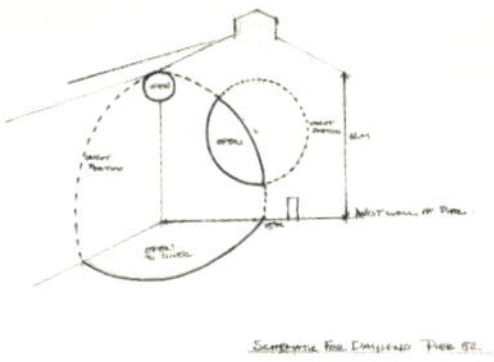

p. 76

p. 170

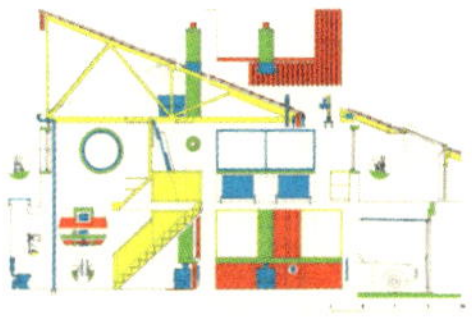

p. 179

p. 226

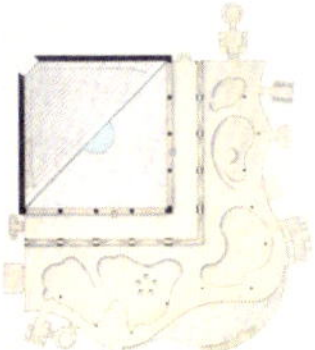

p. 228

## 1976

p. 98

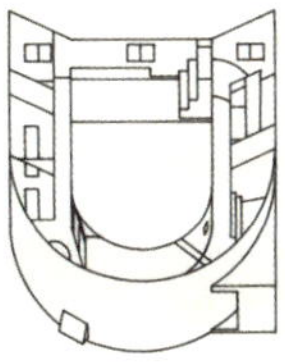

p. 111

## 1977

p. 61

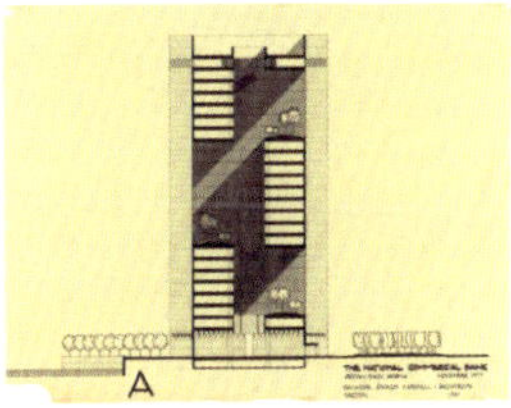

p. 293

## 1978

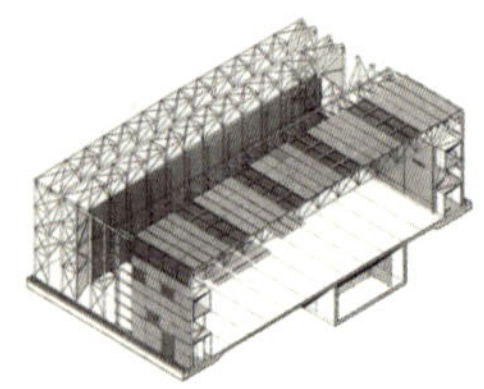
p. 42

p. 157

p. 211

p. 268

## 1979

p. 148

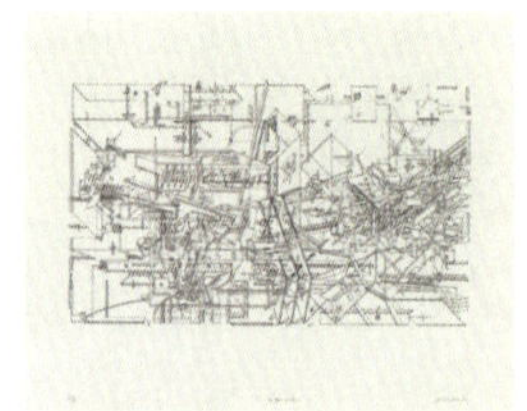
p. 162

## 1980

p. 218

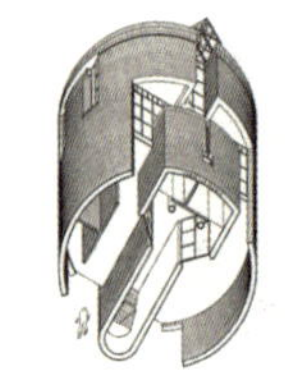

p. 241

## 1981

p. 247

p. 294

## 1982

p. 114

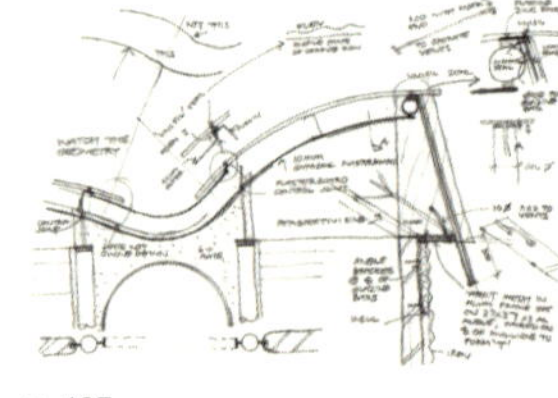
p. 127

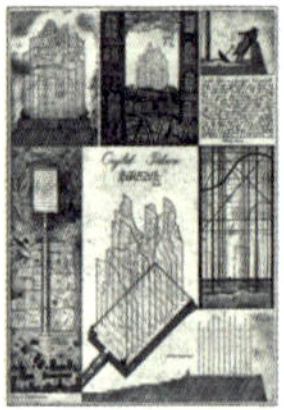
p. 278

## 1983

p. 161

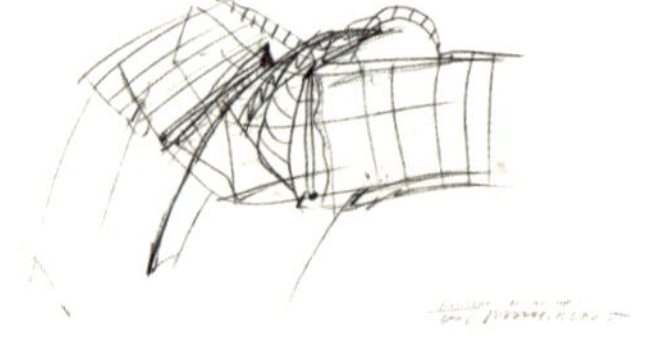
p. 239

## 1984

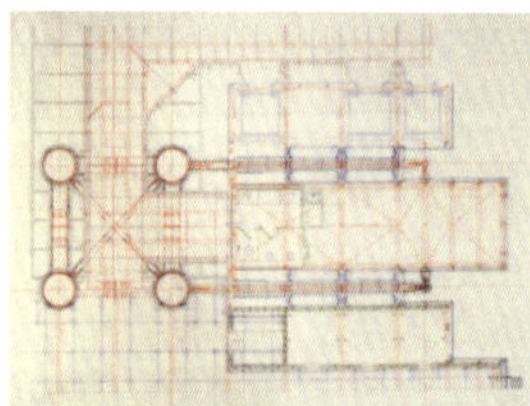
p. 39

p. 124

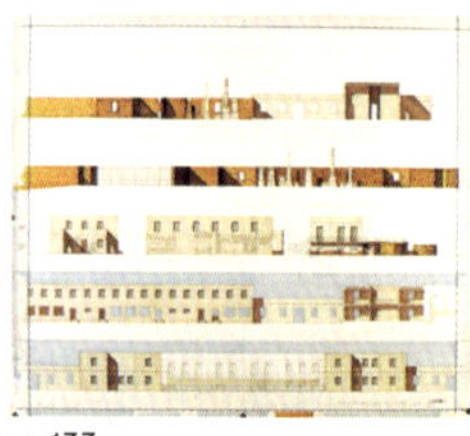
p. 177

## 1985

p. 25

## 1986

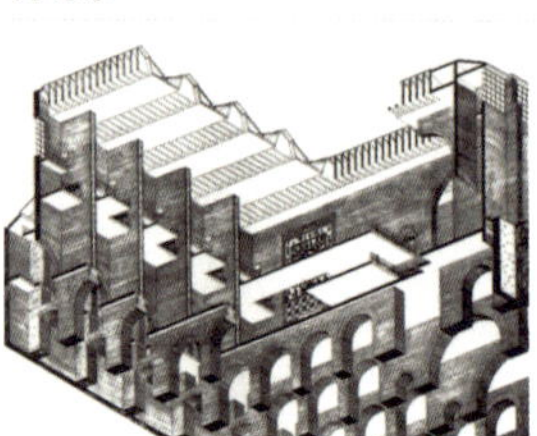
p. 150

## 1987

p. 290

## 1989

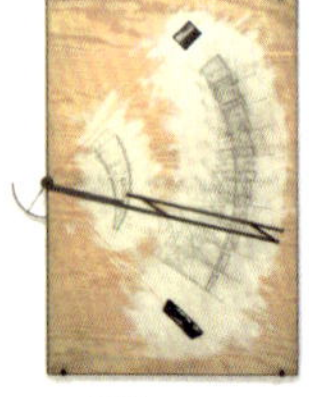
p. 222

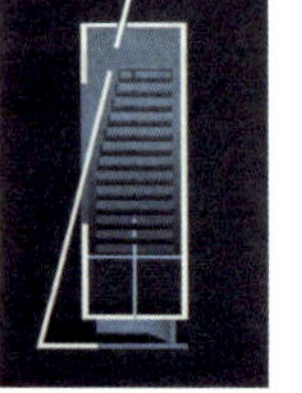
p. 292

## 1990

p. 89

p. 92

## 1992

p. 19

p. 199

## 1993

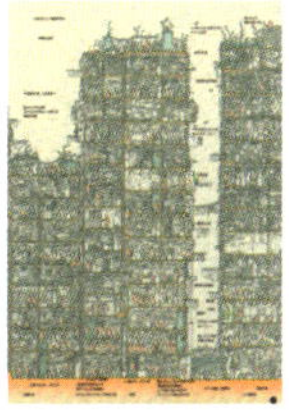

p. 36

## 1994

p. 275

## 1995

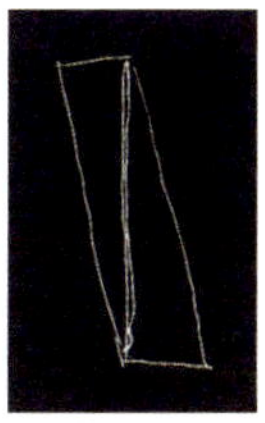

p. 185

p. 195

## 1999

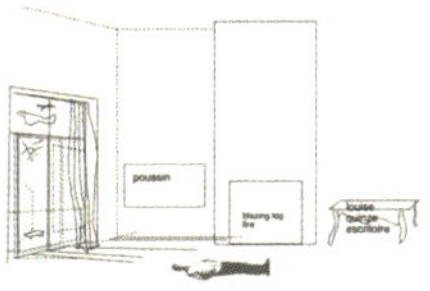

p. 63

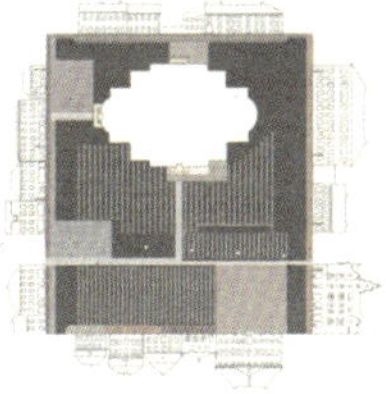

p. 66

p. 172

## 2001

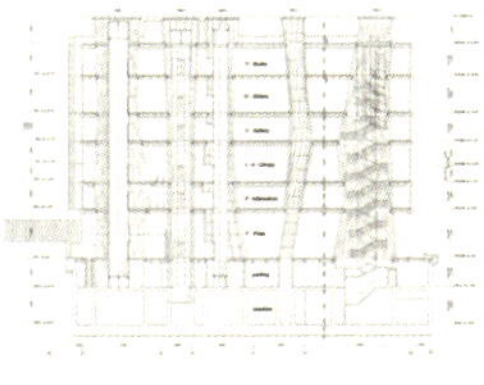

p. 233

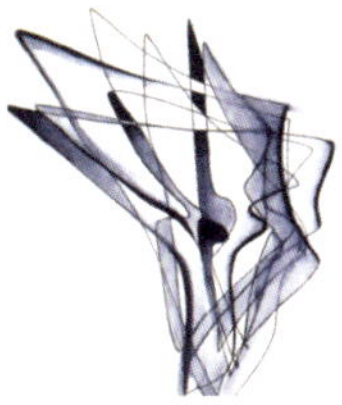

p. 260

## 2002

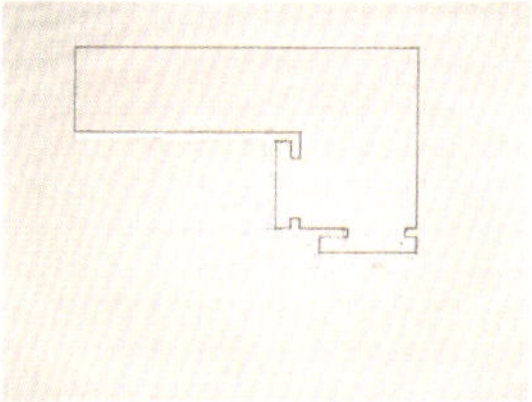

p. 33

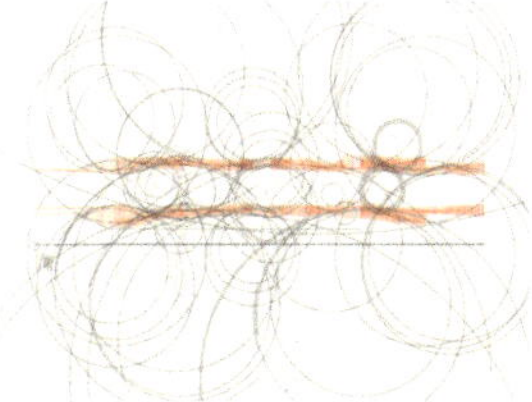

p. 187

## 2004

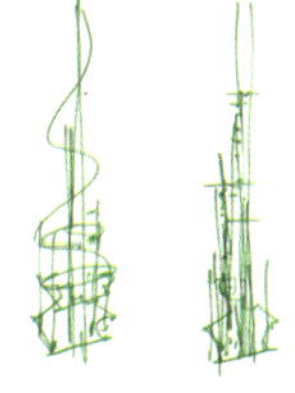
p. 45

p. 51

## 2005

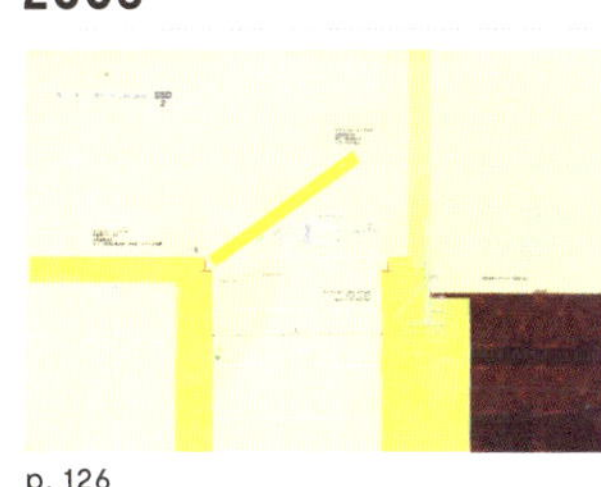
p. 126

p. 143

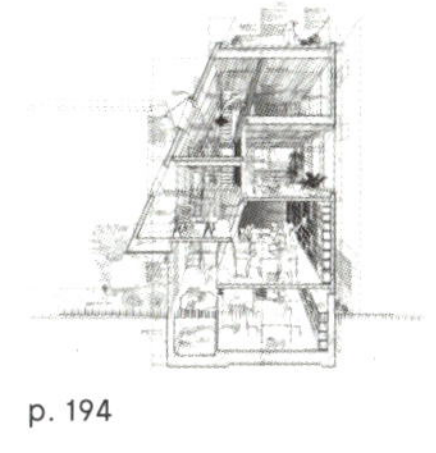
p. 194

## 2007

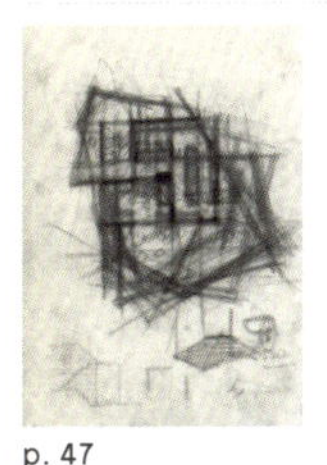
p. 47

## 2008

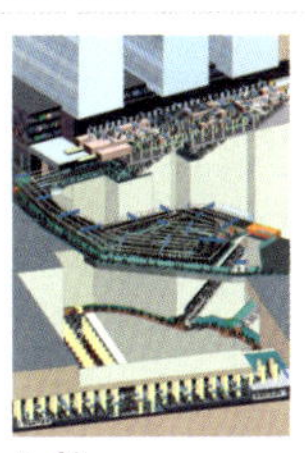
p. 41

p. 159

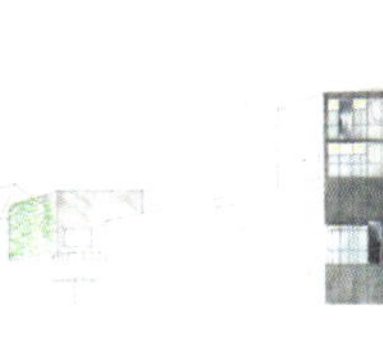

p. 189

p. 277

## 2009

p. 29

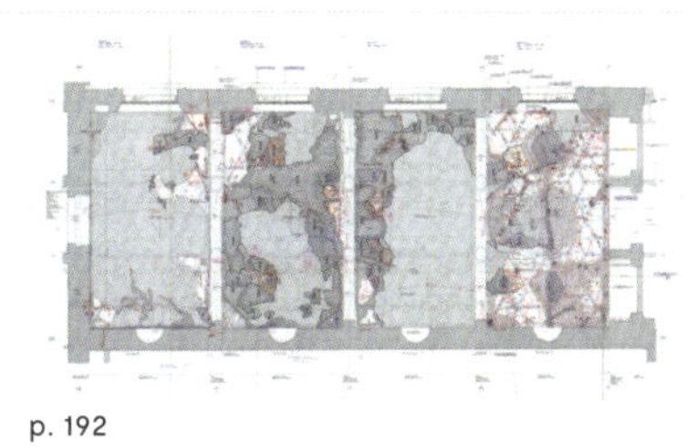
p. 192

## 2010

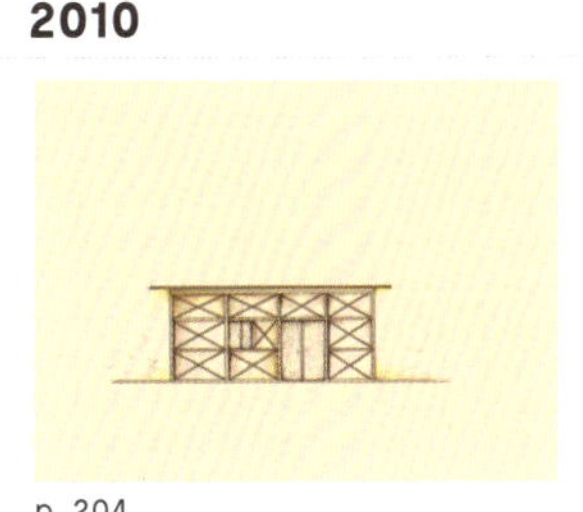
p. 204

## 2011

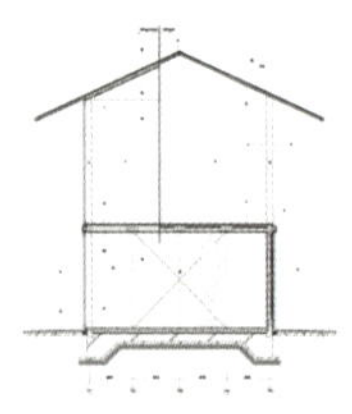
p. 95

## 2012

p. 86

p. 97

p. 220

## 2013

p. 20

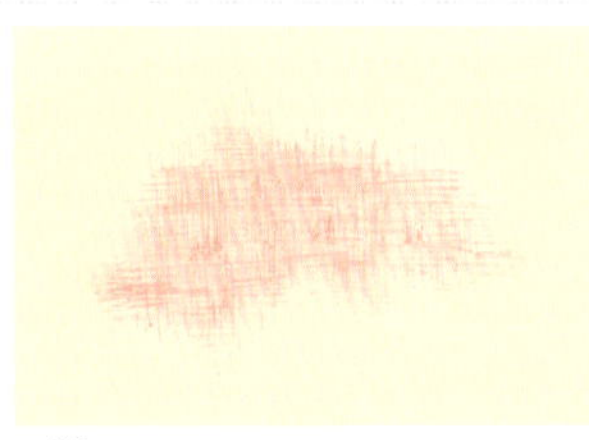
p. 32

p. 55

p. 81

p. 243

p. 261

## 2015

p. 109

## 2016

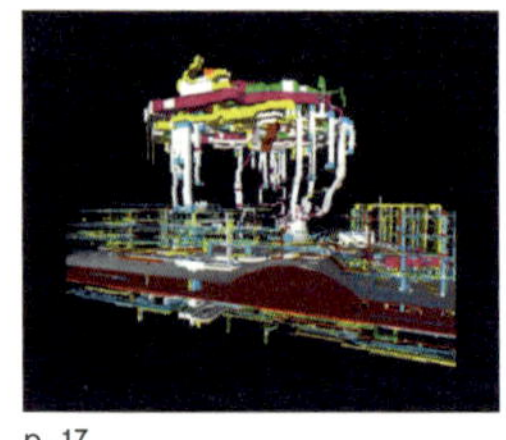
p. 17

p. 34

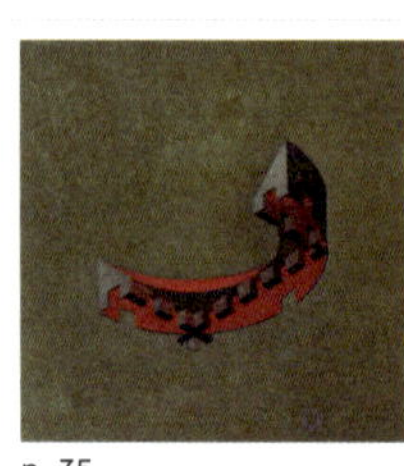
p. 75

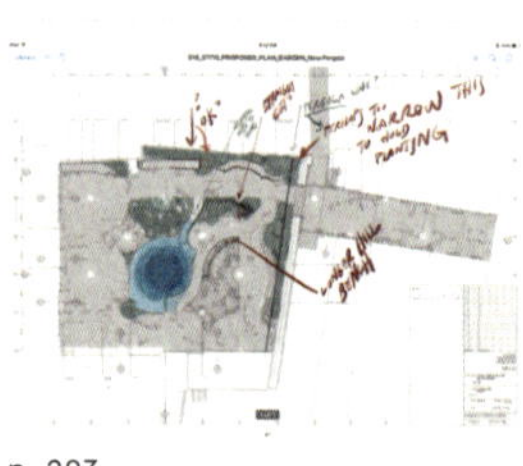
p. 297

## 2017

p. 288

## 2018

p. 121

## Further Reading


Ackerman, James. *Origins, Imitation, Conventions* (Cambridge, Mass.; London: MIT Press, 2002)

Benedik, Christian. *Masterworks of Architectural Drawing from the Albertina Museum* (Munich: Prestel, 2017)

Bingham, Neil Robert. *100 Years of Architectural Drawing: 1900-2000* (London: King, 2012)

Blau, Eve and Kaufman, Edward, eds. *Architecture and Its Image: Four Centuries of Architectural Representation* (Montreal: Canadian Centre for Architecture; Cambridge, Mass., 1989)

Chung, Anita. *Drawing Boundaries: Architectural Images in Qing China* (Honolulu: University of Hawai Press, 2004)

Cook, Peter. *Drawing: The Motive Force of Architecture* (Chichester: Architectural Design Primer, 2013)

Evans, Robin. *Translations from Drawing to Building and Other Essays* (London: AA Documents, 1996)

Fraser, Ian and Henmi, Rod. *Envisioning Architecture: An Analysis of Drawing* (London: John Wiley and Sons, 1993)

Gebhard, David and Nevins, Deborah. *200 Years of American Architectural Drawing* (New York: Whitney Library of Design, 1977)

Kemper, Alfred. *Drawings by American Architects* (New York: John Wiley and Sons, 1973)

Klotz, Heinrich, ed. *Postmodern Visions: Drawings, Paintings and Models by Contemporary Architects* (New York: Abbeville Press, 1985)

Lampugnani, Vittorio. *Visionary Architecture of the 20th Century: Master Drawings from Frank Lloyd Wright to Aldo Rossi* (London: Thames and Hudson, 1982)

Lewis, Tsurumaki. *Manual of the Section* (New York: Princeton Architectural Press, 2016)

Lever, Jill and Richardson, Margaret. *Great Drawings from the Collection of the Royal Institute of British Architects* (London: Trefoil for the Drawing Center, New York, 1983)

Lipstadt, H. 'Architecture and Its Image' *Architectural Design* vol. 59, no. 3/4, Mar./Apr. 1989: pp. 1-89

Lotz, Wolfgang. *Studies in Italian Renaissance Architecture* (Cambridge, Mass.; London: MIT Press, 1977)

McQuaid, Matilda and Riley, Terence. *Envisioning Architecture: Drawings from the Museum of Modern Art* (New York: MoMA, 2002)

Millon, Henry ed. *The Triumph of the Baroque: Architecture in Europe 1600-1750* (Milan: Bompiani, 1999)

Millon, Henry and Lampugnani, Vittorio, eds. *The Renaissance from Brunelleschi to Michelangelo: The Representation of Architecture* (Milan: Bompiani, 1994)

Panofsky, Erwin. *Perspective as Symbolic Form* (New York: Zone Books, 1991)

Perez-Gomez, Alberto and Pelletier, Louise. *Architectural Representation and the Perspective Hinge* (Cambridge MA: MIT Press, 1997)

Powell, Helen and Leatherbarrow, David. *Masterpieces of Architectural Drawing* (London: Abbeville Press, 1983)

Scolari, Massimo. *Oblique Drawing: A History of Anti-perspective* (Cambridge, Mass.; London: MIT Press, 2012)

Sowa, Axel, ed. *Architecture d'aujourd'hui* no. 371, 2007 July/Aug., pp. 42-113

Spiller, Neil. ed. 'AD Profile: 225' *Architectural Design* vol. 83, no. 5, Sept./Oct. 2013: pp. 5-135

Spiro, Annette and Ganzoni, David. *The Working Drawing: The Architect's Tool* (Zurich: Park Books, 2014)

Treib, Marc, ed. *Representing Landscape Architecture* (Abingdon: Taylor & Francis, 2008)

Wilson Jones, Mark. *Principles of Roman Architecture* (London: Yale University Press, 2003)

Yerkes, Carolyn. *Drawing after Architecture: Renaissance Architectural Drawings and their Reception* (Vicenza: Centro Internazionale di Studi di Architettira Andrea Palladio, 2017)

## Index

Illustrations appear in *italics*.

**Acknowledgements**

Thank you to my friends and colleagues, especially Niall Hobhouse and Helen Mallinson at Drawing Matter for their essential contributions. Suggestions and advice were sought and kindly given by Adam Caruso, Maarten Delbeke, Nicholas Olsberg, Markus Lahteenmakhi, Oliver Lütyens, Thomas Padmadabhan, Cara Rachele, Peter St John, Robert Tavernor, Thomas Weaver and Xun Zhou. Adam Caruso and Nina Kidron read and critiqued the texts, and the RIBA Library, still a free and valuable resource open to anyone interested in architecture, was the perfect place for research and writing. Many archives, libraries and collections were generous in their collaboration and advice. These include: Bruno Moser and Filine Wagner, gta Archiv; Elena Lingeri, Archivio Lingeri; Caroline Dagbert, Canadian Centre for Architecture; Chris Macdonald and Peter Salter; Nicholas Boyarsky and the RISD Museum; Susannah Carroll, The Franklin Institute; Meredith Steinfels, Hood Museum of Art, Dartmouth College; Stefania Canta, Renzo Piano Building Workshop; Sheila Schwartz, Research and Archives Director; The Saul Steinberg Foundation; Valentina Bandelloni, Scala Archives; Nadja Bartels, Director of the Tchoban Foundation's Museum for Architectural Drawing; Heather Isbell Schumacher, Archivist, Architectural Archives University of Pennsylvania; Craig Stevens, Drawing Matter; David Owen and Tony Fretton; and David Robson. Thanks also to Emilia Terragni for commissioning me to write the book and acting as a wise colleague throughout; to Belle Place, a calm, efficient and imaginative project editor; and Milena Harrison-Gray, consummate picture researcher and negotiator.

## Picture Credits

Courtesy of National Academy of San Luca, Rome: 210; Courtesy of Accademia Nazionale di San Luca, Roma. Archivio del Moderno e del Contemporaneo, Fondo Ridolfi-Frankl-Malagricci: 223; © ADAGP, Paris and Erede Ettore Sottsass DACS, London 2025: 98; IHF1598 © Aga Khan Trust for Culture: 158; akg-images / Erich Lessing: 163; akg-images / Pictures From History: 130; akg-images: 71; FLHC 26 / Alamy Stock Photo: 116; World History Archive / Alamy Stock Photo: 242; The Albertina Museum, Vienna: 123, 166; The Albertina Museum, Vienna / Courtesy of Susanne Eisenkolb: 196; © Alexander Daxböck: 34; Alvar Aalto Foundation: 102, 253; © ADA: 20; © architecten de vylder vinck taillieu bvba: 189; Louis I. Kahn Collection, University of Pennsylvania and Pennsylvania Historical and Museum Commission.: 90; The Architectural Archives, University of Pennsylvania by the gift of Robert Venturi and Denise Scott Brown: 84; Architectural Archives of the University of Pennsylvania | Venturi, Scott Brown Collection (225): 237; Drawing by Glenn Murcutt courtesy Architecture Foundation Australia: 127; © Architekturmuseum der Technischen Universität in Berlin: 73; Archivo Williams, Claudio Williams Director: 155; © Archives Bordeaux Métropole, BORDEAUX XXI H 272 planche 18: 203; ASSi, Capitoli, 3, cc. 25v-26r: 181; © Archivio Lingeri, Via G.Sacchi 12 Milano: 112; © Ministerio de Educación, Cultura y Deporte. Archivo General de Indias.: 110; ARKM.1973-05-06539, courtesy of ArkDes Collection: 119; Livro das Fortalezas 83, Miranda do Douro by Igor Zyx is licensed under CC-BY-SA-3.0: 197; © 2018. The Art Institute of Chicago / Art Resource, NY / Scala, Florence: 227; © Julia Fish. Courtesy Rhona Hoffman Gallery, Chicago; David Nolan Gallery, New York. Image suppy: © 2018. The Art Institute of Chicago / Art Resource, NY / Scala, Florence: 33; © Atelier Bow-Wow: 194; Library of the Escuela Técnica Superior de Arquitectura, Universidad Politécnica de Madrid: 151; © Banca Monte dei Paschi di Siena S.p.A. Photograph © Foto LENSINI Siena: 235; Julia Morgan architectural drawings, BANC MSS 71/156 c:74b. Courtesy of The Bancroft Library, University of California, Berkeley: 160; © Barragan Foundation / DACS 2025: 62; Akademie der Künste, Berlin, Hans-Scharoun-Archiv Nr. 2696: 72; © original work: Dieter Urbach; © photo: unknown; © reproduction photo: Berlinische Galerie.: 134; © Bernard Tschumi: 247; Courtesy of Biblioteca de la Universidad de Navarra: 279; Courtesy of the Bibliothèque Nationale de France, Paris: 16, 85, 132, 281, 287; Noah's Ark / Natural History Museum, London, UK / Bridgeman Images: 153; Massachusetts Historical Society, Boston, MA, USA / Bridgeman Images: 165; Photo © Christie's Images / Bridgeman Images: 142; Ashmolean Museum, University of Oxford, UK / Bridgeman Images: 35; Wien Museum Karlsplatz, Vienna, Austria / Bridgeman Images: 282; © The Trustees of the British Museum: 27, 53, 65, 141, 269; Collection Centre Canadien d'Architecture / Canadian Centre for Architecture, Montréal: 105, 117, 218, 286; James Stirling / Michael Wilford fonds. Collection Centre Canadien d'Architecture / Canadian Centre for Architecture, Montréal: 217; Canadian Centre for Architecture. Gift of Estate of Gordon Matta-Clark. © Estate of Gordon Matta-Clark / Artists Rights Society (ARS), New York, DACS London 2025: 76; James Stirling / Michael Wilford fonds. Collection Centre Canadien d'Architecture / Canadian Centre for Architecture, Montréal © CCA: 209; Courtesy of Politecnico di Torino, Archivi biblioteca Roberto Gabetti, Fondo Carlo Mollino: 267; Courtesy of The Archive Carlos Diniz / Family of Carlos Diniz & UCSB Art Design & Architecture Museum: 246; Gaudí Chair, Barcelona School of Architecture, Universitat Politècnica de Catalunya: 280; © The Celsing Archive: 152; © Chris Macdonald and Peter Salter. Image courtesy RISD Museum and Nicholas Boyarsky:161; Collection Agnes Gund, New York City, USA. Photo: André Grossmann © 1994 Christo: 275; Fonds Beaudouin et Lods. Académie d'architecture/Cité de l'architecture et du patrimoine/Archives d'architecture du XXe siècle: 107; From the Collections of The Franklin Institute: 115; © COOP HIMMELB(L)AU: 239; The Samuel Courtauld Trust, The Courtauld Gallery, London: 13; Photo courtesy of CSAC, Università di Parma. © ADAGP, Paris and Erede Ettore Sottsass DACS, London 2025: 40; Photo courtesy of CSAC, Università di Parma © Pier Luigi Nervi: 207; © DACS 2025: 26, 37, 88, 175, 178, 190, 213; © Drawing Architecture Studio: 41; © ProDenkmal, Berlin, and David Chipperfield Architects Berlin: 192; © Rob Krier-Archiv, Deutsches Architekturmuseum, Frankfurt am Main; Foto: Uwe Dettmar, Frankfurt am Main: 61; © Dieste y Montañez S.A.: 77; © DOGMA: 97; © Hohe Domkirche Köln, Dombauhütte Köln, Foto: Matz und Schenk: 262; Image courtesy of Drawing Matter Collections. Photographer: Craig Stevens. Copyright: © Architects estate: 30, 70, 92, 99, 137, 139, 147, 179, 268, 274, 276; Courtesy, The Estate of R. Buckminster Fuller. Image courtesy of Drawing Matter Collections. Photographer: Craig Stevens: 226; Image courtesy Drawing Matter Somerset. © Eredi Aldo Rossi, courtesy Fondazione Aldo Rossi: 157; © 2018 Emilio Ambasz: 228; Vitruvius: L' architettura di M. Vitruvio Pollione: dedicata alla Maestà di Carlo Re delle due Sicilie... In Napoli: nella stamperia Simoniana, MDCCLVIII. [1758]. ETH-Bibliothek Zürich, Rar 9798 / Public Domain Mark: 87; Courtesy of Farshid Moussavi Architecture: 187; © FLC / ADAGP, Paris and DACS, London 2025: 104, 144, 257; © Foster + Partners: 39, 42; Image courtesy of Collection Frac Centre-Val de Loire, Photographer: Olivier Martin-Gambier © Madelon Vriesendorp: 12; © 2007 Phillips Auctioneers LLC. All Rights Reserved. © NIEMEYER, Oscar / DACS 2025: 125; © Fundacion Rogelio Salmona: 48; Courtesy of Gehry Partners, LLP: 19; © Geoffrey Bawa Trust. Image courtesy of David Robson: 54; Inc. 8° 36045 © Germanishes Nationalmuseum: 38; Photo by Fine Art Images/Heritage Images/Getty Images: 46; Photo by © Historical Picture Archive/CORBIS/Corbis via Getty Images: 101; Photo by Fine Art Images/Getty Images: 59; Photo by The Print Collector/Getty Images: 18; Photo by Fine Art Images/Heritage Images/Getty Images / RIBA Collections: 176; De Agostini Picture Library / Getty Images: 265; Gift of Ray Kappe. The Getty Research Institute, Los Angeles (2008.M.36). © J. Paul Getty Trust: 258; © Giorgio Grassi: 177; © Go Hasegawa and Associates: 95; © Grafton Architects: 55; gta Archives / ETH Zurich, Gottfried Semper: 183; gta Archives / ETH Zurich, Karl Moser: 291; Imaging Department © President and Fellows of Harvard College: 96; Imaging Department © President and Fellows of Harvard College: 256; Staatliche Museen zu Berlin. Preußischer Kulturbesitz, Kunstbibliothek, Heinrich Tessenow Archiv: 58, 100; © Caruso St John: 66, 121; Image courtesy of the Heritage Foundation of Pakistan © Yasmeen Lari: 204; © Gabriel Orozco / 6a Architects: 297; © Herzog & de Meuron: 17, 290; Collection Het Nieuwe Instituut / BLOM, 33-2: 50; Hood Museum of Art, Dartmouth College: Gift of George Herman, Class of 1941, in memory of those who died in the War against Japan: 289; MS Typ 1096 (BL A1), Houghton Library, Harvard University: 198; © Hopkins Architects: 199; © Ilya Utkin and Alexander Brodsky: 278; Illustration copyright © Hitomi Terasawa. Reproduced by permission of the Proprietor c/o Iwanami Shoten, Publishers, Tokyo: 36; © 2018 James Wines: 294; © junya.ishigami+associates: 277; © Kisho Kurokawa architect & associates. Localisation: Paris, Centre Pompidou - Musée national d'art moderne - Centre de création industrielle. Photo © Centre Pompidou, MNAM-CCI, Dist. RMN-Grand Palais / Georges Meguerditchian: 140; © OPA (Open Platform for Architecture) & LAAV Architects: 109; Courtesy of Liaoning Provincial Museum: 295; Courtesy of the Library of Congress: 283; Courtesy of the Paul Rudolph Archive, Library of Congress Prints and Photographs Division: 259; Library of Congress, Prints & Photographs Division, [LC-USZ62-135212]: 238; Library of Congress, Geography and Map Division: 231; © Acervo Lucio Costa: 254; Courtesy of the University of Hong Kong Libraries © Luke Him Sau: 49; © Marie-José Van Hee architecten: 47; © Mario Botta: 241; Image courtesy of MAXXI Museo nazionale delle arti del XXI secolo, Rome. MAXXI Architettura Collection. Aldo Rossi Archive. © Eredi Aldo Rossi, courtesy Fondazione Aldo Rossi: 93; MAXXI Museo nazionale delle arti del XXI secolo, Rome. MAXXI Architettura Collection, Carlo Scarpa archive: 113; © Moon Hoon: 29; Courtesy of Museo Archeologico Nazionale di Napoli: 229; Image courtesy Museum of Finnish Architecture: 82; © NAA: A710, 39: 171; Courtesy National Gallery of Art, Washington: 186; © Istituto Nazionale di Archeologia e Storia dell'Arte, Rome: 149; Courtesy of the National Library of Sweden (Kungliga Biblioteket): 188; © Sverre Fehn. Image courtesy of The National Museum of Art, Architecture and Design: 133; Courtesy National Museum of Ireland: 83; National Museum, Stockholm: 154; Photo: © Cecilia Heisser / Nationalmuseum: 251; Dimitris Pikionis Archive © 2018 Neohellenic Architecture Archives Benaki Museum: 285; Image courtesy of NSW State Archives: 23; Image courtesy Drawing Matter Somerset. © Niall Hobhouse Ltd / Alvaro Siza: 148; © OFFICE Kersten Geers David Van Severen: 143; © OMA: 211; © Ove Arup / Tecton: 221; Cosanti Foundation: 128; © Gottfried Böhm: 14; Images courtesy of the Petrie Museum, UCL Culture - UCL: 57; © Pezo von Ellrichshausen: 75; © Gallerie degli Uffizi: 156, 212; Courtesy of The Provost and Fellows of Worcester College, Oxford. Photography by Colin Dunn (Scriptura Ltd): 164; Courtesy, The Estate of R. Buckminster Fuller: 266; © Rafael Moneo: 150; RIBA Collections: 64, 67, 120, 174, 191, 201; John Maltby / RIBA Collections: 248; RIBA Collections: 129; © Ricardo Bofill/Taller de Arquitectura: 68; Photo © RMN-Grand Palais (Château de Fontainebleau) / Adrien Didierjean: 135; Photo © Ministère de la Culture, Médiathèque du Patrimoine, Dist. RMN-Grand Palais / image RMN-GP: 208; Photo © National Palace Museum, Taipei, Taïwan, Dist. RMN-Grand Palais / image NPM: 79; Photo © RMN-Grand Palais (musée d'Orsay) / image RMN-GP: 43; © Robbrecht en Daem architecten: 243; © Rogers Stirk Harbour + Partners and DACS 2025: 205; Image courtesy of the Richard Nickel Archive, Ryerson & Burnham Archives, Art Institute of Chicago: 26; Image courtesy of the Ryerson and Burnham Libraries, Art Institute of Chicago: 122; © San Rocco magazine: 261; © SANAA: 51; Collection: Museu de Arte de São Paulo Assis Chateaubriand. Photo by MASP: 270; © The Saul Steinberg Foundation/Artists Rights Society (ARS), NY/DACS, London 2025: 273; © 2018. Digital image, The Museum of Modern Art, New York/Scala, Florence and DACS 2025: 215; © 2018. Photo Scala, Florence/bpk, Bildagentur fuer Kunst, Kultur und Geschichte, Berlin: 103, 167, 249; © 2018. Digital image, The Museum of Modern Art, New York/Scala, Florence: 271; © 2018 Burle Marx & Cia.Ltda Credit: Gift of Roblee McCarthy, Jr. Fund and Lily Auchincloss Fund Digital image, The Museum of Modern Art, New York/Scala, Florence: 24; © The Frank Lloyd Wright Fdn, AZ / Art Resource, NY/Scala, Florence and ARS, NY and DACS, London 2025: 28, 182, 216; © 2018. Digital image, The Museum of Modern Art, New York/ Scala, Florence: 200; © Skidmore, Owings & Merrill. © 2018. Digital image, The Museum of Modern Art, New York/Scala, Florence: 293; © 2018. Digital image, The Museum of Modern Art, New York/Scala, Florence. © Bruce Nauman / Artists Rights Society (ARS), New York and DACS, London 2025: 124; © 2018. Digital image, The Museum of Modern Art, New York/Scala, Florence. © The Easton Foundation/VAGA at ARS, NY and DACS, London 2025: 236; © 2018 Thom Mayne. Digital image, The Museum of Modern Art, New York/Scala, Florence: 89; © Clorindo Testa. Courtesy of Fundación Clorindo Testa. © 2018. Digital image, The Museum of Modern Art, New York/Scala, Florence: 195; © 2018 Lebbeus Woods. Digital image, The Museum of Modern Art, New York/Scala, Florence: 172; © 2018. Digital image, The Museum of Modern Art, New York/ Scala, Florence: 126; © 2018. DeAgostini Picture Library/Scala, Florence: 136; Photograph: Jörg P. Anders. Berlin, Kupferstichkabinett - Staatliche Museen zu Berlin. © 2018. Photo Scala, Florence/bpk, Bildagentur fuer Kunst, Kultur und Geschichte, Berlin: 214; Photographer: Volker-H. Schneider. Berlin, Kupferstichkabinett - Staatliche Museen zu Berlin. © 2018. Photo Scala, Florence/bpk, Bildagentur fuer Kunst, Kultur und Geschichte, Berlin: 52; © 2018 Zaha Hadid. Digital image, Photo Scala, Florence: 114; © 2018. Photo Scala, Florence, courtesy of the Ministero Beni e Att. Culturali e del Turismo: 74; © 2018. Photo Scala, Florence: 184; Photo: Jozsa Denes. © 2018. The Museum of Fine Arts Budapest/Scala, Florence: 21; White Images/Scala, Florence: 240; Digital image, The Museum of Modern Art, New York/ Scala, Florence: 94; Digital image, The Museum of Modern Art, New York/Scala, Florence: 44; Digital image, The Museum of Modern Art, New York/Scala, Florence: 219; Digital image, The Museum of Modern Art, New York/Scala, Florence: 234; Digital image, The Museum of Modern Art, New York/Scala, Florence. © Ron Herron Archive. All Rights Reserved, DACS 2025: 180; © Private Archive Hollein. Digital image, The Museum of Modern Art, New York/Scala, Florence: 169; © 2018 Massimo Scolari. Digital image, The Museum of Modern Art, New York/Scala, Florence: 170; © 2018 Daniel Libeskind. Digital image, The Museum of Modern Art, New York/Scala, Florence: 162; © Tadao Ando. 2018 Digital image, The Museum of Modern Art, New York/Scala, Florence: 292; © 2018 Diller + Scofidio. Digital image, The Museum of Modern Art, New York/ Scala, Florence: 222; Photo Josse/Scala, Florence, © Musée Carnavalet / Roger-Viollet / TopFoto: 145; Album/Scala, Florence. © Estate of Juan O'Gorman / ARS, NY and DACS, London 2025: 60; © 2018 Arata Isozaki Digital image, The Museum of Modern Art, New York/Scala, Florence: 250; © Scenic Architecture office © Zhu Xiaofeng: 220; The Schøyen Collection MS 3031, Oslo and London: 272; © Courtesy of the Seokdang Museum of Dong-A University: 69; © Shchusev State Museum of Architecture: 31, 173, 225, 244; Courtesy of the Trustees of Sir John Soane's Museum, London / Bridgeman Images: 193; © Sou Fujimoto Architects: 32; Courtesy of Steven Holl: 159; © Studio Märkli. Private collection. Courtesy Betts Project: 86; Courtesy the artist, Drawing Matter and Betts Project. Photo: © Betts Project: 81; Digital image © Tate, London 2014: 15; © Tatiana Bilbao: 288; © Iakov Chernikhov. Image source: Tchoban Foundation, Berlin (Inv. TF0655): 106; © Archigram 1964: 131; © Tony Fretton Architects: 63; © Roger-Viollet / Topfoto: 224; Topkapi Palace Museum: 296; © Toyo Ito: 111, 233; © The State Tretyakov Gallery: 108; © Victoria and Albert Museum, London. Given by Mr John Harvey, FSA, FRSL, son of the Artist: 202; © Victoria and Albert Museum, London: 146; Courtesy of the Vastushilpa Foundation: 25; © Zaha Hadid Foundation: 260; Museum of the City of New York: 263; By kind permission of Philip Johnson / Alan Ritchie Architects: 185. Every reasonable effort has been made to acknowledge the ownership of copyright for photographs included in this volume. Any errors that may have occurred are inadvertent, and will be corrected in subsequent editions provided notification is sent in writing to the publisher.

Phaidon Press Limited
2 Cooperage Yard
London E15 2QR

Phaidon Press Inc.
111 Broadway
New York, NY 10006

Phaidon SARL
55, rue Traversière
75012 Paris

phaidon.com

First published 2018
Second edition published 2025


ISBN 978 1 83729 105 2

A CIP catalogue record for this book
is available from the British Library
and the Library of Congress.



Commissioning Editor: Emilia Terragni
Project Editor: Belle Place
Production Controller: Adela Cory
Cover designer: Julia Hasting
Book designer: Hans Stofregen
Artworker: Albino Tavares

The Publisher would also like to thank
Alison Cowan, Diane Fortenberry, Taahir
Husain, Ian McDonald, Rosie Minney,
Eddie Royle and Phoebe Stephenson for
their contributions to the book.

Printed in China